Second Edition

PUBLIC POLICY ANALYSIS: An Introduction

William N. Dunn
University of Pittsburgh

Prentice Hall
Englewood Cliffs, New Jersey 07632

Library of Congress Cataloging-in-Publication Data

Dunn, William N.
    Public policy analysis : an introduction / William N. Dunn. -- 2nd
  ed.
      p.   cm.
    Includes bibliographical references and index.
    ISBN 0-13-738550-1
    1. Policy sciences.   2. Political planning--Evaluation.
  I. Title.
  H61.D882 1994
  361.6'1--dc20   92-44303
                                                           CIP

Editorial/production supervision and
  interior design: Marielle Reiter
Cover design: Arminé Altiparmakian
Manufacturing buyer: Mary Ann Gloriande
Prepress buyer: Kelly Behr
Acquisitions editor: Julie Berrisford
Editorial assistant: Nicole Signoretti
Copy editor: Barbara Zeiders

Printed in the United States of America
10 9 8 7 6 5 4 3

ISBN 0-13-738550-1

PRENTICE-HALL INTERNATIONAL (UK) LIMITED, London
PRENTICE-HALL OF AUSTRALIA PTY. LIMITED, Sydney
PRENTICE-HALL CANADA INC., Toronto
PRENTICE-HALL HISPANOAMERICANA, S.A., Mexico
PRENTICE-HALL OF INDIA PRIVATE LIMITED, New Delhi
PRENTICE-HALL OF JAPAN, INC., Tokyo
SIMON & SCHUSTER ASIA PTE. LTD., Singapore
EDITORA PRENTICE-HALL DO BRASIL, LTDA., Rio de Janeiro

For Marija, Alex, and Liz

Contents

Preface

This volume is designed both as a textbook and as a critical synthesis of the field of public policy analysis. The primary audience for the book is upper-division and masters-level students completing their first course in multi-disciplinary public policy analysis. Because the book addresses the concerns of several disciplines, it provides illustrations and applications of policy analysis to problems faced by political scientists, economists, sociologists, planners, and public managers in several policy arenas:

- Energy and Environment
- Foreign Affairs
- Health
- Criminal Justice
- Social Welfare
- Science and Technology

- Education
- Urban Affairs
- Transportation
- Employment and Labor
- Economic and Social Development
- Communications

The orientation of the book is pragmatic, critical, and multi-disciplinary. One of its major assumptions is that the theory, methodology, and aims of policy analysis must be distinguished from the content of the disciplines in which policy analysis originates. Although policy analysis builds upon political science, economics, and philosophy, it also transforms them. Consequently, policy analysis is viewed as *an applied social science disci-*

pline that employs multiple methods of inquiry, in contexts of argumentation and public debate, to create, critically assess, and communicate policy-relevant knowledge. This book recognizes that many of the concepts and methods of this multi-disciplinary field are likely to be unfamiliar to students taking their first course in public policy analysis. For this reason special instructional devices and learning strategies are used throughout the book:

1. *Advance organizers.* The book makes extensive use of advance organizers, especially visual displays, that introduce students to the logical structure of conceptual frameworks and analytic routines. The advance organizer for the book as a whole is the information-processing model of policy analysis introduced in the first chapter and used throughout the book. This and other advance organizers help students grasp complex relationships and critically assess the assumptions that underlie particular theories, methods, and techniques.

2. *Key principles and generalizations.* At the end of each chapter there is a summary of key principles and generalizations discussed in that chapter. The summaries help students identify and critically assess the central points made in the book.

3. *Glossaries.* Key terms are italicized and defined when first introduced in the text. End-of-chapter glossaries provide a compact summary of these terms and their definitions, along with examples of how they are used.

4. *Balanced examples.* The text attempts to strike a balance between examples that accentuate the complexity of conducting policy analysis in real-life contexts, and examples that simplify the process of applying particular methods. The first type of example helps counteract tendencies to idealize economic, technical, and political rationality ("blackboard policy analysis"), while the second helps empower students to apply methods, not simply read or talk about them. In this second edition, both types of examples have been updated to reflect current practice.

5. *Study suggestions.* Knowledge and skills in policy analysis do not stick unless students have frequent opportunities to apply them. For this reason, study suggestions are provided at the end of each chapter. The study suggestions address two kinds of problems: conceptual problems that develop knowledge and skills in defining, interpreting, explaining, and evaluating; and technical problems that develop knowledge and skills in communicating, calculating, estimating, and computing. Study suggestions may be used by students for self-study and by instructors who are developing written assignments and examinations.

6. *Suggested readings.* In addition to literature contained in the footnotes, each chapter is accompanied by suggested readings keyed to the substance of the chapter. In this edition, the suggested readings have been updated to include many of the most important recent developments in policy analysis.

7. *Practical guidelines.* Students who master particular methods of policy analysis, especially statistical or econometric techniques, frequently experience severe difficulties when they must not only obtain an appropriate analytic solution, but also translate and communicate this solution in the form of a policy issue paper, policy memorandum, or oral briefing. To overcome this kind of difficulty, newly written or revised appendices present step-by-step guidelines on how to prepare policy issue papers (Appendix 1), executive summaries (Appendix 2), letters of transmittal (Appendix 3), and policy memo-

randa (Appendix 4). Additional appendices present guidelines on planning oral briefings and presentations (Appendix 5), including critical and much neglected skills in visually displaying information in graphic, tabular, and matrix forms.

8. *The political context of policy analysis.* A new introductory chapter addresses the role of policy analysis in the policy-making process. This chapter, which treats policy analysis as an *intellectual* activity embedded in a *political* process, shows the various ways in which the process of policy analysis and the process of policy-making are interrelated and interdependent. The emphasis in this chapter, and throughout the book, is on the use of policy analysis to improve processes and products of policy-making.

9. *Statistical software.* The present edition comes with a relatively powerful and user-friendly statistical program called MYSTAT. MYSTAT, which is contained on one disk (5.25″ or 3.5″), can be used with any IBM-compatible computer. For this reason, access to a mainframe computer or special computer laboratory is not necessary. MYSTAT routines are applied at appropriate places in the book to demonstrate how policy-relevant information may be analyzed and interpreted. Many useful statistical routines may be carried out with MYSTAT. These include standard descriptive statistics; bar charts, histograms, stem-and-leaf displays, and scatterplots; time-series analysis with transformations of nonlinear data; analysis of tabular data with nonparametric statistics; and multiple regression analysis. Guidelines on the use of MYSTAT, including sample applications, are provided in Appendix 6.

In the past 10 years this book has been used and evaluated in regular degree programs in many types of disciplinary departments and professional programs. The book has also been used and evaluated in training programs sponsored by government agencies. The extensive revisions incorporated in this second edition reflect much of what I have learned from these evaluations, from my own teaching experiences, and from doing policy analyses and other applied research projects for agencies at the local, state, national, and international levels. This 10-year experience has reaffirmed my belief that the process of problem definition lies at the heart of real-world policy analysis. For this reason, the book is now organized around what I have called *problem-centered policy analysis.* In addition, the original emphasis on communication, argumentation, and public debate has been retained and strengthened. This emphasis stems from the conviction that policy analysts should serve the public (not merely officials) by contributing to processes of argumentation and debate. By focusing on policy argumentation, policy communication, and public discourse, even the most complex technical analyses may be understood as policy arguments in disguise. Finally, an important unstated aim is to help bridge the gap between what scholarly works say about policy analysis and what practitioners of policy analysis actually do. The more we are able to bridge this gap, the more we will achieve a major goal of public policy analysis—to improve the process and products of policy making.

By now there are so many students and colleagues whose reactions have improved this book that the full list is too long to present here. Let me say only that students in the MPA Program in Public Management and Policy and the Ph.D. Program in Public Policy Research and Analysis, both in the University of Pittsburgh's Graduate School of Public and International Affairs, have provided insights, criticisms, and suggestions which have improved this book. In addition, colleagues in Pittsburgh and elsewhere have offered helpful advice on various parts of the book, directly and through discussions of journal articles and papers I have written on aspects of policy analysis in recent years. These colleagues include Anthony Cahill, Donald Campbell, Louise Comfort, Hector Correa, Buzz Fozouni, Donald Goldstein, Doris Gow, Andrea Hegedus, Burkart Holzner, Kevin Kearns, Rita Kelly, Phil Kronenberg, Frans Leeuw, Steven Linder, Duncan MacRae, William Mangum, Gene Meehan, Ian Mitroff, Goktug Morcol, Sam Myers, Stuart Nagel, Sam Overman, Guy Peters, Sigmund Smith, Nelson Teixeira, Mark van de Vall, Jyotsna Vasudev, Alex Weilenmann, and Carol Weiss. I also wish to acknowledge those who reviewed this manuscript at various stages and provided helpful suggestions, criticism, and comments. These include David Nice of Washington State University and David Houston of the University of Tennessee at Knoxville. Sheila Kelly, Lien Rung-Kao and Sujatha Raman assisted in preparing this edition of the book. Marielle Reiter, Production Editor for the Social Sciences at Prentice Hall, guided the manuscript through its various stages with great professional competence. I am very grateful to Julia Berrisford, Political Science Editor at Prentice Hall, for suggesting important substantive improvements in the book and for her wisdom, tact, and firmness in keeping the project on schedule.

William N. Dunn
Graduate School of Public and
International Affairs
University of Pittsburgh

1

Introduction: Policy Analysis in the Policy-Making Process

To say that policy formation is a social process in which an intellectual process is embedded does not mean that the relative effectiveness of the intellectual process cannot be increased, or that the social process cannot be "improved" . . .*

—RAYMOND A. BAUER, *The Study of Policy Formation* (1968)

Policy analysis is the activity of creating knowledge *of* and *in* the policy-making process.[1] In creating knowledge of policy-making processes policy analysts investigate the causes, consequences, and performance of public policies and programs. Such knowledge remains incomplete, however, unless it is made available to policymakers and the public they are obligated to serve. Only when knowledge *of* is linked to knowledge *in* can members of executive, legislative, and judicial bodies, along with citizens who have a stake in public decisions, use the results of policy analysis to improve the policy-making process and its performance. Because the effectiveness of policy making depends on access to the stock of available knowledge, the

---

* From *The Study of Policy Formation* edited by Raymond A. Bauer and Kenneth J. Gergen. Copyright © 1968 by The Free Press, a Division of Macmillan, Inc. Reprinted with the permission of the publisher.

[1] Harold D. Lasswell, *A Pre-view of Policy Sciences* (New York: American Elsevier Publishing Co., 1971), p. 1. Lasswell uses the term *policy sciences* rather than *policy analysis*. For overviews of Lasswell's seminal contributions to policy analysis and the policy sciences, see Gary D. Brewer and Peter de Leon, *Foundations of Policy Analysis* (Homewood, IL: The Dorsey Press, 1983); and Ronald D. Brunner, "The Policy Movement as a Policy Problem," in *Advances in Policy Studies Since 1950*, Vol. 10 of *Policy Studies Review Annual*, ed. William N. Dunn and Rita Mae Kelly (New Brunswick, NJ: Transaction Books, 1992), pp. 155–97.

communication and use of policy analysis are central to the practice and theory of public policy making.[2]

THE PROCESS OF POLICY INQUIRY

This book provides a methodology for policy analysis. Methodology, as used here, is a system of standards, rules, and procedures for creating, critically assessing, and communicating policy-relevant knowledge. Methodology, in this sense, is closely related to those intellectual and practical activities that John Dewey called the *logic of inquiry*, that is, "the operations of the human understanding in solving problems."[3] Problem solving is a key element of the methodology of policy analysis. Equally important, however, policy analysis is a methodology for formulating problems as part of a search for solutions. By asking "right" questions, problems that initially appear to be insoluble sometimes may be reformulated so that previously undetected solutions become visible. When this occurs, the dictum "No solution, no problem" may be replaced with its opposite: "A problem well formulated is a problem half solved" (Box 1–1).

Methodology of Policy Analysis

The methodology of policy analysis draws from and integrates elements of multiple disciplines: political science, sociology, psychology, economics, philosophy. Policy analysis is partly descriptive, drawing on traditional disciplines (for example, political science) that seek knowledge about causes and consequences of public policies.[4] Yet policy analysis is also normative; an additional aim is the creation and critique of knowledge claims

---

[2] Lasswell, A *Pre-view of Policy Sciences*. The classic statements of this problem are Charles E. Lindblom and David K. Cohen, *Usable Knowledge: Social Science and Social Problem Solving* (New Haven, CT: Yale University Press, 1979); and Carol H. Weiss, *Social Science Research and Decision Making* (New York: Columbia University Press, 1980). For recent statements, see David J. Webber, "The Distribution and Use of Policy Knowledge in the Policy Process," in Dunn and Kelly, *Advances in Policy Studies Since 1950*, pp. 415–41; and Duncan MacRae, Jr., "Policy Analysis and Knowledge Use," *Knowledge and Policy: The International Journal of Knowledge Transfer and Utilization*, 4, No. 3 (Fall 1991), 36–50.

[3] Abraham Kaplan, *The Conduct of Inquiry: Methodology for Behavioral Science* (San Francisco: Chandler Publishing Co., 1964), p. 7. On the logic of inquiry, see David C. Paris and James F. Reynolds, *The Logic of Policy Inquiry* (New York: Longman, 1983); and the synthesis of work in this genre by Rita Mae Kelly, "Trends in the Logic of Policy Inquiry: A Comparison of Approaches and a Commentary," *Policy Studies Review*, 5, No. 3 (1986), 520–28.

[4] See, for example, Thomas R. Dye, *Understanding Public Policy*, 3rd ed. (Englewood Cliffs, NJ: Prentice Hall, 1978); Thomas D. Cook and Donald T. Campbell, *Quasi-experimentation: Design and Analysis Issues for Field Settings* (Boston: Houghton Mifflin, 1979); and Donald T. Campbell, *Methodology and Epistemology for Social Science: Selected Papers*, ed. E. Samuel Overman (Chicago: University of Chicago Press, 1988).

BOX 1-1   No Solution, No Problem

Aaron Wildavsky observes that creativity in policy analysis consists of finding problems about which something can and ought to be done.* Emphasizing that the solution is part of defining the problem, he recounts the story of a soldier in New Zealand who did not have sufficient personnel or material to build a bridge across a river. Staring along the bank and looking glum, he was approached by a Maori woman, who asked: "Why so sad, soldier?" Explaining that he was faced with a problem that had no solution, she responded: "Cheer up! No solution, no problem."

Watzlawick, Weakland, and Fisch recount the story of the commandant of the castle of Hochosterwitz, who in 1334 was under prolonged siege by the forces of the Duchess of Tyrol, Margareta Maultasch.† The commandant and his soldiers were down to their last ox, had only two bags of barley corn left, and could not hold out much longer. They were faced with a problem that had no solution.

Reformulating the problem, the commandant arrived at a solution that must have seemed utterly irrational to his troops. He "had the last ox slaughtered, its abdominal cavity filled with the remaining barley, and ordered the carcass thrown down the steep cliff onto a meadow in front of the enemy camp. Upon receiving this scornful message from above, the discouraged duchess abandoned the siege and moved on."

* Aaron Wildavsky, *Speaking Truth to Power: The Art and Craft of Policy Analysis* (Boston: Little, Brown, 1978), p. 3.

† Paul Watzlawick, John Weakland, and Richard Fisch, *Change: Principles of Problem Formation and Problem Resolution* (New York: W. W. Norton, 1974), p. xi.

---

about the value of public policies for past, present, and future generations.[5] This normative, or value-critical, aspect of policy analysis becomes evident once we recognize that policy-relevant knowledge involves a dynamic between dependent variables (ends) and independent variables (means) which are *valuative* in character.[6] The choice of variables therefore often amounts

---

[5] See, for example, Frank Fischer, *Politics, Values, and Public Policy: The Problem of Methodology* (Boulder, CO: Westview Press, 1980). For a review of descriptive, normative, and metaethics in policy analysis, see William N. Dunn, "Values, Ethics, and Standards in Policy Analysis," in *Encyclopedia of Policy Studies*, ed. Stuart S. Nagel (New York: Marcel Dekker, 1983), pp. 831–66.

[6] Duncan MacRae, Jr., *The Social Function of Social Science* (New Haven, CT: Yale University Press, 1976), Chap. 4.

to choosing among competing values: health, wealth, security, peace, justice, equality, freedom. To choose or prioritize one value over another is not a technical judgment, merely; it is also a judgment requiring moral reasoning, and for this reason, policy analysis represents a form of applied ethics. Finally, policy analysis seeks to create knowledge that improves the efficiency of choices among alternative policies—for example, alternative policies for providing affordable health care, redistributing income among the poor, eliminating race and sex discrimination in employment, promoting international economic competitiveness, or maintaining national military security.

The methodology of policy analysis, as noted above, aims at creating, critically assessing, and communicating policy-relevant knowledge. In this context, knowledge refers to plausibly true beliefs, as distinguished from beliefs that are certainly true, or even true with a particular statistical probability. The complexity of processes of policy formation and implementation virtually guarantee that the necessary and sufficient conditions for establishing the certainty of knowledge claims are rarely, if ever, satisfied.[7] Statistical probability, in turn, has no direct bearing on the plausibility of knowledge claims, including causal inferences.[8] Indeed, the establishment of a knowledge claim such as "Raising the minimum wage will result in decreased employment" is a precondition for raising questions about the probability of this result occurring. Although the plausibility of claims may be supplemented or reinforced by statistical evidence, probability as such performs an ancillary role in establishing plausibly true beliefs.[9]

The evolution of policy analysis over the past 50 years has produced a partially codified body of standards, rules, and procedures on which there is broad agreement among practitioners. In this respect the development of policy analysis, along with related specialties such as statistical decision theory, is analogous to the development of psychotherapy as a clinical science.[10] Since the 1930s both have grown rapidly, developing new modes of analysis and intervention to help clients function in complex and difficult environments. Similar to the growth of psychotherapy, policy analysis has developed a core of moderately coherent underlying theories, a variety of methods that enjoy reasonably broad assent among practitioners, a tradition

---

[7] The joint satisfaction of necessary and sufficient conditions is what Cook and Campbell (*Quasi-experimentation*, Chap. 1) call "essentialism," a doctrine that is particularly inappropriate for policy analysis and other applied social sciences.

[8] See Nicholas Rescher, *Induction* (Pittsburgh, PA: University of Pittsburgh Press, 1980), pp. 26–29. Similar conceptions of plausibility have been advanced by Donald T. Campbell, "Can We Be Scientific in Applied Social Research?" in Overman, *Methodology and Epistemology for Social Science: Selected Papers*, pp. 315–33; and Ian I. Mitroff and Richard O. Mason, *Creating a Dialectical Social Science* (Dordrecht: The Netherlands: D. Reidel, 1980).

[9] "Probabilistic argumentation of itself is not a tool of sufficient power to underwrite the validation of induction, because we already need to have induction in hand to make any applicative use of it." Rescher, *Induction*, p. 203.

[10] Baruch Fischhoff, "Clinical Policy Analysis," in *Policy Analysis: Perspectives, Concepts, and Methods*, ed. William N. Dunn (Greenwich, CT: JAI Press, 1986), pp. 111–28.

of criticism directed at political, ideological, and ethical issues raised by the uses of policy analysis, and systematic as well as anecdotal evidence of having improved the capacities of clients to solve problems.[11]

Notwithstanding significant progress in the development of the policy sciences,[12] the application of policy-analytic methods in real-world contexts continues to involve discretionary choices for which the methodology of policy analysis supplies only general guidance. As yet, there is no fully codified body of unequivocally reliable knowledge directing analysts

> when to use formal models and when to rely on intuitive judgments, how to approach decision makers and how to coax from them their true problems, which elicitation methods to use and when to trust their results, which parameters should be subjected to sensitivity analysis and what range of alternative values should be used, how to make certain that the assumptions and conclusions of an analysis are understood and heeded, or when a given method is likely to improve the understanding of a decision problem and when it may cause more trouble than it is worth. Such knowledge as does exist regarding these topics is largely anecdotal. It is acquired by trial and error in the field, perhaps aided by apprenticeship with a veteran practitioner.[13]

Despite the need to make such discretionary judgments in contexts of practice, a growing consensus on core methodological principles is evident in historical changes in the practice of policy research and analysis. This methodological core, drawn from multiple disciplines, is applicable to a range of problems facing governments, and there is a substantial body of knowledge on the strengths and limitations of policy-analytic methods when they have been applied in contexts of practice (see Chapters 6 to 9). To be sure, policy analysis has not replaced the political process, although it seems abundantly clear that this has not been the aim of well-informed and competent analysts. Indeed, policy analysis has come to represent a systematic methodology for problem solving in the face of complexity, an aim that runs directly counter to misguided notions that policy making involves well-in-

---

[11] This evaluation of the development of policy analysis is more positive than Fischhoff's, which was written in late 1979. For recent assessments of the field, see Brunner, "The Policy Movement as a Policy Problem"; Peter de Leon, *Advice and Consent: The Development of the Policy Sciences* (New York: Russell Sage Foundation, 1988); and Bernard Barber, *Effective Social Science: Eight Cases in Economics, Political Science, and Sociology* (New York: Russell Sage Foundation, 1987).

[12] The defining characteristic of any science, as Laudan convincingly shows, is whether it succeeds in producing reliable knowledge in its domain, not whether it conforms to any of the criteria advanced since Aristotle to distinguish nonscience and "true" science. Accordingly, policy analysis and the policy sciences properly may be viewed, along with physics or biology, as sciences in their own right. See Larry Laudan, "The Rise and Demise of the Demarcation Problem," in *Physics, Philosophy, and Psychoanalysis*, ed. Robert S. Cohen and Larry Laudan (Dordrecht, The Netherlands: D. Reidel, 1983), pp. 111–27. A similar argument is made by Ronald D. Brunner, "The Policy Sciences as Science," *Policy Sciences*, 19 (1982), 115–35.

[13] Fischhoff, "Clinical Policy Analysis," p. 112. Fischhoff supports the importance of apprenticeship by citing the work of Michael Polanyi, *Personal Knowledge* (London: Routledge & Kegan Paul, 1962).

formed calculations by economically, politically, or organizationally "rational" actors who seek, respectively, to maximize economic utility, political power, or organizational effectiveness.[14]

A key feature of research and analysis on social problems over the past 40 and more years is the growing recognition of complexity. This historical development has been accompanied by the use of multiple perspectives, theories, and methods, along with the inclusion of multiple policy stakeholders, in the process of creating, critically assessing, and communicating policy-relevant knowledge (Box 1–2). The methodological core of policy analysis today can be broadly characterized as a form of critical multiplism.[15] The basic methodological injunction of critical multiplism is triangulation: If analysts seek to improve policy-relevant knowledge, they should employ multiple perspectives, methods, measures, data sources, and communications media.[16] Multiplism has an important methodological advantage over its rivals: "Approximating the ultimately unknowable truth through the use of processes that critically triangulate from a variety of perspectives on what is worth knowing and what is known."[17]

Critical multiplism is a response to the inadequacies of logical positivism as a theory of knowledge and an effort to develop new procedures on the basis of lessons learned from doing policy analysis during the era of the Great Society.[18] Multiplism is not so much a new methodology as it is a creative synthesis of a broad range of research and analytic practices advocated and used by a cross section of the policy science community. For critical multiplism, inductive plausibility, not certainty, is the defining characteristic of knowledge and a major standard of success in policy inquiry.[19] Inductive plausibility is not established by enumerating cases that support or confirm conclusions, but by identifying, evaluating, and eliminating or

---

[14] See the classic discussion of rationality by Paul Diesing, *Reason in Society* (Urbana, IL: University of Illinois Press, 1962); and David Silverman, *The Theory of Organisations* (New York: Basic Books, 1971).

[15] See Thomas D. Cook, "Postpositivist Critical Multiplism," in *Social Science and Social Policy*, ed. R. Lane Shotland and Melvin M. Mark (Beverly Hills, CA: Sage Publications, 1985), pp. 21–62.

[16] The methodology of triangulation is analogous to practices employed in geodesic surveys, cartography, navigation, and more recently, satellite tracking. The position or location of an object is found by means of bearings from two or more fixed points or electronic signals a known distance apart.

[17] Cook, "Postpositivist Critical Multiplism," p. 57.

[18] For an exposition and critique of positivism and other epistemological orientations in policy analysis, see Mary E. Hawkesworth, "Epistemology and Policy Analysis," in Dunn and Kelly, *Advances in Policy Studies Since 1950*, pp. 293–328; and Hawkesworth, *Theoretical Issues in Policy Analysis* (Albany, NY: State University of New York Press, 1988).

[19] The standard of plausibly true beliefs rather than certain or even probabilistic knowledge, combined with a critical stance toward the applied social sciences and a corresponding positive orientation toward knowledge originating in practice, has been a continuing emphasis in the history of contributions by Donald T. Campbell. See Campbell, *Methodology and Epistemology for Social Science*; and Cook and Campbell, *Quasi-experimentation*. This point is widely misunderstood by policy-oriented social scientists.

BOX 1-2 The Caravan Rolls On

In an article titled "The Caravan Rolls On: Forty Years of Social Problem Research" Gregg and associates explore questions about the effects of institutional frameworks (extrascientific factors) on biases toward "blaming the victim." They studied 40 years of social problem research in six areas: substance abuse, suicide, delinquency, job satisfaction, rape, and race relations. A sample of 698 articles published in 1936, 1956, and 1976 was coded on 80 dimensions, which included types of journals, articles, independent variables, causal attributions, relevance to theory or practice, and types of theory or practice. They then constructed profiles of independent variables (for example, person, milieu, and system variables) and attributions of causes of problems (combinations of person, milieu, and system causes).

In the sample as a whole there was little change in causal attributions over the 40 years, with person attributions (blaming the victim) dominating throughout the period. In the three problem areas of job satisfaction, rape, and race relations, however, there were significant changes toward more complex causal attributions involving milieu and system variables and causal attributions. Research on rape and race relations, the two problem areas with the most balanced approach to causal attribution over the 40-year period, have several important characteristics: (1) a movement from bivariate to multivariate analysis; (2) a change from person attributions to complex person, milieu, and system attributions; and (3) the involvement of those affected by problems in the criticism of research, the formulation of problems and solutions, and the conduct of research and analysis. Progress in social problem research and analysis—including the critical analysis of problem definitions and solutions, a movement toward theories, methods, and data drawn from multiple disciplines, and the participation of multiple stakeholders in setting and carrying out research agendas— "appears to take a social movement, however—or at least the presence of a constituency group of social problem 'victims' within the research community—to push social science toward its ideal." *

* Gary Gregg, Thomas Preston, Alison Geist, and Nathan Caplan, "The Caravan Rolls On: Forty Years of Social Problem Research," *Knowledge: Creation, Diffusion, Utilization*, 1, No. 1 (1979), 54.

synthesizing (where possible) rival theories, perspectives, and hypotheses that challenge the analyst's conclusions. The other major standard is policy relevance, which governs the usability of policy analysis in contexts of practice. Accordingly, policy-relevant knowledge is knowledge that assists in formulating and solving problems, as these problems are *experienced* by policymakers and citizens on whom policies have an impact, including citizens whose rights and opportunities in democratic political systems either have not been realized or have been violated or abridged.[20]

The methodological rules of critical multiplism represent general guidelines for policy inquiry rather than specific prescriptions for the conduct of policy research and analysis.[21] These guidelines for creating, critically assessing, and communicating policy-relevant knowledge span several important areas of policy analysis:

- *Multiple operationism.* The use of multiple measures of policy constructs and variables—or, as Campbell so aptly puts it, "multiple measures of independent imperfection"—enhances the plausibility of knowledge claims by triangulating on the same object with two or more metrics. Examples of multiple operationism include the simultaneous use of paired comparison and forced-choice scales, or measures of costs and benefits based on consumer spending (revealed preferences) and multiple attribute scaling. Multiple operationism avoids the bias of single operational definitions legitimized by early logical positivism.[22]

- *Multimethod research.* The use of multiple methods to observe policy processes and outcomes—for example, the concurrent use of organizational records, mailed questionnaires and ethnographic interviews—promotes the plausibility of knowledge claims by triangulating on the same object with data obtained from two or more instruments. Multimethod research moves beyond positivism, at least as this term is conventionally understood, by rejecting the ideal of quantification and, instead, systematically integrating quantitative and qualitative observations.[23]

- *Multiple analytic synthesis.* The synthesis and critical assessment of available analyses of similar policies and programs—for example, early childhood edu-

---

[20] See Frank Fischer, "Participatory Expertise: Toward the Democratization of Policy Science," in Dunn and Kelly, *Advances in Policy Studies Since 1950*, pp. 349–74; and Rita Mae Kelly, "Policy Inquiry and a Policy Science of Democracy," in Dunn and Kelly, *Advances in Policy Studies Since 1950*, pp. 329–48.

[21] The following list draws on Cook, "Postpositivist Critical Multiplism"; William N. Dunn, "Evaluating the Effects of Policy Analysis: Toward a Theory of Applications," in *Research on Public Policy and Management: A Research Annual*, Vol. 3, ed. Stuart S. Nagel (Greenwich, CT: JAI Press, 1986), pp. 193–209; and Arnold Meltsner, "Don't Slight Communication: Some Problems of Analytical Practice," *Policy Analysis*, 5, No. 3 (1979), 367–92.

[22] The key source on multiple operationism is Donald T. Campbell and Donald W. Fiske, "Convergent and Discriminant Validation by the Multitrait–Multitrait Matrix," *Psychological Bulletin*, 56, No. 2 (March 1959), 81–105; reprinted in Campbell, *Methodology and Epistemology for Social Science*, pp. 37–61.

[23] See, for example, Thomas D. Cook and Charles S. Reichardt, eds., *Quantitative and Qualitative Methods in Evaluation* (Beverly Hills, CA: Sage Publications, 1979); and Mathew B. Miles and A. Michael Huberman, *Qualitative Data Analysis: A Sourcebook of New Methods* (Beverly Hills, CA: Sage Publications, 1984).

cation programs for the poor under Head Start or job training programs for the unemployed under the Job Training and Partnership Act—enhances the plausibility of knowledge claims by examining the stock of knowledge about the effects of policies on different populations in different contexts. The multiple analytic synthesis, also known as the research synthesis, integrative research review, or metaanalysis, challenges the notion of the single, authoritative analysis by accentuating the collective nature of policy-relevant knowledge.[24]

- *Multivariate analysis.* The inclusion of multiple variables in policy models— for example, causal models based on path analysis or case-study analyses based on multiple sources of evidence—enhances the plausibility of knowledge claims by systematically testing and ruling out or synthesizing, where possible, the effects of extrapolicy variables on policy outcomes. Multivariate analysis also may be employed to test the plausibility of rival theories of the policy-making process, for example, competing theories of policy implementation or the uses of policy-relevant knowledge by policymakers.[25]

- *Multiple stakeholder analysis.* The investigation of the interpretive frameworks and perspectives of multiple policy stakeholders—that is, individuals and groups who affect and are affected by the policy-making process—adds plausibility to knowledge claims by triangulating among competing causal and ethical representations of problems and solutions found in real-life (naturalistic) policy settings.[26] Multiple stakeholder analysis draws attention to individuals and groups who participate in formulating and implementing policies as a source of policy-relevant knowledge and directs attention to the public interest by requiring that analysts not only serve "officials," but also the "public," including politically marginal and disadvantaged groups.

- *Multiple perspective analysis.* The incorporation into policy analysis of multiple perspectives—ethical, political, organizational, economic, social, cultural, psychological, technological—promotes plausibility by triangulating among competing representations of problems and solutions. In real-life (naturalistic) policy settings, multiple perspective analysis presupposes the prior conduct of stakeholder analysis. In settings where the primary concern is aca-

---

[24] See Richard J. Light and David B. Pillemer, *Summing Up: The Science of Reviewing Research* (Cambridge, MA: Harvard University Press, 1984); and U.S. General Accounting Office, *The Evaluation Synthesis* (Washington, DC: U.S. Government Printing Office, 1983).

[25] See, for example, Daniel A. Mazmanian and Paul A. Sabatier, *Implementation and Public Policy* (Lanham, MD: University Press of America, 1989); Paul A. Sabatier, "An Advocacy Coalition Framework of Policy Change and the Role of Policy-Oriented Learning Therein," *Policy Sciences*, 21 (1988), 129–68; and Benny Hjern and David Porter, "Implementation Structures: A New Unit of Administrative Analysis," *Organization Studies*, 2 (1981), 211–27. On complex case analysis designs incorporating multiple variables, see Robert K. Yin, *Case Study Analysis* (Beverly Hills, CA: Sage Publications, 1985). On policy models in the traditions of optimal choice and systems dynamics, see Martin Greenberger, Matthew Crenson, and Brian Crissey, *Models in the Policy Process* (New York: Russell Sage Foundation, 1976). An accessible introduction to multivariate analysis, including path analysis in LISREL (Linear System of Relations), is Fred W. Kerlinger, *Foundations of Behavioral Research*, 3rd ed. (New York: Holt, Rinehart and Winston, 1986).

[26] On stakeholder analysis, see Richard O. Mason and Ian I. Mitroff, *Challenging Strategic Planning Assumptions* (New York: Wiley, 1981); and Ian I. Mitroff, *Stakeholders of the Organizational Mind: Toward a New View of Organizational Policy Making* (San Francisco: Jossey-Bass, 1983).

demic or discipline-based perspectives, including formal theories and models, multiple perspective analysis can be accomplished without stakeholder analysis. There is no assurance, however, that formal theories and models adequately represent the frames of reference or mental maps that affect the judgments and behavior of policy stakeholders.[27]

- *Multimedia communications.* The use by policy analysts of multiple communications media is essential for ensuring that knowledge is policy relevant, that is, used by policymakers and other intended beneficiaries. The single medium of communication employed by most discipline-based policy analysts is the scholarly article or book, a medium that is profoundly ineffective in communicating with policymakers who are accustomed to policy issue papers, policy memoranda, executive summaries, news releases, and op-ed articles in newspapers. Since the reading time available to most policymakers is severely limited (30 minutes or less daily), there is a strong preference for interactive communication in one-on-one meetings, telephone conversations, conferences, briefings, and hearings. Finally, different media and documents are more effective with some policy stakeholders than others, since specialized terminology and methods must be used extensively for some groups ("experts") and translated into ordinary language for others ("laypersons"). Triangulating with multiple communications media and alternative knowledge transfer strategies enhances the policy relevance of knowledge and its potential use.[28]

It is seldom possible to observe all these guidelines in a single analysis or study, given typical constraints on time and financial resources. Fortunately, in many instances a number of guidelines are neither necessary nor desirable—for example, cases in which the task of analysis is to structure various dimensions of a policy problem and assess its scope and severity rather than make recommendations for its solution. In such cases, several guidelines (for example, multiple analytic synthesis and multivariate analysis) are likely to be premature and unnecessary. Critical multiplism, however, does not guarantee success in policy analysis, since any methodology "can only bring us reflective understanding of the means which have demonstrated their value in practice by raising them to a level of explicit consciousness."[29] Nevertheless, critical multiplism has an important benefit not provided by rival methodologies: If analysts follow guidelines of critical multiplism, they are less likely to commit preventable errors that stem from the analyst's own limited perspectives of a problem (Box 1–3).

---

[27] The classic example of multiple perspective analysis is Graham Allison, *Essence of Decision: Conceptual Models and the Cuban Missile Crisis* (Boston: Little, Brown, and Company, 1962). Among the many approaches to multiple perspective analysis available to policy analysts (see Chapter 6), see the synthesis by Harold A. Linstone, Arnold J. Meltsner, Marvin Adelson, Arnold Mysior, Linda Umbdenstock, Bruce Clary, Donna Wagner, and Jack Shuman, "The Multiple Perspective Concept: With Applications to Technology Assessment and Other Decision Areas," *Technological Forecasting and Social Change*, 20 (1981), 275–325.

[28] See Meltsner, "Don't Slight Communication . . . "; William N. Dunn and Burkart Holzner, "Knowledge in Society; Anatomy of an Emergent Field," *Knowledge in Society: The International Journal of Knowledge Transfer*, 1, No. 1 (1988), 1–26; and Appendix 5, this volume.

[29] Max Weber, *The Methodology of the Social Sciences*, trans. Edward A. Shils and Henry A. Finch (Glencoe, IL: The Free Press, 1949), p. 115.

BOX 1–3   Preventable Errors of Policy Analysis

Brunner and others have cautioned that most preventable errors of policy analysis stem from the analyst's limited perspective.* As the analyst simplifies and trims the problem to make it analytically tractable, important parts of the relevant context are misconstrued or overlooked altogether.

At the beginning of the Reagan Administration cutbacks in eligibility for Aid to Families with Dependent Children (AFDC) were intended to reduce social welfare costs. The unintended outcome of the cutbacks was an increase in overall costs for one service covered by AFDC—day care. The cutbacks provided incentives for recipients to obtain day care services from another program, Social Security, which also covered day care but at higher costs. The analytical error was that analysts and public officials reduced the problem to one program, overlooking interactions among programs.

In considering four options for meeting rising energy demand, a public utility company undertook four major engineering and cost–benefit analyses. The preferred alternative, a 60-megawatt hydropower facility, represented an environmentally safe source of energy. The construction of the new facility required consultation with community groups in the region.

The process of planning for the new facility coincided with the appointment of a new president, who initiated major changes in organization and decision processes. The choice of the hydropower facility would not have been feasible without these changes, which reflected the managerial style and values of the new president. The same changes also resulted in the establishment of a citizens' task force to participate in the decision. The meetings were dominated by fishermen who strongly opposed construction of the facility. The project was canceled, notwithstanding the favorable conclusions of the engineering and cost–benefit analyses, which did not take into account the personal and organizational factors contributing to the project's demise.

* See Ronald D. Brunner, "The Policy Movement as a Policy Problem," in *Advances in Policy Studies Since 1950,* ed. William N. Dunn and Rita Mae Kelly (New Brunswick, NJ: Transaction Books, 1991), p. 157; Gordon H. Lewis, "The Day Care Tangle: Unexpected Outcomes When Programs Interact," *Journal of Policy Analysis and Management,* 2 (1983), 531–47; and Linstone and others, "The Multiple Perspective Concept," *Technological Forecasting and Social Change,* 20 (1981), 312–13.

Policy-Relevant Information

The methodology of policy analysis provides information that is useful in answering five kinds of questions: What is the nature of the problem? What present and past policies have been established to address the problem, and what are their outcomes? How valuable are these outcomes in solving the problem? What policy alternatives are available to address the problem, and what are their likely future outcomes? What alternatives should be acted on to solve the problem? Answers to these questions yield information about policy problems, policy futures, policy actions, policy outcomes, and policy performance. The five types of information are shown as shaded rectangles in Figure 1–1.

The five types of policy-relevant information shown in Figure 1–1 are interrelated and interdependent. The arrows connecting each informational component depict a dynamic process whereby one type of information is transformed into another by using appropriate policy-analytic procedures (Figure 1–2). Policy-relevant information is the basis for making knowledge claims of many kinds, the starting point in reasoned arguments which establish the plausibility of knowledge claims in the face of criticisms, challenges, or rebuttals (see Chapter 4). Policy argumentation and debate is one of the principal vehicles for converting information into knowledge and, occasionally, even wisdom (Box 1–4).

FIGURE 1–1   Five types of policy-relevant information.

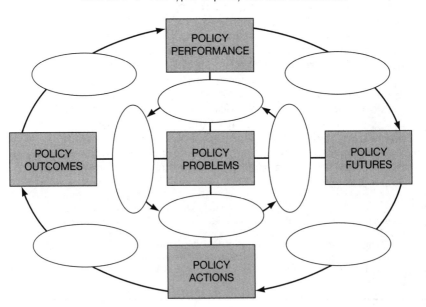

FIGURE 1–2   Five policy-analytic procedures.

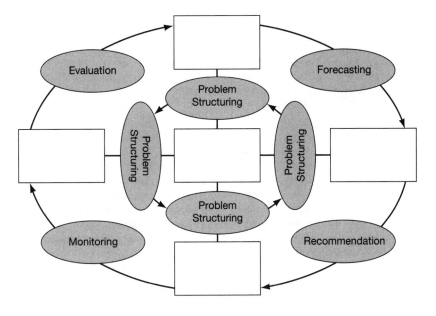

BOX 1–4   The Croissant Connection

Most people have great difficulty distinguishing among data, information, knowledge, and wisdom. Part of this difficulty stems from the fact that these four concepts involve higher and higher levels of cognitive organization, with each succeeding level incorporating the preceding level in a complex hierarchy.

Information scientists sometimes use the following metaphor to capture the complexity of distinctions among data, information, knowledge, and wisdom. In baking bread, the data used are molecules of carbon, hydrogen, and oxygen. In turn, the information at our disposal is starch, flour, water, and yeast. We have knowledge, however, only when we get to the next level, which is using the information to bake bread. Wisdom may be viewed as using knowledge to create a delicious croissant.

Data, information, knowledge, and wisdom are interdependent. To produce and use policy-relevant data or information, however, is not the same thing as producing and using knowledge—or wisdom. The standards for evaluating success are distinctly different at each level.

Policy-Analytic Procedures

In approaching policy analysis as a process of inquiry it is important to distinguish methodology, methods, and techniques. As we have seen, the methodology of policy analysis incorporates standards, rules, and procedures. But it is the standards and rules that govern the selection and use of procedures and the critical assessment of their results. Procedures are thus subordinate to standards of plausibility and policy relevance, and to the general guidelines or rules of critical multiplism; the role of procedures is confined to the production of information about policy problems, policy futures, policy actions, policy outcomes, and policy performance. Procedures alone do not yield policy-relevant knowledge.

The methodology of policy analysis incorporates five general procedures that are common to most efforts at human problem solving: definition, prediction, prescription, description, and evaluation. In policy analysis these procedures have been given special names. *Problem structuring* (definition) yields information about the conditions giving rise to a policy problem. *Forecasting* (prediction) supplies information about future consequences of acting on policy alternatives, including doing nothing. *Recommendation* (prescription) provides information about the relative value or worth of these future consequences in solving or alleviating the problem. *Monitoring* (description) yields information about the present and past consequences of acting on policy alternatives. *Evaluation*, which has the same name as its ordinary language counterpart, provides information about the value or worth of these consequences in solving or alleviating the problem. These five policy-analytic procedures are represented as shaded ovals in Figure 1–2.

The five policy-analytic procedures shown in Figure 1–2 serve as a means for organizing particular methods and techniques of policy analysis discussed in Part II. *Methods* of policy analysis are general procedures for producing and transforming policy-relevant information in a wide variety of contexts. For example, in the area of forecasting, these general procedures range from methods of forecasting based on expert judgment (Delphi methods) to methods based on multivariate analysis (causal modeling) and the extrapolation of historical time series (time-series analysis). Each of these methods is supported by a number of *techniques*, that is, relatively specialized procedures used in concert with particular methods to answer a more restricted range of questions. For example, there are several techniques for estimating serial correlation in time-series data, including the Durbin–Watson statistic. Similarly, the method of benefit–cost analysis is supported by several important techniques, including procedures for discounting benefits and costs to their present value and calculating internal rates of return for projects and programs. In sum, the five policy-analytic procedures are supported by a range of methods and techniques that are useful for producing and transforming policy-relevant information. Figure 1–3 shows the complete framework for problem-centered policy analysis, which is detailed in Chapter 3 and used throughout the book.

FIGURE 1–3   Problem-centered policy analysis.

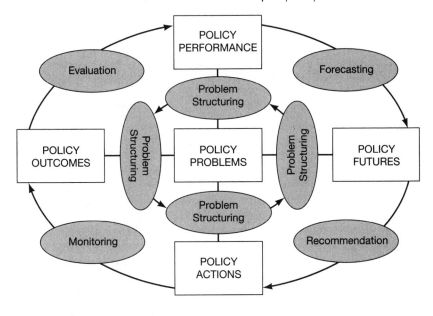

THE PROCESS OF POLICY MAKING

The process of policy analysis is a series of *intellectual* activities carried out within a process comprised of activities that are essentially *political*. These political activities can be described usefully as the *policy-making process* and visualized as a series of interdependent phases arrayed through time: agenda setting, policy formulation, policy adoption, policy implementation, policy assessment (Table 1–1). Policy analysts may produce information relevant to one, several, or all phases of the policy-making process, depending on the type of problem faced by the client for policy analysis.

Policy analysis seeks to create, critically assess, and communicate policy-relevant knowledge within one or more phases of the policy-making process. These phases represent ongoing activities that occur through time. Each phase is related to the next, and the last phase (policy assessment) is linked to the first (agenda setting), as well as to the intermediate phases, in a non-linear cycle or round of activities.[30] The application of policy-analytic

---

[30] On the dynamics of phases of the policy-making process, see Charles O. Jones, *An Introduction to the Study of Public Policy*, 2nd ed. (North Scituate, MA: Duxbury Press, 1977); J. A. Anderson, *Public Policy Making* (New York: Praeger, 1975); and Gary Brewer and Peter de Leon, *Foundations of Policy Analysis* (Homewood, IL: The Dorsey Press, 1983). The classic statement of policy-making phases (or functions) which forms a basis for the works cited above is Harold D. Lasswell, *The Decision Process: Seven Categories of Functional Analysis* (College Park, MD: Bureau of Governmental Research, University of Maryland, 1956). In contrast to Lasswell, Brewer and de Leon, and Jones, the simple framework used above has five rather than seven (or more) phases.

TABLE 1–1   Phases of the Policy-Making Process

PHASE	CHARACTERISTICS	ILLUSTRATION
AGENDA SETTING	Elected and appointed officials place problems on the public agenda. Many problems are not acted on at all, while others are addressed only after long delays.	A state legislator and her co-sponsor prepare a bill that goes to the Health and Welfare Committee for study and approval. The bill stays in committee and is not voted on.
POLICY FORMULATION	Officials formulate alternative policies to deal with a problem. Alternative policies assume the form of executive orders, court decisions, and legislative acts.	A state court considers prohibiting the use of standardized achievement tests such as the SAT on grounds that the tests are biased against women and minorities.
POLICY ADOPTION	A policy alternative is adopted with the support of a legislative majority, consensus among agency directors, or a court decision.	In *Roe* v. *Wade* Supreme Court justices reach a majority decision that women have the right to terminate pregnancies through abortion.
POLICY IMPLEMENTATION	An adopted policy is carried out by administrative units which mobilize financial and human resources to comply with the policy.	The city treasurer hires additional staff to ensure compliance with a new law which imposes taxes on hospitals that no longer have tax-exempt status.
POLICY ASSESSMENT	Auditing and accounting units in government determine whether executive agencies, legislatures, and courts are in compliance with statutory requirements of a policy and achieving its objectives.	The General Accounting Office monitors social welfare programs such as Aid to Families with Dependent Children (AFDC) to determine the scope of welfare fraud.

procedures may yield policy-relevant knowledge that directly affects assumptions, judgments, and actions in one phase, which in turn indirectly affects performance in subsequent phases. Activities involving the application of policy-analytic procedures are appropriate for particular phases of the policy-making process, as shown by the rectangles (policy-making phases) and shaded ovals (policy-analytic procedures) in Figure 1–4. There are a number of ways that applications of policy analysis may improve the policy-making process and its performance.

FIGURE 1–4 Appropriateness of policy-analytic procedures to different phases of policy-making.

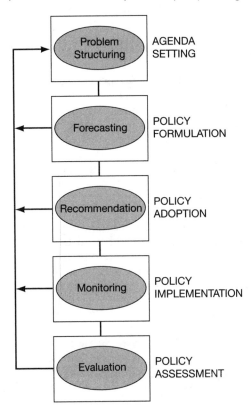

Problem Structuring

Problem structuring can supply policy-relevant knowledge that challenges the assumptions underlying the definition of problems reaching the policy-making process through *agenda setting*. Problem structuring can assist in discovering hidden assumptions, diagnosing causes, mapping possible objectives, synthesizing conflicting views, and designing new policy options. For example, the problem of race and sex bias in the some 20 million standardized tests administered annually in the United States was placed on the legislative agendas of several states throughout the late 1980s. In Pennsylvania, the assumption that test bias is a problem requiring legislative action (prohibition of standardized tests) was challenged by analysts who, after synthesizing and evaluating available research on test bias recommended by multiple stakeholders, reformulated the problem. The large discrepancies in minority and white test scores was not formulated as a problem of test bias, but as an indicator of continuing gross inequalities of educational opportunity between minority and white students. The continued use of standardized tests to monitor and mitigate these gross inequalities was recommended.[31]

Forecasting

Forecasting can provide policy-relevant knowledge about future states of affairs which are likely to occur as a consequence of adopting alternatives, including doing nothing, that are under consideration at the phase of *policy formulation*. Forecasting can examine plausible, potential, and normatively valued futures, estimate the consequences of existing and proposed policies, specify probable future constraints on the achievement of objectives, and estimate the political feasibility (support and opposition) of different options. Analysts in the Health Care Finance Administration, for example, recently employed forecasting methods (statistical projection) to estimate that unless additional revenues are generated, the trust fund for Medicare will be exhausted by the year 2005. In the absence of new health care policy initiatives, benefits under Medicare in 2005 would need to be reduced by $46 billion and, ultimately, the program would need to be cut by more than 50 percent. In the meantime, those 33 to 38 million persons who have no health insurance are likely to increase in number.[32]

Recommendation

Recommendation yields policy-relevant knowledge about the benefits and costs of alternatives the future consequences of which have been estimated through forecasting, thus aiding policymakers in the *policy adoption* phase. Recommendation helps estimate levels of risk and uncertainty, identify externalities and spillovers, specify criteria for making choices, and assign administrative responsibility for implementing policies. For example, recommendations to change speed laws (national maximum speed limit) have focused on the costs per fatality averted under the 55 mph and 65 mph options. One recommendation, based on the conclusion that the 55 mph speed limit will continue to account for no more than 2 to 3 percent of fatalities averted, proposes the expenditure of existing funds on smoke detectors and other preventive health and safety measures.[33] By 1990 some 40 states had abandoned the 55 mph speed limit.

---

[31] William N. Dunn and Gary Roberts, *The Role of Standardized Tests in Minority-Oriented Curricular Reform*, policy paper prepared for the Legislative Office for Research Liaison, Pennsylvania House of Representatives, February 1987.

[32] Sally T. Sonnefeld, Daniel R. Waldo, Jeffrey A. Lemieux, and David R. McKusick, "Projections of National Health Expenditures through the Year 2000," *Health Care Financing Review*, 13, No. 1 (Fall 1991), 1–27.

[33] See, for example, Charles A. Lave and Lester B. Lave, "Barriers to Increasing Highway Safety," in *Challenging the Old Order: Towards New Directions in Traffic Safety Theory*, ed. J. Peter Rothe (New Brunswick, NJ: Transaction Books, 1990), pp. 77–94.

Monitoring

Monitoring provides policy-relevant knowledge about the consequences of previously adopted policies, thus assisting policymakers in the *policy implementation* phase. Many agencies regularly monitor the outcomes and impacts of policies by means of various policy indicators in areas of health, education, housing, welfare, crime, and science and technology.[34] Monitoring helps to assess degrees of compliance, discover unintended consequences of policies and programs, identify implementational obstacles and constraints, and locate sources of responsibility for departures from policies. For example, economic and social welfare policies in the United States were recently monitored by analysts in the Bureau of the Census. Their analysis concludes that real median household income in the United States grew by merely 2 percent between 1969 and 1989. In the same period the share of national income by the top fifth of households grew from 43 percent to 46.7 percent. *All* other income groups experienced a decline, thus accentuating a marked increase in income inequality, an erosion of the middle class, and a decline in the standard of living in the last twenty years.[35]

Evaluation

Evaluation yields policy-relevant knowledge about discrepancies between expected and actual policy performance, thus assisting policymakers in the *policy assessment* phase of the policy-making process. Monitoring not only results in conclusions about the extent to which problems have been alleviated; it also may contribute to the clarification and critique of values driving a policy, aid in the adjustment or reformulation of policies, and establish a basis for restructuring problems. A good example of evaluation is the type of analysis that contributes to the clarification, critique, and debate of values by challenging the dominant mode of technical reasoning which underlies environmental policies in the European Community and other parts of the world.[36]

---

[34] The most thorough and insightful source on the use of policy indicators for policy monitoring is Duncan MacRae, Jr., *Policy Indicators: Links between Social Science and Public Debate* (Chapel Hill, NC: University of North Carolina Press, 1985).

[35] Gordon Green, Paul Ryscavage, and Edward Welniak, "Factors Affecting Growing Income Inequality: A Decomposition," paper presented at the 66th Annual Conference of the Western Economic Association International, Seattle, Washington, July 2, 1991.

[36] See, for example, Silvio O. Funtowicz and Jerome R. Ravetz, "Global Environmental Issues and the Emergence of Second Order Science" (Luxembourg: Commission of the European Communities, Directorate-General for Telecommunications, Information Industries, and Innovation, 1990). See also Funtowicz and Ravetz, "A New Scientific Methodology for Global Environmental Issues," in *Ecological Economics*, ed. Robert Costanza (New York: Columbia University Press, 1991), pp. 137–52.

THE PROCESS OF POLICY COMMUNICATION

Policy analysis is the beginning, not the end, of efforts to improve the policy-making process and its outcomes. This is why policy analysis has been defined as the communication, as well as the creation and critical assessment, of policy-relevant knowledge. To be sure, the quality of policy analysis is essential to potential improvements in policies and their outcomes. But good policy analysis is not necessarily utilized by intended beneficiaries, and even when policy analysis is utilized, this does not guarantee better policies. In fact, there is often a large gap between the conduct of policy analysis and its utilization in the policy-making process, a gap that can be visualized in terms of problems faced by a poorly managed lumber mill (Box 1–5).

The communication of policy-relevant knowledge may be viewed as a four-stage process involving policy analysis, materials development, interactive communication, and knowledge utilization. As Figure 1–5 shows, policy analysis is initiated on the basis of requests for information or advice from stakeholders situated at the various stages of the policy-making process discussed in the preceding section. In responding to these requests, policy analysts create and critically assess knowledge which is relevant to policy problems, policy futures, policy actions, policy outcomes, and policy performance. To communicate such knowledge, however, analysts also de-

---

BOX 1–5   Poorly Managed Lumber Mill

"The social science researchers have gone into the forest of knowledge, felled a good and sturdy tree, and displayed the fruits of their good work to one another. A few enterprising, application-minded lumberjacks have dragged some logs to the river and shoved them off downstream ('diffusion' they call it). Somewhere down the river the practitioners are manning the construction companies. They manage somehow to piece together a few make-shift buildings with what they can find that has drifted down the stream, but on the whole they are sorely lacking lumber in the various sizes and forms they need to do their work properly. The problem is that someone has forgotten to build the mill to turn the logs into lumber in all its usable forms. The logs continue to pile up at one end of the system while the construction companies continue to make due at the other end. . . . There has been governmental and foundation support for the logging operation. There has also been some support for the construction companies. There has been almost nothing, however, for the planning and running of the mill."*

* Jack Rothman, *Social R&D: Research and Development in the Human Services* (Englewood Cliffs, NJ: Prentice Hall, 1980), p. 16.

FIGURE 1–5   The process of policy communication.

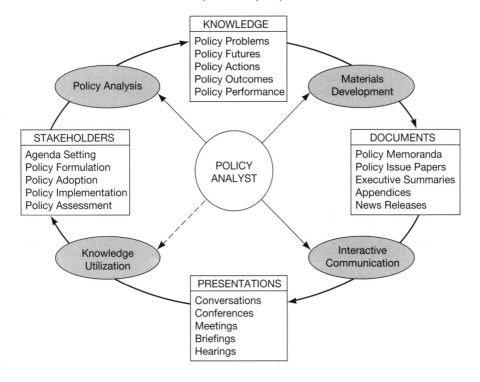

velop multiple policy-relevant documents—policy memoranda, policy issue papers, executive summaries, appendices, and news releases. In turn, these documents serve as a basis for multiple strategies of interactive communication in conversations, conferences, meetings, briefings, formal hearings, and other kinds of oral presentations. The purpose of developing policy-relevant documents and making oral presentations is to enhance prospects for the utilization of knowledge and open-ended debate among stakeholders situated at the several phases of the policy-making process.

The broken line in Figure 1–5 indicates that the influence of analysts on the process of knowledge utilization is limited and indirect. The solid lines indicate that policy analysts directly affect the plausibility of conclusions and recommendations reached by applying policy-analytic procedures, as well as the form, content, and appropriateness of policy-relevant documents and presentations.

Policy-Relevant Documents

The knowledge and skills appropriate for conducting policy analysis are distinctly different from those needed to develop policy-relevant documents (see Appendixes 1 through 4). The development of policy-relevant documents—that is, documents conveying usable knowledge—requires knowledge and skills in synthesizing, organizing, translating, simplifying, displaying, and summarizing information.

- *Synthesis.* Analysts typically work with hundreds of pages of previously published reports, newspaper and journal articles, notes summarizing interviews with key informants or stakeholders, copies of existing and "model" legislation, and tables of statistical series. On the basis of guidelines for triangulation, this information must be synthesized into documents ranging from a maximum of three pages (policy memoranda) to 10 to 20 pages in length (policy issue papers). Information also must be synthesized when preparing summaries of policy issue papers (executive summaries) or materials appropriate for the media (news releases).

- *Organization.* Analysts must be able to organize information in a coherent, logically consistent, and economical manner. Although "document triangulation" means that policy documents vary in style, content, and length, they typically have certain common elements: overview or summary, background of previous efforts to solve the problem, diagnosis of the scope, severity, and causes of the problem, identification and evaluation of alternative solutions to the problem, recommendations for actions that will contribute to a solution of the problem. Policy issue papers, as contrasted with policy memos, usually include additional elements—for example, tables and graphs placed in the body of the policy issue paper and technical appendices.

- *Translation.* The specialized terminology and procedures of policy analysis must be translated into the languages of policy stakeholders. In many cases this requires the conversion of abstract theoretical concepts and complex analytical and statistical routines into ordinary language and arguments employed by nonexperts. Since the audience may also include experts on the problem (for example, other analysts and staff specialists), a detailed exposition of theoretical concepts and analytical and statistical routines can be incorporated in appendices to policy issue papers and other backup documents.

- *Simplification.* Potential solutions for a problem are often broad in scope, interdependent, and complex. The combinations and permutations of policy alternatives, criteria, and likely outcomes can easily exceed one hundred. In such cases, alternatives may be simplified by reducing the larger set to a smaller set of major or strategic options displayed in the form of a matrix.[37] The simplification of complex quantitative relationships also can be accomplished by selecting and presenting in ordinary language cases that typify quantitative profiles.[38]

- *Visual displays.* The availability of advanced, user-friendly computer graphics has increased dramatically the capacity for effective visual communication. The visual display of quantitative information—bar charts, histograms, pie

---

[37] The scorecard or matrix displays developed by Bruce F. Goeller of the RAND Corporation are useful as means for simplifying a large set of interdependent alternatives. For an overview of the Goeller scorecard or matrix, see Bruce F. Goeller, "A Framework for Evaluating Success in Systems Analysis." Santa Monica, CA: The RAND Corporation, 1988.

[38] See Ronald D. Brunner, "Case-Wise Policy Information Systems: Redefining Poverty," *Policy Sciences*, 19 (1986), 201–23.

charts, line graphs, sociodemographic maps—is an essential tool of policy communication.[39]

Summaries. Policymakers with crowded agendas operate under severe time constraints that limit their reading to no more than a few minutes every day.[40] Under these constraints policymakers are far more likely to read an executive summary or condensed memorandum than a full policy issue paper. Skills in preparing summaries are essential for effective policy communication (see Appendix 2).

The most comprehensive and detailed document that may be developed by the analyst is the policy issue paper. A policy issue paper typically addresses many of the following questions: In what ways can the policy problem be formulated? What is the scope and severity of the problem? To what extent does it require public action? If no action is taken, how is the problem likely to change in coming months or years? Have other units of government addressed the problem, and if so, what were the consequences? What goals and objectives should be pursued in solving the problem? What major policy alternatives are available to achieve these goals and objectives? What criteria should be employed to evaluate the performance of these alternatives? What alternative(s) should be adopted and implemented? What agency should have the responsibility for policy implementation? How will the policy be monitored and evaluated?

Analysts are seldom requested to provide answers to all these questions. Instead, they are typically asked to address a smaller set of these questions that have arisen in one or several phases of the policy-making process—for example, questions about the future costs, benefits, and availability of health care which arise in phases of policy formulation or agenda setting. Policy issue papers, it should be noted, are less frequently requested than short policy memoranda or policy briefs ranging from one to several pages in length. Policy memoranda and briefs nevertheless draw on and synthesize the substance, conclusions, and recommendations of multiple policy issue papers, research reports, and other source documents. News releases, in turn, usually summarize the conclusions and recommendations of a major policy issue paper or report.

The multiplicity of policy documents draws attention to the fact that there are many ways to develop appropriate written materials on the basis of the same policy analysis. There are also multiple audiences for the policy-relevant information conveyed in multiple documents. Immediate "clients" are often only one audience, and effective communication may demand that analysts develop different documents for different audiences, thus thinking strategically about opportunities for policy improvement. Meltsner

---

[39] Among the excellent graphics software now available is Harvard Graphics (SPC Software, Mountain View, CA). The outstanding source on the methodology of graphic displays is Edward R. Tufte, *The Visual Display of Quantitative Information* (Cheshire, CT: Graphics Press, 1983).

[40] In a personal communication Ray C. Rist of the U.S. General Accounting Office reports on the basis of GAO surveys that policymakers read an average of 12 minutes daily.

states the case concisely: "Thinking strategically about the composition of the audience is essential for effective communication. The selection of the audience is not something to be left solely to the immediate client. . . . There are many clients to be reached; some may be peripheral, some remote, some in the future, yet all are part of a potential audience."[41] For example, when the preparation of news releases is permitted under standard operating procedures, the news release is the most appropriate vehicle for reaching stakeholder groups in the general public.[42] A policy issue paper is not. If the aim is to communicate with the immediate client, however, it is the executive summary or policy memorandum that is likely to be most effective. Thus, the usability of knowledge conveyed in a policy document is governed by the characteristics of stakeholders in the audience for policy analysis and the contexts in which they affect or are affected by the policy-making process.

Policy Presentations

Just as procedures for conducting policy analysis are different from procedures for developing policy-relevant documents, so are procedures for developing these documents different from procedures for their communication. A common medium of communication is the mailed document, an impersonal means of reaching clients and other policy stakeholders by physically transmitting the original version and copies of a policy-relevant document. The major limitation of this medium is the probability that a document will reach intended beneficiaries but then sit on the shelf. The probability of utilization is enhanced when the substance of policy documents is communicated through policy presentations. Policy presentations—conversations, conferences, briefings, meetings, hearings—constitute an interactive mode of communication that is positively associated with the utilization of policy-relevant knowledge.[43]

There is no codified body of rules for making oral presentations. Nevertheless, experience has shown that a number of general guidelines are important for effective policy communication (see Appendix 5). These guide-

---

[41] See Meltsner, "Don't Slight Communication."

[42] On the role of the mass media in communicating social science knowledge, see Carol H. Weiss and Eleanor Singer, with the assistance of Phyllis Endreny, *Reporting of Social Science in the National Media* (New York: Russell Sage Foundation, 1987). A much neglected area, the role of academic and commercial publishing in communicating ideas emanating from the sciences and humanities, is addressed in Irving Louis Horowitz, *Communicating Ideas: The Crisis of Publishing in a Post-industrial Society* (New York: Oxford University Press, 1986).

[43] The efficacy of the "interactive" model of knowledge utilization vis-à-vis its main rivals—for example, "knowledge-driven" and "decision-driven" models—has been reported in literature for at least 20 years. See Ronald G. Havelock, *Planning for Innovation: Through Dissemination and Utilization of Knowledge* (Ann Arbor, MI: Institute for Social Research, Center for the Utilization of Scientific Knowledge, 1969); Carol H. Weiss, "Introduction," in *Using Social Research in Public Policy Making* (Lexington, MA: D.C. Heath, 1977), pp. 1–22; Lindblom and Cohen, *Usable Knowledge*; and Michael Huberman, "Steps toward an Integrated Model of Research Utilization," *Knowledge: Creation, Diffusion, Utilization*, 8, No. 4 (June 1987), 586–611.

lines offer multiple communications strategies appropriate for the various contingencies encountered in complex practice settings. Among these contingencies are the size of the group, the number of specialists in the problem area addressed, the familiarity of group members with methods employed in the analysis, the credibility of the analyst to the group, and the extent to which the presentation is critical to policies under active consideration. In such contexts, multiple communications strategies are essential: There is no "universal policymaker" who applies the same standards of assessment ("reality tests") for evaluating the plausibility, relevance, and usability of policy analysis. Effective policy communication is contingent on matching communications strategies to characteristics of the audience for policy analysis (Box 1–6).

BOX 1–6   Contingent Communication

Policy presentations are sometimes made under conditions of strong receptivity to analytic methods and conclusions and firm beliefs in the authority of the analyst as a source of policy-relevant knowledge. But policy analyses are frequently presented to groups that have few experts in the problem area, minimum familiarity with policy-analytic methods, limited confidence in analysts and their conclusions, and little time for meetings that seem to interfere with key policy decisions already under consideration. What communications strategies are likely to be effective under these conditions?*

- Make sure that the presentation addresses the needs of key decision makers and recognizes audience diversity.
- Avoid giving too much background information.
- Focus on conclusions. Use simple graphics to convey data and discuss methods only if necessary to support conclusions.
- Pinpoint reasons for your lack of credibility, choosing a strategy to overcome the problem—for example, arrange to be introduced by a credible associate or present as part of a team.
- Be sensitive to time constraints and the probability that the group is committed to a course of action.
- Position your supporters next to people with anticipated negative reactions.
- Prioritize your points so that you present those that are most critical to the group's preferred decision.

* Adapted from Version 2.0 of *Presentation Planner*, a software package developed by Eastman Technology, Inc. and distributed by The Software Butler, Inc. See Appendix 5.

Uses of Policy-Relevant Knowledge

The aim of policy analysis is to improve policies by creating, critically assessing, and communicating policy-relevant knowledge. The improvement of policies, however, requires that policymakers use such knowledge, a complex process that stems from the intersection of three major dimensions of knowledge utilization:[44]

- *Composition of users.* Policy analysis is used by individuals as well as collective entities—for example, agencies, bureaus, and legislatures. When using policy analysis involves gains (or losses) in the expected utility of knowledge for decision making, the process of knowledge utilization constitutes an aspect of individual decision making (individual use).[45] By contrast, when the process of utilization involves public enlightenment or collective learning, the use of policy-relevant knowledge is an aspect of collective decisions—that is, *policies* (collective use).[46]

- *Effects of use.* The use of policy analysis has cognitive as well as behavioral effects. Conceptual effects include the use of policy analysis to think about problems and solutions (conceptual use), or legitimize preferred formulations of problems and solutions by invoking the authority of experts (symbolic use). By contrast, behavioral effects involve the use of policy analysis as a means or instrument for carrying out observable policy-making activities or functions (instrumental use).[47] Conceptual and behavioral uses of policy-relevant knowledge occur among individual and collective users.

- *Scope of knowledge used.* The scope of knowledge utilized by policymakers ranges from the specific to the general. The use of "ideas in good currency" is general in scope (general use), while the use of a particular policy recommendation is specific (specific use).[48] Knowledge that varies in scope is used

---

[44] See William N. Dunn, "Measuring Knowledge Use," *Knowledge: Creation, Diffusion, Utilization* 5, No. 1 (1983), 120–33. See also Carol H. Weiss and Michael J. Bucuvalas, "Truth Tests and Utility Tests: Decision Makers' Frames of Reference for Social Science Research," *The American Sociological Review*, 45 (1980), 302–13; and Jack Knott and Aaron Wildavsky, "If Dissemination Is the Solution, What Is the Problem?" in *The Knowledge Cycle*, ed. Robert F. Rich (Beverly Hills, CA: Sage Publications, 1981), pp. 99–136.

[45] For example, Duncan MacRae, Jr., and John A. Wilde, *Policy Analysis for Public Decisions* (North Scituate, MA: Duxbury Press, 1979).

[46] See, respectively, Carol H. Weiss, "Research for Policy's Sake: The Enlightenment Function of Social Science Research," *Policy Analysis*, 3 (1977); Weiss, "The Circuitry of Enlightenment," *Knowledge: Creation, Diffusion, Utilization*, 8, No. 2 (1986), 274–81; and David Dery, *Problem Definition in Policy Analysis* (Lawrence, KS: University Press of Kansas, 1984).

[47] On distinctions between conceptual, instrumental, and symbolic use, see Nathan Caplan, Andrea Morrison, and Roger Stambaugh, *The Use of Social Science Knowledge in Policy Decisions at the National Level* (Ann Arbor, MI: Institute for Social Research, Center for the Utilization of Scientific Knowledge, 1975); Robert F. Rich, "Uses of Social Science Information by Federal Bureaucrats: Knowledge for Action versus Knowledge for Understanding," in Weiss, *Using Social Research in Public Policy Making*, pp. 199–211; and Karin D. Knorr, "Policymakers' Use of Social Science Knowledge: Symbolic or Instrumental?" in Weiss, pp. 165–82.

[48] The concept of "ideas in good currency" is discussed by Donald A. Schon, "Generative Metaphor: A Perspective on Problem Setting in Social Policy," in *Metaphors and Thought*, ed. A. Ortony (Cambridge: Cambridge University Press, 1979), pp. 254–83.

by individuals and collectives with effects that are conceptual as well as behavioral.

These three dimensions of knowledge use are interdependent. As we shall see in Chapter 9, the intersections among these dimensions—composition, effects, scope—provide a basis for assessing and improving the practice of policy analysis and its impact on the policy-making process. The goal of improving the role of policy analysis, it should be emphasized, is not part of some fatuous plan to establish a "technocratic" elite which, invoking the authority of science to justify its position, seeks to replace the judgments of elected and appointed officials and the public they are obligated to serve. On the contrary, the vision of policy analysis that shapes this book is one in which policy analysts, as members of one of the leading technical communities in today's society,[49] promote reflective individual and collective learning as a vehicle for improving public policy. Quite apart from the desirability of limiting the political authority of policy analysts and other applied social scientists in avowedly democratic societies, it seems more than a little doubtful that moves toward technocratic political domination could be accommodated by the cognitive impairments, disjointed decision processes, tangled systems of interpretation, and organized anarchy which tend to characterize much policy-making today.[50] Indeed, the historical evolution of the applied social sciences, as we shall see in Chapter 2, suggests that policy analysis frequently has performed an informative and critical role rather than one of technocratic political guidance. In short, the aim of policy analysis is to facilitate improved policies by creating, critically assessing, and communicating policy-relevant knowledge, an aim designed to promote individual and collective learning through policy discourse and debate.

SUMMARY

This chapter has presented an overview of the methodology of policy analysis and its role, aims, and functions in the policy-making process. At this

---

[49] A technical community, in contrast to communities of traditional discipline-bound social scientists, career politicians and administrators, or organized policy advocates, is a group of experts who address standard and ethical problems that arise in practice contexts, interact with laypersons to generate knowledge about such problems and their solutions, conduct and disseminate to potential users the results of research and analysis, and subject the activities of the community to mutual quality control. See Duncan MacRae, Jr., "Building Policy-Related Technical Communities," *Knowledge: Creation, Diffusion, Utilization,* 8, No. 3 (March 1987), 431–62; and MacRae, "Technical Communities and Political Choice," *Minerva,* 14, No. 2 (1976), 169–90.

[50] See, for example, James G. March and Johan P. Olsen, "The New Institutionalism: Organizational Factors in Political Life," *The American Political Science Review,* 78, No. 3 (September 1984), 734–49; John W. Kingdon, *Agendas, Alternatives, and Public Policies* (Glenview, IL: Scott, Foresman and Co., 1984); and Charles E. Lindblom, *Inquiry and Change: The Troubled Attempt to Understand and Shape Society* (New Haven, CT: Yale University Press, 1990).

point you should be able to discuss the following principles and generalizations:

1. The communication and use of policy-relevant knowledge are central to the practice and theory of policy analysis. Only when knowledge *of* the policy-making process is communicated *in* that process can policy stakeholders use knowledge to improve public policies.
2. The methodology of policy analysis is a system of standards, rules, and procedures for creating, critically assessing, and communicating policy-relevant knowledge. The methodology of policy analysis has several important characteristics: a concern with formulating as well as solving problems, a commitment to descriptive as well as value-critical inquiry, and a desire to improve the efficiency of choices among alternative policies.
3. Knowledge is defined as plausibly true belief rather than certainty. Statistical probability plays a secondary and supportive role in establishing the plausibility of knowledge claims.
4. The evolution of policy analysis over the past 50 years has produced broad consensus on an appropriate methodology. This is evident in historical changes in the conduct of research on social problems, the dissatisfaction with logical positivism as a theory of knowledge, and responses to lessons learned from research conducted on social programs during the Great Society.
5. Based on these and other experiences, the methodology of policy analysis has been transformed from a series of individual social science disciplines into a multidisciplinary synthesis called critical multiplism. Critical multiplism is based on the principle of triangulation and several important guidelines or rules: multiple operationism, multimethod research, multiple analytic synthesis, multivariate analysis, multiple stakeholder analysis, multiple perspective analysis, and multimedia communications. All guidelines need not be observed in every policy analysis.
6. Five types of information are produced by policy analysts: policy problems, policy futures, policy actions, policy outcomes, and policy performance. These five types of information are obtained by means of five policy-analytic procedures: problem structuring, forecasting, recommendation, monitoring, and evaluation. These policy-analytic procedures are related to particular methods and techniques helpful in producing specific types of information. Information is the basis for knowledge claims that become knowledge (plausibly true belief) when they withstand criticisms, challenges, and rebuttals offered in the course of policy debates.
7. Policy analysis is an intellectual activity carried out within a political process. This process can be visualized as the policy-making process, which has five major phases: agenda setting, policy formulation, policy adoption, policy implementation, and policy assessment. Particular policy-analytic procedures are appropriate for creating information in particular phases of the policy-making process.
8. Policy analysis is the beginning, not the end, of efforts to improve the policy-making process. Before policy-relevant information can be used by intended beneficiaries it must be converted into policy-relevant documents and communicated in presentations of different kinds. The entire process of policy communication has four stages: policy analysis, materials development, interactive communication, and knowledge utilization. Skills needed to develop policy documents and give oral presentations are distinctly different from skills needed to conduct policy analysis.

9. The utilization of knowledge by policy stakeholders is a complex process involving interdependencies among three dimensions: composition of users, effects of use, and scope of knowledge used. The intersection among these three dimensions provides a basis for assessing and improving the role of policy analysis in the policy-making process.

10. Policy analysis does not seek to replace politics by establishing some kind of technocratic elite. This aim is not only undesirable in democracies; it is also unlikely to occur in present-day institutions characterized by various forms of cognitive impairment, disjointed decisions, tangled systems of interpretation, and organized anarchy.

11. In promoting the utilization of policy-relevant knowledge, policy analysis seeks to facilitate individual and collective learning, including improved policies, through communicative interaction and public debate.

GLOSSARY

Critical Multiplism: A methodology of policy analysis (and the social sciences) based on triangulation as a strategy for improving policy-relevant knowledge. Critical multiplism, a response to the inadequacies of logical positivism, enjoins the use of multiple perspectives, multiple methods, multiple measures, multiple data sources, and multiple communications media.

Descriptive Policy Analysis: The aspect of policy analysis directed toward the creation, critique, and communication of knowledge claims about the causes and consequences of policies.

Knowledge Utilization: The use of policy analysis by policy stakeholders to improve the process and outcomes of policy making. The use of policy analysis is a complex process that varies in composition, scope, and effects.

Methodology: A system of standards, rules, and procedures for creating, critically assessing, and communicating policy-relevant knowledge.

Normative Policy Analysis: The aspect of policy analysis directed toward the creation, critique, and communication of knowledge claims about the value of policies to past, present, and future generations.

Policy Analysis: An intellectual and practical activity aimed at creating, critically assessing, and communicating knowledge *of* and *in* the policy-making process. The process of policy analysis has five interdependent phases that together form complex, nonlinear cycles or rounds of intellectual activities. These activities are ordered in time and embedded in a policy-making process that is complex, nonlinear, and essentially political.

Policy-Analytic Methods: Relatively general procedures for producing and transforming policy-relevant information in a variety of contexts. Cost-benefit analysis, time-series analysis, and research synthesis (meta-analysis) are methods.

Policy-Analytic Procedures: General intellectual operations that constitute the logic of policy inquiry. Policy-analytic procedures are problem structuring, forecasting, recommendation, monitoring, and evaluation.

Policy-Analytic Techniques: Relatively specialized procedures used in concert with policy-analytic methods to answer a more restricted range of questions. The estimation of serial correlation in time-series data by calculating the Durbin–Watson statistic is a technique.

Policy-Making Process: A political process incorporating interdependent phases of policy making: policy agenda setting, policy formulation, policy adoption, policy implementation, and policy assessment. The policy-making process may be represented as a nonlinear cycle or round of activities ordered in time.

Policy Presentations: An interactive mode of communicating policy-relevant knowledge that includes conversations, conferences, meetings, briefings, and hearings.

Policy-Relevant Communication: A process incorporating activities of policy analysis, materials development, interactive communication, and knowledge utilization.

Policy-Relevant Documents: Written materials that describe the process and conclusions of policy analysis, including any recommendations for action. Major forms of policy-relevant documents are the policy issue paper, the policy memorandum, the executive summary, the appendix, and the news release.

Policy-Relevant Information: Data that have been selectively interpreted and organized into categories that inform analysts and other stakeholders about policy problems, policy futures, policy actions, policy outcomes, and policy performance. Policy-relevant information is transformed into knowledge claims by means of policy arguments.

Policy-Relevant Knowledge: Information that has been critically assessed and transformed into plausibly true beliefs about the process and outcomes of policy. Plausibly true beliefs are expressed as knowledge claims that are uncertain, contestable, and, where appropriate, supplemented (but never established) by statistical probability.

SUGGESTED READINGS

BARBER, BERNARD, *Effective Social Science: Eight Cases in Economics, Political Science, and Sociology.* New York: Russell Sage Foundation, 1987.

CAMPBELL, DONALD T., *Methodology and Epistemology for Social Science: Collected Papers,* ed. E. Samuel Overman. Chicago: University of Chicago Press, 1988.

COOK, THOMAS D., "Postpositivist Critical Multiplism," in *Social Science and Social Policy,* ed. R. Lane Shotland and Melvin M. Mark. Beverly Hills, CA: Sage Publications, 1985, pp. 21–62.

DE LEON, PETER, *Advice and Consent: The Development of the Policy Sciences.* New York: Russell Sage Foundation, 1988.

DUNN, WILLIAM N. and BURKART HOLZNER, "Knowledge in Society: Anatomy of an Emergent Field," *Knowledge in Society: The International Journal of Knowledge Transfer,* 1, No. 1 (1988), 1–26.

DUNN, WILLIAM N. and RITA MAE KELLY, eds., *Advances in Policy Studies Since 1950,* Vol. 10 of *Policy Studies Review Annual.* New Brunswick, NJ: Transaction Books, 1992.

HAWKESWORTH, MARY E., *Theoretical Issues in Policy Analysis,* Albany, NY: State University of New York Press, 1988.

HOROWITZ, IRVING L., ed., *The Use and Abuse of Social Science: Behavioral Science and Policy Making,* 2nd ed. New Brunswick, NJ: Transaction Books, 1985.

KINGDON, JOHN W., *Agendas, Alternatives, and Public Policies.* Glenview, IL: Scott, Foresman and Company, 1984.

LINDBLOM, CHARLES E., *Inquiry and Change: The Troubled Attempt to Understand and Change Society.* New Haven, CT: Yale University Press, 1990.

LINDBLOM, CHARLES E., and DAVID K. COHEN, *Usable Knowledge: Social Science and Social Problem Solving.* New Haven, CT: Yale University Press, 1979.

MACRAE, DUNCAN, JR., *The Social Function of Social Science.* New Haven, CT: Yale University Press, 1976.

MARCH, JAMES G. and JOHAN P. OLSEN, "The New Institutionalism: Organizational Factors in Political Life," *The American Political Science Review,* 78, No. 3 (September 1984), 734–49.

NAGEL, STUART S., ed., *Encyclopedia of Policy Studies.* New York: Marcel Dekker, 1983.

WEISS, CAROL H., *Social Science Research and Decision Making.* New York: Columbia University Press, 1980.

PART ONE

Methodology for Policy Analysis

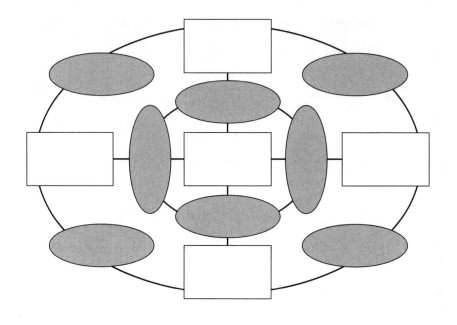

Part I of this book extends the discussion of methodology begun in Chapter 1. The chapters in this part are guided by three aims:

- To sketch the historical development of policy analysis as a methodological response to recurrent practical problems and crises.
- To elaborate the problem-centered model of policy analysis as a framework for understanding the process of creating and transforming different kinds of policy-relevant information.
- To present a methodology of policy argumentation and debate as a means for creating and critically assessing knowledge claims based on this information.

The purpose of Part I as a whole is to show how the methodology of policy analysis facilitates the creation, critical assessment, and communication of policy-relevant knowledge, that is, plausibly true beliefs about the processes, products, and performance of public policy-making.

2

Historical Context
of Policy Analysis

The social sciences have developed very largely through the criticism
of proposals for social improvements or, more precisely, through
attempts to find out whether or not some particular economic or
political action is likely to produce an expected, or desired, result.

—Karl R. Popper, *The Poverty of Historicism* (1960)

As we saw in Chapter 1, policy analysis may be understood as the process
of producing knowledge *of* and *in* policy processes.[1] In this broad sense
policy analysis is as old as civilization itself, and includes diverse forms of
inquiry, from mysticism and the occult to modern science. The advantage
of this general formulation is that it permits us to explore the variety of
meanings that in past times have been attached to the process of producing
policy-relevant knowledge. Etymologically, the term *policy* comes to us from
Greek, Sanskrit, and Latin languages. The Greek and Sanskrit root *polis*
(city-state) and *pur* (city) evolved into the Latin *politia* (state) and later, into
the Middle English *policie*, which referred to the conduct of public affairs
or the administration of government. The etymological origins of policy are
the same for two other important words: *police* and *politics*. This is one of
the reasons why many modern languages, for example, German and Russian, have only one word (*Politik, politika*) to refer to both policy and
politics. It is also one of the factors contributing to the present-day ambiguity
surrounding the boundaries of such disciplines as political science, public

---

[1] Harold D. Lasswell, *A Pre-view of Policy Sciences* (New York: American Elsevier Publishing Co., 1971), p. 1. Knowledge *of* refers to "systematic, empirical studies of how policies
are made and put into effect," while knowledge *in* refers to understanding that "the realism
of a decision depends in part on access to the stock of available knowledge" (pp. 1–2).

33

administration, and the policy sciences, each of which is heavily committed to the study of politics and policy.[2]

The term *policy analysis* need not be restricted to its contemporary meaning, where analysis is either equated with the separation or breaking up of a problem into its basic elements or constituent parts, much as we disassemble a clock or machine,[3] or is identified with the use of particular quantitative techniques associated with systems analysis, econometrics, and applied mathematics.[4] On the contrary, there are many different ways to produce knowledge *of* and *in* policy processes. Some of these emerged in the earliest civilizations, while others arose only in the period following the social transformation which accompanied the Industrial Revolution in eighteenth-century Europe. Thus, policy analysis is not altogether new; nor may it simply be equated with the growth of the empirico-analytic sciences in the past 200 years.[5]

EARLY ORIGINS

Understood in its widest sense, policy analysis may be traced to that point in the evolution of human societies where knowledge of and in policy processes was *consciously* cultivated, thus permitting an explicit and self-reflective examination of links between knowledge and action. The exact time at which policy-relevant knowledge was first produced is debatable and perhaps unknowable. Nevertheless, it is generally believed that the development of specialized procedures for analyzing public policies was related to "the relatively sudden emergence of civilization from the largely autonomous sea of tribal or folk societies" and "the expansion and differentiation of urban civilization in world history."[6] Policy analysis as a specialized activity therefore followed changes in social organization that accompanied new forms of production technology and relatively stable patterns of human settlement.

The Hammurabian Code

The earliest recorded examples of conscious efforts to analyze public policy are found in Mesopotamia. The ancient Mesopotamian city of Ur,

---

[2] See, for example, Ira Sharkansky, *Policy Analysis in Political Science* (Chicago: Markham Publishing Co., 1970); H. George Frederickson and Charles Wise, eds., *Public Administration and Public Policy* (Lexington, MA: D.C. Heath, 1977); and Yehezkel Dror, *Ventures in Policy Sciences: Concepts and Applications* (New York: American Elsevier Publishing Co., 1971).

[3] See, for example, Robert D. Behn and James W. Vaupel, "Teaching Analytical Thinking," *Policy Analysis*, 2 (Fall 1976), 663–92.

[4] See, for example, Edith Stokey and Richard Zeckhauser, *A Primer for Policy Analysis* (New York: W.W. Norton, 1978).

[5] See Duncan MacRae, Jr., *The Social Function of Social Science* (New Haven, CT: Yale University Press, 1976), pp. 54–77; and Martin Rein, *Social Science and Public Policy* (New York: Penguin Books, 1976).

[6] Lassweil, *A Pre-view of Policy Sciences*, pp. 9, 13.

situated in what is now southern Iraq, produced one of the first legal codes in the twenty-first century B.C., some 2000 years before Aristotle (384–322 B.C.), Confucius (551–479 B.C.), and Kautilya (circa 300 B.C.) produced their classic treatises on government and politics. The Code of Hammurabi, written by the ruler of Babylon in the eighteenth century B.C., expressed a need to establish a unified and just public order in a period when Babylon was in transition from a small city-state to a large territorial state. Hammurabi's Code, which has its parallel in Mosaic laws, reflected economic and social requirements of stable urban settlements in which rights and obligations were defined according to social position. The code covered criminal procedures, property rights, trade and commerce, family and marital relations, physicians' fees, and what we now call public accountability. For example, procedures designed to hold governors, magistrates, and other officials accountable included the following provisions:[7]

33. If a governor or a magistrate take possession of the men of levy (or, pardon a deserter) or accept and send a hired substitute on an errand of the king, that governor or magistrate shall be put to death.

34. If a governor or magistrate take the property of an officer, let an officer for hire, present an officer in a judgment to a man of influence, take the gift which the king has given to an officer, that governor or magistrate shall be put to death.

35. If a man buy from an officer the cattle or sheep which the king has given to that officer, he shall forfeit his money.

36. In no case shall one sell the field or garden or house of an officer, constable, or tax-gatherer.

Symbol Specialists

The early Mesopotamian legal codes may be viewed as a response to the growing complexities of fixed urban settlements and to a new pattern of social organization designed for the distribution of commodities and services, record keeping, and the maintenance of internal security and external defense. Concurrently, a growing consciousness of relations between knowledge and action fostered the growth of educated strata who specialized in the production of policy-relevant knowledge. These "symbol specialists," as Lasswell calls them, were responsible for forecasting the consequences of policies, for example, at the onset of the planting season or in times of war.[8] While the primary means for producing policy-relevant knowledge was unscientific by present-day standards, since analysts used mysticism, ritual, and the occult to forecast the future, such procedures were in part dependent on evidence acquired through experience. Policy recommendations, whether produced through magic, mysticism, or ritualistic purification, were ultimately tested on pragmatic grounds. Hence, the authority of early producers of specialized knowledge was based partly on whether their advice

---

[7] *The Code of Hammurabi*, trans. Robert F. Harper (Chicago: University of Chicago Press, 1904).

[8] Lasswell, *A Pre-view of Policy Sciences*, p. 11.

resulted in a better policy, and not simply on the procedures by which such advice was produced.

The recorded history of specialists in the production of policy-relevant knowledge is somewhat fragmentary until the fourth century B.C. In India Kautilya's Arthashastra, one of the first systematic guides to policy-making, statecraft, and government administration, summarized much that had been written up to that time (300 B.C.) on material success, or what we now call economics. Kautilya, who served as an adviser to the Mauryan Empire in northern India, has been compared to Plato (427–327 B.C.), Aristotle (384–322 B.C.), and Machiavelli (1469–1527), all of whom were deeply involved in practical aspects of government policy-making in addition to their work as social thinkers. Plato had served as adviser to the rulers of Sicily, while Aristotle tutored Alexander of Macedonia from the time the latter was 14 years old until he ascended the throne at the age of 20. Aristotle, who like many contemporary social thinkers found practical politics repugnant, seems to have accepted his assignment because he wished to bring knowledge to bear on the public problems of the day:

> Aristotle accepted the proposal because in this respect at least he was a good Platonist. Plato had said that there would be no very good government until philosophers were kings or kings philosophers. If then the opportunity came to a philosopher of guiding the policy of a state, either directly or by instructing a young prince, he could not in conscience reject it.[9]

In ancient times there is perhaps no better illustration of the conscious cultivation of links between knowledge and action than that found in the works of Kautilya, Plato, and Aristotle; nor is there a more persuasive way to show the essentially practical character of early policy analysis than to refer to parts of Kautilya's Arthashastra or Aristotle's Politics and Ethics. Yet these were the products of individual producers of specialized knowledge, not those of entire classes of educated persons who in succeeding historical periods in Europe and Asia would influence policy-making.

Specialized Knowledge in Medieval Society

The gradual expansion and differentiation of urban civilization in the Middle Ages brought with it an occupational structure which facilitated the development of specialized knowledge. Various groups of policy specialists were recruited by princes and kings to provide advice and technical assistance in areas where rulers were least able to make effective decisions: finance, war, and law. The historical evolution of a trained class of specialists in various areas of public policy has been described in the following terms by the German sociologist Max Weber:

---

[9] J. A. K. Thompson, The Ethics of Aristotle: The Nichomachean Ethics Translated (Baltimore: Penguin Books, 1955), p. 11.

In Europe, expert officialdom, based on the division of labor, has emerged in a gradual development of half a thousand years. The Italian cities and seigniories were the beginning, among the monarchies, and states of the Norman conquerors. But the decisive step was taken in connection with the administration of the finances of the prince. . . . The sphere of finance could afford least of all a ruler's dilettantism—a ruler who at that time was still above all a knight. The development of war technique called forth the expert and specialized officer; the differentiation of legal procedure called forth the trained jurist. In these three areas—finance, war, and law—expert officialdom in the more advanced states was definitely triumphant during the sixteenth century.[10]

The growth of expert officialdom, or what Weber called "professional politicians," assumed a variety of forms in different areas of the world. In medieval Europe, India, China, Japan, and Mongolia the clergy were literate and therefore technically useful. Christian, Brahmin, Buddhist, and Lamaist priests, much like some modern social and behavioral scientists, earned a reputation for impartiality and disinterestedness insofar as they stood above practical politics and temptations of political power and economic gain. Humanistically educated men of letters, whose modern counterpart is the presidential speech writer, also exerted a limited but important influence on policy-making until they were replaced in Europe by court nobles who gradually came to dominate the political and diplomatic service. In England, petty nobles and urban rentiers (investors) were recruited without compensation to manage local government in their own interests. Finally, university-trained jurists exerted a decisive influence on policy-making, particularly in Continental Europe. Jurists trained in Roman law and jurisprudence were largely responsible for the transformation of the late medieval state, punctuating every step in the development of modern government.

The Industrial Revolution

In ancient and medieval times the growth of policy-relevant knowledge closely followed the evolution of urban civilization and the rise and expansion of the territorial state. Yet it was not until the onset of the Industrial Revolution in the latter part of the eighteenth century that the production of policy-relevant knowledge became a relatively autonomous activity guided by its own special procedures and insulated from the interests and prejudices of everyday politics. The age of the Industrial Revolution was also that of the Enlightenment, a period in which the belief in common human progress through science and technology became ever more dominant among policymakers and those advising them. It is in this period that the development and testing of scientific theories of nature and society were gradually seen to constitute the only objective means to understand and resolve social problems. Mysticism, magic, and divination gave way to mod-

---

[10] Max Weber, "Politics as a Vocation," in *From Max Weber: Essays in Sociology*, ed. Hans C. Gerth and C. Wright Mills (New York: Oxford University Press, 1946), p. 88.

ern science. In the realm of policy analysis, this meant the production of policy-relevant knowledge according to the canons of empiricism and the scientific method.

THE NINETEENTH-CENTURY BACKGROUND

In 1850, Mr. Mackenzie, the Secretary to Great Britain's National Philanthropic Association, submitted a research proposal to the London Statistical Society (later the Royal Statistical Society) requesting funds to undertake an empirical study of "the quantities of horse-dung deposited daily in the streets of the Metropolis."[11] The proposal was firmly but politely declined on grounds that its subject matter lay outside the Society's current funding priorities. This isolated incident in the transactions of one of Europe's major nineteenth-century centers for policy research illustrates the exaggerated lengths to which empiricism and quantitative methods could be taken. Yet the incident also points to fundamental changes in attitudes toward knowledge that emerged in the nineteenth century.

The Growth of Empirical Research

In Europe a new breed of specialists in the production of policy-relevant knowledge began to base their activities on the systematic recording of empirical data. Prior to this time there had been many efforts, some of them by preeminent philosophers and statesmen, to offer systematic explanations of policy-making and its role in society. Yet for several thousand years there was an essential continuity in methods of inquiry used to solve human problems. When evidence for a particular point of view was solicited at all, it was typically in the form of appeals to authority, ritual, or philosophical principles. What was new in the nineteenth century was a basic change in the procedures used to understand society and its problems, a change reflected in the growth of empirical, quantitative, and policy-related research.[12]

In this period the concern with the systematic collection of facts may be illustrated in many ways. For example, at the turn of the century the first censuses were conducted in the United States (1790) and England (1801). It was at this time that statistics ("state arithmetic") and demography began to develop as specialized fields. The Manchester and London Statistical Societies, both established in the 1830s, were instrumental in shaping a new orientation toward the production of policy-relevant knowledge. These societies, organized by bankers, industrialists, and scholars, sought

---

[11] *Annals of the Royal Statistical Society, 1834–1934* (London, 1934), p. 79. Quoted in Nathan Glazer, "The Rise of Social Research in Europe," in *The Human Meaning of the Social Sciences,* ed. Daniel Lerner (New York: World Publishing Co., 1959), p. 70.

[12] See Daniel Lerner, "Social Science: Whence and Whither?" in *The Human Meaning of the Social Sciences,* pp. 13–23.

to replace traditional ways of thinking about social problems with systematically collected evidence pertaining to the effects of urbanization and industrial employment on the lives of workers and their families.

In the Manchester Society an enthusiasm for quantitative data was coupled with a commitment to social reform. As the first annual report of the society announced: "The [Society] owes its origin to a strong desire felt by its projectors to assist in promoting the progress of social improvement in the manufacturing population by which they were surrounded."[13] The London Society, under the influence of academics such as Thomas Malthus (1766–1834), took a more disinterested and value-neutral approach to social problems. In the words of its prospectus: "The Statistical Society will consider it to be the first and most essential rule of its conduct to exclude carefully all opinions from its transactions and publications—to confine its attention rigorously to facts—and, as far as it may be found possible, to facts which can be stated numerically and arranged in tables."[14] The London and Manchester societies, which used questionnaires to carry out studies whose counterpart is the modern sample survey, also used "paid agents" who were the functional equivalent of the professional interviewer. There were similar developments, although on a lesser scale, in France, Germany, and Holland.

Nineteenth-century contributors to empirical, quantitative, and policy-relevant research came from every part of Europe. The emerging discipline of statistics, references to which may be found in eighteenth-century German and French texts, found one of its first concrete expressions in Sir John Sinclair's *Statistical Account of Scotland* (1791–1799). Yet the most prominent and influential contributor to the methodology of statistics was Adolphe Quetelet (1796–1874), a Belgian mathematician and astronomer who was the major scientific adviser to the Dutch and Belgian governments. The extent of Quetelet's concern with the methodology and techniques of empirical inquiry may be seen in the following description of his work:

> [Quetelet] gave careful consideration to the collection of data, both as to the blank forms to be used and as to the nature of the questions to be asked, to the tabulation and forms of presentation of the material, to methods of averaging and summarizing data, and to the criticism, both of the sources and the results of the investigation. . . . [He held there should be] inquiry into the influences under which the data are collected and the nature of their sources.[15]

In France one of the major empirical studies of the nineteenth century was published by Frederic Le Play (1806–1882). *Les Ouvriers Europeans [The European Workers]*, published in 1855, was a detailed investigation of family income and expenditures of European workers in several countries. In Ger-

---

[13] Quoted in Glazer, "The Rise of Social Research in Europe," p. 51.

[14] Quoted in Glazer, ibid., pp. 51–52.

[15] Frank H. Hankins, "Adolphe Quetelet as Statistician," *Columbia University Studies in History, Economics, and Public Law*, 31, No. 4 (1908), p. 42.

many the work of Ernst Engel (1821–1896) sought to derive laws of "social economics" from empirical data expressed in statistical form. In England the work of Henry Mayhew and Charles Booth, both of whom directly observed the life and employment conditions of the urban poor, represents a formidable contribution to the empirical study of social problems. Mayhew's *London Labour and the London Poor* (1851) contains vivid descriptions of the laborers, peddlers, performers, and prostitutes who comprised London's urban underclass in the 1850s. Booth's *Life and Labour of the People in London* (1891–1903) surpassed Mayhew's account in its attention to detail and the comprehensiveness of its findings. Booth, who compiled evidence by using school inspectors as key informants, also lived among the urban poor to gain firsthand experience of actual living conditions. His studies, designed to show "the numerical relation which poverty, misery, and depravity bear to regular earnings and comparative comfort,"[16] involved millions of people and produced enormous quantities of empirical data. Booth, who was eventually named to the Royal Commission on the Poor Law, influenced the revision of policies on old-age pensions. His work also served as something of a model for policy-related research in the United States, including the *Hull House Maps and Papers* (1895) and W.E.B. Dubois's *The Philadelphia Negro* (1899), both of which sought to document the scope and severity of poverty in urban areas.

In the nineteenth century, methods for producing policy-relevant knowledge clearly underwent a major transformation. Knowledge of nature and society was no longer judged according to its conformity with authority, ritual, or philosophical principle but was assessed in terms of its consistency with empirical observations. Yet this transformation was not so much a result of formal commitments to the canons of empiricism and the scientific method as a consequence of the growing uncertainty that came with the transition from agrarian to industrial civilization. The complexity of society was far greater than it had been at any point in history. There was a rapid acceleration in the geographic and social mobility of the population, most of whom were flocking to already overcrowded urban areas. Coupled with changes in social structures was a gradual transformation of social consciousness, such that individuals and social classes began to see themselves as agents of their own futures.

The Growth of Political Stability

For thousands of years the social organization of urban civilization had changed gradually. The irony of the nineteenth century is that

> political instability in Europe before the Industrial Revolution went hand in hand with exceptional social stability. For the majority of the population knew only an unchanging world in which the patterns of belief, of work, of family life and social habits changed with glacier-like slowness. Wild political conflicts

---

[16] Lerner, "Social Science: Whence and Whither?" p. 20.

and instability had curiously little effect on this immobility of social habit. But industry, and particularly scientific industry, requires a politically stable world in which to operate with anything like efficiency. . . .[17]

By the middle of the eighteenth century, particularly in England, political stability and control rapidly emerged as a consequence of single-party government, a legislature under firm executive control, and the development of a common identity among those who wielded economic, social, and political power. Significantly, some half a century *before* the Industrial Revolution, political stability was associated with profound social instability. This imbalance between the political and social spheres is important for understanding the growth of empirical, quantitative, and policy-relevant research in the succeeding century. Modern science and technology did not shape the growth of the new centralized system of political control and government policy-making; it was the other way around. The new empirical approach to the production of policy-relevant knowledge was less a consequence of the self-conscious emulation of the natural sciences than it was a response to the needs of the state for reliable information on the basis of which policymakers could shape legislation and administer affairs of state. The slowly evolving and relatively stable societies of the period before 1750 gave way in subsequent periods to accelerated societal complexity and unpredictability.

Practical Sources of Specialized Knowledge

In the nineteenth century the production of specialized knowledge was prompted by a concern with practical problems of the day as these were defined by dominant social groups. Government leaders, capitalists, and the managers of the emerging factory system required information that would permit an extension of control over the human and material environment. The urban proletariat, which had grown throughout the eighteenth century in London, Manchester, and Paris, represented an unknown and alien culture whose domestication required that it be understood. Henry Mayhew's account of the lives of the London poor reads very much like descriptions of the colonized peoples of Asia, Africa, and Latin America produced a half a century later:

> We, like the Kaffirs, Fellahs, and Finns, are surrounded by wandering hordes . . . paupers, beggars, and outcasts, possessing nothing but what they acquire by depredation from the industrious, provident, and civilized portion of the community—that heads of these nomads are remarkable for the greater development of the jaws and the cheekbones rather than those of the head— and that they have a secret language of their own . . . for the concealment of their designs: these are points of coincidence so striking that, when placed

---

[17] J. H. Plumb, *The Growth of Political Stability in England, 1675–1725* (Baltimore: Penguin Books, 1973), p. 12.

before the mind, make us marvel that the analogy should have remained thus long unnoticed.[18]

It was in this context that applied social science, first in the form of statistics and demography and later in the form of established disciplines of sociology, economics, political science, and public administration, rose as a challenge to practical problems of understanding and controlling the complexities of society. The development of empirical, quantitative, and policy-relevant research was, first of all, a response to problems of an industrial civilization. But more than this, it was a reflection of dominant cultural values. The growth of new methods of inquiry was much less a product of the desire to attain new scientific "truths" or "objectivity" than it was an attempt by dominant social groups to use products of scientific research for purposes of political and administrative control. In the sphere of nineteenth-century factory production, for example, the political organization of work preceded scientific and technological developments which later culminated in complex machinery and the specialization of tasks.[19] In the sphere of public policy we see a parallel development: New methods of inquiry were products of the recognition by bankers, industrialists, and the Victorian middle class that older methods and techniques for understanding the natural and human environment were no longer adequate.

Industrial civilization had spawned a newly uprooted, uneducated, and displaced class of urban workers and their families. The key questions of the day were practical ones: How much did members of the urban proletariat need to earn to maintain themselves and their families? How much did they have to earn before there was a taxable surplus? How much did they have to save from their earnings to pay for medical treatment and education? In turn, how much should capitalist owners and the state invest in daycare facilities in order to guarantee that the mothers of infants might put in an effective day's work? How much investment in public works projects—sanitation, sewage, housing—was required to maintain adequate public health standards and protect the middle and upper classes from infectious diseases cultivated in urban slums? In modern market economies, as money became the standard measure of value, "the determination of such quanta became a critical need of private and public policy. The roots of social science lie in its responsiveness to these needs of modern society for empirical, quantitative, policy-related information about itself."[20]

The nineteenth-century background of contemporary policy analysis shows how applied social science was fused with the goals of dominant social groups. While the central motif of Western civilization, from ancient times

---

[18] Henry Mayhew, *London Labour and the London Poor* (London, 1851), Vol. I, pp. 1–2. Quoted in Glazer, "The Rise of Social Research in Europe," p. 57.

[19] See Stephen A. Marglin, "What Do Bosses Do? The Origins and Functions of Hierarchy in Capitalist Production," *Review of Radical Political Economics*, 6, No. 2 (1974), 33–60.

[20] Lerner, "Social Science: Whence and Whither?" p. 19.

onward, had been the attempt to repeal limitations on the exercise of reason to dominate nature and society, this process culminated with modern science and technology only in the nineteenth century.[21] From this time onward the use of science to discover and test laws of nature and society was viewed as the only route to objective knowledge. This highly developed form of instrumental reason meant that science came to be regarded as the only legitimate *means* for the production of knowledge. Thereafter, questions about *ends* were gradually set aside as nonrational or arbitrary expressions of personal interests or partisan political values which, by definition, lay outside the bounds of scientific inquiry. It was in the nineteenth century that the production of specialized knowledge was established as "science."

THE TWENTIETH CENTURY

In his 1910 presidential address to the American Political Science Association, the holder of the Chair in the Science of Government at Harvard University, A. Lawrence Lowell, called on his colleagues to adopt a more empirical and practical approach to the study of politics. Lowell brought to the study of politics that same mixture of empiricism, quantification, and policy-relevance which had guided the founders of the Manchester Society in the 1830s. Speaking to professional political scientists Lowell warned:

> We are apt to err in regard to the things to be observed. We are inclined to regard the library as the laboratory of political science, the storehouse of original sources, the collation of ultimate material. . . . But for the most purposes books are no more the original sources for the physiology of politics than they are for geology or astronomy. The main laboratory for the actual working of political institutions is not a library, but the outside world of public life. It is there that phenomena must be sought. It is there that they must be observed at first hand. It is by studying them there that the greatest contributions to the sciences must be expected.[22]

The Professionalization of Social Science

A striking feature of the twentieth century, as compared with the nineteenth, is the professionalization of political science, public administration, sociology, economics, and related social science disciplines. Twentieth-century producers of policy-relevant knowledge were no longer the heterogeneous group of bankers, industrialists, journalists, and scholars who guided the early statistical societies and other institutions for policy research. They were, rather, university professors who specialized in teaching and research and were increasingly called upon by governments to provide practical ad-

---

[21] See Max Horkheimer, *Eclipse of Reason* (New York: Oxford University Press, 1947); and William Leiss, *The Domination of Nature* (New York: George Braziller, 1972).
[22] A. Lawrence Lowell, "The Physiology of Politics," *The American Political Science Review*, 4 (February 1910), 7.

vice on policy-making and government administration. In background, experience, and motivation they were members of social science professions.[23]

Professional social scientists, like their nineteenth-century predecessors, exerted important influences on the practice of public policy-making. Social scientists played an active role in the administration of Woodrow Wilson, particularly during World War I. Later, under the Republican administration of Herbert Hoover, two major social surveys, *Recent Economic Trends* and *Recent Social Trends*, were carried out by social scientists. The greatest influx of social scientists into government came, however, with Franklin Roosevelt's New Deal. The various agencies established during the New Deal (National Recovery Administration, Work Projects Administration, Public Works Administration, Securities and Exchange Commission, Federal Housing Administration) were staffed by large numbers of social scientists.

The primary function of social scientists in this period was to investigate policy problems and broad sets of potential solutions, and not, as in later periods, the testing of policy alternatives by constructing policy models or conducting social experiments. The Roosevelt administration's National Planning Board (later the National Resources Planning Board), a majority of whose members were professional social scientists, provides a good illustration of the general approach to policy questions that was characteristic of the 1930s. The board was conceived as "a general staff gathering and analyzing facts, observing the interrelation and administration of broad policies, proposing from time to time alternative lines of national procedure, based on thorough inquiry and mature consideration."[24] This same general orientation was also present among economists working for the Department of Agriculture, political scientists involved in the reorganization of the executive branch, and anthropologists conducting studies for the Bureau of Indian Affairs. Social scientists also contributed to methodological innovations, as, for example, when the Department of Agriculture assumed leadership in developing the sample survey as a new research tool and instrument of government policy.[25]

The events of World War II and problems of postwar readjustment provided social scientists with opportunities to demonstrate their value in resolving practical problems. Interwar accomplishments in the area of survey research had laid a foundation for the use of interviews by the Office

---

[23] For histories of policy professions, see Bernard Crick, *The American Science of Politics: Its Origins and Conditions* (Berkeley and Los Angeles: University of California Press, 1959); Arthur Somit and James Tannenhaus, *The Development of Political Science* (Boston: Allyn and Bacon, 1967); and John Madge, *The Origins of Scientific Sociology* (New York: The Free Press, 1962).

[24] Quoted in Gene Lyons, *The Uneasy Partnership: Social Science and the Federal Government in the Twentieth Century* (New York: Russell Sage Foundation, 1969), p. 65.

[25] Harry Alpert, "The Growth of Social Research in the United States," in *The Human Meaning of the Social Sciences*, ed. Daniel Lerner (Cleveland, OH: World Publishing Co., 1959), pp. 79–80.

of War Information, the War Production Board, and the Office of Price Administration. Military and civilian agencies relied on social scientists to illuminate problems of national security, social welfare, and defense. Policy research in the war years was addressed to many important problems:[26] soldier orientation and morale; development of psychiatric screening devices; venereal disease control; personal adjustment and combat performance of troops; responses of soldiers to mass communications; evaluation of Japanese morale; estimation of war production requirements; regulation of prices and rationing. In addition, policy-relevant information was produced by the Office of War Information, the Foreign Broadcast Intelligence Service, the Library of Congress, the Department of Justice, and the Office of Strategic Services. The activities of these agencies were continued after the war by the Office of Naval Research, the Department of the Air Force, and, later, by the Research and Development Board of the Department of Defense. Special research institutes were also established by the federal government, including the Operations Research Office of The Johns Hopkins University and the Human Resources Research Office at George Washington University.

Among the many contributions to policy research produced in this period, three warrant special mention. Gunnar Mydral's *An American Dilemma* (1944) made a basic contribution to the study of race relations in the United States and elsewhere, while *The Authoritarian Personality* (1950), prepared by Theodore Adorno and his collaborators, exerted a decisive influence on the study of prejudice for many years to come. *The American Soldier*, a four-volume study reported in 1949 and 1950, was produced by many of the most competent social researchers in the country. Under the general direction of sociologist Samuel Stouffer, this large-scale research project was originally commissioned by the Director of the Army Morale Division in 1941. The project is significant, not only because of its enormity, but also because it illustrates an emerging pattern of extensive governmental support for applied research. Equally important, the project was initiated by policymakers who were involved in day-to-day decisions:

> This aspect of the research was truly innovative, because it was clearly a case where policymakers—commanding officers throughout the world—turned to the social researcher, even if only as a last resort. They wanted not only facts but also inferences and conclusions, as a basis for making decisions about the everyday life of millions of men in uniform.[27]

This project contributed in significant ways to the development and refinement of a variety of quantitative techniques which are now widely used by researchers in all the social science disciplines.

---

[26] Ibid., p. 80.
[27] Howard E. Freeman and Clarence C. Sherwood, *Social Research and Social Policy* (Englewood Cliffs, NJ: Prentice Hall, 1970), 25.

The Policy Sciences Movement

In the years following World War II one of the first systematic efforts to develop a special policy orientation within social science disciplines was *The Policy Sciences: Recent Developments in Scope and Method* (1951), edited by political scientists Daniel Lerner and Harold D. Lasswell.[28] The "policy sciences," as Lasswell observed in his introduction, were not confined to theoretical aims of science but also had a fundamentally practical orientation. Moreover, the purpose of the policy sciences was not simply to contribute to the making of more efficient decisions, but also to provide knowledge "needed to improve the practice of democracy. In a word, the special emphasis is upon the policy sciences of democracy, in which the ultimate goal is the realization of human dignity in theory and fact."[29]

Here we find the older emphasis on science as a means to human progress, but also a clear commitment to particular human values: democracy and human dignity. While some observers have branded this dual emphasis on science and values as a contradiction in terms,[30] it may also be regarded as an attempt to reintroduce ethical and moral discourse into applied social sciences. Rather than assume that social science is the handmaiden of human progress, as philosophers and scientists had generally done since the turn of the nineteenth century, it was necessary to specify the values which defined "progress." In this respect, the early work on the policy sciences bears some striking similarities to earlier efforts to outline the foundations of a critical social science.[31] The aim was not merely to predict through scientific research what *must* happen, but to contribute to the establishment of conditions for the gratification of human existence.[32]

As a programmatic orientation within the social sciences the policy sciences were not wholly unprecedented. For example, early contributions by the German sociologists Max Weber (1864–1920) and Karl Mannheim (1893–1947) might well be regarded as foundational studies in the policy sciences, although they were not titled as such. Mannheim's *Ideology and Utopia: An Introduction to the Sociology of Knowledge* (1929) and *Man and*

---

[28] Brunner points out that the first published statement of the policy sciences is Harold D. Lasswell and Abraham Kaplan, *Power and Society: A Framework for Political Inquiry* (New Haven, CT: Yale University Press, 1950). Lasswell developed a statement on the policy sciences as early as 1943 in a memorandum. See Ronald D. Brunner, "The Policy Movement as a Policy Problem," in *Advances in Policy Studies since 1950*, Vol. 10 of *Policy Studies Annual Review*, ed. William N. Dunn and Rita Mae Kelly (New Brunswick, NJ: Transaction Books, 1991), p. 189, note 2.

[29] Harold D. Lasswell, "The Policy Orientation," in *The Policy Sciences: Recent Developments in Scope and Method*, ed. Daniel Lerner and Harold D. Lasswell (Stanford, CA: Stanford University Press, 1951), p. 15.

[30] Crick, *The American Science of Politics*, pp. 192–93.

[31] See Martin Jay, *The Dialectical Imagination: A History of the Frankfurt Institut for Social Research, 1919–1939* (Boston: Little, Brown and Co., 1973).

[32] See Max Horkheimer, *Critical Theory* (New York: Herder and Herder, 1972).

Society in an Age of Reconstruction (1940) were chiefly concerned with the social organization, determinants, and consequences of knowledge, including forms of specialized knowledge produced for planners and policy-makers. Weber's methodological works also contributed to the analysis of public policy. Contrary to much scholarly opinion, Weber did not conceive of social science as a value-free enterprise and was himself engaged in a number of controversial policy research projects in the 1890s, as a member of the German Association for Social Policy.[33] Weber did insist, nevertheless, on a rigorous distinction between empirical knowledge and value judgments, precisely because so much of the scholarly work of his day contained value judgments masquerading as value-free science.[34]

Weber, in an article titled " 'Objectivity' of Knowledge in Social Science and Social Policy" (1904), offered a critique of economics which is as appropriate today as it was in his own time.[35] Economics, observed Weber, cannot and should not pretend to derive value judgments from a specifically "economic" point of view, since the ideals and norms which underlie such practical activities as economic policy-making can never be derived from empirical science. Yet it was not Weber's aim to create a gulf between social science and social policy, the latter of which inevitably involved value judgments; it was rather to show the various ways that empirical science can help to clarify value questions.[36] Social science, in Weber's view, can help make clear that every action, and also every inaction, implies the acceptance of certain values and the rejection of others. Social science can also assist in the clarification of the meaning attached to action by interpreting the ends of social life. Finally, science can assess the internal consistency of value judgments, laying bare the axioms or ultimate principles from which they are derived. Yet this marked the limits of empirical science: "An empirical science cannot tell anyone what he *ought* to do, but rather what he *can* do, and under certain circumstances what he wishes to do."[37]

In a subsequent article on "The Meaning of Ethical Neutrality" (1917) Weber disavowed any connection between his work and "relativism," that is, the doctrine that no value is demonstrably superior to any other. Here he set forth scientific procedures intended to contribute to the understanding of value questions:[38]

---

[33] Vernon K. Dibble, "Political Judgments and the Perception of Social Relationships: An Analysis of Some Applied Social Research in Late 19th-Century Germany," in *Varieties of Political Expression in Sociology* (Chicago: University of Chicago Press, 1972), pp. 158–59.

[34] Arnold Brecht, *Political Theory: The Foundations of Twentieth-Century Political Thought* (Princeton, NJ: Princeton University Press, 1959), pp. 221–31.

[35] See Edward A. Shils and Henry A. Finch, eds., *Max Weber on the Methodology of the Social Sciences* (Glencoe, IL: The Free Press, 1949); and Brecht, *Political Theory*, pp. 221–27.

[36] Brecht, *Political Theory*, p. 225.

[37] Quoted in Brecht, ibid., p. 225.

[38] See Shils and Finch, *Max Weber on the Methodology of the Social Sciences*; and Brecht, *Political Theory*, pp. 227–29.

1. The elaboration of ultimate value axioms, from which evaluations are derived, and the examination of the internal consistency of these axioms or ultimate principles.
2. The deduction of the implications for other value judgments of given axioms.
3. The examination of the factual consequences that result from the adoption of value judgments because certain means are indispensable for their realization, or undesirable consequences ("by-products") necessarily follow their realization.
4. The discovery of conflicts among value judgments that had not previously been taken into account.

More than a few contemporary contributors to policy analysis have recommended the use of essentially the same procedures.[39]

The development of the policy sciences in the postwar era thus owes much to such early methodological contributors as Weber and Mannheim. Yet the systematic study of public policy also grew out of public administration, then a field within political science. In the interwar period, programs with an emphasis on public policy were established in major universities, notably Harvard's Graduate School of Public Administration, which was established in 1937. In the late 1940s an interuniversity committee was established to develop public policy curricular materials, a major product of which was Harold Stein's *Public Administration and Policy Development: A Case-Book* (1952). The interuniversity committee, composed of teachers and practitioners of public administration, speaks for the close relationship between policy analysis and public administration before and after World War II.[40]

Growth of an "Analycentric" Perspective

The greatest impetus for the development of policy analysis in the years after World War II did not come, however, from the activities of social scientists. Rather the growth of policy analysis occurred largely as a result of the activities of engineers, operations researchers, systems analysts, and applied mathematicians who had received their formal training outside the social sciences. World War II had prompted the involvement of specialists whose orientation toward policy problems was frequently analytical, in the narrow sense of that term. The idea of "analysis" came to be associated with efforts to separate or decompose problems into their fundamental components; for example, decomposing problems of national defense into mutually exclusive alternatives (nuclear warheads, manned bombers, conventional ground troops) whose consequences for the attainment of given objectives might be predicted. Insofar as analysis in this narrow "analycentric" sense[41]

---

[39] See, for example, MacRae, *The Social Function of Social Science*, pp. 77–106.

[40] See Frederickson and Wise, *Public Administration and Public Policy*.

[41] Allen Schick, "Beyond Analysis," *Public Administration Review*, 37, No. 3 (1977), 258–63.

precludes or restricts one's concern with political, social, and administrative aspects of public policy—for example, concerns with the political feasibility of alternatives or their implications for the maintenance of democratic processes—then policy analysis in its new form might well be regarded as a movement *away* from traditions established in the nineteenth century and carried forward in the twentieth. If, however, this new orientation toward policy analysis simply added to traditional concerns rigorous procedures for testing alternatives, then recent changes may be regarded as a consistent and potentially useful supplement to established traditions.[42]

Whatever the verdict on this particular issue, there is no doubt that there was a shift in the aims of policy analysis after World War II. This shift is represented in part by the growing influence of such nongovernmental organizations as the Rand Corporation, which has done a great deal to foster the spread of systems analysis and related techniques in government and the academic community.[43] The development of program–planning–budgeting systems (PPBS) was in large measure due to the efforts of operations researchers and economists working under the direction of Charles Hitch at the Rand Corporation in the 1950s. Hitch and his colleagues wanted to find out "how the country could 'purchase' national security in the most efficient manner—how much of the national wealth should be devoted to defense, how the funds allocated to defense should be distributed among different military functions, and how to assure the most effective use of these funds."[44] Although PPBS was introduced into the Department of Defense in 1965 and was later mandated for use in all federal agencies, after 1971 it became discretionary and soon fell into disuse in most agencies. Despite mixed conclusions about its success as a tool for policy analysis, PPBS seems nevertheless to have diffused among government practitioners and much of the academic community systematic procedures for rigorously testing policy alternatives.[45]

In the postwar period the shift toward an "analycentric" perspective was partly counterbalanced by the rapid growth of private foundations whose mission was to support research in the social sciences and humanities. Approximately 70 percent of all such foundations, which numbered some 5500 in 1969, were established after 1950.[46] During the same period, the

---

[42] See Martin Greenberger, Matthew A. Crenson, and Brian L. Crissey, *Models in the Policy Process: Public Decision Making in the Computer Era* (New York: Russell Sage Foundation, 1976), pp. 23–46.

[43] See Bruce L. R. Smith, *The Rand Corporation: A Case Study of a Nonprofit Advisory Corporation* (Cambridge, MA: Harvard University Press, 1966).

[44] Greenberger, Crenson, and Crissey, *Models in the Policy Process*, p. 32.

[45] See, for example, Alice Rivlin, *Systematic Thinking for Social Action* (Washington, DC: The Brookings Institution, 1971); and Walter Williams, *Social Policy Research and Analysis: The Experience in the Federal Social Agencies* (New York: American Elsevier Publishing Co., 1971).

[46] Irving Louis Horowitz and James E. Katz, *Social Science and Public Policy in the United States* (New York: Praeger Publishers, 1975), p. 17.

federal government began to set aside funds for applied and policy-related research in the social sciences, although the natural sciences continued to receive a lion's share of total government research support. In 1972, the social sciences received approximately 5 percent of all available federal research funds. In the period 1980–1989, funding for applied and basic research in the social sciences fell by approximately 40 percent in constant dollars.[47]

By the mid-1970s Lasswell's earlier call for a policy orientation within the social sciences had been very largely institutionalized. Each of the social science disciplines have established special organizations expressly committed to applied and policy-related research, including the Policy Studies Organization (Political Science), the Society for the Study of Social Problems (Sociology), and the Society for the Psychological Study of Social Issues (Psychology).

In the 1980s the process of institutionalization was carried one step further by the creation of multidisciplinary professional associations such as the Association for Public Policy and Management (Economics and Political Science) and the Society for Socio-Economics (Sociology and Economics). Both associations held regular annual research conferences and one established a journal of record, the *Journal of Policy Analysis and Management*, which merged two journals created earlier (*Public Policy* and *Policy Analysis*). The new journal added range and depth to the mainstream policy journals established in the late 1970s and early 1980s, including *Policy Sciences*, the *Policy Studies Journal*, and *Policy Studies Review*. In addition to these journals were several hundred others that focused on health, welfare, education, criminal justice, science and technology, and other policy issue areas.[48]

In the 1970s new graduate programs and degrees in policy analysis were established in major universities, partly through financial support provided by the Ford Foundation's Program in Public Policy and Social Organization. Most major research universities have policy centers or institutes that are listed in the *Encyclopedia of Associations* along with several thousand nonuniversity policy research organizations, the majority of which were established after 1950. In Washington and most state capitals "policy analyst" became an official job description, while special units devoted to policy analysis have been established throughout the federal government, in most states, and in many larger municipalities. Special policy analysis units have been developed by such bodies as the National Governor's Association and the National League of Cities. Policy analysis is one of the established knowledge industries in late twentieth-century America.

---

[47] National Science Foundation, *Federal Funds for Research, Development, and Other Scientific Activities* (Washington, DC: NSF, 1973); and National Science Board, *Science and Engineering Indicators—1989* (Washington, DC: NSB, 1989).

[48] Michael Marien, the editor of *Future Survey Annual*, estimates the number of policy journals to exceed 400. See Marien, "The Scope of Policy Studies: Reclaiming Lasswell's Lost Vision," in Dunn and Kelly, *Advances in Policy Studies Since 1950*, pp. 445–88.

TOWARD POSTINDUSTRIAL SOCIETY

The main contrast between the nineteenth and twentieth centuries does not lie so much in the methods used to produce policy-relevant knowledge. For some two hundred years there has been a more or less steady growth in the use of empirical and analytic methods to produce information of potential worth to policymakers, together with marked improvements in techniques for the collection, aggregation, and summarization of empirical data. Indeed, many contemporary research institutes would do well to reach the standards of methodological excellence already present at the time Quetelet, Le Play, and Mayhew carried out their various projects. The main cutting point between the two centuries is, therefore, social and not methodological. It is to be found in the social organization and practical uses to which knowledge is put in the twentieth century.

Institutionalization of Policy Advice

The rapid expansion of policy research in the nineteenth century occurred in a social context that was a great deal more diffuse than the specialized networks for producing, criticizing, and distributing knowledge that developed in the twentieth century. Early statistical societies and research institutes, for example, typically included members with no direct ties to scientific disciplines and little sense of professional identity. Moreover, producers of policy research were far fewer in numbers, and the scope of advice to policymakers was comparatively limited by present-day standards. The professionalization of policy research did not become evident on a large scale until the twentieth century.

Even with the growth and professionalization of science in the first half of the twentieth century, the direct involvement of scientists in policy-making was largely a response to social, economic, and political crises.[49] Thus, scientists and other professionals were ad hoc and irregular participants in government throughout the years of social dislocation, economic depression, and war which extended from 1930 to the late 1940s. Only in succeeding years did members of scientific disciplines and other professions—social work, public administration, planning, and policy analysis itself—assume institutionalized roles within government and the academic community. For the first time governments recruited on a regular basis specialists who had received their training and had been certified by the respective disciplines. For many observers this profound change in the social organization and uses of science signified a new era of the "knowledge society," a society in which public policy-making and societal guidance were

---

[49] See Rowland Egger, "The Period of Crises: 1933 to 1945," in *American Public Administration: Past, Present, Future*, ed. Frederick C. Mosher (University, AL: University of Alabama Press, 1975), pp. 49–96.

critically dependent on specialized knowledge and technologies created and applied by members of the various professions.[50]

Policy Analysis in Postindustrial Society

One way to visualize the historical development of policy analysis is to consider the evolution of specialized knowledge as part of a movement toward "postindustrial society," that is, a society which is increasingly dominated by an educated professional-technical class.[51] Postindustrial society, which is an extension of patterns of policy-making and social organization of industrial society, may be characterized in terms that are of direct relevance for assessing the historical evolution and significance of policy analysis:[52]

1. *Centrality of theoretical knowledge.* Although the earliest civilizations (for example, Mesopotamia) relied on specialized knowledge, only in the late twentieth century are innovations in "soft" (social) and "hard" (materials) technologies directly dependent on the codification of theoretical knowledge provided by the social, physical, and biological sciences.

2. *Creation of new intellectual technologies.* The improvement in mathematical and econometric techniques has made it possible to use modeling, simulation, and various forms of systems analysis (for example, PPBS) to find more efficient and "rational" solutions to public problems.

3. *Spread of a knowledge class.* The most rapidly expanding group in the United States is composed of technicians and professionals. This group, including professional managers, represented 25 percent of a labor force of 8 million persons in 1975 and, by the year 2000, may well be the largest group in society.

4. *Change from goods to services.* In 1975 more than 65 percent of the active labor force was engaged in the production and delivery of services, a figure that exceeded 70 percent by 1990. Services are primarily human (for example, health, education, social welfare) and professional-technical (for example, research, evaluation, systems analysis, computer programming).

5. *Instrumentalization of sciences.* Although the natural and social sciences have been used for several hundred years as instruments for the control of the human and material environment, they have been essentially open to internal criticism and protected by norms of objectivity, neutrality, and disinterestedness. In the present period science has become increasingly bureaucratized, subordinated to government goals, and assessed in terms of its instrumental payoffs to society.

6. *Production and use of information.* Information is increasingly becoming one of society's most scarce resources. Information is a collective, not a private good, and cooperative rather than competitive strategies for its production and use are required if optimal results are to be achieved.

---

[50] Fritz Machlup, *The Production and Distribution of Knowledge in the United States* (Princeton, NJ: Princeton University Press, 1962).

[51] Daniel Bell, *The Coming of Post-industrial Society: A Venture in Social Forecasting* (New York: Basic Books, 1976).

[52] Bell, *The Coming of Post-industrial Society*, pp. xvi-xviii.

The development of policy analysis in the latter half of this century, when viewed in light of its nineteenth-century background, seems to lend support to the idea of an emerging "postindustrial" society. Yet what do these historical changes mean? How much influence do producers of policy-relevant knowledge have in present-day society? Although theoretical knowledge is undoubtedly more central than it has been in other historical periods, what does this mean for the distribution of political power? Does the proliferation of new intellectual technologies mean also that the structure of policy-making has changed? Is the spread of a "knowledge class" commensurate with its power and influence? If policy analysis is the production of knowledge for practical purposes, whose purposes are being served? In short, how are we to interpret the historical transformation of policy analysis from its earliest beginnings to the present-day "knowledge society?"

Technocratic Guidance vs. Technocratic Counsel

There are two contending perspectives on these questions.[53] One perspective, dominant among proponents of PPBS and other systems technologies, holds that the professionalization of policy analysis has meant a shift in power from policymakers to policy analysts.[54] This perspective, *technocratic guidance*, is closely associated with an analycentric bias which holds that "the surest way to improve the quality of public choice is to have more analysts producing more analyses."[55] By contrast a contending perspective, *technocratic counsel*, holds that the professionalization of policy analysis and related activities signifies new and more effective ways to enhance the power of policymakers and other dominant groups whose social positions continue to rest on wealth and privilege.[56]

Strictly speaking, neither of these perspectives is wholly accurate in its interpretation of events surrounding the movement toward postindustrial society; each contains a one-sided emphasis on particular characteristics of contemporary society to the exclusion of others. Yet just as the development of nineteenth-century policy analysis was a practical response to problems of the day as viewed by dominant groups, so too is contemporary policy analysis a consequence of changes in the structure and role of government as it has attempted to grapple with new problems. "The contemporary boom in policy analysis," observes Allen Schick, "has its primary source in the huge growth of American governments, not in the intellectual development

---

[53] See Jeffrey D. Straussman, "Technocratic Counsel and Societal Guidance," in *Politics and the Future of Industrial Society*, ed. Leon N. Lindberg (New York: David McKay Co., 1976), pp. 126–66.

[54] See, for example, Amitai Etzioni, *The Active Society* (New York: The Free Press, 1968).

[55] Schick, "Beyond Analysis," p. 259.

[56] See, for example, Guy Benveniste, *The Politics of Expertise* (Berkeley, CA: Glendessary Press, 1972).

of the social sciences."[57] Throughout the twentieth century major expansions of government activity were followed by demands for more policy-relevant information. As government has grown, so too has the market for policy analysis.[58]

The development of policy analysis in this century has followed fits and starts in the growth of federal executive agencies.[59] In 1900 there were some 90 federal executive agencies. By 1940 this total had grown to 196 and, by 1973, the total number of federal executive agencies had jumped to 394. The greatest percentage increase occurred after 1960 in the era of the postindustrial society; of some 394 agencies in existence in 1973, roughly 35 percent were created after 1960. The rapid growth of the federal government was mainly a response to new problems in areas of national defense, transportation, housing, health, education, welfare, and crime. In this same period many commentators on postindustrial society identified a number of new "challenges" to policy-making:[60] participation overload; mobilization of service sector workers; transformation of basic social values; realignment of interest groups; growing cleavages between urban and suburban citizens; and recurrent fiscal crises. Some observers, notably policy scientist Yehezkel Dror, went so far as to formulate the relationship between such problems and policy analysis in the form of "laws": "While the difficulties and dangers of problems tend to increase at a geometric rate, the number of persons qualified to deal with these problems tends to increase at an arithmetic rate."[61]

The growth of policy analysis is a consequence, not a cause, of changes in the structure of government and the nature and scope of social problems. According to the *technocratic guidance* perspective policy-relevant knowledge is an increasingly scarce resource whose possession inevitably enhances the power and influence of policy analysts. The technocratic guidance perspective may be summarized in terms of five major propositions:[62]

1. The growing interdependencies, complexity, and pace of change of contemporary society make existing knowledge obsolete, thus increasing the demand for new forms of policy-relevant knowledge.

---

[57] Schick, "Beyond Analysis," p. 258.

[58] Some argue that a new "scientific state" is replacing the former "administrative state." See Jurgen Schmandt and James E. Katz, "The Scientific State: A Theory with Hypotheses," *Science, Technology, and Human Values*, 11 (1986), 40–50.

[59] Herbert Kaufman, *Are Government Organizations Immortal?* (Washington, DC: The Brookings Institution, 1976), pp. 34–63.

[60] See Andrea L. Weber, "Policy Analysis in the Post-Industrial Society," paper presented at the 1975 Annual Meeting of the Western Political Science Association, Seattle, Washington, March 21, 1975; Samuel P. Huntington, "Postindustrial Politics: How Benign Will It Be?" *Comparative Politics*, VI (January 1974), 163–92; Ronald Inglehart, "The Silent Revolution in Europe: Intergenerational Change in Post-industrial Societies," *The American Political Science Review*, 65 (December 1971), 991–1017; and James O'Connor, *The Fiscal Crisis of the State* (New York: St. Martin's Press, 1973).

[61] Dror, *Ventures in Policy Sciences*, p. 2.

[62] See Straussman, "Technocratic Counsel . . .," pp. 150–51.

2. The problems of contemporary society may be resolved with specialized knowledge produced by professional policy analysts.

3. The technical complexity of policy choices prompts higher levels of direct involvement of professional policy analysts.

4. Higher levels of direct involvement of professional policy analysts enhance their power to make and influence key policy decisions.

5. The growing dependence of politicians on professional policy analysts erodes their political power.

A contending perspective, that of *technocratic counsel*, begins from the assumption that professional policy analysts operate in settings in which policymakers, as the consumers of specialized knowledge, determine to a large extent the activities of producers. In this context the primary role of policy analysts is to legitimize—that is, justify in scientific and technical terms—policy decisions made by the real holders of power. The technocratic counsel perspective may also be summarized in terms of several key propositions.[63]

1. Major policy alternatives reflect conflicting values held by different segments of the community.

2. Value conflicts are associated with disparities of political power in the political system.

3. The choice of a given policy alternative symbolizes the victory of one segment of the community over another.

4. Policymakers use scientific and technical justifications produced by policy analysts to suppress conflicts and legitimize choices after they have been made on political grounds.

5. The effective use of scientific and technical justification requires the maintenance of an image of policy analysis as a set of value neutral, impartial, and apolitical techniques.

6. Professional policy analysts, as the source of scientific and technical justifications, are expendable and therefore serve as convenient scapegoats for policies which fail.

An Assessment

The recent history of policy analysis suggests that parts of both perspectives may be used to characterize the activities of policy analysts. In some cases policy analysts have exercised a large measure of "technocratic guidance." For example, the New York City–Rand Corporation's analysis of factors influencing the response time of city firefighters to reported fires has been credited with unusual success, even though other Rand efforts have been less effective in shaping decisions.[64] On the other hand, the utilization of specialized knowledge to make policy choices appears to be highly uneven. For example, in a study of 204 top federal policymakers

---

[63] Ibid., pp. 151–52.
[64] See Greenberger, Crenson, and Crissey, *Models in the Policy Process*, pp. 231–318.

conducted in 1973–1974, analyses which actually provided a basis for choosing among policy alternatives were ranked least in importance.[65] Moreover, levels of utilization depend on essentially *nontechnical* factors: "the level of knowledge utilization is not so much the result of a slow flow of relevant and valid knowledge from knowledge producers to policymakers, but is due more to factors involving values, ideology, and decision-making styles."[66] In short, there is little to support the technocratic guidance perspective in this and other empirical studies of the use of policy analysis to make key policy choices.[67]

The finding that policy analysis is used for political purposes adds a measure of credibility to the technocratic counsel perspective, as does the prevalent conservative character of many analyses. Policy analysis, for example, has been characterized as a conservative and superficial kind of social science which fails to pose radical questions about basic social values and institutions and neglects policy alternatives that depart significantly from existing practices.[68] Moreover, some observers see in policy analysis an ideology in disguise which suppresses ethical and value questions in the name of science.[69] Under such conditions it is understandable that professional policy analysts may be used as instruments of everyday politics. At the same time it is not altogether clear that policy analysis actually provides a "scientific" justification of policy choices made by the real holders of power, since a large number of analyses have departed significantly from accepted canons of scientific method.[70] Finally, there are questions as to whether policy analysis is capable of legitimizing policy choices in an era when the social value attached to science and technology may be waning.[71]

In conclusion, there are reasons to believe that the technocratic guid-

---

[65] Nathan Caplan and others, *The Use of Social Science Knowledge in Policy Decisions at the National Level* (Ann Arbor, MI: Institute for Social Research, Center for Research on the Utilization of Scientific Knowledge, 1975).

[66] Nathan Caplan, "Factors Associated with Knowledge Use among Federal Executives," *Policy Studies Journal*, 4, No. 3 (1976), 233.

[67] See, for example, Robert F. Rich, *Social Science Information and Public Policy Making* (San Francisco: Jossey-Bass, 1981); and David J. Webber, "The Production and Use of Knowledge in the Policy Process," in Dunn and Kelly, *Advances in Policy Studies Since 1950*.

[68] Charles E. Lindblom, "Integration of Economics and the Other Social Sciences through Policy Analysis," in *Integration of the Social Sciences through Policy Analysis*, ed. James C. Charlesworth (Philadelphia: The American Academy of Political and Social Sciences, 1972), p. 1.

[69] See Laurence H. Tribe, "Policy Science: Analysis or Ideology?" *Philosophy and Public Affairs*, 2, No. 1 (1972), pp. 66–110.

[70] Ilene N. Bernstein and Howard E. Freeman, *Academic and Entrepreneurial Research: The Consequences of Diversity in Federal Evaluation Studies* (New York: Russell Sage Foundation, 1975).

[71] See, for example, L. Vaughn Blankenship, "Public Administration and the Challenge to Reason," in *Public Administration in a Time of Turbulence*, ed. Dwight Waldo (San Francisco: Chandler Publishing Co., 1971), pp. 188–213. But compare Jurgen Habermas, *Toward a Rational Society: Student Protest, Science and Politics* (Boston: Beacon Press, 1970), and Aaron Wildavsky, *Speaking Truth to Power: The Art and Craft of Policy Analysis* (Boston: Little, Brown, 1979).

ance perspective represents an exaggerated assessment of the power and influence of professional policy analysts. Yet the technocratic counsel perspective contains its own one-sided emphasis. Whereas the technocratic guidance perspective overestimates the influence of policy analysis in shaping political choices, the technocratic counsel perspective perhaps exaggerates the symbolic importance of policy analysts in legitimizing policy decisions made on political grounds. Whatever verdict is eventually rendered on these two perspectives, one fact seems clear: The professionalization and growth of policy analysis in the years since World War II reflects fundamental changes in the nature of contemporary society and its problems, changes which have prompted new forms of specialized knowledge. Yet the remedy for poorly executed or inappropriately used policy analysis is not to abandon efforts to produce policy-relevant knowledge, but to create new and better procedures for producing information that may be used to improve public policies. The history of policy analysis demonstrates that these tasks are not simply scientific or intellectual ones; they are fundamentally practical in nature. Throughout history and up to the present day, policy analysis has grown out of political processes that reflect the conflicting values of different segments of the community as they have attempted to pursue alternative visions of social improvement.

SUMMARY

This chapter has presented a broad and selective survey of major landmarks in the evolution of applied social sciences. Its main purpose has been to create greater awareness of the origins and variability of the methodology, methods, and techniques of policy analysis, subjects to which we shall return in later chapters. At this point you should be able to discuss the following generalizations:

1. Policy analysis, in its widest sense, involves the production of knowledge of and in policy processes. Early attempts at legal codification (for example, the Code of Hammurabi), the activities of princely advisors in the Middle Ages (for example, the clergy), the work of nineteenth-century statisticians (for example, Adolphe Quetelet), and contemporary applications of systems analysis (for example, PPBS) fit this broad definition of policy analysis.

2. Historically, the aim of policy analysis has been to provide policy makers with information that could be used to exercise reasoned judgment in finding solutions for policy problems. Thus, policy analysis has a fundamentally practical orientation that makes it similar in most respects to applied social science.

3. The methodology, methods, and techniques of policy analysis have changed markedly throughout history. Yet policy analysis became explicitly empirical and quantitative only in the period following the Industrial Revolution. While twentieth-century policy analysis continued traditions established a century before, the past fifty years have seen the increasing professionalization of policy analysis and its institutionalization in government. In the period after World War II an "analycentric" perspective came to dominate policy analysis.

4. The evolution of policy analysis has generally followed changes in societies. One of the first major changes in societies was the growth of fixed urban settlements in Mesopotamia and, later, in India, China, and Greece. In the medieval period urban civilization became more complex, with an attendant differentiation and specialization of policy-analysis roles, particularly in areas of finance, war, and law. A major transformation in the production of policy-relevant knowledge occurred in the aftermath of the Industrial Revolution and Enlightenment, both of which followed the growth of political stability amidst social turmoil. In the twentieth century policy analysis grew, first, in response to economic dislocation and war, and then as a reaction to the dramatic growth of governments. After World War II we see the emergence of a "postindustrial" society in which an educated technical-professional class has attained a position of prominence unknown in previous periods.

5. There are at least two major ways to explain the historical evolution of policy analysis from earliest times to the present day. According to one perspective (technocratic guidance) policy-relevant knowledge is an increasingly scarce resource whose possession inevitably enhances the power and influence of professional policy analysts. A contending perspective (technocratic counsel) holds that the primary role of policy analysts is to legitimize policy decisions made by the real holders of power. Each perspective helps in some way to explain historical changes, but both tend to exaggerate the power and influence of policy analysts, for different reasons. Whereas the technocratic guidance perspective overestimates the influence of analysts in shaping key policy choices, the technocratic counsel perspective miscalculates the symbolic importance of analysts in legitimizing policy decisions made on political grounds.

6. Whatever verdict is finally rendered on this controversy, it is clear that the nature of contemporary society and its problems have changed dramatically. Efforts to develop new and better procedures for the production of information that will contribute to a resolution of public problems are not simply scientific or intellectual tasks but are fundamentally political in nature. Policy analysis is embedded in political processes that reflect conflicting values of different segments of the community as they have pursued their own visions of social improvement.

GLOSSARY

Analycentric Perspective: A perspective according to which the meaning of "analysis" is implicitly restricted to the decomposition of a problem into its component parts, which are assigned numerical values (utilities and probabilities) for purposes of comparing, evaluating, and prescribing solutions for problems. This restricted perspective tends to preempt other approaches to policy analysis, including those based on complex-adaptive systems thinking, multiple perspectives, informed judgment, intuition, ethics, and argumentation and public discourse.

Critical Social Science: An orientation toward the social sciences which, originated by Theodore Adorno, Max Horkheimer, Jurgen Habermas, and other leading members of the pre–World War II Frankfurt Schule in Germany, contends that knowledge claims should be examined from standpoints that are hermeneutic (What does a claim mean to particular persons?), technical (What forms of social control result from beliefs that science and technology are value free and universally valid?), and critical (What beliefs must be critically examined, challenged, and rejected in order to extend human freedom?). Critical social science, sometimes simply called critical theory, resembles in many respects the orientation of the policy sciences as developed by Harold Lasswell.

Empirical Policy Research: Originating at the outset of the nineteenth century in the work of demographers, statisticians, and survey researchers, empirical and quantitative policy research was directed toward problems of unemployment, urban squalor, disease, and political control. Empirical policy research, as contrasted with older traditions of philosophical speculation, mysticism, superstition, and religious authority, relies primarily (not exclusively) on observations based on sense experience to justify knowledge claims.

Instrumental Reason (Rationality):   A world view according to which science is regarded as the only means for creating authentic knowledge. In the nineteenth century questions about the ends that might justify policies were gradually taken for granted, or set aside as arbitrary, incorrigible, and therefore nonrational expressions of values, which were seen to lie outside the bounds of legitimate scientific inquiry.

Policy Analysis: In its widest historical sense, policy analysis as an approach to social problem solving began at that point in history when knowledge was consciously cultivated so as to permit the explicit and reflective examination of potentialities for linking knowledge and action.

Policy Sciences: The policy sciences, a term and an orientation toward the social sciences originated by Harold D. Lasswell and colleagues before and immediately after World War II, are problem oriented, contextual, multidisciplinary, and explicitly normative. The policy sciences are designed to address fundamental and frequently neglected problems arising in the adjustment of citizens and policymakers to societal changes and the continuous transformation of politics and policies to serve democratic ends.

Political Control: The thesis that empirical, quantitative, and policy-oriented research (and, later, policy analysis) was a consequence, not a cause, of political consolidation and political control established in the eighteenth century.

Postindustrial Society: A society dominated by an educated technical-professional class. Postindustrial societies have several major characteristics: centrality of theoretical knowledge; creation of new intellectual technologies; spread of a knowledge class; change from goods to services; instrumentalization of science; and production and use of information as a scarce resource. The postindustrial society is an extension of industrial society and is a development of the past twenty years.

Symbol Specialists: Educated persons in every historical period who engaged in the production of specialized knowledge that could be used by policymakers to exercise reasoned judgment in seeking solutions for policy problems. Symbol specialists include the clergy and literati in the Middle Ages, but also statisticians and systems analysts in later periods.

Technocratic Counsel: A perspective which holds that the primary role of policy analysts is to legitimize policy decisions made by the real holders of power, whose social position continues to be determined by power, wealth, and privilege.

Technocratic Guidance: A perspective of the historical evolution of policy analysis, particularly since the advent of the "postindustrial" society, which holds that policy-relevant knowledge is an increasingly scarce resource whose possession enhances the power and influence of professional policy analysts.

STUDY SUGGESTIONS

1. Policy analysis was described in this chapter and in Chapter 1 as the process of producing knowledge *of* and *in* the policy-making process. Considering the three dimensions of knowledge use presented in Chapter 1, what problems arise when attempts are made to get policy analysis "in" the policy-making process?

2. Returning again to Chapter 1, what do you think is likely to happen if policy analysts use "critical multiplism" when their clients are policymakers who expect analysis to legitimize their positions by creating an image of "scientific" decision making?

3. One view of organizations is that they are "organized anarchies" or "garbage

cans" which discover preferences through action rather than take action on the basis of preexisting preferences. Organizations, according to this view, are "a collection of choices looking for problems, issues and feelings looking for decision situations in which they might be aired, solutions looking for issues to which they might be the answer, and decision makers looking for work" [Michael Cohen, James March, and Johan Olsen, "A Garbage Can Model of Organizational Choice," *Administrative Science Quarterly* 17 (March 1972), p. 2]. Indicate several ways that policy analysis might improve such organizations. Explain your answer.

4. Carol Weiss and others (see Suggested Readings for Chapter 1) have contrasted several explanations (models) of the ways that policy-relevant knowledge affects policy-making: (a) a *knowledge-driven* model claims that new knowledge has a strong effect on policy decisions, (b) a *decision-driven* model claims that the need for knowledge relevant to policy decisions strongly affects the creation of new knowledge, and (c) a *social interaction* model claims that there is continuous interaction between multiple sources of knowledge and multiple decision makers. How do these three models help evaluate the relative merits of the "technocratic guidance" and "technocratic counsel" perspectives?

5. The growth of policy analysis has been viewed as a response to practical problems and crises. Considering the current situation in this and other countries, would you expect further growth? Decline? Justify your answer.

6. Is the idea of a postindustrial society a valid and useful one? Justify your response.

7. Policy analysis has been described as a four-stage process of analysis, development, communication, and utilization (Chapter 1). This process seems to assume a process of means–end reasoning ("instrumental reason") where the end justifies the means. If policy analysis is the means, what is the end? Explain your response. [*Note:* This question requires a definition of the purpose of policy analysis.]

SUGGESTED READINGS

DE LEON, PETER, *Advice and Consent: The Development of the Policy Sciences.* New York: Russell Sage Foundation, 1988.

FREIDSON, ELLIOT, *Professional Powers: A Study of the Institutionalization of Formal Knowledge.* Chicago: University of Chicago Press, 1986.

LERNER, DANIEL, ed., *The Human Meaning of the Social Sciences.* Cleveland, OH: World Publishing Company, 1959.

MACHLUP, FRITZ, *Knowledge: Its Creation, Distribution, and Economic Significance,* Vol. 1, *Knowledge and Knowledge Production.* Princeton, NJ: Princeton University Press, 1980.

RAVETZ, JEROME, *Science and Its Social Problems.* Oxford: Oxford University Press, 1971.

SCHMANDT, JURGEN and JAMES E. KATZ, "The Scientific State: A Theory with Hypotheses," *Science, Technology, and Human Values,* 11 (1986), 40–50.

3

A Framework
for Policy Analysis

Even the dogs may eat of the crumbs which fall from the rich man's table; and in these days, when the rich in knowledge eat such specialized food at such specialized tables, only the dogs have a chance of a balanced diet.

— Sir Geoffrey Vickers, *The Art of Judgment: A Study of Policy Making* (1965)

THE MEANING OF POLICY ANALYSIS

A description of policy analysis offered by the late E. S. Quade, former head of the Mathematics Department at the Rand Corporation, provides a convenient point of departure for defining policy analysis. Policy analysis is

any type of analysis that generates and presents information in such a way as to improve the basis for policy-makers to exercise their judgment. . . . In policy analysis, the word analysis is used in its most general sense; it implies the use of intuition and judgment and encompasses not only the examination of policy by decomposition into its components but also the design and synthesis of new alternatives. The activities involved may range from research to illuminate or provide insight into an anticipated issue or problem to evaluation of a completed program. Some policy analyses are informal, involving nothing more than hard and careful thinking whereas others require extensive data gathering and elaborate calculation employing sophisticated mathematical processes.[1]

This characterization, emphasizing multiple methods of inquiry, helps outline the several meanings of "analysis." If policy analysis may involve

---

[1] E. S. Quade, *Analysis for Public Decisions* (New York: American Elsevier Publishing Co., 1975), p. 4.

any type of analysis, what are these types? How may different types of analysis contribute to improved judgment among policymakers? On what basis can we distinguish among intuition, decomposition, and synthesis? Do these methods exhaust the range of possible alternatives open to the policy analyst? In short, what are the specific methodological features of policy analysis?

Policy Analysis: A Definition

The broad conception of policy analysis presented in Chapter 2 accentuates the practical character of policy analysis as a response to recurrent problems and crises facing governments. In this chapter we narrow this broad conception by offering a more concrete definition of policy analysis and its characteristics as an applied social science discipline.

For these reasons policy analysis is not confined to the development and testing of general descriptive theories, for example, political and sociological theories of policy-making elites or economic theories of the determinants of public expenditures. Policy analysis goes beyond traditional disciplinary concerns with the explanation of empirical regularities by seeking not only to combine and transform the substance and methods of several disciplines, but also to produce policy-relevant information that may be utilized to resolve problems in specific political settings. Moreover, the aims of policy analysis extend beyond the production of "facts"; policy analysts seek also to produce information about values and preferable courses of action. Policy analysis therefore includes policy evaluation as well as policy recommendation.

An Applied Social Science Discipline

Policy analysis draws from a variety of disciplines and professions whose aims are descriptive, evaluative, and prescriptive. As an applied discipline policy analysis borrows not only from the social and behavioral sciences, but also from public administration, law, philosophy, ethics, and various branches of systems analysis and applied mathematics.[2] The policy analyst may therefore be expected to produce information and plausible arguments about three kinds of questions: (1) *values* whose attainment is the main test of whether a problem has been resolved, (2) *facts* whose presence may limit or enhance the attainment of values, and (3) *actions* whose adoption may result in the attainment of values.

In producing information and plausible arguments about these three types of questions, the analyst may employ one or more of three approaches to analysis: empirical, valuative, and normative (Table 3–1). The empirical approach is concerned primarily with describing the causes and effects of given public policies. Here the primary question is factual (Does something

---

[2] The classic discussion of policy analysis as an applied discipline is Duncan MacRae, Jr., *The Social Functions of Social Science*, (New Haven, CT: Yale University Press, 1976), pp. 277–307.

TABLE 3-1   Three Approaches to Policy Analysis

APPROACH	PRIMARY QUESTION	TYPE OF INFORMATION
Empirical	Does it and will it exist? (*facts*)	Descriptive and predictive
Valuative	Of what worth is it? (*values*)	Valuative
Normative	What should be done? (*action*)	Prescriptive

exist?) and the type of information produced is descriptive in character. The analyst, for example, may describe, explain, or predict public expenditures for health, education, or roads.[3] By contrast, the valuative approach is mainly concerned with determining the worth or value of some policy. Here the question is one of value (Of what worth is it?) and the type of information produced is valuative in character. For example, after providing descriptive information about various kinds of taxation policies, the analyst may evaluate different ways of distributing tax burdens according to their ethical and moral consequences.[4] Finally, the normative approach is concerned with recommending future courses of action that may resolve public problems. In this case the question is one of action (What should be done?) and the type of information produced is prescriptive. For example, a policy of guaranteed minimum annual incomes may be recommended as a way to resolve problems of poverty.

To the degree that policy analysis includes these three aims it includes but goes beyond the aims of traditional social science disciplines. These disciplines have so far tended to avoid valuative and normative approaches, in part because of deep-seated beliefs in the desirability of separating values and facts in science. This belief in the separability of facts and values has sometimes contributed to misunderstandings about the methodology and aims of policy analysis. Prescriptions or recommendations are identified with policy advocacy, which is often viewed as a way to make emotional appeals and ideological pronouncements or to engage in political activism, rather than as a way to produce policy-relevant information and plausible arguments about possible solutions for public problems.

This mistaken view of policy advocacy as a nonrational process is closely related to value relativism, that is, the belief that values are purely subjective and relative to the person who holds them. Value relativism leads to the position that values can neither be debated rationally nor studied with the methods of science.[5] The belief that values have no rational content

---

[3] See, for example, Thomas Dye, *Policy Analysis: What Governments Do, Why They Do It, and What Difference It Makes* (University, AL: The University of Alabama Press, 1976).

[4] See, for example, Peter G. Brown, "Ethics and Policy Research," *Policy Analysis*, 2 (1976), 325–40.

[5] Value statements and value judgments, observes Abraham Kaplan, "are relative but nevertheless objective . . . [they] affirm something whose truth does not depend on the state of mind which evoked the affirmation." See Abraham Kaplan, *The Conduct of Inquiry: Methodology for Behavioral Science* (San Francisco: Chandler Publishing Company, 1964), p. 392. Kaplan calls this position "objective relativism," as distinguished from its subjective counterpart.

is related to the tendency to confuse prescriptive statements with unconditional imperatives, commands, pronouncements, or emotional appeals of various kinds (the original Latin meaning of "to prescribe" refers to acts of directing, ordering, or commanding in accordance with authority). Yet the act of recommending what people *should do* is not the same as telling or exhorting them *to do* it; it is rather "purporting to give them sound solutions to their practical problems."[6]

Finally, the belief in the desirability of separating facts and values in scientific inquiry has also reinforced the view that analysis in the valuative and prescriptive modes runs counter to the development of science. Progress in the development of policy analysis is seen to stand in the same relation to the social and behavioral sciences as that of engineering to the physical sciences. The difficulty with this position is that progress in the disciplines has often been a consequence of applied research, rather than its cause:

> The argument goes that applied research is radically different from basic scientific work and therefore detracts talent and resources from true progress in the discipline. This implies a false comparison with the natural sciences. It is true that technical engineers could not succeed without the knowledge provided by abstract research in mathematics and laboratory experiments of the "pure" sciences. But it is misleading to draw an analogy between the natural and social sciences. Nowhere in the social realm are there unconditional laws and basic theories already well established. Quite to the contrary, it is the study of concrete and circumscribed practical problem-areas that has contributed a good part of the present-day general sociological knowledge.[7]

Multiple Methods of Inquiry

The production of policy-relevant information, whether descriptive, valuative, or prescriptive in character, takes place by employing definite analytical procedures.[8] These procedures differ not only in terms of the kinds of questions for which they are appropriate, but also in terms of their temporal relation to action. Thus, prediction and prescription typically come into use *before* an action has been adopted (*ex ante*), whereas description and evaluation are normally employed *after* an action has occurred (*ex post*). Prediction and prescription deal with the future, while description and evaluation are concerned with the past.[9]

In policy analysis, as we saw in Chapter 1, these general analytical

---

[6] Kurt Baier, "What Is Value? An Analysis of the Concept," in *Values and the Future: The Impact of Technological Change on American Values*, ed. Kurt Baier and Nicholas Rescher (New York: The Free Press, 1969), p. 53.

[7] Paul F. Lazarsfeld and Jeffrey Reitz, *An Introduction to Applied Sociology* (New York: American Elsevier Publishing Co., 1975), p. 10. See also footnote 2.

[8] For a useful discussion of inquiry as a decision-making process, see John O'Shaughnessy, *Inquiry and Decision* (London: George Allen & Unwin, Ltd., 1972).

[9] For similar distinctions, see William D. Coplin, *Introduction to the Analysis of Public Policy from a Problem-Solving Perspective* (New York: Learning Resources in International Studies, 1975); and Charles O. Jones, "Why Congress Can't Do Policy Analysis (or words to that effect)," *Policy Analysis*, 2, No. 2 (1976), 251–64.

procedures have been given special names: (1) *monitoring* (description) permits us to produce information about the past causes and consequences of policies, (2) *forecasting* (prediction) enables us to produce information about the future consequences of policies, (3) *evaluation* (evaluation) involves the production of information about the value or worth of past and future policies, and (4) *recommendation* (prescription) permits us to produce information about the likelihood that future courses of action will result in valued consequences. In addition to these four procedures there is one that cannot be directly translated from those so far discussed. This procedure is (5) *problem structuring.* To do any kind of analysis, one must first be aware of the existence of a problem. *Problem structuring* is that phase in the process of inquiry where the analyst, confronted with information about the consequences of some policy, experiences a "troubled, perplexed, trying situation, where the difficulty is, as it were, spread throughout the entire situation, infecting it as a whole."[10]

To analyze a policy, one must first have some sense of a policy problem and its possible solutions. Problems seldom emerge fully defined; rather, they are structured in different ways as the analyst continuously analyzes and reanalyzes them. Problem structuring, which affects the use and assessment of the other four procedures, is really a *metamethod* (method of methods) that functions as central regulator of the overall process of policy analysis.

One of the important characteristics of policy-analytic procedures is their hierarchical relationship—it is not possible to use some methods without first having used others. Thus, it is possible to monitor policies without forecasting their consequences; but it is seldom possible to forecast policies without first monitoring them.[11] Similarly, the analyst can monitor policies without evaluating them, but it is not possible to evaluate a policy without first having monitored it. Finally, to recommend a policy normally requires that the analyst has already engaged in monitoring, forecasting, and evaluation.[12] This is another way of saying that all policy recommendations are based on factual as well as value premises.

Policy Argumentation

Policy analysis does not stop with the use of multiple methods to produce and transform information. Although information production and

---

[10] John Dewey, *How We Think* (Boston: D.C. Heath and Company, 1933), p. 108.

[11] The explanation of policies is not a necessary condition for forecasting them. For example, it is not necessary to understand the causal factors underlying variations in expenditure patterns to forecast their increase in the future. In a strict sense, however, prediction requires causal knowledge, whereas a "rational forecast" does not.

[12] The exception to the rule again involves monitoring. In making a policy recommendation, causation may be assumed, but not understood. Recipes are among the kinds of recommendations that claim only that a desired result is a consequence of a recommended action. See Joseph L. Bower, "Descriptive Decision Theory from the 'Administrative' Viewpoint," in *The Study of Policy Formation*, ed. Raymond A. Bauer and Kenneth J. Gergen (New York: The Free Press, 1968), p. 105.

transformation are essential to policy analysis, equally important are the creation and critical assessment of knowledge claims based on this information.[13] Knowledge claims, advanced as the conclusions of policy arguments, reflect the reasons why different stakeholders disagree about alternative policies.

Policy arguments, the main vehicle for conducting debates about public policy issues, have six elements (Figure 3–1).[14]

1. *Policy-relevant information.* Policy-relevant information (*I*) produced by multiple methods constitutes the evidence at an analyst's disposal. Information about policy problems, policy futures, policy actions, policy outcomes, and policy performance may be provided in various forms. For example, the outcomes of government energy policy might be expressed in the form of a statistical generalization ("Results of federal demonstration projects show that nuclear power plants are more efficient than conventional power plants"); as the conclusions of experts ("The panel of experts report that nuclear energy is the most practical and efficient form of energy now available"); or as an expressed value or need ("The construction of more nuclear power plants is needed to ensure continued economic growth"). However expressed, policy-relevant information is the point of departure in all policy arguments.

2. *Policy claim.* A policy claim (*C*) is the conclusion of a policy argument. Policy claims—for example, the claim that the government should invest in the construction of more nuclear power plants—are typically the subject of disagreement or conflict among different segments of the community. When a policy claim follows the presentation of information, the claim implies "therefore." For example, if nuclear energy is more efficient (*I*) it follows (therefore) that the government should invest in the construction of more nuclear power plants (*C*). Hence, policy claims are the logical consequence of policy-relevant information.

3. *Warrant.* A warrant (*W*) is an assumption in a policy argument which permits the analyst to move from policy-relevant information to policy claim. A warrant may contain assumptions of several kinds: authoritative, intuitive, analycentric, causal, pragmatic, and value critical (see Chapter 4). For example, a pragmatic warrant for the claim that the government should invest in the construction of more nuclear power plants might be expressed simply as "More energy is needed." The role of the warrant is to carry policy-relevant information to a policy claim about which there is disagreement or conflict, thus providing a *reason* for accepting the claim.

4. *Backing.* The backing (*B*) for a warrant consists of additional assumptions or

---

[13] On policy argumentation see, for example, Charles W. Anderson, "Political Philosophy, Practical Reason, and Policy Analysis," pp. 22–42 in *Confronting Values in Policy Analysis*, ed. Frank Fischer and John Forester (Beverly Hills, CA: Sage Publications, 1987); William N. Dunn, "Policy Reforms as Arguments," in *The Argumentative Turn in Policy Analysis and Planning*, ed. John Forester and Frank Fischer (Durham, NC: Duke University Press, 1993): 293–326; Donald T. Campbell, "Experiments as Arguments," *Knowledge: Creation, Diffusion, Utilization* 3 (1982): 327–47; and Duncan MacRae, Jr., "Professional Knowledge for Policy Discourse: Argumentation versus Reasoned Selection of Proposals," *Knowledge in Society: The International Journal of Knowledge Transfer* 1 (3) (1988): 6–24. See also Chapter 4.
[14] These six elements are based on Stephen Toulmin, *The Uses of Argument* (Cambridge: Cambridge University Press, 1958).

FIGURE 3–1   Elements of a policy argument.

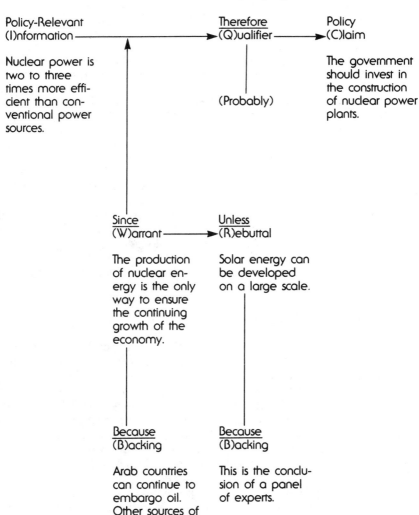

arguments that may be used to support warrants which are not accepted at face value. The backing for warrants may also take various forms, including scientific laws, appeals to the authority of experts, or ethical and moral principles. The backing for warrants allows the analyst to go one step further backward and state underlying assumptions.

5. *Rebuttal.* A rebuttal (R) is a second conclusion, assumption, or argument that states the conditions under which an original claim is unacceptable, or under which it may be accepted only with qualifications. Taken together, policy

claims and rebuttals form the substance of policy issues, that is, disagreements among different segments of the community about alternative courses of government action. The consideration of rebuttals helps the analyst anticipate objections and serves as a systematic means for criticizing one's own claims, assumptions, and arguments.

6. *Qualifier.* A qualifier (*Q*) expresses the degree to which the analyst is certain about a policy claim. In policy analysis, qualifiers are often expressed in the language of probability ("probably," "very likely," "at the 0.01 level of confidence"). When the analyst is completely certain about a claim—that is, when conclusions are wholly deterministic in nature and contain no error—no qualifier is necessary.

The structure of policy arguments illustrates how analysts may use information to recommend solutions for policy problems. The relations among the six elements of a policy argument also demonstrate how policy-relevant information may be interpreted in different ways, depending on the frame of reference, ideology, or worldview of different groups. Policy arguments enable us to go beyond the mere production of information and transform it into plausibly true beliefs (knowledge). Accordingly, analysts may employ multiple methods in a way that is open to challenges, is self-critical, and is directed toward the resolution of problems rather than the justification of favored policy alternatives.

Types of Policy-Relevant Information

Any effort to recommend a course of action depends in part on how well we are able to describe policy problems. To recommend a solution to problems of crime, for example, depends partly on our ability to identify factors presumed to be its causes (unemployment, poverty, inadequate law enforcement). Yet recommendation also depends on whether we have identified the right values to pursue, which means that policy analysis is based as much on the production of ethical as empirical knowledge. For example, not everyone agrees that government should invest resources in crime control activities, since some groups believe that values of social justice should take precedence over those of security. Indeed, many hold that failures to achieve social justice are the source of present-day problems of crime.

The importance of ethical knowledge in policy analysis has perhaps been best described by a former undersecretary in the Department of Housing and Urban Development: "Our problem is not to do what is right. Our problem is to know what is right."[15] Knowledge of what is (*facts*), what is right (*values*), and what to do (*action*) requires the production of five types of information. Policy analysis uses multiple methods of inquiry to produce information about policy problems, policy futures, policy actions, policy outcomes, and policy performance.

A *policy problem* is an unrealized value, need, or opportunity for im-

---

[15] Robert C. Wood, "Foreward" to *The Study of Policy Formation,* p. v. Mr. Wood is here quoting President Lyndon Johnson.

provement which, however identified, may be attained through public action.[16] Knowledge of what problem to solve requires information about a problem's antecedent conditions (for example, school dropouts as an antecedent condition of unemployment), as well as information about values (for example, better schools or full employment) whose attainment may lead to a problem's solution. The provision of information about policy problems is the most critical task of policy analysis, since the way a problem is defined governs our ability to search out and identify appropriate solutions. Inadequate or faulty information at this stage of analysis may result in a fatal error: solving the wrong formulation of a problem when instead one should have solved the right one.[17]

A *policy future* is a consequence of a course of action that may contribute to the attainment of values and, hence, the resolution of a policy problem. Information about the conditions that gave rise to a problem is essential to the identification of policy futures. Yet such information is usually insufficient; the past may not repeat itself, and values themselves change over time. For these reasons the analyst must be concerned with producing information about futures that are not "given" by the existing situation. To produce such information requires creativity, insight, and what many have called "intuition," "judgment," or "tacit knowledge."[18]

A *policy action* is a move or series of moves guided by a policy alternative that is designed to achieve valued future outcomes.[19] In order to recommend a policy action, it is necessary to have information about the positive and negative consequences of acting on different alternatives, including information about the political, legal, and economic constraints on action. Yet it is also essential to know which alternative courses of action are preferable on evaluative grounds, which requires information about which policy alternatives are valued and why. Hence, information about policy actions is produced by forecasting and evaluating the expected consequences of actions. In short, policy recommendation presupposes forecasting and evaluation.

A *policy outcome* is an observed consequence of policy actions. The consequences of policy actions cannot be fully stated or known in advance of action; nor are all observed consequences of action intended or anticipated. Policy analysis therefore produces information about policy actions both before and after they have occurred. In other words, information about

---

[16] Compare Charles O. Jones, *An Introduction to the Study of Public Policy*, 2nd ed. (North Scituate, MA: Duxbury Press, 1977), p. 15; and David Dery, *Problem Definition in Policy Analysis* (Lawrence, KS: University of Kansas Press, 1984).

[17] See Ian I. Mitroff and Thomas R. Featheringham, "On Systematic Problem Solving and the Error of the Third Kind," *Behavioral Sciences*, 19, No. 6 (1974), 383–93.

[18] See, for example, Yehezkel Dror, *Venture in Policy Sciences: Concepts and Applications* (New York: American Elsevier Publishing Co., 1971); Sir Geoffrey Vickers, *The Art of Judgment: A Study of Policy Making* (New York: Basic Books, 1965); and C. West Churchman, *The Design of Inquiring Systems: Basic Concepts of Systems and Organization* (New York: Basic Books, 1971).

[19] Compare James F. Reynolds, "Policy Science: A Conceptual and Methodological Analysis," *Policy Sciences*, 6 (1975), 7.

the consequences of alternative courses of action is produced *ex ante* as well as *ex post*.

Policy performance is the degree to which a given policy outcome contributes to the attainment of values. In reality, policy problems are seldom "solved"; they are most often resolved, reformulated, or even "unsolved."[20] Yet to know whether a problem has been solved, resolved, or unsolved not only requires information about policy outcomes; it is also essential to know whether these outcomes have contributed to the attainment of values that originally gave rise to a problem. Information about policy performance may be used to forecast policy futures or to restructure policy problems.

Policy Systems

Policy analysts are but one among many different types of actors in a policy system. A *policy system*, or the overall institutional pattern within which policies are made, involves interrelationships among three elements: public policies, policy stakeholders, and policy environments (Figure 3–2). *Public policies*, which are long series of more or less related choices (including decisions not to act) made by governmental bodies and officials,[21] are formulated in *issue areas* which range from defense, energy, and health to education, welfare, and crime. In any one of these areas there are many different policy issues, that is, actual or potential courses of government action that involve conflicts among different segments of the community. A given policy issue is usually the result of conflicting definitions of a policy problem. For example, most segments of society view crime as a policy issue; yet crime as a problem involving unattained values of law, order, and security may be defined as a social problem, an economic problem, an educational problem, or a problem of individual motivation. In reality, crime is all of these problems and more.

The definition of a policy problem depends on the pattern of involvement of particular *policy stakeholders*, that is, individuals or groups which have a stake in policies because they affect and are affected by governmental decisions. Policy stakeholders—for example, citizens' groups, labor unions, political parties, government agencies, elected leaders, and policy analysts themselves—often respond in markedly different ways to the same information about a policy environment. A *policy environment*, which is the specific context in which events surrounding a policy issue occur, influences and is in turn influenced by policy stakeholders and public policies. Hence, policy systems contain processes which are *dialectical* in nature, meaning that objective and subjective dimensions of policy-making are inseparable in practice. Policy systems are subjective human products created by the conscious choices of policy stakeholders; policy systems are an objective

---

[20] Russell A. Ackoff, "Beyond Problem Solving," *General Systems*, XIX (1974), 237–39.

[21] Richard Rose, ed., *The Dynamics of Public Policy: A Comparative Analysis* (London and Beverly Hills: Sage Publications, 1976), pp. 9–10. On decisions not to act see Peter Bachrach and Morton S. Baratz, "Decisions and Non-decisions: An Analytic Framework," *The American Political Science Review*, 57 (1963), 632–42.

FIGURE 3–2   Three elements of a policy system.

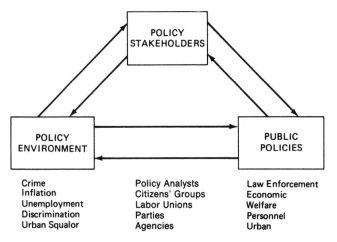

POLICY ENVIRONMENT	POLICY STAKEHOLDERS	PUBLIC POLICIES
Crime	Policy Analysts	Law Enforcement
Inflation	Citizens' Groups	Economic
Unemployment	Labor Unions	Welfare
Discrimination	Parties	Personnel
Urban Squalor	Agencies	Urban

Source: Adapted from Thomas R. Dye, *Understanding Public Policy,*
3rd ed. (Englewood Cliffs, NJ: Prentice Hall, 1978), p. 9.

reality manifested in observable actions and their consequences; policy stakeholders are products of policy systems.[22] Policy analysts, no less than other policy actors, are both creators and products of policy systems.[23]

POLICY ANALYSIS: AN INTEGRATED FRAMEWORK

Policy analysis may be viewed as a process of inquiry that involves five *policy-informational components* that are transformed into one another by using five *policy-analytic procedures,* as illustrated by the framework presented in Figure 3–3.[24] This framework provides a summary of the ideas discussed so far in this chapter and serves as a preview of the contents of Part II, where in each chapter we examine in detail all information components and the methods used to produce and transform them. The use of policy-analytic procedures (problem structuring, forecasting, monitoring, evaluation, rec-

---

[22] Compare Peter L. Berger and Thomas Luckmann, *The Social Construction of Reality: A Treatise in the Sociology of Knowledge* (New York: Doubleday Books, 1967): "Society is a human product. Society is an objective reality. Man is a social product" (p. 6).

[23] This dialectical assumption about policy processes is consistent with the caution that "the term policy needs to be able to embrace both what is intended and what occurs as the result of the intention. . . ." See Hugh H. Heclo, "Review Article: Policy Analysis," *British Journal of Political Science,* 2 (January 1972), 84–85; and Jones, *An Introduction to the Study of Public Policy,* p. 4.

[24] The structure of this framework was suggested by Walter Wallace, *The Logic of Science in Sociology* (Chicago: Aldine Books, 1971). The framework has undergone several transformations since the first edition of this book.

FIGURE 3–3   Problem-centered policy analysis.

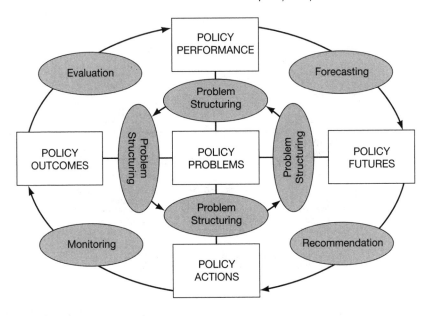

ommendation) permits the analyst to transform one type of information into another. Information and procedures are interdependent; they are linked in a dynamic process of *policy-informational transformations.* Hence, policy-informational components (policy problems, policy futures, policy actions, policy outcomes, policy performance) are transformed one into the other by the use of policy-analytic procedures. The entire process is regulated by problem structuring, which is situated at the center of the framework.

An Illustration from Criminal Justice

Relationships among the five policy-informational components and five policy-analytic methods may be illustrated by considering how a policy analyst in the Law Enforcement Assistance Administration (LEAA) might employ information provided by the Federal Bureau of Investigation. The FBI publishes statistics in the form of *Uniform Crime Reports,* an annual compilation providing information on the number of serious offenses known to federal, state, and local authorities per 100,000 population. Information contained in these reports (Table 3–2) may be used to monitor crime control policies, to evaluate their outcomes, to structure policy problems, to forecast policy futures, and to recommend courses of action to resolve problems of crime.

Information about increases in various categories of crime may be used to monitor the outcomes of federal, state, and local crime control policies.

TABLE 3–2   Reported Offenses Known to the Police (per 100,000 Population)

CATEGORY	YEAR				
	1970	1975	1980	1985	1989
Murder and nonnegligent manslaughter	7.9	9.6	10.6	7.9	8.7
Forcible rape	18.7	26.3	36.8	36.7	38.1
Robbery	172	218	251	209	233
Aggravated assault	165	227	299	303	383
Burglary	1085	1526	1684	1287	1276
Larceny theft	2079	2805	3167	2901	3171
Auto theft	457	469	502	462	630
Total	3985	5282	5950	5207	5740

Source: Federal Bureau of Investigation, Uniform Crime Reports.

This information about policy outcomes may then be transformed into new information about policy performance which tells us the extent to which a given policy has achieved its goals. Information about reported increases in crime, when combined with additional information about policies implemented in the same period—for example, information about the passage of new and more aggressive crime control legislation, or about increases in the unemployment rate—may also be used to structure policy problems. Thus, increased crime may be defined as a problem stemming from the ineffective enforcement of existing legislation or as an economic problem that cannot be resolved without also alleviating problems of unemployment. Through problem structuring, which occurs continually in the process of policy analysis, the analyst may generate new types of information.

Information about crime as a policy problem (and often there are many different and conflicting formulations of the "same" problem) may be used as a basis for forecasting changes in crime rates in the future. For example, assuming that there are no changes in existing policies—that is, that policies remain the same—crime rates may simply be projected into the future on the basis of information about past trends. By contrast, if we assume that existing legislation will be more effectively implemented, then we might forecast a reduction in crime rates over time. Similarly, if crime is formulated as an economic problem we may forecast that an expected upswing in employment will contribute to falling crime rates in future periods. In any one of these cases, forecasting permits the analyst to transform information about policy problems into information about sets of policy alternatives that may contribute in some way to the resolution of the problem of crime. By comparing these alternatives and assessing their probable results in terms of given values, for example, the value of reducing crime by a certain amount per year, the analyst may make recommendations about courses of action that may contribute to the resolution of the problem of crime. Finally, problem structuring may be used to identify unanticipated policy outcomes or to redefine standards of policy performance.

Reconstructed Logic vs. Logic-in-Use

The process of policy analysis illustrated in Figure 3–3 is designed for *methodological* purposes, that is, for studying the strengths and weaknesses of different methods and techniques of policy analysis. As such, Figure 3–3 is a *logical reconstruction* of the process of policy analysis; the actual process of doing policy analysis may or may not conform to this logical reconstruction, which is an abstraction from many concrete descriptions of the practices of policy analysts.[25] The *logic-in-use* of practicing analysts, as distinguished from this logical reconstruction, may reflect variations that stem both from personal characteristics of analysts and the institutional settings in which they work.

Among the factors that influence variations in the logic-in-use of analysts are:

1. *Cognitive styles.* The cognitive styles—relatively stable personal dispositions toward different modes of thinking—affect the practice of policy analysis.[26]
2. *Analytic roles.* Policy analysts perform roles as "entrepreneurs," "politicians," and "technicians."[27]
3. *Institutional incentive systems.* Different orientations toward analysis—the "humanistic-value-critical" and the "scientific"—have been found in a cross section of policy research institutes.[28] Mechanisms for institutional quality control also differ, affecting the validity or plausibility of conclusions and recommendations.[29]
4. *Institutional time constraints.* Analysts working under tight time constraints—for example, a limit of three to seven days to prepare a policy paper for a legislator—proceed through the process of analysis much faster than university-based analysts who have few time constraints. The two groups also use different methods and data sources.[30]
5. *Professional socialization.* Different disciplines socialize members into more traditional "basic" orientations toward policy analysis, while others socialize members into a more "applied" orientation that involves providing advice or recommendations.[31]

---

[25] On reconstructed logic versus logic-in-use, see Kaplan, *The Conduct of Inquiry*, pp. 3–11.

[26] Studies using the Myers–Briggs type indicator (Jungian personality types) suggest distinct cognitive styles among scientists. For a summary, see Ian I. Mitroff and Ralph H. Kilmann, *Methodological Approaches to Social Science* (San Francisco: Jossey-Bass, 1978).

[27] See Arnold Meltsner, *Policy Analysts in the Bureaucracy* (Berkeley, CA: University of California Press, 1976).

[28] See Pamela Doty, "Values in Policy Research," in *Values, Ethics, and the Practice of Policy Analysis*, ed. William N. Dunn (Lexington, MA: D.C. Heath, 1983).

[29] See, for example, Donald T. Campbell, "Guidelines for Monitoring the Scientific Competence of Preventive Intervention Research Centers: An Exercise in the Sociology of Scientific Validity," *Knowledge: Creation, Diffusion, Utilization*, 8, No. 3 (1987), 389–430.

[30] See P. J. Cook and J. W. Vaupel, "What Policy Analysts Do: Three Research Styles," *Journal of Policy Analysis and Management*, 4, No. 3 (1985), 427–28.

[31] See, for example, J. A. Schneider, N. J. Stevens, and L. G. Tornatzky, "Policy Research and Analysis: An Empirical Profile, 1975–1980," *Policy Sciences* 15 (1982), 99–14; and

The process of policy analysis may also diverge from Figure 3-3 in another way. Although the central direction of the outer ring of methods conforms to a series of clockwise transformations, the process of analysis may also involve forward and backward movement between methods and informational components on the outer ring. The inner ring of problem structuring methods moves in a counterclockwise direction, since it is typical that policy analysts return to restructure the problem many times in the course of an analysis. For example, analysts may move back and forth between problem structuring and informational components; analysts may also restructure the problem many times by moving counterclockwise, correcting errors in the process. In any case, problem structuring is the center of the process of policy analysis.

Our awareness of discrepancies between the reconstructed logic and logic-in-use of policy analysis should not raise serious doubts about the suitability of Figure 3-3 as a methodological guide, any more than our knowledge of differences in writing styles should cast doubt on the suitability of a dictionary as one among several guides to the use of language. The reason for noting such discrepancies is to point to inevitable discrepancies between any reconstructed logic and logic-in-use, while at the same time showing how methodology may be a powerful aid in studying, criticizing, and developing particular methods and techniques. In the last analysis, however, solutions to public policy problems do not depend solely on methodological self-awareness but also on the creativity of the analyst. Policy-analytic methods are no panacea, and there is no assurance that the practice of policy analysis will not become routinized, rigid, and sterile.

FORMS OF POLICY ANALYSIS

Prospective Policy Analysis

The relationship between policy-informational components and policy-analytic methods (Figure 3-4) provides a basis for distinguishing three major forms of policy analysis: prospective, retrospective, and integrated analysis. Prospective policy analysis, which involves the production and transformation of information *before* policy actions are initiated and implemented, tends to characterize the operating styles of economists, systems analysts, and operations researchers. Prospective policy analysis is perhaps best illustrated by the description of policy analysis provided by Walter Williams, former chief of the Research and Plans Division of the Office of Economic Opportunity. Policy *analysis*, observes Williams, "is a means of synthesizing information to draw from it policy alternatives and preferences stated in comparable, predicted quantitative and qualitative terms as a basis or guide for policy decisions; conceptually it does not include the *gathering* of information." Policy *research*, by contrast, refers to "all studies using

---

David M. Hedge and Jin W. Mok, "The Nature of Policy Studies: A Content Analysis of Policy Journal Articles," *Policy Studies Journal*, 16, No. 1 (1987), 49–62.

FIGURE 3–4   Forms of policy analysis.

RETROSPECTIVE (Ex Post):   PROSPECTIVE (Ex Ante):
What happened and what   What will happen and what
difference does it make?   should be done?

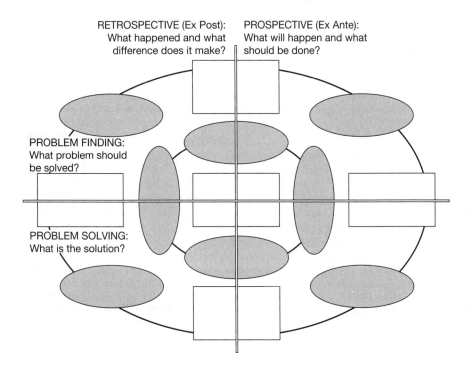

PROBLEM FINDING:
What problem should
be solved?

PROBLEM SOLVING:
What is the solution?

scientific methodologies to describe phenomena and/or determine relation-ships among them."[32]

Prospective analysis often creates large gaps between preferred solu-tions to problems and the efforts of governments to resolve them.[33] Thus, for example, political scientist Graham Allison estimates that perhaps no more than 10 percent of the work required to achieve a desired set of policy outcomes is carried out *before* policy actions are initiated:

> It is not that we have too many good analytic solutions to problems. It is, rather, that we have more good solutions than we have appropriate ac-tions. . . . This perspective suggests that the central questions of policy anal-ysis are quite different from the kinds of questions analysts have traditionally asked.[34]

[32] Walter Williams, *Social Policy Research and Analysis: The Experience in the Federal Social Agencies* (New York: American Elsevier Publishing Co., 1971), p. 13.

[33] See Allen Schick, "Beyond Analysis," *Public Administration Review*, 37, No. 3 (1977), 262.

[34] Graham T. Allison, *Essence of Decision: Explaining the Cuban Missile Crisis* (Boston: Little, Brown and Company, 1971), pp. 267–68.

Retrospective Policy Analysis

Retrospective policy analysis conforms in major respects to the description of policy *research* offered earlier. Retrospective analysis, which is confined to the production and transformation of information *after* policy actions have been taken, typifies the operating styles of three major groups of analysts:

1. *Discipline-oriented analysts.* This group, comprised largely of political scientists and sociologists, seeks primarily to develop and test discipline-based theories and describe the causes and consequences of policies. This group seldom attempts to identify specific goals and objectives of policymakers and makes no effort to distinguish "policy variables which are subject to policy manipulation, and situational variables which are not."[35] For example, the analysis of the effects of party competition on levels of government expenditures provides no information about specific goals and objectives of policymakers; nor is party competition a manipulable variable that policymakers may use to produce changes in expenditures.

2. *Problem-oriented analysts.* This group, also composed largely of political scientists and sociologists, likewise seeks to describe the causes and consequences of policies. Problem-oriented analysts, however, are less concerned with the development and testing of theories deemed important in social science disciplines than with identifying variables that may be manipulated by policymakers to resolve problems. Yet problem-oriented analysts seldom provide information about specific goals and objectives of policymakers, chiefly because the practical problems they analyze are usually of a general nature. For example, the analysis of the effects of public investments in education on the achievement levels of students in the United States provides information about potentially manipulable policy variables (public investment) but does not provide information about the specific goals and objectives of policymakers and other stakeholders who affect and are affected by educational policies.

3. *Applications-oriented analysts.* This third group of analysts includes sociologists and some political scientists but also persons from professions such as social work and public administration and such fields as evaluation research. This group also seeks to describe the causes and consequences of public policies and programs but is not concerned with the development and testing of discipline-based theories. Moreover, this group is not only concerned with policy variables but also with the identification of goals and objectives of policymakers and other stakeholders. Information about these goals and objectives provides a basis for monitoring and evaluating specific policy outcomes, which may in turn be used by practitioners of *ex ante* analysis to structure policy problems, develop new policy alternatives, and recommend courses of action to resolve problems. For example, applications-oriented analysts may provide a rich account of the many factors that influence the success and failure of early childhood educational programs, even though their analysis ends just short of restructuring problems and developing and synthesizing new solutions for policy problems.

---

[35] James S. Coleman, "Problems of Conceptualization and Measurement in Studying Policy Impacts," in *Public Policy Evaluation*, ed. Kenneth M. Dolbeare (Beverly Hills and London: Sage Publications, 1975), p. 25.

The operating styles of these three groups of retrospective analysts reflect characteristic strengths and weaknesses. Discipline-oriented policy analysts seldom produce information which is directly useful for devising solutions for policy problems, chiefly because variables of most relevance for the construction and testing of general scientific theories are rarely capable of manipulation by policymakers. Even when problem-oriented analysts investigate such important problems as educational opportunity, energy, or crime, the resultant information may be macronegative. *Macronegative* information describes the broad causes and consequences of policies and uses aggregate data to show why certain policies and programs do *not* work, as distinguished from *micropositive* information which shows what policies and programs *do* work and under what specific circumstances.[36] It does the policymaker little good to know that the frequency of crime is greater in urban than rural areas; but it may be very useful to know that a specific form of gun control legislation reduces the commission of serious crimes, or that intensive police patrolling is a deterrent to crime.

Even where applications-oriented policy analysis results in micropositive information, there still may be wide communications gaps between practitioners of retrospective and prospective policy analysis. In specific agency settings those analysts charged with identifying, comparing, and recommending alternative solutions for problems may have limited access to information produced by practitioners of retrospective analysis. Similarly, practitioners of prospective analysis may fail to specify in sufficient detail the kinds of policy-relevant information that will be most useful for monitoring and evaluating the results of their recommendations. Finally, the intended outcomes of a policy "are often so vaguely stated that almost any evaluation of it may be regarded as irrelevant because it missed the 'problem' toward which the policy was directed."[37] Policy problems are often formulated in deliberately obscure terms in order to gain acceptance and forestall opposition from various policy stakeholders and the general public.

Contrasts among the operating styles of policy analysts suggest that discipline- and problem-oriented analysis is inherently less useful than applications-oriented analysis and that retrospective analysis as a whole is perhaps less relevant to the resolution of policy problems than prospective analysis. While this conclusion has merit from the point of view of policymakers who must make decisions and take actions, it overlooks several benefits of retrospective policy analysis. Retrospective analysis, whatever its shortcomings, places primary emphasis on the results of action and is not content with information about the goals and objectives of policy, as is often the case with prospective analysis. Moreover, discipline- and problem-oriented analysis may offer new frameworks for understanding policy-making processes, result in challenges to conventional formulations of problems, upend various social myths, and shape the climate of opinion in an entire

---

[36] Williams, *Social Policy Research and Analysis*, p. 8.

[37] Williams, p. 13; and Alice Rivlin, *Systematic Thinking for Social Action* (Washington, DC: The Brookings Institution, 1971).

society. Retrospective analysis "has been most important in its impact on intellectual priorities and understandings, and not nearly so effective in offering solutions for specific political problems."[38]

Integrated Policy Analysis

Integrated policy analysis is a more comprehensive form of analysis which combines the operating styles of practitioners concerned with the production and transformation of information both *before* and *after* policy actions have been taken. Integrated policy analysis not only requires that analysts link retrospective and prospective phases of inquiry but also demands that analysts continuously produce and transform information over time. This means that the analyst may engage in the clockwise transformation of policy-informational components many times before a satisfactory resolution of a policy problem is found. Integrated analysis is therefore continuous, iterative, and unlimited, at least in principle. The analyst may initiate the production and transformation of information at any point in the analytic cycle, either before or after action, and the relation between any two "phases" of policy analysis—for example, between problem structuring and forecasting—is best viewed as a dialectical "moment" where it is impossible to say with certainty where the use of one policy-analytic method begins and another ends.[39]

Integrated analysis may be illustrated by contrasting retrospective evaluations of public policies, on the one hand, and policy-program experiments on the other. Retrospective evaluation of policies and programs in areas such as education, health, and social welfare typically assesses the performance of *existing* policies and programs. Policy and program experiments, by contrast, assess the performance of *new* policies and programs in terms of their actual outcomes.[40] In order to assess new forms of policy action under realistic political and administrative conditions, it is necessary to produce information at each phase of policy analysis: problem structuring, forecasting, recommendation, monitoring, and evaluation. Prospective and retrospective policy analysis, although initiating and terminating analysis at different points, require merely that the analyst complete part of the analytic cycle.

Integrated policy analysis has all the methodological advantages of prospective and retrospective analysis but none of their weaknesses. Integrated analysis provides for the continuous monitoring and evaluation of policies over time. This is not the case with prospective and retrospective analysis, which provide significantly less information. For example, pro-

---

[38] Janet A. Weiss, "Using Social Science for Social Policy," *Policy Studies Journal,* 4, No. 3 (Spring 1976), p. 237.
[39] This point was suggested by Burkhart Holzner, Evelyn M. Fisher, and John H. Marx, "Paul Lazarsfeld and the Study of Knowledge Applications," *Sociological Focus,* 10, No. 2 (April 1977), p. 107.
[40] See, for example, George W. Fairweather and Louis G. Tornatzky, *Experimental Methods for Social Policy Research* (New York: Pergamon Press, 1977).

spective policy analysis typically suffers from inadequate or unreliable information about changes in values, goals, and objectives which occur after policies have been implemented. By contrast, retrospective policy analysis suffers from an inability to shape policy actions, since it is largely confined to the passive reporting of information about the consequences of policies after they have been implemented. Finally, integrated analysis builds on the strengths of disciplines that have specialized in prospective analysis (economics, systems engineering, operations research), as well as those which have placed primary emphasis on retrospective analysis (political science, sociology, law). Hence, integrated analysis is multidisciplinary in the full sense of the word.

Descriptive and Normative Decision Theory

The framework of elements of the process of policy analysis not only helps us visualize interdependencies between information and methods but also assists in showing how different methods are related to major forms of policy analysis: retrospective, prospective, and integrated policy analysis. When we divide this same framework into four parts we find that the left-hand portion contains methods that are normally used by practitioners of retrospective policy analysis (Figure 3–4). By contrast, the right-hand portion of the framework contains methods typically used by practitioners of prospective policy analysis. In effect, the left side of the framework is concerned with the analysis of policy *after* action, whereas the right side deals with the analysis of policy *before* action.

This particular contrast helps to understand several important distinctions made in contemporary debates about the methodology of policy analysis. For example, distinctions between descriptive decision theory and normative decision theory may be captured by the framework. *Descriptive decision theory*, which may be defined as a set of logically consistent propositions that describe action,[41] is essentially concerned with methods for retrospective analysis found on the left-hand side of the framework. The analyst who is concerned with describing the causes and consequences of policy actions must of necessity conduct analyses after action has occurred. Here the primary aim of analysis is to understand a policy problem rather than to solve it.

By contrast, *normative decision theory* is a set of logically consistent propositions that provide a basis for improving the consequences of action.[42] Normative decision theory (sometimes referred to as statistical decision theory, or the theory of rational choice in complex situations) is largely concerned with the use of prospective methods (forecasting and recommendation) found in the right-hand portion of the framework. These methods, as we have seen, are appropriate for predicting and recommending different courses of action before they have occurred. In a larger sense, that is what is meant when policy analysis is described as a "problem-solving" meth-

---

[41] Bower, "Descriptive Decision Theory from the 'Administrative' Viewpoint," p. 104.
[42] Ibid., pp. 104–5.

odology.[43] Whereas descriptive decision theory is oriented toward the understanding of problems, normative decision theory is largely concerned with their solution.

Problem Finding and Problem Solving

When we look at the upper and lower portions of the framework we are able to understand another set of distinctions made in present-day debates about the methodology of policy analysis. The upper portion of the framework deals with methods which are usually described in terms of problem finding, while the lower portion is typically described in terms of problem solving. Problem finding is essentially a conceptual and theoretical activity. Here the primary concern is with questions about the nature of problems and not so much with choosing courses of action that may contribute to their resolution. How well do we understand the problem? Have we identified the right objectives? Are we solving the wrong formulation of a problem when we should be solving the right one?

By contrast, problem solving involves the execution and steering of a course of action over time. Problem solving is essentially a practical activity, as distinguished from problem finding, which is essentially theoretical. Here the primary concern is with choosing a course of action and seeing that it is properly followed over time and not with inquiring into the nature of problems. Analysts working in the lower half of the framework already take problems as "given," seeking at this stage merely to select and implement the right choices. The greatest danger at this stage of analysis is choosing the "right" alternative to solve the "wrong" problem.

The Complexity of Information

The framework also assists in understanding the complexity of information in policy analysis. Note that the vertical and horizontal lines in Figure 3–4 bisect each of the informational components, suggesting that the production of information has a dualistic character. The vertical line, for example, cuts through policy problems, policy performance, and policy actions. The marginal position occupied by policy problems serves to emphasize that policy problems are as much a product of past events as they are a function of future expectations. The production of information about policy problems therefore depends not only on our ability to document the existence of a problem in the past but also on expectations that the problem can and should be resolved by government. Similarly, information about policy performance—that is, the extent to which unattained values have been realized—is governed both by beliefs about the past and expectations about the future. Finally, the marginal position of policy actions helps to stress the important point that the consequences of action are never fully statable or knowable in advance of action itself.

---

[43] For example, as used by Jacob B. Ukeles, "Policy Analysis: Myth or Reality?" *Public Administration Review*, 37, No. 3 (1977), 223–28.

The horizontal line emphasizes the marginality of policy outcomes, policy problems, and policy futures. Information about policy outcomes is as much a result of the way that problems are structured as it is a consequence of the ways that policies are implemented. Information about policy problems is similarly conditioned not only by the way a problem was originally structured—for example, problems typically contain objectives that are later used as criteria for evaluating policy performance—but also by the ways that a course of action is put into practice. Finally, policy futures are influenced both by the theoretical assumptions that underlie the formulation of a problem and by the degree to which policy alternatives are devised with a view toward their implementability. The structuring of a policy problem and the development and synthesis of new alternatives are essentially theoretical activities; yet alternatives must also be chosen and acted upon, which means that the production of information about policy futures is also practical. In short, theory is a guide to action, and action is a test of theory.

In conclusion, the integrated framework for policy analysis presented in this chapter permits us to study the assumptions, uses, and limitations of particular policy-analytic methods. In subsequent chapters this same framework will also prove useful in studying particular techniques of policy analysis used today. Second, the framework systematically and explicitly relates major elements of the process of policy analysis, enabling us to see the many ways that methods of inquiry and argument permit the analyst to produce and transform information. Third, the framework helps to distinguish major forms of policy analysis used today. It provides us with a classification scheme that will later prove helpful once we consider methods and techniques in more detail. Finally, the framework may serve as a means for synthesizing diverse assumptions and approaches to policy analysis. Integrated policy analysis may thus serve as a vehicle for bridging current gaps between approaches to policy analysis as different as descriptive and normative decision theory, disjointed incrementalism and systems analysis, and empirical, valuative, and normative approaches to policy analysis.[44]

SUMMARY

In this chapter we have defined policy analysis, described its characteristics and role in solving problems, and outlined elements of policy analysis as a process of inquiry. The purpose of this chapter has been to develop a framework that may be used to examine the assumptions, strengths, and limitations of particular methods and techniques. At this point you should be able to discuss the following key principles and generalizations:

---

[44] On the problem of synthesizing approaches see, for example, contributions to Bauer and Gergen, *The Study of Policy Formation*; and Kathleen A. Archibald, "Three Views of the Expert's Role in Policy-Making: Systems Analysis, Incrementalism, and the Clinical Approach," *Policy Sciences*, 1, No. 1 (1970), 73–86.

1. As an applied discipline policy analysis draws from a variety of disciplines whose purposes are descriptive, evaluative, and normative. Policy analysis borrows, not only from the social and behavioral sciences, but also from public administration, law, philosophy, ethics, and branches of systems analysis and applied mathematics.

2. Policy analysts are expected to produce and transform information about values, facts, and actions. These three types of information are associated with three approaches to policy analysis: empirical, valuative, and normative.

3. Recommendation is a rational process whereby analysts produce information and reasoned arguments about potential solutions for public problems. Policy advocacy should not be confused with emotional appeals, ideological platforms, or simple political activism.

4. The most general procedures for solving human problems (description, prediction, evaluation, prescription) may be compared and contrasted according to the time when they are used (before versus after action) and the kinds of questions for which they are appropriate (empirical, valuative, normative). These general procedures correspond to policy-analytic procedures of monitoring, forecasting, evaluation, and recommendation. In addition one policy-analytic method has no direct correspondence to any single general procedure: problem structuring. Problem structuring is a metamethod.

5. Policy-analytic methods are hierarchically related and interdependent. Some policy-analytic methods (for example, monitoring) may be used by themselves, while others (for example, evaluation) require the prior use of another method. Recommendation requires the prior use of monitoring, evaluation, and forecasting. Every recommendation is a combination of factual and value premises.

6. Knowledge of what is (facts), what is right (values), and what to do (action) requires the use of multiple methods of inquiry and argument to produce and transform information about policy problems, policy futures, policy actions, policy outcomes, and policy performance.

7. Policy analysts seek not only to produce information but also to transform it as part of knowledge claims and arguments about policy. Policy arguments reflect the reasons why different segments of the community disagree about alternative courses of action open to governments and are the main vehicle for conducting debates about public issues.

8. Every policy argument has six elements: policy-relevant information, policy claim, warrant, backing, rebuttal, and qualifier. Relations among these elements show how information may be transformed into plausibly true beliefs (knowledge).

9. Policy analysis is essentially a cognitive process, while policy-making is a political one. Many factors other than methodology shape the ways that policy analysis is utilized in the policy-making process. Policy analysts are but one among many different types of stakeholders in a policy system.

10. A given policy issue is typically a result of conflicting definitions of a policy problem. Definitions of policy problems are shaped by the pattern of involvement of different stakeholders and their response to common policy environments.

11. Policy systems are dialectical in nature. Policy systems are subjective creations of stakeholders; policy systems are an objective reality; stakeholders are products of policy systems.

12. As a process of inquiry policy analysis involves three kinds of elements: policy-analytic methods, policy-informational components, and policy-informational transformations. Methods and information are interdependent.
13. The process of policy analysis may be described in terms of reconstructed logic and logic-in-use. The logic-in-use of particular analysts may be influenced by their time and resource constraints, cognitive styles, and professional socialization.
14. There are three main forms of policy analysis: retrospective, prospective, and integrated. Contrasts among these main forms help us understand key unresolved issues of policy analysis: the importance of time, the relation of descriptive and normative decision theory, the role of theory and practice, and the meaning of problem solving.
15. The integrated framework provides us with a methodology for policy analysis—that is, a means for applying standards, rules, and procedures in doing policy analysis. The framework also serves as a medium for synthesizing diverse assumptions and approaches to policy analysis used today.

GLOSSARY

Descriptive Decision Theory: A set of logically consistent propositions that describes the causes and consequences of policy actions.

Evaluation: The policy-analytic procedure used to produce information about the value or worth of past and/or future courses of action.

Forecasting: The policy-analytic procedure used to produce information about the probability of occurrence of policy futures.

Integrated Policy Analysis: The production and transformation of information both *before* and *after* policy actions have been adopted.

Logic-in-Use: The rules and procedures actually used by policy analysts, sometimes referred to as *cognitive style.*

Macronegative Information: Information that describes the broad causes and consequences of policies and uses aggregate (macro) data to show why policies and programs will *not* work.

Micropositive Information: Information that describes specific causes and consequences of policies and uses disaggregated (micro) data to show why policies and programs *will* work under specified circumstances.

Monitoring: The policy-analytic procedure used to produce information about the past causes and consequences of policies.

Normative Decision Theory: A set of logically consistent propositions that provides a basis for improving the consequences of policy actions.

Policy Action: A complex series of moves guided by a policy alternative that is designed to achieve certain values.

Policy Advocacy: The use of policy-relevant information to make plausible knowledge claims based on reasoned arguments about possible solutions for problems. Policy advocacy is a way to make normative statements, not to issue prescriptions, commands, or orders of various kinds.

Policy Alternative: A potentially available course of action that may contribute to the attainment of values and the resolution of a policy problem.

Policy Analysis: An applied social science discipline that uses multiple methods of inquiry in contexts of argumentation and public debate, to create, critically assess, and communicate policy-relevant knowledge.

Policy-Analytic Procedure: One or more of five procedures for solving policy problems: problem structuring, forecasting, recommendation, monitoring, and evaluation.

Policy Argument: Claims and underlying assumptions that provide reasons why information should be transformed in a particular way. Policy arguments have six main elements: policy-relevant information, policy claim, warrant, backing, qualifier, and rebuttal.

Policy Environment: The specific context in which events surrounding a policy issue occur.

Policy Formulation: The development and synthesis of alternative solutions for policy problems.

Policy Implementation: The execution and steering of policy actions over time.

Policy-Informational Component: A methodological concept used to describe one of five types of policy-relevant information: policy problems, policy futures, policy actions, policy outcomes, and policy performance.

Policy-Informational Transformation: A methodological concept used to describe the process whereby policy-informational components are transformed into one another by using multiple methods of inquiry and argument.

Policy Issue: A disagreement or conflict among policy actors about an actual or potential course of government action.

Policy Outcome: An observed consequence of a policy action.

Policy Performance: The degree to which a given policy outcome contributes to the attainment of values.

Policy Problem: An unrealized need, value, or opportunity which, however identified, may be attained through public action.

Policy Stakeholders: Individuals or groups who have a stake in a policy because they affect and are affected by government decisions.

Policy System: The overall institutional pattern within which policies are made. The three elements of a policy system are public policies, policy stakeholders, and policy environments.

Problem Structuring: The policy-analytic method used to produce information about the nature of a problem and its potential solutions.

Prospective Policy Analysis: The production and transformation of information *before* policy actions have been adopted.

Public Policy: A complex pattern of interdependent collective choices, including decisions not to act, made by governmental bodies and officials.

Recommendation: The policy-analytic procedure used to produce information about the probable consequences of future courses of action and their value or worth.

Reconstructed Logic: A set of rules or procedures which, based on the synthesis of a great many concrete descriptions of the practice of policy analysis, provides an abstract representation of the process of policy analysis.

Retrospective Policy Analysis: The production and transformation of information *after* policy actions have been adopted.

STUDY SUGGESTIONS

1. Following is a list of public policy issues. Pick one of these issues and describe three alternative formulations of policy problems that might underlie the issue.

   (a) Should the Law Enforcement Assistance Administration (LEAA) support high-impact police patrols in urban areas?

   (b) Should the State Department support the visa application of a head of state of a country whose policies run counter to the Universal Declaration of Human Rights?

   (c) Should Congress pass legislation to socialize medical and health services?

   (d) Should the government regulate the price of natural gas?

   (e) Should the government strictly enforce pollution standards?

   (f) Should the Food and Drug Administration prohibit the sale of drugs and other substances that have been found to cause physical harm to laboratory animals?

(g) Should a publicly funded university admit minority students who have achieved lower entrance examination scores than have white students?

2. Pick one of the policy issues from the previous list. Provide examples of descriptive, predictive, valuative, and prescriptive information that might be used to structure the problem(s) that underlie the issue.

3. A now-classic report on American education by sociologist James S. Coleman and his colleagues has generated intense debate on educational policy since its publication in 1966. The Coleman Report, published under the title *Equality of Educational Opportunity* (Washington, DC: U.S. Government Printing Office, 1966), suggested that such factors as pupils per teacher, investments in school equipment and facilities, teachers' salaries, and the quality of curricula have *no significant influence* on student learning and achievement. Instead, it was found that family backgrounds of students and their peers were closely related to scholastic aptitude scores, attitudes toward education, and scholastic achievement. Further, the report found that black schools were not physically inferior to white schools, and that black teachers have about the same education, experience, and salaries as white teachers.

The U.S. Civil Rights Commission used many of the conclusions of the Coleman Report to support policy recommendations designed to achieve racial balance in schools through busing. Since the appearance of the Coleman Report and subsequent government efforts to implement school busing policies, a number of policy actors—including professional educators, social scientists, black leaders, and white neighborhood groups—have disagreed continuously and intensely about the report and its implications for educational policies.

Listed below are some typical statements from this debate. Identify each statement as primarily descriptive, predictive, valuative, or prescriptive. Note that some statements may be descriptive and valuative at the same time, depending on whether values are used to *characterize* something (for example, "He is a good Nazi") as well as to *appraise* it (for example, "Nazis are bad"). Only the context in which a statement is made may enable us to distinguish between characterizing value judgments (descriptive statements) and appraisals (valuative statements).

(a) "Since schools in large urban areas are primarily black, the hopes of blacks for higher educational achievement cannot be realized."

(b) "The Coleman Report is a racist document based on the myth of white supremacy."

(c) "Educational reform will not bring about economic equality, since research shows that there is no relation between school achievement and earnings, either for whites or for blacks."

(d) "Black students bused to predominantly white schools do not improve their performance relative to white students."

(e) "School busing is a failure, since it doesn't help black students, and perhaps even results in increased community conflict."

(f) "In the long run, school busing is the only available alternative for correcting racial imbalances, and should therefore be adopted as the only viable solution consistent with democratic values."

(g) "True social equality can only be achieved through a radical redistribution of societal resources."

(h) "A national policy of compulsory school busing ought to be abandoned as soon as possible."

(i) "Radical educational reforms, including massive investments in special programs for the disadvantaged, should be adopted to alter inequalities of educational opportunity."

(j) "Community control of schools is a more important objective than any abstract liberal commitment to goals of social equality."

4. Beside each statement below list the policy-analytic method(s) appropriate for producing the information.

(a) "Approximately two-thirds of all citizens are satisfied with the quality of municipal services."

(b) "By 1995 the percentage of the population below the poverty line will have dropped to 6 percent."

(c) "Policy analysts and other producers of specialized knowledge are increasingly exerting decisive influence on the policy-making process in the United States and other postindustrial societies."

(d) "The ratio of benefits to costs for program A is twice that of program B."

(e) "Crime is an economic, social, political, and psychological phenomenon that permits only comprehensive solutions."

(f) "Nuclear energy is many times more efficient in meeting the country's energy needs than is solar energy."

(g) "If Congress values equality of opportunity it will pass the Equal Rights Amendment."

(h) "The reading scores of children who completed the Head Start Program were not significantly different from scores of children who attended no early childhood education program."

5. Using all six elements described in the text, diagram a policy argument that results in a normative claim. Begin your argument with the following policy-relevant information: "In larger municipalities (over 25,000 persons), the greater the number of families below the poverty line, the greater the number of reported criminal offenses." Be sure to include a rebuttal in your argument and pay careful attention to the way you formulate the problem.

SUGGESTED READINGS

BEHN, ROBERT D. and JAMES W. VAUPEL, *Quick Analysis for Busy Decision Makers.* New York: Basic Books.

BOBROW, DAVIS B. and JOHN S. DRYZEK, *Policy Analysis by Design.* Pittsburgh, PA: University of Pittsburgh Press, 1987.

BREWER, GARY D. and PETER DELEON, *The Foundations of Policy Analysis.* Homewood, IL: The Dorsey Press, 1983.

DROR, YEHEZKEL, *Public Policymaking Re-examined.* 2nd ed. San Francisco, CA: Chandler Publishing Company, 1984.

DUNN, WILLIAM N. and RITA MAE KELLY (eds.), *Advances in Policy Studies Since 1950.* New Brunswick, NJ: Transaction Books, 1992.

GUESS, GEORGE M. and PAUL G. FARNHAM, *Cases in Public Policy Analysis.* New York: Longman, 1989.

HOUSE, PETER W. and ROGER D. SHULL, *Rush to Policy: Using Analytic Techniques in Public Sector Decision Making.* New Brunswick, NJ: Transaction Books, 1988.

LASSWELL, HAROLD D., *A Pre-View of Policy Sciences.* New York: American Elsevier, 1971.

MACRAE, DUNCAN, JR. and JAMES A. WILDE, *Policy Analysis for Public Decisions.* North Scituate, MA: Duxbury Press, 1979.

MEEHAN, EUGENE, *The Thinking Game.* Chatham, NJ: Chatham House Publishers, 1988.

NAGEL, STUART S., *Basic Literature in Policy Studies: A Comprehensive Bibliography.* Greenwich, CT: JAI Press, 1984.

———, *Contemporary Policy Studies: Integration and Evaluation.* Westport, CT: Greenwood Press, 1988.

———, *Encyclopedia of Policy Studies.* New York: Marcel Dekker, 1983.

PARIS, DAVID C. and JAMES F. REYNOLDS, *The Logic of Policy Inquiry.* New York: Longman, 1983.

PATTON, CARL V. and DAVID S. SAWICKI, *Basic Methods of Policy Analysis and Planning.* Englewood Cliffs, NJ: Prentice Hall Publishers, 1986.

QUADE, EDWARD S. *Analysis for Public Decisions,* 3rd rev. ed. by Grace M. Carter. New York: North-Holland Publishing Company, 1989.

STARLING, GROVER, *Strategies for Policy Making.* Chicago, IL: The Dorsey Press, 1988.

STOKEY, EDITH and RICHARD ZECKHAUSER, *A Primer for Policy Analysis.* New York: W. W. Norton and Company, 1978.

WEIMER, DAVID L. and ALAN VINING, *Policy Analysis: Concepts and Practice.* Englewood Cliffs, NJ: Prentice Hall, 1989.

4

The Functions
of Policy Argument

Substantial arguments serve to redeem or to criticize validity claims,
whether the claims to truth implicit in assertions or the claims to
correctness connected with norms (of action or evaluation) or implied
in recommendations and warnings. They have the force to convince
the participants in a discourse . . . *to provide rational grounds* for the
recognition of validity claims.

—JURGEN HABERMAS, *Legitimation Crisis* (1975)

In Chapter 3 we learned how five general procedures of policy analysis may
be used to produce and transform five types of policy-relevant information.
We also saw that such information is the starting point in processes of policy
argumentation and debate, the catalyst for creating, critically assessing, and
communicating plausibly true beliefs about public policy. Policy argumentation and debate are major vehicles for generating usable knowledge.[1]

In this chapter we examine in greater detail the role of policy argumentation and debate in transforming policy-relevant information into usable knowledge. We begin by defining and characterizing usable knowledge,
focusing on contrasts between "essentialist" and "plausibilist" views of policy
causation. We then examine the structure of policy arguments and their
role in creating, critically assessing, and communicating usable knowledge.
Since usable knowledge must meet standards required of knowledge in general, we also outline a process of truth estimation based on a system of
criteria for assessing the plausibility of competing knowledge claims offered
as the conclusions of policy arguments. We then contrast multiple modes
of policy argument, showing how the analysis of these modes permits the
development of knowledge claims and the critical assessment of their underlying assumptions. In the concluding section we examine the role of

---

[1] Charles E. Lindblom and David K. Cohen, *Usable Knowledge: Social Science and Social
Problem Solving* (New Haven, CT: Yale University Press, 1979).

values and ethics in policy analysis, showing how implicit value premises and ethical commitments can be made explicit by incorporating them in policy arguments and debates.

USABLE KNOWLEDGE IN POLICY ANALYSIS

Data, information, knowledge, and wisdom are interdependent but distinguishable elements in a nested hierarchy of cognitive processes (see Box 1–4). Information is data that have been interpreted and organized for the achievement of some goal or purpose associated with changing the thoughts or actions of policymakers. A good example is information disseminated by the Educational Resources Information Center (ERIC) or the National Criminal Justice Reference Service (NCJRS). Both information systems are designed to change the thoughts and actions of policymakers by informing them about research in different areas of education and criminal justice. By contrast, knowledge is information that has been communicated to some policymaker who transforms it into plausibly true beliefs that enable the pursuit of goals under changing circumstances.[2] For example, legislators may be said to know—as distinguished from simply being informed—when they transform information communicated by ERIC into plausibly true beliefs about the effects of class size on achievement and act on such beliefs to support (or oppose) packages of school-reform initiatives that change in form and content throughout the legislative session.

To count as knowledge, beliefs need not be certain. For example, beliefs need not be definitive statements about the level of student achievement that will be produced as a consequence of altering class sizes through school-reform legislation. Thus, the term knowledge is not restricted to those occasions when "policymakers are certain that manipulating these variables will produce the expected effects—that is, if x is done, y will follow with a known probability. . . ."[3] Nor is knowledge confined to formal statistical probability, which plays a supporting but ancillary role in the establishment of plausibly true beliefs. In this respect, the first step is to estimate the plausibility that a policy will have certain consequences—for example, that reducing class size will have a weak effect in improving student achievement—and only then assign a probability that this effect will occur by chance (for example, the weak positive effect of x on y is expected to occur by chance 1 time out of 1000).[4]

---

[2] Churchman defines knowledge as "the ability to pursue goals though the world about us changes. . . ." C. West Churchman, *The Design of Inquiring Systems: Basic Concepts of Systems and Organization* (New York: Basic Books, 1971), p. 12.

[3] Jack Knott and Aaron Wildavsky, "If Dissemination Is the Problem, What Is the Solution?" in *The Knowledge Cycle*, ed. Robert F. Rich (Beverly Hills, CA: Sage Publications, 1981), p. 108.

[4] The confusion of statistical significance, association, and causation is still common in the social sciences. See, for example, the review by Thomas J. Duggan and Charles W. Dean, "Common Misinterpretations of Significance Levels in Sociological Journals," *American So-*

The idea of plausibility originates in the recognition that it is rarely possible under real-life circumstances to make knowledge claims of the form "doing x will lead to y" that are immune to criticism, challenge, or rebuttal. If it were possible to make unequivocal claims of this kind, they would meet the following requirements, usually called the "essentialist" view of causation:[5]

1. The policy (x) must precede the policy outcome (y) in time.
2. The occurrence of the policy (x) must be necessary for the occurrence of the outcome (y)—that is, the outcome (y) must not occur in the absence of the policy (x).
3. The occurrence of the policy (x) must be sufficient for the occurrence of the outcome (y)—that is, the outcome (y) must occur when the policy (x) is present.

If these requirements were satisfied, the relation between a policy and one or more outcomes would be certain. The policy would be both necessary and sufficient for the occurrence of the outcome, a requirement that is seldom if ever met in complex policy settings. Instead, what typically occurs is that other conditions, factors, or variables—rival explanations that challenge or rebut the claim that the policy is or has been responsible for the outcome—make it impossible to know definitively whether the policy is necessary or sufficient for the occurrence of the outcome. Here the best that may be expected is an optimally plausible claim about the outcome of a policy in a particular context.

Policy analysis may be seen as a process of engaging in argumentation and debate in order to create, critically assess, and communicate plausibly true beliefs about the performance of policy-making processes. The creation and critical assessment of knowledge claims is essential for establishing optimally plausible truth claims; the communication of competing knowledge claims and their underlying warrants is equally important, since it is the process of communication which assures that contending claims are not only relevant to individuals and groups with a stake in policies, but perceived as such. To be sure, the role of the analyst in these processes is seldom direct, since direct involvement is rarely feasible under typical real-world constraints. Nevertheless, policy analysts can and do engage in these processes as vicarious participants. *Usable or policy-relevant knowledge, then, consists of optimally plausible truth claims that are created by engaging,*

ciologist, 3 (February 1968), 45–46. Path analysis and other forms of causal modeling involving correlation coefficients, regression weights, and levels of statistical significance "are not a method for discovering causes, but a method applied to a causal model formulated . . . on the basis of knowledge and theoretical considerations." Fred W. Kerlinger and Elazar J. Pedhazur, *Multiple Regression in Behavioral Research* (New York: Holt, Rinehart and Winston, 1973), p. 305.

[5] Readable discussions of the essentialist view may be found in Thomas D. Cook and Donald T. Campbell, *Quasi-experimentation: Design and Analysis Issues for Field Settings* (Boston: Houghton Mifflin, 1979), Chap. 1; and Yvonne S. Lincoln and Egon G. Guba, *Naturalistic Inquiry* (Beverly Hills, CA: Sage Publications, 1985), Chap. 6.

directly and vicariously, in processes of policy communication, argumentation, and debate.

THE STRUCTURE OF POLICY ARGUMENTS

The understanding of processes of policy communication, argumentation, and debate is facilitated by employing a structural model of argument developed by Stephen Toulmin.[6] The structural model of argument is a powerful medium for representing processes of practical reasoning the conclusions of which are less than deductively certain. From Aristotle to the present such practical arguments have been viewed as rhetorical syllogisms (enthymemes) consisting of premises that either have not been explicitly stated or, if so stated, are incomplete and inconclusive. In contrast to the standard logic of deductive reasoning, practical reasoning yields conclusions "about which we are not entirely confident by relating them back to other information about which we have greater assurance. . . ."[7] Practical arguments are never certain and seldom, if ever, are they deductive or analytical.

Types of Knowledge Claims

Knowledge claims are the conclusions of policy arguments. There are three types of knowledge claims: designative, evaluative, and advocative. These three types of claims (Figure 4–1) correspond to the three approaches to policy analysis discussed in Chapter 3. Designative claims, associated with the empirical approach to policy analysis, are concerned with questions of *fact*: "What are the outcomes of a particular policy?" Evaluative claims, closely related to the valuative approach to policy analysis, are concerned with questions of value: "Was the policy worthwhile?" Advocative claims, which correspond to the normative approach to policy analysis, are concerned with questions of *action*: "Which policy should be adopted?" (Figure 4–1).

Whereas *approaches* to policy analysis represent general orientations toward the production and transformation of information, policy *claims* are highly specific; they represent the conclusions of a policy argument or debate. Policy arguments, as we saw in the last chapter, contain six elements: policy-relevant information (*I*), policy claim (*C*), warrant (*W*), backing (*B*), rebuttal (*R*), and qualifier (*Q*) (see Figure 3–1). The first three of these elements are present in all genuine policy arguments; the combination of information and warrant provides the reasons why one should accept the conclusion. Additional elements may be introduced for specific purposes. A backing, for example, is introduced as a way to add persuasiveness to an

---

[6] Stephen Toulmin, *The Uses of Argument* (Cambridge: Cambridge University Press, 1958). See also Stephen Toulmin, Robert Rieke, and Alan Janik, *An Introduction to Reasoning* (New York: Macmillan, 1979).

[7] Toulmin, *The Uses of Argument*, p. 127.

FIGURE 4–1 Three types of policy claims.

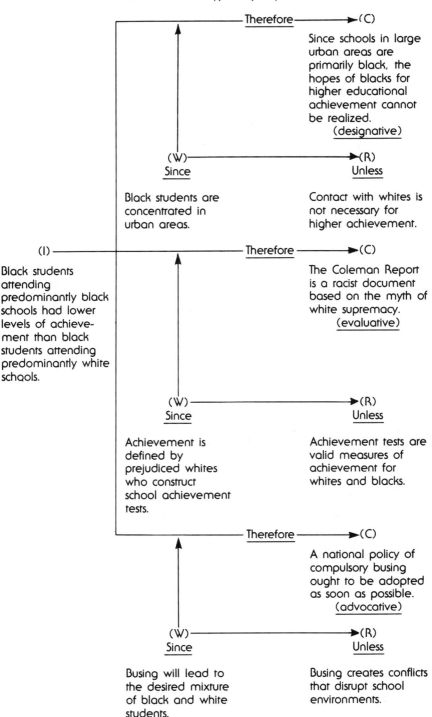

Therefore ————▶(C)

Since schools in large urban areas are primarily black, the hopes of blacks for higher educational achievement cannot be realized.
(designative)

(W) ————————————▶(R)
Since   Unless

Black students are concentrated in urban areas.   Contact with whites is not necessary for higher achievement.

(I) ————————————— Therefore ————▶(C)

Black students attending predominantly black schools had lower levels of achievement than black students attending predominantly white schools.

The Coleman Report is a racist document based on the myth of white supremacy.
(evaluative)

(W) ————————————▶(R)
Since   Unless

Achievement is defined by prejudiced whites who construct school achievement tests.   Achievement tests are valid measures of achievement for whites and blacks.

Therefore ————▶(C)

A national policy of compulsory busing ought to be adopted as soon as possible.
(advocative)

(W) ————————————▶(R)
Since   Unless

Busing will lead to the desired mixture of black and white students.   Busing creates conflicts that disrupt school environments.

argument that is not well accepted. By contrast, a rebuttal supplies the essential ingredient in any genuine debate—that is, disagreement or conflict surrounding a course of public action. By definition, there are no policy issues without a rebuttal.

One of the important features of policy analysis is that the same information may lead to altogether different knowledge claims. For example, a highly important document in the recent history of policy analysis, the Coleman Report, provided information about similarities and differences between black and white school children (see Chapter 3, Study Suggestion 3). The same information, however, led to (1) the *designative claim* that "Since schools in large urban areas are primarily black, the hopes of blacks for higher educational achievement cannot be realized"; (2) the *evaluative claim* that "The Coleman Report is a racist document based on the myth of white supremacy"; and (3) the *advocative claim* that "a national policy of compulsory busing ought to be adopted as soon as possible." Note carefully that each of these claims begins with the same information, namely that "black students attending predominantly black schools had lower levels of achievement than black students attending predominantly white schools" (Figure 4–1).[8]

For this same information to lead to such very different knowledge claims, certain assumptions must provide the grounds for making the transition from information to competing claims. These assumptions, represented by warrants, show why the same information may be interpreted in markedly different ways. The example of the Coleman Report shows not only that identical information may lead to all three types of knowledge claims, but that the plausibility of any one type of claim (for example, the advocative claim about compulsory busing) may be challenged in the form of rebuttals.[9] Thus, specific types of arguments permit diverse interpretations of the same information. These arguments—which represent the frame of reference, theory, ideology, or worldview brought to bear on information—are the principal vehicles for carrying information to claim in a policy argument or debate.

The Process of Knowledge Critique

The structural model of argument is a powerful medium for understanding the critical functions of reason in advancing and challenging knowledge claims made in fields as diverse as philology, physics, literary criticism, and strategic planning and management.[10] The structural model,

---

[8] In the original Coleman Report this finding was qualified by showing that differences in achievement levels persisted when socioeconomic differences between black and white families were taken into account.

[9] Rebuttals may be attached to information (*I*), warrants (*W*), backings (*B*), or to the claim (*C*) itself.

[10] On the following features of the structural model, see Wayne Brockriede and Douglas Ehninger, "Toulmin on Argument: An Interpretation and Application," *The Quarterly Journal of Speech*, XLVI (1960), 45–53; Nicholas Rescher, *Induction* (Pittsburgh, PA: University of Pittsburgh Press, 1980), pp. 33–37; Ian I. Mitroff and Richard O. Mason, *Creating a Dialectical*

first, shows that knowledge claims are *ampliative*. Knowledge claims are not definitive statements that follow with certainty from policy-relevant information, but truth estimates that transcend or leap beyond the information at hand. Second, the model is *erotetic*, since all elements of an argument are carefully scrutinized and subjected to a process of questioning and answering. The process of argumentation begins with questions, not answers. Third, the structural model recognizes the diversity of contexts in which arguments are made. Knowledge claims are optimally plausible, given the *contextual* norms and standards employed to challenge or rebut claims. The norms and standards employed in contexts of social science research, for example, are fundamentally different from those employed in medicine, law, politics, or physics. Fourth, argumentation is a *dynamic* process that involves movements from information via warrants to claims. In subsequent chains of argument, claims become information in new sequences and complex networks of argumentation and debate. Finally, arguments are *systemic*, since they represent an interdependent configuration of reasoners who bring differing norms and standards to the task of assessing knowledge claims.

The structural model of argument is particularly appropriate as an instrument for representing complex patterns of policy argumentation and debate based on multiple forms of critical reasoning. These multiple forms of reasoning, which represent a concrete manifestation of the methodology of critical multiplism discussed in Chapter 1, include the logics-in-use of professional analysts who have been trained in rules, standards, and procedures of the social sciences, as well as the logics-in-use of policymakers and citizens who employ rules, standards, and procedures which have been acquired experientially. Because the structural model accommodates these multiple forms of reasoning it is responsive to the problematic offered by Lindblom and Cohen, who correctly argue that policy analysts are "engaged in producing inconclusive evidence and argument. Problem complexity denies the possibility of proof and reduces the pursuit of fact to the pursuit of those selective facts which, if appropriately developed, constitute evidence in support of relevant argument."[11]

The structural model has several comparative advantages when contrasted with the standard analytic reasoning outlined in texts and handbooks of public policy analysis:[12]

Social Science (Dordrecht, The Netherlands: D. Reidel, 1981), Chap. 6; and Toulmin, Rieke, and Janik, *An Introduction to Reasoning*, Chap. 1.

[11]Lindblom and Cohen, *Usable Knowledge*, p. 81.

[12] On these and related advantages, see Mitroff and Mason, *Creating a Dialectical Social Science*; Hayward R. Alker, "Historical Argumentation and Statistical Inference: Towards More Appropriate Logics for Historical Research," *Historical Methods*, 17, No. 3 (1984), 164–73; Alker, "The Dialectical Logic of Thucydides' Melian Dialogue," *The American Political Science Review*, 82, No. 3, (1988), 805–20; William N. Dunn, "Reforms as Arguments," *Knowledge: Creation, Diffusion, Utilization*, 3 (1982), 293–326; Dunn, "Justifying Policy Arguments: Criteria for Practical Discourse," *Evaluation and Program Planning*, 13 (1990), 321–29; and Frank Fischer, *Politics, Values, and Public Policy: The Problem of Methodology* (Boulder, CO: Westview Press, 1980).

1. Whereas standard-form policy analysis tends to assume that reliable and valid information (I) yields unambiguous policy claims (C), the structural model of policy argument stresses the ubiquity of multiple interpretations of the same data. These multiple interpretations are products of conflicting assumptions used to warrant (W) the ampliative leap from information (I) to claim (C), backings (B) employed to justify warrants (W), and rebuttals (R) introduced to dispute one or more elements of a policy argument.

2. Whereas standard-form policy analysis tends to assume a correspondence between the economic, technical, or political rationality of analysts and the processes of reasoning of policymakers, the structural model of policy argument compels a thorough examination of processes of reasoning and forms of rationality exhibited by all important stakeholders in the policy-making process. These processes of reasoning and forms of rationality are evident in the content of warrants (W) and backings (B) put forth to justify a policy claim (C).

3. Whereas standard-form policy analysis frequently obscures the rationale for moving from information (I) to policy claim (C), for example, by suppressing the assumption or premise which would justify this movement, the structural model requires that such assumptions or premises be critically examined as aspects of the overall structure of policy reasoning.

4. Whereas standard-form policy analysis frequently assumes that policy analysis is the product of a single expert, the structural model stipulates that policy arguments are social processes involving at least two contending parties, each of whom transacts claims (C) through a natural process of comparing the strengths and weaknesses of the various elements that constitute a policy argument.

5. Whereas standard-form policy analysis typically excludes ethical considerations as extraneous to the process of policy inquiry, the structural model explicitly accommodates ethical claims (C), warrants (W), backings (B), and rebuttals (R) as essential elements of policy debates.

6. Whereas standard-form policy analysis is often confined to several dominant modes of argument—for example, modes of argument based on the authority of policy experts or on presumed causal relations embodied in theories of policy-making—the structural model of argument incorporates multiple modes of policy argument: authoritative, statistical, causal, methodological, intuitive, comparative, analogical, motivational, ethical. Modes of policy argument are defined by differences in the content of warrants (W) and backings (B).

In short, the structural model of argument, when extended to the domain of public policy, is a powerful instrument for representing the content and structure of policy arguments and debates.[13] The structural model of policy argument is *interpretive* (conflicting interpretations of the same information are systematically evoked), *multirational* (many forms of reasoning are systematically represented), *critical* (suppressed or unexamined premises are raised to a level of explicit consciousness), *transactive* (arguments change as a consequence of natural social processes involving the comparison, evaluation, and revision of claims), *ethical* (arguments include

---

[13] Portions of the foregoing argument are drawn from Dunn, "Justifying Policy Arguments."

processes of ethical as well as causal reasoning), and *multimodal* (many modes of policy argument warrant the movement from information to claim). The structural model, by providing a visual representation of policy arguments and argument chains (Figure 4–1), compels a reflective examination of the frames of reference, worldviews, and ideologies of stakeholders who advance and contest knowledge claims, and appropriately affirms that the creation, critical assessment, and communication of policy analysis are symbolic or communicative acts. The essential feature of such communicative acts is that they involve two or more parties who reciprocally affect, through processes of rational persuasion and debate, the acceptance and rejection of knowledge claims that are at best optimally plausible rather than certain.

Criteria for Plausibility Assessment

The structural model is useful as a framework for naturalistic inquiry.[14] In contrast to other naturalistic or qualitative methodologies, however, the analysis of policy arguments is responsive to important methodological questions surrounding the justification of knowledge claims.[15] How does practical reasoning work when it is properly executed? How does one make a successful practical argument? What criteria are available to distinguish between plausible and implausible policy arguments? If the capacity to persuade is a key feature of policy arguments, what makes one argument more persuasive than another? In short, are there rational standards for appraising policy arguments?

These questions may be approached as a problem of justifying inductive reasoning.[16] Induction may be characterized in its traditional sense as a movement to general principles from specific instances, but also as a process of nondemonstrative reasoning that does not culminate in conclusions which are certain. In this context, policy arguments are frequently based on implicit or incomplete premises called enthymemes. Rather than dismiss policy arguments with implicit or incomplete premises as fatally flawed deductive arguments, we may view such arguments as a process of *enthymematic deduction.* Here, uncertain inductive arguments are transformed into deductive ones by searching for the maximally plausible premise that can certify a deductively valid argument. Policy arguments with implicit, unstated, or incomplete premises (that is, enthymemes) need not be seen as aspiring but failed attempts to achieve certainty through deductive

---

[14] See Yvonna S. Lincoln and Egon G. Guba, *Naturalistic Inquiry* (Beverly Hills, CA: Sage Publications, 1985).

[15] On these questions as they pertain to policy argumentation and debate, see Donald T. Campbell, "Experiments as Arguments," *Knowledge: Creation, Diffusion, Utilization,* 3, No. 3 (1982), 327–38; Duncan MacRae, Jr., "Professional Knowledge for Policy Discourse: Argumentation versus Reasoned Selection of Proposals," *Knowledge in Society,* 1, No. 3 (1988), 6–24; and Carol H. Weiss, "Policy Research as Advocacy: Pro and Con," *Knowledge and Policy,* 4, No. 1–2 (1991), 37–55.

[16] See Rescher, *Induction.*

inferences—or as unsuccessful attempts to provide policymakers with definitive knowledge claims stating which policy variables to manipulate to produce particular outcomes. Rather, policy arguments may be viewed as ways to produce relatively plausible truth estimates.

These truth estimates are produced by moving from a given question (Q) to a body of background knowledge (K) relevant to the question, and then searching for alternative answers $(A_1, A_2, \ldots, A_n)$ that approximate the universe of potential answers. The aim is to identify "the contextually most plausible enthymematic (because information-extending) premise E_i—that is, the (maximally plausible) supplemental supposition which can underwrite a deductively valid argument leading from K to A_i."[17] The outcome of this process is a series of practical arguments that yield answers (A_i) to the inductive question (Q). If we relabel elements of this process with terms used in the structural model of argument, we can represent a series of plausible knowledge claims as follows:

$$
\begin{array}{cccc}
[I] & [I] & [I] & [I] \\
\langle W_1 \rangle & \langle W_2 \rangle & \langle W_3 \rangle & \langle W_n \rangle \\
\hline
[C]_1 & [C]_2 & [C]_3 & [C]_n
\end{array}
$$

In each of the cases above the warrant $[W]_i$ has been bracketed to show that it is a tacit or incomplete premise needed to make the argument plausible. Warrants $[W_i]$ supplement information $[I]$ by supplying premises that plausibly might certify the deductive transition from information $[I]$ to knowledge claim $[C_i]$. Alternative warrants also perform the same critical function as rebuttals in the structural model of argument. They state: *unless* W_j is more plausible than W_i. When warrants are equally plausible $(W_i = W_j)$, the plausibility of their backings $[B_i]$ can be used to choose among claims.[18]

The inductive task is to determine which of several policy claims is the most plausible answer to a policy question (Q) such as: What should the policy be, given data that such and such is or ought to be so? The structure of reasoning in this and other cases provides that the question (Q) can result in a range of possible claims $(C_1, C_2, \ldots, C_n)$. Corresponding to each claim is an appropriate warrant (W_i) which, combined with the information (I), yields an argument that is deductively valid. Since several deductively valid arguments may be present at the same time, it is the argument yielding the most plausible claim (C^*) that best answers the question (Q), given the information (I) available in a particular context.

A central question remains: What governs the plausibility of claims (C_i) such as to make one of them (C^*) optimally plausible? The answer is that induction is a process of truth estimation guided by criteria of plau-

---

[17] Ibid., p. 11.
[18] See Mitroff and Mason, *Creating a Dialectical Social Science*, pp. 87–102.

sibility assessment.[19] Applicable to policy arguments and to practical reasoning in general, these criteria include:

- *Completeness.* Elements of an argument should comprise a genuine whole that encompasses all appropriate considerations. For example, the plausibility of arguments about the effects of a policy depends on whether such arguments encompass a full range of plausible rival explanations similar in form and perhaps content to the several dozen rival hypotheses (threats to validity) elaborated by Campbell and colleagues.[20]
- *Consonance.* Elements of an argument should be internally consistent and compatible. For example, ethical arguments concerning the justice or fairness of a policy are plausible to the degree that they incorporate a system of internally and externally consistent ethical hypotheses.[21]
- *Cohesiveness.* Elements of an argument should be operationally connected. For example, the plausibility of an ethical argument depends on whether responses to several levels of descriptive and valuative questions—levels ranging from verification and validation to vindication—are operationally linked.[22]
- *Functional regularity.* Elements of an argument should conform to an expected pattern. For example, statistical arguments that offer estimates of parameters of unobserved (and often unobservable) populations are plausible to the degree that patterns in the sample and the population from which it is drawn are claimed to be functionally regular or uniform, not irregular or discordant, on the basis of sample data and background knowledge at our disposal.[23]
- *Functional simplicity, economy, and efficacy.* Elements of an argument should be arranged in a simple and parsimonious way, contributing to the effective and efficient attainment of goals. For example, simple and readily understandable policy models, particularly those that may be displayed graphically, tend to be more plausible than those which are highly complicated and interpretable only by specialists.

This system of criteria permits assessments of different modes of policy argument based on premises that incorporate but are not exhausted by the standards, rules, and procedures of the (social) sciences. For example, criteria of plausibility assessment may be applied to modes of argument based on premises that are authoritative, intuitive, analogical, and ethical, as well as those that are causal, methodological, and statistical. The system of criteria is thus applicable to the modes of argument typically employed by

---

[19] See Rescher, *Induction*, pp. 31–47. I have substituted the term *criteria of plausibility assessment* for what Rescher calls *criteria of cognitive systematization.*

[20] Donald T. Campbell and Julian C. Stanley, *Experimental and Quasi-experimental Designs for Research* (Chicago: Rand McNally, 1966); and Thomas D. Cook and Donald T. Campbell, *Quasi-experimentation: Design and Analysis Issues for Field Settings* (Boston: Houghton Miffin, 1979).

[21] See, for example, Duncan MacRae, Jr., *The Social Function of Social Science* (New Haven, CT: Yale University Press, 1976), pp. 92–93.

[22] See, for example, Fischer, *Politics, Values, and Public Policy*, Table 10, pp. 207–10.

[23] Rescher, *Induction*, p. 41.

experts and citizens alike. Finally, it should be noted that any claim about the plausibility of policy arguments based on these criteria is itself subject to argumentation and debate. Any *ex ante* claim about the future performance of policy argumentation in generating optimally plausible truth estimates is itself plausible rather than certain.

MODES OF POLICY ARGUMENT

Modes of policy argument are vehicles for transforming policy-relevant information into policy claims. There are at least eight different ways of transforming information into policy claims:[24] *authoritative, statistical, classificational, intuitive, analycentric, explanatory, pragmatic,* and *value critical.* These eight modes may be contrasted according to the types of arguments used to carry information to claim:

1. *Authoritative mode.* In the authoritative mode policy claims are based on arguments from *authority.* Information is carried to claim on the basis of assumptions about the achieved or ascribed statuses of producers of policy-relevant information. For example, the testimony of scientific experts or seasoned political observers might be used as part of an argument to accept a policy recommendation.

2. *Statistical mode.* In the statistical mode policy claims are based on arguments from *samples.* Information is carried to claim on the basis of the assumption that what is true of members of a sample will also be true of members of the population not included in the sample. For example, random samples of 30 or more individuals are generally taken to be representative of the (unobserved and often unobservable) population from which they were drawn. Nonprobability (for example, purposive) samples may also be assumed to be representative of a population.

3. *Classificational mode.* In the classificational mode policy claims are based on arguments from *membership.* Information is carried to claim on the basis of the assumption that what is true of the class of persons or groups included in the information is also true of individuals or groups which are (or are believed to be) members of the class described in the warrant. For example, classificational arguments may claim that a person has a given attribute, since she is a member of the class of persons the majority of which are assumed to have that attribute. Arguments involving race and sex discrimination, or perceived enemies or ideologies, often take the form of classificational arguments.

4. *Intuitive mode.* In the intuitive mode claims are based on arguments from *insight.* Information is carried to policy claim on the basis of assumptions about the inner mental states of producers of policy-relevant information. For example, the insight, judgment, or "tacit knowledge" of policymakers might be adduced as part of an argument to accept a particular recommendation.

---

[24] These modes of argument are based in part on Brockriede and Ehninger, "Toulmin or Argument." The value-critical mode is an addition to their scheme and that of Toulmin, while other types of argument (motivation, parallel case, analogy) have been regrouped under the pragmatic mode.

5. *Analycentric mode.* In the analycentric mode policy claims are based on arguments from *method*. Information is carried to claim on the basis of assumptions about the validity of methods or rules employed by analysts. For example, a policy claim might be put forth on the basis of arguments that a policy analyst used "universal selection rules" derived from mathematics, systems analysis, or economics.

6. *Explanatory mode.* In the explanatory mode claims are based on arguments from *cause*. Information is carried to claim on the basis of assumptions about the presence of certain generative powers ("causes") and their results ("effects"). For example, a policy claim might be established on the basis of general propositions or "laws" contained within theories about organizational behavior or political decision making.

7. *Pragmatic mode.* In the pragmatic mode policy claims are based on arguments from *motivation, parallel case,* or *analogy*. Information is carried to claim on the basis of assumptions about the motivating power of goals, values, and intentions; assumptions about the similarities among two or more cases of policy-making; or assumptions about similarities among relationships found in two or more policy settings. For example, a policy claim that the government should strictly enforce pollution standards might be based on arguments that citizens are motivated by the desire to achieve the goal of a clean environment or on the basis of arguments that parallel or analogous policies have been successfully implemented in other settings.

8. *Value-critical mode.* In the value-critical mode claims are based on arguments from *ethics*. Information is carried to claim on the basis of assumptions about the rightness or wrongness, goodness or badness of policies and their consequences. For example, a policy claim might be established on the basis of moral principles (equality) or ethical norms (right to privacy) which are deemed to be valid irrespective of the motivations of particular groups.

These eight modes of policy argument, as may be seen, differ in terms of the types of arguments used to establish policy claims. The warrants (W) contained in these arguments also have different characteristics. The six modes of policy argument, the bases of arguments, and the foci of associated warrants are summarized in Table 4–1.

Arguments from Authority

In the authoritative mode, policy claims are based on arguments from *authority*. Policy-relevant information consists of factual reports or expressions of opinion. The function of the warrant in an authoritative argument is to affirm the reliability of the source of the information. The policy claim often simply reiterates information that has been certified by the warrant.[25] To illustrate, let us imagine that a policy analyst advising the National Security Council at the height of the Cold War made the following designative claim (C): "Soviet leaders calculate that a minor buildup of nuclear power in the NATO countries will add only marginally to American striking

---

[25] See Brockriede and Ehninger, "Toulmin on Argument," p. 48.

TABLE 4-1   Modes of Policy Argument

MODE	BASIS	FOCUS OF WARRANT
Authoritative	Authority	Achieved or ascribed statuses of actors ("experts," "insiders")
Statistical	Samples	Estimation of characteristics of an unobserved or unobservable population by means of a sample assumed to be representative due to the operation of some rule (central limit theorem)
Classificational	Membership	Similarity of characteristics of a member of a class on the basis of characteristics of the majority of other members of that class ("Russia is capitalist and must be democratic, since most capitalist countries are democratic")
Intuitive	Insight	Inner mental states of actors (insight, judgment, "tacit knowledge")
Analycentric	Method	Validity of analytic methods or rules ("universal selection rules" of mathematics, economics, systems analysis)
Explanatory	Cause	Generative powers ("causes") and their results ("effects") (general propositions and "laws" within theories of organizational behavior)
Pragmatic	Motivation	Motivating power of goals, values, intentions (desires of policy stakeholders)
	Parallel case	Similarities among cases (parallel policies)
	Analogy	Similarities among relations (analogous policies)
Value critical	Ethics	Rightness or wrongness, goodness or badness of policies and their consequences ("equality" as moral principle)

power." The policy-relevant information (I) is available in the form of a statement from a leading analyst of foreign affairs, Klaus Knorr. "Soviet leaders calculate that a minor buildup of nuclear power in the NATO countries . . . will add only marginally [to the danger of American striking power]."[26] The warrant (W) affirms Knorr's reliability and is backed (B) by additional assumptions that add to the persuasiveness of the argument. The rebuttal (R) challenges the initial assumptions and creates a policy issue, that is, disagreement or conflict over a course of government action (Figure 4-2).

The function of an authoritative argument remains basically the same whether the source of information is an outside expert or the analyst making the argument. Authoritative arguments are not limited to designative claims but may also carry information to evaluative and advocative claims. In each case claims are based on assumptions about the achieved or ascribed status of producers of policy-relevant information. The authority of these persons is established through socially accepted definitions of what it is to be a

---

[26] Ibid., p. 51.

FIGURE 4–2   Structure of authoritative argument.

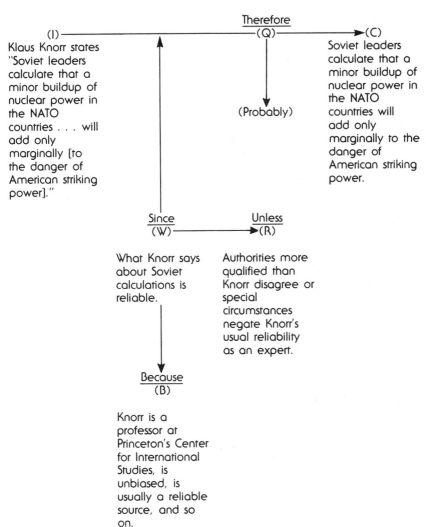

Therefore

(I) ——————————————————(Q)———————————→(C)

Klaus Knorr states
"Soviet leaders
calculate that a
minor buildup of
nuclear power in
the NATO
countries . . . will
add only
marginally [to
the danger of
American striking
power]."

(Probably)

Soviet leaders
calculate that a
minor buildup of
nuclear power in
the NATO
countries will
add only
marginally to the
danger of
American striking
power.

Since   Unless
(W) ——————————→(R)

What Knorr says
about Soviet
calculations is
reliable.

Authorities more
qualified than
Knorr disagree or
special
circumstances
negate Knorr's
usual reliability
as an expert.

Because
(B)

Knorr is a
professor at
Princeton's Center
for International
Studies, is
unbiased, is
usually a reliable
source, and so
on.

qualified producer of information. Depending on the social context, authorities may be kings, magicians, or religious leaders, or they may occupy roles as presidents, legislators, agency heads, scientists, or professors.

The inner mental states of authorities may be important, as in the intuitive mode, although this is rarely the case in arguments about the expertise of producers of information. In contrast to the analycentric mode, the role of methods in authoritative arguments is marginal. Methods may influence the way that information is expressed—for example, in footnotes to government reports, expert testimony, or expert (Delphi) forecasts—but they are unlikely to affect the cogency of authoritative arguments. Finally, arguments developed in the explanatory, pragmatic, and value-critical modes may serve as rebuttals to authoritative arguments, undermining the authority of experts by raising doubts about their qualifications.

Arguments from Samples

In the statistical mode policy claims are based on arguments from *samples*. Policy-relevant information consists of events, conditions, persons, groups, organizations, or societies that are taken to be representative of a larger population of the same elements. The function of the warrant is to affirm that what is true of the elements in the sample is also true of the unobserved (and often unobservable) elements in the population. The policy claim states that the sample is an adequate or satisfactory representation of the population.

To illustrate an argument from a sample, consider the director of a community food bank who wanted to know whether persons receiving food are receiving an adequate daily allowance of calcium, one of the most important minerals in the body (Figure 4–3). The director's claim (C) is that Food Bank clients are receiving 755 milligrams (mg) of calcium, which is less than the Recommended Daily Allowance (RDA) of 800 mg, an amount prescribed by the Food and Nutrition Board of the National Academy of Sciences. In this case the information (I) describes the average daily intake of calcium (755 mg) in a random sample of 50 clients. The information also indicates that this average daily intake could occur by chance 9 times out of 100, a conclusion reached on the basis of a statistical estimate (Z test) and included in the qualifier (Q). The warrant (W) that justifies the transition from information (I) to claim (C) is the principle—often employed habitually, as a rule of thumb, rather than by explicit reference to sampling theory—that a random sample of 30 or more is usually adequate for generalizing to the population from which the sample is selected. When pressed for additional justification the director also checks her statistics text to find the appropriate theoretical backing (B), which is the central limit theorem.

A member of the director's staff responsible for distributing the food is particularly sensitive to criticism and resistant to the idea that clients served by the Food Bank have nutritional deficiencies. The staff member challenges the claim with several rebuttals (R): A 9 percent margin of error leaves too much room for chance; another sample may result in another conclusion; and in any case, the difference between 755 and 800 mg of calcium is not *practically* significant. This last part of the rebuttal is not very plausible, since it is not consistent with the fact that the RDA of 800 mg is a minimum, and any amount less than this would appear to be practically significant. The first two parts of the rebuttal are somewhat more plausible. Additional samples can always lead to different results (after all, the samples are random); and one can always seek greater confidence in making conclusions. On balance, however, it appears that the director's argument is relatively more plausible than that of the staff member, par-

FIGURE 4–3   Structure of statistical argument.

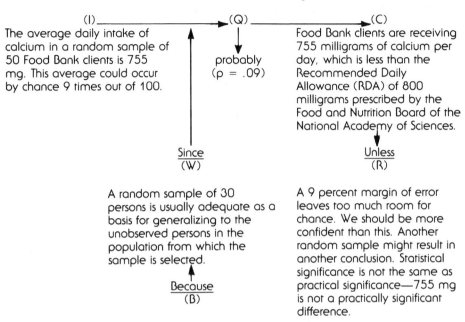

(I)_____→(Q)_____→(C)
The average daily intake of   Food Bank clients are receiving
calcium in a random sample of   755 milligrams of calcium per
50 Food Bank clients is 755   probably   day, which is less than the
mg. This average could occur   (p = .09)   Recommended Daily
by chance 9 times out of 100.   Allowance (RDA) of 800
                    milligrams prescribed by the
                    Food and Nutrition Board of the
                    National Academy of Sciences.

            Since   Unless
            (W)   (R)

A random sample of 30   A 9 percent margin of error
persons is usually adequate as a   leaves too much room for
basis for generalizing to the   chance. We should be more
unobserved persons in the   confident than this. Another
population from which the   random sample might result in
sample is selected.   another conclusion. Statistical
                    significance is not the same as
            Because   practical significance—755 mg
            (B)   is not a practically significant
                    difference.

The central limit theorem (CLT) states that a
random sample equal to or greater than 30
will have a mean which can be considered as
a value from a normal distribution centered
on the population mean with a standard error
equal to the population standard deviation
divided by the square root of the sample size.
The CLT provides a basis for estimating the
probability that the sample mean lies within a
designated margin for error about the
population mean (level of confidence).

ticularly if we consider that additional expenses to conduct research will deplete a limited budget that is supposed to go for food.

Arguments from samples are not always statistical, in the strict sense that statistics are estimates of population values (called parameters). Several types of nonrandom samples, while they do not permit statistical estimates, are nevertheless useful in making claims about populations—for example, purposive samples, theoretical samples, and sociometric (snowball) samples.[27] Even case studies (a sample of one) may be used to generalize to

---

[27] See Delbert C. Miller, *Handbook of Research Design and Social Measurement*, 4th ed. (Newbury Park, CA: Sage Publications, 1991).

wider populations, provided a well-articulated theory is available as a basis for matching patterns in a population with those discovered through case-study research.[28]

Arguments from Membership

In the classificational mode claims are based on arguments from *membership*. Information is carried to claim on the basis of a warrant which asserts that what is true of the class of members included in the information (persons, groups, organizations, states) is also true of members of the class described in the warrant. To illustrate, consider the following argument about the relationship between regime type and the control of terrorism (Figure 4-4). The information (*I*) is that history shows that most authoritarian regimes exercise firm control over terrorists and other armed groups situated within their borders. The claim (*C*) is that Iran, Syria, and Libya can control terrorism. The warrant (*W*) carrying the information to claim is that what is true of most authoritarian regimes is also true of a subset of authoritarian regimes, Iran, Syria, and Libya. The backing (*B*) in this case is the implicit assumption that the class of authoritarian regimes has important shared characteristics, for example, ideological cohesiveness among leaders, centralized political control, effective military intelligence, and so on. The rebuttal (*R*) is that one or more of the Middle Eastern states lacks characteristics—for example, ideological cohesiveness or effective military intelligence—which justify its placement in the class of authoritarian states.

The plausibility of classificational arguments depends heavily on the completeness and internal consistency of the characteristics or properties employed to define the class. Various classes of political regimes—authoritarian, totalitarian, dictatorial, democratic—are typically much less homogeneous and internally consistent than the classification suggests. The same is true with classes of policies (for example, "privatization"), organizations (for example, "public," "private," "nonprofit"), political doctrines (for example, "liberal," "conservative," "reactionary"), and people (for example, "lower class," "middle class," "upper class"). Many apparently simple classifications turn out to be complex, not simple, with multiple dimensions which are frequently inconsistent.

Arguments from Insight

In the intuitive mode policy claims are based on arguments from *insight*. Policy-relevant information consists of factual reports or expressions of opinion. The function of the warrant is to affirm that inner mental states (insight, judgment, understanding) of producers of information make them specially qualified to offer opinions or advice. The policy claim may simply

---

[28] See, for example, Donald T. Campbell, " 'Degrees of Freedom' and the Case Study," in *Methodology and Epistemology for Social Science: Selected Papers*, ed. E. Samuel Overman (Chicago: University of Chicago Press, 1988), pp. 377–87; and Robert K. Yin, *Case Study Analysis* (Beverly Hills, CA: Sage Publications, 1985).

FIGURE 4–4   Structure of classificational argument.

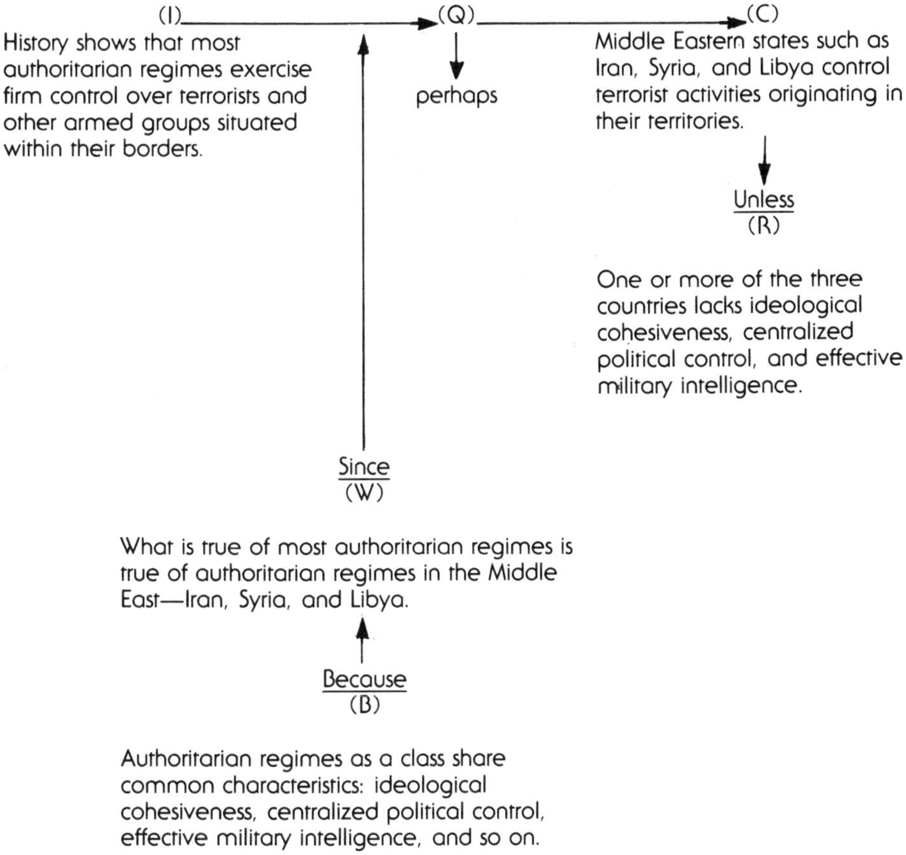

(I)_____→(Q)_____→(C)

History shows that most   Middle Eastern states such as
authoritarian regimes exercise   Iran, Syria, and Libya control
firm control over terrorists and   perhaps   terrorist activities originating in
other armed groups situated   their territories.
within their borders.

Unless
(R)

One or more of the three
countries lacks ideological
cohesiveness, centralized
political control, and effective
military intelligence.

Since
(W)

What is true of most authoritarian regimes is
true of authoritarian regimes in the Middle
East—Iran, Syria, and Libya.

Because
(B)

Authoritarian regimes as a class share
common characteristics: ideological
cohesiveness, centralized political control,
effective military intelligence, and so on.

reiterate the report or opinion supplied in the information. The intuitive
mode of policy analysis may be illustrated by the account of early military
policy making considered earlier:

When in 1334 the Duchess of Tyrol, Margareta Maultasch, encircled the castle
of Hochosterwitz in the province of Carinthia, she knew only too well that
the fortress, situated on an incredibly steep rock rising high above the valley
floor, was impregnable to direct attack and would yield only to a long siege.
In due course, the situation of the defenders became critical: they were down
to their last ox and had only two bags of barley corn left. Margareta's situation
was becoming equally pressing, albeit for different reasons: her troops were
beginning to be unruly, there seemed to be no end to the siege in sight, and
she had similarly urgent military business elsewhere. At this point the commandant of the castle decided on a desperate course of action which to his
men must have seemed sheer folly; he had the last ox slaughtered, had its

abdominal cavity filled with the remaining barley, and ordered the carcass thrown down the steep cliff onto a meadow in front of the enemy camp. Upon receiving this scornful message from above, the discouraged duchess abandoned the siege and moved on.[29]

In this illustration (Figure 4–5) the policy claim (C) is: "We should throw down the last ox." Policy-relevant information (I) is available in the form of the commandant's inner mental states or thoughts as he analyzed the problem: "The commandant believes that the last slaughtered ox, when

FIGURE 4–5   Structure of intuitive argument.

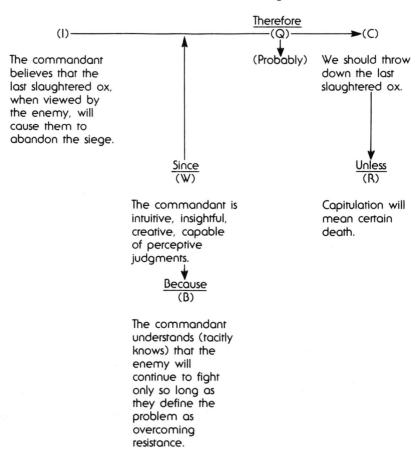

---

[29] Quoted in Paul Watzlawick, John Weakland, and Richard Fisch, *Change: Principles of Problem Formation and Problem Resolution* (New York: W.W. Norton & Company, 1974), p. xi.

viewed by the enemy, will cause them to abandon the siege." The warrant (W) affirms that the commandant has special capabilities (insight, judgment), and the backing (B) adds cogency to the argument by describing what the commandant understands or tacitly knows about the nature of the problem. The rebuttal (R), which is here attached to the claim (C), challenges the commandant's recommendation by offering a counterargument. Note that the rebuttal cannot be attached to the warrant in this case, since we are dealing with an inner mental state that is by definition private and unknown to others.

This example of fourteenth-century military policy-making serves to emphasize the unique advantages of insight, judgment, and tacit knowledge in developing creative resolutions of policy problems. Yet it also points to the difficulties and weaknesses of the intuitive mode of policy analysis. For there is perhaps no concept in contemporary policy analysis that is more difficult to grasp than that of "intuition." While many commentators on policy analysis urge that intuition, judgment, and tacit knowledge be incorporated in the analysis of policy problems,[30] the difficulty with intuitive policy analysis, as compared with other modes, is that it seems impossible to specify in advance the methods or forms of reasoning that are likely to yield insight or creativity. A creative act, observes Churchman, "is an act that cannot be designed beforehand, although it may be analyzable in retrospect. If this is the correct meaning of creativity, then no intelligent technician can be creative."[31]

The intuitive mode places primary reliance on the inner mental states of producers of information as a means for developing policy arguments. Although warrants in the intuitive and authoritative modes affirm something about producers of information, arguments in the authoritative mode are concerned with publicly accepted definitions of expertise, and not with the inner mental states of qualified occupants of various social roles. Insight, understanding, and judgment may come from direct personal experiences with policy-making, as when policymakers and policy analysts discern the meaning of "serial acts of conscious choice which punctuate and seem to modify [their] course."[32] But in this case intuition must become "public" if it is to serve as a basis for arguments in the pragmatic mode. Further, intuition often provides basic assumptions for arguments in the analycentric, explanatory, and value-critical modes, although this is seldom recognized and less often acknowledged. Although intuitive policy analysis is a neglected area, it is also elusive. For while insight, understanding, and judg-

---

[30] For example, Yehezkel Dror, *Ventures in Policy Sciences* (New York: American Elsevier Publishing Co., 1971), p. 52; Sir Geoffrey Vickers, *The Art of Judgment: A Study of Policy Making* (New York: Basic Books, 1965); and Edgar S. Quade, *Analysis for Public Decisions* (New York: American Elsevier, 1975), pp. 4–5. Some observers have also commented favorably on the possibility of drug-induced changes in the mental states of policymakers. See Kenneth B. Clark, "The Pathos of Power: A Psychological Perspective," *American Psychologist*, 26, No. 12 (1971), 1047–57.
[31] Churchman, *The Design of Inquiring Systems*, p. 17.
[32] Vickers, *The Art of Judgment*, p. 13.

ment may be difficult to describe, it does not help to know simply that mental states are inner, private, and inaccessible to others. What is needed are publicly available methods for identifying and somehow learning how to practice creative acts.[33]

Arguments from Method

In the analycentric mode policy claims are based on arguments from *method*. Policy-relevant information may consist of factual statements or reports and the function of the warrant is to provide a reason for accepting the claim by associating it with the use of approved analytic methods or rules. The claim is that the event, condition, or object described in the information should be regarded as valuable, or worthless, or adopted as a desirable course of action. To illustrate, let us consider the following public investment problem. Imagine that an analyst has information (I) that the production of energy per dollar is greater in nuclear power plants than in hydroelectric plants, which in turn produce more energy per dollar than solar power plants. The claim (C) is that the government should invest in nuclear energy rather than solar energy. The warrant (W) associates information with claim by invoking the transitivity rule of mathematical economics.[34] The warrant is backed (B) by the assumption that transitivity is a "universal selection rule" which guarantees the rationality of choice. The rebuttal (R) and its backing (B) challenge the original assumption about the universal validity of transitivity and create the grounds for a methodological debate (Figure 4–6).

In the analycentric mode policy claims are assessed primarily in terms of the methods and rules whereby they are produced. The sense of "analysis" in the analycentric mode is best conveyed by a dictionary definition of the term as "the separation or breaking up of a whole into its fundamental elements or constituent parts." Methods themselves are derived from rules of formal logic. Once a policy problem has been decomposed or broken up into its constituent parts (for example, projects with different benefits and costs), then these parts provide a basis for comparing and choosing the alternative which is "optimal," that is, results in the greatest benefit in re-

---

[33] Ibid., p. 17. The common distinctions among types of intuitive experiences, particularly those of a "secular," "religious," and "mystical" nature, should not be overdrawn. Churchman, in illustrating the power of religious imagery as a source of intuition, recalls the story of the French mathematician, Henri Poincaré, who for a long period had been grappling with a difficult mathematical problem. "Suddenly, when he was in the midst of the very mundane act of stepping on a bus, the whole solution flashed in his mind . . . he not only knew the solution, he knew he knew it. But what was the flash of insight? It's not very helpful to label it 'intuition,' nor to say that it was the result of 'unconscious thinking.' It seems far more revealing to say . . . that God spoke to him." Churchman goes on to argue that any source of intuition or creative thought, from supreme beings to astrology, provides an accessible point of reference from which one can begin to learn about intuition and creativity, rather than talk in more vague or general terms, pp. 243–44.

[34] On rules expressing transitive and cyclical preferences, see, for example, Norman Frohlich and Joe A. Oppenheimer, *Modern Political Economy* (Englewood Cliffs, NJ: Prentice Hall, 1978), pp. 6–13.

FIGURE 4–6   Structure of analycentric argument.

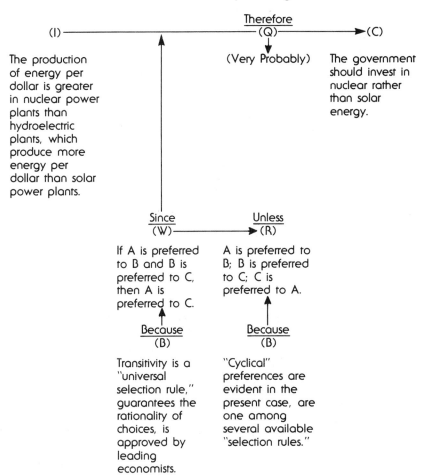

lation to costs. In the analycentric mode analysts tend to believe that the use of approved methods "sets the policy agenda and its directions, that useful analysis will be used analysis."[35]

The analycentric mode is related to the authoritative and intuitive modes, insofar as authority and intuition may serve as sources of approved methods. Professional and scientific communities, for example, create and maintain definitions of the purpose, scope, methods, and problem orientation of policy analysis and other applied disciplines.[36] Intuition may also

---

[35] Allen Schick, "Beyond Analysis," *Public Administration Review*, 37, No. 3 (1977), 259.

[36] See, for example, Thomas Kuhn, *The Structure of Scientific Revolutions*, 2nd ed. (Chicago: University of Chicago Press, 1971), p. 103.

serve as a source of approved methods. The acceptance of basic axioms of mathematical economics, for example, may be a product of intuition:

> Consider . . . the axiom which asserts the transitivity of preference: if A is preferred to B, and B to C, then A is (or rationally must be) preferred to C. The intuitive appeal of this assertion is so great that few if any economists feel the urge to build formal economic systems in which the axiom fails. Geometry . . . is the classic example; the intuitive strength of Euclid's "postulates" was so great that for two thousand years geometers played their games strictly within the domain . . . which Euclid had laid down. Even when non-Euclidean geometries were discovered in the early ninteenth century, most mathematicians never thought of them as valid.[37]

In the analycentric mode the adherence to approved methods is frequently believed to provide guarantees that policy decisions will be "rational." A rational choice is thought to be possible (1) if the analyst can order all consequences associated with action, (2) if the ordering of consequences is transitive, and (3) if the analyst can consistently and in a transitive fashion choose the alternative which will bring the greatest benefit in relation to cost.[38]

Challenges to this argument may be made on authoritative, intuitive, pragmatic, and ethical grounds. Thus, for example, new schools of analysis may serve as a source of approved methods, new axioms providing for nontransitive preferences may come to be accepted on intuitive grounds, and rules which run counter to moral principles and ethical norms may be replaced with new ones.[39] Challenges may also be made on pragmatic grounds, for example, by arguing that "universal selection rules" do not actually promote better decisions in policy settings characterized by incomplete information, value conflicts, and multiple competing objectives.[40] Yet it is difficult to challenge such rules on explanatory grounds, since a successful argument from method must demonstrate only that the results of using particular rules of choice are superior to those which occur without them, and that the observed improvement bears some relation to the change in action prescribed by the rule.[41] To show that improved results are a consequence of the use of a particular rule (for example, transitivity), the analyst need not certify or prove that the relation between rule and claim is a causal one. Rather it is pragmatic arguments, that is, those which assess

[37] Churchman, *The Design of Inquiring Systems*, p. 25.

[38] Joseph L. Bower, "Descriptive Decision Theory from the 'Administrative' Viewpoint," in *The Study of Policy Formation*, ed. Raymond A. Bauer and Kenneth J. Gergen (New York: The Free Press, 1968), pp. 104–6.

[39] See, for example, the discussion of the evolution of welfare economics in MacRae, *The Social Function of Social Science*, pp. 107–57.

[40] See, for example, Raymond Bauer's Introduction to *The Study of Policy Formation*, pp. 11–12.

[41] Joseph Bower, "Descriptive Decision Theory from the 'Administrative' Viewpoint," p. 106.

claims in terms of their observed consequences, which have the greatest capacity to overturn policy claims made in the analycentric mode.

Arguments from Cause

In the explanatory mode analysts are primarily concerned with determining the causes and effects of public policies.[42] Analysts typically use arguments from *cause* to transform policy-relevant information into policy claims. In causal arguments information consists of one or more factual statements or reports about a policy environment, policy stakeholder, or a public policy. The warrant transforms these statements or reports by relating them to generative powers (causes) and their results (effects). The policy claim then relates these causes and effects back to the information supplied.

The role of causal arguments in transforming policy-relevant information into policy claims may be illustrated by political scientist Graham Allison's account of the role of conceptual models in explaining foreign policy behavior during the Cuban Missile Crisis in October, 1962.[43] Showing how different conceptual models result in alternative explanations of foreign policy, Allison argues that (1) government policy analysts think about problems of foreign policy in terms of implicit conceptual models that shape their thought; (2) most analysts explain the behavior of governments in terms of one basic model which assumes the rationality of political choices (*rational policy model*); and (3) alternative conceptual models, including those which emphasize organizational processes (*organizational process model*) and bureaucratic politics (*bureaucratic politics model*), provide bases for improved explanation and prediction of foreign policy behavior.

In this effort to compare and contrast alternative conceptual models, Allison uses the explanatory mode of policy analysis. The main purpose of the analysis is to assess various advocative claims about the proper direction of U.S. foreign policy by reviewing explanatory arguments derived from the three conceptual models. The policy alternatives open to the United

---

[42] For works representative of the explanatory mode, see, for example, James E. Anderson, *Public Policy-Making* (New York: Praeger Publishers, 1975); Thomas R. Dye, *Understanding Public Policy*, 3rd ed. (Englewood Cliffs, NJ: Prentice Hall, 1978); Robert Eyestone, *The Threads of Public Policy: A Study in Policy Leadership* (Indianapolis, IN: Bobbs-Merrill, 1971); Jerald Hage and J. Rogers Hollingsworth, "The First Steps toward the Integration of Social Theory and Public Policy," *The Annals of the American Academy of Political and Social Science*, 434 (November 1977), 1–23; Richard I. Hofferbert, *The Study of Public Policy* (Indianapolis, IN: Bobbs-Merrill, 1974); Charles O. Jones, *An Introduction to the Study of Public Policy*, 2nd ed. (North Scituate, MA: Duxbury Press, 1977); Robert L. Lineberry, *American Public Policy: What Government Does and What Difference It Makes* (New York: Harper & Row, 1977); Austin Ranney, ed., *Political Science and Public Policy* (Chicago: Markham, 1968); Richard Rose, ed., *The Dynamics of Public Policy: A Comparative Analysis* (Beverly Hills, CA: Sage Publications, 1976); Ira Sharkansky, ed., *Policy Analysis in Political Science* (Cambridge, MA: Markham, 1970); and Peter Woll, *Public Policy* (Cambridge, MA: Winthrop Publishers, 1974).

[43] Graham T. Allison, "Conceptual Models and the Cuban Missile Crisis," *The American Political Science Review*, LXIII, No. 3 (1969), 689–718.

States—from no action to diplomatic pressures, secret negotiations, invasion, surgical air strike, and blockade—are examined in terms of alternative explanations of foreign policy behavior. The structure of these explanations is of the classical (deductive-nomological) type, which means that valid explanations are possible only when general theoretical propositions or laws link prior circumstances with subsequent events.[44]

Among the several advocative claims made at the time of the Cuban Missile Crisis let us consider that policy recommendation actually adopted by the United States government: "The United States should blockade Cuba." In this case the policy-relevant information is "The Soviet Union is placing offensive missiles in Cuba." To carry information (*I*) to policy claim (*C*), a warrant (*W*) answers the question: What makes it possible, given the information provided, to claim that the United States should blockade Cuba? The warrant provides the answer, which is *since* "The blockade will force the withdrawal of missiles by showing the Russians that the United States is determined to use force." In providing additional cogency to the argument the backing (*B*) answers the question: Why would the blockade have this effect? The backing answers the question by stating *because* "An increase in the cost of an alternative reduces the likelihood of that alternative being chosen."[45] Note that the backing represents a general theoretical proposition or law within the rational policy model (Figure 4–7).

The primary purpose of Allison's account is not to demonstrate the inherent superiority of one or another of the three conceptual models; it is rather to show that the use of multiple competing models can result in improved explanations of foreign policy behavior. The use of multiple models moves policy analysis from a self-contained argument about the relation between information and claim to a new stage where a reasoned debate about policy issues may occur. In this context, the organizational process model provides a rebuttal (*R*) in the form of a competing causal argument. The rebuttal states *unless* "Russian leaders are unable to force their own organizational units to depart from assigned tasks and routines." This might occur *because* "Major lines of organizational behavior are straight, that is, behavior at one time is marginally different from that behavior at *t* − 1."[46] The backing (*B*) for the rebuttal is once more a general proposition or law within the organizational process model.

The use of causal arguments is essential for the interpretation of information in the explanatory mode. Information is carried to claim by means of assumptions about nonhuman generative powers (causes) and their results (effects).[47] Yet the case of policy arguments during the Cuban Missile Crisis also illustrates some of the difficulties and limitations of policy analysis in the explanatory mode. First, several competing causal arguments may serve equally well in carrying information to policy claim. These arguments,

---

[44] See Carl G. Hempel, *Aspects of Scientific Explanation* (New York: The Free Press, 1965) and the discussion below.

[45] Allison, "Conceptual Models," p. 694.

[46] Ibid., p. 702.

[47] Brockriede and Ehninger, "Toulmin on Argument," p. 48.

FIGURE 4–7   Structure of explanatory argument.

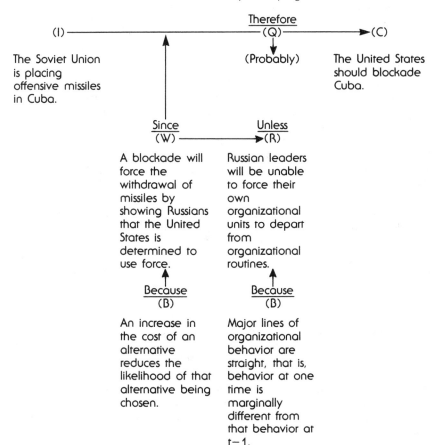

whether or not they are backed by scientific theories, can seldom be corroborated or refuted on the basis of the available information.[48] Second, a given causal argument, however persuasive, cannot directly lead to an advocative claim or recommendation, since traditional causal explanations do not themselves contain value premises.[49] In the example above there is a

[48] See Georg H. von Wright, *Explanation and Understanding* (Ithaca, NY: Cornell University Press, 1970), p. 145; and Kuhn, *The Structure of Scientific Revolutions.*

[49] This is not to say that these explanations do not imply values, since all empirical theories in the social as well as natural sciences rest on certain unstated value premises. See, for example, M. Gunther and K. Reshaur, "Science and Values in Political 'Science,'" *Philosophy of Social Sciences*, 1, (1971), 113–21; J. W. Sutherland, "Axiological Predicates in Scientific Enterprise," *General Systems*, XIX (1974), 3–14; and Ian I. Mitroff, *The Subjective Side of Science: A Philosophical Inquiry into the Psychology of the Apollo Moon Scientists* (New York: American Elsevier Publishing Co., 1974).

suppressed value premise, which is that United States leaders are motivated by a desire to achieve the value of security from Soviet military presence in the western hemisphere. If some other values had motivated policymakers, either one of the causal arguments might have supported altogether different claims, for example, that the United States should invade and occupy Cuba.

Compared with other modes the explanatory mode transforms information primarily in terms of nonhuman generative powers (causes) and their results (effects); rarely does the explanatory mode focus on intentions, goals, or desires, factors which are essential for analysts working in the pragmatic mode. Indeed, analysts working in the explanatory mode tend to avoid subjective factors of any kind, preferring instead to emphasize empirically observable effects of decisions taken by policy actors.[50] In the explanatory mode analysts generally avoid case studies and analogies, since neither provides explanations that are valid over time and in a variety of settings.[51]

Explanatory policy analysis may accept intuition, judgment, or "tacit knowledge" as appropriate constituents of policy analysis.[52] Yet when such subjective factors are included as legitimate aspects of policy analysis, it is by considering inner subjective states as a possible vehicle for "discovering" policy-relevant information; subjective factors are not regarded as appropriate bases for "validating" policy claims. Therefore, subjective factors are received with great suspicion until they have been made public through observational methods (for example, interobserver agreement and replicability) that permit the intersubjective confirmation of experience. Intersubjective agreement serves as a check on the subjectivity of policy analysts, making them epistemologically accountable for their claims.[53]

Analysts working in the explanatory mode attach only secondary importance to the proper use of accepted analytic methods or to the authority attached to policy-relevant information. Explanatory policy analysis, for example, reflects a general skepticism about the use of methods or rules for making "optimal" policy decisions. The primary criticism of optimization methods developed in economics, mathematics, operation research, and systems analysis is that they bear little if any resemblance to the ways that policies are actually made.[54] Finally, if authoritative arguments are used at all, it is to further certify causal arguments, rather than to argue that the achieved characteristics (expertise) or ascribed statuses (social position) of producers of policy-relevant information are valued in their own right.[55]

---

[50] See, for example, Hofferbert, *The Study of Public Policy*, p. 4, who writes that policies are "the visible products of decisions taken by identifiable actors for public purposes."

[51] See, for example, Dye, *Understanding Public Policy*, pp. 7–8.

[52] See, for example, Dror, *Ventures in Policy Sciences;* and Sheldon Wolin, "Political Theory as a Vocation," *The American Political Science Review*, 63 (1969), 1062–82. The term "tacit knowledge" comes from Michael Polanyi, *Personal Knowledge* (Chicago: University of Chicago Press, 1958).

[53] The best discussion of these points is Martin Landau, *Political Theory and Political Science* (New York: The Macmillan Company, 1972), pp. 43–77.

[54] See Bower, "Descriptive Decision Theory from the 'Administrative' Viewpoint."

[55] For a parallel argument, see Walter Wallace, *The Logic of Science in Sociology* (Chicago: Aldine Publishing Company, 1971), p. 12.

The ultimate aim of analysts working in the explanatory mode is to develop and test general propositions that explain public policy.[56] Explanations are generally sought by employing traditional causal reasoning, sometimes known as deductive-nomological explanation. This particular form of explanation is that described by philosopher Carl Hempel:

> We divide explanation into two major constituents, the *explanandum* and the *explanans*. By the explanandum, we understand the sentence describing the phenomenon to be explained (not that phenomenon itself); by the explanans the class of those sentences which are adduced to account for the phenomenon. . . . [Scientific explanation] answers the question, "Why did the explanandum-phenomenon occur?" by showing that the phenomenon resulted from particular circumstances, specified in C_1, C_2, . . . , C_k, in accordance with laws L_1, L_2, . . . , L_r. By pointing this out, the argument shows that, given the particular circumstances and the laws in question, the occurrence of the phenomenon was to be *expected*; and it is in this sense that the explanation enables us to understand why the phenomenon occurred.[57]

A simple example can serve to illustrate traditional causal explanation.[58] If I leave my car outside over night and the temperature drops below freezing, my full radiator (without antifreeze) will burst. Why will this happen? "My radiator burst" (*explanandum*). "My radiator was full of water, the cap was tightly fastened, and the temperature outside dropped below freezing" (circumstances, or C_k, in the *explanans*). Finally, "the volume of water expands when it freezes" (general proposition or law, L_r, in the explanans).[59] In this example knowledge of prior circumstances and the appropriate law permit us to predict the resultant event with certainty.

Although this is an example of one type of explanation, there are serious questions about its suitability for the kinds of problems historians, social scientists, and policy analysts investigate.[60] This is so, among other reasons, because policy analysis is partly evaluative and advocative in character. Every advocative claim contains both factual and value premises, whereas in traditional causal explanations we find only factual premises. Traditional causal explanations also require that the *explanans* precede or accompany the *explanandum*. Yet many advocative claims often reverse this sequence, insofar as circumstances that explain an action are often situated in the future. Future circumstances, including intentions, goals, and desires, explain present actions to the extent that actions cannot occur without the motivation provided by such intentions, goals, and desires.[61] Finally, any correspondence between the results of acting on an advocative

---

[56] Allison, "Conceptual Models," notes on p. 690 (note 4), for example, that Hempel's description of classical (deductive-nomological) explanation is used as the basis for his arguments.

[57] Hempel, *Aspects of Scientific Explanation*, pp. 247, 337.

[58] See von Wright, *Explanation and Understanding*, p. 12.

[59] Ibid. p. 12.

[60] Ibid. p. 11.

[61] Ibid. pp. 74–124; G. E. M. Anscombe, *Intention* (London: Basil Blackwell, 1957); and W. H. Dray, *Laws and Explanation in History* (London: Oxford University Press, 1957).

claim and the conclusions of a causal argument may be purely accidental. In matters of public policy, predictions made on the basis of deductive-nomological explanations will fail if policy actors decide on the basis of intelligent reflection to change their behavior, or if "unpredictable factors deriving from creative intellectual innovation intervene."[62]

Pragmatic Arguments

In the pragmatic mode policy claims are based on arguments from *motivation, parallel case,* and *analogy.* Information may consist of statements of fact or opinion that have been established as claims in a previous argument. The warrant in an argument from motivation interprets these statements in terms of the motivating power of intentions, goals, or values of policy stakeholders. The warrant in arguments from parallel case or analogy asserts that instances of policy reported in the information bear an essential similarity either to a second instance believed to be in the same category or to a second instance which is believed to evidence a similar relationship. Policy claims either assert that a course of action should be adopted because of the motivating power of intentions, goals, or values or because parallel or analogous policies have succeeded in the past.

In the pragmatic mode policy claims are based on the assumption that "the ends of action are seldom *fully* stable and determined until the act is finished or is so completely relegated to automatic routines that it no longer requires consciousness and attention."[63] Hence, advocative claims are rarely based on traditional causal arguments of the kind produced in the explanatory mode, where the function of general propositions and laws is to provide explanations and predictions in which cause and effect are fully stated and determined in advance of action.[64] In the pragmatic mode relationships between action and consequence are only partly known in advance of action, as may be seen by examining the three kinds of arguments used in the pragmatic mode:

1. *Motivational arguments.* In arguments from motivation policy claims are based on assumptions that an action should be adopted because of the motivating power of intentions, goals, or values of policy actors. Such arguments seek to demonstrate that the goals or values underlying a recommended course of action are such as to warrant its acceptance, adoption, or performance. In cases where no parallel or analogous policies are available, it is often sufficient to know that large or important groups actually desire to follow the course of action contained in the claim. Here the principle may be: "We know what's right, but we won't fully know whether it will work until we try it." School

---

[62] Alasdair MacIntyre, "Ideology, Social Science, and Revolution," *Comparative Politics,* 5, No. 3 (1973), p. 334.

[63] Louis Wirth, "Preface" to Karl Mannheim, *Ideology and Utopia: An Introduction to the Sociology of Knowledge* (London: Routledge & Kegan Paul, 1960), p. xxiv.

[64] See, for example, Merton's definition of a scientific law as "a statement of invariance derivable from a theory." Robert Merton, *Social Theory and Social Structure* (Glencoe, IL: The Free Press, 1957), pp. 95–96.

desegregation and the War on Poverty are examples of policies based partly on motivational arguments.

2. *Comparative arguments.* In comparative arguments (or arguments from parallel case), policy claims are based on assumptions that the results of policies adopted in similar circumstances are worthwhile or successful. Government agencies in the United States and abroad often face similar problems, and policy claims may be based on their experiences. The British experience with comprehensive medical care and city planning ("new towns") has influenced debates about policy alternatives in the United States. The experience of certain states in adopting taxation, open housing, and equal employment opportunity policies has been used as a basis for policy recommendations at the federal level.[65] A variation of comparing parallel cases in different settings is an argument based on the experience of the same agency over time. Past policies in the same agency are used as a basis for claims that the agency should adopt particular courses of action, usually those which are marginally different from the status quo. Claims about federal and state budgetary policy typically derive from assumptions about similarities with past policies adopted in the same agency.[66]

3. *Analogical arguments.* In arguments from analogy policy claims are based on assumptions that relationships (not cases themselves) among two or more policies are essentially similar. A large number of policies in many issue areas may be based on arguments from analogy. For example, advocative claims about air pollution policies may be based on assumptions about the success of water pollution policies. In making claims about ways to reduce employment discrimination against women, the analyst may proceed from assumptions about the success or failure of policies designed to reduce discrimination against blacks.[67]

To illustrate the pragmatic mode let us consider the following advocative claim (C): "The Congress should pass the Equal Rights Amendment." The first warrant (W_1) is motivational and affirms the claim by arguing that a formally stated need for action is grounded in a widely shared desire to achieve social equality. The second warrant (W_2) is comparative and affirms the claim by arguing that equal rights legislation has been effective in other similar settings. The analogical warrant (W_3) carries information to claim on the basis of an assumption that legislation against racial discrimination is related to the effective prevention of racial discrimination in the same way that the Equal Rights Amendment is related to the effective prevention of sex discrimination (Figure 4–8).

Each of the three types of pragmatic arguments proceed from the same policy-relevant information (I), which is that the Equal Rights Amendment is needed to prevent discrimination against women. This information might have been established in a previous argument, for example, an argument based on the assumption that existing legislation is ineffective in preventing

---

[65] Lineberry, *American Public Policy*, p. 28.

[66] See, for example, Aaron Wildavsky's now classic treatment of incremental policy-making in *The Politics of the Budgetary Process* (Boston: Little, Brown and Company, 1964).

[67] Lineberry, *American Public Policy*, p. 28.

FIGURE 4–8   Structure of pragmatic argument.

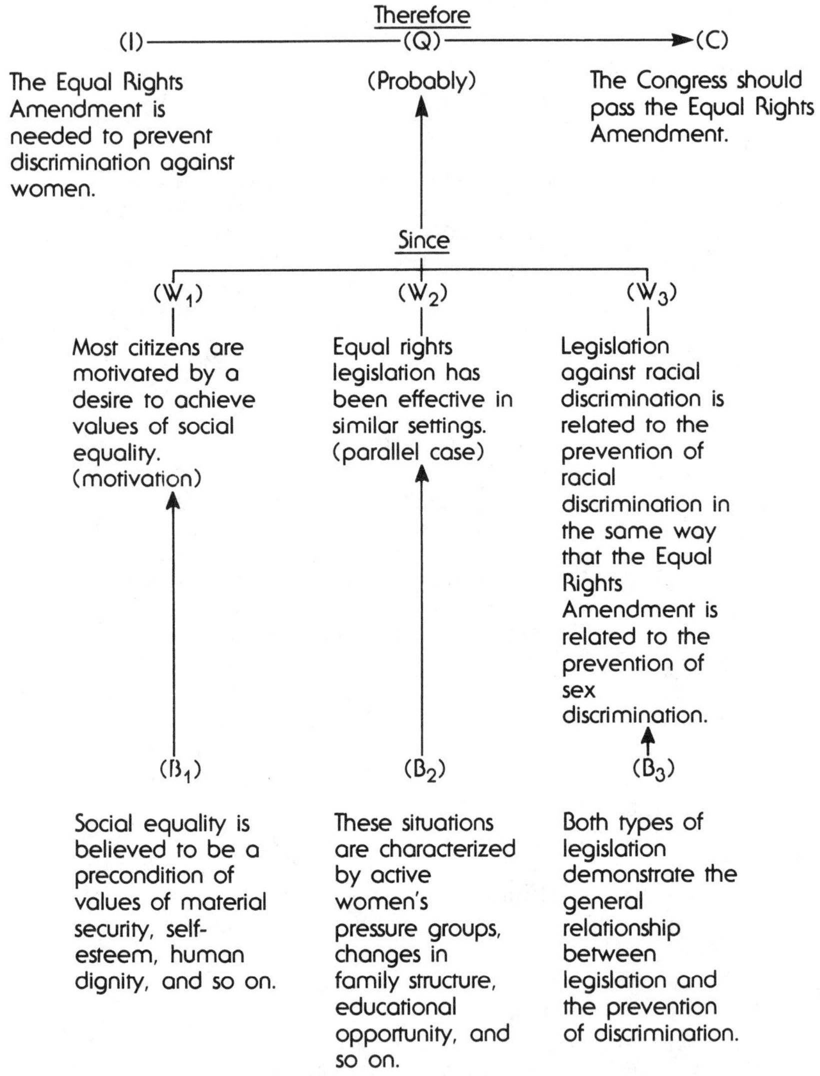

Therefore

(I) ——————————————(Q)———————————————▶(C)

| The Equal Rights Amendment is needed to prevent discrimination against women. | (Probably) | The Congress should pass the Equal Rights Amendment. |

Since

(W_1)   (W_2)   (W_3)

| Most citizens are motivated by a desire to achieve values of social equality. (motivation) | Equal rights legislation has been effective in similar settings. (parallel case) | Legislation against racial discrimination is related to the prevention of racial discrimination in the same way that the Equal Rights Amendment is related to the prevention of sex discrimination. |

(B_1)   (B_2)   (B_3)

| Social equality is believed to be a precondition of values of material security, self-esteem, human dignity, and so on. | These situations are characterized by active women's pressure groups, changes in family structure, educational opportunity, and so on. | Both types of legislation demonstrate the general relationship between legislation and the prevention of discrimination. |

sex discrimination. Note also that the three warrants are backed in different ways. The first backing (B_1) reinforces the cogency of the argument by stating that social equality is believed to be a precondition of fundamental human values (material security, self-esteem, human dignity). The second backing (B_2) strengthens the argument by specifying the characteristics of the situations that make them similar, while the third (B_3) assents the existence of analogous relationships. Although rebuttals (R) have not been provided as part of the illustration, there are many counterassumptions that may be introduced to challenge the claim that Congress should pass the Equal Rights Amendment.[68]

The pragmatic mode differs from the authoritative insofar as the special position or expertise of producers of information does not enter directly into policy arguments. Yet authority may exert an indirect influence on the persuasiveness of policy arguments. The image of countries known for effective policies in certain areas—for example, health policies in socialist countries—may affect the initial selection of cases regarded as suitable for comparison. The fact that persons are speaking for one or another stakeholder group (labor, farmers, corporate business) may itself be sufficient to call into question or dismiss arguments from motivation. Finally, comparative arguments that focus on the same agency or institution may be authoritative arguments in disguise, since tradition, habit, and established governmental routines may serve as the functional equivalents of warrants in the authoritative mode.[69]

The pragmatic mode also differs from the intuitive. In arguments from insight, claims are based on assumptions about the inner mental states of producers of information, while pragmatic arguments stress the consequences of action. Nevertheless, pragmatic arguments may place heavy emphasis on "extrarational" processes as a basis for improved policy-making. Extrarational processes, in Dror's words, make

a positive contribution to better policy making. Intuitive judgment, holistic impressions derived from immersion in a situation, and creative invention of new alternatives are illustrations of extrarational phases of preferable policy-making.[70]

The claim here is not that the mere presence of certain inner mental states among producers of information is alone sufficient, but that the practical consequences of acting on a claim based on insight may be superior. The argument, therefore, is pragmatic and not intuitive, even though the inner mental state of the producer of information affects its eventual success or failure in the field of action.

The pragmatic and intuitive modes are also based on similar conceptions of the meaning of policy. Both emphasize definitions of policy as subjectively guided action and rely heavily on the capacity of analysts to interpret the meaning of policies as seen from the perspectives of policy stakeholders themselves.[71] This is most evident in motivational arguments,

---

[68] For example, most citizens may not be motivated by a desire to achieve values of social equality; or apparently similar settings may not be comparable on one or more dimensions.

[69] For a well-known critique of incremental policy-making partly in terms of its authoritative nature see Yehezkel Dror, "Muddling Through—'Science' or Inertia?" *Public Administration Review*, 24, No. 3, (1964), 153–65.

[70] Dror, *Ventures in Policy Sciences*, p. 261.

[71] For a thorough treatment of subjective understanding, see Fred R. Dallmayr and

where policy claims are based on assumptions about the intentions, goals, and values of stakeholders who affect and are affected by policies. Yet comparative and analogical arguments may also depend heavily on the subjective interpretation of meaning. Thus, to know whether policies represent parallels or analogs, one must also establish that they involve similar goals, values, and intentions.

The pragmatic mode bears a superficial resemblance to the analycentric mode, insofar as both aim at the improvement of policy-making by taking into account the preferences of policy actors. Yet it is one thing to base advocative claims on allegedly "universal" selection rules (that is, the transitivity of preferences) and quite another to base claims on goals and values encountered in specific policy contexts. In specific contexts the presence of value conflicts often negates two major assumptions of analycentric policy analysis; namely, that policy choices "involve an individual decision maker, and value is unidimensional and functionally expressible in dollars."[72] In short, it is not the mere consideration of subjective preferences that distinguishes the pragmatic and analycentric modes, but the way that such subjective factors are taken into account. In the pragmatic mode "preferences" are grounded in the meaning of action to policy actors in specific contexts.[73]

The pragmatic and explanatory modes may be contrasted in terms of different conceptions of the role of science in policy analysis:[74]

1. *Theory-directed vs. problem-oriented analysis.* The ultimate aim of analysis in the explanatory mode is the development and testing of general scientific theories, whereas the pragmatic mode seeks to create policies modified by the results of analysis.

2. *Cumulative vs. time-limited knowledge.* In the explanatory mode analysts strive for complete information after actions have been taken, whereas analysts working in the pragmatic mode are typically satisfied with partial information available at the time actions must be taken.

3. *Methodological precision vs. probable approximation.* In the explanatory mode analysts seek results which are methodologically precise, but perhaps grossly inappropriate, while in the pragmatic mode analysts strive for results which are approximately correct with a high degree of appropriateness to the problem.

Thomas A. McCarthy, eds., *Understanding and Social Inquiry* (Notre Dame, IN: University of Notre Dame Press, 1977). For an extension of principles of subjective understanding to decision making and policy analysis, see Robert A. Gorman, "On the Inadequacies of Nonphilosophical Political Science: A Critical Analysis of Decision-Making Theory," *International Studies Quarterly*, 14, No. 4 (1970), 395–411.

[72] Bower, "Descriptive Decision Theory from the 'Administrative' Viewpoint," p. 107.

[73] See Rein's discussion of idiographic analysis, where narratives, arguments, case studies, and organizational stories are used to develop explanations of values, goals, and preferences which are "always embedded in a specific context." Rein, *Social Science and Public Policy*, pp. 14–15, 139–70.

[74] See James S. Coleman, *Policy Research in the Social Sciences* (Morristown, NJ: General Learning Press, 1972); and Thomas Dye, *Policy Analysis: What Governments Do, Why They Do It, and What Difference It Makes* (University, AL: University of Alabama Press, 1976), pp. 15–19.

4. *Explanatory adequacy vs. manipulability.* In the explanatory mode analysts focus on variables that will provide the most adequate explanations within a discipline-based theory, whereas analysts working in the pragmatic mode seek to identify factors which are subject to policy manipulation.

5. *Scientific vs. everyday communication.* In the explanatory mode analysts use terminology that is valued because it contributes to precise communication among social scientists within disciplines, while analysts working in the pragmatic mode attempt to use language which is part of the policy setting and the everyday lives of policy stakeholders.

6. *Self-corrective vs. planned competitiveness.* In the explanatory mode analysts are subject to self-corrective mechanisms that facilitate organized criticism within scientific disciplines and the scrutiny of research results by colleagues, whereas it is often necessary in the pragmatic mode to introduce competition among analysts with different perspectives as a way to maintain or enhance the validity of findings.

The pragmatic and explanatory modes also differ in terms of their respective approaches to the explanation of policy. In the explanatory mode information has no meaning outside the context provided by general scientific propositions and laws, even though conformity to experience is the final test of any proposition.[75] In the pragmatic mode experience is likewise decisive, with one important difference; claims in the pragmatic mode refer to actions, whereas claims in the explanatory mode refer to events.[76] Explanations of action in the pragmatic mode are typically based on motivational arguments of the form "The government should adopt course action A, since most citizens are motivated by the desire to achieve the ends toward which the action is directed." Although it may appear so, this is not merely a circular argument; rather it is one of the primary means for developing rational explanations of action in the social sciences.[77]

Motivational arguments represent a form of reasoning which philosophers since Aristotle have called *practical syllogism* or practical inference. In practical inference the major premise or warrant (W) describes some desired state or end of action, while the minor premise or information (I) relates a particular course of action to this desired state as a means to an end. The conclusion or claim (C) consists of a recommendation about the use of this particular means as a way to secure the desired state or end. Whereas in *theoretical inference* (arguments from cause) the acceptance of the assumptions leads to an acceptance of the conclusion or claim, in a *practical inference* (argument from motivation) acceptance of the assumptions leads to actions in accordance with them.[78]

Practical reasoning is of great importance to pragmatic modes of ar-

---

[75] On experience as the ultimate test of scientific propositions, see Karl R. Popper, *The Logic of Scientific Discovery* (New York: Science Edition, 1961), pp. 40–41.

[76] For the distinction between *event* and *action*, see von Wright, *Explanation and Understanding*, pp. 22–24.

[77] Ibid., pp. 25–33.

[78] Ibid., p. 27.

gument in policy analysis, where one of the chief problems is to explain actions in terms of goals, values, and intentions:

> the practical syllogism provides the sciences of man with something long missing from their methodology: an explanation model in its own right which is a definite alternative to the subsumption-theoretic covering law model [i.e., deductive-nomological explanation]. Broadly speaking, what the subsumption-theoretical model is to causal explanation and explanation in the natural sciences, the practical syllogism is to teleological explanation and explanation in history and the social sciences.[79]

Motivational arguments not only provide an alternative explanatory model for policy analysis, but also permit us to conceptualize policymaking as a political process. Arguments from motivation force analysts to think in terms of the goals, values, and perceptions of policy actors and "enter the phenomenological world of the policy maker. . . ."[80] Motivational arguments also bring us closer to value questions, which are typically kept separate from "factual" matters in the other modes of policy argument.

Arguments from Ethics

In the value-critical mode, policy claims are based on *ethics*. Policy-relevant information is carried to claim on the basis of assumptions about the rightness or wrongness, goodness or badness of policies and their consequences. The warrant in an argument from ethics provides reasons for accepting a claim by associating it with some moral principle or ethical rule, while information consists of statements which have been established as policy claims in a previous argument. The claim is that the person, situation, or condition referred to in the information should be regarded as valuable or worthless, or that a policy described in the information supplied should or should not be adopted.

To illustrate the value-critical mode let us consider the following evaluative claim (C): "The existing distribution of income in the United States is unjust." In this case the information (I) supplied is that "In 1975 the top 20 percent of American families received 41 percent of all income, while the bottom 20 percent received 5.4 percent. In 1989 the top 20 percent received 46.7 percent, while the bottom 20 percent received 3.8 percent. In 1969–89 real income increased by 2 percent." The warrant (W) is the so-called *Pareto rule*, named after the Italian economist and sociologist Wilfredo Pareto (1848–1923) and regarded by many policy analysts as a simple ethical rule to which most people agree.[81] The rule states that "An optimum distribution of income in society is one where some individuals benefit without others losing." The backing (B) for the warrant is "Pareto optimality

---

[79] Ibid.

[80] Raymond Bauer, *The Study of Policy Formation*, p. 4.

[81] See Peter G. Brown's "Ethics and Policy Research," *Policy Analysis*, 2 (1976), 332–35.

guarantees that all persons will retain income to which they are justly entitled by ability and work." The rebuttal (R) is "Pareto optimality does not reflect unjust entitlements to income based on illegality, fraud, and racial discrimination" (Figure 4–9).

The preceding illustration shows how ethical and moral debates may

FIGURE 4–9   Structure of value-critical argument.

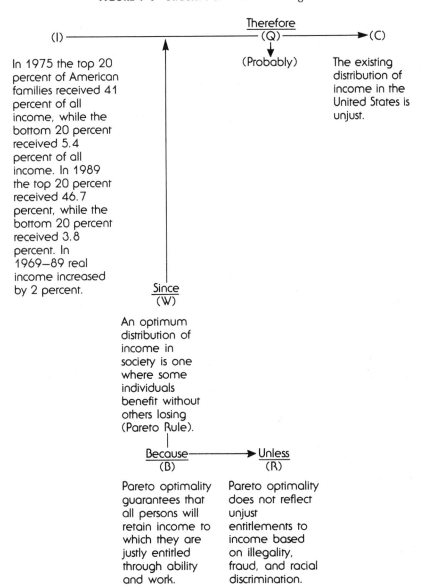

Therefore
(I) —————————————————————— (Q) ——————————→(C)

In 1975 the top 20   (Probably)   The existing
percent of American   distribution of
families received 41   income in the
percent of all   United States is
income, while the   unjust.
bottom 20 percent
received 5.4
percent of all
income. In 1989
the top 20 percent
received 46.7
percent, while the
bottom 20 percent
received 3.8
percent. In
1969–89 real
income increased
by 2 percent.   Since
                             (W)

An optimum
distribution of
income in
society is one
where some
individuals
benefit without
others losing
(Pareto Rule).

Because ——————→ Unless
(B)   (R)

Pareto optimality   Pareto optimality
guarantees that   does not reflect
all persons will   unjust
retain income to   entitlements to
which they are   income based
justly entitled   on illegality,
through ability   fraud, and racial
and work.   discrimination.

be conducted in policy analysis. In the value-critical mode information and assumptions are examined systematically in terms of their underlying ethical implications and consequences. The example of Pareto optimality shows that a widely accepted ethical rule, while it justifies the claim about an unjust society, does not apply to situations involving fraud, illegality, and discrimination. The systematic analysis of underlying ethical and moral justifications forces parties in a debate to clarify the meaning of key concepts, such as "entitlement," which are far more complex than may be apparent at first glance. Finally, parties making a claim may be forced to consider whether a particular ethical rule, such as Pareto optimality, violates their own moral convictions. For example, proponents of the Pareto Rule may see that its application violates their own moral convictions about the necessity of basing principles of entitlement on ability and work. In short, debates conducted within the value-critical mode assist analysts in developing ethical rules which are general in their applicability to various situations and internally consistent.[82] The value-critical mode differs from each of the other modes of policy argument in one essential respect: Whereas each of the other modes takes values as a "given," the value-critical mode attempts to uncover the *reasons* why particular values are held.

REASON AND ETHICS IN POLICY ANALYSIS

The systematic, reasoned, and critical examination of values is an essential element of policy analysis. As we have seen, the same policy-relevant information may be interpreted in markedly different ways, depending on assumptions contained in the frame of reference, theory, or ideology of policy analysts and other policy stakeholders. While most policy analysts recognize that values can be studied with the methods of social science— for example, public opinion surveys may be used to describe the values of different social groups—many also believe that disagreements about values cannot be debated rationally. This view, known as *value relativism*, holds that statements about such values as equality, justice, and freedom cannot be "proved" empirically, and, for this reason, are best considered as nonrational expressions of individual desires or emotions.[83] The most that policy analysts can do, according to this view, is to treat values as "data" which can be subjected to analysis, much in the same way as one analyzes data in chemistry, physics, or biology.

Value relativism is associated with another view widely shared by policy analysts, namely, that methods of policy analysis can be used for good or ill, depending only on the purposes that analysis is supposed to serve. This view, known as *scientific instrumentalism*, holds that methods of policy

---

[82] MacRae, *The Social Function of Social Science*, pp. 92–94.

[83] See Arnold Brecht, *Political Theory* (Princeton, NJ: Princeton University Press, 1959), pp. 132–35.

analysis are neutral instruments that may be used by analysts who are disinterested and detached from policy problems.[84] "Facts" and "values," according to this view, should be strictly separated in the course of analyzing policy problems. The analyst should and must accept certain values as "given," since values themselves cannot be debated rationally. The role of policy analysis is therefore confined to discovering the best *means* to realize ends which are given and thus lie beyond the realm of reasoned debate.

There are many philosophical and practical problems associated with value relativism and scientific instrumentalism. As we have already seen, there are reasons to doubt that policy analysis is or can be "value free." The definition of policy problems, for example, is typically dependent on competing values held by different policy stakeholders. Similarly, the same information is often used to support radically different policy claims, often because of competing value assumptions. Finally, evaluative and advocative claims, each of which is directly dependent on value assumptions, may be justified with policy arguments that provide *reasons* for holding one value or another. In short, policy analysis is value dependent; but it may also be value critical, which means that values as well as facts may be debated rationally.[85]

Values: Contexts and Forms of Communication

To approach policy arguments and debates in a value-critical way requires that we recognize that ethical rules and moral principles are not merely arbitrary psychological preferences or emotive expressions. No doubt it is often true that values are merely *expressions* of individual desires, tastes, or preferences, for example, when an individual expresses a personal commitment to racial equality. Yet this *personal context* of values does not exhaust the range of possible contexts in which values may be debated. Two additional contexts of values, the *standard* and *ideal*, are not simply reflections of arbitrary individual desires.[86]

The standard context involves *value statements* about particular (standard) situations where a typical individual or group is described as holding certain values. For example, a value statement in the standard context is "Compulsory school busing is a bad policy in the eyes of most white middle-class citizens." By contrast, the ideal context involves *value judgments* which are not dependent on expressions of individual desires in the personal context or on statements about the values of a typical group in the standard context. Value judgments depend on the rightness or wrongness, goodness or badness, of policies in all possible contexts, irrespective of who happens to hold or oppose the value in question. Thus, for example, to argue that "All persons have a right to participate in the selection of their own rep-

---

[84] Rein, *Social Science and Public Policy*, pp. 37–95.
[85] MacRae, *The Social Function of Social Science*, pp. 77–106.
[86] Kaplan, *The Conduct of Inquiry*, pp. 387–97.

TABLE 4–2   Contexts and Forms of Communication of Values

CONTEXT	FORM OF COMMUNICATION	EXAMPLE
Personal	Value expression	"I prefer to select my own representative"
Standard	Value statement	"Most citizens are motivated by the desire to select their own representatives"
Ideal	Value judgment	"All citizens have a right to participate in the selection of their own representatives"

resentatives" is a value judgment that requires reasons which go much beyond my own preferences or those of a typical individual or group. Relationships between the context and form of communication of values are illustrated in Table 4–2.

The Basis and Ground of Values

Whatever their context and form of communication, values can be explained as well as justified. There is always some *basis* on which values may be *explained,* that is, where values are shown to be a consequence of the preferences or desires of some person or group.[87] For example, the claim (C) that "The government should establish social programs which provide social services to the poor" may be established with a warrant (W_1) which states that "Most citizens are motivated by the desire to achieve the value of social equity." This warrant may in turn be backed (B_1) by the assumption that "Social equity is believed to be a prerequisite of political stability." This *motivational argument* (Figure 4–8) explains but does not justify the value in question (social equity).

By contrast, an argument from ethics (Figure 4–9) provides a *ground* on which values may be *justified* (Figure 4–10). In this case the warrant (W_2) states that "Social equity is a value worth achieving," while the backing (B_2) justifies the warrant by affirming that "All persons are entitled by birth to share equitably in the consumption of basic social services." Note that arguments from motivation and ethics may be mutually supportive, as in this example. Yet the basis and ground of values may also conflict, which means that any similarity between pragmatic and value-critical modes of policy argument may be purely coincidental. In short, it is essential to distinguish between the basis and ground of values, since each performs a very different function in policy arguments.

In policy analysis, as we have seen, facts and values are interdependent. For policy-relevant information to be regarded as "factual," it is often necessary to filter such information through particular sets of assumptions. Any given empirical generalization—for example, that black students at-

---

[87] Ibid., pp. 387–89.

FIGURE 4–10 Contrasts between the basis and ground of values.

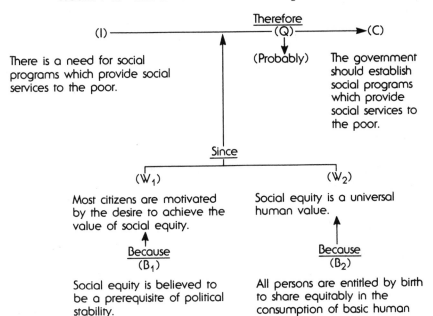

tending predominantly black schools have lower levels of achievement than black students attending predominantly white schools—requires interpretation by means of some theory, frame of reference, worldview, or ideology which itself contains certain values and ethical positions and excludes others.[88] The primary function of theories, frames of reference, worldviews, and ideologies is to interpret and transform policy-relevant information. Information does not "prove" or "validate" theories, frames of reference, worldviews, and ideologies; information can at best "falsify" them, although in the social sciences (as compared with natural sciences) this is more difficult and therefore uncommon.[89] In other words, the same information is often wholly consistent with conflicting policy claims. The underlying assumptions differ.

A recognition of the value-dependent nature of social science is crucial for understanding the role of reason and ethics in policy analysis. No inquiry into a policy problem is or can be free from the influence of values, for all forms of inquiry are ultimately based on beliefs about the nature of human beings, societies, government, and knowledge itself. For this reason, all

---

[88] See Laurence Tribe, "Policy Science: Analysis or Ideology?" *Philosophy and Public Affairs*, 2, No. 1 (1972), 66–110.

[89] von Wright, *Explanation and Understanding*, p. 203.

forms of policy analysis should be treated as potentially "ideological," in the sense that methods of policy analysis may conceal the real values of analysts. The "attempt to eradicate biases by trying to keep out the valuations themselves is a hopeless and misdirected venture. There is no other device for excluding biases in social sciences than to face the valuations and to introduce them as explicitly stated, specific, and sufficiently concretized value premises."[90] In policy analysis the best way to make values explicit is to include them as part of a reasoned ethical argument or debate.

SUMMARY

In this chapter we have examined the structure of policy arguments and their role in transforming policy-relevant information into usable knowledge. The main purpose of the chapter has been to show how the same information may lead to markedly different knowledge claims, depending on the assumptions used to conduct a policy argument or debate. The plausibility of these arguments and debates may be assessed with criteria for making truth estimates. At this point you should be able to discuss the following key principles and generalizations:

1. There are two contending approaches for defining knowledge: the "essentialist" and the "plausibilist." To count as knowledge, beliefs need not be certain; beliefs may be optimally plausible in given contexts and still qualify as knowledge.

2. In real-life contexts of public policy-making it is rarely if ever possible to establish that a policy is both necessary and sufficient for the occurrence of a policy outcome. Usable or policy-relevant knowledge consists of optimally plausible truth claims which are created by engaging, directly and vicariously, in processes of policy communication, argumentation, and debate.

3. When contrasted with standard-form policy analysis, the main advantages of the structural model of argument are that it is interpretive, multirational, critical, transactive, ethical, and multimodal.

4. Criteria for assessing the plausibility of policy arguments include completeness, consonance, cohesiveness, functional regularity, and functional simplicity, economy, and efficacy. This system of criteria is applicable to multiple modes of policy argument and relevant to the standards, rules, and procedures of experts as well as citizens.

5. Designative, evaluative, and advocative claims correspond to the three approaches to policy analysis discussed in Chapter 3, that is, the empirical, valuative, and normative approaches to policy analysis. Policy claims represent the conclusions of a policy argument or debate.

6. The same policy-relevant information may lead to radically different policy claims, depending on the assumptions contained in a policy argument. Assumptions represent the frame of reference, theory, ideology, or worldview of

---

[90] Gunnar Myrdal, *An American Dilemma* (New York: Harper & Row Publishers, 1944), p. 1033.

analysts and are the principal vehicle for carrying information to claim in a policy argument or debate.

7. There are at least eight modes of policy argument which may be contrasted according to their respective assumptions, that is, warrants and backings. These six modes are authoritative, statistical, classificational, intuitive, analycentric, explanatory, pragmatic, and value critical.

8. Policy claims may be made on the basis of one, several, or all modes of policy argument. Claims may be warranted by an argument from method (analycentric mode), backed by an argument from insight (intuitive mode), and rebutted by an argument from motivation (pragmatic mode). There are many possible combinations of warrants, backings, and rebuttals in a policy argument or debate.

9. The systematic, reasoned, and critical examination of values is an essential element of policy analysis. Policy analysis is not value free; it is value dependent and may also be value critical, which means that values as well as facts may be debated rationally.

10. Ethical rules and moral principles are not merely the arbitrary psychological preferences or emotive expressions of individuals. Values may be communicated in the form of expressions, statements, and judgments which correspond, respectively, to the personal, standard, and ideal contexts of values.

11. Whatever their context and form of communication, values may be explained as well as justified. The basis of values explains why they are a consequence of the preferences or desires of some person or group, while the ground of values justifies them in terms of ethical rules or moral principles. The basis and ground of values correspond, respectively, to arguments from motivation and arguments from ethics.

12. All forms of policy analysis should be treated as potentially "ideological," in the sense that methods of policy analysis may conceal the real values of analysts. In policy analysis the best way to make values explicit is to include them as part of a reasoned ethical argument or debate.

GLOSSARY

Advocative Claim: A contestable policy claim that provides warrants, backings, and information to certify a belief that action should be taken to solve a problem.

Analycentric Argument: A policy argument that uses one or more warrants or backings that refer to methodological rules or principles to certify that a claim based on the method is plausibly true.

Authoritative Argument: A policy argument that uses one or more warrants or backings that refer to the achieved or ascribed status of a source of knowledge to certify that a claim made by the source is plausibly true.

Backing: The part of an argument that states the assumption, principle, or supplementary argument used to support or back a warrant that is lacking in plausibility. Backings respond to the question "Why?" with a statement beginning with "Because."

Classificational Argument: A policy argument that uses one or more warrants or backings that refer to membership in some class to certify that a claim about the member is plausibly true.

Designative Claim: A contestable policy claim that provides reasons and evidence for believing that something exists or came about as a result of one or more causative factors.

Enthymematic Deduction: The process of transforming uncertain inductive arguments into deductive ones by identifying the maximally plausible warrants and backings that can certify a deductively valid argument.

Essentialism: The epistemological doctrine according to which a genuine knowledge claim is one that has been certified by demonstrating that the necessary and sufficient conditions for the occurrence of an event are present. An essentialist policy argument is one claiming that policy knowledge, as distinguished from information or data, requires demonstrating that a policy is both necessary and sufficient for the occurrence of a policy outcome.

Evaluative Claim: A contestable policy claim that provides reasons and evidence for believing that some means is right or that some end is good.

Explanatory Argument: A policy argument that uses one or more warrants or backings that refer to the validity of a theory to certify that a claim based on the theory is plausibly true.

Intuitive Argument: A policy argument that uses one or more warrants or backings that refer to the special powers of judgment of a source of knowledge to certify that a claim based on such special powers of judgment is plausibly true.

Knowledge Claim: A contestable claim that provides reasons and evidence for believing that a conclusion is plausibly true.

Mode of Argument: The characteristic feature of a warrant or backing used to certify the plausibility of a policy claim. The principal modes of policy argument are authoritative, intuitive, analycentric, explanatory, pragmatic, classificational, statistical, and value-critical.

Plausibilism: The epistemological doctrine according to which knowledge claims are truth estimates which are more or less plausible, rather than certain. Plausibility takes precedence over statistical probability, since the latter supplements but does not substitute for plausibility.

Plausibility Assessment: A procedure for assessing the plausibility of a knowledge claim by systematically evaluating the completeness, consonance, cohesiveness, functional regularity, and functional simplicity, economy, and efficacy of the entire argument of which the claim is a product.

Policy Claim: The part of a policy argument that states a conclusion or recommendation. Claims follow the term "Therefore."

Policy-Relevant Information: The part of a policy argument that states the information on which a claim is partly based. Information is data that have been selectively chosen, interpreted, and organized for purposes of making a policy argument. Data are the taken-for-granted or "given" conclusions of a previous argument. Information responds to the question "What do you have to go on?" and may be challenged or rebutted with additional information or an entire argument.

Practical Argument: An argument the conclusions of which are less than deductively certain. Practical arguments, also known as rhetorical syllogisms or enthymemes, consist of information, warrants, and backings that are frequently implicit and usually, if not always, contestable.

Pragmatic Argument: A policy argument that uses one or more warrants or backings referring to the motivating purposes of an individual or group, or the directly similar or analogous properties of some situation, to certify the claim that other individuals, groups, or situations will behave or perform in a similar or analogous manner is plausibly true.

Qualifier: The part of an argument that states the relative plausibility or credibility of a knowledge claim and the argument by which the claim was produced.

Rebuttal: The part of an argument that challenges a claim, warrant, backing, or information by stating the conditions that diminish their plausibility. The statement of a rebuttal begins with the term "Unless."

Statistical Argument: A policy argument that uses one or more warrants or backings referring to samples from populations to certify the claim that what is true of the population is plausibly true of the sample.

Structural Model of Argument: A framework developed by Stephen Toulmin for identifying, classifying, organizing, and evaluating elements of any argument, and the argument as a whole. The structural model may be used to examine the underlying assumptions of policy arguments and threats or challenges to their plausibility. The six elements of an argument are: information, qualifier, claim, warrant, backing, and rebuttal.

Usable Knowledge: Optimally plausible truth claims created through processes of policy communication, argumentation, and debate.

Value-Critical Argument: A policy argument that uses one or more warrants or backings drawn from an ethical or meta-ethical theory to certify a claim that an action or state of affairs is plausibly right or good.

Warrant: The part of an argument that states the assumption, principle, or supplementary argument used to certify that a claim is plausibly true, given the information supplied. The warrant responds to the question "Why?" with a statement beginning with "Since."

STUDY SUGGESTIONS

1. Use three of the following policy problems to construct designative, evaluative, and advocative claims about public policy. You should construct nine claims in all.

Crime	Fiscal crisis
Pollution	Human rights
Quality of life	Unemployment
Equality of opportunity	Desegregation

    Note the following examples. "Inflation is a consequence of excessive government spending" (designative claim). "Inflation is one of the negative consequences of government spending" (evaluative claim). "The government should reduce expenditures" (advocative claim).

2. Take two of the problems analyzed above and construct a policy argument. Provide the policy-relevant information (I), policy claim (C), warrant (W), and a backing (B). Label each of your arguments as designative, evaluative, or advocative.

3. Construct a policy debate by providing rebuttals (R) for each argument in Study Suggestion 2.

4. Use three of the following policy issues to construct value expressions, value statements, and value judgments. You should construct nine responses in all.

    — Should abortion be outlawed?

    — Should marijuana be legalized?

    — Should foreign policy be based on the protection of human rights in other countries?

    — Should income be redistributed from the rich to the poor?

    — Should citizens be compelled to reduce energy consumption?

    — Should the right of government employees to strike be curtailed?

5. For each of the value expressions, statements, and judgments constructed above, provide a basis and ground. For example, if the issue was "Should local government reduce spending on municipal services," you might have responded "I am against government spending" (value expression). The basis for the expression might have been "I pay more taxes for municipal services than I actually receive in the form of services." The ground might be "Persons should not be required to pay for services they do not receive."

6. Construct rebuttals for each of the grounds offered in Study Suggestion 5. [*Note:* Study Suggestions 4 to 6 may be answered as part of a class exercise by dividing students into two or more competing groups.]

SUGGESTED READINGS

ALKER, HAYWARD R., JR., "The Dialectical Logic of Thucydides' Melian Dialogue," *The American Political Science Review*, 82, No. 3 (1988), 805–820.

ANDERSON, CHARLES W., "Political Philosophy, Practical Reason, and Policy Analysis," in *Confronting Values in Policy Analysis*, ed. Frank Fischer and John Forester. Newbury Park, CA: Sage Publications, 1987, pp. 22–42.

COX, J. R. and CHARLES A. WILLARD, eds., *Advances in Argumentation Theory and Research.* Carbondale, IL: University of Southern Illinois Press, 1982.

DUNN, WILLIAM N., "Reforms as Arguments," in *The Argumentation Turn in Policy Analysis*, ed. John Forester and Frank Fischer. Durham, NC: Duke University Press, 1993.

FISCHER, FRANK, *Politics, Values, and Public Policy: The Problem of Methodology.* Boulder, CO: Westview Press, 1980.

FORESTER, JOHN and FRANK FISCHER, *The Argumentative Turn in Policy Analysis.* Durham, NC: Duke University Press, 1993.

MACRAE, DUNCAN, JR., "Professional Knowledge for Policy Discourse: Argumentation versus Reasoned Selection of Proposals," *Knowledge in Society*, 1, No. 3 (1988), 6–24.

MAJONE, G., *Evidence, Argument, and Persuasion in the Policy Process.* New Haven, CT: Yale University Press, 1989.

MCCLOSKEY, D. N., *The Rhetoric of Economics.* Madison, WI: University of Wisconsin Press, 1988.

MITROFF, IAN I. and RICHARD O. MASON, *Creating a Dialectical Social Science.* Dordrecht, The Netherlands: D. Reidel, 1981.

RESCHER, NICHOLAS, *Dialectics: A Controversy-Oriented Approach to the Theory of Knowledge.* Albany, NY: State University of New York Press, 1977.

——, *Induction.* Pittsburgh, PA: University of Pittsburgh Press, 1980.

TOULMIN, STEPHEN, R. RIEKE, and A. JANIK, *An Introduction to Reasoning*, 2nd ed. New York: Macmillan, 1984.

WEISS, CAROL H., "Policy Research as Advocacy: Pro and Con," *Knowledge and Policy*, 4, No. 1–2 (1991), 37–55.

PART TWO

Methods
for
Policy Analysis

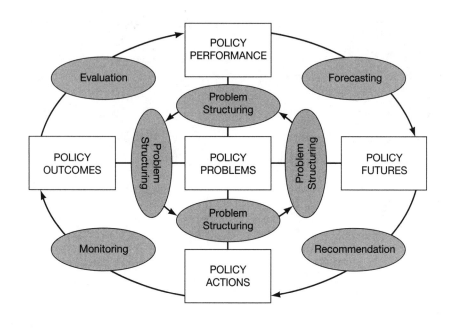

In Part I we provided a methodology for policy analysis, that is, a system of standards, rules, and procedures for producing usable, or policy-relevant, knowledge. The framework for conducting problem-centered policy analysis introduced in Part I has been reproduced above as means for visualizing the content of Part II. In Part II we examine in detail each of the general procedures outlined in this framework: problem structuring, forecasting, recommendation, monitoring, and evaluation. These general procedures are now discussed along with specific methods and techniques that enable analysts to create, critically assess, and communicate policy-relevant knowledge about policy problems, policy futures, policy actions, policy outcomes, and policy performance. Part II, then, covers methods and techniques for:

- Structuring policy problems
- Forecasting policy futures
- Recommending policy actions
- Monitoring policy outcomes
- Evaluating policy performance

5

Structuring Policy Problems

Successful problem solving requires finding the right solution to the right problem. We fail more often because we solve the wrong problem than because we get the wrong solution to the right problem.

—RUSSELL L. ACKOFF, *Redesigning the Future: A Systems Approach to Societal Problems* (1974)

Many people believe that policy problems are objective conditions whose existence may be established simply by determining what the "facts" are in a given case. This naive view of the nature of policy problems fails to recognize that the same facts—for example, government statistics which show that crime, pollution, and poverty are on the upswing—are often interpreted in markedly different ways by different policy stakeholders. Hence, the same policy-relevant information can and often does result in conflicting definitions and explanations of a "problem." This is not so much because the facts of the matter are inconsistent (and often they are), but because policy analysts, policymakers, and other stakeholders hold competing assumptions about human nature, government, and opportunities for social change through public action. Policy problems are partly in the eye of the beholder.

In this chapter we provide an overview of the nature of policy problems and outline major components of the process of problem structuring in policy analysis. After comparing and contrasting different types of policy models, we consider methods for structuring policy problems. Illustrations in the text not only demonstrate the importance of problem structuring in policy analysis but show that problem structuring is embedded in a political process where "the definition of alternatives is the supreme instrument of power."[1]

---

[1] E. E. Schattschneider, *The Semisovereign People* (New York: Holt, Rinehart and Winston, 1960), p. 68.

NATURE OF POLICY PROBLEMS

Policy problems are unrealized needs, values, or opportunities for improvement that may be pursued through public action.[2] As we saw in Chapter 3, information about the nature, scope, and severity of a problem is produced by applying the policy-analytic procedure of problem structuring. Problem structuring, which is a continuously recurring phase of policy inquiry in which analysts search among competing problem formulations of different stakeholders, is no doubt the most important activity performed by policy analysts. Problem structuring is a central guidance system or steering mechanism that affects the success of all subsequent phases of policy analysis. The reason problem structuring is so important is that policy analysts seem to fail more often because they solve the wrong problem than because they get the wrong solution to the right problem.

Beyond Problem Solving

Policy analysis is often described as a problem-solving methodology. Although this is partly correct—and analysts do succeed in finding solutions for public problems[3]—the problem-solving image of policy analysis can be misleading. The problem-solving image wrongly suggests that analysts can successfully identify, evaluate, and recommend solutions for a problem without spending considerable prior time and effort in formulating that problem. In fact, however, policy analysis is a dynamic, multilevel process in which methods of problem structuring take priority over methods of problem solving (see Figure 5–1).

Figure 5–1 shows that methods of problem structuring precede and take priority over methods of problem solving in policy analysis. Methods at one level are inappropriate and ineffective at the next, because the questions are different at the two levels. For example, lower-level questions about the net benefits (benefits minus costs) of alternative solutions for the control of industrial pollution already assume that industrial pollution is the problem. At the next-higher level the question that must be answered involves the scope and severity of pollution, the conditions that contribute to pollution, and potential solutions for its mitigation or elimination. Here the analyst may well find that the most appropriate formulation of the problem is closely related to the driving habits of Americans for whom gasoline and oil are comparatively cheap and heavily subsidized by the government. This is a question of problem structuring; the former is a question of problem solving. In short, it is important to recognize the distinctions among the problem-related processes represented by the flowchart in Figure 1–5:

- *Problem sensing versus problem structuring.* The process of policy analysis does not begin with clearly articulated problems, but a sense of diffuse worries and

---

[2] See David Dery, *Problem Definition in Policy Analysis* (Lawrence, KS: University Press of Kansas, 1984).

[3] See, for example, Bernard Barber, *Effective Social Science: Eight Cases in Economics, Political Science, and Sociology* (New York: Russell Sage Foundation, 1987).

FIGURE 5–1   Priority of problem structuring in policy analysis.

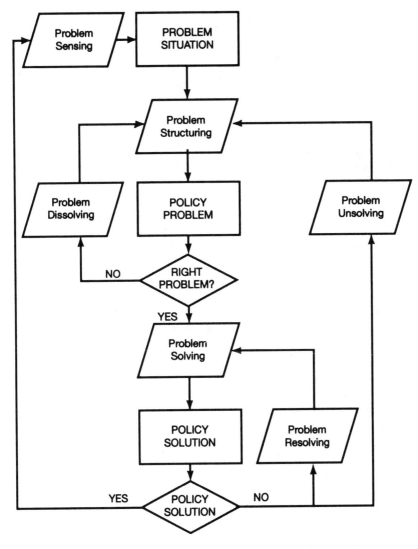

Source: William N. Dunn, "Methods of the Second Type: Coping with the Wilderness of Conventional Policy Analysis," *Policy Studies Review*, 7, No. 4 (1988), 720–37.

inchoate signs of stress.[4] These diffuse worries and inchoate signs of stress are not problems, but *problem situations* that are sensed by policy analysts, policymakers, and citizen stakeholders. Policy problems "are products of thought acting on environments; they are elements of problem situations that are ab-

---

[4] Martin Rein and Sheldon H. White, "Policy Research: Belief and Doubt," *Policy Analysis*, 3, No. 2 (1977), 262.

stracted from these situations by analysis. What we experience, therefore, are *problem situations*, not problems which, like atoms or cells, are conceptual constructs."[5]

- *Problem structuring versus problem solving.* Policy analysis is a multilevel process that includes higher-order methods of *problem structuring* as well as lower-order methods of *problem solving.* These higher-order methods and the questions for which they are appropriate are what some have recently discussed as policy design, or design science.[6] Higher-order methods of problem structuring are *metamethods*—that is, they are "about" and "come before" lower-order methods of problem solving. When analysts use lower-order methods to solve complex problems, they run the risk of committing what Raiffa and others call errors of the third kind: solving the wrong problem.[7]

- *Problem resolving versus problem unsolving and problem dissolving.* The terms *problem resolving, problem unsolving,* and *problem dissolving* refer to three types of error-correcting processes.[8] Although the three terms come from the same root (L. *solvere,* to solve or dissolve), the error-correcting processes to which they refer occur at distinct levels (Figure 5–1). *Problem resolving* involves the reanalysis of a correctly structured problem to reduce calibrational errors, for example, reducing the probability of type I or type II errors in testing the null hypotheses that a policy has no effect on a particular policy outcome. *Problem unsolving,* by contrast, involves the abandonment of a solution based on the wrong formulation of a problem—for example, the policy of urban renewal implemented in central cities during the 1960s—and a return to problem structuring in an attempt to formulate the right problem. In turn, *problem dissolving* involves the abandonment of an incorrectly formulated problem and a return to problem structuring before there is any effort to solve it.

Characteristics of Problems

These examples should make us cautious about taking policy problems for granted, since everyday understanding and common sense are poor guides when we deal with matters as complex as policy problems. In fact, this discussion helps point to several important characteristics of policy problems:

1. *Interdependence of policy problems.* Policy problems in one area (for example, energy) frequently affect policy problems in other areas (for example, health care and unemployment). In reality policy problems are not independent entities; they are parts of whole systems of problems best described as *messes,*

---

[5] Russell A. Ackoff, *Redesigning the Future: A Systems Approach to Societal Problems* (New York: Wiley, 1974), p. 21.

[6] See Stephen H. Linder and B. Guy Peters, "From Social Theory to Policy Design," *Journal of Public Policy,* 4, No. 4 (1985), 237–59; John Dryzek, "Don't Toss Coins into Garbage Cans: A Prologue to Policy Design," *Journal of Public Policy,* 3, No. 3 (1983), 345–67; and Trudi C. Miller, "Conclusion: A Design Science Perspective," in *Public Sector Performance: A Turning Point,* ed. T. C. Miller (Baltimore: Johns Hopkins University Press, 1985).

[7] Howard Raiffa, *Decision Analysis* (Reading, MA: Addison-Wesley, 1968), p. 264.

[8] See Russell L. Ackoff, "Beyond Problem Solving," *General Systems,* XIX (1974); 237–39; and Herbert A. Simon, "The Structure of Ill Structured Problems," *Artificial Intelligence* 4 (1973), 181–201.

that is, systems of external conditions that produce dissatisfaction among different segments of the community.[9] Systems of problems (messes) are difficult or impossible to resolve by using an *analytic approach*—that is, one that decomposes problems into their component elements or parts—since only rarely can problems be defined and resolved independently of one another. Sometimes it is easier "to solve ten interlocking problems simultaneously than to solve one by itself."[10] Systems of interdependent problems require a *holistic approach*, that is, one that views problems as inseparable and unmeasurable apart from the whole system of which they are interlocking parts.[11]

2. *Subjectivity of policy problems.* The external conditions that give rise to a problem are selectively defined, classified, explained, and evaluated. Although there is a sense in which problems are objective—for example, air pollution may be defined in terms of levels of gases and particulates in the atmosphere—the same data about pollution are typically interpreted in markedly different ways. Policy problems "are products of thought acting on environments; they are elements of problem situations that are abstracted from these situations by analysis. What we experience, therefore, are *problem situations*, not problems which, like atoms or cells, are conceptual constructs."[12] In policy analysis it is particularly important not to confuse problem situations with policy problems, since the latter are mental artifacts that come about by transforming experience through human judgment.

3. *Artificiality of policy problems.* Policy problems are possible only when human beings make judgments about the desirability of altering some problem situation. Policy problems are products of subjective human judgment; policy problems also come to be accepted as legitimate definitions of objective social conditions; policy problems are therefore socially constructed, maintained, and changed.[13] Problems have no existence apart from the individuals and groups who define them, which means that there are no "natural" states of society which in and of themselves constitute policy problems.

4. *Dynamics of policy problems.* There are as many different solutions for a given problem as there are definitions of that problem. "Problems and solutions are in constant flux; hence problems *do not stay solved.* . . . Solutions to problems become obsolete even if the problems to which they are addressed do not."[14]

Systems of problems (messes) are not mechanical entities; they are *purposeful (teleological) systems* in which (1) no two members are identical in all or even any of their properties or behaviors; (2) the properties or behavior of each member has an effect on the properties or behavior of the system as a whole; (3) the properties and behavior of each member, and the

---

[9] Russell L. Ackoff, *Redesigning the Future: A Systems Approach to Societal Problems* (New York: Wiley, 1974), p. 21.

[10] Harrison Brown, "Scenario for an American Renaissance," *Saturday Review* (December 25, 1971), 18–19.

[11] See Ian I. Mitroff and L. Vaughan Blankenship, "On the Methodology of the Holistic Experiment: An Approach to the Conceptualization of Large-Scale Social Experiments," *Technological Forecasting and Social Change*, 4 (1973), 339–53.

[12] Ackoff, *Redesigning the Future*, p. 21.

[13] Compare Peter L. Berger and Thomas Luckmann, *The Social Construction of Reality*, 2nd ed. (New York: Irvington, 1980).

[14] Ackoff, *Redesigning the Future*, p. 21.

way each affects the system as a whole, depend on the properties and be-havior of at least one other member of the system; and (4) all possible subgroups of members have a nonindependent effect on the system as a whole.[15] What this means is that systems of problems—crime, poverty, un-employment, inflation, energy, pollution, health—cannot be decomposed into independent subsets without running the risk of producing the right solution to the wrong problem.

A key characteristic of systems of problems is that the whole is greater—that is, qualitatively different—than the simple sum of its parts. A pile of stones may be defined as the sum of all individual stones but also as a pyramid. Similarly, a human being

> can write or run, but none of its parts can. Furthermore, membership in the system either increases or decreases the capabilities of each element; it does not leave them unaffected. For example, a brain that is not part of a living body or some substitute cannot function. An individual who is part of a nation or a corporation is thereby precluded from doing some things he could other-wise do, and he is enabled to do others he could not otherwise do.[16]

Finally, a recognition of the interdependence, subjectivity, artificiality, and dynamics of policy problems alerts us to the possible *unanticipated consequences* that may follow from policies based on the right solution to the wrong problem. Consider, for example, the problem situation con-fronted by Western European governments in the last decade. France and West Germany, seeking to expand the supply of available energy by con-structing nuclear power plants on the Rhine River, defined the energy prob-lem in a way that assumed that the production of nuclear power is inde-pendent of the other problems. Consequently, the relation of energy to wider systems of problems did not enter into the formulation of the problem. One observer, writing in the 1970s, cautioned that

> malaria will arrive as a major epidemic in Europe within the next ten years, thanks to the decision in Germany and France to build atomic generators that utilize river waters for their cooling systems and hence bring the water tem-perature within the range in which anopheles (the malaria-carrying mosquito) breeds.[17]

Problems vs. Issues

If policy problems are really whole systems of problems, it follows that policy issues must be equally complex. Policy issues not only involve dis-agreements about actual or potential courses of action; they also reflect competing views of the nature of problems themselves. An apparently clear-cut policy issue—for example, whether the government should enforce air

---

[15] Mitroff and Blankenship, pp. 341–42.

[16] Ackoff, *Redesigning the Future*, p. 13.

[17] Ivan Illich in conversation with Sam Keen, reported in *Psychology Today* (May 1976).

quality standards in industry—is typically the consequence of conflicting sets of assumptions about the nature of pollution:[18]

1. Pollution is a natural consequence of capitalism, an economic system where the owners of industry seek to maintain and increase profits from their investments. Some damage to the environment is a necessary price to pay for a healthy capitalist economy.

2. Pollution is a result of the need for power and prestige among industrial managers who seek promotions in large career-oriented bureaucracies. Pollution has been just as severe in socialist systems where there are no profit-seeking private owners.

3. Pollution is a consequence of consumer preferences in high mass-consumption society. In order to ensure corporate survival owners and managers must satisfy consumer preferences for high-performance engines and automobile travel.

The ability to recognize differences among problem situations, policy problems, and policy issues is crucial for understanding the different ways that common experiences are translated into disagreements about actual and potential courses of government action. The formulation of a problem is heavily influenced by the assumptions that different policy stakeholders—legislators, agency administrators, business leaders, consumer groups—bring to a given problem situation. In turn, different formulations of the problem shape the ways that policy issues are defined. In the example of environmental pollution above, assumptions about the operation of a healthy capitalist economy will no doubt result in a negative position on government enforcement of air quality standards in industry, while assumptions about corporate managerial behavior are likely to result in an affirmative position. By contrast, the third set of assumptions about consumer preferences and corporate survival may produce the position that government regulation of industrial pollution is a nonissue, since government cannot legislate consumer demand.

The complexity of policy issues may be visualized by considering the organizational levels where they are formulated (Figure 5–2). Policy issues may be classified according to a hierarchy of types: major, secondary, functional, and minor. *Major issues* are those which are typically encountered at the highest levels of government within and between federal, state, and local jurisdictions. Major issues typically involve questions of agency mission, that is, questions about the nature and purposes of government organizations. The issue of whether the Department of Health and Human Services should seek to eliminate the conditions which give rise to poverty is a question of agency mission. *Secondary issues* are those located at the level of agency programs at the federal, state, and local levels. Secondary issues may involve the setting of program priorities and the definition of target groups and beneficiaries. The issue of how to define poverty families is a secondary issue. *Functional issues*, by contrast, are those located at

[18] See Ritchie P. Lowry, *Social Problems: A Critical Analysis of Theories and Public Policy* (Lexington, MA: D.C. Heath and Company, 1974), pp. 23–25.

FIGURE 5–2   Hierarchy of types of policy issues.

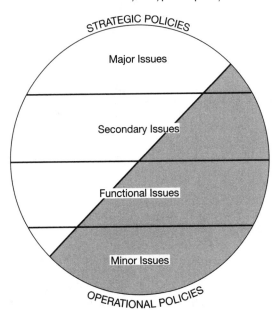

both the program and project levels and which involve such questions as budgeting, finance, and procurement. Finally, *minor issues* are those which are found most frequently at the level of specific projects. Minor issues involve personnel, staffing, employee benefits, vacation times, working hours, and standard operating procedures and rules.

As one moves up the hierarchy of types of policy issues, problems become more and more interdependent, subjective, artificial, and dynamic. Although these levels are interdependent, some issues call for policies which are strategic while others demand operational policies. A *strategic policy* is one where the consequences of decisions are relatively irreversible. Such issues as whether the United States should send troops to the Persian Gulf, or whether the civil service should be reorganized, call for strategic policies because the consequences of action cannot be reversed for many years. By contrast, *operational policies*—that is, policies where the consequences of decisions are relatively reversible—do not involve the risks and uncertainty present at higher levels. While all types of policies are interdependent—for example, the realization of an agency's mission depends in part on the adequacy of its personnel practices—it is important to recognize that the complexity and irreversibility of a policy increases as one moves up the hierarchy of types of policy issues.

Three Classes of Policy Problems

There are three classes of policy problems: well-structured, moderately structured, and ill-structured problems.[19] The structure of each of these three classes is determined by its relative complexity, that is, the degree to which the problem is actually an interdependent system of problems. The differences among well-structured, moderately structured, and ill-structured problems are best illustrated by considering variations in their common elements (Table 5–1).

Well-structured problems are those which involve one or a few decision makers and a small set of policy alternatives. Utilities (values) reflect consensus on goals which are clearly ranked in order of decision makers' preferences. The outcomes of each alternative are either known with complete certainty (deterministically), or within acceptable margins of probable error (risk). The prototype of the well-structured problem is the completely computerized decision problem, where all consequences of all policy alternatives are programmed in advance. Relatively low-level operational problems in public agencies provide illustrations of well-structured problems. For example, problems of replacing agency vehicles are relatively simple ones that involve finding the optimum point at which an old vehicle should be traded for a new one, taking into account average repair costs for older vehicles and purchasing and depreciation costs for new ones.

Moderately structured problems are those involving one or a few decision makers and a relatively limited number of alternatives. Utilities (values) also reflect consensus on clearly ranked goals. Nevertheless, the outcomes of alternatives are neither certain (deterministic) nor calculable within acceptable margins of error (risk); they are uncertain, which means that the probability of error cannot be estimated at all. The prototype of the moderately structured problem is the policy simulation or game, an illustration of which is the so-called "prisoner's dilemma."[20] In this game two prisoners are held in separate cells, where each is interrogated by the prosecuting attorney, who must obtain a confession from one or both prisoners to obtain a conviction. The prosecutor, who has enough evidence to convict each prisoner of a lesser crime, tells each that if neither confesses, they will both be tried for a lesser crime carrying lesser punishment; if both confess to the more serious crime, they will both receive a reduced sentence; but if only one confesses, he will receive probation, while the other will receive a maximum sentence. The "optimal" choice for each prisoner, given that neither can predict the outcome of the other's decision, is to confess.

---

[19] See Ian I. Mitroff and Francisco Sagasti, "Epistemology as General Systems Theory: An Approach to the Design of Complex Decision-Making Experiments," *Philosophy of the Social Sciences*, 3 (1973), 117–34.

[20] See Anatol Rapoport and Albert M. Chammah, *Prisoner's Dilemma* (Ann Arbor, MI: University of Michigan Press, 1965).

TABLE 5-1   Differences in the Structure of Three Classes of Policy Problems

	STRUCTURE OF PROBLEM		
ELEMENT	Well Structured	Moderately Structured	Ill Structured
Decision maker(s)	One or few	One or few	Many
Alternatives	Limited	Limited	Unlimited
Utilities (values)	Consensus	Consensus	Conflict
Outcomes	Certainty or risk	Uncertainty	Unknown
Probabilities	Calculable	Incalculable	Incalculable

Yet it is precisely this choice that will result in a five-year sentence for both prisoners, since both are likely to try to minimize their sentences. This example not only illustrates the difficulties of making decisions when outcomes are uncertain but also shows that otherwise "rational" individual choices may contribute to collective irrationality in small groups, government bureaucracies, and society as a whole.

Ill-structured problems are those which typically involve many different decision makers whose utilities (values) are either unknown or impossible to rank in a consistent fashion. Whereas well-structured and moderately structured problems reflect consensus, the main characteristic of ill-structured problems is conflict among competing goals. Policy alternatives and their outcomes may also be unknown, such that estimates of risk and uncertainty are not possible. The problem of choice is not to uncover known deterministic relations, or to calculate the risk or uncertainty attached to policy alternatives, but rather to define the nature of the problem. The prototype of the ill-structured problem is the completely intransitive decision problem, that is, one where it is impossible to select a single policy alternative that is preferred to all others. Whereas well-structured and moderately structured problems contain preference rankings that are *transitive*—that is, if alternative A_1 is preferred to alternative A_2, and alternative A_2 is preferred to alternative A_3, then alternative A_1 is preferred to alternative A_3—ill-structured problems have preference rankings that are intransitive.

Many of the most important policy problems are ill structured. One of the lessons of political science, public administration, and other disciplines is that well-structured and moderately structured problems are rarely present in complex governmental settings.[21] For example, it is unrealistic to assume the existence of one or a few decision makers with uniform preferences (utilities), since public policies are sets of interrelated decisions

---

[21] See, for example, David Braybrooke and Charles E. Lindblom, A *Strategy of Decision* (New York: The Free Press, 1963); and Herbert A. Simon, "Theories of Decision-Making in Economic and Behavioral Science," *American Economic Review*, XLIX (1959), 255–57.

made and influenced by many policy stakeholders over long periods of time. Consensus is rare, since public policy-making typically involves conflicts among competing stakeholders. Finally, it is seldom possible to identify the full range of alternative solutions for problems, in part because of constraints on the acquisition of information, but also because it is frequently difficult to reach a satisfactory formulation of the problem. The reasons why ill-structured problems are so critical for public policy analysis have been ably summarized by a number of social scientists.[22]

PROBLEM STRUCTURING IN POLICY ANALYSIS

The requirements for solving ill-structured problems are not the same as those for solving well-structured problems. Whereas well-structured problems permit analysts to use conventional methods, ill-structured problems demand that *the analyst take an active part in defining the nature of the problem itself.*[23] In actively defining the nature of the problem, analysts must not only impose part of themselves on the problem situation but must also exercise creative judgment and insight. This means that policy analysis is properly devoted to problem structuring as well as problem solving. In fact, problem solving is only one part of the work of policy analysis:

> The problem-solving image holds that the work of policy begins with articulated and self-evident problems. Supposedly, policy begins when recognizable problems appear, problems about which one can hypothesize possible courses of action and in relation to which one can articulate goals. . . . It is not clear problems, but diffuse worries, that appear. Political pressure groups become unusually active, or their activities become more telling; formal and informal social indicators give signs of unfavorable trends, or of trends that may be interpreted as unfavorable. There are signals, then, of a problem, but no one knows yet what the problem is. . . . In other words, the situation is such that the problem itself is problematic. Policy analysis contains processes for finding and construing problems; it involves problem setting [structuring] in order to interpret inchoate signs of stress in the system.[24]

Creativity in Problem Structuring

The criteria for determining the success of problem structuring are also different from those used to judge the success of problem solving. Suc-

---

[22] See, for example, Thomas R. Dye, *Understanding Public Policy*, 3rd ed. (Englewood Cliffs, NJ: Prentice Hall, 1978), pp. 30–31; Richard O. Mason and Ian I. Mitroff, *Creating a Dialectical Social Science* (Dordrecht, The Netherlands: D. Reidel, 1981); and James G. March and Johan P. Olsen, "The New Institutionalism: Organizational Factors in Political Life," *The American Political Science Review*, 78, No. 3 (1984), 739–49.

[23] See John R. Hayes, *Cognitive Psychology* (Homewood, IL: Dorsey Press, 1978), pp. 210–13.

[24] Martin Rein and Sheldon H. White, "Policy Research: Belief and Doubt," *Policy Analysis*, 3, No. 2 (1977), 262.

cessful problem solving requires that analysts obtain correct technical solutions for clearly formulated problems. By contrast, successful problem
structuring requires that analysts obtain creative solutions for ambiguous
and ill-defined problems. In fact, the criteria for judging creative acts in
general are also applicable to creativity in problem structuring. Problem
structuring is creative to the extent that one or more of the following conditions are satisfied:[25] (1) the product of analysis is sufficiently *novel* that
most people could not or would not have arrived at the same solution; (2)
the process of analysis is sufficiently *unconventional* that it involves the
modification or rejection of previously accepted ideas; (3) the process of
analysis requires sufficiently *high motivation and persistence* that analysis
takes place with high intensity or over long periods of time; (4) the product
of analysis is regarded as *valuable* by analysts, policymakers, and other stakeholders, since it provides an appropriate solution for the problem; and (5)
the problem as initially posed is so *ambiguous, vague, and ill defined* that
part of the task is to formulate the problem itself.

Phases of Problem Structuring

As we saw above (Figure 5–1), problem structuring takes priority over
problem solving in policy analysis. Problem structuring may be viewed as
a process with four interdependent phases: *problem search, problem definition, problem specification,* and *problem sensing* (Figure 5–3). A prerequisite of problem structuring is the recognition or "felt existence" of a *prob-
lem situation.* In moving from problem situation the analyst engages in
problem search. At this stage, the goal is not the discovery of a single problem
(for example, that of the client or the analyst); it is rather the discovery of
the many problem representations of multiple policy stakeholders. Practicing analysts normally face a large, tangled network of competing problem
formulations which are dynamic, socially constructed, and distributed
throughout the policy-making process. In effect, analysts are faced with a
metaproblem[26]—a problem-of-problems that is ill structured because the
domain of problem representations held by diverse stakeholders seems unmanageably huge.[27] The central task is to structure a metaproblem, that is,
a second-order problem that may be defined as the class of all first-order
problems, which are its members. Unless these two levels are clearly distinguished, analysts run the risk of formulating the wrong problem by con-
fusing member and class. By failing to distinguish these levels, analysts

---

[25] See Alan Newell, J. C. Shaw, and Herbert A. Simon, "The Process of Creative Thinking," in *Contemporary Approaches to Creative Thinking,* ed. H. E. Gruber, G. Terrell, and M.
Wertheimer (New York: Atherton Press, 1962), pp. 63–119; see also the excellent monograph
by James L. Adams, *Conceptual Blockbusting* (Stanford, CA: Stanford Alumni Association,
1974).

[26] See Yehezkel Dror, *Design for Policy Sciences* (New York: Elsevier, 1971).

[27] Another distinguishing feature of an ill-structured problem is that its boundaries are
unmanageably huge. See P. Harmon and D. King, *Expert Systems: Artificial Intelligence in
Business* (New York: Wiley, 1985).

FIGURE 5-3   Phases of problem structuring.

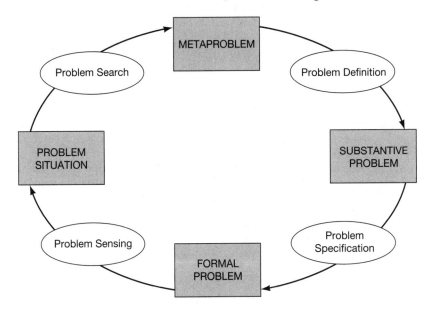

violate the rule that "whatever involves *all* of a collection must not be one of the collection."[28]

In moving from metaproblem to *substantive problem*, the analyst attempts to *define* the problem in its most basic and general terms. For example, the analyst may decide whether the problem is one of economics, sociology, or political science. If the substantive problem is conceptualized as an economic one, the analyst will treat it in terms of factors related to the production and distribution of goods and services—for example, market prices as a determinant of costs and benefits of public programs. Alternatively, if the problem is viewed as political or sociological, the analyst will approach it in terms of the distribution of power and influence among competing interest groups, elites, and other social strata. The choice of a conceptual framework is often similar to the choice of a worldview, ideology, or popular myth and indicates a commitment to a particular view of reality.[29]

To illustrate the importance of worldviews, ideologies, and popular

---

[28] Alfred North Whitehead and Bertrand Russell, *Principia Mathematica*, 2nd ed., Vol. I (Cambridge: Cambridge University Press, 1910), p. 101. See also Paul Watzlawick, John Weakland, and Richard Fisch, *Change: Principles of Problem Formation and Problem Resolution* (New York: W. W. Norton), p. 6.

[29] Ian Mitroff and Ralph H. Kilmann, *Methodological Approaches to Social Science* (San Francisco: Jossey-Bass, 1978). See also Thomas Kuhn, *The Structure of Scientific Revolutions*, 2nd ed. (Chicago: University of Chicago Press, 1971); and Ian G. Barbour, *Myths, Models and Paradigms* (New York: Harper & Row, 1976).

myths in conceptualizing substantive problems, consider the various ways to define the problem of poverty. Poverty may be defined as a consequence of accidents or inevitable states of society, of the actions of evil persons, or of imperfections in the poor themselves.[30] These definitions of poverty contain elements of a worldview, myth, or ideology insofar as each involves a selective perception of elements of a problem situation. Worldviews, ideologies, and myths are partly true and partly false, which means that they are useful and dangerous at the same time. In this example the attribution of poverty to historical accidents or to inevitability represents a *naturalistic perspective* of social problems which distorts reality by claiming that questions about the distribution of wealth are pointless; but this same myth may also sensitize analysts to the relative nature of definitions of poverty by pointing to the fact that no known society has wholly resolved the problem. Similarly, the attribution of poverty to evil or morally corrupt capitalists distorts their actual motivations. Yet this same *moralistic perspective*, which explains poverty in terms of presumed moral weaknesses, also directs attention to the ways in which private ownership promotes waste, exploitation, and social irresponsibility. Finally, to attribute poverty to imperfections in the poor themselves not only results in blaming the victim rather than responsible social forces, but also points to the fact that some poor persons choose to live under conditions that the rest of society defines as "poverty." This *environmentalist perspective*, which attributes poverty and other social problems to characteristics of the immediate environment of victims, often results in a self-contradictory brand of humanitarianism known as "blaming the victim." The humanitarian can

> concentrate his charitable interest on the defects of the victim, condemn the vague social and environmental stresses that produced the defect (some time ago), and ignore the continuing effect of victimizing social forces (right now). It is a brilliant ideology for justifying a perverse form of social action designed to change, not society, as one might expect, but rather society's victim.[31]

Once a substantive problem has been defined, a more detailed and specific *formal problem* may be constructed. The process of moving from substantive to formal problem is carried out through *problem specification*, which typically involves the development of a formal mathematical representation (model) of the substantive problem. At this point difficulties may occur, since the relationship between an ill-structured substantive problem and a formal representation of that problem may be tenuous.[32] Most methods for specifying problems in formal mathematical terms are inappropriate for ill-structured problems, where the main task is not to obtain the correct mathematical solution but to define the nature of the problem itself.

---

[30] Lowry, *Social Problems*, pp. 19–46.

[31] William Ryan, *Blaming the Victim* (New York: Pantheon Books, 1971), p. 7.

[32] See Ralph E. Strauch, "A Critical Look at Quantitative Methodology," *Policy Analysis*, 2 (1976), 121–44.

Errors of the Third Type (E_{III})

A critical issue of problem structuring is how well substantive and formal problems actually correspond to the original problem situation. If most problem situations in fact contain whole systems of problems (messes), then a central requirement of policy analysis is the formulation of substantive and formal problems that adequately represent that complexity. The degree of correspondence between a given problem situation and a substantive problem is determined at the problem definition phase. Here the analyst compares characteristics of the problem situation and the substantive problem, which is often based on implicit assumptions or beliefs about human nature, time, and the possibilities for social change through government action. Equally important, however, is the degree of correspondence between the problem situation and the formal problem, which is often specified in the form of a mathematical formula or set of equations.

In the first instance (problem search), analysts who fail to engage in search, or stop searching prematurely, run the risk of choosing the wrong boundaries of the metaproblem. Important aspects of the metaproblem— for example, the formulations of problems held by those who are or will be charged with implementing the policy—simply may be left outside the boundaries of the metaproblem. In the second instance (problem definition), analysts run the risk of choosing the wrong worldview, ideology, or myth to conceptualize a problem situation when they should have chosen the right one. In the third case (problem specification), the main risk is to choose the wrong formal representation (model) of the substantive problem when the right one should have been chosen. In any case, analysts may commit *errors of the third type* (E_{III}).[33] Type III error has been described by decision theorist Howard Raiffa in the following terms:

> One of the most popular paradigms in . . . mathematics describes the case in which a researcher has either to accept or reject a so-called null hypothesis. In a first course in statistics the student learns that he must constantly balance between making an error of the first kind (that is, rejecting the null hypothesis when it is true) and an error of the second kind (that is, accepting the null hypothesis when it is false) . . . practitioners all too often make errors of a third kind: solving the wrong problem.[34]

The process of problem structuring raises a number of issues that are central to the methodology of policy analysis and science in general. Each phase of problem structuring requires different kinds of methodological skills and implies different standards of rationality. For example, the kinds

---

[33] See Ian I. Mitroff and Frederick Betz, "Dialectical Decision Theory: A Meta-Theory of Decision-Making," *Management Science*, 19, No. 1 (1972), 11–24. Kimball defines type III error as "the error committed by giving the right answer to the wrong problem." See A. W. Kimball, "Errors of the Third Kind in Statistical Consulting," *Journal of the American Statistical Association*, 52 (1957), 133–42.

[34] Howard Raiffa, *Decision Analysis* (Reading, MA: Addison-Wesley, 1968), p. 264.

of skills most appropriate for discovering metaproblems and defining substantive problems are observational and conceptual, respectively. Mathematical and statistical subjects (economics, operations research, systems analysis) are primarily relevant for specifying formal problems. Problem structuring also raises questions about different meanings of rationality, since rationality is not simply a matter of finding an adequate formal representation of a problem situation. This is the standard technical definition of rationality criticized for its formal oversimplification of complex processes.[35] Rationality may be defined at more fundamental levels, where the unconscious or uncritical choice of a worldview, ideology, or myth may seriously distort the conceptualization of a substantive problem and its potential solutions. In this case, policy analysis may be an ideology in disguise.[36] Finally, the search for metaproblems is based on a process of questioning and answering best described as *erotetic rationality*.

TYPES OF POLICY MODELS

Policy models are simplified representations of selected aspects of a problem situation constructed for particular purposes.[37] Just as policy problems are mental constructs based on the conceptualization and specification of elements of a problem situation, policy models are artificial reconstructions of reality in issue areas that range from energy and the environment to poverty, welfare, and crime. Policy models may be expressed as concepts, diagrams, graphs, or mathematical equations and may be used not only to describe, explain, and predict elements of a problem situation but also to improve it by recommending courses of action to resolve particular problems. Policy models are never literal descriptions of a problem situation. Like policy problems, policy models are artificial devices for imaginatively ordering and interpreting our experience of problem situations.

Policy models are useful and even necessary. They simplify systems of problems (messes) by helping to reduce and make manageable the complexities encountered by policy analysts in their work. Policy models may help distinguish essential from nonessential features of a problem situation, highlight relationships among important factors or variables, and assist in explaining and predicting the consequences of policy choices. Policy models may also play a self-critical and creative role in policy analysis by forcing

---

[35] See, for example, Ida R. Hoos, *Systems Analysis in Public Policy: A Critique* (Berkeley, CA: University of California Press, 1972).

[36] Laurence Tribe, "Policy Science: Analysis or Ideology? *Philosophy and Public Affairs*, 2, No. 1 (1972), 66–110; and "Ways Not to Think about Plastic Trees," in *When Values Conflict: Essays on Environmental Analysis, Discourse, and Decision*, ed. Laurence Tribe, Corinne S. Schelling, and John Voss (Cambridge, MA: Ballinger Publishing Co., 1976).

[37] See Saul I. Gass and Roger L. Sisson, eds., *A Guide to Models in Governmental Planning and Operations* (Washington, DC: Office of Research and Development, Environmental Protection Agency, 1974); and Martin Greenberger, Mathew A. Crenson, and Brian L. Crissey, *Models in the Policy Process* (New York: Russell Sage Foundation, 1976).

analysts to make their own assumptions explicit and to challenge conventional ideas and methods of analysis. Finally, the use of policy models is not a matter of choice, since everyone uses some kind of model. In the words of policy modeler Jay Forrester:

> Each of us uses models constantly. Every person in his private life and in his business life instinctively uses models for decision-making. The mental image of the world around you which you carry in your head is a model. One does not have a city or a government or a country in his head. He has only selected concepts and relationships which he uses to represent the real system. A mental image is a model. All of our decisions are taken on the basis of models. The question is not to use or ignore models. The question is only a choice among alternatives.[38]

By simplifying problem situations, models inevitably contribute to the selective distortion of reality. Models themselves cannot tell us how to discriminate between essential and nonessential questions; nor can they explain, predict, evaluate or recommend, since these judgments are external to the model and not part of it. While models may help us to undertake these analytic tasks, the key word is "us," for it is we and not the model who provide the assumptions necessary to interpret features of reality described by a model. Finally, policy models—particularly those expressed in mathematical form—are frequently difficult to communicate to policymakers and other stakeholders for whom models are designed as an aid to better decision making.

Descriptive Models

Policy models may be compared and contrasted according to a large number of dimensions, the most important of which help to distinguish among the purposes, forms of expression, and methodological functions of models. Two of the main forms of policy models are descriptive and normative. The purpose of *descriptive models* is to explain and/or predict the causes and consequences of policy choices. Descriptive models are used to monitor the outcomes of policy actions—for example, the annual list of social indicators published by the Office of Management and the Budget—as well as to forecast economic performance. For example, the Council of Economic Advisers prepares an annual economic forecast for inclusion in the President's Economic Report.

Normative Models

By contrast, the purpose of *normative models* is not only to explain and/or predict but also to provide rules and recommendations for optimizing the attainment of some utility (value). Among the many types of normative

---

[38] Jay W. Forrester, "Counter-intuitive Behavior of Social Systems," *Technological Review*, 73 (1971), 3.

models used by policy analysts are those that help determine optimum levels of service capacity (queuing models), the optimum timing of service and repairs (replacement models), the optimum volume and timing of orders (inventory models), and the optimum return on public investments (benefit–cost models). Normative decision problems are usually of the form: Find the values of the controllable (policy) variables which will produce the greatest utility (value), as measured by the value of outcome variables that policymakers wish to change.

One of the simplest and most familiar normative models is compound interest. At one point or another in their lives many persons have used some variation of this model to find the values of policy variables (for example, a bank versus a savings and loan association) which will produce the greatest interest income (utility) on savings, as measured by the amount of money that one may expect after a given number of years (value of outcome variable that the individual wishes to change). The analytical model for compound interest is

$$S_n = (1 + r)^n S_0$$

where S_n is the amount to which savings will accumulate in a given (n) number of years, S_0 is the initial savings, and $(1 + r)^n$ is a constant return on investment (1) plus the rate of interest (r) in the given time period (n). If an individual (policymaker) knows the interest rates of different savings institutions and wishes to optimize the return on savings, this simple normative model should permit a straightforward choice of that institution offering the highest rate of interest, provided there are no other important considerations (for example, the security of deposits or special privileges for patrons) that should be taken into account. Note, however, that this normative model also predicts the accumulation of savings under different alternatives, thus pointing to a characteristic of all normative models: They not only permit us to estimate past, present, and future values of outcome variables but also allow us to optimize the attainment of some value.

Verbal Models

Policy models, whether descriptive or normative, may also be distinguished according to the forms in which they are expressed. Normative and descriptive models may be expressed in three main forms: verbally, symbolically, and procedurally.[39] *Verbal models* are expressed in everyday language, rather than the language of symbolic logic or mathematics, and are the equivalent of what we described earlier as substantive problems. In using verbal models the analyst typically relies on reasoned judgments to make predictions and offer recommendations. Reasoned judgment produces pol-

---

[39] Models may also be expressed physically, as when various materials are used to construct representations of human organs, cities, or machines. The basic limitation of such models is that they cannot represent human action, which involves communication processes, social learning, and choice.

icy arguments, rather than results presented in the form of precise numerical values. Verbal models are relatively easily communicated among experts and laypersons alike, and their costs are low. A limitation of verbal models is that the reasons offered for predictions and recommendations may be implicit or hidden, making it difficult to reconstruct and critically examine arguments as a whole. The arguments for and against a blockade of the Soviet navy during the Cuban Missile Crisis of 1962 are a good example of verbal policy models. President Kennedy's own verbal model of the crisis argued, in effect, that a blockade was the United States's only real option:

> Above all, while defending our own vital interests, nuclear powers must avert those confrontations which bring an adversary to a choice of either a humiliating retreat or a nuclear war. To adopt that kind of course in the nuclear age would be evidence only of the bankruptcy of our policy—of a collective death wish for the world.[40]

Symbolic Models

Symbolic models use mathematical symbols to describe relationships among key variables that are believed to characterize a problem. Predictions or optimal solutions are obtained from symbolic models by employing mathematical, statistical, and logical methods. Symbolic models are difficult to communicate among laypersons, including policymakers, and even among expert modelers there are frequent misunderstandings about basic elements of models.[41] The costs of symbolic models are probably not much greater than those of verbal models, provided one takes into account the enormous time and effort expended on public debate, which is the main vehicle for expressing verbal models. A practical limitation of symbolic models is that their results may not be easily interpretable, even among specialists, since the assumptions of models may not be adequately spelled out. Symbolic models may improve policy decisions, but only if

> the premises on which models are constructed are made explicit. . . . All too frequently what purports to be a model based on theory and evidence is nothing more than a scholar's preconception and prejudices cloaked in the guise of scientific rigor and embellished with extensive computer simulations. Without empirical verification there is little assurance that the results of such exercises are reliable, or that they should be applied for normative policy purposes.[42]

Although we have already considered a simple symbolic model designed for normative purposes (compound interest), there are many sym-

---

[40] Quoted in Graham T. Allison, "Conceptual Models and the Cuban Missile Crisis," *The American Political Science Review*, 63, No. 3 (1969), 698.

[41] See Greenberger and others, *Models in the Policy Process*, pp. 328–36.

[42] Gary Fromm, "Policy Decisions and Econometric Models," cited by Greenberger and others, *Models in the Policy Process*, p. 72.

bolic models whose primary aim is descriptive. One of the most frequently used symbolic models is the simple linear equation

$$Y = a + bX$$

where Y is a variable that the analyst seeks to predict and X is a policy variable that is potentially manipulable by policymakers. The relation between X and Y is known as a linear function, which means that relations between X and Y will form a straight line when plotted on a graph (Figure 5–4). In this model the symbol b denotes the amount of change in Y due to changes in X, which may be depicted by the slope of the straight line when plotted on a piece of paper (the steeper the slope, the greater the effect of X on Y). The symbol a (called an *intercept constant*) denotes the point where the straight line intercepts the vertical or Y-axis when X is zero. In Figure 5–4 all values of Y are one-half those of X along the broken line (that is, $Y = 0 + 0.5X$), while along the solid line, they are equal (that is, $Y = 0 + 1.0X$). This linear model permits the analyst to determine how much change in the policy variable (X) will be necessary to produce a given value of the outcome variable (Y).

Procedural Models

Procedural models represent dynamic relationships among variables believed to characterize a policy problem. Predictions and optimal solutions

FIGURE 5–4   A symbolic model.

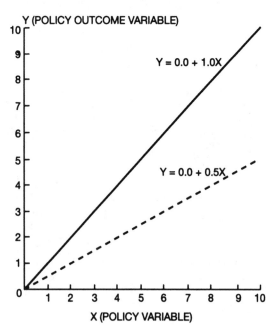

Y (POLICY OUTCOME VARIABLE)

$Y = 0.0 + 1.0X$

$Y = 0.0 + 0.5X$

X (POLICY VARIABLE)

are obtained by simulating and searching through sets of possible relation-ships—for example, economic growth, energy consumption, and food sup-plies in future years—that cannot be adequately described because reliable data are unavailable. Simulation and search procedures are generally (al-though not necessarily) performed with the aid of a computer, which is programmed to yield alternative predictions under different sets of as-sumptions.

Procedural models, it should be noted, also make use of symbolic modes of expression. The main difference between symbolic and procedural models is that the former use actual data to estimate relationships among policy and outcome variables, whereas procedural models assume (simulate) such relationships. The costs of procedural models are relatively high, as compared with verbal and symbolic models, largely because of the time required to develop and run computer programs. At the same time pro-cedural models may be written in reasonably nontechnical language, thus facilitating communication among laypersons. While the strength of pro-cedural models is that they permit creative simulation and search, their weakness is that it is frequently difficult to find data or arguments that justify model assumptions.

One of the simplest forms of procedural models is the decision tree, which is created by projecting policy decisions and their possible conse-quences into the future. Figure 5–5 illustrates a simple decision tree that estimates the probability that each of several policy alternatives will reduce pollution.[43] Decision trees are useful in comparing subjective estimates of

FIGURE 5–5   Simulation model.

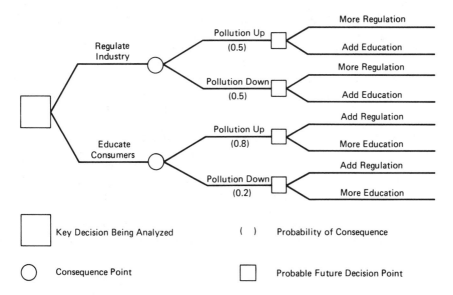

[43] See Gass and Sisson, *A Guide to Models in Governmental Planning and Operations*, pp. 26–27.

the possible consequences of various policy choices under conditions where it is difficult to calculate risk and uncertainty on the basis of existing data.

Models as Surrogates and Perspectives

A final important dimension of policy models relates to their assumptions. Policy models, irrespective of their purpose or mode of expression, may be viewed as surrogates or perspectives.[44] A *surrogate model* is assumed to be a substitute for substantive problems. Surrogate models proceed, consciously or unconsciously, from the assumption that the formal problem is a valid representation of the substantive problem. By contrast, *perspective models* are viewed as one among many possible ways to structure substantive problems. Perspective models are based on the assumption that the formal problem can never serve as a wholly valid representation of substantive problems.

The distinction between surrogate and perspective models is particularly important in public policy analysis, where, as we have seen, many of the most important problems are ill structured. The structure of most public policy problems is sufficiently complex that the use of surrogate models significantly increases the probability of errors of the third type (E_{III}), that is, solving the wrong formulation of a problem when one should have solved the right one. This point may be clarified by considering two illustrations of formal modeling in policy analysis. The first of these illustrations is concerned with the use of symbolic models, while the second deals with verbal models.[45]

Suppose that an analyst has constructed a simple symbolic model expressed in the form of a single linear equation such as that described earlier in Figure 5-5. Using the equation $Y = a + bX$ the analyst makes a series of observations that permit her to plot actual values of X and Y, as shown in Figure 5-6. Suppose also that an implicit assumption leads the analyst to conclude that the observed values of X and Y constitute a causal relationship, where the policy variable (X) is believed to produce significant changes in an outcome variable (Y). At this point the analyst will very likely interpret the results of the formal symbolic model as a confirmation of the structure of the substantive problem. For example, the analyst will no doubt interpret the slope of the line as a measure of the effects of X on Y, while the correlation between observed values of Y (data points) and those predicted by the equation (those lying on the straight line) will be taken as an estimate of the accuracy of the prediction. The probable conclusion is that any change in the policy variable will result in a corresponding unit change in the value of the outcome variable.

The point of this illustration is that the formal symbolic model itself provides no guidance in answering the question of whether X causes Y. If

---

[44] Strauch, "A Critical Look at Quantitative Methodology," pp. 136–44.

[45] These illustrations are adapted from Strauch, "A Critical Look at Quantitative Methodology," pp. 131–33; and Watzlawick, Weakland, and Fisch, *Change*.

FIGURE 5–6   Assumed effects of X on Y.

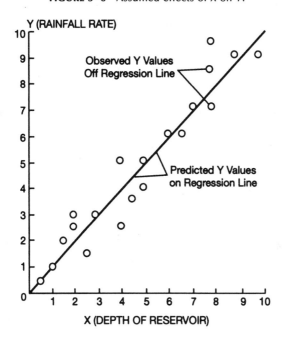

X happens to be unemployment and Y poverty there may be a case for the predicted relation, provided the substantive problem has been defined in such a way as to provide plausible reasons for believing that unemployment causes poverty. Yet this information is not contained in the symbolic model; it comes from *outside* the model. The observed relation between X and Y might just as easily be interpreted as evidence of the effects of poverty on unemployment, provided the substantive problem has been defined in terms of the assumption that poverty is not an economic phenomenon but a cultural one. Poverty, for example, may be defined in terms of a "culture of poverty" that depresses the motivation to work.

The lesson of this illustration is that the conceptualization of substantive problems governs the interpretation of symbolic models. Formal representations of substantive problems are perspectives and not surrogates. To clarify this point further, let us return to the formal symbolic model previously discussed:

> Suppose, for example, that X is the mean annual depth of a reservoir and that Y is the annual rainfall in the area. . . . Because reservoir-management policies can be changed, reservoir depth is a policy variable subject to policy manipulation. Annual rainfall is a variable we might be interested in controlling, and common sense clearly suggests that the relationship between rainfall and reservoir depth is nonspecious. . . . In spite of this, however, the conclusion suggested by the analysis—that we can decrease rainfall by draining

water more rapidly from the reservoir . . . seems ludicrous. This is because the causal relationship assumed in the analysis—reservoir depth causes rainfall—runs counter to our common sense understanding that rainfall determines reservoir depth.[46]

Consider now a second illustration of the difficulties that arise when we confuse surrogate and perspective models. This time we will use an illustration that makes the same point about verbal models, that is, models that are expressed in everyday language. Suppose that you are a policy analyst confronted with the following problem situation: The director of the state department of transportation has requested that a study be undertaken to recommend the least costly way to connect nine key transportation points in the central region of the state. As the agency's policy analyst you are directed to show how all nine points may be connected by four sections of highway. You are also told that these four sections of highway must be straight (no curves will be permitted); and that each new section must begin at the point where the last section stopped (the construction team will not be permitted to retrace its steps). You are then shown a map of the region (Figure 5–7) and asked to make a recommendation that will solve the director's problem.

Unless you were already familiar with this classic conceptual problem (called simply the "nine-dot problem"), it is very unlikely that you were able to solve it. Few people manage to find the solution by themselves, not because the problem is technically complicated (in fact it is simple), but because they almost always commit an error of the third type (E_{III}), solving the wrong formulation of a problem when they should have solved the right one. This is because most people approach the problem situation with implicit assumptions that make it impossible to solve the problem. The central point, however, is that these assumptions are introduced by analysts themselves; they are *not* part of the problem situation. In other words, analysts themselves create a substantive problem that cannot be solved.

FIGURE 5–7   Map of transportation points in central region.

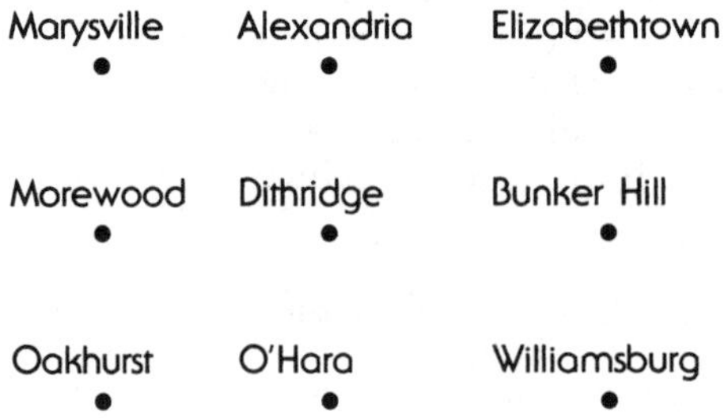

Marysville   Alexandria   Elizabethtown
•   •   •

Morewood   Dithridge   Bunker Hill
•   •   •

Oakhurst   O'Hara   Williamsburg
•   •   •

---

[46] Strauch, "A Critical Look at Quantitative Methodology," p. 132.

FIGURE 5–8   Solution for nine-dot problem.

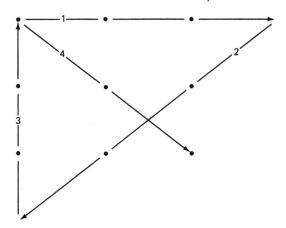

The solution for the nine-dot problem is presented in Figure 5–8. The solution appears surprisingly simple, novel, and unconventional; that is, it has several of the key characteristics of creative policy analysis discussed earlier. Why is this so? First, and most important, it becomes suddenly clear that we have been solving the wrong problem. So long as we assume that the solution must be found within the boundaries set by our verbal model— that is, the square composed of the nine dots—then a solution is not possible. Yet this condition is imposed, not by the formal verbal model, but by the implicit assumption of "squareness" that unconsciously shaped our definition of the substantive problem. Imagine what would have occurred if we had transformed the verbal model into a symbolic one, for example, by using plane geometry to derive quantitative estimates of the distance between points. This would not only have led us further and further away from the solution; it may have also created an aura of scientific rigor and precision that would lend authority to the conclusion that the problem is "insoluble." Finally, this illustration helps convey a simple but important point about the use of verbal, symbolic, and procedural models in policy analysis. Formal models cannot themselves tell us whether we are solving the wrong formulation of a problem when we should be solving the right one: The map is *not* the territory.

METHODS OF PROBLEM STRUCTURING

Problem structuring is the process of generating and testing alternative conceptualizations of a problem situation. As we saw in Figure 5–3, problem structuring involves four interrelated phases: problem sensing, problem search, problem definition, and problem specification. A number of methods and related techniques are helpful in carrying out problem-structuring

TABLE 5–2 Methods of Problem Structuring

METHOD	AIM	PROCEDURES	SOURCE OF KNOWLEDGE	PERFORMANCE CRITERION
Boundary analysis	Estimation of metaproblem boundaries	Saturation sampling, problem elicitation, and cumulation	Knowledge system	Correctness-in-limit
Classificational analysis	Clarification of concepts	Logical division and classification of concepts	Individual analyst	Logical consistency
Hierarchy analysis	Identification of possible, plausible, and actionable causes	Logical division and classification of causes	Individual analyst	Logical consistency
Synectics	Recognition of similarities among problems	Construction of personal, direct, symbolic, and fantasy analogies	Individual analyst or group	Plausibility of comparisons
Brainstorming	Generation of ideas, goals, and strategies	Idea generation and evaluation	Group	Consensus
Multiple perspective analysis	Generation of insight	Joint use of technical, organizational, and personal perspectives	Group	Improved insight
Assumptional analysis	Creative synthesis of conflicting assumptions	Stakeholder identification, assumption surfacing, challenging, pooling, and synthesis	Group	Conflict
Argumentation mapping	Assumption assessment	Plausibility and importance rating and graphing	Group	Optimal plausibility and importance

activities in each phase. These methods, along with their respective aims, procedures, source of knowledge, and criteria of performance, are displayed in Table 5–2.

Boundary Analysis

An important task of problem structuring is estimating whether the system of individual problem formulations that we have called a *metaproblem* is relatively complete. This task is similar to the situation of the homesteaders described by Kline in his essays on the myth of certainty in mathematics.[47] The homesteaders, while clearing their land, are aware that enemies lurk in the wilderness that lies just beyond the clearing. To increase their security, the homesteaders clear a larger and larger area but never feel completely safe. Frequently, they must decide whether to clear more land or attend to their crops and domesticated animals within the boundaries of the clearing. They do their best to push back the wilderness but know full well that the enemies lurking beyond the clearing could surprise and destroy them. They hope that they will not choose to tend the crops and livestock when, instead, they should have chosen to clear more land.

The analogy of the homesteaders accentuates a key problem of problem structuring in policy analysis. Policy analysts are rarely faced with a single, well-defined problem; rather, they are faced with multiple problems which, distributed throughout the policy-making process, are defined in distinctly different ways by stakeholders whose perspectives and actions are interdependent. Under these circumstances analysts appear as homesteaders working within unmanageable boundaries, or perhaps as modern counterparts of Diogenes, engaged in "a never-ending discourse with reality, to discover yet more facets, more dimensions of action, more opportunities for improvement."[48]

To make effective use of the methods and techniques of problem structuring described in this chapter, it is important to conduct a problem boundary analysis. Methods of problem structuring just discussed, along with related methods which presuppose that the problem has already been structured,[49] do not themselves provide any way to know whether a set of prob-

---

[47] Morris Kline, *Mathematics: The Loss of Certainty* (New York: Oxford University Press, 1980). See also the critical essays on uncertainty and creativity in modern mathematics by Michael Guillen, *Bridges to Infinity* (Ithaca, NY: Cornell University Press, 1988).

[48] Dery, *Problem Definition in Policy Analysis*, pp. 6–7.

[49] These other methods include the analytic hierarchy process, interpretive structural modeling, policy capturing, and Q-methodology. See, respectively, Thomas L. Saaty, *The Analytic Hierarchy Process* (New York: McGraw-Hill, 1980); John N. Warfield, *Societal Systems: Planning, Policy, and Complexity* (New York: Wiley, 1976); Kenneth R. Hammond, *Judgment and Decision in Public Policy Formation* (Boulder, CO: Westview Press, 1977); and Stephen R. Brown, *Political Subjectivity: Applications of Q-Methodology in Political Science* (New Haven, CT: Yale University Press, 1980). Computer software is available for applications of these methods.

lem formulations is relatively complete. The relative completeness of a set of problem formulations may be estimated by means of a three-step process:[50]

1. *Saturation sampling.* A saturation (or snowball) sample of stakeholders may be obtained by a multistage process that begins with a set of individuals and groups known to differ on a policy. Stakeholders in this initial set may be contacted, face-to-face or by telephone, and asked to name two additional stakeholders who agree most and least with the arguments and claims discussed. The process is continued until no *new* stakeholders are named. Provided that the set of stakeholders is not a subsample from a larger population, there is no sampling variance, because all members of the working universe of policy-relevant stakeholders in a specific area (for example, a bill addressing health care reform or a court decision protecting the environment) have been contacted.[51]

2. *Elicitation of problem representations.* This second step is designed to elicit the alternative problem representations which Heclo has described as the "ideas, basic paradigms, dominant metaphors, standard operating procedures, or whatever else we choose to call the systems of interpretation by which we attach meaning to events."[52] The evidence required to characterize these problem representations may be obtained from face-to-face interviews or, more realistically under the time constraints facing most analysts, from telephone conversations and documents requested from stakeholders in the saturation sampling phase.

3. *Boundary estimation.* The third step is to estimate the boundaries of the metaproblem. Here the analyst constructs a cumulative frequency distribution where stakeholders are arrayed on the horizontal axis and the number of *new* problem elements—ideas, concepts, variables, assumptions, objectives, policies—are plotted on the vertical axis (Figure 5–9). As the new and nonduplicative problem elements of each stakeholder are plotted, the slope of the curve displays different rates of change. An initial rapid rate of change is followed by slow change and eventually stagnation, which is the point at which the curve becomes flat. After this point, the collection of additional information about the nature of the problem is unlikely to improve the accuracy of the collective problem representation, because the boundary of the metaproblem has been estimated.

The estimation procedures described satisfy requirements for sound inductive estimates in general: character, coordination, cost-effectiveness, and correctness-in-the-limit.[53] Applications of similar procedures in other complex areas—for example, estimates of boundaries of scientific literature,

---

[50] See William N. Dunn, "Methods of the Second Type: Coping with the Wilderness of Conventional Policy Analysis," *Policy Studies Review,* 7, No. 4 (1988), 720–37.

[51] On these points as they apply to sociometric and saturation sampling in general, see Seymour Sudman, *Applied Sampling* (New York: Academic Press, 1976).

[52] Hugh Heclo, "Policy Dynamics," in *The Dynamics of Public Policy,* ed. Richard Rose (Beverly Hills, CA: Sage Publications, 1976), pp. 253–54.

[53] See Nicholas Rescher, *Induction* (Pittsburgh, PA: University of Pittsburgh Press, 1980), pp. 24–26. For the detailed argument relating these requirements to problem structuring in policy analysis, see Dunn, "Methods of the Second Type."

FIGURE 5-9   Boundaries of a metaproblem.

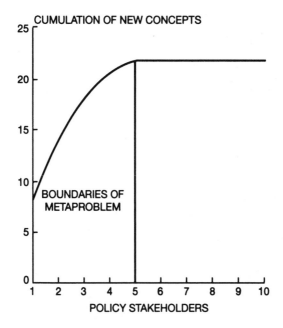

CUMULATION OF NEW CONCEPTS

POLICY STAKEHOLDERS

library holdings, languages, literary works, consumer preferences—suggest lawful regularities in the patterns and limits of growth in knowledge systems.[54] Boundary analysis, like other policy-analytic procedures, yields results that are plausible and not certain. In conjunction with other problem structuring methods and techniques, these boundary estimation procedures reduce the likelihood of type III errors in policy analysis.

Classificational Analysis

Classificational analysis is a technique for clarifying concepts used to define and classify problem situations.[55] In sensing a problem situation, policy analysts must somehow classify their experiences. Even the most simple descriptions of problem situations are based on the classification of experience through inductive reasoning, a process where general (abstract) concepts, such as poverty, crime, and pollution, are formed by experiencing particular (concrete) objects or situations. When we classify a problem sit-

---

[54] For a brief but provocative essay on these regularities, see Herbert A. Simon, "The Sizes of Things," in *Statistics: A Guide to the Unknown*, ed. Judith M. Tanur and others (San Francisco: Holden-Day, 1972), pp. 195–202.

[55] See John O'Shaughnessy, *Inquiry and Decision* (New York: Harper & Row, 1973), pp. 22–30.

uation in one way, we often foreclose opportunities to classify it in another way, as the nine-dot problem illustrates so well.

Classificational analysis is based on two main procedures: logical division and logical classification. When we select a class and break it down into its component parts the process is called *logical division;* the reverse process, which involves the combination of situations, objects, or persons into larger groups or classes, is called *logical classification.* The basis of any classification depends on the analyst's purpose, which in turn depends on substantive knowledge about a problem situation.

Consider, for example, the analysis of poverty in the United States. All families in the United States may be broken down into two subclasses: those whose incomes are above and below a poverty line established by the U.S. Social Security Administration. If an analyst stops at this point in the process of logical division, he or she will reach the conclusion that poverty in the United States is gradually declining and perhaps claim that the progressive reduction of poverty is a consequence of the operation of a healthy capitalist economy. Yet when the process of logical division is carried one step further, and poverty families are divided into two additional subclasses on the basis of income before and after government transfer payments, the analyst will reach an altogether different conceptualization of the problem. Here the analyst will no doubt conclude that the reduction of poverty is a consequence of public welfare and social security programs and probably claim that problems of poverty cannot be resolved by the private enterprise system, since the number of families below the poverty line increased absolutely and relative to the total population between 1968 and 1972 (Table 5–3).

Although there is no way to know with certainty whether the bases of a classification system are the right ones, there are several rules that help ensure that a classification system is both relevant to a problem situation and logically consistent:

1. *Substantive relevance.* The basis of a classification should be developed according to the analyst's purpose and the nature of the problem situation. This rule, deceptively simple in theory, means that classes and subclasses should conform as closely as possible to the "realities" of the problem situation. Yet since what we know about a situation is partly a function of the concepts we use to experience it, there are no absolute guidelines that tell us when we have perceived a problem correctly. Poverty, for example, may be classified as a problem of inadequate income, cultural deprivation, or psychological motivation—it may be all of these and more.

2. *Exhaustiveness.* Categories in a classification system should be exhaustive. This means that all subjects or situations of interest to the analyst must be "used up," so to speak. In the above example all families in the United States must fit into one or another of the various categories. If we discover that some families have no income, either from their own efforts or government transfers, a new category might be created.

3. *Disjointness.* Categories must be mutually exclusive. Each subject or situation must be assigned to one and only one category or subcategory. In classifying families, for example, they must fall into one or the other of the two main

TABLE 5–3 Number of Households Living below Poverty Level, 1965–1972[1]

	1965		1968		1972	
CATEGORY	Number (millions)	Percent-age of Total	Number (millions)	Percent-age of Total	Number (millions)	Percent-age of Total
Pretransfer households[2]	15.6	25.7	14.9	23.2	17.6	24.8
Posttransfer households[3]	10.5	17.3	10.1	15.7	10.0	14.1

Notes:
[1] The U.S. Social Security Administration defined poverty as falling below the following income levels: $3223 (1965), $3553 (1968), $4275 (1972). These levels are established for the annual cash income of a nonfarm family of four.
[2] Excludes government transfers in the form of cash payments (Social Security, Public Assistance), nutrition (Food Stamps), housing, health (Medicaid, Medicare), social services (OEO), employment and manpower, and education.
[3] Includes government transfers of all forms.
Source: R. D. Plotnick and F. Skidmore, *Progress against Poverty: Review of the 1964–1974 Decade,* Institute for Research on Poverty, Poverty Policy Analysis Series No. 1 (New York: Academic Press, 1975).

subcategories (income above and below the poverty line), which means that no family can be "double-counted."

4. *Consistency.* Each category and subcategory should be based on a single classificational principle. A violation of this rule leads to overlapping subclasses and is known as the fallacy of cross-division. For example, we commit the fallacy of cross-division if we classify families according to whether they are above the poverty line or receiving welfare payments, since many families fall into both categories. This rule is actually an extension of rules of exhaustiveness and disjointness.

5. *Hierarchical distinctiveness.* The meaning of levels in a classification system (categories, subcategories, sub-subcategories) must be carefully distinguished. This rule, which is really a guideline for interpreting classification systems, is derived from the simple but important rule discussed previously: Whatever involves *all* of a collection must not be one of the collection. Humankind is the class of all individuals; but it is not itself an individual. Similarly, poverty as a characteristic of 14 million families cannot be understood in terms of the behavior of one family multiplied by 14 million. A population of 14 million poor families is not just quantitatively different from a single family; it is also qualitatively different since it involves a whole system of interdependent economic, social, and political characteristics.

The rule of hierarchical distinctiveness deserves further elaboration, since it is central to problem structuring. In structuring policy problems it frequently happens that analysts ignore the distinction between member and class and that a class cannot be a member of itself. This point is best illustrated by returning to the nine-dot problem (Figure 5–7). When a person first attempts to solve this problem his

> assumption is that the dots compose a square and that the solution must be found *within* that square, a self-imposed condition which the instructions do not contain. His failure, therefore, does not lie in the impossibility of the task, but in his attempted solution. Having now created the problem it does not matter in the least which combination of four lines he now tries, and in what order; he always finishes with at least one unconnected dot. This means that he can run through the totality of first-order change possibilities [i.e., those that are confined to the level of members of the class defined as a square] . . . but will never solve the task. The solution is a second-order change [i.e., one that involves *all* of the class] which consists in leaving the field and which cannot be contained within itself because . . . it involves all of a collection and cannot, therefore, be part of it.[56]

One of the most useful approaches to classificational analysis is set thinking.[57] Set thinking involves the study of relations of sets to each other and to subsets, where a *set* is defined as a clearly delimited collection of objects or elements. Sets and subsets are the equivalents of classes and subclasses in a classification system and are expressed visually with aid of Venn diagrams.[58] In the Venn diagram in Figure 5–10, the rectangle might be used to represent all families in the United States. In set language it is known as the *universal set (U)*. Two of its component sets, shown as circles A and B in the rectangle, might be used to represent families above and below the poverty line. If we apply rules of exhaustiveness, disjointedness, and consistency, all families will be divided into one or the other of the sets, A and B, so that the two sets reflect distinct levels of income which do not overlap. In set language the *union* of A and B is equal to the *universe (U)* of all families. The symbol for union is ∪, read as "union" or "cup."

Two sets often intersect to form a subset, so that the properties of the

FIGURE 5–10   Set union.

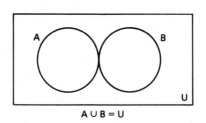

A ∪ B = U

---

[56] Watzlawick and others, *Change*, p. 25. See also Gregory Bateson, *Steps to an Ecology of Mind* (New York: Ballantine Books, 1972).

[57] Set theory, created by the German mathematician-logician Georg Canter (1874–1897), is the mathematical theory of collections of aggregates of entities.

[58] Venn diagrams, used extensively to illustrate set problems, are named after the English logician, John Venn (1834–1923).

FIGURE 5-11   Set intersection.

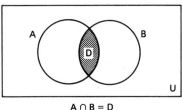

A ∩ B = D

original two sets overlap, as shown in Figure 5-11. For example, the intersection (D) of nonpoverty (A) and poverty (B) families might be used to illustrate that some families in each group receive government transfer payments. In set language the intersection of A and B is equal to D, which is expressed symbolically as A ∩ B = D and read "A intersect (or cap) B equals D." Union and intersection are the two most important set operations and may be used to construct classification schemes (Figure 5-12) and crossbreaks (Figure 5-13). Crossbreaks are a basic form of logical division used to organize data in tables.

Venn diagrams, classification schemes, and crossbreaks are important

FIGURE 5-12   Classificational scheme.

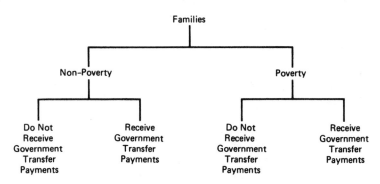

FIGURE 5-13   Crossbreak.

	A_1	A_2
B_1	B_1A_1	B_1A_2
B_2	B_2A_1	B_2A_2

A_1 = nonpoverty families
A_2 = poverty families
B_1 = do not receive transfer payments
B_2 = receive transfer payments

techniques for structuring policy problems. Procedures of classificational analysis, however, focus on the individual policy analyst, rather than groups, and use logical consistency as the primary criterion of performance in assessing how well an analyst has conceptualized the problem. While the consistency of a classification scheme is an important aspect of its adequacy, there is no way to know with confidence that the substantive basis of any category or subcategory is the right one. Since different analysts frequently disagree about substantive bases of categories, the individual focus of classificational analysis may foreclose opportunities to generate alternative classification schemes. In short, classificational analysis is a technique for improving the clarity of given concepts and their relationships. Classificational analysis does not guarantee that concepts will have substantive relevance.

Hierarchy Analysis

Hierarchy analysis is a technique for identifying possible causes of a problem situation.[59] Regrettably, formal logic and many social science theories provide little guidance in identifying possible causes. There is no certain way to deduce causes from effects, or effects from causes, and social science theories are frequently so general or abstract as to be of little direct help in specific situations. In order to identify the possible causes contributing to a problem situation, it is useful to have conceptual frameworks that outline the many causes that may be operating in a given situation.

Hierarchy analysis helps the analyst to identify three kinds of causes: possible causes, plausible causes, and actionable causes. *Possible causes* are events or actions that, however remote, may contribute to the occurrence of a given problem situation. For example, resistance to work, unemployment, and the distribution of power and wealth among elites may all be taken as possible causes of poverty. By contrast, *plausible causes* are those that, on the basis of scientific research or direct experience, are believed to exert an important influence on the occurrence of a situation judged to be problematic. In the preceding example resistance to work is unlikely to be regarded as a plausible cause of poverty, at least among experienced observers, whereas unemployment and elites are. Finally, the distribution of power and wealth among elites is unlikely to be viewed as an *actionable cause*—that is, one which is subject to control or manipulation by policymakers—since no single policy or set of policies intended to resolve problems of poverty can alter the social structure of an entire society. In this example unemployment is both a plausible and actionable cause of poverty.

Political scientists Stuart Nagel and Marian Neef provide a good example of the potential uses of hierarchy analysis to structure policy problems. Many observers have been ready to accept the explanation that the major cause of overcrowded jails is the large number of persons arrested and detained in jail while awaiting trial. For this reason a policy of pretrial release—that is, a policy that provides for the release of a certain number

---

[59] See O'Shaughnessy, *Inquiry and Decision*, pp. 69–80.

of those arrested (usually for less serious offenses) prior to a formal trial—has been favored by many reformers.

The difficulty with this policy, as well as the causal explanation on which it is based, is that it overlooks plea bargaining as one among several plausible causes of jail overcrowding. In plea bargaining, which is widely practiced in the U.S. judicial system, a defendant agrees to plead guilty in return for a prosecutor's agreement to reduce the charge or the sentence. When plea bargaining is taken into account along with pretrial release the following consequences may occur:

> If the percentage of defendants released prior to trial goes up, then the percentage of successful plea bargains will probably go down. . . . Now, if guilty pleas go down as a result of increased pretrial release, then the number of trials will probably go up. . . . And if the number of trials increases, then the delay in going to trial will also increase, unless the system increases its quantity of prosecutors, judges, and public defenders. . . . If this delay in going to trial increases for cases in general, including defendants in jail, then the jail population may increase, since its size depends on the length of time that defendants are kept in jail as well as on the quantity of defendants who go there. Any decrease in the jail population as a result of increased pretrial release may be more than offset by the increased delay and length of pretrial detention caused by the increased pretrial release and the consequent reduction in guilty pleas and increase in trials.[60]

This example not only illustrates the potentially creative role of hierarchy analysis in structuring policy problems but also shows how hierarchy analysis can contribute to the discovery of possible unanticipated consequences of public policies whose effects seem self-evident. What could be more obvious than that pretrial release will result in a reduction of the jail population? The answer depends on having a satisfactory understanding of the plausible causes that contribute to the original problem situation. Figure 5–14 provides a simple illustration of hierarchy analysis applied to possible, plausible, and actionable causes of fires.

The rules for conducting a hierarchy analysis are the same as those used for classificational analysis: substantive relevance, exhaustiveness, disjointness, consistency, and hierarchical distinctiveness. Similarly, procedures of logical division and classification also apply to both types of analysis. The major difference between classificational analysis and hierarchy analysis is that the former involves the division and classification of concepts in general, whereas hierarchy analysis builds particular concepts of possible, plausible, and actionable causes. Nevertheless, both forms of analysis focus on the individual analyst and use logical consistency as the primary criterion for assessing how well a problem has been conceptualized, and neither guarantees that the correct substantive basis for concepts will be found. Thus, hierarchy analysis may also foreclose opportunities to generate al-

---

[60] Stuart S. Nagel and Marian G. Neef, "Two Examples from the Legal Process," *Policy Analysis*, 2, No. 2 (1976), 356–57.

FIGURE 5-14   Hierarchy analysis of the causes of fires.

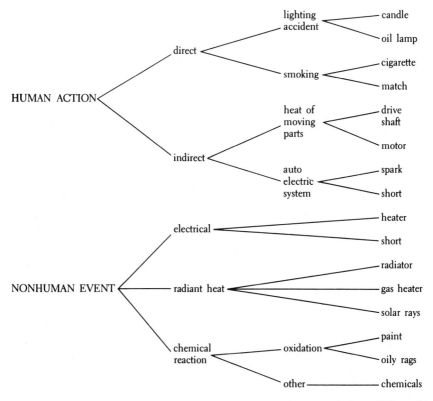

Source: John O'Shaughnessy, *Inquiry and Decision* (New York: Harper & Row, 1973), p. 76.

ternative causal explanations by relying on the individual analysts, rather than on groups, as a source of knowledge.

Synectics

Synectics is a method designed to promote the recognition of analogous problems.[61] Synectics, which refers broadly to the investigation of similarities, helps analysts make creative use of analogies in structuring policy problems. Many studies show that people frequently fail to recognize that what appears to be a new problem is really an old one in disguise, and that old problems may contain potential solutions for problems that appear to be new. Synectics is based on the assumption that an awareness of identical

---

[61] See W. J. Gordon, *Synectics* (New York: Harper & Row, 1961); and Hayes, *Cognitive Psychology*, pp. 72, 241.

or similar relationships among problems will greatly increase the problem-solving capacities of analysts.

In structuring policy problems analysts may produce four types of analogies:

1. *Personal analogies.* In constructing personal analogies, analysts attempt to imagine themselves experiencing a problem situation in the same way as does some other policy stakeholder, for example, a policymaker or client group. Personal analogies are especially important in uncovering political dimensions of a problem situation, for "unless we are willing and able to think 'politically'—if only as a matter of role playing—we will not be able to enter the phenomenological world of the policymaker and understand the policy process."[62]
2. *Direct analogies.* In making direct analogies, the analyst searches for similar relationships among two or more problem situations. In structuring problems of drug addiction, for example, analysts may construct direct analogies from experiences with the control of contagious diseases.[63]
3. *Symbolic analogies.* In making symbolic analogies, the analyst attempts to discover similar relationships between a given problem situation and some symbolic process. For example, symbolic analogies are often drawn between servomechanisms of various kinds (thermostats, automatic pilots) and policy processes. In each case analogous processes of adaptation are viewed as consequences of continuous feedback from the environment.[64]
4. *Fantasy analogies.* In making fantasy analogies, analysts are completely free to explore similarities between a problem situation and some imaginary state of affairs. Defense policy analysts, for example, have sometimes used fantasy analogies to structure problems of defense against nuclear attack.[65]

Synectics relies on individual analysts and groups to make appropriate analogies. The main criterion for assessing how well a problem has been conceptualized is the plausibility of comparisons, that is, the degree to which a given problem situation is actually similar to others taken as analogies.

Brainstorming

Brainstorming is a method for generating ideas, goals, and strategies that help identify and conceptualize problem situations. Originally designed by Alex Osborn as a means to enhance creativity, brainstorming may be

---

[62] Raymond A. Bauer, "The Study of Policy Formation: An Introduction," in *The Study of Policy Formation*, ed. R. A. Bauer and K. J. Gergen (New York: The Free Press, 1968), p. 4.

[63] See, for example, Mark H. Moore, "Anatomy of the Heroin Problem: An Exercise in Problem Definition," *Policy Analysis*, 2, No. 4 (1976), 639–62.

[64] See, for example, David Easton, *A Framework for Political Analysis* (Englewood Cliffs, NJ: Prentice Hall, 1965).

[65] See, for example, Herman Kahn, *On Thermonuclear War* (Princeton, NJ: Princeton University Press, 1960). For a critique, see Philip Green, *Deadly Logic: The Theory of Nuclear Deterrence* (Columbus, OH: Ohio State University Press, 1966).

used to generate a large number of suggestions about potential solutions for problems.[66] Brainstorming involves several simple procedures:

1. Brainstorming groups should be composed in accordance with the nature of the problem situation being investigated. This usually means the selection of persons who are particularly knowledgeable about the given situation, that is, experts.

2. Processes of idea generation and idea evaluation should be kept strictly apart, since intense group discussion may be inhibited by premature criticism and debate.

3. The atmosphere of brainstorming activities should be kept as open and permissive as possible in the idea-generating phase.

4. The idea-evaluating phase should begin only after all ideas generated in the first phase have been exhausted.

5. At the end of the idea-evaluating phase, the group should prioritize ideas and incorporate them in a proposal that contains a conceptualization of the problem and its potential solutions.

Brainstorming is a highly versatile procedure which may involve relatively structured or unstructured activities, depending on the analyst's aims and the practical constraints of the situation. Relatively unstructured brainstorming activities occur frequently in government agencies and public and private "think tanks." Here discussions of policy problems are informal and largely spontaneous, involving the interaction of generalists and specialists from several scientific disciplines or fields.[67] Brainstorming activities may also be relatively structured, with various devices used to coordinate or focus group discussions. These devices include the establishment of *continuous decision seminars* which, seeking to avoid the restrictive atmosphere of conventional committees, involve a team of highly motivated experts who meet with high frequency over a number of years.[68]

Another device for coordinating and focusing brainstorming activities is the construction of *scenarios*, which are outlines of hypothetical future events that may alter some problem situation. Scenario writing, which has been used to explore potential military and political crises, involves the constructive use of the imagination to describe some aspect of a future situation. There are two major types of scenarios: operations-analytical and free-form. In constructing a free-form scenario the analyst is "an iconoclast, a model breaker, a questioner of assumptions, and—in rare instances—a

---

[66] Alex F. Osborn, *Your Creative Power* (New York: Charles Scribner, 1948).

[67] See Edgar F. Quade, *Analysis for Public Decisions* (New York: American Elsevier Publishing Co., 1975), pp. 186–88; and Olaf Helmer and Nicholas Rescher, *On the Epistemology of the Inexact Sciences* (Santa Monica, CA: The Rand Corporation, February, 1960).

[68] Harold D. Lasswell, "Technique of Decision Seminars," *Midwest Journal of Political Science*, 4, No. 2 (1960), 213–26; and Lasswell, *The Future of Political Science* (New York: Atherton Press, 1963).

fashioner of new criteria."[69] By contrast, an operations-analytical scenario has limited aims:

. . . instead of building up a picture of unrestrained fiction or even of constructing a utopian invention that the author considers highly desirable, an operations-analytical scenario starts with the present state of the world and shows how, step by step, a future state might evolve in a plausible fashion out of the present one.[70]

A good example of a relatively structured brainstorming effort is the Year 2000 Planning Program, a two and one-half year project carried out in the U.S. Bureau of the Census.[71] In this project 120 self-selected participants from all levels and branches of the Bureau, from secretaries to division heads and the director, were asked to think as freely as possible about the future and to construct free-form scenarios which to them indicated what the bureau should be like in the year 2000. Participants were asked to write group reports that were later integrated in a final report by an executive group composed of representatives of the individual groups. The final report was subsequently presented to the executive staff of the Census Bureau, as well as to the advisory committees of the American Statistical Association, the American Marketing Association, and the American Economic Association.

The Year 2000 Planning Program was successful on several counts. The report was received with moderate approval by all groups, and most members thought that the program should be continued in some form, perhaps permanently. Two creative products of the project were suggestions to establish an ombudsman to protect the interests of users of Census data and to create a Census University to develop and execute the bureau's continuing education programs. Those who were most positive about the report were oriented toward strategic concerns involving ill-structured problems; less positive reactions came from persons with tactical or operational orientations toward well-structured problems. The program itself was made possible by a recognition among top-level bureau staff, including the director, that the bureau was confronted by important long-range problems whose structure was highly complex and "messy." Finally, although the program involved significant resource allocations, there did not appear to be major risks in executing the program.

The main difference between brainstorming and other techniques for

---

[69] Seyon H. Brown, "Scenarios in Systems Analysis," in *Systems Analysis and Policy Planning: Applications in Defense*, ed. E. S. Quade and W. I. Boucher (New York: American Elsevier Publishing Co., 1968), p. 305.

[70] Olaf Helmer, *Social Technology* (New York: Basic Books, 1966), p. 10. Quoted in Quade, *Analysis for Public Decisions*, p. 188.

[71] See Ian I. Mitroff, Vincent P. Barabba, and Ralph H. Kilmann, "The Application of Behaviorial and Philosophical Technologies to Strategic Planning: A Case Study of a Large Federal Agency," *Management Science*, 24, No. 1 (1977), 44–58.

problem structuring is that the focus is on groups of knowledgeables rather than individual experts. Moreover, brainstorming activities are assessed, not in terms of logical consistency or the plausibility of comparisons, but according to consensus among members of brainstorming groups. The major limitation of consensus as a criterion of performance in problem structuring is that conflicts about the nature of problems may be suppressed, thus foreclosing opportunities to generate and evaluate potentially appropriate ideas, goals, and strategies. While the Year 2000 Planning Program sought to create an open and permissive atmosphere, the final evaluation of the program's success was based on consensus among authoritative decision makers (agency executive staff) and experts (advisory committees of professional associations). In short, this program and other relatively structured brainstorming activities provide no explicit procedures to promote the creative use of conflict in structuring policy problems.

Multiple Perspective Analysis

Multiple perspective analysis is a method for obtaining greater insight into problems and potential solutions by systematically applying personal, organizational, and technical perspectives to problem situations.[72] Seen as an alternative to the near-exclusive emphasis on so-called rational-technical approaches in planning, policy analysis, technology assessment, social impact assessment, and other areas, multiple perspective analysis is expressly designed to address ill-structured policy problems. Although there are many characteristics of each of the three perspectives, their major features are as follows:

1. *Technical perspective.* The technical (T) perspective views problems and solutions in terms of optimization models and employs techniques based on probability theory, benefit–cost and decision analysis, econometrics, and systems analysis. The technical perspective, said to be based on a scientific–technological worldview, emphasizes causal thinking, objective analysis, prediction, optimization, and qualified uncertainty. A good example of the T perspective is provided by the decision to drop the atomic bomb on Japan. The problem was seen to be composed of five alternatives—bombing and blockade, invasion, atomic attack without warning, atomic attack after warning, and dropping the bomb on an uninhabited island. Given the goal of unconditional surrender with a minimum loss of Allied lives and destruction of Japan, the third alternative (atomic attack without warning) was the preferred alternative.

2. *Organizational perspective.* The organizational (O) perspective views problems and solutions as part of an orderly progression (with minor but temporary crises) from one organizational state to another. Standard operating proce-

---

[72] See Harold A. Linstone, *Multiple Perspectives for Decision Making: Bridging the Gap between Analysis and Action* (New York: North-Holland Publishing Company, 1984); and Linstone and others, "The Multiple Perspective Concept: With Applications to Technology Assessment and Other Decision Areas," *Technological Forecasting and Social Change*, 20 (1981), 275–325.

dures, rules, and institutional routines are major characteristics of the O perspective, which is often resistant to the T perspective and only minimally concerned with achieving goals and improving performance. The decision to drop the atomic bomb provides a good example of the O perspective and how it differs from the T perspective. From an O perspective, a decision not to use the bomb raised profound organizational fears, since $2 billion in funding was expended without congressional approval. Dropping the bomb showed Congress that the funds were not wasted, and at the same time, inaugurated the Cold War by challenging the perceived Soviet threat.

3. *Personal perspective.* The personal (P) perspective views problems and solutions in terms of individual perceptions, needs, and values. Major characteristics of the personal perspective are an emphasis on intuition, charisma, leadership, and self-interest as factors governing policies and their impacts. The example of the atomic bomb also shows how the P perspective supplies insights not available from either the T or the O perspectives. In 1945 the new President, Harry Truman, was an outsider to the FDR establishment, which had grown and solidified during Roosevelt's three terms in office. Truman lacked the legitimacy and influence necessary to challenge the establishment, including entrenched bureaucratic interests and policies, so early in his presidency. A decision not to drop the atomic bomb would be perceived as a sign of weakness to contemporaries and to future historians. Truman, who had a strong sense of history, wanted to appear as a bold and decisive leader.

Multiple perspective analysis is relevant to any sociotechnological problem found in areas of public policy-making, corporate strategic planning, regional development, and other domains. To employ multiple perspective analysis, Linstone and colleagues have developed some of the following guidelines:

- *Interparadigmatic mix.* Form teams on the basis of an interparadigmatic rather than interdisciplinary mix. For example, a team composed of a businessperson, lawyer, and writer is preferred to a team with an economist, a political scientist, and a psychologist. The interparadigmatic mix is preferable because it maximizes opportunities to find an appreciation for T, O, and P perspectives in the team.

- *Balance among perspectives.* In advance of planning and policy analysis activities it is not possible to decide how much emphasis to place on T, O, and P perspectives. As the team engages in its work, the discovery of the proper balance among the three perspectives will permit assignments to T, O, and P tasks. In the meantime, an equal distribution is preferable.

- *Uneven replicability.* The T perspective typically employs methods (for example, experimental design) which are replicable. The O and P perspectives are not replicable. Like a jury trial, or even a retrial, the process is not replicable; nor are nonroutine executive decisions.

- *Appropriate communications.* Adapt the medium of communication to the message. Summaries, oral briefings, scenarios, and vignettes are appropriate for communicating with those who hold O and P perspectives. Models, data, lists of variables, and analytical routines are appropriate for those with a T perspective.

- *Deferred integration.* Leave the integration of perspectives to the client or policymaker, but point out linkages among the T, O, and P perspectives and the differing conclusions they yield.

Multiple perspective analysis has been employed extensively in the domain of technology assessment and other areas of public policy. Methods of multiple perspective analysis, developed on the basis of earlier work in foreign policy and the design of knowledge systems,[73] is a way to deal with the complexity of ill-structured problems that originate in sociotechnological systems with high scientific and technical content.

Assumptional Analysis

Assumptional analysis is a technique that aims at the creative synthesis of conflicting assumptions about policy problems.[74] In many respects assumptional analysis is the most comprehensive of all problem structuring methods, since it includes procedures used in conjunction with other techniques and may focus on groups, individuals, or both. The most important feature of assumptional analysis is that it is explicitly designed to treat ill-structured problems, that is, problems where policy analysts, policymakers, and other stakeholders cannot agree on how to formulate a problem. The main criterion for assessing the adequacy of a given formulation of a problem is whether conflicting assumptions about a problem situation have been surfaced, challenged, and creatively synthesized.

Assumptional analysis is designed to overcome four major limitations of policy analysis: (1) policy analysis is often based on the assumption of a single decision maker with clearly ordered values that may be realized at a single point in time, (2) policy analysis typically fails to consider in a systematic and explicit way strongly differing views about the nature of problems and their potential solutions, (3) most policy analysis is carried out in organizations whose "self-sealing" character makes it difficult or impossible to challenge prevailing formulations of problems, and (4) criteria used to assess the adequacy of problems and their solutions often deal with surface characteristics (for example, logical consistency), rather than with basic assumptions underlying the conceptualization of problems.

Assumptional analysis explicitly recognizes the positive as well as the negative features of conflict and commitment. "Conflict is needed to permit the existence of maximally opposing policies to ferret out and to challenge the underlying assumptions that each policy makes. Commitment on the

---

[73] The antecedent works in foreign policy and knowledge systems design are, respectively, Graham Allison, *Essence of Decision: Conceptual Models and the Cuban Missile Crisis* (Boston, Little, Brown and Company, 1962); and C. West Churchman, *The Design of Inquiring Systems* (New York: Basic Books, 1971).

[74] See Ian I. Mitroff and James R. Emshoff, "On Strategic Assumption-Making: A Dialectical Approach to Policy and Planning," *Academy of Management Review*, 4, No. 1 (1979): 1–12; Richard O. Mason and Ian I. Mitroff, *Challenging Strategic Planning Assumptions: Theory, Cases, and Techniques* (New York: Wiley, 1981); and Ian I. Mitroff, Richard O. Mason, and Vincent P. Barabba, *The 1980 Census: Policymaking amid Turbulence* (Lexington, MA: D.C. Heath, 1983).

other hand is also necessary if the proponents for each policy are to make the strongest possible case (not necessarily the best) for their respective points of view."[75] Assumptional analysis involves the use of five procedures used in successive phases:

1. *Stakeholder identification.* In the first phase policy stakeholders are identified, ranked and prioritized. The identification, ranking, and prioritization of stakeholders is based on an assessment of the degree to which they influence and are influenced by the policy process. This procedure results in the identification of stakeholders—for example, dissident groups of administrators or clients—who are usually excluded in the analysis of policy problems.

2. *Assumption surfacing.* In this second phase analysts work backwards from a recommended solution for a problem to the selective set(s) of data that support the recommendation and the underlying assumptions that, when coupled with the data, allow one to deduce the recommendation as a consequence of the data. Each recommended solution put forth by policy stakeholders should contain a list of assumptions that explicitly and implicitly underlie the recommendation. By listing all assumptions—for example, that poverty is a consequence of historical accidents, elite domination, unemployment, cultural deprivation, and so on—there is an explicit specification of the problem to which each recommendation is addressed.

3. *Assumption challenging.* In the third phase analysts compare and evaluate sets of recommendations and their underlying assumptions. This is done by systematically comparing assumptions and counterassumptions which differ maximally from their counterparts. During this process each assumption previously identified is challenged by a counterassumption. If a counterassumption is implausible, it is eliminated from further consideration; if it is plausible, it is examined to determine if it might serve as a basis for an entirely new conceptualization of the problem and its solution.

4. *Assumption pooling.* When the assumption-challenging phase has been completed, the diverse proposed solutions generated in previous phases are pooled. Here assumptions (rather than recommendations) are negotiated by prioritizing assumptions in terms of their relative certainty and importance to different stakeholders. Only the most important and uncertain assumptions are pooled. The ultimate aim is to create an acceptable list of assumptions on which as many stakeholders as possible agree.

5. *Assumption synthesis.* The final phase is the creation of a composite or synthetic solution for the problem. The composite set of acceptable assumptions can serve as a basis for the creation of a new conceptualization of the problem. When issues surrounding the conceptualization of the problem and its potential solutions have reached this point, the activities of stakeholders may become cooperative and cumulatively productive.

The last four phases of assumptional analysis are illustrated in Figure 5–15, which helps visualize important features of the technique. First, the method begins with recommended solutions for problems rather than assumptions themselves. This is because most policy stakeholders are aware of proposed solutions for problems but seldom conscious of underlying as-

---

[75] Mitroff and Emshoff, "On Strategic Assumption-Making," p. 5.

FIGURE 5–15   The process of assumptional analysis.

Original Solutions	→	Common Data	→	Assumption Surfacing
Counter Solutions	←	Common Data	←	Assumption Challenging
Solutions Pool	→	Common Data	→	Assumption Pooling
"Best" Solutions	←	Common Data	←	Assumption Synthesis

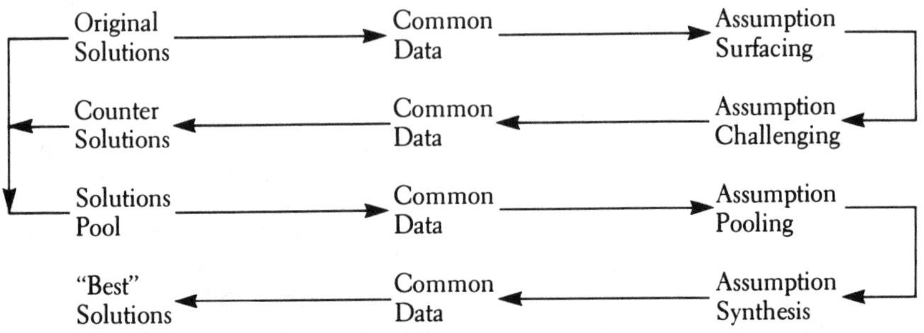

Source: Adapted from Ian I. Mitroff and James R. Emshoff, "On Strategic Assumption-Making: A Dialectical Approach to Policy and Planning." *Academy of Management Review* (1979).

sumptions. By starting with recommended solutions, the method builds on what is most familiar to stakeholders but then goes on to use familiar solutions as a point of reference for forcing an explicit consideration of underlying assumptions. A second important feature of the technique is that it attempts, as far as possible, to focus on the *same* set of data or policy-relevant information. The reason for this is that conflicts surrounding the conceptualization of policy problems are not so much matters of "fact" but matters involving conflicting interpretations of the same data. Although data, assumptions, and recommended solutions are interrelated, it is not so much the problem situation (data) that governs the conceptualization of problems but the assumptions that analysts and other stakeholders bring to the problem situation. Finally, assumptional analysis systematically addresses a major problem of policy analysis, which is that of applying some set of procedures to deal with conflict in a creative manner.

The aims and procedures of assumptional analysis are intimately related to the modes of policy argument presented in Chapter 4.[76] Each mode of policy argument contains characteristically different kinds of assumptions that may be used to produce alternative conceptualizations of problem situations. Assumptional analysis is therefore a major vehicle for conducting reasoned debates about the nature of policy problems. Assumptional analysis may be used with groups of policy stakeholders who actually participate in structuring policy problems or by an individual analyst who simulates the assumptions of stakeholders in order to conduct a reasoned debate with herself. Assumptional analysis can help reduce errors of the third type (E_{III}).

Argumentation Mapping

Methods of assumptional analysis are closely related to the modes of policy argument presented in Chapter 4. Each mode of policy argument—

---

[76] For an elaboration of assumptional analysis using the structural model of argument presented in Chapter 4, see Mitroff, Mason, and Barabba, *The 1980 Census, passim.*

authoritative, statistical, classificational, analycentric, causal, intuitive, pragmatic, and value critical—is based on distinctly different assumptions. These assumptions, when combined with the same policy-relevant information, yield conflicting knowledge claims.

An important technique of assumptional analysis is the use of graphic displays to map the plausibility and importance of elements of policy arguments. The first step in this process is to rate these elements—that is, warrants, backings, and rebuttals—on two ordinal scales. For example, recommendations to abandon the 55 mph speed limit (National Maximum Speed Law of 1973) have been based on the warrant that the opportunity costs of time lost driving at slower speeds increases risky driving among motorists with higher incomes. Conversely, it has been argued that the frequency of accidents is less among younger motorists, a claim that is based on the warrant that younger drivers earn less income, have lower opportunity costs, take fewer risks, and therefore have fewer accidents. This warrant may be rated by different stakeholders on nine-point plausibility and importance scales (1 = low, 9 = high) and plotted on a graph such as that shown in Figure 5–16.[77]

FIGURE 5–16   Distribution of warrant by plausibility and importance.

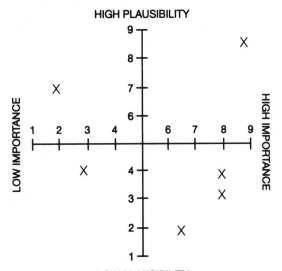

HIGH PLAUSIBILITY

LOW PLAUSIBILITY

WARRANT: The opportunity costs of driving time are less for younger drivers, who earn less income. Younger drivers therefore take fewer risks.

---

[77] Computer software called *Claim Game* provides capabilities for entering, saving, storing, and accessing a system of complex policy arguments. The program enables analysts to rate each element of an argument on nine-point plausibility and importance scales and plot stakeholders and their assumptions on the coordinates formed by the intersection of the two scales.

Figure 5–16 displays the plausibility and importance ratings for six stakeholders. The graph shows that stakeholders are distributed across the four quadrants, indicating substantial disagreement about the plausibility and importance of the warrant. If stakeholders are participants in a problem-structuring group, the disagreements evident in the right half of the graph (that is, high importance) can be discussed and perhaps resolved in favor of an optimally plausible knowledge claim. The typical situation, however, is one where the analyst must identify a range of stakeholders and, on the basis of telephone interviews and documents stating the stakeholders' arguments and assumptions, make judgments about the plausibility and importance that stakeholders probably would attach to a warrant, backing, or rebuttal. For example, a review of documents on the 55 mph speed limit indicates that the stakeholder rating the warrant as highly plausible (P = 9) is an economist, while the stakeholder who ranks the warrant as having low plausibility (P = 2) is an ethnographer who specializes in the culture of young drivers and bases his analyses on interviews with young drivers, parents, teachers, law enforcement personnel, and other stakeholders.[78]

On the basis of reasoned arguments and evidence provided by these two sources—along with information about the assumptions of various stakeholders and available statistics on accident and fatality rates by age group—the analyst would apply plausibility criteria presented in Chapter 4 and no doubt conclude that this particular warrant has low plausibility. The warrant also has high importance—whether it is plausible or implausible, it is highly relevant to the conclusions of the argument.

SUMMARY

In this chapter we have provided an overview of the nature of policy problems, outlined components of the process of problem structuring, distinguished among different types of policy models, and described and illustrated techniques for structuring policy problems. At this point you should be able to discuss the following key principles and generalizations:

1. Problem structuring is the most crucial but least understood aspect of policy analysis. The process of structuring policy problems does not seem to follow definable rules while problems themselves are frequently so complex that they seem to defy systematic treatment.

2. Policy analysts fail more often because they solve the wrong problem than because they get the wrong solution to the right problem. The fatal error in policy analysis is E_{III}, solving the wrong formulation of a problem when one should have solved the right one.

---

[78] See Thomas H. Forrester, Robert F. McNown, and Larry D. Singell, "A Cost–Benefit Analysis of the 55 mph Speed Limit," *Southern Economic Journal*, 50 (1984), reviewed by George M. Guess and Paul G. Farnham, *Cases in Public Policy Analysis* (New York: Longman, 1989), p. 199. For an ethnographic analysis of younger drivers and the meanings they attach to accidents and fatalities—which are different from those predicted by economic theory—see J. Peter Rothe, *Challenging the Old Order* (New Brunswick, NJ: Transaction Books, 1990).

3. Policy problems are really systems of interdependent problems or "messes" (Ackoff). The main characteristics of policy problems are interdependence, subjectivity, artificiality, and dynamics. Policy problems may rarely be decomposed into independent, discrete, and mutually exclusive parts; problems are really systems of problems with teleological (purposive) properties, such that the quality of the whole is different than the quantitative sum of the parts.

4. Policy issues that appear to be simple are frequently just as complex as the systems of problems (messes) from which they arise. Policy issues are the result of prior disputes about the nature of policy problems, which are in turn based on selective interpretations of problem situations.

5. The relative complexity of problems determines the kinds of methods and techniques appropriate for their resolution. The relative complexity and strategic versus operational nature of policies and issues are associated with hierarchical levels within organizations.

6. The structural complexity of problems varies according to the characteristics and relationships among five elements: decision maker(s), alternatives, utilities (values), outcomes, and probabilities of outcomes. Well-structured, moderately structured, and ill-structured problems may be arranged along a continuum proceeding from the relatively simple to the complex.

7. Many of the most important policy problems are ill structured because they are really complex systems of problems that involve high levels of conflict among competing stakeholders. It is unrealistic to assume the existence of one or a few decision makers with uniform preferences; consensus on goals and objectives is rare; and it is seldom possible to identify the full range of alternative solutions and their consequences.

8. The requirements for solving ill-structured problems are not the same as those for solving well-structured problems. Whereas well-structured problems permit the use of conventional analytic methods designed to produce solutions for clearly defined problems, ill-structured problems require that the analyst take an active part in defining the nature of the problem itself. This demands creative judgment and insight.

9. Policy analysis is properly devoted to problem structuring as well as problem solving. Criteria for evaluating the success of problem structuring are essentially the same as those for assessing creativity in general.

10. Problem structuring is a process with four interdependent phases: problem sensing, problem search, problem definition, and problem specification. Each of these phases results in the production of information about problem situations, metaproblems, substantive problems, and formal problems.

11. Substantive and formal problems are often a result of unexamined worldviews, ideologies, popular myths, and paradigms. A critical issue in policy analysis is how well problem situations, substantive problems, and formal problems correspond to one another. A lack of correspondence among the three may mean that an analyst has committed an error of the third type (E_{III})—providing the wrong substantive or formal representation of a problem when one should have provided the right one.

12. Each phase of problem structuring requires different skills, some philosophical and conceptual and others technical. The use of these different skills is related to different meanings of "rationality" in policy analysis. Rationality is not simply a matter of finding an adequate formal representation of a problem through technical procedures (for example, mathematical modeling) but is also concerned with finding an adequate conceptual representation of a problem,

which requires self-conscious and critical choices among competing world-views, ideologies, and myths.

13. Policy models are simplified representations of selected aspects of a problem situation. Policy models are useful and necessary; their use is not a matter of choice, since everyone uses some kind of model to simplify problem situations.

14. Policy models selectively distort problem situations. Models cannot discriminate between essential and nonessential questions; nor can they explain, predict, evaluate, or recommend, since these judgments are external to the model and not part of it.

15. The most important dimensions of policy models are their purpose (descriptive versus normative), form of expression (verbal, symbolic, procedural), and methodological assumptions (surrogate versus perspective). Policy models are perspectives and not surrogates; the use of models as surrogates increases the probability of E_{III} in attempting to solve ill-structured problems.

16. Methods for structuring policy problems include boundary analysis, classificational analysis, hierarchy analysis, synectics, brainstorming, multiple perspective analysis, assumptional analysis and argumentation mapping. Although each of these methods has distinct aims, procedures, foci, and criteria of performance, all are designed to reduce the probability of E_{III}.

GLOSSARY

Argumentation Mapping: A graphic technique used in conjunction with assumptional analysis to display on a set of coordinates the plausibility and importance of warrants, backings, and rebuttals.

Analytic Approach: An approach to problem structuring that decomposes problems into component elements or parts which are typically regarded as independent entities.

Boundary Analysis: A method of ensuring the relative completeness of a set of problem representations (metaproblem) by means of a three-step process of saturation sampling, elicitation of problem representations, and boundary estimation.

Creativity: A property of problem structuring where the product of analysis is novel and valuable; the process of analysis is unconventional and requires high motivation and persistence; and the problem as initially posed is ambiguous, vague, and ill defined.

Descriptive Model: A model constructed for purposes of explaining and/or predicting the consequences of policy choices.

Environmental Perspective: A point of view which assumes that social problems are a consequence of factors present in the immediate environment of victims of problems. This perspective often results in "blaming the victim."

Error of the Third Type (E_{III}):   The formulation of the wrong substantive or formal representation of a problem when one should have formulated the right one. Type III errors should be distinguished from type I and type II errors, that is, rejecting the null hypothesis when it is true (E_I) and accepting the null hypothesis when it is false (E_{II}).

Holistic Approach: An approach to problem structuring that views problems as inseparable and unmeasurable apart from the whole system of which they are interlocking parts.

Ill-Structured Problem: A problem involving many decision makers; utilities (values) which are conflictual or unknown; alternatives which are unknown or impossible to order transitively; and outcomes which are unknown.

Mess: A term coined by philosopher-operations researcher Russell Ackoff to describe systems of interdependent problems that produce dissatisfaction among different segments of the community.

Moderately Structured Problem: A problem involving one or a few decision makers; a small number of alternatives; consensus on utilities (values); and uncertain outcomes whose consequences cannot be estimated probabilistically.

Moralistic Perspective: A point of view which assumes that social problems are a consequence of presumed moral weaknesses or flaws of particular persons or groups.

Multiple Perspective Analysis: A method for obtaining greater insight into problems and potential solutions by applying personal, organizational, and technical perspectives of a problem situation.

Naturalistic Perspective: A point of view which assumes that social problems are inevitable or the products of historical accidents.

Normative Model: A model constructed for purposes of optimizing the attainment of some utility (value).

Perspective Model: A model that functions as one among many possible ways to structure substantive problems.

Policy Model: A simplified representation of selected aspects of a problem situation constructed for particular purposes.

Policy Problem: A set of mental or conceptual constructs abstracted from a problem situation by stakeholders.

Problem Definition: The process of characterizing a substantive problem in its most basic and general terms.

Problem Dissolving: The abandonment of an incorrectly formulated problem and a return to problem structuring before there is any further attempt to solve the problem.

Problem Resolving: The reanalysis of a correctly structured problem in order to reduce calibrational or measurement errors.

Problem Search: The process of discovering and bounding the many problem representations, or metaproblem, produced by multiple stakeholders.

Problem Sensing: A phase of problem structuring where the analyst experiences diffuse worries and inchoate signs of stress by recognizing a problem situation.

Problem Situation: A situation or set of external conditions which, once experienced, gives rise to dissatisfaction, uneasiness, and a felt recognition that something is wrong (John Dewey).

Problem Solving: The use of lower-order methods to alleviate or eliminate a problem after it has been correctly structured.

Problem Specification: A phase of problem structuring where the analyst develops a formal (logical or mathematical) representation of a substantive problem.

Problem Structuring: The use of higher-order methods (metamethods) to discover the critical elements of a problem, their causal arrangement, and value implications.

Problem Unsolving: The abandonment of a solution based on the incorrect formulation of a problem and a return to problem structuring in order to formulate the right problem.

Procedural Model: A model expressed in the form of elementary procedures designed to represent dynamic relationships.

Purposeful (Teleological) System: A system where no two members are identical in all or any properties; the properties of each member affect the properties of the system as a whole; the properties of each member, and the way each affects the system as a whole, depend on the properties of at least one other member of the system; and all possible subgroups of members have a nonindependent effect on the system as a whole.

Strategic Issue: An issue involving decisions whose consequences are relatively irreversible, as distinguished from an operational issue, where consequences are easily reversed.

Surrogate Model: A model that functions as a substitute for substantive problems and the problem situations from which substantive problems arise.

Symbolic Model: A model expressed in the language of symbolic logic or mathematics; the equivalent of a formal problem.

Transitivity: The property of a set of alternatives where A_1 is preferred to A_2, A_2 is preferred to A_3, and A_1 is (therefore) preferred to A_3.

Unanticipated Consequences: Consequences (positive and/or negative) that are known only after an action has been taken.

Verbal Model: A model expressed in everyday language rather than symbolic logic or mathematics; the equivalent of a substantive problem.

Well-Structured Problem: A problem involving one or a few decision makers; a small set of policy alternatives; consensus on utilities (values); and outcomes known with complete certainty (deterministically) or within acceptable margins of probable error (risk).

STUDY SUGGESTIONS

1. "Our problem is not to do what is right," stated Lyndon Johnson during his years in the White House. "Our problem is to know what is right." Considering the major characteristics and types of policy problems discussed in this chapter, to what extent can we know in advance which policy is the "right" one?
2. A commonly accepted viewpoint among many policy analysts in government and in universities is that policy analysis can be objective, neutral, and impartial. Given the characteristics of ill-structured problems, consider the extent to which this viewpoint is plausible.
3. Provide two or three examples from your own experience of ways that world-views, ideologies, and popular myths shape the formulation of policy problems.
4. There are several broad types of organizational structures in which policy formation occurs. One type is the "bureaucratic" structure, whose characteristics include centralization, hierarchical chain of command, specialization of tasks, and complete information. The bureaucratic form of organization requires consensus on preferred policy outcomes as well as certainty that alternative courses of action will result in certain preferred outcomes (J. D. Thompson, *Organizations in Action*, New York: McGraw-Hill, 1967, pp. 134–35). If many of our most important policy problems are ill-structured ones, what does this say about the appropriateness of the bureaucratic form of organization for formulating and resolving such problems?
5. If many of our most important problems are ill-structured ones, to what extent is it possible to hold individual policymakers, policy analysts, and planners politically and morally responsible for their actions? (For a provocative discussion of this point see M. M. Webber and H. W. J. Rittel, "Dilemmas in a General Theory of Planning," *Policy Sciences*, 4, No. 2 (1973), 155–69.)
6. The ill-structured problems described below are taken from illustrations published in the journal *Policy Analysis* (now the *Journal of Policy Analysis and Management*) under the title "Department of Unintended Consequences."

    — For several thousand years, Egyptian agriculture depended on the fertilizing sediment deposited by the flood of the Nile. No longer, however. Due to expensive modern technology intended to improve the age-old lot of the peasant, Egypt's fields must be artificially fertilized. John Gall, writing in the *New York Times Magazine* (December 26, 1976), reports that the Nile sediment is now deposited in the Aswan Dam's Lake Nasser. Much of the dam's electrical output is used to supply enormous amounts of electricity to new fertilizer plants made necessary by the construction of the dam.
    — University of Illinois ecologists can explain how certain harmful field mice spread from their native regions into areas where they had never before been found. They are using the new, limited-access, cross-country highways, which turn out to be easy escape routes with few barriers. Older highways and roads, as well as railroad rights-of-way, run into towns and villages every few miles and effectively deter mice migration. The Illinois group found that before interstate highways ran through central Illinois, one type of mouse was limited to a single county. But in six years of super-highways the 4-inch-long creatures have spread 60 miles south through the center of the state. The ecologists are concerned

lest the mice, a species that loves to chew on trees, become a threat in central and southern counties where apple orchards abound (*Wall Street Journal*, December 1, 1977).

— Edward J. Moody . . . argues persuasively that worship of Satan has the effect of normalizing abnormal people. Thus, to "keep secret" from ordinary people their satanic power and existence, such persons are urged to behave as straight as possible. The effect, of course, is more effective social relations—the goal for which Satan's name has been invoked in the first place! (P. E. Hammond, "Review of Religious Movements in Contemporary America," *Science*, May 2, 1975, p. 442).

— Residents of San Francisco's North Beach areas must now pay $10 for the privilege of parking in their own neighborhood. A residential parking plan was recently implemented to prevent commuters from using the area as a daytime parking lot. But according to a story in the *San Francisco Bay Guardian* (March 14, 1978), the plan has in no way improved the residential parking situation. Numbers of commuters from outlying districts of the city have simply been changing their car registrations to North Beach addresses. A North Beach resident—now $10 poorer—still spends a lot of time driving around the block.

Choose one of these problems and write a short essay on how classificational analysis, hierarchy analysis, and synectics might be used to structure this problem.

7. Construct a scenario on the state of one of the following problem situations in the year 2050:

— Availability of public mass transit
— Arms control and national security
— Crime prevention and public safety
— Quality of the public school system
— State of the world's ecological system

8. Select an editorial on a current issue of public policy from a newspaper (for example, *The New York Times*, *The Washington Post*, *The Economist*, *Le Monde*) or news magazine (for example, *Newsweek*, *The New Republic*, *National Review*). After reading the editorial:

(a) Use the procedures for argumentation analysis (Chapter 4) to display contending positions and underlying assumptions.
(b) Rate the assumptions and plot them according to their plausibility and importance (Figure 5–17).
(c) Which arguments are the most plausible?

9. Give members of the class the following question: "The prison population in the United States is increasing by approximately 10 percent annually. List five reasons for the increase." Collect the lists and create a cumulative frequency distribution by plotting the *new* reasons offered by each student. Use the third step in boundary analysis described in this chapter (see Figure 5–10).

(a) Does the curve flatten out?
(b) Does the curve help estimate the boundaries of the "metaproblem"?

(c)   What explains the tendency of such curves to flatten out?
(d)   Would your formulation of the problem be different if you had stopped considering reasons after a small number of students?
(e)   Is problem definition in policy analysis a "never-ending discourse with reality"?

SUGGESTED READINGS

ACKOFF, RUSSELL L., *Redesigning the Future*. New York: Wiley, 1974.

ADAMS, JAMES L., *Conceptual Blockbusting*. Stanford, CA: Stanford Alumni Association, 1974.

ADELMAN, L., T. R. STEWART, and K. R. HAMMOND, "A Case History of the Application of Social Judgment Theory to Policy Formulation," *Policy Sciences*, 6 (1975), 137–59.

BOBROW, DAVIS B. and JOHN S. DRYZEK, *Policy Analysis by Design*. Pittsburgh, PA: University of Pittsburgh Press, 1986.

BRUNNER, RONALD D., "The Policy Movement as a Policy Problem," in *Advances in Policy Studies Since 1950*, Vol. 10 of *Policy Studies Review Annual*, ed. William N. Dunn and Rita Mae Kelly. New Brunswick, NJ: Transaction Books, 1992.

CHURCHMAN, C. WEST, *The Design of Inquiring Systems*. New York: Basic Books, 1971.

DERY, DAVID, *Problem Definition in Policy Analysis*. Lawrence, KS: University Press of Kansas, 1984.

DROR, YEHEZKEL, *Public Policy Making Reexamined*, rev ed. New Brunswick, NJ: Transaction Books, 1983.

DRYZEK, JOHN S., "Policy Analysis as a Hermeneutic Activity," *Policy Sciences*, 14 (1982), 309–29.

DUNN, WILLIAM N., "Methods of the Second Type: Coping with the Wilderness of Conventional Policy Analysis," *Policy Studies Review*, 7, No. 4 (1988), 720–37.

——and ARI GINSBERG, "A Sociocognitive Approach to Organizational Analysis," *Human Relations*, 39, No. 11 (1986), 955–75.

FISCHHOFF, BARUCH, "Clinical Policy Analysis," in *Policy Analysis: Perspectives, Concepts, and Methods*, ed. William N. Dunn. Greenwich, CT: JAI Press, 1986.

——, "Cost–Benefit Analysis and the Art of Motorcycle Maintenance," *Policy Sciences*, 8 (1977), 177–202.

GEORGE, ALEXANDER, "Criteria for Evaluation of Foreign Policy Decision Making," *Global Perspectives*, 2 (1984), 58–69.

HAMMOND, KENNETH R., "Introduction to Brunswickian Theory and Methods," *New Directions for Methodology of Social and Behavioral Science*, 3 (1980), 1–12.

HOFSTADTER, RICHARD, *Godel, Escher, Bach*. New York: Random House, 1979.

HOGWOOD, BRIAN W. and B. GUY PETERS, *The Pathology of Public Policy*. Oxford: Clarendon Press, 1985.

LINDER, STEPHEN H. and B. GUY PETERS, "A Metatheoretic Analysis of Policy Design," in *Advances in Policy Studies Since 1950*, Vol. 10 of *Policy Studies Review Annual*, ed. William N. Dunn and Rita Mae Kelly. New Brunswick, NJ: Transaction Books, 1992.

LINSTONE, HAROLD A., *Multiple Perspectives for Decision Making*. New York: North-Holland, 1984.

MASON, RICHARD O. and IAN I. MITROFF, *Challenging Strategic Planning Assumptions*. New York: Wiley, 1981.

MEEHAN, EUGENE J., *The Thinking Game*. Chatham, NJ: Chatham House, 1988.

MITROFF, IAN I., RICHARD O. MASON, and VINCENT P. BARABBA, *The 1980 Census: Policy-making amid Turbulence*. Lexington, MA: D.C. Heath, 1983.

SAATY, THOMAS L., *The Analytic Hierarchy Process*. New York: McGraw-Hill, 1980.

SCHON, DONALD A., *The Reflective Practitioner*. New York: Basic Books, 1983.

SIEBER, SAM, *Fatal Remedies*. New York: Plenum Press, 1981.

WARFIELD, JOHN N., *Societal Systems: Planning, Policy, and Complexity*. New York: Wiley, 1976.

WATZLAWICK, PAUL, JOHN WEAKLAND, and RICHARD FISCH, *Change: Principles of Problem Formation and Problem Resolution*. New York: W.W. Norton, 1974.

6

Forecasting Policy Futures

> . . . as long as the structure of society is simple and static, established valuations will last for a very long time, but if society changes this will immediately be reflected in the changing valuations. Revaluations and re-definitions of the situation will necessarily accompany the changed structure of society.
>
> —KARL MANNHEIM, *Diagnosis of Our Time* (1944)

Problem structuring yields policy-relevant information that is essential for the next phase of policy analysis—forecasting policy futures. By structuring a policy problem analysts create new knowledge about the boundaries of a problem, the conditions that contribute to its occurrence, the actions that might be taken for its solution or alleviation, and the perceived opportunities for improvement which make it a problem in the first place.

Knowledge about the structure of a problem is essential for forecasting and all subsequent phases of policy analysis. As we learned in Chapter 5, however, problem structuring is provisional, not final—problem structuring methods are applied and reapplied throughout the process of policy analysis. A given problem formulation—for example, that pollution is a consequence of unrestrained profit maximization in capitalist economies—usually involves errors that are detected and corrected by cycling backwards to problem dissolving, problem unsolving, and problem resolving (see Figure 5–1). Thus, while forecasting, recommendation, monitoring, and evaluation are ordered in a clockwise fashion, the process of problem structuring moves backward in a counterclockwise direction.

The capacity to forecast policy futures is critical to the success of policy analysis and the improvement of policy-making. Through forecasting we can obtain a prospective vision, or foresight, thereby enlarging capacities for understanding, control, and societal guidance. As we shall see, however, forecasts of all kinds—whether based on expert judgment, the simple extrapolation of historical trends, or on technically sophisticated econometric models—are prone to errors based on faulty or implausible assumptions, on the error-amplifying effects of institutional incentive systems, and on the accelerating complexity of policy issue areas ranging from health, welfare, and education to science, technology, and the environment.

We begin this chapter with an overview of the forms, functions, and performance of forecasting in policy analysis, stressing a range of criteria for assessing the strengths and limitations of different forecasting methods. We then compare and contrast three major approaches to creating information about policy futures: extrapolative forecasting, theoretical forecasting, and judgmental forecasting. We conclude with a presentation of methods and techniques of forecasting employed in conjunction with these three approaches.

FORECASTING IN POLICY ANALYSIS

Forecasting is a procedure for producing factual information about future states of society on the basis of prior information about policy problems. Forecasts take three principal forms: projections, predictions, and conjectures.

1. A *projection* is a forecast which is based on the extrapolation of current and historical trends into the future. Projections put forth designative claims based on arguments from method and parallel case, where assumptions about the validity of particular methods (for example, time-series analysis) or similarities between cases (for example, past and future policies) are used to establish the cogency of claims. Projections may be supplemented by arguments from authority (for example, the opinions of experts) and cause (for example, economic or political theory).

2. A *prediction* is a forecast based on explicit theoretical assumptions. These assumptions may take the form of theoretical laws (for example, the law of diminishing utility of money), theoretical propositions (for example, the proposition that civil disorders are caused by the gap between expectations and capabilities), or analogies (for example, the analogy between the growth of government and the growth of biological organisms). The essential feature of a prediction is that it specifies the generative powers ("causes") and consequences ("effects"), or the parallel processes or relations ("analogs") believed to underlie a relationship. Predictions may be supplemented by arguments from authority (for example, informed judgment) and method (for example, econometric modeling).

3. A *conjecture* is a forecast based on informed or expert judgments about future states of society. These judgments may take the form of intuitive arguments, where assumptions about the insight, creative intellectual power, or tacit knowledge of stakeholders (for example, "policy insiders") are used to support designative claims about the future. Judgments may also be expressed in the form of motivational arguments where present or future goals, values, and intentions are used to establish the plausibility of claims, as when conjectures about future societal values (for example, leisure) are used to claim that the average work week will be reduced to 30 hours in the next 20 years. Conjectures may be supplemented by arguments from authority, method, and cause.

Aims of Forecasting

Policy forecasts, whether based on extrapolation, theory, or informed judgment, have several important aims. First, and most important, forecasts provide information about future changes in policies and their consequences. The aims of forecasting are similar to those of much scientific and social scientific research, insofar as the latter seek both to understand and control the human and material environment. Nevertheless, efforts to forecast future societal states are "especially related to control—that is, to the attempt to plan and to set policy so that the best possible course of action might be chosen among the possibilities which the future offers."[1]

Forecasting permits greater control through understanding past policies and their consequences, an aim which implies that the future is determined by the past. Yet forecasts also enable us to shape the future in an active manner, irrespective of what has occurred in the past. In this respect the future-oriented policy analyst must ask what values can and should guide future action. But this leads to a second and equally difficult question: How can the analyst evaluate the future desirability of a given state of affairs?

> Even if the values underlying current actions could be neatly specified, would these values still be operative in the future? As Ikle has noted, " 'guiding predictions' are incomplete unless they evaluate the desirability of the predicted aspects of alternative futures. If we assume that this desirability is to be determined by our future rather than our present preferences . . . then we have to predict our values *before* we can meaningfully predict our future."[2]

This concern with future values may complement traditional social science disciplines that emphasize predictions based on past and present values. While past and present values may determine the future, this will hold true only if intellectual reflection by policy stakeholders does not lead them to change their values and behavior, or if unpredictable factors do not intervene to create profound social changes, including irreversible processes of chaos and emergent order.[3]

Limitations of Forecasting

In the years since 1985 there have been a number of unexpected, surprising, and counterintuitive political, social, and economic changes—for example, the formal abandonment of socialism in the Soviet Union, the dissolution of communist parties in Eastern Europe, the fall of the Berlin Wall, the growing uncertainty surrounding policies to mitigate global warm-

---

[1] Irene Taviss, "Futurology and the Problem of Values," *International Social Science Journal*, XXI, No. 4 (1969), 574.

[2] Ibid.; and Fred Charles Ikle, "Can Social Predictions Be Evaluated?" *Daedalus*, 96 (Summer 1967), 747.

[3] See Alasdair MacIntyre, "Ideology, Social Science, and Revolution," *Comparative Politics*, 5, No. 3 (1973); and Ilya Prigogine and Isabelle Stengers, *Order Out of Chaos* (New York: Bantam Books, 1984).

ing. These changes at once call attention to the importance and the difficulties of forecasting policy futures under conditions of increasingly complex, rapid, and even chaotic changes. The growing difficulty of forecasting,
however, should be seen in light of limitations and strengths of various types
of forecasts over the past three decades and more.[4]

1. *Forecast accuracy.* The accuracy of relatively simple forecasts based on the
   extrapolation of trends in a single variable, as well as relatively complex forecasts based on models incorporating hundreds of variables, has been limited.
   In the five-year period ending in 1983, for example, the Office of Management
   and Budget underestimated the federal budget deficit by an annual average
   of $58 billion. A similar record of performance tends to characterize forecasts
   of the largest econometric forecasting firms, which include Chase Econometrics, Wharton Econometric Forecasting Associates, and Data Resources,
   Inc. For example, average forecasting error as a proportion of actual changes
   in GNP was approximately 50 percent in the period 1971–1983.[5]
2. *Comparative yield.* The accuracy of predictions based on complex theoretical
   models of the economy and of the energy resource system has been no greater
   than the accuracy of projections and conjectures made, respectively, on the
   basis of simple extrapolative models and informed (expert) judgment. If one
   of the important advantages of such models is sensitivity to surprising or counterintuitive future events, simple models have a comparative advantage over
   their technically complex counterparts, since developers and users of complex
   models tend to employ them mechanistically. Ascher's question is to the point:
   "If the implications of one's assumptions and hypotheses are obvious when
   they are 'thought out' without the aid of a model, why use one? If the implications are surprising, the strength of the complex model is in drawing from
   a set of assumptions these implications. . . ."[6] Yet precisely these assumptions
   and implications—for example, the implication that a predicted large increase
   in gasoline consumption may lead to changes in gasoline taxes, which are
   treated as a constant in forecasting models—are overlooked or discarded because they are inconsistent with the assumptions of models.
3. *Context.* The assumptions of models and their results are sensitive to three
   kinds of contexts: institutional, temporal, and historical. Variations in institutional incentive systems are a key aspect of differences in institutional contexts, as represented by government agencies, businesses, and nonprofit research institutes. Forecasting accuracy tends to be greater in nonprofit
   research institutes than in businesses or government agencies (Figure 6–1a).
   In turn, the temporal context of a forecast, as represented by the length of
   time over which a forecast is made (for example, one quarter or year vs. five
   years ahead), affects forecast accuracy. The longer the time frame, the less
   accurate the forecast. Finally, the historical context of forecasts affects ac-

---

[4] The seminal work on forecasting is William Ascher, *Forecasting: An Appraisal for Policy Makers and Planners* (Baltimore and London: Johns Hopkins University Press, 1978). Also see Ascher, "The Forecasting Potential of Complex Models," *Policy Sciences* 13 (1981), 247–67; and Robert McNown, "On the Use of Econometric Models: A Guide for Policy Makers," *Policy Sciences* 19 (1986), 360–80.

[5] McNown, "On the Use of Econometric Models," pp. 362–67.

[6] Ascher, "The Forecasting Potential of Complex Models," p. 255.

curacy. The relatively greater complexity of recent historical periods dimin-
ishes forecast accuracy, a pattern that is evident in the growth of forecasting
errors since 1965 (Figure 6–1b).

Forecasting accuracy and comparative yield are thus closely related
to the institutional, temporal, and historical contexts in which forecasts are
made. The accuracy and comparative yield of forecasts are also affected,
as we might expect, by the assumptions that people bring to the process.
As Ascher notes, one of the difficulties of assessing the performance of
forecasts lies in identifying the assumptions of forecast developers and users.
In many forecasts, there is a serious problem of "assumption drag,"[7] that
is, a tendency among developers and users of forecasting models to cling
to questionable or plainly implausible assumptions built into a model—for
example, the assumption that the pricing policies as well as the governments
of petroleum-producing countries will remain stable. An important impli-

FIGURE 6–1 Contexts affecting forecast accuracy.

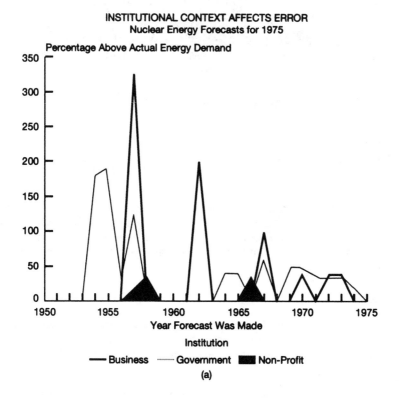

INSTITUTIONAL CONTEXT AFFECTS ERROR
Nuclear Energy Forecasts for 1975

(a)

---

[7] See Ascher, *Forecasting*, Chap. 1.

FIGURE 6–1   *(Continued)*

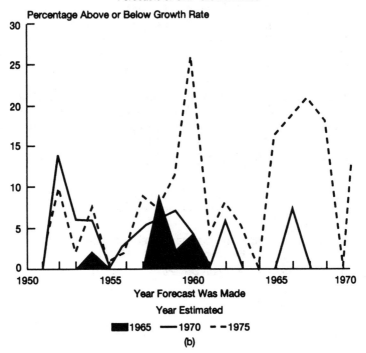

HISTORICAL CONTEXT AFFECTS ERROR
Forecasts of GNP Growth Rates

Note: Percentages are normalized errors.

Source: Adapted from William Ascher, *Forecasting: An Appraisal for Policy Makers and Planners* (Baltimore: Johns Hopkins University Press, 1978).

cation may be derived from the phenomenon of assumption drag—namely, that the task of structuring policy problems is central to the performance of forecasters. Indeed, the correction of errors by dissolving or unsolving problems is quite as important to forecasting as it is to other phases of policy analysis.

Types of Futures

Policy forecasts, whether made in the form of projections, predictions, or conjectures, are used to estimate three types of future societal states: potential futures, plausible futures, and normative futures.[8] *Potential fu-*

---

[8] See David C. Miller, "Methods for Estimating Societal Futures," in *Methodology of Social Impact Assessment*, ed. Kurt Finsterbusch and C. P. Wolf (Stroudsburg, PA: Dowden, Hutchinson & Ross, 1977), pp. 202–10.

tures (sometimes called *alternative futures*) are future societal states that may occur, as distinguished from societal states that eventually do occur. A future state is never certain until it actually occurs, and there are many potential futures. *Plausible futures* are future states which, on the basis of assumptions about causation in nature and society, are believed to be likely if policymakers do not intervene to redirect the course of events. By contrast, *normative futures* are potential and plausible futures which are consistent with an analyst's conception of future needs, values, and opportunities. The specification of normative futures narrows the range of potential and plausible futures, thus linking forecasts to specific goals and objectives (Figure 6–2).

Goals and Objectives of Normative Futures

An important aspect of normative futures is the specification of goals and objectives. But today's values are likely to change in the future, thus making it difficult to define normative futures on the basis of existing preferences. The analyst must, therefore, be concerned with future changes in the ends as well as means of policy. In thinking about the ends of policy it is useful to contrast goals and objectives. Although goals and objectives are both future oriented, goals express broad purposes while objectives set forth specific aims. Goals are rarely expressed in the form of operational definitions—that is, definitions which specify the set of operations necessary to measure something—while objectives are. Relatedly, goals are not quantifiable; but objectives may be and often are. Statements of goals usually do not specify the time period in which policies are expected to achieve desired consequences, while statements of objectives do. Finally, goals define target populations in broad terms, while objectives define target populations specifically. Contrasts between goals and objectives are illustrated in Table 6–1.

The definition of normative futures not only requires that we clarify goals and objectives; it also requires that we identify which sets of policy

FIGURE 6–2   Three types of societal futures: potential, plausible, and normative.

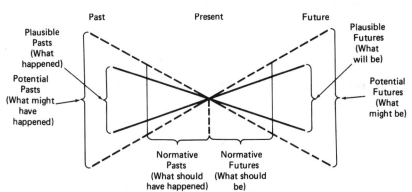

TABLE 6–1   Contrasts between Goals and Objectives

CHARACTERISTIC	GOALS	OBJECTIVES
Specification of purposes	1. Broadly stated (. . . to upgrade the quality of health care . . .)	1. Concrete (. . . to increase the number of physicians by 10 percent . . .)
Definition of terms	2. Formal (. . . the quality of health care refers to accessibility of medical services . . .)	2. Operational (. . . the quality of health care refers to the number of physicians per 100,000 persons . . .)
Time period	3. Unspecified (. . . in the future . . .)	3. Specified (. . . in the period 1990–2000 . . .)
Measurement procedure	4. Nonquantitative (. . . adequate health insurance . . .)	4. Frequently quantitative (. . . the number of persons covered per 1000 persons . . .)
Treatment of target groups	5. Broadly defined (. . . persons in need of care . . .)	5. Specifically defined (. . . families with annual incomes below $19,000 . . .)

alternatives are relevant for the achievement of aims. Although these questions may appear simple, they are in fact difficult. Whose goals and objectives should the analyst use as a focal point of forecasts? How does an analyst choose among a large number of alternatives to achieve given goals and objectives? If analysts use existing policies to specify goals, objectives, and alternatives, they run the risk of applying a conservative standard. If, on the other hand, they propose new goals, objectives, and alternatives, they may be charged with imposing their own beliefs and values or making choices that are closer to the positions of one stakeholder than another.

Sources of Goals, Objectives, and Alternatives

One way to select goals, objectives, and alternatives is to consider their possible sources. Alternatives imply goals and objectives, just as goals and objectives imply policy alternatives. Sources of policy alternatives, goals, and objectives may be found by returning to problem structuring procedures in Chapters 4 and 5.

1. *Authority*. In searching for alternatives to resolve a problem, analysts may appeal to experts. For example, the President's Commission on the Causes and Prevention of Violence may be used as a source of policy alternatives (registration of firearms, restrictive licensing, increased penalties for the use of guns to commit crime) to deal with the problem of gun controls.[9]
2. *Insight*. The analyst may also appeal to the intuition, judgment, or tacit knowledge of persons believed to be particularly insightful about a problem. These

---

[9] See National Commission on the Causes and Prevention of Violence, Final Report, *To Establish Justice, To Ensure Domestic Tranquility* (Washington, DC: U.S. Government Printing Office, 1969).

"knowledgeables," who are not experts in the ordinary sense of the word, are an important source of policy alternatives. For example, various stakeholders from the Office of Child Development, a division of the Department of Education, have been used as a source of informed judgments about policy alternatives, goals, and objectives in the area of child welfare.[10]

3. *Method.* The search for alternatives may benefit from innovative methods of analysis. For example, new techniques of systems analysis may be helpful in identifying alternatives and rank-ordering multiple conflicting objectives.[11]

4. *Scientific theories.* Explanations produced by the natural and social sciences are also an important source of policy alternatives. For example, social psychological theories of learning have served as one source of early childhood education programs, such as Head Start and Follow Through.

5. *Motivation.* The beliefs, values, and needs of stakeholders may serve as a source of policy alternatives. Alternatives may be derived from the goals and objectives of particular occupational groups, for example, workers whose changing beliefs, values, and needs have created a new "work ethic" involving demands for leisure and flexible working hours (flex-time).

6. *Parallel case.* Experiences with policy problems in other countries, states, and cities are an important source of policy alternatives. The experiences of New York and California with financial reforms have served as a source of financial policies in other states.

7. *Analogy.* Similarities between different kinds of problems are a source of policy alternatives. Legislation designed to increase equal employment opportunities for women has been based on analogies with policies adopted to protect the rights of minorities.

8. *Ethical systems.* Another important source of policy alternatives is ethical systems. Theories of social justice put forward by philosophers and other social thinkers serve as a source of policy alternatives in a variety of issue areas.[12]

APPROACHES TO FORECASTING

Once goals, objectives, and alternatives have been identified, it is possible to select an approach to forecasting. By selecting an approach we mean three things. The analyst must (1) decide what to forecast, that is, determine what the *object* of the forecast is to be; (2) decide how to make the forecast, that is, select one or more *bases* for the forecast; and (3) choose *techniques* that are most appropriate for the object and base selected.

---

[10] See, for example, Ward Edwards, Marcia Guttentag, and Kurt Snapper, "A Decision-Theoretic Approach to Evaluation Research," in *Handbook of Evaluation Research*, Vol. 1, ed. Elmer L. Struening and Marcia Guttentag (Beverly Hills, CA: Sage Publications, 1975), pp. 159–73.

[11] An excellent example is Thomas L. Saaty and Paul C. Rogers, "Higher Education in the United States (1985–2000): Scenario Construction Using a Hierarchical Framework with Eigenvector Weighting," *Socio-Economic Planning Sciences*, 10 (1976), 251–63. See also Saaty, *The Analytic Hierarchy Process* (New York: Wiley, 1980).

[12] John Rawls, *A Theory of Justice* (Cambridge, MA: Harvard University Press, 1971). On ethical systems as a source of policy alternatives see Duncan MacRae, Jr., *The Social Function of Social Science* (New Haven, CT: Yale University Press, 1976).

Objects

The *object* of a forecast is the point of reference of a projection, prediction, or conjecture. Forecasts have four objects:[13]

1. *Consequences of existing policies.* Forecasts may be used to estimate changes that are likely to occur if no new government actions are taken. The status quo, that is, doing nothing, is an existing policy. Examples are population projections of the U.S. Bureau of the Census and projections of female labor force participation in 1985 made by the U.S. Bureau of Labor Statistics.[14]

2. *Consequences of new policies.* Forecasts may be used to estimate changes in society that are likely to occur if new policies are adopted. For example, energy demand in 1995 may be projected on the basis of assumptions about the adoption of new policies to regulate industrial pollution.[15]

3. *Contents of new policies.* Forecasts may be used to estimate changes in the content of new public policies. The Congressional Research Service, for example, forecasts the possible adoption of a four-week annual paid vacation on the assumption that the government and labor unions will follow the lead of European countries, most of which have adopted four- or five-week annual paid vacations for workers.[16]

4. *Behavior of policy stakeholders.* Forecasts may be used to estimate the probable support (or opposition) to newly proposed policies. For example, techniques for assessing political feasibility may be used to estimate the probability that different stakeholders will support a policy at various stages of the policy process, from adoption to implementation.[17]

Bases

The *basis* of a forecast is the set of assumptions or data used to establish the plausibility of estimates of consequences of existing or new policies, the content of new policies, or the behavior of stakeholders. There are three major bases of forecasts: trend extrapolation, theoretical assumptions, and informed judgment. Each of these bases is associated with one of the three forms of forecasts previously discussed.

Trend extrapolation is the extension into the future of trends observed in the past. Trend extrapolation assumes that what has occurred in the past

---

[13] See William D. Coplin, *Introduction to the Analysis of Public Policy Issues from a Problem-Solving Perspective* (New York: Learning Resources in International Studies, 1975), p. 21.

[14] See, for example, Howard N. Fullerton, Jr. and Paul O. Flaim, "New Labor Force Projections to 1990." *Monthly Labor Review* (December 1976).

[15] See Barry Hughes, *U.S. Energy, Environment and Economic Problems: A Public Policy Simulation* (Chicago: American Political Science Association, 1975).

[16] See Everett M. Kassalow, "Some Labor Futures in the United States," Congressional Research Service, Congressional Clearing House on the Future, Library of Congress (January 31, 1978).

[17] See Michael K. O'Leary and William D. Coplin, *Everyman's "Prince."* (North Scituate, MA: Duxbury Press, 1976).

will also occur in the future, provided that no new policies or unforeseen events intervene to change the course of events. Trend extrapolation is based on *inductive logic*, that is, the process of reasoning from particular observations (for example, time-series data) to general conclusions or claims. In trend extrapolation we usually start with a set of time-series data, project past trends into the future, and then invoke assumptions about regularity and persistence that justify the projection. The logic of trend extrapolation is illustrated in Figure 6–3.

Theoretical assumptions are systematically structured and empirically testable sets of laws or propositions which make predictions about the occurrence of one event on the basis of another. Theoretical assumptions are causal in form, and their specific role is to explain and predict. The use of theoretical assumptions is based on *deductive logic*, that is, the process of reasoning from general statements, laws, or propositions to particular sets of information and claims. For example, the proposition that in "postindustrial" society the knowledge of policy analysts is an increasingly scarce resource which enhances their power may be used to move from information about the growth of professional policy analysis in government to

FIGURE 6–3 The logic of extrapolation: inductive reasoning.

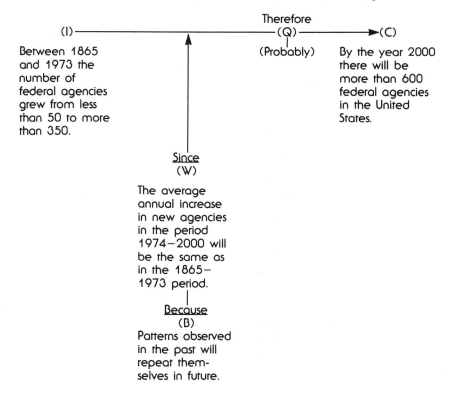

the predictive claim that policy analysts will have more power than policy-makers in coming years (Figure 6–4).

Informed judgments refer to knowledge based on experience and insight, rather than inductive or deductive reasoning. These judgments are usually expressed by experts or knowledgeables and are used in cases where theory and/or empirical data are unavailable or inadequate. Informed judgments are often based on *retroductive logic*, that is, the process of reasoning that begins with claims about the future and then works backward to the information and assumptions necessary to support claims. A good example of informed judgment as a basis of forecasts is the use of scientists or other knowledgeables to make conjectures about future changes in technology. Through retroductive logic experts may construct a scenario which claims that there will be automated highways with adaptive automobile autopilots

FIGURE 6–4   The logic of theoretical prediction: deductive reasoning.

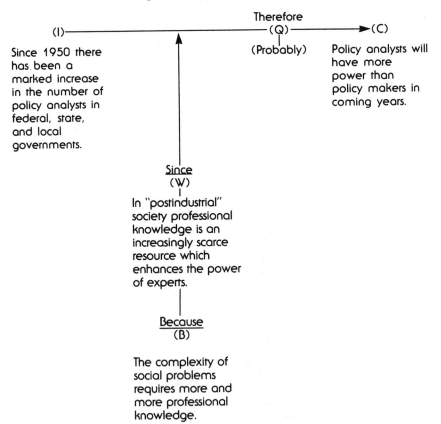

in the year 2000. Experts then work backwards to the information and assumptions needed to establish the plausibility of the claim (Figure 6–5). In practice the boundaries between inductive, deductive, and retroductive reasoning are often blurred. Retroductive reasoning is often a creative way to explore ways that potential futures may grow out of the present, while inductive and deductive reasoning yield new information and theories that lead to claims about future societal states. Nevertheless, inductive and deductive reasoning are potentially conservative, since the use of information about past events or the application of established scientific theories may restrict consideration of potential (as distinguished from plausible) futures. A good example of the restrictive influence of past events and established scientific theories comes from the well-known astronomer William H. Pickering (1858–1938):

> The popular mind pictures gigantic flying machines speeding across the Atlantic and carrying innumerable passengers in a way analogous to our modern

FIGURE 6–5 The logic of informed judgment: retroductive reasoning.

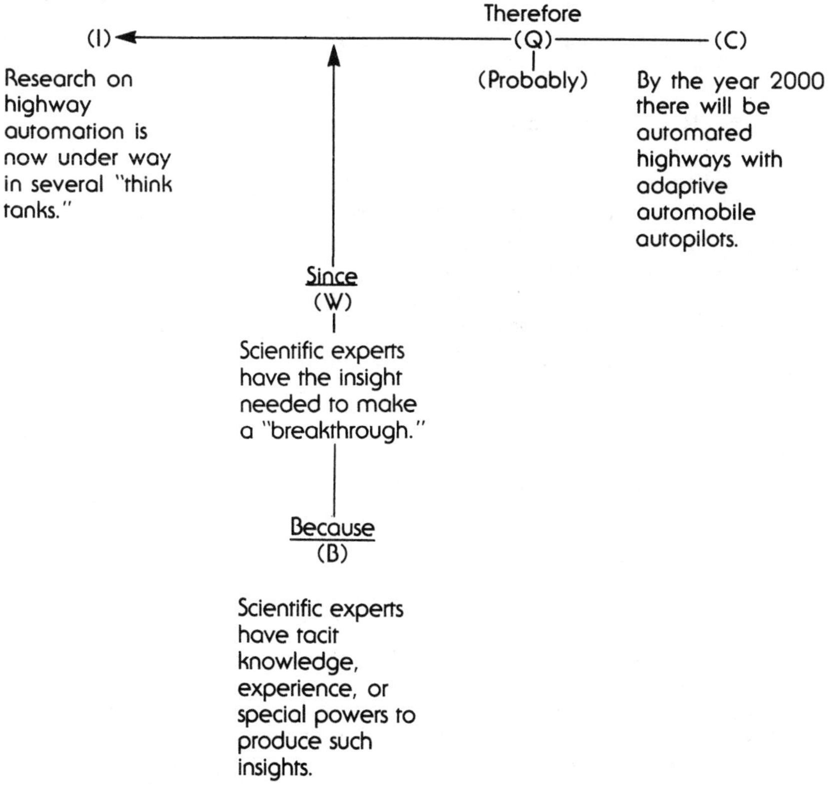

TABLE 6–2   Three Approaches to Forecasting with Their Bases, Appropriate Methods and Techniques, and Products

APPROACH	BASIS	APPROPRIATE TECHNIQUE(S)	PRODUCT
Extrapolative forecasting	Trend extrapolation	Classical time-series analysis Linear trend estimation Exponential weighting Data transformation Catastrophe methodology	Projections
Theoretical forecasting	Theory	Theory mapping Causal modeling Regression analysis Point and interval estimation Correlational analysis	Predictions
Judgmental forecasting	Informed judgment	Conventional Delphi Policy Delphi Cross-impact analysis Feasibility assessment	Conjectures

steamships. . . . It seems safe to say that such ideas must be wholly visionary, and even if a machine could get across with one or two passengers the expense would be prohibitive. . . .[18]

Methods and Techniques

While the selection of an object and basis helps guide the analyst toward appropriate methods and techniques, there are literally hundreds of forecasting methods and techniques to choose from.[19] A useful way to think about these methods and techniques is to group them according to the bases of forecasts discussed above. Table 6–2 outlines the three approaches to forecasting, their bases, appropriate methods, and products. This table serves as an overview of the rest of the chapter.

EXTRAPOLATIVE FORECASTING

Methods and techniques of extrapolative forecasting enable analysts to make projections of future societal states on the basis of current and historical data. Extrapolative forecasting is usually based on some form of *time-series*

---

[18] Quoted in Brownlee Haydon, *The Year 2000* (Santa Monica, CA: The Rand Corporation, 1967).

[19] See, for example, Daniel P. Harrison, *Social Forecasting Methodology* (New York: Russell Sage Foundation, 1976); Denis Johnston, "Forecasting Methods in the Social Sciences," *Technological Forecasting and Social Change*, 2 (1970); Arnold Mitchell and others, *Handbook of Forecasting Techniques* (Fort Belvoir, VA: U.S. Army Engineer Institute for Water Resources, December 1975); and Miller, "Methods for Estimating Societal Futures."

analysis, that is, on the analysis of numerical values collected at multiple points in time and presented chronologically. Time-series analysis provides summary measures (averages) of the amount and rate of change in past and future years. Extrapolative forecasting has been used to project economic growth, population decline, energy consumption, quality of life, and agency workloads.

When used to make projections, extrapolative forecasting rests on three basic assumptions:

1. *Persistence*. Patterns observed in the past will persist in the future. If energy consumption has grown in the past, it will do so in the future.
2. *Regularity*. Past variations in observed trends will regularly recur in the future. If wars have occurred every twenty or thirty years in the past, these cycles will repeat themselves in the future.
3. *Reliability and validity of data*. Measurements of trends are reliable (that is, relatively precise or internally consistent) and valid (that is, measure what they purport to be measuring). For example, crime statistics are relatively imprecise measures of actual criminal offenses.

When these three assumptions are met, extrapolative forecasting may yield insights into the dynamics of change and greater understanding of potential future states of society. When any one of these assumptions is violated, extrapolative forecasting techniques are likely to yield inaccurate or misleading results.[20]

Classical Time-Series Analysis

When making extrapolative forecasts we may use *classical time-series analysis*, which views any time series as having four components: secular trend, seasonal variations, cyclical fluctuations, and irregular movements. *Secular trend* is a smooth long-term growth or decline in a time series. Figure 6–6 shows a secular trend in the growth of crimes per 1000 persons in Chicago over a 30-year period. By convention the time-series variable is plotted on the Y-axis (also called the *ordinate*) and years are plotted on the X-axis (also called the *abscissa*). A straight-line trend has been used to summarize the growth of total arrests per 1000 persons between 1940 and 1970. In other cases (for example, mortality) the straight-line trend shows a long-term decline, while still other cases (for example, consumption of coal oil) shows a *curvilinear trend*, that is, a trend where the numerical values in a time-series display a convex or concave pattern.

Seasonal variation, as the term suggests, is the variation in a time series which recurs periodically within a one-year period or less. The best examples of seasonal variations are the ups and downs of production and sales that

---

[20] Fidelity to these and other methodological assumptions is no guarantee of accuracy. In this author's experience, the *less* accurate of two or more forecasts is frequently based on strict adherence to technical assumptions. This is why judgment is so important to all forms of forecasting, including complex modeling. See Ascher, *Forecasting*, Chap. 1.

FIGURE 6–6   Demonstration of secular trend: total arrests per 1000 population in Chicago, 1940–1970.

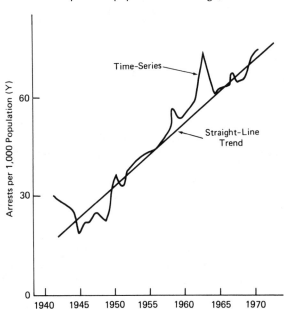

Source: Adapted from Ted R. Gurr, "The Comparative Analysis of Public Order," in *The Politics of Crime and Conflict,* ed. Ted R. Gurr, Peter N. Grabosky, and Richard C. Hula (Beverly Hills, CA: Sage Publications, 1977), p. 647.

follow changes in weather conditions and holidays. The workloads of social welfare, health, and public utilities agencies also frequently display seasonal variations as a result of weather conditions and holidays. For example, the consumption of home heating fuels increases in the winter months and begins to decline in March of each year.

Cyclical fluctuations are also periodic but may extend unpredictably over a number of years. Cycles are frequently difficult to explain, since each new cyclical fluctuation may be a consequence of unknown factors. Total arrests per 1000 population in Chicago, displayed over a period of more than 100 years, show at least three cyclic fluctuations (Figure 6–7). Each of these cycles is difficult to explain, although the third cyclical fluctuation coincides with the Prohibition Era (1919–1933) and the rise of organized crime. This example points to the importance of carefully selecting an appropriate time frame, since what may appear to be a secular trend may in fact be part of some larger long-term pattern of cyclical fluctuations. Note also that total arrests per 1000 persons were higher in the 1870s and 1890s than in most years from 1955 to 1970.

FIGURE 6–7   Demonstration of cyclical fluctuations:
total arrests per 1000 population in Chicago, 1868–1970.

Source: Ted R. Gurr, "The Comparative Analysis of Public
Order," in *The Politics of Crime and Conflict*, ed. Ted R. Gurr,
Peter N. Grabosky, and Richard C. Hula (Beverly Hills, CA: Sage
Publications, 1977), p. 647.

The interpretation of cyclic fluctuations is frequently made more difficult by the presence of *irregular movements*, that is, unpredictable variations in a time series that appear to follow no regular pattern. Irregular
movements may be the result of many factors (changes in government,
strikes, natural disasters). As long as these factors are unaccounted for they
are treated as random error, that is, unknown sources of variation that
cannot be explained in terms of secular trend, seasonal variations, or cyclical
fluctuations. For example, the irregular movement in total arrests that occurred after 1957 (Figure 6–7) might be regarded as an unpredictable variation in the time series that follows no regular pattern. On closer inspection,
however, the sharp temporary upswing in arrests may be explained by the
changes in record keeping that came into effect when Orlando Wilson was
appointed chief of police.[21] This example points to the importance of un-

---

[21] See Donald T. Campbell, "Reforms As Experiments," in *Readings in Evaluation
Research*, ed. Francis G. Caro (New York: Russell Sage Foundation, 1971), pp. 240–41.

derstanding the sociohistorical and political events underlying changes in a time series.

Linear Trend Estimation

A standard technique for extrapolating trends is *linear trend estimation*, a procedure that uses regression analysis to obtain mathematically precise estimates of future societal states on the basis of observed values in a time series. Linear regression is based on assumptions of persistence, regularity, and data reliability. When linear regression is used to estimate trend, it is essential that observed values in a time series are not curvilinear, since any significant departure from linearity will produce forecasts with sizable errors. Nevertheless, linear regression may also be used to remove the linear trend component from a series that displays seasonal variations or cyclical fluctuations.

There are two important properties of regression analysis:

1. *Deviations cancel.* The sum of the differences between observed values in a time series and values lying along a computed straight-line trend (called a *regression line*) will always equal zero. Thus, if the trend value (Y_t) is subtracted from its corresponding observed value (Y) for all years in a time series, the total of these differences (called *deviations*) will equal zero. When the observed value for a given year lies *below* the regression line, the deviation ($Y - Y_t$) is always *negative*. By contrast, when the observed value is *above* the regression line, the deviation ($Y - Y_t$) is always *positive*. These negative and positive values cancel each other out, such that $\sum(Y - Y_t) = 0$.

2. *Squared deviations are a minimum.* If we square each deviation (that is, multiply each deviation value by itself) and add them all up, the sum of these squared deviations will always be a minimum or least value. This means that linear regression minimizes the distances between the regression line and all observed values of Y in the series. In other words, it is the most efficient way to draw a trend line through a series of observed data points.

These two properties of regression analysis are illustrated with hypothetical data in Figure 6–8.

The computation of linear trend with regression analysis is illustrated in Table 6–3 with data on energy consumption. In column (3) note that years in the time series are coded by calculating the numerical distance (x) of each year from the middle of the entire period (that is, 1973). The middle of this series is given a coded value of zero and treated as the origin. The values of x range from -3 to $+3$ and are deviations from the origin. Observe also the computational procedures used in columns (4) and (5) of Table 6–3. The value of xY is calculated by multiplying values of energy consumption (Y) by each coded time value (x), as shown in column (4). The value of x^2, shown in column (5), is calculated by multiplying each value of x by itself, that is, squaring all the x values in column (3). Finally, column (6) contains trend values of the time-series variable (Y_t). These trend values, which form the straight line graphed in Figure 6–8, are calculated according to the

FIGURE 6–8 Two properties of linear regression.

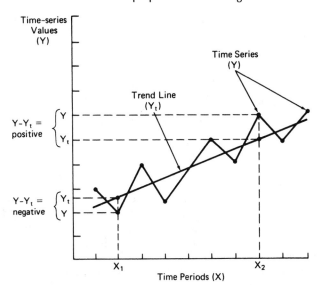

Note: $\sum(Y - Y_t) = 0$; $\sum(Y - Y_t)^2 = $ a minimum (least) value.

TABLE 6–3 Time-Series Data on Total Energy Consumption Used in Linear Regression

YEARS (X) (1)	ENERGY CONSUMPTION (Y) (2)	CODED TIME VALUE (x) (3)	COLUMNS (2) BY (3) (xY) (4)	COLUMN (3) SQUARED (x^2) (5)	TREND VALUE FOR ENERGY CONSUMPTION (Y_t) (6)
1970	66.9	-3	-200.7	9	68.35
1971	68.3	-2	-136.6	4	69.31
1972	71.6	-1	-71.6	1	70.27
1973	74.6	0	0	0	71.24
1974	72.7	1	72.7	1	72.20
1975	70.6	2	141.2	4	73.17
1976	74.0	3	222.0	9	74.13
$n = 7$	$\sum Y = 498.7$	$\sum x = 0$	$\sum(xY) = 27.0$	$\sum(x^2) = 28$	$\sum Y_t = 498.7$

$$Y_t = a + b(x)$$

$$a = \frac{\sum Y}{n} = \frac{498.7}{7} = 71.24$$

$$b = \frac{\sum(xY)}{\sum(x^2)} = \frac{27.0}{28.0} = 0.964$$

$$Y_t = 71.24 + 0.964(x)$$

$$Y_{t(1980)} = 71.24 + 0.964(7) = 77.99 \text{ quadrillion BTUs}$$

following equation:

$$Y_t = a + b(x)$$

where

Y_t = the trend value for a given year

a = the value of Y_t when $X = 0$

b = the slope of the trend line representing the change in Y_t for each unit of time

x = the coded time value for any year, as determined by its distance from the origin

Once the values of a and b have been calculated, estimates of total energy consumption may be made for any year in the *observed* time series or for any *future* year. For example, Table 6–3 shows that the trend value for energy consumption in 1972 is 70.27 quadrillion Btu. To project total energy consumption for 1980, we set the value of x at 7 (that is, seven time periods away from 1973, the origin) and solve the equation $Y_{t(1980)} = a + b(x)$. The formula for computing the value of a is

$$a = \frac{\sum Y}{n}$$

where

$\sum Y$ = the sum of observed values in the series

n = the number of years in the observed time series

The formula for computing the value of b is

$$b = \frac{\sum(xY)}{\sum(x^2)}$$

where

$\sum(xY)$ = the sum of the products of the coded time values and the observed values in the series [see column (4) of Table 6–3]

$\sum(x^2)$ = the sum of the squared coded time values [see column (5) of Table 6–3]

The calculations in Table 6–3 not only permit us to compute trend values for energy consumption in the observed series; they also enable us to project total energy consumption for any given year in the future. Thus, the estimate of total energy consumption in 1980 [$Y_{t(1980)}$] is 77.99 quadrillion BTUs.

In illustrating the application of linear regression we have used a time series with an odd number of years. We treated the middle of the series as the origin and coded it as zero. Obviously, there are many time series that contain an even number of years, and a different procedure must be used for determining each coded time value (x), since there is no middle year. The procedure used with even-numbered time series is to divide the series into two equal parts and code the time values in intervals of two (rather than in intervals of one, as in odd-numbered series). Each year in Table 6–4 is exactly two units away from its neighbor, and the highest and lowest coded time values are $+7$ and -7, rather than $+3$ and -3. Note that the size of the interval need not be 2; it could be 3, 4, 5 or any number provided that each year is equidistant from the next one in the series. Increasing the size of the interval will not affect the computation of results.

Despite its precision in extrapolating secular trend, linear regression is limited by several conditions. First, the time series must be *linear*, that is, display a constant increase or decrease in values along the trend line. If the pattern of observations is *nonlinear* (that is, where the amounts of change increase or decrease from one time period to the next), other techniques must be used. Some of these techniques require fitting various types of curves to nonlinear time series. Second, plausible arguments must be offered to show that historical patterns will *persist* in the future, that is,

TABLE 6–4   Linear Regression with an Even-Numbered Series

YEARS (X) (1)	ENERGY CONSUMPTION (Y) (2)	CODED TIME VALUE (x) (3)	COLUMNS (2) BY (3) (xY) (4)	COLUMN (3) SQUARED (x^2) (5)	TREND VALUE FOR ENERGY CONSUMPTION (Y_t) (6)
1969	64.4	-7	-450.8	49	66.14
1970	66.9	-5	-334.5	25	67.36
1971	68.3	-3	-204.9	9	68.57
1972	71.6	-1	-71.6	1	69.78
1973	74.6	1	74.6	1	71.00
1974	72.7	3	218.1	9	72.21
1975	70.6	5	353.0	25	73.43
1976	74.0	7	518.0	49	74.64
$n = 8$	$\sum Y = 563.1$	$\sum x = 0$	$\sum(xY) = 101.9$	$\sum(x^2) = 168$	$\sum Y_t = 563.1$

$$Y_t = a + b(x)$$

$$a = \frac{\sum Y}{n} = \frac{563.1}{8} = 70.39$$

$$b = \frac{\sum(xY)}{\sum(x^2)} = \frac{101.9}{168} = 0.607$$

$$Y_t = 70.39 + 0.607(x)$$

$$Y_{t(1980)} = 70.39 + 0.607(15) = 79.495 \text{ quadrillion BTUs}$$

continue in much the same form in subsequent years as they have in past ones. Third, patterns must be *regular*, that is, display no cyclical fluctuations or sharp discontinuities. Unless all of these conditions are present, linear regression should not be used to extrapolate trend.

The MYSTAT output for the regression analyses computed by hand in Tables 6–3 and 6–4 is displayed in Exhibit 6–1. The MYSTAT output was obtained by, first, entering and saving the time-series data according to procedures in the MYSTAT manual. Second, the files in which the data were saved were called up for analysis with the USE command. Third, the commands necessary to execute the regression analysis (MODEL) and obtain the results (ESTIMATE) were used. For example, after naming and saving the file in the EDIT mode and changing to the MAIN mode, the MYSTAT sequence for Table 6–3 was as follows:

> USE "A: TABLE63.MYS"
> MODEL ENERGY = CONSTANT + YEAR
> ESTIMATE

As may be seen by comparing Table 6–3 in the text with the MYSTAT output (Table 6–3 in Exhibit 6–1) the results are identical.[22] The first line of the MYSTAT output identifies the dependent variable (which was named "ENERGY"), the number of observations in the sample (N: 7), the correlation coefficient expressing the strength of the relationship between time and energy consumption (MULTIPLE R: .729), and the squared correlation coefficient (SQUARED MULTIPLE R: .531), which expresses the proportion of variance in the dependent variable ("ENERGY") explained by the independent variable ("YEAR").

For present purposes the most important part of the MYSTAT output is lines 4 and 5. Line 4 gives the coefficient for the constant, *a*, which is 71.243—this is the value of Y, energy consumption, when X equals zero. Line 5 gives the coefficient for the slope of the regression line, *b*, which is 0.964—this is the amount of change in Y, energy consumption, for each unit change in X, the years. This part of the MYSTAT output enables us to write the regression equation and, using the coefficients in this equation, forecast the value of energy consumption for any future year. The regression equation for Table 6–3 is

$$Y_t = 71.243 + 0.964(X)$$

The regression equation for Table 6–4, which has eight rather than seven years in the time series, is

$$Y_t = 70.388 + 0.607(X)$$

---

[22] Here we consider only part of the MYSTAT output. Later, in this and subsequent chapters, we examine other parts of the output of the MYSTAT regression program as well as other routines. An overview of MYSTAT routines and how to use them is presented in Appendix 6.

EXHIBIT 6–1   MYSTAT Output for Tables 6–3 and 6–4

Table 6–3

```
DEP VAR: ENERGY      N:   7   MULTIPLE R: .729   SQUARED MULTIPLE R:  .531
ADJUSTED SQUARED MULTIPLE R: .437      STANDARD ERROR OF ESTIMATE:      2.146


 VARIABLE   COEFFICIENT   STD ERROR   STD COEF TOLERANCE    T    P(2 TAIL)
 CONSTANT        71.243       0.811      0.000  .        87.843    0.000
     YEAR         0.964       0.406      0.729  .100E+01   2.378    0.063



                          ANALYSIS OF VARIANCE


  SOURCE   SUM-OF-SQUARES   DF   MEAN-SQUARE    F-RATIO      P


 REGRESSION       26.036    1      26.036       5.655      0.063
 RESIDUAL         23.021    5       4.604
```

Table 6–4

```
DEP VAR: ENERGY      N:   8   MULTIPLE R: .829   SQUARED MULTIPLE R:  .687
ADJUSTED SQUARED MULTIPLE R: .634      STANDARD ERROR OF ESTIMATE:      2.169


 VARIABLE   COEFFICIENT   STD ERROR   STD COEF TOLERANCE    T    P(2 TAIL)
 CONSTANT        70.388       0.767      0.000  .        91.796    0.000
     YEAR         0.607       0.167      0.829  .100E+01   3.625    0.011



                          ANALYSIS OF VARIANCE


  SOURCE   SUM-OF-SQUARES   DF   MEAN-SQUARE    F-RATIO      P


 REGRESSION       61.807    1      61.807      13.140      0.011
 RESIDUAL         28.222    6       4.704
```

Note how much of a difference there is in the slopes after adding only one year to the series.

Many time-series data of concern to policy analysts—for example, data on crime, pollution, public expenditures, urbanization—are nonlinear. A variety of techniques have been developed to fit nonlinear curves to patterns of change that do not display a constant increase or decrease in the values of an observed time series. Although these techniques are not presented in detail, we discuss some of their properties and underlying assumptions. Readers who wish to investigate these forecasting techniques in greater depth should consult advanced texts on time-series analysis.[23]

Nonlinear Time Series

Time series that do not meet conditions of linearity, persistence, and regularity fall into five main classes (Figure 6–9):

1. *Oscillations.* Here there are departures from linearity, but only *within* years, quarters, months, or days. Oscillations may be persistent and regular (for example, most police arrests occur between 11 P.M. and 2 P.M. throughout the year) but not show a constant increase or decrease within the period under examination (Figure 6–9a). Oscillations *within* years may occur in conjunction with long-term secular trends *between* years. Examples include seasonal variations in unemployment, monthly variations in agency workloads, and daily variations in levels of pollutants.

2. *Cycles.* Cycles are nonlinear fluctuations that occur between years or longer periods of time. Cycles may be unpredictable, or occur with persistence and regularity. While the overall pattern of a cycle is always nonlinear, segments of a given cycle may be linear or curvilinear (Figure 6–9b). Examples are business cycles and the "life cycles" of academic fields, scientific publications, and civilizations.

3. *Growth curves.* Departures from linearity occur *between* years, decades, or some other unit of time. Growth curves evidence either cumulative *increases* in the rate of growth in a time series, cumulative *decreases* in this rate of growth, or some *combination* of the two (Figure 6–9c). In the latter case growth curves are S-shaped and called *sigmoid* or *logistic* curves. Growth curves, which developed out of studies of biological organisms, have been used to forecast the growth of industry, urban areas, population, technology, and science. Although growth curves are not linear, they are nevertheless persistent and regular.

4. *Decline curves.* Here departures from linearity again occur *between* years, decades, or longer periods. In effect, decline curves are the counterpart of growth curves. Decline curves evidence either cumulative increases or decreases in the rate of decline in a time series (Figure 6–9d). Increasing and decreasing rates of decline may be combined to form curves with different shapes. Patterns of decline are sometimes used as a basis for various dynamic or "life-cycle" perspectives of the decline of civilizations, societies, and urban areas. Decline curves are nonlinear but regular and persistent.

---

[23] See G. E. P. Box and G. M. Jenkins, *Time Series Analysis: Forecasting and Control* (San Francisco: Holden-Day, 1969); and S. C. Wheelwright and S. Makridakis, *Forecasting Methods for Management* (New York: Wiley, 1973).

FIGURE 6–9   Five classes of nonlinear time series.

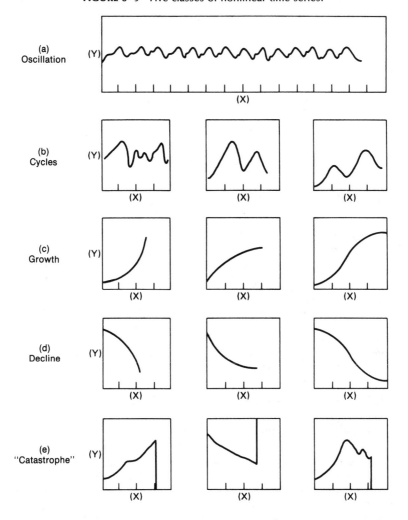

5. *"Catastrophes."* The main characteristic of time-series data that are "catastrophic" is that they display sudden and sharp discontinuities. The analysis of catastrophic change, a field of study founded by the French mathematician René Thom, not only involves nonlinear changes over time; it also involves patterns of change that are discontinuous (Figure 6–9e). Examples include sudden shifts in government policy during war (surrender or withdrawal), the collapse of stock exchanges in times of economic crisis, and the sudden change in the density of a liquid as it boils.[24]

---

[24] See C. A. Isnard and E. C. Zeeman, "Some Models from Catastrophe Theory in the Social Sciences," in *The Use of Models in the Social Sciences*, ed. Lyndhurst Collins (Boulder, CO: Westview Press, 1976), pp. 44–100.

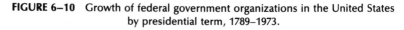

FIGURE 6–10   Growth of federal government organizations in the United States by presidential term, 1789–1973.

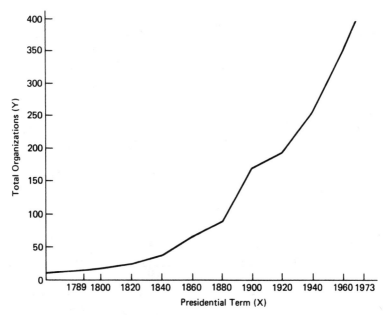

Source: Herbert Kaufman, *Are Government Organizations Immortal?* (Washington, DC: The Brookings Institution, 1976), p. 62.

The growth and decline curves illustrated in Figure 6–9c and d cannot be described by a straight-line trend. Patterns of growth and decline display little or no cyclical fluctuation, and the trend is best described as *exponential growth* or *decline,* that is, growth or decline where the values of some quantity increase or decrease at an increasing rate. The growth of federal government organizations between 1789 and 1973 (Figure 6–10) is an example of exponential growth. After 1789 the total number of organizations began to grow slowly, until about 1860 when the growth rate began to accelerate. Clearly, this growth trend is very different from the secular trends and cyclical variations examined so far.[25]

Techniques for fitting curves to processes of growth and decline are more complex than those used to estimate secular trend. While many of these techniques are based on linear regression, they require various transformations of the time-series variable (Y). Some of these transformations of the time-series variable (Y) involve roots ($\sqrt[n]{Y}$), while others require logarithms (log Y) or exponents (e^x). In each case the aim is to express mathematically changes in a time series that increase by increasing or decreasing amounts (or, conversely, decrease by increasing or decreasing amounts).

---

[25] The outstanding work on processes of growth in science and other areas is Derek de Sólla Price, *Little Science, Big Science* (New York: Columbia University Press, 1963).

While these techniques will not be presented here, their logic is sufficiently important for public policy analysis to warrant further illustration.

A simple illustration will serve best to clarify techniques for curve fitting. Recall the model of compound interest presented in Chapter 5. This model states that

$$S_n = (1 + r)^n S_0$$

where

S_n = the amount to which a given investment will accumulate in a given (n) number of years

S_0 = the initial amount of the investment

$(1 + r)^n$ = a constant return on investment (1.0) plus the rate of interest (r) in a given (n) number of years

Imagine that the manager of a small municipality of 10,000 persons is confronted by the following situation. In order to meet immediate out-of-pocket expenses for emergencies, it was decided in 1970 that a sum of $1000 should be set aside in a special checking account. The checking account is very handy but earns no interest. In 1971 and subsequent years, because of rising inflation, the manager began to increase the sum in the special account by $100 per year. The increase in funds, illustrated in Figure 6–11a, is a good example of the kind of linear trend we have been examining. The time series increases by constant amounts ($100 per year) and, by 1980, there was $2000 in the special account. In this case the time-series values (Y) are identical to the trend values ($Y_t = Y$), since all values of Y are on the trend line.

Now consider what would have occurred if the manager had placed the funds in a special interest-bearing account (we will assume that there are no legal restrictions and that withdrawals can be made without penalties). Assume that the annual rate of interest is 10 percent compounded annually. Assume also that only the original $1000 was left in the account for the 10-year period, that is, no further deposits were made. The growth of city funds, illustrated in Figure 6–11b, is a good example of the kind of growth trend we have been discussing. City funds increased by increasing amounts over the 10-year period (but at a constant interest rate compounded annually), and the total funds available at the end of 1980 was $2594, as compared with $2000 in the non-interest-bearing account. Note also that in the first case (no interest) it takes 10 years to double the original amount, and that no accumulation above the original $1000 comes from interest. In the second case, however, it takes a little more than seven years to double the original amount, and all of the additional ($1594) accumulation comes from interest. The values used to calculate accumulation at the end of 1980 are

$$S_n = (1 + r)^n S_0$$
$$= (1 + r)^{10}(\$1000) = (2.5937)(\$1000)$$
$$S_{10} = \$2594.00$$

FIGURE 6–11   Linear versus growth trends.

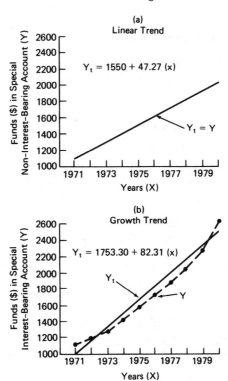

Note that accumulation for any given year (for example, 1975 as the fifth year) may be calculated simply by substituting the appropriate values in the formula $S_5 = (1 + r)^5(\$1000) = (1.6105)(\$1000) = \$1610.51$.

Consider now the limitations of linear regression in estimating growth trends such as that illustrated in Figure 6–11b. The linear regression equation of Figure 6–11b [$Y_t = 1753.30 + 82.31(x)$] will produce an inaccurate forecast. For example, a 1990 forecast using the linear regression equation yields a trend estimate of $4140.29 [$Y_{t(1990)} = 1753.30 + 82.31(29) = \$4140.29$]. By contrast, the compound interest formula, which exactly represents the growth in accumulated funds, produces a 1990 estimate of $6727.47 [$S_{20} = (1.1)^{20}(\$1000) = \$6727.47$].[26] The linear regression estimate is therefore highly inaccurate.

Fortunately, the linear regression technique may be adapted to estimate growth trends. For regression to do this, however, it is necessary to change our original linear equation [$Y_t = a + b(x)$] to a nonlinear one.

---

[26] Note that the compound interest formula is not a technique for extrapolating growth trends. It is used here merely as an illustration.

Although there are many ways to do this, two of the most common procedures are exponential weighting and data transformation.

Exponential Weighting

In *exponential weighting* the analyst may raise one of the terms in the regression equation to a power, for example, square the value of $b(x)$; or add another term, also raised to a power, to the equation [for example, $c(x^2)$]. The more pronounced the increase (or decrease) in the observed growth pattern, the higher the power necessary to represent it. For example, if we have slowly increasing amounts of change, such as those illustrated by the compound interest formula (Figure 6–11b), we might add to the original linear regression equation $[Y_t = a + b(x) = 1753.30 + 82.31(x)]$ a third term $[c(x^2)]$ that has been raised to a power by squaring the coded time value (x). The equation (called a second degree parabola) then reads

$$Y_t = a + b(x) + c(x^2)$$
$$= 1753.30 + 82.31(x) + 1.8(x^2)$$

Note that the only part of this equation that is not linear is the squared time value (x^2). This means that any value of x computed for given years will increase by a power of 2 (for example, coded values of -5 and $+9$ become 25 and 81, respectively). The higher the original x value, the greater the amount of change, since the squares of larger numbers produce disproportionately larger products than do the squares of smaller numbers. Whereas a coded time value (x) of 9 is three times the value of 3 in the linear regression equation, in the second-degree parabola the same year is nine times the value of the corresponding year

$$\frac{9}{3} = 3 \quad \text{and} \quad \frac{9^2}{3^2} = 9$$

It is now easier to visualize what it means to say that growth processes exhibit increasing increases in a time series.

Data Transformation

A second procedure used to adapt linear regression techniques to processes of growth and decline is *data transformation*. Whereas exponential weighting involves the writing of a new and explicitly nonlinear regression equation [for example, $Y_t = a + b(x) + c(x^2)$], the transformation of data permits analysts to work with the simple linear equation $[Y_t = a + b(x)]$, but only after values of the time-series variable (Y) have been appropriately transformed. One way to transform the time-series variable is to take its square root $(\sqrt{Y})$. Another way to transform data is to take either the common or the natural *logarithm* of values of the time-series variable. The common (base 10) logarithm of a number is the power to which 10 must be raised to produce that number. For example, 2 is the logarithm of 100, since 10 must be raised to the power of 2 to produce 100 ($10 \times 10 = 10^2 = 100$). The natural (base e) logarithm of a number is the power to which the base e, which equals 2.71828, must be raised to produce that number. For example, the natural logarithm of 100 is 4.6052, since 2.71828 raised to the power 4.6052 equals 100. The abbreviation for base 10 logarithms is log, and the abbreviation for base e logarithms is ln. For readers with no experience with logarithms and roots, it is easier to grasp the nature of these transformations if we study a hypothetical time series which exhibits extremely rapid growth (Table 6–5). We can then observe the consequences of taking roots and logarithms of the time-series variable before solving the simple linear regression equation.

Note that all computations used in Table 6–5 are identical to those already used in applying linear regression to estimate trend. The only difference is that values of Y have been transformed, either by taking their square roots or their common (base 10) logarithms. Observe that the linear regression procedure is wholly inappropriate for describing the sharp growth trend that progresses by multiples of 10 in each period [column (2), Table 6–5]. The linear equation [$Y_t = a + b(x)$] produces a 1981 forecast of 85,227, when the actual value of the series will be 1,000,000! (We are assuming, of course, that the series will grow by a factor of 10 in 1981 and subsequent years.) The linear equation based on the square root transformation [$\sqrt{Y_t} = a + b(x)$] helps very little with this explosive time series. The transformation results in a 1981 estimate of 94,249, hardly much of an improvement.

Only the logarithmically transformed linear equation [log $Y = a + b(x)$] gives us the exact value for 1981. In effect, what we have done is "straighten out" the growth trend by taking the common logarithm of Y, thus permitting the use of linear regression to extrapolate trend. This does *not* mean that the trend is actually linear (obviously, it is not). It only means that we can use linear regression to make a precise forecast of the value of the *nonlinear* trend in 1981 or any other year. Note, however, that to make a trend estimate for 1981 we must convert the logarithmic value (6.0) back into the original value of the Y variable. This is done (Table 6–5) by taking the *antilogarithm* of 6.0 (abbreviated "antilog 6.0"), which is 1,000,000 (an antilogarithm is the number corresponding to the logarithm, for example, antilog 2 = 100, antilog 3 = 1000, antilog 4 = 10,000, and so on). Note also that roots must also be reconverted by raising the trend estimate by the appropriate power (see Table 6–5).

Now that we understand some of the fundamentals of estimating growth trends, let us return to our example of the manager of the small municipality and the problem of compound interest. We know from the compound interest model that $1000 invested at an interest rate of 10 percent (compounded annually) will accumulate to $6727.47 by the end of 1990. That is,

$$S_n = (1 + r)^n S_0$$
$$= (1 + 0.10)^{20}(\$1000)$$
$$S_{20} = \$6727.47$$

TABLE 6–5 Square Root and Logarithm of a Time-Series Exhibiting Rapid Growth

YEAR (X) (1)	ORIGINAL VALUE OF TIME-SERIES VARIABLE (Y) (2)	SQUARE ROOT OF TIME-SERIES VARIABLE $(\sqrt{Y})_t$ (3)	LOGARITHM OF TIME-SERIES VARIABLE (log Y) (4)	CODED TIME VALUE (x) (5)	TIME VALUE SQUARED (x^2) (6)	COLUMNS (2) BY (5) (xY) (7)	COLUMNS (3) BY (5) $(x\sqrt{Y})_t$ (8)	COLUMNS (4) BY (5) (x log Y) (9)	TREND ESTIMATES Y_t (10)	TREND ESTIMATES $\sqrt{Y_t}$ (11)	TREND ESTIMATES log Y_t (12)
1976	10	3.16	1.0	−2	4	−20	−6.32	−2	−19,718	−51.0	1.0
1977	100	10.0	2.0	−1	1	−100	−10.0	−2	1,271	20.6	2.0
1978	1,000	31.62	3.0	0	0	0	0	0	22,260	92.2	3.0
1979	10,000	100.0	4.0	1	1	10,000	100.0	4	43,249	163.8	4.0
1980	100,000	316.23	5.0	2	4	200,000	632.46	10	64,238	235.4	5.0
5	111,300	461.01	15.0	0	10	209,880	716.14	10.0	11,300	461.01	15.0

$Y_t = a + b(x)$

$a = \dfrac{\sum Y}{n} = \dfrac{111,300}{5} = 22,260$

$b = \dfrac{\sum(xY)}{\sum(x^2)} = \dfrac{209,880}{10} = 20,988$

$Y_t = 22,260 + 20,988(x)$

$Y_{t(1981)} = 22,260 + 20,988(3)$

$= 85,224$

$\sqrt{Y_t} = a + b(x)$

$a = \dfrac{\sum \sqrt{Y}}{n} = \dfrac{461.01}{5} = 92.2$

$b = \dfrac{\sum(x\sqrt{Y})}{\sum(x^2)} = \dfrac{716.14}{10} = 71.6$

$\sqrt{Y_t} = 92.2 + 71.6(x)$

$Y_{t(1981)} = [92.2 + 71.6(3)]^2$

$= 94,249$

$\log Y = a + b(x)$

$a = \dfrac{\sum \log Y}{n} = \dfrac{15}{5} = 3.0$

$b = \dfrac{\sum(x \log Y)}{\sum(x^2)} = \dfrac{10}{10} = 1.0$

$\log Y = 3.0 + 1.0(x)$

$Y_{t(1981)} = $ antilog $3.0 + 1.0(3)$

$= $ antilog 6.0

$= 1,000,000$

If we use the linear regression equation to extrapolate to 1990, we will obtain $4140.29. This is $2587.18 in error ($6727.47 − 4140.29 = $2587.18). But what can we do about this sizable error, given that we would like to use the linear regression model to forecast the growth trend? The easiest way to deal with this problem is to find the base 10 logarithms of all values of Y and use these with the linear regression equation. This has been done in Table 6–6, which shows that the 1990 trend estimate based on the logarithmic transformation is $logY_{t(1990)} = 3.829$. When we take the antilogarithm of this value (antilog 3.829), we find that it equals $6745.27, an estimate that is very close to that produced by the compound interest formula. Hence, through a logarithmic transformation of the time-series variable, we have successfully applied linear regression to a nonlinear growth process. The same kinds of logarithmic transformations are regularly used in public policy analysis to extrapolate other important growth trends, including national income, population, and government expenditures.

Catastrophe Methodology

No matter how successfully we adapt linear regression to problems of forecasting growth and decline, there is one condition that must be present: The processes we seek to understand and extrapolate must be smooth and continuous. Yet as we have seen (Figure 6–9e), many time series are discontinuous. It is here where catastrophe methodology, a field within the special branch of mathematics called topography, provides useful insights. *Catastrophe methodology*, which involves the systematic study and mathematical representation of discontinuous processes, is specifically designed to forecast trends where small changes in one variable (for example, time) produce sudden large changes in another variable. The point where a small change in one variable results in a sudden and dramatic shift in another variable is called a *catastrophe*, a term that refers to a mathematical theorem that classifies discontinuous processes into five major types rather than to any sense of impending doom or disaster. According to its founder, René Thom, it is a methodology (not a theory) for studying the elementary types of discontinuity in nature and society.[27]

Catastrophe methodology is much too complex to survey here. We should nevertheless be aware of some of its major assumptions and applications to public policy analysis:

1. *Discontinuous processes.* Many of the most important physical, biological, and social processes are not only curvilinear; they are also abrupt and discontinuous. An example of discontinuous processes in the social realm is the sudden shift in public policy that sometimes follows smooth and gradually evolving changes in public opinion on specific policy issues.

---

[27] See Isnard and Zeeman, "Some Models from Catastrophe Theory in the Social Sciences." René Thom's major work is *Stabilite structurelle et morphogenese*, trans. D. H. Fowler (New York: W.A. Benjamin, 1975). Related to catastrophe methodology is work on chaos theory. See Prigogine and Stengers, *Order Out of Chaos*.

TABLE 6–6 Linear Regression with Logarithmic Transformation of Time Series

YEARS (X) (1)	TIME-SERIES VARIABLE (Y) (2)	LOGARITHM OF TIME-SERIES VARIABLE (log Y) (3)	CODED TIME VALUE (x) (4)	SQUARED TIME VALUE (x^2) (5)	COLUMNS (3) BY (4) (x log Y) (6)	TREND ESTIMATE (log Y_t) (7)
1971	1100	3.041	−9	81	−27.369	3.0413
1972	1210	3.083	−7	49	−21.581	3.0827
1973	1331	3.124	−5	25	−15.620	3.1241
1974	1464	3.165	−3	9	−9.495	3.1655
1975	1611	3.207	−1	1	−3.207	3.2069
1976	1772	3.248	1	1	3.248	3.2483
1977	1949	3.290	3	9	9.870	3.2897
1978	2144	3.331	5	25	16.655	3.3311
1979	2358	3.373	7	49	23.611	3.3725
1980	2594	3.414	9	81	30.726	3.4139
10	17533	32.276	0	330	6.838	32.2760

$$\log Y_t = a + b(x)$$

$$a = \frac{\sum \log Y}{n} = \frac{32.276}{10} = 3.2276$$

$$b = \frac{\sum (x \log Y)}{\sum (x^2)} = \frac{6.838}{330} = 0.0207$$

$$\log Y_t = 3.2276 + 0.0207(x)$$

$$\log Y_{t(1990)} = 3.2276 + 0.0207(29) = 3.829$$

$$Y_{t(1990)} = \text{antilog } 3.829 = \$6745.27$$

2. *Systems as wholes.* Social systems as a whole frequently exhibit changes that are not the simple sum of their parts. Sudden shifts may occur in the structure of a social system as a whole, even though the system's parts may have changed gradually and smoothly. For example, public opinion on major policy issues may suddenly diverge, making for an intense debate or confrontation, while at the same time the opinions of individual citizens evolve gradually. Similarly, public policies may shift abruptly, even though the direction of public opinion has changed gradually.

3. *Incremental delay.* In attempting to maintain or build public support, policymakers tend to choose policies that involve incremental changes of existing routines and practices. Incremental choice involves "the continual successive comparison of the adopted policy with all nearby alternatives."[28] Delay is a consequence of many factors: incomplete information; the prevalence of in-

---

[28] Isnard and Zeeman, "Some Models from Catastrophe Theory," p. 52. Incremental delay is normally labelled the "Delay Rule" (Change policy in the direction that locally increases support). Other rules are "Maxwell's Rule" (Change policy to where support is maximum) and the "Voting Rule" (change policy to where the *base*, rather than the maximum, support is greatest).

tuitive (ordinary common sense) forms of analysis; political loyalties and commitments; institutional inertia; and historical precedent.

4. *Catastrophic policy change.* Incremental policy-making delays catastrophic change until the last possible moment, partly because smoothly evolving changes in the opinion of contending groups do not appear to require abrupt changes of direction. At a given point in time policymakers are compelled to make sudden and discontinuous shifts in policy in order to retain popular support.

So far, the primary application of catastrophe methodology in public policy analysis has been to the area of public opinion.[29] A sudden and discontinuous shift in West German energy policy, for example, has been explained by using catastrophe methodology to show how gradual changes in public opinion, together with incremental delay, produced a decision to suddenly terminate plans for the construction of a nuclear power plant in Kaiserstuhl, an agricultural area situated on the Rhine River in the state of Baden Wurttemberg.[30] Following public hearings construction was begun on the plant, only to be followed by sit-ins and the forcible removal of demonstrators from the site. Throughout this period public opinion gradually shifted in favor of the farming population in the region. Finally, after a number of incremental policy changes and considerable cost to the government, the project was abruptly abandoned.[31]

Catastrophe methodology provides concepts and techniques for understanding discontinuous policy processes. Yet it is a set of concepts and methods, rather than a "theory." As such it rests on the assumption that discontinuous processes observed in the past will repeat themselves in the future. While catastrophe methodology attempts to provide sound theoretical reasons for the occurrence of future events (as contrasted with simple beliefs that patterns observed in the past will repeat themselves in the future), catastrophe methodology is best viewed, at least for the time being, as a form of extrapolative forecasting. It is more a way to think about discontinuous policy futures than to make predictions derived from theory.

THEORETICAL FORECASTING

Theoretical forecasting methods help analysts to make *predictions* of future societal states on the basis of theoretical assumptions and current and historical data. In contrast to extrapolative forecasting, which uses assumptions

---

[29] See Isnard and Zeeman, "Some Models from Catastrophe Theory," pp. 45–60.

[30] See Rob Coppock, "Decision-Making When Public Opinion Matters," *Policy Sciences,* 8 (1977), 135–46.

[31] For a similar case, although presented in terms of "speculative augmentation" rather than catastrophe methodology, see Charles O. Jones, *Clean Air* (Pittsburgh, PA: University of Pittsburgh Press, 1975). Interestingly, Jones challenges the explanatory value of "disjointed incrementalism" (see Chapter 1), while Isnard and Zeeman see it as a major factor contributing to catastrophic change.

about historical recurrence to make *projections*, theoretical forecasting is based on assumptions about cause and effect contained in various theories. Whereas the logic of extrapolative forecasting is essentially inductive, the logic of theoretical forecasting is essentially deductive.

Deductive logic, as you will recall, is a form of reasoning where certain general statements (axioms, laws, propositions) are used to show the truth or falsity of other more specific statements, including predictions. In policy analysis deductive reasoning is most frequently used in connection with arguments from cause that seek to establish that if one event (X) occurs, another event (Y) will follow it. While the distinguishing feature of theoretical forecasting is that predictions are deduced from theoretical assumptions, it should be emphasized that deduction and induction are interrelated. The persuasiveness of a deductive argument is considerably increased if theoretically deduced predictions are observed time after time through empirical research. Similarly, an isolated empirical generalization ("The enemy chose to withdraw when threatened") is much more persuasive if backed by one or more assumptions contained in a theory ("The greater the costs of an alternative, the less likely that it will be chosen").[32]

In this section we consider several procedures that assist analysts in making theoretical forecasts: theory mapping, causal modeling, regression analysis, point and interval estimation, and correlational analysis. Some of these procedures (theory mapping) are concerned with ways to identify and systemize theoretical assumptions, while others (regression) provide better estimates of future societal states predicted from theory. Before we begin, however, it is essential to recognize that none of these techniques actually makes predictions; only theory can make predictions. In the words of a key contributor to the area of theoretical modeling:

> Owing to the inherent nature of the scientific method, there is a gap between the languages of theory and research. Causal inferences belong on the theoretical level, whereas actual research can only establish covariations and temporal sequences. . . . As a result, we can never actually demonstrate causal laws empirically.[33]

Theory Mapping

Theory mapping is a technique that helps analysts to identify and arrange key assumptions within a theory or causal argument.[34] Theory mapping can assist in uncovering four types of causal arguments: convergent,

---

[32] The classic discussion of relations between theory and empirical data (generalizations) in the social sciences is Robert K. Merton, *Social Theory and Social Structure*, rev. ed. (Glencoe, IL: The Free Press, 1957), pp. 95–99.

[33] Hubert M. Blalock, Jr., *Causal Inferences in Nonexperimental Research* (Chapel Hill, NC: University of North Carolina Press, 1964), p. 172.

[34] Adapted from John O'Shaughnessy, *Inquiry and Decision* (New York: Harper & Row, 1973), pp. 58–61; and M. C. Beardsley, *Thinking Straight* (Englewood Cliffs, NJ: Prentice-Hall, 1950).

divergent, serial, and cyclic. *Convergent arguments* are those in which two or more assumptions about causation are used to support a conclusion or claim. *Divergent arguments* are those in which a single assumption supports more than one claim or conclusion. By contrast, in *serial arguments* one conclusion or claim is used as an assumption to support a series of further conclusions or claims. Finally, *cyclic arguments* are serial arguments in which the last conclusion or claim in a series is connected with the first claim or conclusion in that series. The consequences of a cyclic argument may be positively or negatively self-reinforcing. These four types of causal arguments are illustrated in Figure 6–12.

A theory may contain a mixture of convergent, divergent, serial, and cyclic arguments. Several procedures may be used to uncover the overall structure of an argument or theory: (1) separate and number each assumption, which may be an axiom, law, or proposition; (2) underline the words that indicate claims ("therefore," "thus," "hence") or assumptions used to warrant claims ("since," "because," "for"); (3) when specific words ("therefore," and so on) have been omitted, but are clearly implied, supply the appropriate logical indicators in brackets; and (4) arrange numbered assumptions and claims in an arrow diagram that illustrates the structure of the causal argument or theory.

Let's apply these procedures to an important theory about public policy

FIGURE 6–12   Four types of causal arguments.

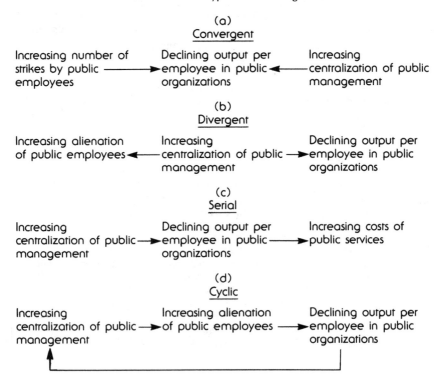

making. This theory, called "public choice," is concerned with the institutional conditions underlying efficient (and inefficient) government administration.[35] Public choice theorists have attempted to show on theoretical grounds how various institutional arrangements, particularly democratic forms of administration, will result in greater efficiency and public accountability. Public choice theory is also controversial, since it suggests that major problems of American government (inefficiency, inequity, unresponsiveness) are partly a consequence of the teachings of public administration, a discipline that for 50 and more years has emphasized centralization, hierarchy, and the consolidation of administrative powers.

In an effort to explain the inefficiency of governmental institutions one public choice theorist, Vincent Ostrom, offers the following argument, which has been mapped by underlining key words and supplying logical indicators in brackets:

> Gordon Tullock in *The Politics of Bureaucracy* (1965) analyzes the consequences which follow when [IT IS ASSUMED THAT] rational, self-interested individuals pursue maximizing strategies in very large public bureaucracies. Tullock's "economic man" is [THEREFORE] an ambitious public employee who seeks to advance his career opportunities for promotions within a bureaucracy. Since career advancement depends upon favorable recommendations by his superiors, a career-oriented public servant will act so as to please his superiors. [THEREFORE] Favorable information will be forwarded; unfavorable information will be repressed. [SINCE] Distortion of information will diminish control and create expectations which diverge from events generated by actions. Large-scale bureaucracies will thus become error-prone and cumbersome in adapting to rapidly changing conditions. [SINCE] Efforts to correct the malfunctioning of bureaucracy by tightening control will simply magnify errors. A decline in return to scale can [THEREFORE] be expected to result. [BECAUSE] The larger the organization becomes, the smaller the percent of its activities will relate to output and the larger the proportion of its efforts will be expended on management.[36]

In the argument just quoted we have already used procedures (2) and (3) of theory mapping. We have underlined words that indicate claims or assumptions underlying claims and supplied missing logical operators in brackets. Observe that the argument begins with an assumption about human nature ("economic man"), an assumption so fundamental that it is called an axiom. Axioms are regarded as true and self-evident; that is, they are believed to require no proof. Note also that this is a complex argument whose overall structure is difficult to grasp simply by reading the passage.

The structure of the argument can be more fully described when we complete steps (1) and (4). Using procedure (1) we separate and number

---

[35] See Vincent Ostrom, *The Intellectual Crisis in American Public Administration*, rev. ed. (University, AL: The University of Alabama Press, 1974).

[36] Ibid., p. 60. Underlined words and bracketed insertions have been added for purposes of illustrating theory mapping procedures.

each claim and its warranting assumption, changing some of the words to improve the clarity of the original argument.

[SINCE]	1. Public employees working in very large public bureaucracies are rational, self-interested individuals who pursue maximizing strategies ("economic man").
[AND]	2. The desire for career advancement is a consequence of rational self-interest.
[THEREFORE]	3. Public employees strive to advance their career opportunities.
[SINCE]	4. The advancement of career opportunities is a consequence of favorable recommendations from superiors.
[AND]	5. Favorable recommendations from superiors are a consequence of receiving favorable information from subordinates.
[THEREFORE]	6. Subordinates striving to advance their careers will forward favorable information and suppress unfavorable information.
[SINCE]	7. The repression of unfavorable information creates errors by management, reducing their flexibility in adapting to rapidly changing conditions.
[AND]	8. The repression of unfavorable information diminishes managerial control.
[THEREFORE]	9. Managers compensate for their loss of control by attempting to tighten control. Compensatory attempts to tighten control further encourage the repression of unfavorable information and (6) the magnification of management errors (7). Further (8) loss of control produces attempts to tighten control.
[AND]	10. Compensatory tightening of control is a consequence of the size of public bureaucracies.
[SINCE]	11. Compensatory tightening of control requires the expenditure of a larger proportion of effort on management activities, and a smaller proportion of output activities.
[THEREFORE]	12. The larger the public bureaucracy the smaller the proportion of effort expanded on output activities in relation to size, that is, the less the return to scale.

By separating and numbering each claim and warranting assumption, we have begun to expose the logical structure of the argument. Note that there are different types of causal arguments in this theory of governmental inefficiency. The first part of the quotation contains a serial argument that emphasizes the influence of employee motivation on information error and managerial control. The second part of the quotation contains another serial argument, but one that stresses the importance of the size of public bureaucracies. In addition, there is one cyclic argument (error magnification) and several divergent and convergent arguments.

The structure of the overall argument cannot be satisfactorily exposed until we complete procedure (4) and draw an arrow diagram that depicts the causal structure of the argument (Figure 6–13). Observe, first, that there are two serial arguments: (1, 2, 3) and (5, 4, 3). The second of these (5, 4, 3) can stand by itself and does not require the first (1, 2, 3), which rests exclusively on deductions from the axiom of "economic man." Second, there is one divergent argument (5, 4, 6) which indicates that the same factor (5) has multiple consequences. There are also three convergent arguments, (4, 2, 3), (3, 5, 6), and (8, 10, 9), which suggest in each case that there are two factors that explain the occurrence of the same event.

The arrow diagram also exposes two central features of this theoretical argument. It makes explicit an important potential relationship, denoted by the broken line between (10) and (6), which suggests that the size of public bureaucracies may independently affect the tendency to forward or suppress information. At the same time the arrow diagram helps identify a cyclic argument [6, 7, 8, 9] that is crucial to this theory. This part of the theory argues, in effect, that we may expect a cumulative increase in the amount

FIGURE 6–13   Arrow diagram illustrating the causal structure of an argument.

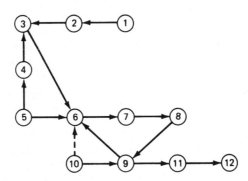

1. Rational Self-Interest (RSA)
2. Desire for Career Advancement (DCA)
3. Striving to Advance Career Opportunities (SAC)
4. Favorable Recommendations for Superiors (FRS)
5. Favorable Information from Subordinates (FIS)
6. Suppression of Unfavorable Information (SUI)
7. Management Error (ME)
8. Loss of Managerial Control (LMC)
9. Compensatory Tightening of Control (CTC)
10. Size of Public Bureaucracies (SPB)
11. Expenditures on Management (EM)
12. Return to Scale (RS)

of management error as a result of the self-reinforcing relationship among information suppression (6), management error (7), loss of management control (8), compensatory tightening of control (9), consequent further encouragement of information suppression (6), and so on. This cyclic argument, also known as a *positive feedback loop* (positive because the values of variables in the cycle continue to grow), suggests that any forecast based on public choice theory will predict a curvilinear pattern of growth in management error and government inefficiency.

If we had not used theory mapping procedures, it is doubtful that we would have uncovered the mixture of convergent, divergent, serial, and cyclic arguments contained in the structure of the theory. Particular causal assumptions—for example, the assumption that the size of public bureaucracies may combine with compensatory tightening of control to repress unfavorable information—are not clearly stated in the original passage. Because theory mapping makes the structure of claims and assumptions explicit it provides us with opportunities to use techniques of theoretical modeling.

Theoretical Modeling

Theoretical modeling refers to a broad range of techniques and assumptions for constructing simplified representations (models) of theories. Modeling is an essential part of theoretical forecasting, since analysts seldom make theoretical forecasts directly from theory. While analysts may begin with theories, they must develop models of these theories before they can actually forecast future events. Theoretical modeling is essential because theories are frequently so complex that they must be simplified before they may be applied to policy problems, and because the process of analyzing data to assess the plausibility of a theory involves constructing and testing models of theories, not the theories themselves.

In the last chapter we compared and contrasted models in terms of their aims (descriptive, normative), forms of expression (verbal, symbolic, procedural) and methodological functions (surrogates, perspectives). The majority of theoretical forecasting models are primarily descriptive, since they seek to predict rather than optimize some valued outcome. For the most part these models are also expressed symbolically, that is, in the form of mathematical symbols and equations. Note that we have already used several symbolic models in connection with extrapolative forecasting, for example, the regression equation or model $[Y_t = a + b(x)]$. Although it is not a causal model (since no explicit causal arguments are offered), it is nevertheless expressed symbolically.

In public policy analysis there are a number of standard forms of symbolic models which assist in making theoretical forecasts: causal models, linear programming models, input–output models, econometric models, microeconomic models, and system dynamics models.[37] As it is beyond the

---

[37] For a discussion of these and other standard model forms, see Martin Greenberger and others, *Models in the Policy Process* (New York: Russell Sage Foundation, 1976), Chap.

scope of this book to detail each of these model forms, we confine our attention to causal models. In our review we will outline the major assumptions, strengths and limitations, and applications of causal modeling.

Causal Modeling

Causal models are simplified representations of theories that attempt to explain and predict the causes and consequences of public policies. The basic assumption of causal models is that covariations between two or more variables—for example, covariations which show that increases in per capita income occur in conjunction with increases in welfare expenditures in American states—are a reflection of underlying generative powers (causes) and their consequences (effects). The relation between cause and effect is expressed by laws and propositions contained within a theory and modeled by the analyst. Returning to our illustration from public choice theory, observe that the statement "The proportion of total effort invested in management activities is determined by the size of public organizations" is a theoretical proposition. A model of that proposition might be $Y = a + b(X)$, where Y is the ratio of management to nonmanagement personnel, a and b are constants, and X is the total number of employees in public organizations of different sizes.

The strength of causal models is that they force analysts to make causal assumptions explicit. The limitation of causal models lies in the tendency of analysts to confuse covariations uncovered through statistical analysis with causal arguments. Causal inferences always come from *outside* a model, that is, from laws, propositions, or assumptions within some theory. In the words of Sewall Wright, one of the early pioneers in causal modeling, causal modeling procedures are "not intended to accomplish the impossible task of deducing causal relations from the values of the correlation coefficients."[38]

Causal modeling has been used to identify the economic, social, and political determinants of public policies in issue areas ranging from transportation to health, education and welfare.[39] One of the major claims of research based on causal modeling is that differences in political structures (for example, single vs. multiparty polities) do not directly affect such policy outputs as educational and welfare expenditures. On the contrary, differences in levels of socioeconomic development (income, industrialization,

---

4; and Saul I. Gass and Roger L. Sisson, eds., *A Guide to Models in Governmental Planning and Operations* (Washington, DC: U.S. Environmental Protection Agency, 1974). While these models are here treated as descriptive and symbolic (using the definitions of these terms provided in Chapter 5), some (for example, linear programming) are often treated as normative. Similarly, others (for example, system dynamics) are typically treated as procedural (or simulation) models. This should accentuate the point that the distinctions among types of models are relative and not absolute.

[38] Sewall Wright, "The Method of Path Coefficients," *Annals of Mathematical Statistics*, 5 (1934), 193; quoted in Fred N. Kerlinger and Elazar J. Pedhazur, *Multiple Regression in Behavioral Research* (New York: Holt, Rinehart and Winston, 1973), p. 305.

[39] For a review see Thomas R. Dye and Virginia H. Gray, "Symposium on Determinants of Public Policy: Cities, States, and Nations," *Policy Studies Journal*, 7, No. 4 (Summer 1979).

urbanization) determine differences in political structures, which in turn affect expenditures for education and welfare. This conclusion is controversial because it appears to contradict the commonly shared assumption that the content of public policy is determined by structures and processes of politics, including elections, representative mechanisms, and party competition.

One of the main statistical procedures used in causal modeling is *path analysis,* a specialized approach to linear regression that uses multiple (rather than single) independent variables. In using path analysis we hope to identify those independent variables (for example, income) which singly and in combination with other variables (for example, political participation) determine changes in a dependent variable (for example, welfare expenditures). An independent variable is presumed to be the cause of a dependent

FIGURE 6–14   Path diagram illustrating
a model of public choice theory.

1—Employees Per Public Organization (EPO)
2—Ratio of Managers to Non-Managers (RMN)
3—Costs in Tax Dollars Per Unit of Service (CUS)

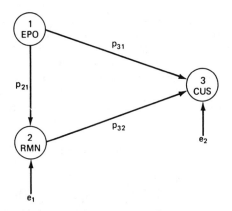

Note: The symbol p designates a causal path and the subscripts specify the direction of causation. p_{31} means that variable 3 is caused by variable 1. Variables that have no antecedent cause are called exogenous variables (that is, their cause is external to the system), while all others are called endogenous (that is, their cause is internal to the system). The symbol e (sometimes designated as u) is an error term, defined as the unexplained (residual) variance in an endogenous variable that is left over after taking into account the effects of the endogenous variable that precedes it in the path diagram. Error terms should be uncorrelated with each other and with other variables.

variable, which is presumed to be its effect. Estimates of cause and effect are called path coefficients, which express one-directional (recursive) causal relationships among independent and dependent variables. A standard way of depicting causal relationships is the path diagram. A path diagram looks very much like the arrow diagram used to map public choice theory, except that a path diagram contains estimates of the strength of the effects of independent on dependent variables. A path diagram has been used to model part of public choice theory in Figure 6–14. The advantage of path analysis and causal modeling is that they permit forecasts which are based on explicit theoretical assumptions about causes (the number of employees in individual public organizations) and their consequences (the ratio of managerial to nonmanagerial staff and costs in tax dollars per unit of public service). The limitation of these procedures, as already noted, is that they are not designed for the impossible task of inferring causation from estimates of relationships among variables. Although the absence of a relationship may be sufficient to infer that causation is *not* present, only theory permits us to make causal inferences and, hence, predictions.

Regression Analysis

A useful technique for estimating linear relationships among variables in theoretical forecasting models is regression analysis. *Regression analysis*, which has already been considered in slightly modified form in our discussion of trend estimation, is a general statistical procedure that yields precise estimates of the pattern and magnitude of a relationship between a dependent variable and one or more independent variables. When regression analysis is performed with one independent variable, it is called *simple regression*; if there are two or more independent variables it is called *multiple regression*. While many theoretical forecasting problems require multiple regression, we will limit ourselves to simple regression in the remainder of this section.[40]

Regression analysis is particularly useful in theoretical modeling. It provides summary measures of the pattern of a relationship between an independent and dependent variable. These summary measures include a regression line, which permits us to estimate values of the dependent variable simply by knowing values of the independent variable, and an overall measure of the vertical distances of observed values from the regression line. A summary measure of these distances, as we shall see, permits us to calculate the amount of error contained in a forecast. Since regression analysis is based on the principle of *least squares* it has a special advantage already noted in connection with linear trend estimation. It provides the one best "fit" between data and the regression line by ensuring that the squared distances between observed and estimated values represent a minimum or least value.[41]

---

[40] For a thorough and readable treatment of multiple regression and related techniques, see Kerlinger and Pedhazur, *Multiple Regression in Behavioral Research*.

[41] If this point is not clear you should return to the section on extrapolative forecasting and review Figure 6–8.

A second advantage of regression analysis is that it forces the analyst to decide which of two (or more) variables is the cause of the other, that is, to specify the independent (cause) and dependent (effect) variable. To make decisions about cause and effect, however, analysts must have some theory as to why one variable should be regarded as the cause of another. Although regression analysis is particularly well suited to problems of predicting effects from causes, the best that regression analysis can do (and it does this well) is to provide precise *estimates* of relationships predicted by a theory. Yet it is the theory and its simplified representation (model), and not regression analysis, that do the predicting. Regression analysis can only provide estimates of relationships between variables that, because of some theory, have been stated in the form of predictions.[42] For this reason analysts should employ theory-mapping procedures before using regression analysis.

To illustrate the application of regression analysis to problems of theoretical forecasting, let us suppose that municipal policymakers wish to determine the future maintenance costs of police patrol vehicles under two alternative policies. One policy involves regular police patrols for purposes of traffic and crime control. In 1980 the total maintenance costs for the 10 patrol cars were $18,250, or $1825 per vehicle. The total mileage for the 10 vehicles was 535,000 miles, that is, 53,500 miles per vehicle. A new policy now being considered is one that would involve "high-impact" police patrols as a way to create greater police visibility, respond more rapidly to citizens' calls for assistance, and ultimately, deter crime by increasing the probability that would-be offenders are apprehended.[43]

Local policymakers are interested in any means that will reduce crime. Yet there are increasing gaps between revenues and expenditures, and several citizens' groups have pressed for a cutback in municipal employees. Policymakers need some way to forecast, on the basis of their own mileage and maintenance records, how much it will cost if several of the ten vehicles are driven an additional 15,000 miles per year.

This forecasting problem may be effectively dealt with by using regression analysis. The relationship between cause and effect is reasonably clear, and the primary determinant of maintenance costs is vehicle usage as measured by miles driven.[44] A municipal policy analyst might therefore plot the values of the independent (X) and dependent (Y) variables on a *scatter*

---

[42] Recall the distinction between surrogate and perspective models in Chapter 5 and the example of the annual rainfall rate and reservoir depth. This and other examples show vividly that regression analysis, apart from its superiority in making precise estimates, cannot answer questions about which variable predicts another.

[43] Under the sponsorship of the Law Enforcement Assistance Administration high-impact patrolling has been used, with mixed success, in a number of large municipalities. See Elinor Chelimsky, "The Need for Better Data to Support Crime Control Policy," *Evaluation Quarterly*, 1, No. 3 (1977), 439–74.

[44] The question of causation is never certain, as illustrated by this example. Under certain conditions maintenance costs may affect miles driven, for example, if cost-conscious managers or policemen limit vehicle use in response to knowledge of high expenses. Similarly, annual mileage for certain vehicles may mean larger patrol areas, which in turn may be situated where road conditions are better (or worse) for cars.

diagram (*scatterplot*) which will show the pattern of the relationship (linear–nonlinear), the direction of the relationship (positive–negative), and the strength of the relationship (strong–moderate–weak) between annual mileage per vehicle and annual maintenance costs per vehicle (Figure 6–15). We assume that the pattern, direction, and strength of the relationship is linear, positive, and strong, as shown in Figure 6–15a.

Regression analysis assumes that variables are related in a linear pattern. While linear regression analysis may also be used with negative linear relationships (Figure 6–15b), it will produce serious errors if applied to curvilinear patterns such as those illustrated in Figure 6–15c and d. In such cases, as we saw earlier in the discussion of curve fitting, we must either

FIGURE 6–15   Scattergram illustrating different patterns and relationships between hypothetical annual maintenance costs and annual mileage per vehicle.

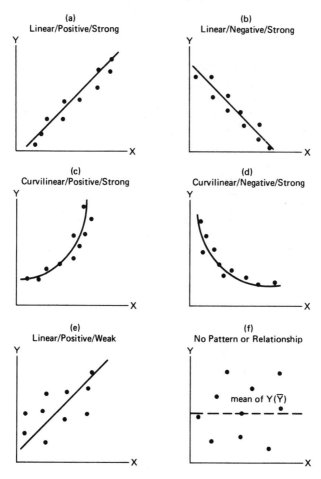

use nonlinear regression or transform values of variables (for example, by taking their logarithms) prior to applying conventional linear regression techniques. Regression analysis will yield less reliable estimates when data are widely scattered, as in Figure 6–15e. If data indicate no pattern or relationship (Figure 6–15f), the best estimate of changes in Y due to X is the average (mean) of values of Y.

Recall from our discussion of trend estimation that the straight line describing the relationship between X and Y variables is called a *regression line*. The equation used to fit the regression line to observed data in the scatter diagram is identical to that used to estimate linear trend, with several minor differences. The symbol Y_t (the subscript *t* refers to a trend value) is replaced with Y_c (the subscript *c* refers to a computed value). These different subscripts remind us that here, regression is applied to two substantive variables, whereas in linear trend estimation one of the variables is time. The formula for the regression equation is

$$Y_c = a + b(X)$$

where

a = the value of Y_c when X = 0, called the Y *intercept* because it shows where the computed regression line intercepts the Y-axis

b = the value of changes in Y_c due to a change of one unit in X, called the *slope* of the regression line because it indicates the steepness of the straight line

X = a given value of the independent variable

A second minor difference between the regression and trend equations is the computation of values of a and b. In regression analysis we do not work with original values of Y and coded time values of X but with *mean deviations*. A mean deviation is simply the difference between a given value of X or Y and the average (mean) of all values of X or Y. The formulas necessary to calculate the mean and mean deviations for X and Y are

$$\text{mean of X} = \overline{X} = \frac{\sum X}{n}$$

$$\text{mean of Y} = \overline{Y} = \frac{\sum Y}{n}$$

$$\text{mean deviation of X} = x = X - \overline{X}$$

$$\text{mean deviation of Y} = y = Y - \overline{Y}$$

The values of a and b in the regression equation are computed with the following formulas:

$$b = \frac{\sum(xy)}{\sum(x^2)}$$

$$a = \overline{Y} - b(\overline{X})$$

Let us now return to the forecasting problem facing our municipal policy analyst. All data needed to solve the regression equation are provided in Table 6–7. Observe that column (1) lists the 10 vehicles in the municipal fleet. Annual mileage (X) and maintenance costs (Y) are expressed in thousands of miles and dollars [columns (2) and (3)] for ease of calculation. At the bottom of columns (1) and (2) we have also calculated the sums of X $(\sum X)$ and Y $(\sum Y)$ and their respective means $(\overline{X} = \sum X/n = 53.6$ and $\overline{Y} = \sum Y/n = 1.785)$. Columns (4) and (5) contain the deviations of each X and Y value from its respective mean. These mean deviations $(x = \overline{X} - X$ and $y = Y - \overline{Y})$ show us the spread of each X and Y value about its own mean. Note that the values of the mean deviation sum to zero [bottom of columns (4) and (5)]. This is because the means of X and Y are averages, which guarantee that values above the mean will cancel those below the mean.

The mean deviations $(x$ and $y)$ exhibit the spread of each value around the X and Y means. Nevertheless, they cannot be used as a summary measure of this spread, since they sum to zero. For this reason mean deviations are squared [columns (7) and (8)], thus eliminating negative signs, and summed. These sums, called the *sums of squares* (which is a shortened form of "sums of the squares of mean deviations"), provide an overall summary of the spread of X and Y values around their means. Finally, in column (6) we have multiplied the mean deviations $(x$ and $y)$, obtaining *deviation cross-products* (xy). These cross-products are an expression of the pattern and strength of relationship between X and Y, but one that takes into account the spread of X and Y scores.

To estimate future maintenance costs under the high-impact police patrol program we first solve the regression equation

$$Y_c = a + b(X)$$

by substituting calculations from the worksheet into formulas for a and b. Hence

$$b = \frac{\sum(xy)}{\sum(x^2)} = \frac{179.54}{5610.5} = 0.032$$
$$a = \overline{Y} - b(\overline{X}) = 1.785 - 0.032(53.6) = 0.07$$
$$Y_c = 0.07 + 0.032(X)$$

This regression equation means that the regression line intercepts the Y axis at 0.07 thousand dollars (that is, $70); and that maintenance costs increase by 0.032 thousand dollars (that is, $32) for every 1000 miles driven. On the basis of this information we can make precise estimates of maintenance costs on the basis of knowledge of annual miles per vehicle. Computed values (Y_c) for each original value of X (column (9)) may be plotted on a graph to create the regression line. Finally, our forecast indicates that the city will incur an additional $4870 in expenses by adopting high-impact patroling, since an additional 150 thousand miles will result in $Y_{150} = 0.07 + 0.032(150) = 4.87 thousand dollars.

TABLE 6–7 Worksheet for Estimating Future Maintenance Costs from Annual Mileage per Vehicle

VEHICLE NUMBER (1)	MILEAGE PER VEHICLE (THOUSANDS OF MILES) (X) (2)	MAINTENANCE COSTS PER VEHICLE (THOUSANDS OF DOLLARS) (Y) (3)	X MEAN DEVIATION $(X - \bar{X})$ (x) (4)	Y MEAN DEVIATION $(Y - \bar{Y})$ (y) (5)	DEVIATION CROSS-PRODUCT (xy) (6)	X MEAN DEVIATION SQUARED (x^2) (7)	Y MEAN DEVIATION SQUARED (y^2) (8)	ESTIMATED VALUE OF Y (Y_c) (9)
1	24	0.45	−29.5	−1.335	39.38	870.25	1.782	0.838
2	23	1.2	−30.5	−0.585	17.84	930.25	0.342	0.806
3	30	0.8	−23.5	−0.985	23.15	552.25	0.970	1.030
4	40	1.1	−13.5	−0.685	9.25	182.25	0.469	1.400
5	48	1.9	−5.5	0.115	−0.633	30.25	0.013	1.606
6	65	1.8	11.5	0.015	0.173	132.25	0.0002	2.150
7	65	2.3	11.5	0.515	5.923	132.25	0.265	2.150
8	60	2.6	6.5	0.815	5.298	42.25	0.664	1.990
9	90	2.5	36.5	0.715	26.098	1332.25	0.511	2.950
10	91	3.2	37.5	1.415	53.063	1406.25	2.002	2.982
$n = 10$	$\sum X = 536$ $\bar{X} = 53.6$	$\sum Y = 17.85$ $\bar{Y} = 1.785$	0.0	0.0	$\sum(xy) = 179.54$	$\sum(x^2) = 5610.5$	$\sum(y^2) = 7.02$	$\sum Y_c = 17.85$

$$b = \frac{\sum(xy)}{\sum(x^2)} = \frac{179.54}{5610.50} = 0.032$$

$$a = \bar{Y} - b(\bar{X}) = 1.785 - 0.032(53.6) = 0.0698 \text{ or } 0.07$$

$$Y_c = a + b(X) = 0.07 + 0.032(X)$$

$$Y_{150} = 0.07 + 0.032(150) = 4.87 = \$4870$$

Point and Interval Estimation

Regression analysis, as we have seen, enables us to fit a regression line to data in such a way that the squared distances between data points and the regression line are a minimum or least value (see Figure 6–8). This means that regression analysis not only uses (rather than loses) information about variations in costs and mileage; it also permits us to make a sound estimate of the central tendency in a relationship and compare this estimate with observed values in a scatter diagram. Because the distances between the regression line and individual data points are minimized, the regression estimate contains less error than other kinds of estimates, for example, those calculated on the basis of average costs per mile driven. Regression analysis also allows us to calculate the probable error in our estimate. This may be done in several ways (Table 6–8). One way is simply to subtract each value of Y_c [column (3)] from its corresponding observed value [column (2)]. This tells us how much distance there is between each pair of estimated and observed values. The error of a regression estimate, expressed by the distance between values of Y and Y_c, increases in direct proportion to the amount of scatter. The greater the scatter, the less accurate the estimate.

TABLE 6–8   Calculation of Standard Error of Estimated Maintenance Costs

VEHICLE NUMBER (1)	OBSERVED MAINTENANCE COSTS (Y) (2)	ESTIMATED MAINTENANCE COSTS (Y_c) (3)	OBSERVED MINUS ESTIMATED COSTS ($Y - Y_c$) (4)	OBSERVED MINUS ESTIMATED COSTS SQUARED ($Y - Y_c)^2$ (5)
1	0.45	0.838	−0.388	0.151
2	1.2	0.806	0.394	0.155
3	0.8	1.030	−0.230	0.053
4	1.1	1.400	−0.300	0.090
5	1.9	1.606	0.294	0.086
6	1.8	2.150	−0.350	0.123
7	2.3	2.150	0.150	0.023
8	2.6	1.990	0.610	0.372
9	2.5	2.950	−0.450	0.203
10	3.2	2.982	0.218	0.048
$n = 10$	$\sum Y = 17.85$	$\sum Y_c = 17.85$	$\sum(Y - Y_c) = 0$	1.304

$$S_{y \cdot x} = \sqrt{\frac{\sum(Y - Y_c)^2}{n}} = \sqrt{\frac{\sum(Y - Y_c)^2}{10}} = \sqrt{\frac{1.304}{10}} = 0.36111$$

$$Y_i = Y_c \pm Z(S_{y \cdot x})$$

$$Y_{i(150)} = 4.87 \pm 2(0.3611) = 4.87 \pm 0.72222$$

$$= 4.14778 \text{ to } 5.59222$$

$$= \$4147.78 \text{ to } \$5592.22$$

Another way to calculate error is to sum and average these distances. Because one of the properties of linear regression is that these distances equal zero when they are added up [that is, $\sum(Y - Y_c) = 0$], we must square them before we divide by the number of cases to find the average. Column (4) of Table 6–8 shows that the average squared error (also called the variance of an estimate) is 1.304. This expression of error, while useful for certain calculations to be described in a moment, is difficult to interpret. Fortunately, the square root of this value is a good approximation of the error that will occur about two-thirds of the time in a regression estimate.[45] The square root of the average squared error, called the *standard error of estimate,* is calculated with the following formula:[46]

$$S_{y \cdot x} = \sqrt{\frac{\sum(Y - Y_c)^2}{n}}$$

where

$(Y - Y_c)^2$ = the squared difference between observed and estimated values of the dependent variable

n = the number of cases

In the example above the standard error of estimate is

$$S_{y \cdot x} = \sqrt{\frac{\sum(Y - Y_c)^2}{n}} = \sqrt{\frac{1.304}{10}}$$

$$= \sqrt{.1304} = 0.3611 \text{ thousand}$$

$$= \$361.11 \text{ in annual maintenance costs}$$

What this means is that any actual value of maintenance costs is likely to be $361.11 above or below an estimated value about two-thirds of the time. The figure of $361.11 is one standard error ($1 \times \$361.11$); two standard errors are $722.22 ($2 \times \$361.11$); and three standard errors are $1,083.33 ($3 \times \$361.11$). The standard error gives us a *probability interpretation* of these values, since one standard error unit will occur about two-thirds (actually 68.3 percent) of the time; two standard error units will occur about 95 percent (actually, 95.4 percent) of the time; and three standard error units will occur about 99 percent (actually 99.7 percent) of the time.

---

[45] For readers who recall the normal curve, the standard error is the standard deviation of the average squared error. One standard error is one standard deviation unit to the left or right of the mean of a normal distribution and therefore includes the middle 68.3 percent of all values in the distribution. In the example above we have assumed for purposes of illustration that data are normally distributed.

[46] Note that we divide by n, because the 10 vehicles constitute the entire population of vehicles under analysis. If we were working with a sample we would divide by $n - 1$. This is a way of providing an unbiased estimate of the variance in the population sampled. Most packaged computer programs use $n - 1$, even though sampling may not have occurred.

The standard error of estimate allows us to make estimates that take error into account systematically. Rather than make simple *point estimates*—that is, estimates that produce a single value of Y_c—we can make *interval estimates* that yield values of Y_c expressed in terms of one or more standard units of error. If we want to be 95 percent confident that our estimate is accurate (this is usually regarded as a minimum standard of accuracy), we will want to express our estimate in terms of two intervals above and below the original point estimate. We can use the following formula to find out how much error we might expect in our point estimate of $4870 [Y_{150} = 0.07 + 0.032(150) = 4.87$ thousand dollars] 95 percent of the time:

$$Y_i = Y_c + Z(S_{y \cdot x})$$
$$= 4.87 \pm 2(0.3611)$$
$$= 4.87 \pm 0.72222 = 4.14778 \text{ to } 5.59222$$
$$= \$4147.78 \text{ to } \$5592.22$$

where

Y_c = the point estimate of Y

Z = a standard error unit which takes the value of 2 (95 percent confidence) in this case

$S_{y \cdot x}$ = the value (0.3611) of one standard error unit

Y_i = an interval estimate of Y ($\pm$ 0.72222)

Correlational Analysis

Regression analysis has an additional feature of importance to theoretical forecasting: It permits us to use *correlational analysis* to interpret relationships. Recall that different scatter diagrams not only exhibit the pattern of a relationship but also its direction and strength (see Figure 6–15). Yet it is desirable that we have measures of the direction and strength of these relationships, not just the visual images contained in scatter diagrams. Two measures that yield such information can be calculated from the worksheet already prepared for estimating future maintenance costs (Table 6–7). The first of these measures is the *coefficient of determination* (r^2), which is a summary measure or index of the amount of variation in the dependent variable explained by the independent variable. The second is the *coefficient of correlation* (r), which is the square root of the coefficient of determination. The coefficient of correlation, which varies between -1.0 and $+1.0$, tells us whether the direction of the relationship is positive or negative and how strong it is. If r is 0, there is no relationship, whereas a value of $\pm$ 1.0 (that is, positive or negative) indicates a maximal relationship. Unlike the coefficient of correlation (r), the coefficient of determination (r^2) takes a positive sign only and varies between 0.0 and 1.0. The formulas for both coefficients are applied below to our data on maintenance costs and mileage (see Table 6–7).

$$r^2 = \frac{b(\sum xy)}{\sum(y^2)} = \frac{0.032(179.54)}{7.02} = 0.818 \text{ or } 0.82$$

$$r = \sqrt{r^2} = \sqrt{0.818} = 0.90$$

The same analysis carried out by hand in Tables 6–7 and 6–8 has been done with MYSTAT (Exhibit 6–2). The same coefficients and measures have been obtained with MYSTAT but with much greater efficiency. When we inspect the MYSTAT output we see that the first line identifies the dependent variable, maintenance costs per vehicle, which has been labeled MAINCOST. The first line also gives the number of observations, N: 10, and provides the correlation coefficient (r), designated as MULTIPLE R: .905. At the end of the first line of output we see the coefficient of determination (r^2), designated as SQUARED MULTIPLE R: .818. All these coefficients are in agreement with our hand calculations.

At the end of the second line we find the STANDARD ERROR OF ESTIMATE: 0.399. This value is somewhat larger than that obtained in Table 6–7, because MYSTAT uses $n - 1$ in the denominator. This is appropriate for samples but increases the standard error of estimate ($S_{x \cdot y}$). The fourth line of the MYSTAT output also provides us with the value of the intercept (CONSTANT = 0.070), which conforms to the output in Table 6–7. The slope of the regression line is also given in MILEAGE = 0.032, which is also identical. Finally, the table marked ANALYSIS OF VARI-

---

EXHIBIT 6–2   MYSTAT Output for Table 6–7

DEP VAR:MAINCOST   N: 10   MULTIPLE R: .905   SQUARED MULTIPLE R: .818
ADJUSTED SQUARED MULTIPLE R: .796   STANDARD ERROR OF ESTIMATE: 0.399

VARIABLE	COEFFICIENT	STD ERROR	STD COEF	TOLERANCE	T	P(2 TAIL)
CONSTANT	0.070	0.312	0.000	.	0.223	0.829
MILEAGE	0.032	0.005	0.905	.100E+01	6.005	0.000

ANALYSIS OF VARIANCE

SOURCE	SUM-OF-SQUARES	DF	MEAN-SQUARE	F-RATIO	P
REGRESSION	5.746	1	5.746	36.058	0.000
RESIDUAL	1.275	8	0.159		

ANCE provides a breakdown of that part of the total SUM-OF-SQUARES due to the effects of regressing the dependent variable on the independent variable (REGRESSION = 5.746). The output also provides that part of the sum of squares due to error, that is, RESIDUAL = 1.275. If we add the REGRESSION and RESIDUAL sum of squares and divide this sum into the REGRESSION sum of squares we will obtain the coefficient of determination (SQUARED MULTIPLE R). Thus

$$\frac{5.746}{5.746 + 1.275} = 0.818 = 0.82$$

These coefficients tell us that 82 percent of the variance in annual maintenance costs is explained by annual mileage ($r^2 = 0.82$) and that the direction and strength of the relationship between these two variables is positive and strong ($r = 0.90$). Note that the size of these coefficients decreases in direct proportion to the distances of observed values from the regression line. Stated in another way, the size of the coefficients of determination and correlation are negatively related to the standard error of estimate. The more the error, the weaker the relationship. Regression analysis, when supplemented by interval estimation and coefficients of determination and correlation, provides much more information of direct relevance to policymakers than other forms of estimation. For example, simple estimates of average costs per mile, apart from their relative inaccuracy, neither provide summary measures of the direction and strength of relationships; nor do they anticipate forecasting errors in a systematic way. In this and many other cases regression analysis can assist policymakers in dealing with the uncertainties that accompany efforts to predict the future.

JUDGMENTAL FORECASTING

In contrast to extrapolative and theoretical forecasting techniques, where empirical data and/or theories play a central role, judgmental forecasting techniques attempt to elicit and synthesize informed judgments. Judgmental forecasts are often based on arguments from insight, since assumptions about the creative powers of persons making the forecast (and not their social positions per se) are used to warrant claims about the future. The logic of intuitive forecasting is essentially retroductive, since analysts begin with a conjectured state of affairs (for example, a normative future such as world peace) and then work their way back to the data or assumptions necessary to support the conjecture. Nevertheless, inductive, deductive, and retroductive reasoning are never completely separable in practice. Judgmental forecasting is therefore often supplemented by various extrapolative and theoretical forecasting procedures.[47]

[47] In fact, even large-scale econometric models are dependent on judgmental forecasting. The best sources on this point are Ascher, *Forecasting*; Ascher, "The Forecasting Potential of Complex Models"; and McNown, "On the Use of Econometric Models."

In this section we review three intuitive forecasting techniques: Delphi technique, cross-impact analysis, and the feasibility assessment technique. These and other techniques, most of which have been widely used in government and industry, are particularly well suited to the kinds of problems we described (Chapter 5) as messy, ill structured, or squishy. Since one of the characteristics of ill-structured problems is that policy alternatives and their consequences are unknown, it follows that in such circumstances there are no relevant theories and/or empirical data to make a forecast. Under these conditions judgmental forecasting techniques are particularly useful and even necessary.

The Delphi Technique

Delphi technique is a judgmental forecasting procedure for obtaining, exchanging, and developing informed opinion about future events. Delphi technique (named after Appollo's shrine at Delphi, where Greek oracles sought to foresee the future) was developed in 1948 by researchers at the Rand Corporation and has since been used in many hundreds of forecasting efforts in the public and private sectors. Originally, the technique was applied to problems of military strategy, but its application gradually shifted to forecasts in other contexts: education, technology, marketing, transportation, mass media, medicine, information processing, research and development, space exploration, housing, budgeting, and the quality of life.[48] While the technique originally emphasized the use of experts to verify forecasts based on empirical data, Delphi began to be applied to problems of values forecasting in the 1960s.[49] The Delphi technique has been used by analysts in countries ranging from the United States, Canada, and the United Kingdom to Japan and the Soviet Union.

Early applications of Delphi were motivated by a concern with the apparent ineffectiveness of committees, expert panels, and other group processes. The technique was designed to avoid several sources of distorted communication found in groups: domination of the group by one or several persons; pressures to conform to peer group opinion; personality differences and interpersonal conflict; and the difficulty of publicly opposing persons in positions of authority. To avoid these problems early applications of the Delphi technique emphasized five basic principles: (1) *anonymity*: all experts or knowledgeables respond as physically separated individuals whose anonymity is strictly preserved; (2) *iteration*: the judgments of individuals are aggregated and communicated back to all participating experts in a series of two or more rounds, thus permitting social learning and the modification

---

[48] Thorough accounts may be found in Harold Sackman, *Delphi Critique* (Lexington, MA: D.C. Heath and Company, 1975); and Juri Pill, "The Delphi Method: Substance, Contexts, a Critique and an Annotated Bibliography," *Socio-Economic Planning Sciences*, 5 (1971), 57–71.

[49] See, for example, Nicholas Rescher, *Delphi and Values* (Santa Monica, CA: The Rand Corporation, 1969).

of prior judgments; (3) *controlled feedback:* the communication of aggregated judgments occurs in the form of summary measures of responses to questionnaires; (4) *statistical group response:* summaries of individual responses are presented in the form of measures of central tendency (usually the median), dispersion (the interquartile range), and frequency distributions (histograms and frequency polygons); and (5) *expert consensus:* the central aim, with few exceptions, is to create conditions under which a consensus among experts is likely to emerge as the final and most important product.

These principles represent a characterization of conventional Delphi. *Conventional Delphi*, which dominated the field well into the late 1960s, should be contrasted with policy Delphi. *Policy Delphi* is a constructive response to the limitations of conventional Delphi and an attempt to create new procedures which match the complexities of policy problems. In the words of one of its chief architects:

> Delphi as it originally was introduced and practiced tended to deal with technical topics and seek a consensus among homogeneous groups of experts. The Policy Delphi, on the other hand, seeks to generate the strongest possible opposing views on the potential resolution of a major policy issue . . . a policy issue is one for which there are no experts, only informed advocates and referees.[50]

While policy Delphi is based on two of the same principles as conventional Delphi (iteration and controlled feedback), it also introduces several new ones:

1. *Selective anonymity.* Participants in a policy Delphi remain anonymous only during the initial rounds of a forecasting exercise. After contending arguments about policy alternatives have surfaced, participants are asked to debate their views publicly.

2. *Informed multiple advocacy.* The process for selecting participants is based on criteria of interest and knowledgeableness, rather than "expertise" per se. In forming a Delphi group investigators therefore attempt to select as representative a group of informed advocates as may be possible in specific circumstances.

3. *Polarized statistical response.* In summarizing individual judgments, measures that purposefully accentuate disagreement and conflict are used. While conventional measures may also be used (median, range, standard deviation), policy Delphi supplements these with various measures of polarization among individuals and groups.

4. *Structured conflict.* Starting from the assumption that conflict is a normal feature of policy issues, every attempt is made to use disagreement and dissension for creatively exploring alternatives and their consequences. In addition, efforts are made to surface and make explicit the assumptions and arguments that underlie contending positions. The outcomes of a policy Del-

---

[50] Murray Turoff, "The Design of a Policy Delphi," *Technological Forecasting and Social Change*, 2, No. 2 (1970), 149–71. See also Harold A. Linstone and Murray Turoff, eds., *The Delphi Method: Techniques and Applications* (New York: Addison-Wesley, 1975).

phi are nevertheless completely open, which means that consensus as well as a continuation of conflict might be results of the process.

5. *Computer conferencing.* Where possible, computer consoles are used to structure a continuous process of anonymous interaction among physically separated individuals. Computer conferencing eliminates the need for a series of separate Delphi rounds.

A policy Delphi may be conducted in a number of different ways, depending on the context and the skill and ingenuity of the persons using the technique. Since policy Delphi is a major research undertaking, it involves a large number of technical questions, including sampling, questionnaire design, reliability and validity, and data analysis and interpretation. Although these questions are beyond the scope of this chapter,[51] it is important to obtain an overall understanding of the process of conducting a policy Delphi. A policy Delphi can best be visualized as a series of interrelated steps.[52]

Step 1. Issue specification. Here the analyst must decide what specific issues should be addressed by informed advocates. For example, if the area of concern is national drug abuse policy, one of the issues might be "The personal use of marijuana should or should not be legalized." One of the central problems of this step is deciding what proportion of issues should be generated by participants, and what proportion should be generated by the analyst. If the analyst is thoroughly familiar with the issue area, it is possible to develop a list of issues prior to the first round of the Delphi. These issues may be included in the first questionnaire, although respondents should be free to add or delete issues.

Step 2. Selection of advocates. Here the key stakeholders in an issue area should be selected. To select a group of advocates who represent conflicting positions, however, it is necessary to use explicit sampling procedures. One way to do this is to use "snowball" sampling. Here the analyst begins by identifying one advocate, usually someone who is known to be influential in the issue area, and asking that person to name two others who agree and disagree most with his or her own position. These two persons are asked to do the same thing, which results in two more persons who agree and disagree maximally, and so on (hence the term "snowball" sample). Advocates should be as different as possible, not only in terms of positions attributed to them, but also in terms of their relative influence, formal

---

[51] Unfortunately, there are few shortcuts to developing methodologically sound questionnaires for use in policy Delphis. On questionnaire construction the best short introduction is Earl R. Babbie, *Survey Research Methods* (Belmont, CA: Wadsworth, 1973). On reliability and validity see Fred N. Kerlinger, *Foundations of Behavioral Research*, 3rd ed. (New York: Holt, Rinehart and Winston, 1985), pp. 442–78. A useful general purpose handbook on these questions is Delbert C. Miller, *Handbook of Research Design and Social Measurement*, 5th ed. (Newbury Park, CA: Sage Publications, 1991).

[52] See Turoff, "The Design of a Policy Delphi," pp. 88–94.

authority, and group affiliation. The size of the sample might range from 10 to 30 persons, although this depends on the nature of the issue. The more complex the issue, and hence the more heterogeneous the participants, the larger the sample must be to be representative of the range of advocates.

Step 3. Questionnaire design.   Since a policy Delphi takes place in a series of rounds, analysts must decide which specific items will go in questionnaires to be used in the first and subsequent rounds. Yet the second-round questionnaire can only be developed after the results of the first round are analyzed; the third-round questionnaire must await results of the second round; and so on. For this reason only the first-round questionnaire can be drafted in advance. Although the first-round questionnaires may be relatively unstructured (with many open-ended items), they may also be relatively structured, provided the analyst has a good idea of the major issues. First-round questionnaires may include several types of questions: (1) *forecasting items* requesting that respondents provide subjective estimates of the probability of occurrence of particular events, (2) *issue items* requesting respondents to rank issues in terms of their importance, (3) *goal items* that solicit judgments about the desirability and/or feasibility of pursuing certain goals, and (4) *options items* requesting that respondents identify alternative courses of action that may contribute to the attainment of goals and objectives.

Several types of scales are available to measure responses to each of these four types of items. One procedure is to use different scales with different types of items. For example, a certainty scale may be used primarily with forecast items; an importance scale with issue items; desirability and feasibility scales with goal items; and some combination of these scales with options items. The best way to show what is involved is to illustrate the way that items and scales are presented in a policy Delphi questionnaire. This has been done in Table 6–9.

Observe that the scales in Table 6–9 do not permit neutral answers, although "No Judgment" responses are permitted for all items. This restriction on neutral responses is designed to bring out conflict and disagreement, an important aim of the policy Delphi. An important part of the construction of questionnaires is pretesting among a sample of advocates and determining the reliability of responses.

Step 4. Analysis of first-round results.   When the questionnaires are returned after the first round, analysts attempt to determine the initial positions on forecasts, issues, goals, and options. Typically, some items believed to be desirable or important are also believed to be unfeasible, and vice versa. Since there will be conflicting assessments among the various advocates, it is important to use summary measures that not only express the central tendency in the set of responses but also describe the extent of dispersion or polarization. These summary measures are used, not only to eliminate items that are uniformly important, undesirable, unfeasible and/or

TABLE 6–9 Types of Items and Scales Used in a Policy Delphi Questionnaire

TYPE OF ITEM	ITEM	SCALE				
Forecast	According to a recent projection by researchers at the National Institute of Mental Health the number of marijuana users per 1000 persons in the general population will double between 1980 and 1990. How certain are you that this projection is reliable?	Certainly Reliable 1 [ ]	Reliable 2 [ ]	Risky 3 [ ]	Unreliable 4 [ ]	No Judgment 0 [ ]
Issue	The personal use of marijuana *should/should not* be legalized. [Circle one.] How important is this issue relative to others?	Very Important 1 [ ]	Important 2 [ ]	Slightly Important 3 [ ]	Unimportant 4 [ ]	No Judgment 0 [ ]
Goal	One goal of national policy might be to increase public awareness of the difference between drug use (responsible) and abuse (irresponsible). How *desirable* is this objective?	Very Desirable 1 [ ]	Desirable 2 [ ]	Undesirable 3 [ ]	Very Undesirable 4 [ ]	No Judgment 0 [ ]
Options	It has been suggested that drug abuse education programs contribute to the reduction of potential users in the general population. How *feasible* is this policy option?	Definitely Feasible 1 [ ]	Possibly Feasible 2 [ ]	Possibly Unfeasible 3 [ ]	Definitely Unfeasible 4 [ ]	No Judgment 0 [ ]

Note: For additional information, see Irene Ann Jillson, "The National Drug Abuse Policy Delphi: Progress Report and Findings to Date," in *The Delphi Method: Techniques and Applications*, ed. Harold A. Linstone and Murray Turoff (New York: Addison-Wesley, 1975), pp. 124–59.

uncertain, but also serve in the second-round questionnaire as a means to communicate to participants the results of the first round. The calculation and subsequent presentation of these summary measures of central tendency, dispersion, and polarization are best illustrated graphically. Assume for purposes of illustration that ten advocates in the first round of a hypothetical policy Delphi provided different assessments of the desirability and feasibility of two drug-control goals: to reduce the supply of illicit drugs and to increase public awareness of the difference between responsible and irresponsible drug use. Let us imagine that the responses were those presented in Table 6–10.

Observe that some respondents (advocates 2, 8, and 9) believe that the goal of reducing the supply of illicit drugs is very undesirable but possibly or definitely feasible, while others (advocates 1, 5, 7, and 10) believe that this goal is very desirable but definitely unfeasible. When we compare these inconsistencies between desirability and feasibility with responses under goal 2 (public awareness), we find much less inconsistency in the latter set of scores. All of this suggests that the responses to goal 1, while much lower in average desirability and feasibility, also reflect the kinds of important conflicts that policy Delphi is specially designed to address. In this case analysts would not want to eliminate this item. Rather they would want to

TABLE 6–10 Hypothetical Responses in First-Round Policy Delphi: Desirability and Feasibility of Drug-Control Objectives

ADVOCATE	GOAL 1 (REDUCE SUPPLY)		GOAL 2 (PUBLIC AWARENESS)	
	Desirability	*Feasibility*	*Desirability*	*Feasibility*
1	1	4	1	1
2	4	1	2	2
3	3	3	2	1
4	4	2	1	2
5	1	4	2	1
6	2	3	2	1
7	1	4	1	1
8	4	2	1	2
9	4	1	2	2
10	1	4	1	2
	$\Sigma = 25$	$\Sigma = 28$	$\Sigma = 15$	$\Sigma = 15$
	Md = 2.5	Md = 3.0	Md = 1.5	Md = 1.5
	Mn = 2.5	Mn = 2.8	Mn = 1.5	Mn = 1.5
	Range = 3.0	Range = 3.0	Range = 1.0	Range = 1.0

Note: The median (Md) in a set of scores is the value of the score that falls in the middle when the scores are arranged in order of magnitude. If the number of scores is even (as above) the median is the value of the score which is halfway between the two middle scores. The median is normally used in place of the mean (Mn) when we do not know if the intervals between measures (for example, the intervals between 1 and 2 and 3 and 4) are equidistant.

report these conflicts as part of the second-round instrument, requesting that respondents provide the reasons, assumptions, or arguments that led them to positions that were so different. Another way to bring out such disagreements is to construct and report an average *polarization measure*, which may be defined as the absolute difference among scores for all combinations of respondents answering a particular question.[53]

Step 5. Development of subsequent questionnaires. Questionnaires must be developed for second, third, fourth, or fifth rounds (most policy Delphis involve three to five rounds). As indicated previously, the results of prior rounds are used as a basis for subsequent ones. One of the most important aspects of policy Delphi occurs in these rounds, since it is here that advocates have an opportunity to observe the results of immediately preceding rounds and offer explicit reasons, assumptions, and arguments for their respective judgments. Note that later rounds do not simply include information about central tendency, dispersion, and polarization; they also include a summary of arguments offered for the most important conflicting judgments. In this way the policy Delphi promotes a reasoned debate and maximizes the probability that deviant and sometimes insightful judgments are not lost in the process. By the time the last round of questionnaires is completed, all advocates have had an opportunity to state their initial positions on forecasts, issues, goals, and options; to examine and evaluate the reasons why their positions differ from those of others; and to reevaluate and change their positions.

Step 6. Organization of group meetings. One of the last tasks is to bring advocates together for a face-to-face discussion of the reasons, assumptions, and arguments that underlie their various positions. This face-to-face meeting, since it occurs after all advocates have had a chance to reflect on their positions and those of others, may create an atmosphere of informed confidence that would not be possible in a typical committee setting. Face-to-face discussions also create conditions where advocates may argue their positions intensely and receive immediate feedback.

Step 7. Preparation of final report. There is no guarantee that respondents will have reached consensus but much reason to hope that creative ideas about issues, goals, options, and their consequences will be the most important product of a policy Delphi. The report of final results will therefore include a review of the various issues and options available, taking care that all conflicting positions and underlying arguments are presented

---

[53] Ibid., p. 92; and Jerry B. Schneider, "The Policy Delphi: A Regional Planning Application," *Technological Forecasting and Social Change*, 3, No. 4 (1972). The total number of combinations (C) is calculated by the formula $C = k(k - 1)/2$, where k is the number of responses to a particular item. The average difference is obtained by computing the numerical distance between all combinations, adding them up, and dividing by the number of respondents. This requires that we ignore the signs (plus or minus). Another procedure is to retain the signs, square each difference (eliminating minus signs), sum and average.

fully. This report may then be passed on to policymakers, who may use the results of the policy Delphi as one source of information in arriving at decisions.

Cross-Impact Analysis

Delphi technique is closely related to another widely used judgmental forecasting technique called cross-impact analysis. *Cross-impact* analysis, developed by the same Rand Corporation researchers responsible for early applications of conventional Delphi,[54] is a technique that elicits informed judgments about the probability of occurrence of future events on the basis of the occurrence or nonoccurrence of related events. The aim of cross-impact analysis is to identify events that will facilitate or inhibit the occurrence of other related events. Cross-impact analysis was expressly designed as a supplement to conventional Delphi. In the words of two of its early developers:

> A shortcoming of [Delphi] and many other forecasting methods . . . is that potential relationships between the forecasted events may be ignored and the forecasts might well contain mutually reinforcing or mutually exclusive items. [Cross-impact analysis] is an attempt to develop a method by which the probabilities of an item in a forecasted set can be adjusted in view of judgments relating to the potential interactions of the forecasted items.[55]

The basic analytical tool used in cross-impact analysis is the *cross-impact matrix*, a symmetrical table that lists potentially related events along row and column headings (Table 6–11). The type of forecasting problem for which cross-impact analysis is particularly appropriate is one involving a series of interdependent events. Table 6–11, for example, expresses the interdependencies among events that follow the mass production of automobiles. Observe the string of direct positive effects (represented by plus (+) signs) directly above the blank cells in the main diagonal. These effects are first-, second-, third-, fourth-, fifth-, and sixth-order impacts of mass automobile production. Note also the positive feedback effects of $(E_2–E_1)$, $(E_3–E_1)$, $(E_7–E_4)$, and $(E_7–E_5)$. These positive feedback effects suggest that ease of travel and patronization of large suburban stores may themselves affect the mass production of automobiles, for example, by increasing demand. Similarly, various forms of social deviance may intensify existing levels of alienation from neighbors and create even greater social-psychological dependence on family members.

This illustration purposefully oversimplifies linkages among events. In many other situations the linkage of one event with another is not unam-

---

[54] These researchers include Olaf Helmer, T. J. Gordon, and H. Hayward. Helmer is credited with coining the term *cross-impact*. See T. J. Gordon and H. Hayward, "Initial Experiments with the Cross-Impact Matrix Method of Forecasting," *Futures*, 1, No. 2 (1968), 101.

[55] Ibid., p. 100.

TABLE 6–11   Cross-Impact Matrix Illustrating Consequences of Mass Automobile Use

		E_1	E_2	E_3	E_4	E_5	E_6	E_7
					EVENTS (E)			
EVENTS (E)	E_1		+	0	0	0	0	0
	E_2	$\oplus$		+	0	0	0	0
	E_3	$\oplus$	0		+	0	0	0
	E_4	0	0	0		+	0	0
	E_5	0	0	0	0		+	0
	E_6	0	0	0	0	0		+
	E_7	0	0	0	$\oplus$	$\oplus$	0	

E_1 = mass production of automobiles

E_2 = ease of travel

E_3 = patronization of large suburban stores

E_4 = alienation from neighbors

E_5 = high social-psychological dependence on immediate family members

E_6 = inability of family members to meet mutual social-psychological demands

E_7 = social deviance in form of divorce, alcoholism, juvenile delinquency

Note: A plus (+) indicates direct one-way effects; a zero (0) indicates no effect; a circled plus sign $\oplus$ indicates positive feedback effects.

Source: Adapted from Joseph Coates, "Technology Assessment: The Benefits, the Costs, the Consequences," *The Futurist*, 5, No. 6 (December 1971).

biguously positive; nor do events follow one another so neatly in time. Moreover, many events may be negatively linked. For this reason cross-impact analysis takes into account three aspects of any linkage:

1. *Mode (direction) of linkage.* This indicates whether one event affects the occurrence of another event and if so, whether the direction of this effect is positive or negative. Positive effects occur in what is called the *enhancing mode*, while negative ones fall into a category called the *inhibiting mode*. A good example of linkages in the enhancing mode is increased gasoline prices provoking research and development on synthetic fuels. The arms race and its effects on the availability of funds for urban redevelopment is an illustration of linkages in the inhibiting mode. The *unconnected mode* refers to unconnected events.

2. *Strength of linkage.* This indicates how strongly events are linked, whether in the enhancing or inhibiting mode. Some events are strongly linked, meaning that the occurrence of one event substantially changes the likelihood of another's occurring, while other events are weakly linked. In general, the weaker the linkage, the closer it comes to the unconnected mode.

3. *Elapsed time of linkage.* This indicates the amount of time (weeks, years, decades) between the occurrence of linked events. Even though events may be strongly linked, either in the enhancing or inhibiting modes, the impact of

one event on the other may require a considerable period of time. For example, the linkage between the mass production of automobiles and social deviance required an elapsed time of several decades.

Cross-impact analysis works on the principle of conditional probability. Conditional probability states that the probability of occurrence of one event is dependent on the occurrence of some other event, that is, the two events are not independent. Conditional probabilities may be denoted by $P(E_1/E_2)$, which is read "The probability of the first event (E_1), given the second event (E_2)." For example, the probability (P) of being elected president (E_1) after a candidate has received the party nomination (E_2) may be 0.5, that is, there is a fifty-fifty chance of winning the election $[P(E_1/E_2) = 0.50]$. However, the probability (P) of being elected (E_1) without the party's nomination (E_3) is low, since party nomination is almost a prerequisite for the presidency $[P(E_1/E_3) = 0.20]$.

This same logic is extended to cross-impact analysis. The construction of a cross-impact matrix begins with the question: "What is the probability that a certain event (E) will occur prior to some specified point in time?" For example, an extrapolative forecast using time-series analysis may provide an interval estimate which claims that there is a 90 percent (0.9) probability that total energy consumption will exceed 100.0 quadrillion BTUs by 1995. The next question is: "What is the probability that this event (E_2) will occur, given that another event (E_1) is certain to precede it?" For example, if presently unpredictable factors (new agreements, political turmoil, accidents) result in a doubling of oil prices (E_1) by 1995, the probability of energy consumption at the level of 100.0 quadrillion BTUs may be reduced to 0.5. In this case, note that "objective" data used to make the original extrapolative forecast are combined with a "subjective" judgment about the conditional probability of the originally projected event, given the prior occurrence of the first.

The construction of a cross-impact matrix for any reasonably complex problem involves many thousands of calculations and requires a computer. Many applications of cross-impact analysis in areas of science and technology policy, environmental policy, transportation policy, and energy policy have involved more than 1000 separate iterations (called "games" or "plays") to determine the consistency of the cross-impact matrix; that is, to make sure that every sequence of conditional probabilities has been taken into account before a final probability is calculated for each event. Despite the technical complexity of cross-impact analysis, the basic logic of the technique may be readily grasped by considering a simple illustration.

Suppose that a panel of experts assembled for a conventional Delphi provides estimates of the probability of occurrence of four events $(E_1 \cdots E_4)$ for future years. Suppose further that these four events are an increase in the price of gasoline to \$3 per gallon (E_1), the "gentrification" of central city neighborhoods by former suburbanites (E_2), a doubling of reported crimes per capita (E_3), and the mass production of short-distance battery-powered autos (E_4). The probabilities attached to these four events are, respectively, $P_1 = 0.5$, $P_2 = 0.5$, $P_3 = 0.6$, and $P_4 = 0.2$. Given these

TABLE 6–12   Hypothetical Illustration of the First Round (Play) in a Cross-Impact Matrix

IF THIS EVENT OCCURS (P = 1.0)	THEN THE CHANGED PROBABILITY OF OCCURRENCE OF THESE EVENTS IS:			
	E_1	E_2	E_3	E_4
E_1 Gas to $3 per gallon		0.7	0.8	0.5
E_2 "Gentrification"	0.4		0.7	0.4
E_3 Crime doubles	0.5	0.4		0.1
E_4 Electric autos	0.4	0.5	0.7	

EVENTS	ORIGINAL PROBABILITIES (P)
E_1	$P_1 = 0.5$
E_2	$P_2 = 0.5$
E_3	$P_3 = 0.6$
E_4	$P_4 = 0.2$

subjective estimates, the forecasting problem is: Given that one of these events occurs (that is, P = 1.0, or 100%) how will the probabilities of other events change?[56]

Table 6–12 illustrates the first round (play) in the construction of a cross-impact matrix. Observe that the assumption that gasoline per gallon will go to $3 produces revised subjective probabilities for "gentrification" (an increase from 0.5 to 0.7), reported crimes per capita (an increase from 0.6 to 0.8), and the mass manufacture of electric autos (an increase from 0.2 to 0.5). These changes reflect the *enhancing linkages* discussed earlier. By contrast, other linkages are *inhibiting*. For example, the gentrification of central cities makes it less likely that gasoline will increase to $3 per gallon (note the decrease from 0.5 to 0.4), on the assumption that oil companies will become more price competitive when former suburbanites drive less. Finally, there are also *unconnected linkages*. Increased crime and mass-produced electric autos exert no influence on the probability of gas prices increasing to $3 per gallon or on the process of gentrification (note that original probabilities remain constant at 0.5).

The advantage of the cross-impact matrix is that it enables the analyst to discern interdependencies that otherwise may have gone unnoticed. Cross-impact analysis also permits the continuous revision of prior probabilities on the basis of new assumptions or evidence. If new empirical data become available for some of the events (for example, crime rates), the

---

[56] Alternatively, we can ask the same question about the *nonoccurrence* of an event. Therefore, it is usually necessary to construct two matrices: one for occurrences and one for nonoccurrences. See James F. Dalby, "Practical Refinements to the Cross-Impact Matrix Technique of Technological Forecasting," in *Industrial Applications of Technological Forecasting* (New York: Wiley, 1971), pp. 259–73.

matrix may be recalculated. Alternatively, different assumptions may be introduced—perhaps as a consequence of a policy Delphi that yields conflicting estimates and arguments—to determine how sensitive certain events are to changes in other events. Finally, information in a cross-impact matrix may be readily summarized at any point in the process.

Cross-impact matrices may be used to uncover and analyze those complex interdependencies that we have described as ill-structured problems. The technique is also consistent with a variety of related approaches to intuitive forecasting, including technology assessment, social impact assessment, and technological forecasting.[57] As already noted, cross-impact analysis is not only consistent with conventional Delphi, but actually represents its adaptation and natural extension. For example, while cross-impact analysis may be done by single analysts, the accuracy of subjective judgments may be increased by using Delphi panels.

Cross-impact analysis, like the other forecasting techniques discussed in this chapter, has its limitations. First, the analyst can never be sure that all potentially interdependent events have been included in the analysis, which again calls attention to the importance of problem structuring (Chapter 5). There are other techniques to assist in identifying these events, including variations of theory mapping (see Table 6–9) and the construction and graphic presentation of networks of causally related events called *relevance trees* (see Figure 5–14). Second, the construction and "playing" of a cross-impact matrix is a reasonably costly and time-consuming process, even with the advent of packaged computer programs and high performance computer technology. Third, there are technical difficulties associated with matrix calculations (for example, nonoccurrences are not always analyzed), although many of these problems have been resolved.[58] Finally, and most important, existing applications of cross-impact analysis suffer from one of the same weaknesses as conventional Delphi, namely, an unrealistic emphasis on consensus among experts. Most of the forecasting problems for which cross-impact analysis is especially well suited are precisely the kinds of problems where conflict, and not consensus, is widespread. Problem structuring methods are needed to surface and debate the conflicting assumptions and arguments that underlie subjective conditional probabilities.

Feasibility Assessment

The final judgmental forecasting procedure we will consider in this chapter is one that is expressly designed to produce conjectures about the future behavior of policy stakeholders. This procedure, most simply described as the *feasibility assessment technique*, assists analysts in producing forecasts about the probable impact of stakeholders in supporting or op-

---

[57] On these related approaches see François Hetman, *Society and the Assessment of Technology* (Paris: Organization for Economic Cooperation and Development, 1973); and Kurt Finsterbusch and C. P. Wolf, eds., *Methodology of Social Impact Assessment* (Stroudsburg, PA: Dowden, Hutchinson & Ross, 1977).

[58] See Dalby, "Practical Refinements to Cross-Impact Matrix Technique," pp. 265–73.

posing the adoption and/or implementation of different policy alternatives.[59] The feasibility assessment technique is particularly well suited for problems requiring estimates of the probable consequences of attempting to legitimize policy alternatives under conditions of political conflict and the unequal distribution of power and other resources.

The feasibility assessment technique may be used to forecast the behavior of stakeholders in any phase of the policy-making process, including policy adoption and implementation. What makes this technique particularly useful is that it responds to a key problem which we have already encountered in reviewing other intuitive forecasting techniques: Typically, there is no relevant theory or available empirical data that permits us to make predictions or projections about the behavior of policy stakeholders. While social scientists have proposed various theories of policy-making behavior that are potentially available as a source of predictions, most of these theories are insufficiently concrete to apply in specific contexts.[60]

The feasibility assessment technique is one way to respond to a number of concerns about the lack of attention to questions of political feasibility and policy implementation in policy analysis. While problems of policy implementation play a large part in most policy problems, much of contemporary policy analysis pays little attention to this question. What is needed is a systematic way to forecast "the capabilities, interests, and incentives of organizations to implement each alternative. . . ."[61] In practical terms this means that the behavior of relevant stakeholders must be forecasted along with the consequences of policies themselves. Only in this way can the analyst ensure that organizational and political factors which may be critical to the adoption and implementation of a policy are adequately accounted for.

The feasibility assessment technique, like other intuitive forecasting procedures, is based on subjective estimates. The feasibility assessment technique may be used by single analysts, or by a group of knowledgeables, much as in a Delphi exercise. Feasibility assessment focuses on several aspects of political and organizational behavior:

1. *Issue position.* Here the analyst estimates the probability that various stakeholders will support, oppose, or be indifferent to each of two or more policy alternatives. Positions are coded as supporting ($+1$), opposing (-1), or indifferent (0). A subjective estimate is then made of the probability that each

---

[59] The following discussion draws from but modifies Michael K. O'Leary and William D. Coplin, "Teaching Political Strategy Skills with 'The Prince,' " *Policy Analysis*, 2, No. 1 (Winter 1976), 145–60. See also O'Leary and Coplin, *Everyman's "Prince."*

[60] These theories deal with elites, groups, coalitions, aggregates of individuals and leaders. See, for example, Raymond A. Bauer and Kenneth J. Gergen, eds., *The Study of Policy Formation* (New York: The Free Press, 1968); and Daniel A. Mazmanian and Paul A. Sabatier, *Implementation and Public Policy* (Lanham, MD: University Press of America, 1989).

[61] Graham T. Allison, "Implementation Analysis: 'The Missing Chapter' in Conventional Analysis: A Teaching Exercise," in *Benefit–Cost and Policy Analysis: 1974*, ed. Richard Zeckhauser (Chicago: Aldine Publishing Company, 1975), p. 379.

stakeholder will adopt the coded position. This estimate (which ranges from 0 to 1.0) indicates the saliency or importance of the issue to each stakeholder.

2. *Available resources.* Here the analyst provides a subjective estimate of the resources available to each of the stakeholders in pursuing their respective positions. Available resources include prestige, legitimacy, budget, staff, and access to information and communications networks. Since stakeholders nearly always have positions on other issues for which part of their resources are necessary, available resources should be stated as a fraction of total resources held by the stakeholder. The resource availability scale, expressed as a fraction, varies from 0 to 1.0. Note that there may be a high probability that a given stakeholder will support a policy (for example, 0.9), yet that same stakeholder may have little capability to affect the policy's adoption or implementation. This is typically the result of an overcommitment of resources (prestige, budget, staff) to other issue areas.

3. *Relative resource rank.* Here the analyst determines the relative rank of each stakeholder with respect to its resources. Relative resource rank, one measure of the "power" or "influence" of stakeholders, provides information about the magnitude of political and organizational resources available to each stakeholder. A stakeholder who commits a high fraction (say, 0.8) of available resources to support a policy may nevertheless be unable to affect significantly a policy's adoption or implementation. This is because some stakeholders have few resources to begin with.

Since the purpose of feasibility assessment is to forecast behavior under conditions of political conflict, it is essential to identify as representative and powerful a group of stakeholders as possible. The analyst may identify representative stakeholders from various organizations and organizational levels with different constituencies and with varying levels of resources and roles in the policy-making process.

An illustration of the feasibility assessment technique has been provided in Table 6–13. In this example a policy analyst in a large municipality has completed a study which shows that local property taxes must be raised by an average of 1 percent in order to cover expenditures for the next year. Alternatively, expenditures for municipal services must be cut by a comparable amount, an action that will result in the firing of 1500 employees. Since most public employees are unionized, and there has been a threat of a strike for more than two years, the mayor is extremely hesitant to press for a cutback in services. At the same time local taxpayers' groups are known to be strongly opposed to yet another tax increase, even if it means the loss of some services. Under these conditions the mayor has requested that the analyst provide a feasibility assessment of the policy alternatives.

Table 6–13 shows that a tax increase is unfeasible. In fact the negative sign of the indices (simple and adjusted) at the bottom of the table indicates that there is more opposition than support for a tax increase. By contrast, the index of total feasibility (adjusted) for the budget cut is positive and in the weak range. The index of total feasibility ranges from -1.0 to $+1.0$, which means that the feasibility of different policy alternatives is directly comparable. Observe, however, that there is an adjusted total feasibility index. The adjustment is necessary because the maximum value that the

TABLE 6–13 Feasibility Assessment of Two Fiscal Policy Alternatives in a Hypothetical Municipality

(a) Alternative 1
(Tax Increase)

STAKE-HOLDER (1)	CODED POSITION (2)	PROBABILITY (3)	FRACTION OF RESOURCES AVAILABLE (4)	RESOURCE RANK (5)	FEASIBILITY SCORE (6)
Mayor	+1	0.2	0.2	0.4	0.016
Council	−1	0.6	0.7	0.8	−0.336
Taxpayers' association	−1	0.9	0.8	1.0	−0.720
Employees' union	+1	0.9	0.6	0.6	0.324
Mass media	+1	0.1	0.5	0.2	0.010
					$\sum F = -0.706$

Index of total feasibility (TF) $= \dfrac{\sum F}{n} = \dfrac{-0.706}{5} = -0.14$

Adjusted total feasibility $(\text{TF}_{ADJ}) = \text{TF}(5/2) = -0.14(2.5) = -0.35$

(b) Alternative 2
(Budget Cut)

STAKE-HOLDER (1)	CODED POSITION (2)	PROBABILITY (3)	FRACTION OF RESOURCES AVAILABLE (4)	RESOURCE RANK (5)	FEASIBILITY SCORE (6)
Mayor	+1	0.8	0.2	0.4	0.192
Council	+1	0.4	0.5	0.8	0.160
Taxpayers' association	+1	0.9	0.7	1.0	0.630
Employees' union	−1	0.9	0.8	0.6	−0.432
Mass media	−1	0.1	0.5	0.2	−0.010
					$\sum F = 0.54$

Index of total feasibility (TF) $= \dfrac{\sum F}{n} = \dfrac{0.54}{5} = 0.11$

Adjusted total feasibility $(\text{TF}_{ADJ}) = \text{TF}(5/3) = 0.11(5/3) = 0.11(1.66) = 0.183$

index can take depends on its sign (positive or negative) and the number of positive (or negative) positions taken.

In Table 6–13a, for example, the maximum negative value of the index depends on the number of negative positions in relation to positive ones. Imagine that the two negative feasibility scores were "perfect" (that is, −1.0), and that all other stakeholders were indifferent, giving them feasibility scores of 0.0. In this case the maximum value of the sum of individual feasibility scores would be -2.0. If we then divide by the total number of stakeholders ($n = 5$), we produce an index value of -0.40, even though there is maximum opposition to the alternative. For this reason we must compute a maximum value of TF, which in this case is $TF_{MAX} = 2/5 = 0.40$. To find the adjusted value of the index (TF_{ADJ}) we simply divide the original value of TF by its maximum value, that is, $TF/TF_{MAX} = TF_{ADJ} = -0.40/0.40 = -1.0$. The same procedure was used to find the maximum and adjusted positive values of TF in Table 6–13b.

The feasibility assessment technique forces the analyst to make explicit subjective judgments, rather than treat political and organizational questions in a loose or arbitrary fashion. Feasibility assessment also enables analysts to systematically consider the sensitivity of issue positions and available resources to changes in policy alternatives. In the previous example a smaller tax increase, combined with austerity measures and a plan to increase the productivity of municipal employees, would probably evoke altogether different levels of feasibility.

The limitations of the feasibility assessment technique are similar to those already encountered with other judgmental forecasting techniques. The feasibility assessment technique, like conventional Delphi and cross-impact analysis, provides no systematic way of surfacing the assumptions and arguments that underlie subjective judgments. Perhaps the best way to resolve this difficulty is to adopt procedures from policy Delphi, or use assumptional analysis (Chapter 5). A second limitation of the technique is that it assumes that the positions of stakeholders are independent and that they occur at the same point in time. These assumptions are unrealistic, since they ignore processes of coalition formation over time and the fact that one stakeholder's position is frequently determined by changes in the position of another. To capture the interdependencies of issue positions as they shift over time, some adaptation of cross-impact analysis might be employed. Finally, the feasibility assessment technique, like other judgmental forecasting techniques discussed in this chapter, is most useful under conditions where the complexity of a problem cannot easily be grasped by using available theories or empirical data. For this reason any attempt to outline its limitations should also consider its potential as a source of creative insight and surprising or counterintuitive findings.

In concluding this chapter it is important to stress that different approaches to forecasting are complementary. The strength of one approach or technique is very often the weakness or limitation of another, and vice versa. All of this is to say that the logical foundations of each approach are interdependent. Improvements in forecasting are therefore likely to result from the creative combination of different approaches and techniques, that is, from *multimethod forecasting*. Multimethod forecasting combines multiple forms of logical reasoning (inductive, deductive, retroductive), multiple bases (extrapolation, theory, judgment), and multiple objects (the content and consequences of new and existing policies and the behavior of policy stakeholders). Multimethod forecasting recognizes that neither precision nor creativity are ends in themselves. What appears to be a creative or insightful conjecture may lack plausibility and turn out to be pure speculation or quackery, while highly precise projections or predictions may simply answer the wrong question. The ultimate justification for a forecast is whether it provides plausibly true results. In the words of an accomplished policy analyst and former assistant secretary in the Department of Defense: "It is better to be roughly right than exactly wrong."[62]

SUMMARY

In this chapter we have provided an overview of the nature, types, and uses of forecasting in policy analysis, compared three major approaches to forecasting, and described and illustrated a range of forecasting methods and techniques appropriate to each approach. You should now be prepared to discuss the following principles and generalizations:

1. Forecasts may take three principal forms: projections, predictions, and conjectures. Each of these principal forms has a different basis: trend extrapolation, theory, and informed judgment.

2. Supporting arguments used to justify projections, predictions, and conjectures also differ. Projections tend to be justified by arguments from method and parallel case; predictions are typically warranted by arguments from cause and analogy; and conjectures are frequently based on arguments from insight and motivation.

3. Forecasts, irrespective of their form, provide information about future changes in policies and their consequences. While forecasting may promote increased understanding, it is especially related to social control. Forecasts permit us to shape the future in an active and creative manner, rather than passively accept the past as a determinant of the future.

4. Policy forecasting is regularly practiced by government agencies, private corporations, and nonprofit research institutes. The accuracy of all forecasts is sensitive to temporal, historical, and institutional contexts; and complex procedures (for example, econometric modeling) are not necessarily more accurate or useful than simple extrapolative and judgmental forecasts.

5. Forecasting may be used to make estimates of three types of future societal states: potential futures, plausible futures, and normative futures. The specification of normative futures allows the analyst to narrow the range of potential and plausible futures, thus increasing the chance that forecasts are oriented toward specific goals and objectives.

6. Goals and objectives may be compared and contrasted in terms of their breadth of purpose, type of definition, specification of time periods, measurement procedures, and treatment of target groups.

---

[62] Alain C. Enthoven, "Ten Practical Principles for Policy and Program Analysis," in Zeckhauser, *Benefit–Cost and Policy Analysis: 1974*, p. 459.

7. Goals and objectives imply alternatives, while alternatives in turn imply goals and objectives. Available sources for identifying goals, objectives, and alternatives include authority, insight, method, scientific theories, motivation, parallel case, analogy, and ethical systems.

8. Approaches to forecasting may be identified, compared, and contrasted according to their objects, bases, methods, and products. Objects of forecasting include the content and consequences of new and existing policies and the behavior of policy stakeholders. Bases of forecasts (trend extrapolation, theory, subjective judgment) are associated with three distinct but interrelated processes of logical reasoning: induction, deduction, and retroduction. While methods of forecasting may be numbered in the hundreds, applications of these methods result in three types of products: projections, predictions, and conjectures.

9. The understanding and use of forecasting techniques is made much easier if they are grouped according to the three approaches: extrapolative, theoretical, and intuitive. Some of the more important extrapolative forecasting techniques are classical time-series analysis, linear trend estimation, exponential weighting, data transformation, and catastrophe methodology.

10. When extrapolative forecasting techniques are used to estimate linear and nonlinear trend, they rest on assumptions of persistence, regularity, and data reliability. Techniques for linear trend estimation cannot be applied to nonlinear processes without exponential weighting or data transformation. Techniques for nonlinear trend estimation cannot be applied to the kinds of discontinuous processes that are a special focus of catastrophe methodology and chaos theory.

11. Many time series do not meet conditions of linearity, persistence, and regularity. Some time series are also discontinuous. Time series that do not meet one or more of these conditions fall into one of five groups: oscillations, cycles, growth curves, decline curves, and catastrophes.

12. Some of the more important theoretical forecasting techniques are theory mapping, causal modeling, regression analysis, interval estimation, and correlational analysis. Some of these techniques are concerned with ways to identify and explicate theoretical assumptions, while others provide better estimates of future societal states predicted on the basis of theory. None of these techniques actually makes predictions; only theory can do this.

13. Some of the more important judgmental forecasting techniques are conventional Delphi, policy Delphi, cross-impact analysis, and feasibility assessment. Some of these techniques may be used to make subjective estimates of the future consequences of changes in technology and public policies, while others help make estimates of the behavior of policy stakeholders in supporting or opposing the adoption and implementation of policies. The major strength of judgmental forecasting techniques is that they provide estimates of future societal states under conditions where relevant theory or reliable data are unavailable.

14. Different approaches to forecasting are complementary. The strengths of one approach or technique are very often the limitations of another, and vice versa. Improvements in forecasting are likely to result from multimethod forecasting, which combines multiple forms of logical reasoning, multiple bases, and multiple objects.

15. It is better to be roughly right than exactly wrong.

GLOSSARY

Catastrophe: A departure from linearity which exhibits a sudden and discontinuous change in the value of a time-series variable. Examples are the collapse of stock exchanges and the sudden change in the density of a liquid when it boils.

Causal Model: A simplified representation of a theory that attempts to explain and predict the causes and consequences of public policies. Causal models assume that observed covariations are a reflection of underlying causal relationships.

Coefficient of Correlation (r):   A summary measure or index of the direction and strength of association between two variables. The coefficient of correlations is calculated from the value of the coefficient of determination: $r = \sqrt{r^2}$. The range of r is -1.0 to $+1.0$.

Coefficient of Determination (r^2):   A summary measure or index of the amount of variation in a dependent variable explained by an independent variable. The coefficient of determination can be calculated from values in the regression equation: $r^2 = b(\sum xy)/\sum(y^2)$. The range of r^2 is 0.0 to 1.0.

Conjecture: A forecast based on informed subjective judgments about future states of society. Most technological forecasts are conjectures.

Cross-Impact Matrix: A symmetrical table that lists potentially related events along row and column headings. Entries in the cross-impact matrix are conditional probabilities that help to uncover the direction (mode) of linkages (enhancing, inhibiting, unconnected), their strength (expressed as a conditional probability), and the elapsed time between linked events (expressed in years or longer periods).

Cycle: A departure from linearity which evidences upward or downward fluctuations between years or longer periods of time. A good example is business cycles.

Decline Curve: A departure from linearity which evidences cumulative increases (or decreases) in continuously decreasing rates of change.

Deductive Logic: The process of reasoning from general statements (laws, propositions, assumptions) to particular sets of information and claims. Theoretical predictions are based on deductive logic.

Exponential Growth (Decline):   Processes of growth (or decline) where increases in some quantity increase (or decrease) at an increasing rate. A property of growth (and decline) curves.

Growth Curve: A departure from linearity which evidences cumulative increases (or decreases) in continuously increasing rates of change. *Sigmoid (S-shaped)* and *logistic curves* are types of growth curves.

Index of Total Feasibility: An index of the total feasibility of an alternative. The index ranges from -1.0 to $+1.0$ and is composed of four dimensions: a coded issue position; an estimate of the probability of adopting the coded position; an estimate of the fraction of resources available to pursue the position; and relative resource rank. $TF = \sum F/n$, where F is a feasibility score for each stakeholder and n is the number of stakeholders. The index of total feasibility must be adjusted (TF_{ADJ}) for the number of supporters or opponents, or it will not reach its maximum value of ∓ 1.0.

Inductive Logic: The process of reasoning from particular observations (for example, time-series data) to general claims and the assumptions that warrant such claims. Trend extrapolation is based on inductive logic.

Interval Estimate: A probabilistic estimate expressed in terms of the intervals above and below a computed value (Y_c) of a dependent variable. Intervals are calculated from values of the standard error of estimate.

Linear Process: A time series whose values display a constant increase or decrease in the amount of change from one period to the next.

Nonlinear (Curvilinear) Process: A time series whose values display an increase or decrease in the *rate* of change from one time period to the next.

Normative Futures: Potential and plausible futures that are consistent with an analyst's conception of future needs, values, and opportunities. Full employment, disarmament, and zero population growth are normative futures.

Oscillation: A departure from linearity which occurs *within* years, quarters, months, or days. Seasonal variations are oscillations.

Plausible Futures: Possible future states of society which, on the basis of assumptions about causation in nature and society, might conceivably come about if policy makers do not intervene to change the course of events. Widespread environmental degradation by 2000 is a plausible future.

Point Estimate: A nonprobabilistic estimate expressed solely in terms of a computed value (Y_c) of a dependent variable.

Policy Goal: An aim or purpose which is broadly stated, formally defined, unspecified as to time and target groups, and unquantified. Security, welfare, and justice are goals.

Policy Objective: An aim or purpose which is concrete, operationally defined, time- and target group-specific, and frequently measured with quantitative procedures.

Positive (Negative) Feedback Loop: A relation between two variables where the values of both variables continue to grow (or decline) as a consequence of the self-reinforcing influence of each variable on the other.

Potential (Alternative) Futures: Possible societal states that may occur in the future, as distinguished from states that eventually do occur. A society based on solar energy is a potential future.

Prediction: A forecast based on explicit theoretical assumptions. Annual economic forecasts based on economic models are predictions.

Projection: A forecast based on the extrapolation of current and historical trends into the future. Estimates of population growth and energy consumption are projections.

Regression Line: The straight line describing the relation between a dependent and independent variable in a regression equation. The formula for the regression equation is $Y_c = a + b(x)$, where $b = \sum(xy)/\sum(x^2)$ and $a = Y - b(\overline{X})$.

Relevance Tree: A graphic representation of networks of causally related events. Produces results similar to those obtained by *theory mapping* and *hierarchy analysis* (Chapter 5) and assists in identifying events for inclusion in a *cross-impact matrix*.

Retroductive Logic: The process of reasoning backwards from claims about the future to the assumptions and data that warrant such claims. Subjective judgments are typically based on retroductive logic.

Scatter Diagram (Scatterplot):   A graph that shows the pattern, direction, and strength of a relation between a dependent and independent variable. A basic tool of regression analysis.

Standard Error of Estimate ($S_{y,x}$):   An index of the probable error in an estimate, expressed as the square root of the averaged squared error in a regression estimate: $S_{x,y} = \sqrt{\sum(Y - Y_c)^2/n - 1}$. The value of one standard error is a good approximation of the error that will occur about two-thirds of the time in a regression estimate; two and three standard errors approximate the error that will occur about 95 and 99 percent of the time.

STUDY SUGGESTIONS

1. "Those who fail to learn from history are bound to repeat it." Write a critique of this statement on the basis of the three approaches to forecasting discussed in this chapter.

2. How does the way an analyst structures a policy problem affect the selection of an approach to forecasting? Recall that the selection of an approach implies decisions about the basis and object of a forecast.

3. Review the modes of policy argument presented in Chapter 4. Construct authoritative, explanatory, analycentric, intuitive and pragmatic arguments to support the following statement: "Total energy consumption will exceed 150 quadrillion BTUs by 1995."

4. In this chapter subjective judgment is contrasted with theory and the extrapolation of current and historical data. Recalling the distinction between "surrogate" and "perspective" models (Chapter 5), what makes these three bases of forecasts similar as well as different? Are theories and data "surrogates"?

5. Diagram inductive, deductive, and retroductive arguments that might be used to make forecasts about an issue area of your selection. (Review Figures 6–3 to 6–5 before you begin.)

6. Following is a list of policy goals. Convert each of these goals into policy objectives:

   (a) To enhance the national security of the United States.
   (b) To ensure that all Americans have access to adequate health care.
   (c) To provide equal educational opportunity for everyone.
   (d) To make our streets and homes safe.
   (e) To ensure the responsible use of energy in an age of scarcity and non-renewable energy sources.
   (f) To place the management of the city on a sound financial basis.

7. Choose a recent newspaper or magazine editorial on an important public policy issue. Use the five theory-mapping procedures described in the text to uncover the structure of the arguments made in this editorial. Be sure to draw an arrow diagram as your conclusion.

8. Consider the benefits of causal models. (a) For what kinds of forecasting problems are these models most relevant? (b) What are the strengths of these models? (c) What are their limitations?

9. If the path coefficients in Figure 6–14 were $p_{31} = 0.41$, $p_{21} = 0.71$, and $p_{32} = 0.39$, what would this tell us about the possible validity of public choice theory? Is linear regression an appropriate technique for testing the public choice model, given the kinds of arguments offered by public choice theorists to support their claims?

10. Study the following table, which shows the total number of work stoppages in local governments in the United States from 1960 through 1969. (a) Con-

Work Stoppages in Local
Government, 1960–1969

YEAR	NUMBER OF STOPPAGES
1960	33
1961	28
1962	21
1963	27
1964	37
1965	42
1966	133
1967	169
1968	235
1969	372

Source: U.S. Department of Labor, Bureau of Labor Statistics, Work Stoppages in Government, 1974 (Washington, DC: U.S. Government Printing Office, 1976), p. 5.

struct a worksheet for computing the values required to solve for *b* and *a* in the equation $Y_t = a + b(x)$. (b) Compute the Y intercept. (c) Compute the slope of the regression line. (d) Write the regression equation that describes the relation between time and work stoppages. (e) Estimate work stoppages for 1974. (f) The actual number of work stoppages in local government in 1974 was 348. Was your estimate very different from the actual observed value of work stoppages? Why? Why not?

11. Use MYSTAT to complete Study Suggestion 10. Your 1974 estimate will have to be calculated separately, on the basis of the MYSTAT output.

12. Using MYSTAT, construct a scatter diagram for the data used in Study Suggestion 10. Should linear trend estimation be used with these data? Why? Why not?

13. Transform the data on work stoppages, using the base *e* logarithmic transformation in MYSTAT. Then:

    (a) Rerun the regression analysis.
    (b) Compare the new results with those of Study Suggestion 11.

14. The following table summarizes relationships between public investments in five personnel training programs and the numbers of trainees engaged in full-time jobs six months after completing the programs. (a) Construct a worksheet for computing values required to solve for *b* and *a* in the regression equation $Y_c = a + b(X)$. (b) Compute the Y intercept. (c) Compute the slope of the regression line. (d) Write the regression equation that describes the relation between subsequent employment and program investment. (e) What is the estimate of Y when X is 3.5?

Dollar Investment and Subsequent Employment of Trainees in Five Personnel Training Programs

PROGRAM	SUBSEQUENT EMPLOYMENT (HUNDREDS)	INVESTMENT ($ MILLIONS)
1	100	2.0
2	300	3.0
3	200	4.0
4	500	6.0
5	400	5.0

Note: To check your calculations: $a = -60$; $b = 90$.
Source: Fictitious data.

15. Use MYSTAT to complete Study Suggestion 14.

16. For the data in Study Suggestion 14: (a) Construct a worksheet for calculating the standard error of estimate. (b) Compute the standard error of estimate at the 95 percent estimation interval (that is, 2 standard errors). (c) Compute the coefficient of determination and the coefficient of correlation. (d) Interpret $S_{y \cdot x}$, r^2, and r. Write a policy memo to the Secretary of Labor, which interprets results (see Appendix 4).

Chapter 6 / Forecasting Policy Futures

17. Use MYSTAT to check your calculations in Study Suggestion 16.
18. Construct a short policy Delphi questionnaire in an issue area of your choice (for example, crime, energy, health). (a) List the major issues to be addressed by advocates. (b) Write issue, goal, options, and forecasting items (one each). (c) Construct desirability, feasibility, importance, and certainty scales for each item.
19. Following are original probabilities for four future events. (a) Construct a cross-impact matrix on the basis of these original probabilities. (b) Indicate linkages (modes) among events. (c) Interpret the results.

EVENTS (E)	ORIGINAL PROBABILITY (P)
E_1 Solar energy available commercially in 2000	$(P_1 = 0.7)$
E_2 Rate of growth of GNP slows to 1.5 percent by 1995	$(P_2 = 0.4)$
E_3 Synthetic fuel marketed on mass basis by 1995	$(P_3 = 0.5)$
E_4 Air passenger traffic doubles by 2000	$(P_4 = 0.3)$

20. A medium-sized municipality is considering the adoption of high-impact police patrols to deter crime. Although the costs of the new program will be met with federal funds from the Law Enforcement Assistance Administration, the mayor is concerned that an open clash between the local police officers' association and the black community may develop. Further, since the mayor is up for reelection soon, he does not want to risk a defeat of the high-impact patrol proposal in the municipal council, since this will harm his chances for reelection. The four main stakeholders are the mayor, the city council, the police officer's association, and local black leaders. Their positions and resources are summarized in the following table. (a) Calculate the index of total feasibility for this policy alternative. (b) Adjust the index according to its maximum value. (c) Indicate how the index can help the mayor resolve his problem.

STAKEHOLDER	CODED POSITION	PROBABILITY	FRACTION OF RESOURCES AVAILABLE	RESOURCE RANK
Mayor	+	0.2	0.4	0.3
Council	+	0.5	0.2	1.0
Police officers' association	+	0.8	0.6	0.5
Black leaders	−	0.7	0.7	0.8

SUGGESTED READINGS

ALLEN, T. HARRELL, *New Methods in Social Science Research: Policy Sciences and Futures Research*. New York: Frederick A. Praeger, 1978.
ASCHER, WILLIAM, *Forecasting: An Appraisal for Policy Makers and Planners*. Baltimore: Johns Hopkins University Press, 1978.

——, "The Forecasting Potential of Complex Models," *Policy Sciences*, 13 (1981), 247–67.

BARTLETT, ROBERT V., ed., *Policy through Impact Assessment: Institutionalized Analysis as a Policy Strategy.* New York: Greenwood Press, 1989.

BOX, G. E. P. and G. M. JENKINS, *Time Series Analysis: Forecasting and Control.* San Francisco: Holden-Day, 1969.

DROR, YEHEZKEL, *Policymaking under Adversity.* New Brunswick, NJ: Transaction Books, 1986.

FINSTERBUSCH, KURT and C. P. WOLF, eds., *Methodology of Social Impact Assessment.* Stroudsburg, PA: Dowden, Hutchinson & Ross, 1977.

GASS, SAUL I. and ROGER L. SISSON, eds., *A Guide to Models in Governmental Planning and Operations.* Washington, DC: U.S. Environmental Protection Agency, 1974.

GUESS, GEORGE M. and PAUL G. FARNHAM, *Cases in Public Policy Analysis.* New York: Longman, 1989, Chap. 3, "Forecasting Policy Options," pp. 49–67.

HARRISON, DANIEL P., *Social Forecasting Methodology.* New York: Russell Sage Foundation, 1976.

LINER, CHARLES D., "Projecting Local Government Revenue," in *Budget Management: A Reader in Local Government Financial Management*, ed. W. Bartley Hildreth and Gerald J. Miller. Athens, GA: University of Georgia Press, 1983, pp. 83–92.

LINSTONE, HAROLD A. and MURRAY TUROFF, eds., *The Delphi Method: Techniques and Applications.* Reading, MA: Addison-Wesley, 1975.

MARIEN, MICHAEL, *Future Survey Annual: A Guide to the Recent Literature of Trends, Forecasts, and Policy Proposals.* Bethesda, MD: World Future Society, published annually.

——, "The Scope of Policy Studies: Reclaiming Lasswell's Lost Vision," in *Advances in Policy Studies Since 1950*, Vol. 10 of *Policy Studies Review Annual*, ed. William N. Dunn and Rita Mae Kelly. New Brunswick, NJ: Transaction Books, 1992, pp. 445–88.

McNOWN, ROBERT, "On the Use of Econometric Models: A Guide for Policy Makers," *Policy Sciences*, 19 (1986); 360–80.

O'LEARY, MICHAEL K. and WILLIAM D. COPLIN, *Everyman's "Prince."* North Scituate, MA: Duxbury Press, 1976.

SCHROEDER, LARRY D. and ROY BAHL, "The Role of Multi-year Forecasting in the Annual Budgeting Process for Local Governments," *Public Budgeting and Finance*, 4, No. 1 (1984), 3–14.

THOMOPOULOS, NICK T., *Applied Forecasting Methods.* Englewood Cliffs, NJ: Prentice Hall, 1980.

TOULMIN, LLEWELLYN M. and GLENDAL E. WRIGHT, "Expenditure Forecasting," in *Handbook on Public Budgeting and Financial Management*, ed. Jack Rabin and Thomas D. Lynch. New York: Marcel Dekker, 1983, pp. 209–87.

U.S. GENERAL ACCOUNTING OFFICE, *Prospective Evaluation Methods: The Prospective Evaluation Synthesis.* Washington, DC: U.S. General Accounting Office, Program Evaluation and Methodology Division, July 1989.

7

Recommending
Policy Actions

An economist is a man who knows the price of everything and the value of nothing.

—Oscar Wilde

But, Mr. Wilde, prices are values.

—Anonymous Economist[1]

Forecasting, as we saw in Chapter 6, is a procedure for producing factual information about future states of society on the basis of information about the nature of policy problems. Yet forecasting yields factual claims about policy futures. Forecasting does not offer explicit reasons why we should value one future state over another; nor does it permit us to make claims that answer the question: What should be done?

The purpose of this chapter is to address this important question by considering the policy-analytic procedure of recommendation. We first review the nature and role of recommendation in policy analysis. Second, we compare and contrast two major approaches to recommendation: cost–benefit analysis and cost–effectiveness analysis. Finally, we review methods and techniques that enable us to use these approaches to make policy recommendations.

RECOMMENDATION IN POLICY ANALYSIS

The policy-analytic procedure of *recommendation* enables analysts to produce information about the likelihood that future courses of action will

---

[1] Quoted by Robert Dorfman, "An Afterword: Humane Values and Environmental Decisions," in *When Values Conflict: Essays on Environmental Analysis, Discourse, and Decision*, ed. Laurence H. Tribe, Corinne S. Schelling and John Voss (Cambridge, MA: Ballinger Publishing Co. for the American Academy of Arts and Sciences, 1976), p. 153.

result in consequences that are valuable to some individual, group, or society as a whole. The procedure of recommendation involves the transformation of information about policy futures into information about policy actions that will result in valued outcomes. To recommend a particular policy action requires prior information about the future consequences of acting on different alternatives. Yet making policy recommendations requires that we also determine which alternatives are most valuable and why. For this reason the policy-analytic procedure of recommendation is closely related to ethical and moral questions.[2]

Recommendation and Multiple Advocacy

Should the United States increase its economic commitment to less developed countries by raising levels of foreign aid and technical assistance? Should the Congress pass legislation that will strictly curtail the pollution of the atmosphere and waterways by industry? Should state governments provide low-cost home-heating fuel to the poor? Should the city council raise local taxes to build a community recreation center? Should the federal government provide a minimum annual income for all citizens or invest in a cure for cancer?

All of these issues call for policy recommendations that answer the question: What should be done? Any answer to this question requires an approach that is normative, rather than one which is merely empirical or merely evaluative, since the question is one of right action (see Chapter 3). Questions of action demand that analysts choose among multiple advocative claims about what should be done.[3]

Advocative claims have several distinctive characteristics. Advocative claims are:

1. *Actionable.* Advocative claims focus on actions that may be taken to resolve a policy problem. Although advocative claims require prior information about what will occur and what is valuable, they go beyond questions of "fact" and "value" and include arguments about the specific actions that will satisfy needs, values, and opportunities for improvement.

2. *Prospective.* Advocative claims are prospective, since they occur prior to the time that actions are taken (*ex ante*). While policy-analytic procedures of monitoring and evaluation are retrospective, since they are applied after actions are taken (*ex post*), forecasting and recommendation are both applied prospectively (*ex ante*).

3. *Value laden.* Advocative claims depend as much on "facts" as they do on "values." To claim that a particular policy alternative should be adopted requires not only that the action being recommended will have the predicted

---

[2] For a synthesis of literature on ethical aspects of policy analysis, see William N. Dunn, "Values, Ethics, and Standards in Policy Analysis," in *Encyclopedia of Policy Studies*, ed. Stuart S. Nagel (New York: Marcel Dekker, 1983), pp. 831–66.

[3] On multiple advocacy, see Alexander George, *Presidential Decision Making in Foreign Policy: The Effective Use of Information and Advice* (Boulder, CO: Westview Press, 1980).

consequences; it also requires that the predicted consequences are valued by individuals, groups, or society as a whole.

4. *Ethically complex.* The values underlying advocative claims are ethically complex. A given value (for example, health) may be regarded both as intrinsic and extrinsic. *Intrinsic values* are those which are valued as ends in themselves; *extrinsic values* are those which are valued because they will produce some other value. Health may be regarded as an end in itself and as a condition necessary for the attainment of other values, including security, freedom, and self-actualization. Similarly, democratic participation may be valued as an end in itself (intrinsic value) and a means to political stability (extrinsic value).

The idea of multiple advocacy should be sharply contrasted with the view that the function of policy analysis is to support a predetermined political position by mustering as much information as possible on behalf of the client's cause. Multiple advocacy is an approach to the systematic comparison and critical assessment of a number of potential solutions, not a way to defend single positions at any cost. To be sure, analysts eventually arrive at single set of recommendations—but only after critically assessing the pros and cons of multiple potential solutions for a problem. Multiple advocacy, which tacitly employs a process of triangulation which forms the methodological core of critical multiplism (see Chapter 1), is just as much an approach to problem structuring as problem solving.[4] When policy analysts follow guidelines of multiple advocacy, they are less likely to fall into what is commonly known as the *over-advocacy trap* (Box 7-1), a trap that often results in recommending the wrong solution because we have formulated the wrong problem. Indeed, the process of making plausible policy recommendations often requires that we move backward to problem structuring before we can move forward to a solution.

Simple Model of Choice

Advocative claims are possible only when the analyst is confronted by a situation of choice between two or more alternatives. In some situations the choice is between a new course of action and the status quo. In other situations choice may be complex, since there may be many alternatives to choose from.

In its simplest terms choice may be represented as a process of reasoning that involves three interrelated components: (1) the definition of a problem requiring action; (2) the comparison of consequences of two or more alternatives to resolve the problem; and (3) the recommendation of the alternative that will result in a preferred outcome, that is, the alternative that best satisfies some need, value, or opportunity. For example, choice may be described as a process of reasoning where the first alternative (A_1)

[4] Ian I. Mitroff, Richard O. Mason, and Vincent P. Barabba, *The 1980 Census: Policymaking amid Turbulence* (Lexington, MA: D.C. Heath, 1983), see multiple advocacy as a methodology for problem structuring which has features similar to their own dialectical approach.

BOX 7–1   The Over-Advocacy Trap

In *Presidential Decision Making and Foreign Policy: The Effective Use of Information and Advice* (1980), Alexander George has listed many shortcomings and weaknesses of policy advice which, applicable to domestic and foreign policy alike, are best described as the *over-advocacy trap.** The over-advocacy trap occurs when:

- The client and the analyst agree too readily on the nature of the problem and responses to it.
- Disagreements among policy advocates incorporated in an analysis do not cover the full range of policy alternatives.
- The analyst ignores advocates for unpopular policy alternatives.
- The analyst fails to communicate recommendations requiring that the client face up to a difficult or unpopular decision.
- The analyst is dependent on a single source of information.
- The client is dependent on a single analyst.
- Assumptions of a policy are evaluated only by advocates of that policy—including the trapped analyst or client.
- The client dismisses the results of analysis simply because they are perceived as negative or counterintuitive.
- The client or the analyst uncritically accepts consensus findings without probing the basis for the consensus and how it was achieved.

* Alexander George, *Presidential Decision Making in Foreign Policy* (Boulder, CO: Westview Press, 1980), pp. 23–24. I have changed some of George's language to show the relevance of his points to policy analysis (for example, the term *adviser* has been replaced with *analyst*).

---

yields one outcome (O_1), the second alternative (A_2) yields another outcome (O_2), and the value of O_1 is greater than O_2 ($O_1 > O_2$). Having this information the analyst will find no difficulty in recommending A_1 as the preferred alternative. The analyst reasons as follows: The first alternative leads to one result, while the second leads to another. The first result is more valuable than the second. Therefore ($\therefore$), the first course of action should be recommended (Figure 7–1).

This simple process of reasoning contains two essential elements of choice: factual and value premises. The first decision premise states that A_1 will result in O_1 while the second decision premise states that A_2 will result

FIGURE 7–1 Simple model
of choice.

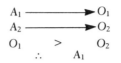

in O_2. These are *factual premises*; that is, assumptions that in principle may be shown to be true or false on the basis of factual knowledge. The third premise, however, is a *value premise*, that is, an assumption that may be shown to be good or bad on the basis of some set of values or system of ethics. This value premise states that O_1 is preferable to O_2 on some scale of values. Such premises cannot be proved right or wrong by appealing to factual premises, since questions of value require reasoned arguments about why the outcome in question is good or right for some person, group, or society as a whole. All choices contain both factual and value premises.

This simple model has the advantage of pointing out that factual and value premises are present in all choice situations. The disadvantage of this simple model is that it obscures the complexity of choice. Consider, for example, the conditions that must be present for this model of choice to be a valid one.[5]

1. *Single decision maker.* The choice must be confined to a single person. If choices are affected by or in turn affect more than one person, there are likely to be conflicting sets of factual and value premises.

2. *Certainty.* The outcomes of choice must be known with certainty. Yet the outcomes of choice are seldom known with certainty. People who affect and are affected by the choice often disagree about factual and value premises. Moreover, alternative courses of action are not the only causes of outcomes since there are many uncontrollable factors that enhance or inhibit the occurrence of a given outcome.

3. *Immediacy of consequences.* Results of a course of action must occur immediately. In most choice situations, however, outcomes of action occur over long periods of time. Because outcomes do not occur immediately the values that originally prompted action change with time.

Imagine now that our simple model of choice involves the issue of whether or not to provide minimum wages to unskilled workers. Assume that unskilled workers are not now covered by minimum wage legislation. On the basis of this information we conclude that maintaining the status quo (no minimum wage laws) will result in an annual average income of $4000 for unskilled workers. We might also forecast that a minimum wage of $4.50 per hour will result in an annual average income of $7000 for

---

[5] See, for example, Richard Zeckhauser and Elmer Schaefer, "Public Policy and Normative Economic Theory," in *The Study of Policy Formation,* ed. Raymond A. Bauer and Kenneth J. Gergen (New York: The Free Press, 1968), p. 28.

unskilled workers covered by the proposed policy. If we assume that more income is better than less income, we will have no difficulty in choosing as follows:

$$A_1 \rightarrow O_1 \ (\$4000)$$
$$A_2 \rightarrow O_2 \ (\$7000)$$
$$O_2 > O_1$$
$$\therefore A_2$$

This case fails to satisfy the three conditions necessary for the simple model of choice. First, there are multiple decision makers, not simply one. Many stakeholders—for example, legislators, voters, administrators, employers—affect and are affected by the issue of minimum wages. Each of these stakeholders brings different factual and value premises to the choice situation, so there is likely to be considerable conflict about what should be done and why. For example, certain legislators may want to increase the income of unskilled workers while constituents may want to reduce the tax burden that will accompany the enactment and implementation of minimum wage legislation. Second, there is considerable uncertainty about the consequences of minimum wage legislation. Many factors other than the legislation—for example, the availability of college students as an alternative source of unskilled labor—may determine whether or not employers will actually pay the minimum wage. Finally, the consequences of the legislation will occur over a relatively long period of time, which means that values may also change. For example, if the cost of living increases dramatically as a result of inflation, some groups who formerly supported a $4.50 per hour minimum wage may decide that such a level will not produce enough of an increase in real wages to justify the effort. If an alternative policy providing for a $5.00 per hour minimum wage is proposed, employers may be much more likely to hire college students than pay their unskilled employees the new minimum wage. In short, the simple model of choice provides a distorted picture of the actual issues involved in setting minimum wages for unskilled workers.

Complex Model of Choice

Suppose that a more thorough effort were made to gather relevant information about the policy issue of minimum wages. In addition to the original alternatives (minimum wages and the status quo), a third alternative may have been identified, for example, personnel training. This third alternative may have been proposed on the assumption that the problem is not low wages but an absence of skills necessary to qualify workers for available higher-paying jobs. After adding this third alternative we might forecast the following consequences: The first alternative (A_1 or the status quo) will produce by 1991 an average annual income of $4000 for some 12,000 unskilled workers; the second alternative (A_2 or a $4.50 per hour minimum wage) will produce by 1991 an average annual income of $7000 for 6000 unskilled workers, with the remaining workers entering the ranks of the unemployed since they will be replaced by college students; the third alternative (A_3 or personnel training) will produce by 1991 an average annual income of $4000 for some 10,000 formerly unskilled workers who will find jobs.

Each of these three alternatives will also have different consequences for stakeholders. For example, Congress members who will vote on the issue must be attentive to their prospects for reelection. Maintaining the status quo will result in the loss of fifty seats in districts where labor and welfare rights organizations are very powerful. Minimum wage legislation will result in no electoral changes, since the costs of the program will be passed on to owners of small businesses, who have little influence in the legislature. Finally, personnel training will result in a loss of ten seats in districts with strong opposition to any new tax increase. Further, the full benefits of training will not be felt for several years, since the real earning capacity of trainees will increase gradually, reaching an average annual level of $5000 for 12,000 workers by 1993. The real incomes of unskilled workers receiving the minimum wage will remain constant and may even decline as a result of inflation. Finally, the three alternatives have different costs that will be borne unequally by various stakeholders. The first alternative (the status quo) involves no new costs, but the second will require that owners of small businesses pay the additional wages. The third alternative will distribute costs among taxpayers who will foot the bill for training programs.

The simple model of choice has quickly become considerably more complex as a result of multiple stakeholders, uncertainty about outcomes, and time. If we diagram the choice situation in its new and complex form (Table 7–1), we find that the choice is more difficult to make. If we are concerned only with immediate monetary results in 1991, there is no difficulty. A_1 is the preferred alternative, since O_1 is greater than O_4 and O_7. But if we consider future monetary results in 1993, A_3 is the preferred alternative, since O_8 is greater than O_2, which in turn is greater than O_5. Finally, if we are concerned with political consequences in 1994, A_2 is the preferred alternative, since O_6 is greater (that is, produces more retained seats) than A_9 and A_3.

The problem with this complex choice is that we cannot make a satisfactory recommendation that combines the values of all stakeholders at multiple points in time. A situation such as this, where it is impossible to consistently rank alternatives according to two or more attributes, is termed *intransitive*. Intransitive choice typically involves multiple conflicting objectives and should be contrasted with situations involving transitive choices. A *transitive* choice is one where alternatives can be consistently ranked according to one or more attributes: If A_1 is preferable to A_2 in the choice set (A_1, A_2) and A_2 is preferable to A_3 in the choice set (A_2, A_3), then A_1 is preferable to A_3 in the set (A_1, A_3). Transitive choices can be constructed by assigning values to each alternative, so that if A_1 is preferred to A_2 and A_3, it is assigned a higher value. The person making a choice is said to maximize utility (value) by selecting the alternative that yields the

TABLE 7–1   Complex Model of Choice

A_1 (status quo)	O_1 ($48,000 income in 1991)	O_2 ($48,000 income in 1993)	O_3 (retain 150 seats in 1994)
A_2 (minimum wages)	O_4 ($42,000 income in 1991)	O_5 ($36,000 income in 1993)	O_6 (retain 200 seats in 1994)
A_3 (personnel training)	O_7 ($40,000 income in 1991)	O_8 ($60,000 income in 1993)	O_9 (retain 190 seats in 1994)

$$O_1 > O_4 > O_7; \therefore A_1$$
$$O_8 > O_2 > O_5; \therefore A_3$$
$$O_6 > O_9 > O_3; \therefore A_2$$

greatest value. Transitive and intransitive choice situations are illustrated in Table 7–2.

Forms of Rationality

In principle, any situation of choice can yield a recommendation that is preferred to all others because it will result in desired outcomes. Yet most choice situations involve multiple stakeholders, uncertainty, and consequences that change over time. In fact, conflict and disagreement are es-

TABLE 7–2   Transitive and Intransitive Choice

(a) Transitive

ALTERNATIVE	1981 Income	1983 Income	1982 Elections
A_1	1st	1st	1st
A_2	2nd	2nd	2nd
A_3	3rd	3rd	3rd

(b) Intransitive

ALTERNATIVE	1981 Income	1983 Income	1982 Elections
A_1	1st	2nd	3rd
A_2	2nd	3rd	1st
A_3	3rd	1st	2nd

sential characteristics of most policy issues:

> Difficult choice problems in which attribute rankings conflict lie at the core of the decisions that must be made by public policy makers. These difficulties may arise because their decisions affect many individuals. Though policy A might be better for one group in our society, policy B might be better for another. If time is a crucial element we may find, for example, that policy B will be better twenty years from today. In a third context, policy A might be superior if some uncertain events turn out favorably but policy B might be a better hedge against disaster.[6]

For these and similar reasons it may appear that the process of making policy recommendations is not and cannot be "rational." Tempting as this conclusion might be, our inability to satisfy the conditions of the simple model of choice does not mean that the process of recommendation is not and cannot be rational. If by *rationality* we mean a self-conscious process of using reasoned arguments to make and defend advocative claims, we will find not only that many choices are rational; we will also see that most are *multirational*. This means that there are multiple rational bases underlying most policy choices:[7]

1. *Technical rationality.* Technical rationality is a characteristic of reasoned choices that involve the comparison of alternatives according to their capacity to promote *effective* solutions for public problems. Choices between solar and nuclear energy technologies are an example of technical rationality.
2. *Economic rationality.* Economic rationality is a characteristic of reasoned choices that involve the comparison of alternatives according to their capacity to promote *efficient* solutions for public problems. Choices involving the comparison of alternative medical care systems in terms of their total costs and benefits to society may be characterized in terms of economic rationality.
3. *Legal rationality.* Legal rationality is a characteristic of reasoned choices that involve the comparison of alternatives according to their *legal conformity* to established rules and precedents. Choices that involve the award of public contracts according to whether companies comply with laws against racial and sexual discrimination are an example of legal rationality.
4. *Social rationality.* Social rationality is a characteristic of reasoned choices that involve the comparison of alternatives according to their capacity to maintain or improve valued social institutions, that is, promote *institutionalization*. Choices involving the extension of rights to democratic participation at work are an example of social rationality.
5. *Substantive rationality.* Substantive rationality is a characteristic of reasoned choices that involve the comparison of *multiple forms of rationality*—technical, economic, legal, social—in order to make the most appropriate choice under given circumstances. For example, many issues of government information policy involve questions about the usefulness of new computer technologies, their costs and benefits to society, their legal implications for rights

---

[6] Ibid., p. 30.

[7] See Paul Diesing, *Reason and Society* (Urbana, IL: University of Illinois Press, 1962).

to privacy, and their consistency with democratic institutions. Debates about these issues may be characterized in terms of substantive rationality.

The Rational-Comprehensive Theory

The main characteristic of these different forms of rationality is that they involve reasoned choices about the desirability of adopting different courses of action to resolve public problems. Yet any of these multiple forms of rationality—technical, economic, legal, social, substantive—is difficult to realize fully in most policy-making settings. In fact, for choices to be rational and comprehensive at the same time, they would have to meet the following conditions, which are described as the *rational-comprehensive theory* of decision making:[8]

1. An individual or collective decision maker must identify a policy problem on which there is consensus among all relevant stakeholders.
2. An individual or collective decision maker must define and consistently rank all goals and objectives whose attainment would represent a resolution of the problem.
3. An individual or collective decision maker must identify all policy alternatives that may contribute to the attainment of each goal and objective.
4. An individual or collective decision maker must forecast all consequences that will result from the selection of each alternative.
5. An individual or collective decision maker must compare each alternative in terms of its consequences for the attainment of each goal and objective.
6. An individual or collective decision maker must choose that alternative which maximizes the attainment of objectives.

The Disjointed-Incremental Theory

There are several important criticisms of the rational-comprehensive theory of decision making. The first of these, known as the *disjointed-incremental theory* of decision making, holds that actual policy choices seldom conform to the requirements of the rational-comprehensive theory.[9] According to the incremental theory individual or collective decision makers:

1. Consider only those objectives that differ incrementally (that is, by small amounts) from the status quo.
2. Limit the number of consequences forecast for each alternative.
3. Make mutual adjustments in goals and objectives, on the one hand, and alternatives on the other.
4. Continuously reformulate problems—and hence goals, objectives, and alternatives—in the course of acquiring new information.

---

[8] See Charles E. Lindblom, *The Policy-Making Process* (Englewood Cliffs, NJ: Prentice Hall, 1968).

[9] See Charles E. Lindblom and David Braybrooke, *A Strategy of Decision* (New York: The Free Press, 1963).

5. Analyze and evaluate alternatives in a sequence of steps, such that choices are continuously amended over time, rather than made at a single point prior to action.
6. Continuously remedy existing social problems, rather than solve problems completely at one point in time.
7. Share responsibilities for analysis and evaluation with many groups in society, so that the process of making policy choices is fragmented or disjointed.

Arrow's Impossibility Theorem

A second important criticism of the rational-comprehensive theory is known as Arrow's impossibility theorem. This theorem, developed by Nobel Prize winner Kenneth Arrow, demonstrates that it is impossible for decision makers in a democratic society to meet conditions of the rational-comprehensive theory.[10] One of Arrow's conclusions is that individual choices cannot be aggregated through majority voting procedures to create a collective decision that will produce a single best solution for all parties. The impossibility of creating, on the basis of aggregated individual choices, a collective decision that involves transitive preferences is described as the voters paradox.

To illustrate the voters paradox, imagine a committee composed of three members: Brown, Jones, and Smith (Table 7–3). The committee is deciding on which of three forms of energy—solar, coal, and nuclear—should be adopted to resolve the energy crisis. Brown, the leader of an energy rights organization, prefers solar to coal and coal to nuclear, reasoning that this ranking creates least risk to citizens. Since Brown's choice is transitive, it conforms to the rule: If A is preferred to B, and if B is preferred to C, then A is preferred to C. Jones and Smith, who are representatives of the coal and nuclear industries, also have transitive preferences. Jones prefers coal to nuclear, nuclear to coal, and coal to solar, reasoning that coal is most feasible from a technological standpoint followed by nuclear and solar. Smith, in turn, prefers nuclear to solar, solar to coal, and nuclear to coal, reasoning that nuclear is most efficient. Solar energy is not as efficient as coal but creates fewer dangers to the environment. Coal is viewed by Smith as the least desirable of the three alternatives.

The three choices are rational and transitive from each individual's point of view. Yet once the three committee members attempt through majority rule to reach a democratic decision about pairs of alternatives, we encounter a paradox. When we ask the committee members to choose between solar and coal, we see that solar is preferred to coal by a margin of 2 to 1 (Brown and Smith versus Jones). Similarly, when we ask members to choose between coal and nuclear, we also observe that coal is preferred to nuclear by a 2 to 1 margin (Brown and Jones versus Smith). If we now

---

[10] See Kenneth J. Arrow, Social Choice and Individual Values (New York: Wiley, 1963). Arrow received the Nobel Prize in Economics in 1972.

TABLE 7-3   The Voter's Paradox

COMMITTEE MEMBER	PREFERENCE
Brown	A (solar) preferred to B (coal) B (coal) preferred to C (nuclear) A (solar) preferred to C (nuclear)
Jones	B (coal) preferred to C (nuclear) C (nuclear) preferred to A (solar) B (coal) preferred to A (solar)
Smith	C (nuclear) preferred to A (solar) A (solar) preferred to B (coal) C (nuclear) preferred to B (coal)
Majority	A (solar) preferred to B (coal) B (coal) preferred to C (nuclear) C (nuclear) preferred to A (solar)

apply the transitivity rule to these *collective* preferences, we should find that if A is preferred to B (solar to coal), and B is preferred to C (coal to nuclear), then A is preferred to C (solar to nuclear). But this is not the collective result, since two committee members (Jones and Smith) have expressly argued that they prefer C to A (nuclear to solar). Hence, individual preferences are transitive, while the collective preference is *cyclic*, which means that alternatives cannot be ranked consistently. For this reason, a rational choice is impossible. The difference between transitive and cyclic choices is illustrated in Figure 7–2.

This example shows that individuals may choose rationally—whether on technical, economic, legal, social, or substantive bases—but majority rule does not yield a rational collective choice. Arrow's impossibility theorem logically proves that it is impossible to apply democratic procedures (for example, majority rule) to reach collective decisions that are transitive. Arrow's impossibility theorem is based on assumptions that there are at least two individuals in any group and that they choose one from among at least three alternatives. Arrow specifies five "reasonable conditions" of any democratic decision procedure: (1) *nonrestriction of choices*, that is, all possible combinations of individual preferences must be fully taken into account in developing a collective choice; (2) *nonperversity of collective choice*, that is, collective choices must consistently reflect individual choices; (3) *independence of irrelevant alternatives*, that is, choices must be confined to a given set of alternatives that are independent of all others; (4) *citizens' sovereignty*, that is, collective choices must not be constrained by prior choices; and (5) *nondictatorship*, that is, no individual or group can determine the outcome of collective choices by imposing their preferences on others.

To avoid the dilemma of cyclic preferences, we might delegate collective choices to a few decision makers (for example, experts) who can be expected to reach consensus and, hence, a transitive choice. While this

FIGURE 7-2   Transitive and cyclic choice.

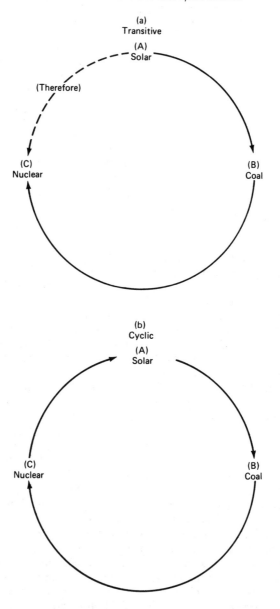

solves the problem of intransitive preferences, it nevertheless violates conditions of citizens' sovereignty and nondictatorship. Alternatively, we might introduce additional alternatives (for example, hydroelectric power) in the hope that this may provide a basis for consensus. This violates the condition of independence of irrelevant alternatives. In practice both of these procedures are employed in political systems formally committed to majority rule.[11] Since they depart from one or more of Arrow's "reasonable conditions," they result in choices that are described as *second-best*.

Bounded Rationality

Comprehensive rationality has also been challenged by Nobel Prize winner Herbert A. Simon. More than twenty-five years ago, Simon developed a theory of *bounded rationality*, according to which decision makers simply avoid the effort to be rational and comprehensive at the same time.[12] While choices are rational, they are nevertheless bounded by the practical circumstances under which choices are made. Simon argues:

> It is impossible for the behavior of a single, isolated individual to reach *any high degree of rationality*. The number of alternatives he must explore is so great, the information he would need to evaluate them so vast that even an approximation to objective rationality is hard to conceive.[13]

This formulation recognizes the bounds or limits of comprehensive rational choice when decision makers seek to maximize some valued outcome. In contrast to this type of *maximizing behavior*, Simon proposes the concept of *satisficing behavior*. Satisficing behavior refers to acts of choice where the decision maker seeks to identify courses of action that are just "good enough," that is, where the combination of *satis*factory and suf*fice* produce a "satisficing" choice. In other words, the decision maker does not need to consider all the many alternatives that, in principle, might produce increases in the benefits of action (that is, maximizing behavior). The decision maker need only consider the most evident alternatives that will produce a reasonable increase in benefits (that is, satisficing behavior).

Rationality as Constrained Maximization

The theory of bounded rationality, and with it the concept of satisficing behavior, emphasizes the limits of comprehensive rational choice. Nevertheless, Simon's theory, while a challenge to the comprehensive-rational theory of decision making, is not an argument for nonrational or irrational behavior. In fact, satisficing behavior may be fully rational, if by "rationality" we mean the process of exercising reason in making choices that take into

---

[11] The setting of the sequence of issues on agendas is an important example of violating conditions of citizens' sovereignty and nondictatorship. See Duncan Black, *The Theory of Committees and Elections* (Cambridge, MA: Cambridge University Press, 1958). For a review of these problems, see Norman Frohlich and Joe A. Oppenheimer, *Modern Political Economy* (Englewood Cliffs, NJ: Prentice Hall, 1978), Chap. 1.

[12] See Herbert A. Simon, *Administrative Behavior* (New York: Macmillan, 1945). Simon received the Nobel Prize in 1978 for his contributions to the study of decision-making in economic organizations. For Simon's other works, see *Models of Man* (New York: Wiley, 1957) and *The Sciences of the Artificial* (New York: Wiley, 1970).

[13] Simon, *Administrative Behavior*, p. 79.

account the costs of acquiring information. Indeed, such behavior can be defined as reasoned choice that attempts to *maximize* valued outcomes while concurrently recognizing *constraints* imposed by the costs of information. In the words of two proponents of rational choice as constrained maximization:

> It is doubtful whether any analyst of rational choice procedures would claim that a decision maker should systematically investigate and evaluate all of the alternatives available to him. Such search is both time-consuming and costly, and an optimal decision procedure should take these factors into account . . . the cost of decision-making should be incorporated into the maximizing model.[14]

This conception of rational choice is one that neither accepts the rational-comprehensive theory of decision making, nor does it accept the notion that constrained choices are somehow less than rational. Instead, rationality is viewed as the exercise of choice under conditions where the costs and benefits of searching for new alternatives and forecasting their consequences have been taken into account.

Mixed Scanning

A final perspective on the issue of rational choice is one provided by sociologist Amitai Etzioni. Etzioni has proposed a strategy of *mixed scanning* as an alternative both to comprehensive rationality and rival viewpoints, including disjointed incrementalism and bounded rationality.[15] While accepting the criticisms of the rational-comprehensive theory of decision making, Etzioni and others have pointed to limitations of the incremental theory.[16] Incrementalism, for example, has a conservative and status quo orientation that is difficult to reconcile with needs for creativity and innovation in policy-making. Incrementalism also suggests that most policy choices will be made by the most powerful interests in society, since it is these interests that have the most to gain from policies that differ as little as possible from the status quo. Finally, incrementalism does not recognize that policy choices differ in scope, complexity, and importance. Major strategic decisions, for example, are basically different from day-to-day operational decisions, a distinction that the disjointed-incremental theory does not adequately take into account.

Mixed scanning distinguishes between the requirements of strategic choices that set basic policy directions and operational choices that help lay the groundwork for strategic decisions and contribute to their implementation. In effect, mixed scanning seeks to adapt strategies of choice to the

---

[14] Zeckhauser and Schaefer, "Public Policy and Normative Economic Theory," p. 92.

[15] See Amitai Etzioni, "Mixed-Scanning: A 'Third' Approach to Decision Making," *Public Administration Review*, XXVII (December 1967), 385–92.

[16] See also Yehezkel Dror, *Ventures in Policy Sciences* (New York: American Elsevier, 1971).

nature of the problems confronted by policymakers. Because what is rational in one context may not be so in another, mixed scanning selectively combines elements of comprehensive rationality and disjointed incrementalism. In Etzioni's words:

> Assume we are about to set up a world-wide weather observation system using weather satellites. The rationalistic approach [that is, the rational-comprehensive theory] would seek an exhaustive survey of weather conditions by using cameras capable of detailed observations and by scheduling reviews of the entire sky as often as possible. This would yield an avalanche of details, costly to analyze and likely to overwhelm our action capabilities (e.g., "seeding" cloud formations that could develop into hurricanes or bring rain to arid areas). Incrementalism would focus on those areas in which similar patterns developed in the recent past and, perhaps, in a few nearby regions; it would thus ignore all formations which might deserve attention if they arose in unexpected areas.[17]

Mixed scanning, in contrast to either of the two approaches taken alone, provides for choices based both on comprehensive rationality and disjointed incrementalism. The precise combination depends on the nature of the problem. The more that problems are strategic in nature, the more that the rational-comprehensive approach is appropriate. Conversely, the more that problems are operational in nature, the more appropriate the disjointed-incremental approach. In all circumstances some combination of the two approaches is necessary, since the problem is not to adopt one approach and reject the other. The problem is rather to combine them in an effective way.

Erotetic Rationality

A challenge to forms of rationality described above is what is best called *erotetic rationality*. Erotetic rationality, which has already been encountered in our review of the functions of policy argument (Chapter 4), refers to a process of questioning and answering or, in a word, reasoned interrogation. Erotetic rationality, which may be deeply unsatisfying to those who demand well-specified criteria for sound recommendations in advance of inquiry, lies at the core of inductive processes of many kinds.[18]

The major principle of erotetic rationality has been stated succinctly by Albert in his critique of the uses of benefit-cost analysis in legal-judicial settings: "Ignorance is the sine qua non of rationality."[19] In many of the most important cases, analysts simply do not know the relationship between policies, policy outcomes, and the values in terms of which such outcomes

---

[17] Etzioni, "Mixed-Scanning," p. 389.

[18] See Nicholas Rescher, *Induction* (Pittsburgh, PA: University of Pittsburgh Press, 1980), pp. 6–7.

[19] Jeffrey M. Albert, "Some Epistemological Aspects of Cost–Benefit Analysis," *The George Washington Law Review* 45, No. 5 (1977), 1030.

should be assessed. This knowledge gap requires the frank acknowledgment of ignorance as a prerequisite of initiating the process of questioning and answering, a process in which an *ampliative* methodology yields rationally optimal answers to questions which "transcend accreted experience and outrun the reach of the information already at our disposal."[20]

Erotetic rationality, in this sense, is closely related to problem structuring as the central guidance system of policy analysis (Chapter 5). It also lies at the core of induction by elimination as found in quasi-experimental policy research, dialectical planning and policy analysis, and policy argumentation analysis.[21] The concept of "usable ignorance" in environmental policy is based on erotetic rationality,[22] as are recent innovations in physics represented by the work of Ilya Prigogine, an originator of chaos theory and recipient of the 1977 Nobel Prize in Chemistry: "Twentieth century physics is no longer the knowledge of certainties, it is one of interrogation. . . . And everywhere, instead of uncovering the permanence and immutability that classical science has taught us to seek out in nature, we have encountered change, instability, and evolution."[23]

Criteria for Policy Recommendation

The several types of rational choice may be viewed in terms of specific decision criteria used to advocate solutions for policy problems. By *decision criteria* we mean explicitly stated values that underlie recommendations for action. Decision criteria are of six main types: effectiveness, efficiency, adequacy, equity, responsiveness, and appropriateness.[24]

Effectiveness refers to whether a given alternative results in the achievement of a valued outcome (effect) of action, that is, an objective. Effectiveness, which is closely related to technical rationality, is often measured in terms of units of products or services or their monetary value. If nuclear generators produce more energy than solar collection devices, the former are regarded as more effective, since nuclear generators produce

---

[20] Rescher, *Induction*, p. 6. Rescher traces the origins of an ampliative methodology of inquiry to the American pragmatist philosopher, Charles Sanders Peirce, who used the term *ampliative* for conclusions which transcend information stipulated in given premises, that is, conclusions which follow from premises only inconclusively.

[21] For a critique and synthesis of these three approaches—represented by the work of Donald T. Campbell, Ian I. Mitroff, and Stephen Toulmin—see William N. Dunn, "Reforms As Arguments," in *The Argumentation Turn in Policy Analysis*, ed. John Forester and Frank Fischer (Durham, NC: Duke University Press, 1993).

[22] See Jerome R. Ravetz, "Usable Knowledge, Usable Ignorance: Incomplete Science with Policy Implications," *Knowledge: Creation, Diffusion, Utilization* 9, No. 1 (1987), 87–116.

[23] Ilya Prigogine, "A New Model of Time, a New View of Physics," in *Models of Reality*, ed. Jacques Richardson (Mt. Airy, MD: Lomond Publications, 1984). Quoted by Rita Mae Kelly and William N. Dunn, "Some Final Thoughts," in *Advances in Policy Studies Since 1950*, ed. Dunn and Kelly (New Brunswick, NJ: Transaction Books, 1992), p. 526.

[24] On decision criteria, see Theodore H. Poister, *Public Program Analysis: Applied Research Methods* (Baltimore: University Park Press, 1978), pp. 9–15.

more of a valued outcome. Similarly, an effective health policy is one that provides more quality health care to more people, assuming that quality health care is a valued outcome (objective).

Efficiency refers to the amount of effort required to produce a given level of effectiveness. Efficiency, which is synonymous with economic rationality, is the relationship between effectiveness and effort, with the latter often measured in terms of monetary costs. Efficiency is often determined by calculating the costs per unit of product or service (for example, dollars per gallon of irrigation water or dollars per medical examination), or by calculating the volume of goods or services per unit of cost (for example, 10 gallons of irrigation water per dollar or 50 medical examinations per $1000). Policies that achieve the greatest effectiveness at least cost are said to be efficient.

Adequacy refers to the extent to which any given level of effectiveness satisfies the needs, values, or opportunities that gave rise to a problem. The criterion of adequacy specifies expectations about the strength of a relationship between policy alternatives and valued outcomes. The criterion of adequacy may refer to four types of problems (Table 7–4):

1. *Type I problems.* Problems of this type involve fixed costs and variable effectiveness. When maximum allowable budgetary expenditures result in fixed costs, the aim is to maximize effectiveness within the limits of available resources. For example, given a fixed budget of $1 million for each of two programs, a health policy analyst will recommend the alternative that results in the greatest improvement in the quality of health care in the community. The response to type I problems is called *equal-cost analysis*, since analysts compare alternatives that vary in effectiveness but whose costs are treated as equal. Here the most adequate policy is one that maximizes the attainment of objectives while remaining within the limits of fixed costs.

2. *Type II problems.* Problems of this type involve fixed effectiveness and variable costs. When the level of valued outcomes is fixed, the aim is to minimize costs. For example, if public transportation facilities must serve at least 100,000 persons annually, the problem is to identify those alternatives—bus, monorail, subways—that will achieve this fixed level of effectiveness at least cost. The response to type II problems is called *equal-effectiveness analysis*, since analysts compare alternatives that vary in costs but whose effectiveness is equal. Here the most adequate policy is one that minimizes costs while achieving fixed levels of effectiveness.

TABLE 7–4 Criteria of Adequacy: Four Types of Problems

	COSTS	
EFFECTIVENESS	*Fixed*	*Variable*
Fixed	Type IV (equal-cost–equal-effectiveness)	Type II (equal-effectiveness)
Variable	Type I (equal-cost)	Type III (variable-cost–variable-effectiveness)

3. *Type III problems.* Problems of this type involve variable costs and variable effectiveness. For example, the choice of an optimal budget to maximize the attainment of agency objectives is a type III problem. The response to type III problems is called *variable-cost-variable-effectiveness analysis*, since costs and effectiveness are free to vary. Here the most adequate policy is one that maximizes the ratio of effectiveness to costs.

4. *Type IV problems.* Problems of this type involve fixed costs as well as fixed effectiveness. Type IV problems, which involve *equal-cost-equal-effectiveness analysis*, are often especially difficult to resolve. Analysts are not only limited by the requirement that costs not exceed a certain level but are also limited by the constraint that alternatives satisfy a predetermined level of effectiveness. For example, if public transportation facilities must serve a minimum of 100,000 persons annually—yet costs have been fixed at an unrealistic level— then any policy alternative must either satisfy both constraints or be rejected. In such circumstances the only remaining alternative may be to do nothing.

The different definitions of adequacy contained in these four types of problems point to the complexity of relationships between costs and effectiveness. For example, two programs designed to provide municipal services (measured in units of service to citizens) may differ significantly in terms both of effectiveness and costs (Figure 7–3). Program I achieves a higher overall level of effectiveness than program II, but program II is less costly at lower levels of effectiveness. Should the analyst recommend the program that maximizes effectiveness (program I), or the program that minimizes costs at the same level of effectiveness (program II)?

To answer this question we must look at the relation between costs and effectiveness, rather than view costs and effectiveness separately. Yet this is where the complications begin (see Figure 7–3). (1) If we are dealing with a type I (equal-cost) problem and costs are fixed at $20,000 ($C_2$), pro- gram II is more adequate because it achieves the highest level of effective- ness while remaining within the fixed-cost limitation. (2) If we are con- fronted with a type II (equal-effectiveness) problem and effectiveness is fixed at 6000 units of service (E_2), program I is more adequate. (3) If, on the other hand, we are dealing with a type III (variable-cost-variable-effective- ness) problem, where costs and effectiveness are free to vary, program II is more adequate, since the ratio of effectiveness to costs (called an *effective- ness–cost ratio*) is greatest at the intersection of E_1 and C_1. Here program II produces 4000 units of service for $10,000, that is, a ratio of 4000 to 10,000 or 0.4. By contrast, program II has an effectiveness–cost ratio of 0.32 (8000 units of service divided by $25,000 $=$ 8000/25,000 $=$ 0.32).[25] Finally, (4) if we are dealing with a type IV (equal-cost-equal-effectiveness) problem, where both effectiveness and costs are fixed at E_2 and C_2, neither program is adequate. This dilemma, which permits no adequate solution, is known as *criterion overspecification.*

---

[25] A simple way to display effectiveness–cost ratios graphically is to draw a straight line from the *origin* (that is, lower left-hand corner) of a graph to the *knee* of the effectiveness– cost curve (that is, the point where the straight line touches the curvature but does not pass through it). The more that the line moves leftwards toward the vertical effectiveness scale, the greater the ratio between effectiveness and costs.

FIGURE 7–3 Cost–effectiveness comparisons using four criteria of adequacy.

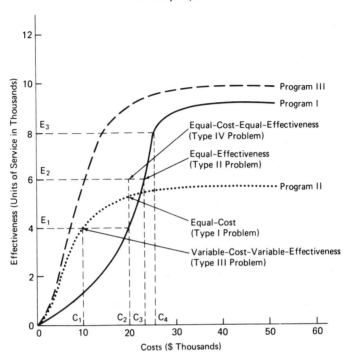

Source: Adapted from E. S. Quade, *Analysis for Public Decisions* (New York: American Elsevier, 1975), p. 93.

The lesson of this illustration is that it is seldom possible to choose between two alternatives on the basis of *either* costs *or* effectiveness. While it is sometimes possible to convert measures of effectiveness into dollar benefits, which permits us to calculate net income benefits by subtracting monetary costs from monetary benefits, it is frequently difficult to establish convincing dollar equivalents for many of the most important policy outcomes. What is the dollar equivalent of a life saved through traffic safety programs? What is the dollar value of international peace and security promoted by United Nations educational, scientific, and cultural activities? What is the dollar value of natural beauty preserved through environmental protection legislation? While such questions will be examined further when we discuss cost–benefit analysis, it is important to recognize that the measurement of effectiveness in dollar terms is a complex and difficult problem.[26]

---

[26] See, for example, Richard Zeckhauser, "Procedures for Valuing Lives," *Public Policy* (Fall 1975), 419–64; and Baruch Fischhoff, "Cost–Benefit Analysis and the Art of Motorcycle Maintenance," *Policy Sciences*, 8 (1977), 177–202.

Sometimes it is possible to identify an alternative that simultaneously satisfies all criteria of adequacy. For example, the broken-line curve in Figure 7–3 might represent a third program that adequately meets fixed-cost as well as fixed-effectiveness criteria and also has the highest ratio of effectiveness to costs. Since this situation is rare, it is almost always necessary to specify the level of effectiveness and costs that are regarded as adequate. Yet this is a matter of reasoned judgment about what constitutes an adequate level of effectiveness, given the costs.

Questions of adequacy cannot be resolved by arbitrarily adopting a single criterion. For example, net income benefits (dollars of effectiveness minus dollar costs) are *not* an appropriate criterion when costs are fixed and a single program with the highest benefit–cost ratio can be repeated many times within total fixed-cost limits. This is illustrated in Table 7–5, where program I can be repeated 10 times up to a fixed-cost limit of $40,000, with total net benefits of $360,000 (that is, $36,000 × 10). Program I, since it can be repeated 10 times, has the highest benefit–cost ratio. But if program I cannot be repeated—that is, if only one of the three programs must be selected—program III should be recommended. Program III produces the greatest net benefits, even though it has the lowest benefit–cost ratio.

The criterion of *equity* is closely related to legal and social rationality and refers to the distribution of effects and effort among different groups in society. An equitable policy is one where effects (for example, units of service or monetary benefits) or effort (for example, monetary costs) are fairly or justly distributed. Policies designed to redistribute income, educational opportunity, or public services are sometimes recommended on the basis of the criterion of equity. A given program might be effective, efficient, and adequate—for example, the benefit–cost ratio and net benefits may be superior to all other programs—yet it might still be rejected on grounds that it will produce an inequitable distribution of costs and benefits. This could happen under several conditions: Those most in need do not receive services in proportion to their numbers; those who are least able to pay bear a disproportionate share of costs; or those who receive most of the benefits do not pay the costs.

The criterion of equity is closely related to competing conceptions of justice or fairness and to ethical conflicts surrounding the appropriate basis

TABLE 7–5 Comparison of Benefit–Cost Ratio and Net Benefits as Criteria of Adequacy (in Thousands of Dollars)

PROGRAM	BENEFITS	COSTS	BENEFIT–COST RATIO	NET BENEFITS
I	40	4	10	36
II	64	8	8	56
III	100	40	2.5	60

Source: Adapted from Richard Zeckhauser and Elmer Schaefer, "Public Policy and Normative Economic Theory," in *The Study of Policy Formation*, ed. R. A. Bauer and K. J. Gergen (New York: The Free Press, 1968), p. 73.

for distributing resources in society. Such problems of "distributive justice," which have been widely discussed since the time of the ancient Greeks, may occur each time a policy analyst recommends a course of action that affects two or more persons in society. In explicitly defining objectives for society as a whole the analyst may actually be seeking a way to measure *social welfare*, that is, the aggregate satisfaction experienced by members of a community. Yet, as we know, individuals and groups have different values. What satisfies one person or group often does not satisfy another. Under these circumstances the analyst must consider a fundamental question: How can a policy maximize the welfare of society, and not just the welfare of particular individuals or groups? The answer to this question may be pursued in several different ways:

1. *Maximize individual welfare.* The analyst can attempt to maximize the welfare of all individuals simultaneously. This requires that a single transitive preference ranking be constructed on the basis of all individual values. *Arrow's impossibility theorem*, as we have seen, demonstrates that this is impossible even in cases where there are two persons and three alternatives.

2. *Protect minimum welfare.* Here the analyst can attempt to increase the welfare of some persons while still protecting the positions of persons who are worst off. This approach is based on the *Pareto criterion*, which states that one social state is better than another if at least one person is better off, and no one is worse off. A *Pareto optimum* is a social state in which it is not possible to make any person better off without also making another person worse off. The Pareto criterion is seldom applicable, since most policy decisions involve the provision of services to persons who are made better off by taxing those who are made worse off.

3. *Maximize net welfare.* Here the analyst attempts to increase net welfare (for example, total benefits less total costs) but assumes that the resulting gains could be used to compensate losers. This approach is based on the *Kaldor–Hicks criterion*: One social state is better than another if there is a net gain in efficiency (total benefits minus total costs) and if those who gain can compensate losers. For all practical purposes this criterion, which does not require that losers actually be compensated, avoids the issue of equity. The Kaldor–Hicks criterion is one of the foundations of traditional cost–benefit analysis.

4. *Maximize redistributive welfare.* Here the analyst attempts to maximize redistributional benefits to selected groups in society, for example, the racially oppressed, poor, or sick. One redistributive criterion has been put forth by philosopher John Rawls: One social state is better than another if it results in a gain in welfare for members of society who are worst off.[27]

Rawls's formulation attempts to provide an ethical foundation for the concept of justice. It does so by requesting that we imagine ourselves in an "original" state, where there is a "veil of ignorance" about the future distribution of positions, statuses, and resources in a civil society yet to be established. In this "original" state, individuals will choose a social order on the basis of the redistributive criterion just described, since it is in everyone's individual interest to establish a society in which they will not be worst off.

---

[27] John Rawls, A *Theory of Justice* (Cambridge, MA: Harvard University Press, 1971).

By postulating this "original" condition, it becomes possible to reach consensus on a just social order. This "original" condition should be contrasted with the conditions of present societies, where vested interests make it impossible to reach consensus on the meaning of justice. The weakness of Rawls's formulation is its oversimplification or avoidance of conflict. The redistributive criterion is appropriate for well-structured problems and not for the types of problems typically encountered by public policy analysts. While this does not mean that the redistributive criterion cannot be used to make choices, it does mean that we have still not reached a single basis for defining social welfare.

None of these criteria of equity is fully satisfactory. The reason is that conflicting views about the rationality of society as a whole (social rationality) or of the appropriateness of legal norms guaranteeing rights to property (legal rationality) cannot be resolved simply by appealing to formal economic rules (for example, the Pareto or Kaldor–Hicks criteria) or to formal philosophical principles (for example, Rawls's redistributive criterion). Questions of equity, fairness, and justice are political ones; that is, they are influenced by processes involving the distribution and legitimation of power in society. While economic theory and moral philosophy can improve our capacity to critically assess competing criteria of equity, they cannot replace the political process.

Responsiveness refers to the extent that a policy satisfies the needs, preferences, or values of particular groups. The criterion of responsiveness is important because an analyst can satisfy all other criteria—effectiveness, efficiency, adequacy, equity—yet still fail to respond to the actual needs of a group that is supposed to benefit from a policy. A recreation program might result in an equitable distribution of facilities but be unresponsive to the needs of particular groups (for example, the elderly). In effect, the responsiveness criterion asks a practical question: Do criteria of effectiveness, efficiency, adequacy, and equity actually reflect the needs, preferences, and values of particular groups?

The final criterion to be discussed here is that of appropriateness. The criterion of *appropriateness* is intimately related to substantive rationality, since questions about the appropriateness of a policy are not concerned with individual sets of criteria but two or more criteria taken together. Appropriateness refers to the value or worth of a program's objectives and to the tenability of assumptions underlying these objectives. While all other criteria take objectives for granted—for example, neither the value of efficiency nor of equity is questioned—the criterion of appropriateness asks whether these objectives are proper ones for society. To answer this question analysts may consider all criteria together—that is, reflect on the relations among multiple forms of rationality—and apply higher-order criteria (metacriteria) that are logically prior to those of effectiveness, efficiency, adequacy, equity, and responsiveness.[28]

---

[28] On similar metacriteria, including generality, consistency, and clarity, see Duncan MacRae, Jr., *The Social Function of Social Science* (New Haven, CT: Yale University Press, 1976).

The criterion of appropriateness is necessarily open ended, since by definition it is intended to go beyond any set of existing criteria. For this reason there is not and cannot be a standard definition of criteria of appropriateness. The best we can do is consider several examples:

1. *Equity and efficiency.* Is equity as redistributional welfare (Rawls) an appropriate criterion when programs designed to redistribute income to the poor are so inefficient that only a small portion of redistributional benefits actually reaches them? When such programs are viewed as a "leaky bucket" used to carry benefits to the poor, analysts may question whether equity is an appropriate criterion.[29]

2. *Equity and entitlement.* Is equity as minimum welfare an appropriate criterion when those who receive additional benefits have not earned them through socially legitimate means? Analysts may question the appropriateness of the Pareto criterion when those who gain (even though none lose) have done so through corruption, fraud, discrimination, and unearned inheritance.[30]

3. *Efficiency, equity, and humanistic values.* Are efficiency and equity appropriate criteria when the means required to achieve an efficient or just society conflict with democratic processes? Analysts may challenge the appropriateness of efficiency or equity when efforts to rationalize decision making for these purposes subvert conditions required for emancipation, individuation, or self-actualization.[31] Efficiency, equity, and humanism are not necessarily equivalent. Alienation, as Marx and other social thinkers have recognized, is not automatically eliminated by creating an abundant society of equals.

4. *Equity and reasoned ethical debate.* Is equity as redistributive welfare (Rawls) an appropriate criterion when it subverts opportunities for reasoned ethical debate? This criterion of equity can be challenged on grounds that it presupposes an individualistic conception of human nature where ethical claims are no longer derived from reasoned arguments but are "the contractual composite of arbitrary (even if comprehensible) values individually held and either biologically or socially shaped. . . . The structure of the Rawlsian argument thus corresponds closely to that of instrumental rationality; ends are exogenous, and the exclusive office of thought in the world is to ensure their maximum realization. . . . [Rawls's premises] reduce all thought to the combined operations of formal reason and instrumental prudence in the service of desire."[32]

APPROACHES TO RECOMMENDATION

In making policy recommendations the analyst typically addresses a number of interrelated questions. Whose needs, values, and opportunities are at issue, and what alternatives are available for their satisfaction? What

---

[29] See Arthur M. Okun, *Equality and Efficiency* (Washington, DC: The Brookings Institution, 1975).

[30] See, for example, Peter Brown, "Ethics and Policy Research," *Policy Analysis,* 2 (1976), 325–40.

[31] See, for example, Jurgen Habermas, *Toward a Rational Society* (Boston: Beacon Books, 1970); and *Legitimation Crisis* (Boston: Beacon Books, 1975).

[32] See Laurence H. Tribe, "Ways Not to Think about Plastic Trees," in Tribe and others, *When Values Conflict,* p. 77.

goals and objectives should be attained, and how should they be measured? How much will it cost to attain objectives and what kinds of constraints—budgetary, legal, administrative, political—may impede their attainment? Are there side effects, spillovers, and other anticipated and unanticipated consequences that should be counted as costs or benefits? How will the value of costs and benefits change over time? How certain is it that forecasted outcomes will occur? What should be done?

Public vs. Private Choice

Answers to these questions are designed to enhance our capabilities for making persuasive policy recommendations. Although these questions are just as relevant for policy-making in the private as in the public sector, there are several important differences between these sectors that should be kept in mind.[33]

1. *Nature of public policy processes.* Policy-making in the public sector involves bargaining, compromise, and conflict among citizens' groups, legislative bodies, executive departments, regulatory commissions, businesses, and many other stakeholders. There is no single producer or consumer of goods and services whose profits or welfare is to be maximized. The presence of numerous stakeholders with competing or conflicting values makes problems of choice more complex in the public than in the private sector.

2. *Collective nature of public policy goals.* Policy goals in the public sector are collective ones which are supposed to reflect society's preferences or some broad "public interest." The specification of these collective goals, as we have seen, often involves multiple conflicting criteria, from effectiveness, efficiency, and adequacy to equity, responsiveness, and appropriateness.

3. *Nature of public goods.* Public and private goods may be divided into three groups: specific goods, collective goods, and quasi-collective goods. *Specific goods* are exclusive, since the person who owns them has the legal right to exclude others from their benefits. The allocation of specific goods (for example, cars, houses, or physicians' services) is often made on the basis of market prices, which are determined by supply and demand. *Collective goods* are nonexclusive, since they may be consumed by everyone. No person can be excluded from the consumption of clean air, water, and roads provided by the government. It is frequently impossible to allocate collective goods on the basis of market prices, since normal relationships between supply and demand do not operate in the public sector. *Quasi-collective goods* are specific goods whose production has significant spillover effects for society. Although elementary education can be provided by the private sector, the spillovers are regarded as so important that the government produces great quantities at a cost affordable by all.

Organizations in the public and private sectors produce each of these three types of goods. Nevertheless, the public sector is primarily occupied

---

[33] See H. H. Hinrichs and G. M. Taylor, *Systematic Analysis: A Primer on Benefit-Cost Analysis and Program Evaluation* (Pacific Palisades, CA: Goodyear Publishing Co., 1972), pp. 4–5.

with the provision of such collective and quasi-collective goods as defense, education, social welfare, public safety, transportation, environmental protection, recreation, and energy conservation. By contrast, the private sector is chiefly concerned with the production of such specific goods as food, appliances, machinery, and housing. Contrasts between the production of these goods in the public and private sectors are illustrated in Figure 7–4.

Because the nature of these three types of goods differs, so do the procedures for estimating their value to producers and consumers. The primary aim of a private firm producing specific goods for the market is to make profits, that is, to maximize the difference between the total revenues earned by selling a product and the total costs required for its production. When a private firm is faced with a choice between two or more products that differ in the revenues they will earn and the costs required for their production, the firm will choose that product that maximizes profits, defined as total revenue minus total costs. If the firm should decide to invest in a product which yields lower profits, either in the short or the long run, we can estimate the opportunity cost of the decision. *Opportunity cost* refers to the benefits sacrificed by investing resources to produce one product when another more profitable alternative might have been chosen.

FIGURE 7–4   Three types of goods in the public and private sectors.

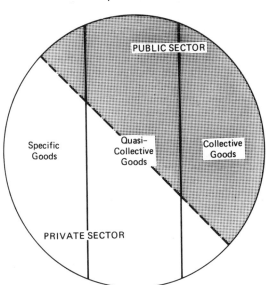

Source: H. H. Hinrichs and G. M. Taylor, *Systematic Analysis: A Primer on Benefit–Cost and Program Evaluation* (Pacific Palisades, CA: Goodyear Publishing Co., 1972), p. 5.

Supply and Demand

Opportunity costs in the private sector can be estimated by using market prices as a measure of costs and benefits. Market prices of specific goods are determined by supply and demand. If we look at various combinations of the price and quantity of a specific good, we observe that (1) consumers will demand greater quantities (Q) of a product as the price (P) for that product decreases; and (2) producers will supply greater quantities (Q) of a product as the price (P) of that product increases (Figure 7–5). Finally, (3) the combination of price and quantity that yields a single level of consumer demand and producer supply—that is, the point where supply and demand intersect (P_eQ_e in Figure 7–5)—indicates the price and quantity of specific goods that will be sold on the market. Graphic representations of the various combinations of price and quantity where consumers and producers are willing to buy and sell a product are called a *demand curve* and *supply curve*, respectively. The point where demand and supply curves intersect is called the *equilibrium price–quantity combination*.

The equilibrium price–quantity combination represents that point where consumers and producers, if they are completely free to choose what they will buy and sell, will produce and consume equal quantities of a good at a given price. If we know the equilibrium price–quantity combination for a specific good (for example, electric toothbrushes), we can determine the profit of a given investment by subtracting the total costs required to produce a specific good from the total revenues earned by selling the product

FIGURE 7–5   Supply and demand curves and the equilibrium price–quantity combination.

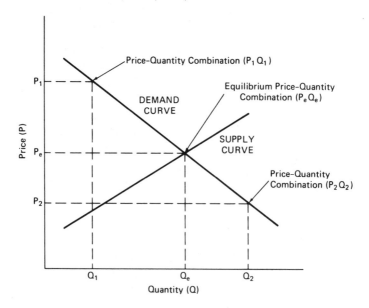

at the equilibrium price (P_e) and equilibrium quantity (Q_e). By knowing the profits that can be earned from alternative investments, it is possible to estimate the benefits sacrificed by investing resources to produce one product when another more profitable investment might have been made. For example, if a firm producing electric toothbrushes (a specific good) and earning an annual profit of $1 million finds that it could have earned a profit of $2 million by producing electric drills at the same cost (including costs for any additional labor, technology, or marketing facilities), the opportunity cost of the investment in electric toothbrush production is $1 million.

The logic of profit maximization in the private sector can be extended to public policy. We can view public programs as if they were private firms attempting to maximize profits on investments. Instead of using profits (total revenue minus total cost) as a criterion for recommending alternatives, we can use net benefits (total benefits minus total costs). We can also apply the concept of opportunity costs by viewing public programs as investments in the production of goods that might have been made by private firms. For example, if government invests $50 million in the construction of a dam that will yield $10 million in net benefits to farmers and other beneficiaries, it must extract these investment resources from private citizens who could have invested the $50 million elsewhere. If private investment would have yielded $20 million in net benefits (profits) to private citizens, the opportunity cost of building the dam is $10 million (net private benefits of $20 million minus net public benefits of $10 million).

Public Choice

This logic begins to break down when we consider differences between public and private choice, including contrasts among specific, quasi-collective, and collective goods. While the logic of profit maximization can be applied to certain kinds of public goods (for example, the production of hydroelectric power), there are important reasons why concepts of profit, net benefits, and opportunity costs are difficult to apply to problems of public choice:

1. *Multiple legitimate stakeholders.* Public policy-making involves multiple stakeholders whose claims on public investments are frequently guaranteed by law. While there are also multiple stakeholders in private policy-making, none except owners and stockholders can legitimately make claims on investments. In the public sector, with its many legitimate stakeholders, it is difficult to know whose benefits should be maximized and who should bear the costs of public investments.

2. *Collective and quasi-collective goods.* Because most public goods are collective (for example, clean air) or quasi-collective (for example, education), it is difficult or impossible to sell them on the market, where transactions are made on the basis of ability to pay. For this reason market prices are frequently unavailable as a measure of net benefits or opportunity costs. Even where prices are based on interview surveys among citizens, some persons may falsely indicate no willingness to pay for a public good but later use the good at a

price lower than that they are actually willing to pay. This is called the *free-rider problem*.

3. *Limited comparability of income measures*. Even when the net benefits of public and private investments can be expressed in dollars as a common unit of measure, private investments with higher net benefits are not always preferable to public ones with lower (or even zero or negative) net benefits. For example, a private investment in a new office building that yields $1 million in net benefits is unlikely to be preferred over a public investment in a cure for cancer that yields zero or negative net benefits. Even where comparisons are confined to public investments, the use of income measures to recommend alternatives implies that the goal of increasing aggregate income "is more important than good health or better education, or the elimination of poverty, and that these other goals are legitimate only to the extent that they increase future income."[34]

4. *Public responsibility for social costs and benefits*. Private firms are responsible for their own *private costs* and *private benefits* but not for social ones, except as prescribed by law (for example, antipollution legislation) or moral convention. By contrast, the costs and benefits of public programs are socialized, thus becoming *social costs* and *social benefits* that go much beyond the need to satisfy private stockholders. Social costs and social benefits (for example, the costs of destroying the natural environment by building highways) are difficult to quantify and often have no market price. Such social costs and social benefits are called intangibles.

Contrasts between public and private choice do not mean that the logic of profit maximization is wholly inapplicable to public problems. Contrasts do mean, however, that there are limitations to such logic when applied to public problems. These strengths and limitations are evident when we consider two of the most important approaches to recommendation in policy analysis: cost–benefit and cost–effectiveness analysis.

Cost–Benefit Analysis

Cost–benefit analysis is an approach to policy recommendation that permits analysts to compare and advocate policies by quantifying their total monetary costs and total monetary benefits. While cost–benefit analysis may be used to recommend policy actions, in which case it is applied prospectively (*ex ante*), it may also be used to evaluate policy performance. In this case (see Chapter 9) it is applied retrospectively (*ex post*). Much of modern cost–benefit analysis is based on that field of economics that treats problems of how to maximize social welfare, that is, the aggregate economic satisfaction experienced by members of a community.[35] This field is called *wel-*

---

[34] Alice Rivlin, *Systematic Thinking for Social Action* (Washington, DC: The Brookings Institution, 1971), p. 56.

[35] For comprehensive treatments of cost–benefit analysis, see, for example, Edward J. Mishan, *Cost–Benefit Analysis* (New York: Frederick A. Praeger, 1976); and Edward M. Gramlich, *Benefit–Cost Analysis of Public Programs*, 2nd ed. (Englewood Cliffs, NJ: Prentice Hall, 1990).

fare economics, since it is especially concerned with the ways that public investments may contribute to the maximization of net income as a measure of aggregate satisfaction (welfare) in society.

Cost–benefit analysis has been applied to many different kinds of public programs and projects. The earliest applications of cost–benefit analysis were in the area of dam construction and the provision of water resources, including efforts to analyze the costs and benefits of hydroelectric power, flood control, irrigation, and recreation. Other more recent applications include transportation, health, manpower training, and urban renewal.

When used to make recommendations in the public sector cost–benefit analysis has several distinctive characteristics:

1. Cost–benefit analysis seeks to measure *all* costs and benefits to society that may result from a public program, including various intangibles that cannot be easily measured in terms of monetary costs and benefits.

2. Traditional cost–benefit analysis epitomizes *economic rationality*, since the criterion most frequently employed is global economic efficiency. A policy or program is said to be efficient if its *net benefits* (that is, total benefits minus total costs) are greater than zero and higher than those net benefits that would have resulted from an alternative public or private investment.

3. Traditional cost–benefit analysis uses the *private marketplace* as a point of departure in recommending public programs. The opportunity costs of a public investment are often calculated on the basis of what net benefits might have been gained by investing in the private sector.

4. Contemporary cost–benefit analysis, sometimes called *social cost–benefit analysis,* can also be used to measure redistributional benefits. Since social cost–benefit analysis is concerned with criteria of equity, it is consistent with *social rationality.*

Cost–benefit analysis has a number of strengths. First, *both* costs and benefits are measured in dollars as a common unit of value. This permits analysts to subtract costs from benefits, a task that is not possible with cost-effectiveness analysis. Second, cost–benefit analysis permits us to go beyond the confines of a single policy or program and link benefits to the income of society as a whole. This is possible because the results of individual policies and programs can be expressed in monetary terms, at least in principle. Finally, cost–benefit analysis allows analysts to compare programs in widely differing areas (for example, health and transportation), since net efficiency benefits are expressed in terms of dollars. This is not possible when effectiveness is measured in terms of units of service, since the number of persons treated by physicians cannot be directly compared with the number of miles of roads built.

Cost–benefit analysis, in both its traditional and contemporary forms, also has several limitations. First, an exclusive emphasis on economic efficiency can mean that criteria of equity are meaningless or inapplicable. In practice, the Kaldor–Hicks criterion simply ignores problems of redistributional benefits, while the Pareto criterion seldom resolves conflicts between efficiency and equity. Second, monetary value is an inadequate measure of responsiveness, since the actual value of income varies from person to person. For example, an extra $100 of income is far more significant to the head of a poverty household than to a millionaire. This problem of *limited interpersonal comparisons* often means that income is an inappropriate measure of individual satisfaction and social welfare. Third, when market prices are unavailable for important goods (for example, clean air or health services), analysts are often forced to estimate *shadow prices*, that is, subjective estimates of the price that citizens might be willing to pay for goods and services. These subjective judgments may simply be arbitrary expressions of the values of analysts.

Cost–benefit analysis, even when it takes into account problems of redistribution and social equity, is closely tied to income as a measure of satisfaction. For this reason it is difficult to discuss the appropriateness of *any* objective that cannot be expressed in monetary terms. The exclusive concentration on net income or redistributional benefits often inhibits reasoned debates about the ethical or moral bases of alternative policies. Cost–benefit analysis is therefore limited in its capacity to consider relations among alternative forms of reason (technical, economic, social, legal) as part of an overall effort to establish the substantive rationality of policies and programs. Hence, cost–benefit analysis may come very close to providing us with "the price of everything and the value of nothing."

Types of Costs and Benefits

In using cost–benefit analysis it is essential to consider *all* costs and benefits that may result from a policy or program. While such a comprehensive inventory of costs and benefits is quite difficult to achieve in practice, it can help reduce errors that occur when we omit some costs and benefits from our analysis. One of the best ways to guard against such errors is to classify costs and benefits: inside ("internal") vs. outside ("external"); directly measurable ("tangible") vs. indirectly measurable ("intangible"); primary ("direct") vs. secondary ("indirect"); and net efficiency ("real") vs. distributional ("pecuniary"). These types of costs and benefits, and the questions they are based on, are illustrated in Figure 7–6.

Inside vs. outside costs and benefits.   Here the question is whether a given cost or benefit is internal or external to a given target group or jurisdiction. Inside or internal costs and benefits are called *internalities*, while outside or external ones are called *externalities*. What is an inside cost or benefit (internality) in one case will be an outside one (externality) in another. The difference depends on how the analyst draws boundaries around the target group or jurisdiction. If the boundary is society as a whole, there may be no externalities. If, however, the boundary is a particular target group or jurisdiction, there will be internalities as well as externalities. Externalities are the positive and negative spillovers outside the boundaries of the jurisdiction or target group. For example, the construction of high-rise apartments in a central-city area as part of an urban renewal program has certain costs and benefits within the urban jurisdiction, including expenditures on construction and income derived from rents. The same urban

FIGURE 7–6   Classification of costs and benefits according to four types of questions.

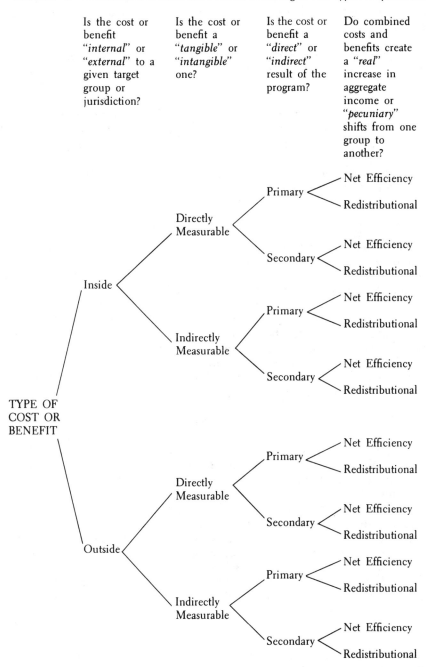

renewal program also has external costs to suburban jurisdictions which must provide additional fire and police services in areas where vagrants or criminals have resettled because they can no longer afford to live in the central-city area.

Directly measurable vs. indirectly measurable costs and benefits. The question here is whether the cost or benefit is a "tangible" or "intangible" one. *Tangibles* are costs and benefits that are directly measurable in terms of known market prices for goods and services, while *intangibles* are costs and benefits that are indirectly measurable in terms of estimates of such market prices. When dealing with intangibles, such as the price of clean air, the analyst may attempt to estimate shadow prices by making a subjective judgment about the dollar value of costs and benefits. In the urban renewal example the analyst may try to estimate the opportunity costs that various groups might be willing to pay for the destruction of the sense of community resulting from urban renewal.

Primary and secondary costs and benefits.   Here the question is whether the cost or benefit is a "direct" or "indirect" result of a program. A *primary cost or benefit* is one that is related to the most highly valued program objectives, while a *secondary cost or benefit* is one that is related to objectives that are less valued. For example, an urban renewal program may have as its most important objective the provision of low-cost housing to the poor, in which case the primary costs and benefits would include expenditures for construction and income from rents. Secondary costs and benefits would involve lesser objectives, including intangible costs, such as the destruction of a sense of community, or tangible benefits, such as reduced costs of police and fire services because of better street lighting and fire-resistant construction.

Net efficiency vs. redistributional benefits.   Here the question is whether combined costs and benefits create an increase in aggregate income or result merely in shifts in income or other resources among different groups. *Net efficiency benefits* are those that represent a "real" increase in net income (total benefits minus total costs), while *redistributional benefits* are those that result in a "pecuniary" shift in the incomes of one group at the expense of another but without increasing net efficiency benefits. Such changes are called *real benefits* and *pecuniary benefits*, respectively. For example, an urban renewal project may produce $1 million in net efficiency benefits. If urban renewal also results in increased sales in small grocery stores in the immediate area—and decreased sales in stores that are more distant from new high-rise apartments—the benefits and the costs of income gained and lost are "pecuniary." They cancel each other out without producing any change in net efficiency benefits.

To call one type of benefit "real" and the other merely "pecuniary" can introduce considerable bias: Is an increase in the disposable income of the poor less "real" than an improvement in the net benefits of the community? For this reason it is best to drop the categories of "real" vs. "pecuniary" altogether, provided that we do not *add* any increase in redistributional benefits to net efficiency benefits without also *subtracting* the costs of redistribution to those whose income or other benefits were reduced. This error, called *double counting*, can produce invalid estimates of net efficiency benefits.

Observe that answers to these four questions can result in many combinations of costs and benefits. A given inside cost or benefit may be directly measurable (tangible) or indirectly measurable (intangible). An intangible cost or benefit may in turn be primary or secondary, depending on the relative importance of different objectives. A primary or secondary objective may itself be defined in terms of net efficiency or redistribution. Typically, either net efficiency or redistribution must be a primary objective, since it is seldom possible to create higher net efficiency benefits *and* redistributional benefits at the same time. In other words, these two types of benefits conflict. They represent a situation requiring *tradeoffs*, that is, conscious efforts to determine how much of one objective should be sacrificed to obtain another.

Tasks in Cost–Benefit Analysis

In conducting a cost–benefit analysis, most of the following tasks (Table 7–6) are important for making maximally plausible recommendations.

Problem structuring. The search for alternative formulations of the problem and the definition of the boundaries of the metaproblem (see Figure 5–9) are essential tasks of cost–benefit analysis. Problem structuring does not occur once, at the beginning of the cost–benefit analysis, but occurs at many points throughout the analysis. Problem structuring yields information about the potentially relevant goals, objectives, alternatives, criteria, target groups, costs, and benefits to guide the analysis. Problem structuring also may result in dissolving, resolving, and unsolving the problem many times during the cost–benefit analysis (see Figure 5–1).

Specification of objectives. Analysts usually begin with general aims or goals, for example, controlling cocaine addiction. Goals, as we have seen, must be converted into objectives that are temporally specific and measurable (see Figure 6–2). The goal of controlling cocaine addiction may be converted into a number of specific objectives, for example, a 50 percent reduction in the supply of cocaine within five years. Objectives usually imply policy alternatives. The reduction in supply implies a policy of drug interdiction, whereas another objective—for example, a 50 percent reduction in the demand for cocaine—not only implies a policy of drug interdiction to raise the price of cocaine and lower demand, but also suggests drug rehabilitation as a way to decrease the number of addicts and, in turn, lower demand. In this and other cases the relation between objectives and policy

TABLE 7–6   Ten Tasks in Conducting a Cost–Benefit Analysis

TASK	DESCRIPTION
Problem structuring	Formulation of metaproblem by defining boundaries of goals, objectives, alternatives, criteria, target groups, costs, and benefits
Specification of objectives	Conversion of general aims (goals) into temporally specific and measurable aims (objectives)
Specification of alternatives	Selection of most promising policy alternatives from a larger set of potential solutions defined at the problem structuring phase
Information search, analysis, and interpretation	Location, analysis, and interpretation of information needed to forecast the outcomes of specified policy alternatives
Identification of target groups and beneficiaries	Listing of all groups (stakeholders) which are a target of action (for example, regulation) or inaction (status quo), or which will benefit from action or inaction
Estimation of costs and benefits	Estimation in units of monetary value the specific benefits and costs of each alternative in all classes (internal and external, directly and indirectly measurable, primary and secondary, efficiency and redistributional)
Discounting of costs and benefits	Conversion of monetary costs and benefits into their present value on the basis of a specified discount factor
Estimation of risk and uncertainty	Use of sensitivity and *a fortiori* analysis to estimate probabilities that benefits and costs will occur in future
Choice of decision criterion	Choice of criterion for selecting among alternatives: Pareto improvement, net efficiency improvement, distributional improvement, internal rate of return
Recommendation	Selection of alternative that is most plausible, considering rival ethical and causal hypotheses

alternatives rests on causal assumptions that may be prove to be questionable or plainly mistaken.

Identification of alternative solutions.   Once objectives have been specified, the analyst's assumptions about the causes of a problem and its potential solutions are almost inevitably transformed into alternative policies to achieve these objectives. The way a problem has been structured—for example, the problem of cocaine may be formulated as a demand problem requiring the interdiction of the flow of drugs from South America—thus governs the policies perceived to be appropriate and effective. If problem search has been severely restricted, inadvertently or for explicit political and ideological reasons, the policy metaproblem will exclude otherwise promising policy alternatives. Eventually, problem unsolving may be necessary (see Figure 5–1).

Information search, analysis, and interpretation.   The task here is to locate, analyze, and interpret information relevant for forecasting the

outcomes of policy alternatives. At this point the principal objects of a forecast are the costs and benefits of policy alternatives already identified at the
previous stage of analysis. Here, information may be acquired from available
data on costs and benefits of similar existing programs. For example, prior
to the establishment of the Drug Enforcement Administration, published
budgetary data on the costs of drug enforcement activities of the U.S. Cus-
toms Service was used to estimate some of the costs of new drug interdiction
policies. The benefits of interdiction in the form of decreased supply and
demand were based on economic and administrative assumptions which
eventually proved to be highly questionable or plainly wrong.[36]

Identification of target groups and beneficiaries. Here the task is
to conduct a stakeholder analysis (Chapter 5) which lists all groups that have
a stake in the policy issue because they will be affected, negatively and
positively, by the adoption and implementation of policy recommendations.
Target groups are the objects of new regulations or restrictions that typically
involve the loss of freedom or resources—for example, regulations restricting the choice of women to terminate pregnancies or new tax schedules
which increase the tax burden on the middle class. By contrast, beneficiaries
are groups that will gain from the adoption and implementation of recommendations, for example, commercial truckers who receive increased
net income as a consequence of some 40 states moving from the 55 mph
to the 65 mph speed limit in the late 1980s.

Estimation of costs and benefits. This task, perhaps the most difficult in cost–benefit analysis, requires the estimation in monetary terms of
all benefits and costs that are likely to be experienced by target groups and
beneficiaries. As we have seen (Figure 7–6), the types of benefits and costs
are several: internal and external, directly and indirectly measurable, primary and secondary, net efficiency and redistributional. In many areas of
public policy it is difficult and even practically impossible to estimate costs
or benefits. For example, the monetary benefits of a fatality averted through
mandatory seat belt laws, obligatory state vehicle inspections, or breast cancer screening programs are subject to broad disagreement, especially when
the costs of these fatality-averting policies are subtracted from the benefits
of a human life. The validity, reliability, and appropriateness of such measures is often disputed.

Discounting of costs and benefits. If a certain level of costs and
benefits is projected for a future time period, estimates must adjust for the
decreasing real value of money due to inflation and future changes in interest rates. The real value of costs and benefits is usually based on the
technique of discounting, a procedure that expresses future costs and ben-

---

[36] See George M. Guess and Paul G. Farnham, *Cases in Public Policy Analysis*, Chap.
5, "Coping with Cocaine" (New York: Longman, 1989), pp. 7–48; and Constance Holden,
"Street-Wise Crack Research," *Science*, 246 (December 15, 1989), 1376–81. As of 1992, the
Bush administration had made no apparent effort to unsolve the problem.

efits in terms of their present value. For example, the value of human life is sometimes expressed as an hourly wage rate multiplied by life expectancy. If the human life being valued is that of a 20-year-old with low earning capacity—and if the discount factor used is 10 percent—the present value of that person's life can amount to no more than a few thousand dollars. This raises critical ethical questions about the comparability of values attached to the lives of young and old, poor and rich, rural and urban populations.

Estimation of risk and uncertainty.   The task here is to employ sensitivity analysis, a generic term that refers to procedures that test the sensitivity of conclusions to alternative assumptions about the probability of occurrence of different costs and benefits, or to different discount factors. It is difficult to develop reliable probabilistic estimates because different forecasts of the same future outcome, as we learned in Chapter 6, often have widely differing levels of accuracy which stem from differences in institutional, temporal, and historical contexts.

Choice of a decision criterion.   Here the task is to specify a decision criterion or rule for choosing between two or more alternatives with different mixes of costs and benefits. These criteria are of six types: efficiency, effectiveness, adequacy, equity, responsiveness, and appropriateness. Among efficiency criteria are net efficiency improvement (the net present value after discounting costs and benefits to their present value must exceed zero) and internal rate of return (the rate of return on a public investment must be greater than that which could be earned at the actual rate of interest paid). Effectiveness criteria include the marginal effectiveness of graduated levels of public investment in producing the greatest volume of some valued good or service (for example, access to medical treatment per dollar invested in health maintenance organizations vs. traditional health care providers). Distributional and redistributional criteria, respectively, include Pareto improvement (at least one group gains while none loses) and Rawlsian improvement (those worst off become better off). The choice of a decision criterion has important ethical implications, since decision criteria are grounded in very different conceptions of moral obligation and the just society.

Recommendation.   The final task in cost–benefit analysis is to make a recommendation by choosing between two or more policy alternatives. The choice of alternatives is seldom clear and unequivocal, which calls for a critical analysis of the plausibility of recommendations, taking into account rival causal and ethical hypotheses which may weaken or invalidate a recommendation. For example, a recommendation based on Pareto improvement may be weakened by establishing that the rich will benefit at the expense of the middle and lower classes. In retrospect, this has been the actual history of social and economic policy in the United States over the last 20 years.[37]

---

[37] See, for example, Frank Levy, *Dollars and Dreams: The Changing American Income Distribution* (New York: Russell Sage Foundation, 1987).

Cost—Effectiveness Analysis

Cost—effectiveness analysis is an approach to policy recommendation that permits analysts to compare and advocate policies by quantifying their total costs and effects. In contrast to cost—benefit analysis, which attempts to measure all relevant factors in a common unit of value, cost—effectiveness analysis uses two different units of value. Costs are measured in monetary units, while effectiveness is typically measured in units of goods, services, or some other valued effect. In the absence of a common unit of value, cost—effectiveness analysis does not permit net effectiveness or net benefit measures, since it makes no sense to subtract total costs from total units of goods or services. It is possible, however, to produce cost—effectiveness and effectiveness—cost ratios, for example, ratios of costs to units of health service or units of health service to costs.

These ratios have an altogether different meaning than cost—benefit ratios. Whereas effectiveness—cost and cost—effectiveness ratios tell us how much of a good or service is produced per dollar expended—or, alternatively, how many dollars are expended per unit produced—benefit—cost ratios tell us how many times more benefits than costs are produced in a given instance. Benefit—cost ratios must be greater than 1 if there are any net benefits at all. For example, if total benefits are $4 million and total costs are $6 million, then the benefit—cost ratio is 4 to 6, or 0.66, and total net benefits are minus $2 million. If total net benefits are zero ($4 million minus $4 million equals zero), then the benefit—cost ratio is always 1 ($4 \div 4 = 1$). By definition, then, a benefit—cost ratio must exceed 1 for there to be any net benefits. This is not true of effectiveness—cost ratios, which have a different meaning from one case to the next.

Cost—effectiveness analysis, like its cost—benefit counterpart, may be applied prospectively (*ex ante*) as well as retrospectively (*ex post*). In contrast to cost—benefit analysis, cost—effectiveness analysis grew out of work done for the Defense Department in the early 1950s, and not from work in the field of welfare economics. Much of the early development of cost—effectiveness analysis was carried out by the Rand Corporation in projects designed to evaluate alternative military strategies and weapons systems. In the same period cost—effectiveness analysis was applied to problems of program budgeting in the Department of Defense and was extended in the 1960s to other government agencies.[38]

Cost—effectiveness analysis is particularly appropriate for questions involving the most efficient way to use resources to attain objectives that cannot be expressed in terms of income. Cost—effectiveness analysis has been used to recommend alternative policies and programs in criminal justice, manpower training, transportation, health, defense, and other areas.

Cost—effectiveness analysis, when used to make recommendations in

---

[38] See, for example, David Novick, *Efficiency and Economy in Government through New Budgeting and Accounting Procedures* (Santa Monica, CA: The Rand Corporation, February 1954); Roland J. McKean, *Efficiency in Government through Systems Analysis* (New York: Wiley, 1958); Charles J. Hitch and Roland J. McKean, *The Economics of Defense in the Nuclear Age* (New York: Atheneum, 1965); and T. A. Goldman, ed., *Cost-Effectiveness Analysis* (New York: Frederick A. Praeger, 1967).

the public sector, has several distinguishing characteristics:

1. Cost–effectiveness analysis, since it avoids problems of measuring benefits in monetary terms, is more easily applied than cost–benefit analysis.
2. Cost–effectiveness analysis epitomizes *technical rationality*, since it attempts to determine the utility of policy alternatives but without relating their consequences to global economic efficiency or aggregate social welfare.
3. Cost–effectiveness analysis, since it relies minimally on market prices, is less dependent on the logic of profit maximization in the private sector. Cost–effectiveness analysis, for example, frequently makes no attempt to determine if benefits exceed costs or if alternative investments in the private sector would have been more profitable.
4. Cost–effectiveness analysis is well suited to the analysis of externalities and intangibles, since these types of effects are difficult to express in dollars as a common unit of measure.
5. Cost–effectiveness analysis typically addresses fixed-cost (type I) or fixed-effectiveness (type II) problems, whereas cost–benefit analysis typically addresses variable-cost-variable-effectiveness (type III) problems.

The strengths of cost–effectiveness analysis are its comparative ease of application, its capacity to treat collective and quasi-collective goods whose values cannot be estimated on the basis of market prices, and its appropriateness for analyzing externalities and intangibles. The main limitation of cost–effectiveness analysis is that recommendations are less easily related to questions of aggregate social welfare. Unlike cost–benefit analysis, efforts to measure costs and effectiveness are confined to given programs, jurisdictions, or target groups and cannot be used to calculate net income benefits as a measure of the aggregate satisfaction experienced by members of a community.

Cost–effectiveness analysis also attempts to consider all costs and benefits of policies and programs, with the exception that benefits are not measured in monetary terms. Many of the same types of costs and benefits as those discussed previously are important in cost–effectiveness analysis: inside vs. outside; directly measurable vs. indirectly measurable; and primary vs. secondary. While it is not possible to calculate net efficiency benefits, redistributional effects may be analyzed.

The tasks in conducting a cost–effectiveness analysis are similar to those required in cost–benefit analysis (Table 7–6), with two exceptions. Only costs are discounted to their present value and criteria of adequacy differ from those normally used in cost–benefit analysis. In cost–effectiveness analysis two criteria of adequacy are most often employed:

1. *Least-cost criterion.* After establishing a desired level of effectiveness, the costs of programs with equal effectiveness are compared. Programs with less than the fixed level of effectiveness are dropped, while the program which meets the fixed level of effectiveness at least cost is recommended.
2. *Maximum-effectiveness criterion.* After establishing an upper level of permissible costs (usually a budgetary constraint), programs with equal costs are compared. Programs which exceed the upper cost limit are dropped, while the

program that meets the fixed-cost level with the maximum effectiveness is recommended.

3. *Marginal effectiveness.* If units of some service or good as well as the costs of that service or good can be expressed on two continuous scales, the marginal effectiveness of two or more alternatives can be calculated. For example, the costs of providing security services by municipal police and by private security firms contracted by municipalities can be expressed on two continuous scales: a graduated scale of costs associated with each hour of patrols and the number of crimes against property reported, deterred, investigated, and cleared. A continuous cost–effectiveness function may be established for each type of service provider. The provider with the highest effectiveness–cost ratio at any point along the function beyond some minimum level of effectiveness has the greater marginal effectiveness—that is, the highest effectiveness achieved at the last dollar expended at the margin between the last dollar and the subsequent dollar cost (see point E_1–C_1 in Figure 7–3).

4. *Cost–effectiveness.* The cost–effectiveness of two or more alternatives is the cost per unit of goods or services. For example, the 55 mph and 65 mph speed limits involve different costs per fatality averted, with the latter ranking slightly lower in cost–effectiveness. If the 55 mph and 65 mph speed limits have approximately equal costs (the denominator), but the latter averts slightly fewer fatalities (the numerator), then the average cost per fatality averted will be greater for the 65 mph speed limit. Effectiveness–cost ratios, in contrast to the benefit–cost ratios used in cost–benefit analysis, may not take into account all costs (for example, the value of lives lost driving at the higher speed limit). For this reason, simple effectiveness–cost ratios may yield biased estimates of the actual costs of a given service or good, although the exclusion of costs is by no means an inherent limitation of cost–effectiveness analysis.

Methods for Recommendation

A range of methods and techniques are available for making recommendations with cost–benefit and cost–effectiveness analysis (Table 7–7). These methods and techniques are most easily understood if they are viewed as tools for carrying out tasks of cost–benefit analysis described above (see Table 7–6). Cost–benefit and cost–effectiveness analysis, as we saw above, differ in certain important respects. These differences, however, are mainly related to the choice of decision criteria—for example, net efficiency improvement cannot be estimated with cost–effectiveness analysis because benefits are not expressed in monetary terms. With few exceptions (for example, calculating the present value of future benefits) methods and techniques of cost–benefit analysis are also appropriate for cost–effectiveness analysis.

Objectives Mapping

A frequent difficulty experienced in making policy recommendations is knowing what objectives to analyze. *Objectives mapping* is a technique used to array goals and objectives and their relationship to policy alternatives. Goals, objectives, and alternatives that have been identified by one or more methods of problem structuring (Chapter 5) may be depicted in

TABLE 7–7   Methods and Techniques for Recommendation Classified by Tasks of Cost–Benefit Analysis

TASK	METHOD/TECHNIQUE
Problem structuring[1]	Boundary analysis
	Classificational analysis
	Hierarchy analysis
	Multiple perspective analysis
	Argumentation analysis
	Argumentation mapping
Specification of objectives	Objectives mapping
	Value clarification
	Value critique
Information search, analysis, and interpretation	Boundary analysis[2]
Identification of target groups and beneficiaries	Boundary analysis
Estimation of costs and benefits	Cost element structuring
	Cost estimation
	Shadow pricing
Discounting of costs and benefits	Discounting
Estimation of risk and uncertainty	Feasibility assessment[3]
	Constraints mapping
	Sensitivity analysis
	A fortiori analysis
Choice of decision criterion	Value clarification
	Value critique
Recommendation	Plausibility analysis

Notes:
[1] See Chapter 5 for these methods and techniques.
[2] See Chapter 5.
[3] See Chapter 6.

the form of an *objectives tree*, which is a pictorial display of the overall structure of objectives and their relationships.[39] The objectives, when mapped in the form of a tree diagram, often form a hierarchy in which certain objectives that are necessary for the attainment of other objectives are arranged vertically. An objectives tree for the development of a national energy policy is illustrated in Figure 7–7.

In constructing an objectives tree the analyst may start with existing objectives or may generate new ones. If it is necessary to generate new objectives, there are several problem-structuring techniques available for this purpose, including hierarchy analysis, classificational analysis, brainstorming, and argumentation analysis (see Chapter 5). Once a set of objectives has been obtained it is possible to arrange them hierarchically in a

---

[39] See T. Harrell Allen, *New Methods in Social Science Research: Policy Sciences and Futures Research* (New York: Frederick A. Praeger, 1978), 95–106.

FIGURE 7–7   Objectives tree for national energy policy.

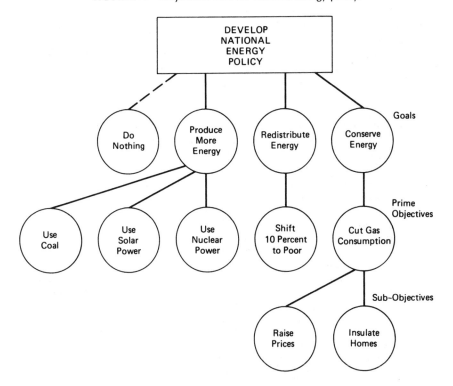

tree such as that provided in Figure 7–7. Objectives trees are more general at the top and progressively more detailed as one moves lower in the hierarchy. Typically, the uppermost part of an objectives tree contains broad purposes, while lower levels represent goals, prime objectives, and subobjectives. Observe that when we read downwards, we answer the question "*How* should we accomplish this objective?" When we read upwards, we answer the question "*Why* should we pursue this objective?" Objectives mapping is therefore useful, not only for purposes of mapping the complexities of policy implementation (that is, "how" questions), but also for clarifying the ends of action (that is, "why" questions). Finally, most objectives can be regarded both as ends and means.

Value Clarification

Value clarification is a procedure for identifying and classifying value premises that underlie the selection of policy objectives. The need for value clarification in making policy recommendations is most evident when we consider competing criteria for recommendation (effectiveness, efficiency, adequacy, responsiveness, equity, appropriateness) and the multiple forms of rationality from which these criteria are derived. Value clarification helps answer such questions as the following: What value premises underlie the choice of policy objectives? Are these value premises those of policy analysts, of policymakers, of particular social groups, or of society as a whole? What circumstances explain the fact that certain groups are committed to these value premises and objectives, while others are opposed? Finally, what reasons are offered to justify particular value premises and objectives?

There are several major steps in value clarification:[40]

1. Identify all relevant objectives of a policy or program. Objectives may simply be listed or displayed in the form of an objectives tree (Figure 7–7).

2. Identify all stakeholders who affect and are affected by the attainment or non-attainment of the objectives. Be sure to include yourself, as policy analyst, in the list of stakeholders.

3. List the value premises that underlie each stakeholder's commitment to objectives. For example, environmentalists may value energy conservation because it preserves the aesthetic qualities of the natural environment, while suburban homeowners may value energy conservation because it provides for a more secure material existence.

4. Classify value premises into those that are simply expressions of personal taste or desire (*value expressions*); those that are statements about the beliefs of particular groups (*value statements*); and those that are judgments about the universal goodness or badness of the actions or conditions implied by the objective (*value judgments*). For example, you as policy analyst may express a personal desire for more energy consumption, environmental groups may state their belief in energy conservation, and oil producers may offer judgments about increased energy production that are based on beliefs in universal rights to use private property as owners see fit.

5. Further classify value premises into those that provide a *basis for explaining* objectives (for example, environmentalists seek to conserve energy because this is consistent with their belief in the inviolability of nature), and those that provide a *ground for justifying* objectives (for example, energy conservation is an appropriate objective because nature and humanity alike are entitled to rights of self-protection).

The advantage of value clarification is that it enables us to go beyond the analysis of objectives as if they were merely expressions of personal desire or taste. Value clarification also takes us one step beyond the explanation of circumstances that explain objectives. While the *bases* of values are important—for example, it is important to know that the poor favor greater social equity—ethical and moral disputes cannot be resolved without examining the *grounds* for justifying objectives.

Value Critique

Value critique is a set of procedures for examining the persuasiveness of conflicting arguments offered in the course of a debate about policy

---

[40] For background material see the section of Chapter 4 on "Reason and Ethics in Policy Analysis."

objectives. Whereas value clarification enables us to classify values according to their form, context, and function, value critique allows us to examine the role of values in policy arguments and debates. Value clarification focuses on the objectives and underlying values of individual stakeholders. By contrast, value critique focuses on conflicts among the objectives and underlying values of different stakeholders. Value clarification also has a static quality, while value critique looks toward changes in values that may result from reasoned debates.

Procedures for value critique are an extension of the value-critical mode of policy argument discussed in Chapter 4. In conducting a value critique it is necessary to:

1. Identify one or more advocative claims, that is, claims that set forth a recommendation for action.
2. List all stakeholders who will affect and be affected by the implementation of the recommendation.
3. Describe each stakeholder's argument for and against the recommendation.
4. Identify each element in the debate: information (*I*), claim (*C*), qualifier (*Q*), warrant (*W*), backing (*B*), and rebuttal (*R*).
5. Assess the *ethical persuasiveness* of each argument and determine whether to retain, alter, or reject the recommendation.

To illustrate the process of value critique, imagine a policy analyst who has completed a cost–benefit analysis of low-cost home insulation. The recommendation or claim (*C*) is that the government should adopt the low-cost home insulation program. Information (*I*) indicates that the net benefits of the program are $50 million and the benefit–cost ratio is 5 to 1. Since the program will result in considerable energy savings, it is almost certainly justified (*Q*). But after the arguments of each stakeholder have been analyzed, the recommendation seems less persuasive (Figure 7–8). The original warrant (*W*) used to support the recommendation is that of increased social welfare, a warrant which in turn might be backed (*B*) by the Pareto or Kaldor–Hicks criteria. The rebuttal (*R*) is that the program will not benefit the poor and the elderly. This rebuttal is backed by the Rawls criterion (*B₂*) that persons who are worst off should gain.

Note that this debate is both economic and ethical, since it involves questions of efficiency and of justice at the same time. One result of the debate might be to modify the recommendation in such a way that the government would provide low-cost home insulation on a graduated-cost basis. Those who cannot afford it might pay nothing, while those in higher income brackets would pay most. Yet this would make the program less attractive to those who use most heat. If equal costs were maintained across the board (with the exception of the poor and the elderly, who would pay nothing), the total net benefits may well be negative. While value critique cannot finally answer the question of how much efficiency should be sacrificed for a given increase in social equity, it does make it possible to conduct a reasoned ethical debate about such questions, rather than expect cost–

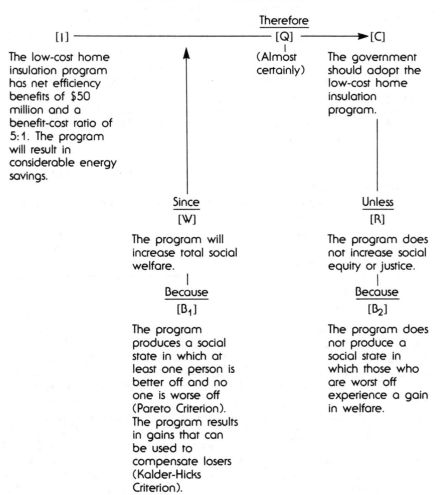

FIGURE 7–8   Value-critical debate.

benefit analysis to provide answers to questions for which it is not suited. Economics is not ethics any more than price is value.

Cost Element Structuring

The concept of cost is central to the process of making policy recommendations, since the pursuit of one objective almost always requires that we sacrifice another. *Opportunity costs*, as we have seen, are the benefits that could otherwise be obtained by investing resources in the attainment of some other objective. In other words, costs are benefits forgone or

TABLE 7–8   Cost Element Structure

I. Primary (direct) costs
  1. One-time fixed costs
    Research
    Planning
    Development, testing, and evaluation
  2. Investment costs
    Land
    Building and facilities
    Equipment and vehicles
    Initial training
  3. Recurring (operating and maintenance) costs
    Salaries, wages, and fringe benefits
    Maintenance of grounds, vehicles, and equipment
    Recurrent training
    Direct payments to clients
    Payments for extended support services
    Miscellaneous materials, supplies, and services
II. Secondary (indirect) costs
  1. Costs to other agencies and third parties
  2. Environmental degradation
  3. Disruption of social institutions
  4. Other

lost, while net benefits (total benefits minus total costs) are a measure of the costs that would have been paid if resources had been invested in the pursuit of some other objective.

Cost element structuring is a procedure for classifying and describing all costs that will be incurred by establishing and operating a program.[41] The cost element structure is a list of functions, equipment, and supplies that require the expenditure of resources. The purpose of cost element structuring is to create a list of functions, equipment, and supplies that is exhaustive and mutually exclusive. If the list is exhaustive, no important costs will be overlooked. If the list contains mutually exclusive items, no costs will be *double counted.*

A cost element structure contains two main divisions: *primary* (direct) and *secondary* (indirect) costs. Primary costs are subdivided into three categories: *one-time fixed costs, investment costs,* and *recurrent* (*operating and maintenance*) *costs.*[42] A typical cost element structure is illustrated in Table 7–8.

[41] See H. G. Massey, David Novick, and R. E. Peterson, *Cost Measurement: Tools and Methodology for Cost-Effectiveness Analysis* (Santa Monica, CA: The Rand Corporation, February 1972).

[42] Poister, *Public Program Analysis*, pp. 386–87; and H. P. Hatry, R. E. Winnie, and D. M. Fisk, *Practical Program Evaluation for State and Local Government* (Washington, DC: The Urban Institute, 1973).

Cost Estimation

Cost estimation is a procedure that provides information about the dollar value of items in a cost element structure. While the cost element structure indicates what elements should be measured, cost estimation actually measures them. A *cost-estimating relationship* is an explicit measure of the relationship between the quantity of functions, materials, or personnel and their costs. The simplest type of cost–estimating relationship is cost per unit, for example, the cost per acre of land, per square foot of facilities, or per worker in a given job category. More complex cost–estimating relationships involve the use of linear regression and interval estimation (Chapter 6). For example, linear regression may be used to provide an interval estimate of vehicle maintenance costs, using miles driven as the independent variable.

Cost–estimating relationships are central to the process of making recommendations, since explicit measures of the relationship between the quantity of functions, materials, or personnel and their costs permit analysts to compare two or more policy alternatives in a consistent manner. Cost-estimating relationships are used to construct cost models that represent some or all of the costs that will be required to initiate and maintain a program. A simplified cost model for initial investment is illustrated in Figure 7–9.

Shadow Pricing

Shadow pricing is a procedure for making subjective judgments about the monetary value of benefits and costs when market prices are unreliable or unavailable. Market prices might be distorted (that is, not represent the actual social value of costs and benefits) for a number of reasons. These reasons include unfair competition, monopolistic or oligopolistic practices, and government price support programs. In such cases upward (or downward) adjustments can be made in the actual market price of a good or service. In other cases market prices are simply unavailable. This is often the case with certain collective goods (for example, clean air or a sense of community) which we discussed earlier as *intangibles*. Analysts can use several procedures to estimate the price of such intangibles.[43]

1. *Comparable prices.* Here the analyst uses prices for comparable or similar items in the market. For example, in estimating the economic benefits of time saved by the construction of a mass rapid transit system, the analyst might use area wage rates as a measure of the monetary value of time saved by using the new transportation facilities. This equation of work time and leisure time is based on the questionable assumption that time saved in travel could have been used to earn income.

2. *Consumer choice.* Here the analyst estimates the value of intangibles (for example, travel time) by observing consumer behavior in situations where in-

---

[43] Poister, *Public Program Analysis*, pp. 417–19.

FIGURE 7–9 Simplified partial cost model for total initial investment.

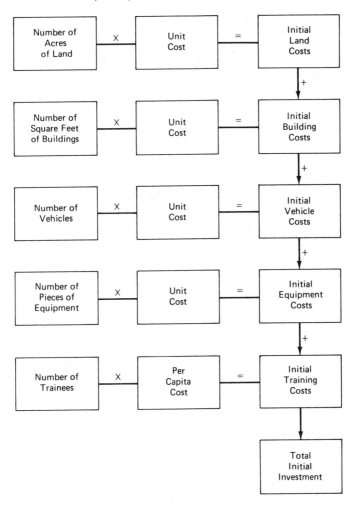

dividuals are forced to choose between a given intangible and money. For example, estimates of the value of time can be made by observing actual choices made between low-cost and time-consuming versus high-cost and time-reducing modes of travel. This may help to determine how much consumers are willing to pay for reduced travel time, although it assumes that consumers have complete information about the relation between time and costs and that both alternatives are equal in all respects, save time and cost.

3. *Derived demand.* Here the value of intangibles for which there are no market prices (for example, satisfaction with government parks and recreation areas that charge no fees) can be estimated on the basis of the indirect costs paid by visitors. A demand curve (that is, a curve that displays the various price–quantity combinations at which consumers will use a service) can be derived

from the costs paid by consumers in traveling to the park. These indirect costs are taken to be actual prices paid for the use of parks and recreation areas. This procedure assumes that the sole purpose of the travel is to use the park or recreation area.

4. *Survey analysis.* Here the analyst surveys citizens by interviewing them or asking them to complete mailed questionnaires. Respondents indicate at what level of costs they will be willing to pay for a given service (for example, bus transportation). One weakness of this procedure is the so-called *free-rider problem*, that is, a situation where consumers will claim that they are not willing to pay for a service in the hope that they will benefit from the service while others pay for it.

5. *Cost of compensation.* Here the analyst estimates the value of intangibles—particularly those that occur in the form of unwanted outside costs (negative externalities)—by obtaining prices for actions required to correct them. For example, the costs of environmental damage might be estimated by basing dollar values on the prices of programs for water purification, noise abatement, or reforestation. Similarly, the benefits of an antipollution enforcement program might be estimated on the basis of medical costs that will be avoided because people contract less lung cancer, emphysema, and other chronic diseases.

Constraint Mapping

Constraint mapping is a procedure for identifying and classifying limitations and obstacles that stand in the way of achieving policy and program objectives. Generally, constraints fall into six categories:

1. *Physical constraints.* The attainment of objectives may be limited by the state of development of knowledge or technology. For example, the reduction of pollution through the use of solar energy is constrained by the present low level of development of solar technology.

2. *Legal constraints.* Public law, property rights, and agency regulations often limit attempts to achieve objectives. For example, social programs designed to redistribute resources to the poor are frequently constrained by reporting requirements.

3. *Organizational constraints.* The organizational structure and processes available to implement programs may limit efforts to achieve objectives. For example, excessive centralization, poor management, and low morale limit the effectiveness and efficiency of public programs.[44]

4. *Political constraints.* Political opposition may impose severe limitations on the implementation as well as the initial acceptance of programs. Such opposition is reflected in organizational inertia and tendencies to avoid problems by practicing incremental decision making. For example, certain problems (consumer protection, environmental protection, energy conservation) may take years even to be placed on the formal agenda of public bodies.[45]

---

[44] For a general treatment of these organizational constraints, see Vincent Ostrom, *The Intellectual Crisis in American Public Administration* (University, AL: University of Alabama Press, 1974).

[45] See, for example, Roger W. Cobb and Charles D. Elder, *Participation in American Politics: The Dynamics of Agenda-Building* (Boston: Allyn and Bacon, 1972).

5. *Distributional constraints.* Public programs designed to provide social services efficiently are often limited by the need to ensure that benefits and costs are equitably distributed among different groups. Programs that achieve the highest net efficiency benefits, as we have seen, are frequently those that produce least social equity, and vice versa.

6. *Budgetary constraints.* Government budgets are limited, thus requiring that objectives be considered in light of scarce resources. Fixed budgets create type I problems, where analysts are forced to consider alternatives that maximize effectiveness within the limits of available resources.

An effective way to identify and classify constraints is to construct a *constraints tree*, which is a graphic display of limitations and obstacles that stand in the way of achieving objectives. A constraints tree involves the superimposition of constraints on an objectives tree (see Figure 7–7). A simplified constraints tree for national energy policy is illustrated in Figure 7–10.

Cost Internalization

Cost-internalization is a procedure for incorporating all relevant outside costs (externalities) into an internal cost element structure. Costs as well as benefits can be internalized by considering significant positive and negative spillovers of public policies and programs. When costs are fully internalized, there are no externalities since, by definition, all costs are internal ones. This means that a variety of important external costs—for example, costs of pollution, environmental degradation, or social dislocation—are explicitly built into the process of recommendation.

In general, there are four kinds of spillovers or externalities to which policy analysts should pay particular attention:[46]

1. *Production-to-production spillovers.* The products of a program serving one target group or jurisdiction may affect (positively or negatively) the products of another. For example, successful alcoholism and drug-treatment programs may result in a decrease of law enforcement activities in the surrounding community.

2. *Production-to-consumption spillovers.* The products of a particular program may affect the quality and quantity of goods consumed by members within another target group or jurisdiction. For example, publicly funded highway projects may displace residents from their homes or change the demand for goods and services in neighboring areas.

3. *Consumption-to-consumption spillovers.* The consumption activities of public programs in one area may affect consumption patterns within adjacent target groups or jurisdictions. For example, the construction of a large government office facility may make it impossible for local citizens to find adequate parking.

4. *Consumption-to-production spillovers.* The consumption activities of public programs in one area may affect the production activities of public and private programs in adjacent areas. For example, the construction of a public housing project may improve the market for local businesses.

---

[46] Hinrichs and Taylor, *Systematic Analysis*, pp. 18–19.

FIGURE 7-10   Constraints map for national energy policy.

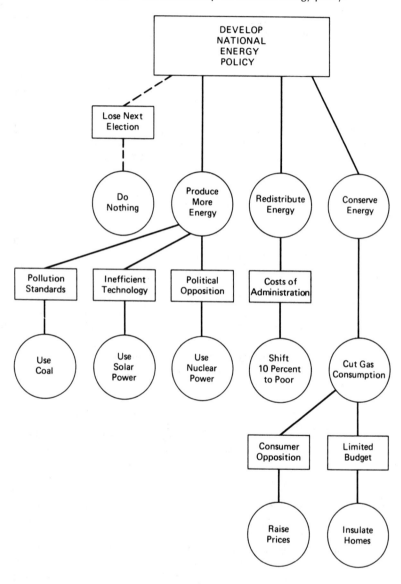

The importance of cost internalization is evident in Table 7–9, which shows total, outside, and inside costs for three programs designed to provide maternal care. If all three programs are equally effective, an analyst at the state level who has not internalized federal cost sharing will recommend program I, since it satisfies the least-cost criterion. If federal costs are internalized, program III will be recommended, since total costs are least.

TABLE 7–9 Internal, External, and Total Costs of Alternative Maternal Care Programs (Costs per Patient)

	PROGRAM					
TYPE OF COST	*Maternal and Infant Care Project* I		*Neighborhood Health Center* II		*Private Physician* III	
Cost to state (internal)	$31	10%	$96	43.3%	$85	48.3%
Cost to federal government (external)	282	90	103	51.7	90	51.7
Total cost	$313	100%	$199	100%	$175	100%

Source: Adapted from M. R. Burt, *Policy Analysis: Introduction and Applications to Health Programs* (Washington, DC: Information Resources Press, 1974), p. 35.

This example calls attention to the relative nature of internal and external costs, since what is an externality to one party is not to another.

Discounting

Discounting is a procedure for estimating the present value of costs and benefits that will be realized in the future. Discounting is a way to take into account the effects of time when making policy recommendations. Time is important because future costs and benefits have less value than present ones. A dollar spent today is more valuable than a dollar spent one or two years from now, since today's dollar can be invested so that it will generate $1.12 one year from now (at 12 percent interest). Apart from interest earnings, many people prefer to consume now rather than later, since the future is uncertain and it is hard to delay the consumption which produces immediate satisfaction.

Many policies and programs generate different levels of costs and benefits that flow forward into time. These flows of costs and benefits, called *cost (or benefit) streams,* are unevenly distributed in time. For this reason, each cost and benefit stream must be discounted to its present value. For example, two health programs with equal effectiveness and identical total costs over a five-year period would appear to be equally recommendable. Yet in one of these programs (program I), costs are heavily concentrated in the first year, while in the other (program II), they are concentrated in the last year. If we assume that the dollar is losing value at the rate of 10 percent per year, then program II achieves the same level of effectiveness at least cost. If we do not take time and the changing value of money into account, there is no basis for distinguishing the two programs (Figure 7–11).

The present value of a future benefit or cost is found by using a *discount factor,* which expresses the amount by which the value of future benefits and costs should be decreased to reflect the fact that present dollars

FIGURE 7–11   Comparison of discounted and undiscounted costs cumulated for two programs with equal effectiveness.

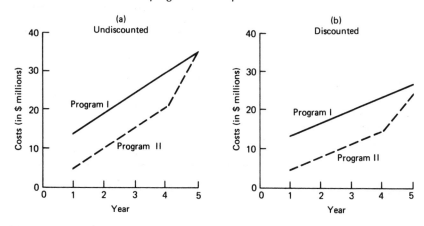

have more value than future ones. Once we know the discount factor we simply multiply this factor by the known dollar value of a future benefit or cost. This was what was done in Figure 7–9. Given a certain *discount rate*, that is, the rate at which the value of future benefits and costs should be reduced, the discount factor may be calculated by knowing the number of years over which future benefits and costs must be discounted. The formula for the discount factor is

$$DF = \frac{1}{(1 + r)^n}$$

where r is the discount rate and n is the number of years over which benefits or costs are discounted.[47] For example, to calculate the discount factor (DF) for a discount rate of 10 percent at five years, we make the following computations:

$$
\begin{aligned}
DF &= \frac{1}{(1 + r)^n} \\
&= \frac{1}{(1 + 0.10)^5} = \frac{1}{(1.1)^5} \\
&= \frac{1}{1.61} \\
&= 0.621
\end{aligned}
$$

---

[47] The discount factor assumes that future dollar values in a cost (or benefit) stream are unequal (for example, heavy costs at the beginning of a period decrease over time). If the future dollar values in a cost (or benefit) stream are identical from year to year (for example, $1 million in costs every year for five years) it is customary to use a shortcut, called an *annuity factor*

TABLE 7–10 Calculation of Present Value of Cost Stream over Five Years at 10 Percent Discount Rate (in Millions of Dollars)

YEAR	FUTURE VALUE (FV)	DISCOUNT RATE (r)	NUMBER OF YEARS (n)	DISCOUNT FACTOR (DF) $1/(1 + r)^n]$	PRESENT VALUE (PV) [FV·DF]
1991	$100	0.10	1	0.909	$ 90.90
1992	50	0.10	2	0.826	41.30
1993	10	0.10	3	0.751	7.51
1994	10	0.10	4	0.683	6.83
1995	10	0.10	5	0.621	6.21
	$180.0				$152.75

If we want to discount the value of $100 in costs incurred in the fifth year, we simply multiply this cost by the discount factor, that is, $100 × 0.621 = $62.10. In other words, the present value of $100 in costs incurred in the fifth year at a discount rate of 10 percent is $62.10. *Present value* is the dollar value of future costs or benefits that have been multiplied by the appropriate discount factor. The formula for the present value of a stream of costs or benefits is

$$PV = \Sigma(FV \cdot DF)$$

where FV designates the future value of costs or benefits, DF is the discount factor, and the symbol Σ (sigma) tells us to sum or add up all the products of costs or benefits times the discount factor for all years in the cost (or benefit) stream.[48]

The calculation of the present value of a cost stream is illustrated in Table 7–10. Observe that the future value of all undiscounted costs is $180 million, while the present value of the discounted cost stream is $152.75 million. Assume that the present value of the *benefit* stream is $175 million. If we were using the net benefit criterion to make a recommendation (that is, net benefits must be greater than zero), the undiscounted costs would

---

(annuity means annually, or regularly over a number of years). The formula for the annuity factor is

$$AF = 1 - \left(\frac{1}{1 + r}\right) n/r.$$

Stated more concisely, $AF = 1 - DF/r$.

[48] Another formula for present value, which gives identical results, is $PV = FV/(1 + r)^n$, where FV is future costs or benefits, r is the discount rate, and n is the number of years over which costs or benefits must be discounted.

result in a rejection of the program ($175 − 180 = −$5). By contrast, when we discount the cost stream our recommendation would be positive, since net benefits are $22.5 million ($175 − 152.75 = $22.5).

Once we know the appropriate discount rate, it is a simple matter to calculate the discount factor and the present value of a cost (or benefit) stream. The problem is that the choice of a discount rate depends on judgments that reflect the ethical values of analysts, policymakers, or particular social groups. For example, the higher the rate at which we discount future benefits, the more difficult it is to obtain net benefits and benefit–cost ratios that justify public programs. If discount rates are uniformly high, this leads to a minimal role for government investments and a maximal one for private ones. If, on the other hand, discount rates are uniformly low, this encourages an expanded role for government in society. For this reason it is important to recognize competing bases for selecting a discount rate:

1. *Private discount rates.* Here the selection of a discount rate is based on judgments about the appropriate rate of interest charged for borrowing money in the private sector. The argument for using private rates is that public investments are made with the tax monies of citizens who could have invested in the private sector. The private rate of discount therefore measures the benefits that would have been obtained if funds had been left in the private sector. These are the opportunity costs of public (versus private) investment. The arguments against private rates are that private rates differ widely (from 5 to 20 percent) because of market distortions; private rates do not reflect the external social costs of private investment (for example, pollution); and private rates reflect narrow individual and group preferences and not those of society as a whole.

2. *Social discount rates.* Here the selection of a discount rate is based on judgments about the social time preference of society as a whole. The *social time preference* refers to the collective value that society attaches to benefits or costs realized in some future time period. This collective value is not simply the sum of individual preferences, since it reflects a collective sense of what is valuable for the community as a whole. The *social rate of discount,* that is, the rate at which future collective benefits and costs should be discounted, is generally lower than the private rate. The arguments for a social rate of discount are that the social rate compensates for the narrowness and short-sightedness of individual preferences; it takes into account external social costs of private investment (for example, the depletion of finite natural resources); and it reflects a concern with the security, health, and welfare of future generations. Arguments against the social rate of discount are that it is economically inefficient or "irrational" and that the social rate of discount should be *higher* than the private rate. The assumption here is that the private rate actually underestimates the value of future benefits, since individuals habitually underestimate the extent to which rapid technological progress promotes future income.

3. *Government discount rates.* Here a discount rate is selected on the basis of the current costs of government borrowing. The problem is that the rate at which federal, state, and local governments may borrow money varies considerably. While the Office of Management and Budget (OMB) has recently advocated a 10 percent discount rate for most government programs, this standard rate does not reflect the opportunity cost of investments when lower interest rates are available within a given state, region, or community.

The selection of a discount rate is a matter of reasoned judgment and ethical discourse. Conflicts surrounding the choice of a discount rate cannot be resolved by pretending that market prices will produce value consensus. The choice of a discount rate is closely connected to competing views of the proper role of government in society and to the different forms of rationality discussed earlier. Under these circumstances the analyst must examine the sensitivity of net benefits and benefit–cost ratios to alternative discount rates and the assumptions that justify their selection. Alternatively, the analyst can calculate the *internal rate of return* on investment, a procedure used to recommend alternatives when the rate of undiscounted benefits returned for each discounted dollar of costs exceeds the actual rate at which investment funds are borrowed. Here, as elsewhere, it is essential to examine the underlying assumptions and ethical implications of any choice based on the internal rate of return.

Sensitivity Analysis

Sensitivity analysis is a procedure for examining the sensitivity of results of cost–benefit or cost–effectiveness analysis to alternative assumptions about the likelihood that given levels of costs or benefits will actually occur. In comparing two or more policy alternatives, there may be considerable uncertainty about the probable outcomes of action, even though a single overall measure of costs and benefits (for example, an effectiveness–cost ratio) may have been calculated. In such circumstances the analyst may introduce alternative assumptions about future costs—for example, assumptions about high, medium, and low costs—and compute separate ratios under each of these assumptions. The point is to see how "sensitive" the ratios are to these different assumptions.

For example, in comparing two personnel training programs, the analyst may examine the sensitivity of transportation costs to possible changes in the price of gasoline. Here the analyst may introduce assumptions that the price of gasoline will increase by 10 percent, 20 percent, and 30 percent over the life of the program. Since program I is situated in a semirural area, trainees must drive a longer distance to reach the training site than trainees in program II, which is located in the city. A marked increase in gasoline prices could result in recommending the most costly of the two programs. An example of this kind of sensitivity analysis is provide in Table 7–11. Another type of sensitivity analysis, and one we already discussed in Chapter 6, involves the use of regression analysis to make interval estimates of the values of costs or benefits.

A Fortiori Analysis

A fortiori analysis is a procedure used to compare two or more alternatives by resolving all uncertainties in favor of an alternative that is generally preferred on intuitive grounds but which appears after preliminary analysis to be the weaker of the two alternatives. The analyst may deliberately resolve a major cost uncertainty in favor of the weaker, but intuitively favored, alternative. If the stronger alternative still dominates the intuitively

TABLE 7–11   Sensitivity Analysis: Effects of Possible Increases in Gasoline Prices on Costs of Two Training Programs (in Thousands of Dollars)

	PRICE INCREASE		
PROGRAM	*10%*	*20%*	*30%*
I. Semirural			
Total costs	$4400	$4800	$5200
Trainees	5000	5000	5000
Costs per trainee	$0.88	$0.96	$1.04
II. Urban			
Total costs	$4500	$4800	$5100
Trainees	5000	5000	5000
Costs per trainee	$0.90	$0.96	$1.02

favored one, there is an even stronger case for the competing alternative. Note that *a fortiori* means "with even greater strength."

Plausibility Analysis

Plausibility analysis is a procedure for testing a recommendation against rival claims. Plausibility analysis, a form of critical multiplism used to examine rival causal and ethical claims, may be presented as a policy debate. There are at least 10 types of rival claims, each of which is a threat to the plausibility of recommendations based on cost–benefit analysis. These threats to the plausibility of policy recommendations are illustrated (Figure 7–12) with examples drawn from debates about the efficacy of the 55 mph speed limit in saving lives.

- *Invalidity.* A policy recommendation is based on an invalid assumption about the causal relation between a policy and its outcomes. For example, debates about the efficacy of the 55 mph speed limit (National Maximum Speed Law of 1973) have focused on the extent to which enforcing a maximum speed on all intercity highways is responsible for the observed decline in traffic fatalities after 1973. The claim that the new maximum speed (55 mph) was responsible for the decline of 9800 fatalities between 1973 and 1975 has been challenged on grounds that the decline was due to the new compressed range or standard deviation of speeds; improvements in automobile and highway safety; the interaction of maximum speed with population density; and the effects of recession, unemployment, and declining gasoline prices on miles driven and, consequently, fatality rates.[49]

---

[49] See Duncan MacRae, Jr., and James Wilde, *Policy Analysis for Public Decisions* (North Scituate, MA: Duxbury Press, 1979), pp. 133–52; Edward R. Tufte, *Data Analysis for Politics and Policy* (Englewood Cliffs, NJ: Prentice Hall, 1974), pp. 5–18; Charles T. Clotfelter and John C. Hahn, "Assessing the National 55 mph Speed Limit," *Policy Sciences* 9 (1978), 281–94; and Charles A. Lave and Lester B. Lave, "Barriers to Increasing Highway Safety," in *Challenging the Old Order: Toward New Directions in Traffic Safety Theory*, ed. J. Peter Rothe (New Brunswick, NJ: Transaction Books, 1990), pp. 77–94. The author has tested the effects of unemployment and gasoline prices on mileage and fatality rates, explaining over 90 percent of the variance in mileage death rates.

FIGURE 7-12   Threats to the plausibility of cost–benefit analysis.

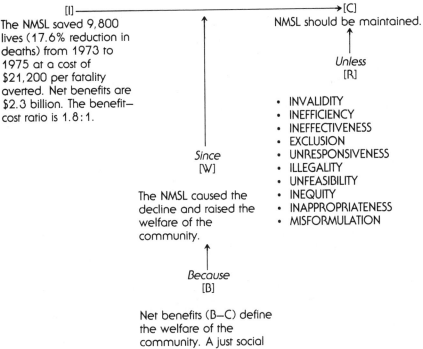

[I]──→[C]
The NMSL saved 9,800 lives (17.6% reduction in deaths) from 1973 to 1975 at a cost of $21,200 per fatality averted. Net benefits are $2.3 billion. The benefit–cost ratio is 1.8:1.

NMSL should be maintained.

Unless
[R]

- INVALIDITY
- INEFFICIENCY
- INEFFECTIVENESS
- EXCLUSION
- UNRESPONSIVENESS
- ILLEGALITY
- UNFEASIBILITY
- INEQUITY
- INAPPROPRIATENESS
- MISFORMULATION

Since
[W]

The NMSL caused the decline and raised the welfare of the community.

Because
[B]

Net benefits (B–C) define the welfare of the community. A just social state is one in which at least one person is better off, and no one is worse off (Pareto optimality).

- *Inefficiency.* Estimates of the net efficiency benefits of the 55 mph speed limit vary markedly, depending on the value attached to human lives and the costs of time lost by driving at 55 mph rather than 65 mph. One estimate of net efficiency benefits is $2.3 billion, while another is minus $3.4 billion.[50]
- *Ineffectiveness.* Estimates of the cost–effectiveness of the 55 mph speed limit also vary markedly. The costs per fatality averted range from approximately $1300 to $21,000, depending on assumptions about what should be included as costs and benefits.[51]
- *Exclusion.* The exclusion of legitimate costs and benefits will produce implausibly high or low net efficiency benefits. For example, costs of time lost by driving at 55 mph or benefits in the form of the monetary value of human lives may be excluded.
- *Unresponsiveness.* The costs of time and other resources are often based on

---

[50] See Grover Starling, *Strategies for Policy Making* (Chicago: The Dorsey Press, 1988), pp. 407–10; and Guess and Farnham, *Cases in Public Policy Analysis*, pp. 177–203.

[51] Starling, *Strategies for Policy Making*, pp. 409–11; see also references in footnote 49.

assumptions that individuals would be willing to pay the average wage rate to engage in a timesaving activity. The average wage rate is typically unresponsive to the price individuals are actually willing to pay. For example, approximately half of drivers are engaged in recreational activities, not commerce or business. The average wage rate, which markedly increases the estimated costs of the 55 mph speed limit, is therefore unresponsive to the perceived costs of driving at 55 mph.

• *Illegality*. In some cases the legality of a recommendation may be challenged. It is not appropriate to count as costs (or benefits) income earned through illegality, fraud, or unlawful discrimination. In cases involving the comparable worth of jobs held by men, women, and minorities, illegality is a major factor. In the case of the 55 mph speed limit, it is not.

• *Unfeasibility*. Policy recommendations can be challenged on grounds that they are not feasible because of political, budgetary, and administrative constraints. The implementation of the 55 mph speed limit varies across states because of differing capacities for implementing or enforcing speed laws. Implementational capacity is generally greater in states with high population density.

• *Inequity*. Recommendations may be challenged on ethical grounds involving alternative conceptions of social equity and justice. The group that pays a disproportionately high cost in terms of lives lost is younger drivers. The median age of traffic fatalities is approximately 29 years, which means that half of traffic deaths are relatively young persons. The Rawlsian conception of justice of fairness—that is, those worst off should benefit—may be used to challenge policies designed to reduce fatalities through speed laws rather than through educational and driver training programs that specially target young drivers.[52]

• *Inappropriateness*. Recommendations based on estimates of the value of human lives sometimes employ discounted lifetime earnings as a measure of value. Efforts to establish the cost (discounted or undiscounted) of a human life may be challenged on grounds that it is inappropriate to calculate a price for human lives, which are not commodities on an open market.[53]

• *Misformulation*. A standing challenge to recommendations based on cost–benefit analysis is that the problem has been misformulated. In the case of the 55 mph speed limit, saving fuel during the oil crisis of 1970–1973 was the original problem for which the National Maximum Speed Law was a recommended solution. The definition of the problem shifted to averting fatalities after the oil crisis passed. The existing formulation of the problem (averting traffic fatalities) may be challenged on grounds that the problem should be formulated as one of saving a nonrenewable resource, mitigating the emission of pollutants, and averting fatalities by a significant increase in taxes on gasoline, which in constant dollars cost less per gallon in 1990 than in 1974.

These threats to the plausibility of policy recommendations do not apply solely to cost–benefit and cost–effectiveness analyses. Since all policy recommendations are based on causal as well as ethical premises, these

---

[52] On this question, see, especially, Rothe, *Challenging the Old Order*.

[53] See the discussion in Guess and Farnham, *Cases in Public Policy Analysis*.

threats to plausibility are relevant to almost any policy that seeks to achieve reforms through the regulation, allocation, or reallocation of resources.[54]

In concluding this chapter it is important to emphasize that the policy-analytic method of recommendation involves many uncertainties. The most important of these has to do with the role of values and ethics in policy analysis. The purpose of a policy recommendation is not simply to forecast or predict some future outcome but to advocate a course of action whose consequences are also *valuable* to members of a community. Yet, as we have seen, there are severe difficulties in using economic theory and the tools of cost–benefit analysis to justify claims about what is best for society as a whole. For this reason, uncertainties about values are best treated as a matter for reasoned ethical argument and debate and not as technical economic questions.

A second source of uncertainty stems from incomplete knowledge about the effects of policies on valued outcomes. Even if there were total consensus on all important social values, we would still not know with certainty which policies and programs work best under different conditions. Some of this uncertainty is a result of the poor quality of data available to measure costs and benefits. Many cost–benefit analyses, for example, are based on incomplete information about the range of costs and benefits that must be considered in a reasonably thorough analysis. An even more important source of uncertainty stems from the inaccuracy of measurement procedures and the consequent need to exercise judgment in matters involving the estimation of shadow prices or the selection of an appropriate discount rate.

SUMMARY

In this chapter we have provided an overview of the nature and role of recommendation in policy analysis, compared and contrasted two major approaches to recommendation, and described specific techniques used in conjunction with these approaches. You should now be able to discuss the following principles and generalizations:

1. The policy-analytic method of recommendation is closely related to ethical and moral questions, since policy recommendations require that we determine which alternatives are most valuable and why.

2. Policy recommendations answer the question: What should be done? For this reason policy recommendations require an approach that is normative, and not one that is merely empirical or merely evaluative. All policy recommendations involve claims about action, rather than claims that are simply designative (as in forecasting) or simply evaluative (as in evaluation).

[52] On this question, see, especially, Rothe, *Challenging the Old Order.*

[53] See the discussion in Guess and Farnham, *Cases in Public Policy Analysis.*

[54] See Dunn, "Policies as Arguments"; and Frank Fischer, *Politics, Values, and Public Policy: The Problem of Methodology* (Boulder, CO: Westview Press, 1980).

3. Claims based on multiple advocacy have several distinctive characteristics. They are actionable, prospective, value laden, and ethically complex.

4. Recommendations involve reasoned choices among two or more alternatives. A simple model of choice involves the definition of a problem requiring action; the comparison of consequences of two or more alternatives to resolve a problem; and the recommendation of the alternative that best satisfies some need, value, or opportunity.

5. The simple model of choice contains two essential elements: factual premises and value premises. Value premises cannot be proved right or wrong by appealing to factual premises, since questions of value or ethics require reasoned arguments about why an outcome is good or right for some person, group, or society as a whole. All choices contain both factual and value premises.

6. The simple model of choice obscures the complexity of most choice situations, since the model is based on three unrealistic assumptions: a single decision maker; certainty; and consequences that occur at one point in time.

7. A complex model of choice is based on alternative assumptions: multiple stakeholders; uncertainty or risk; and consequences that extend through time. This complex model is a more adequate reflection of the realities of public policymaking.

8. In many complex choice situations, it is impossible to consistently rank alternatives according to two or more criteria of choice. These intransitive choices, as distinguished from those which are transitive, involve multiple conflicting objectives held by numerous stakeholders.

9. Our inability to satisfy the conditions of the simple model of choice does not mean that the process of recommendation is not and cannot be rational, if by "rationality" we mean a self-conscious process of making reasoned arguments to make and defend claims.

10. Most policy choices are multirational because they have multiple rational bases. These multiple bases are evident in six types of rationality: technical, economic, legal, social, substantive, and erotetic. The main characteristic of these different types of rationality is that they involve reasoned choices that are based on explicit arguments about the desirability of adopting different courses of action to resolve public problems.

11. For choices to be rational and comprehensive at the same time, they would have to satisfy conditions often described as the rational-comprehensive theory of decision making. Comprehensive rationality has been challenged on grounds that most decisions are actually disjointed and incremental (disjointed incrementalism); that fully democratic choices are impossible (Arrow's impossibility theorem); that choices are bounded by practical constraints (bounded rationality); that choices reflect efforts to maximize objectives under constraints (constrained maximization); and that different choice procedures are used for different kinds of problems (mixed scanning).

12. None of these challenges to comprehensive rationality requires that we abandon the idea of rational choice. We are required, however, to redefine rationality in terms of choices that conform to principles of incrementalism, satisficing behavior, second best, constrained maximization, mixed scanning, and (initial) ignorance.

13. Different types of rational choice may be specified in the form of alternative decision criteria. These are effectiveness, efficiency, adequacy, equity, responsiveness, and appropriateness.

14. It is seldom possible to choose between two alternatives on the basis of *either* costs *or* effectiveness. It is almost always necessary to specify the level of effectiveness and costs that is regarded as adequate. This is largely a matter of reasoned judgment that cannot be resolved by arbitrarily adopting a single criterion of adequacy.

15. Answers to questions about the welfare of society as a whole may be pursued in several different ways: maximize individual welfare; protect minimum welfare (Pareto); maximize net welfare (Kaldor–Hicks); maximize redistributive welfare (Rawls). None of these criteria is wholly satisfactory, since each fails to address problems of conflicting social values.

16. A policy analyst can satisfy criteria of effectiveness, efficiency, adequacy, and equity, yet still fail to satisfy the criterion of responsiveness. Similarly, even after the criterion of responsiveness has been satisfied, it is still possible to question the appropriateness of objectives. The criterion of appropriateness is closely related to substantive rationality.

17. In making recommendations the policy analyst typically addresses questions about objectives, costs, constraints, externalities, time, and risk and uncertainty.

18. Public and private choice differ in three main respects: the nature of public policy processes; the collective nature of public policy goals; and the nature of public goods. The logic of profit maximization in the private sector, while useful for some aspects of policy analysis, is limited when we consider that public policy-making involves multiple legitimate stakeholders, collective and quasi-collective goods, the limited comparability of income measures, and public responsibility for social costs and benefits.

19. Two major approaches to recommendation in policy analysis are cost-benefit analysis and cost–effectiveness analysis. While both approaches seek to measure all costs and benefits to society, only cost–benefit analysis measures costs as well as benefits in dollars as a common unit of value. Costs and benefits are of several types: inside vs. outside; tangible vs. intangible; primary vs. secondary; and real vs. pecuniary.

20. In conducting a cost–benefit analysis it is necessary to complete a series of interrelated tasks: specification of objectives; identification of alternatives; collection, analysis, and interpretation of information; specification of target groups; identification of types of costs and benefits; discounting of costs and benefits; specification of criteria for recommendation; and recommendation itself. The criteria of adequacy most frequently employed in traditional cost-benefit analysis are net benefits and benefit–cost ratios. In contemporary cost-benefit analysis these criteria are supplemented by redistributional criteria.

21. Cost–effectiveness analysis is appropriate when objectives cannot be expressed in terms of income benefits. The tasks in conducting a cost–effectiveness analysis are similar to those required in cost–benefit analysis, with two exceptions. Only costs are discounted to their present value, and the criteria of adequacy most often employed are those of least cost and maximum effectiveness.

22. Several useful methods and techniques are available to complete tasks in cost-benefit analysis. Some of these techniques are designed for structuring problems (boundary analysis, classificational analysis, hierarchy analysis, multiple perspective analysis, argumentation analysis, argumentation mapping). Other methods and techniques are specific to cost–benefit and cost–effectiveness analysis: objectives mapping, value clarification, value critique, cost element structuring, cost estimation, shadow pricing, discounting, feasibility assess-

ment, constraints mapping, sensitivity analysis, *a fortiori* analysis, and plausibility analysis.

23. The policy-analytic method of recommendation involves many uncertainties. The most important of these stems from the absence of consensus about social values and ethical principles. Other important sources of uncertainty are incomplete knowledge of cause–effect relations, poor data, and the inaccuracy of measurement procedures. Uncertainties that stem from value conflict are best treated as a matter for reasoned ethical argument and debate, and not as technical economic questions.

24. Plausibility recognizes these uncertainties by testing recommendations against rival claims. There are at least 10 threats to the plausibility of policy recommendations developed on the basis of cost–benefit analysis and other methods: invalidity, inefficiency, ineffectiveness, exclusion, unresponsiveness, illegality, unfeasibility, inequity, inappropriateness, and misformulation. These threats to plausibility are relevant to almost any policy recommendation which seeks to achieve reforms through the regulation, allocation, or reallocation of resources.

GLOSSARY

Adequacy: A criterion according to which an alternative is recommended if it satisfies a specific level of need that gave rise to a problem.

Advocative Claim: A conclusion of a policy argument that involves facts, values, and a call for action. Advocative claims have an action focus, future orientation, fact-value interdependence, and value duality.

Appropriateness: A criterion according to which an alternative is recommended if it results in an appropriate choice of objectives. The criterion of appropriateness is connected with substantive rationality, since it involves the *substance* (hence, "substantive") of objectives rather than means or instruments to realize them.

Arrow's Impossibility Theorem: A theorem stated by Kenneth Arrow to demonstrate in formal logical terms that it is impossible for decision makers to aggregate individual preferences without violating one or more of five reasonable conditions of democratic decision making.

Bounded Rationality: A theory of decision making developed by Herbert Simon to show that practical conditions of decision making result in rational choices that are bounded, rather than comprehensive, and which promote efforts to "satisfice" rather than "maximize" the attainment of objectives.

Collective Goods: Goods produced mainly by the public sector which are nonexclusive, since their ownership is vested in no particular person and they may be consumed by all.

Constrained Maximization: A theory of decision making which claims that attempts to maximize the attainment of some objective are constrained by the awareness of the costs of information.

Constraints Tree: A pictorial display of limitations and obstacles to the attainment of objectives.

Cost Element Structure: A list of functions, equipment, or supplies that require the expenditure of resources.

Cost-Estimating Relationship: An explicit measure of the relationship between the quantity of functions, materials, and personnel and their costs.

Criterion Overspecification: The setting of cost and effectiveness limits in such a way that no alternative simultaneously satisfies the cost and effectiveness constraints.

Cyclic Preference: A type of intransitive preference where alternatives cannot be ranked consistently. A is preferred to B in the choice set (A, B), B is preferred to C in the choice set (B, C), but C is preferred to A in the set (A, C).

Discount Factor: A quantitative index that expresses the amount by which the value of future benefits or costs should be decreased to reflect the fact that present dollars have more value than future ones. $DF = 1/(1 + r)^n$, where DF is the discount factor, r the discount rate, and n the number of years over which costs or benefits are discounted.

Disjointed-Incremental Theory:　A theory of decision making which claims that actual policy choices are not rational and comprehensive. Instead they involve choices that differ only incrementally from the status quo and processes of analysis and evaluation that are disjointed, remedial, serial, and in continuous flux.

Double Counting:　An error that occurs when benefits which go to one group at the expense of another are incorrectly added to net efficiency benefits without also subtracting the costs to the group that loses.

Economic Rationality:　A characteristic of reasoned choices that involve the comparison of alternatives according to their capacity to provide *efficient* solutions for problems.

Effectiveness:　A criterion according to which an alternative is recommended if it results in maximum achievement of a valued outcome (effect), apart from efficiency considerations.

Efficiency:　A criterion according to which an alternative is recommended if it results in a higher ratio of effectiveness to cost at the margin (marginal efficiency).

Equity:　A criterion according to which an alternative is recommended if it results in a more just or fair distribution of resources in society. Alternative criteria of social equity include those of Pareto, Kaldor–Hicks, Rawls, and others.

Externalities:　Costs or benefits which fall outside a target group or jurisdiction that is the focus of a policy recommendation.

Extrinsic Values:　Events, conditions, or processes that are valued as means to ends rather than ends in themselves. Democratic processes are often regarded as an extrinsic value insofar as democracy is viewed as a means to political stability, economic efficiency, or self-actualization.

Factual Premise:　An assumption that in principle may be shown to be true or false on the basis of factual knowledge. Factual premises *explain* the consequences of an action but do not justify them.

Free-Rider Problem:　A problem that occurs when persons indicate no willingness to pay for a public good but later use the good at a price lower than that they are actually willing to pay.

Intangibles:　Costs or benefits that are not directly measurable in terms of market prices.

Intrinsic Values:　Events, conditions, or processes that are valued as ends in themselves, rather than as means to an end. Human life is often regarded as an intrinsic value, although one person's intrinsic value may be another person's extrinsic value.

Kaldor–Hicks Criterion:　A criterion of equity which states that one social state is better than another if there is a net gain in efficiency (total benefits minus total costs) and if those who gain can compensate losers.

Least-Cost Criterion:　A criterion of adequacy used with *equal-effectiveness analysis* and *type II problems* to recommend an alternative that achieves the same level of effectiveness as other alternatives at a lower cost.

Legal Rationality:　A characteristic of reasoned choices that involve the comparison of alternatives according to their *legal conformity* to established rules and precedents.

Limited Interpersonal Comparison:　A situation which arises when the actual value of a unit of income (for example, $100) varies from person to person, because of education, experience, social status, ethical beliefs, and other factors.

Maximum-Effectiveness Criterion:　A criterion of adequacy used with *equal-cost analysis* and type I problems to recommend an alternative that achieves a higher level of effectiveness than other alternatives at the same cost.

Mixed Scanning:　A theory of decision making developed by sociologist Amitai Etzioni to claim that comprehensive rational choices are appropriate for strategic problems, while incremental choices are appropriate for operational problems.

Multirationality:　Explicit reasoned arguments offered on multiple rational bases: technical, economic, legal, social, or substantive.

Net Efficiency Benefits:　Benefits that represent a "real" increase in net income (total benefits minus total costs), as distinguished from benefits that represent a "pecuniary" (that is, monetary) shift in the income of one group at the expense of another but *without* increasing "real" or net efficiency benefits.

Objectives Tree: A pictorial display of the overall structure of objectives and their relationships.

Opportunity Cost: The benefits foregone by investing resources to produce one product when another more profitable investment might have been made. Opportunity costs are often calculated on the basis of prices for goods and services on the private market.

Pareto Criterion: A criterion of equity which states that one social state is better than another if at least one person is better off, and no one is worse off. A *Pareto optimum* is a social state where it is not possible to make any person better off without also making another person worse off.

Present Value: The dollar value of future costs or benefits that have been multiplied by the appropriate *discount factor.* PV = $\sum$(FV·DF), where PV is the present value of a cost or benefit stream, FV the future value of a stream of costs or benefits, DF the discount factor, and $\sum$ (sigma) a summation sign that tells us to add up all the products of costs or benefits times the discount factor.

Primary Costs (Benefits):   A cost or benefit that is related to the most valued program objectives. Primary costs or benefits (sometimes called *direct* costs or benefits) should be distinguished from *secondary costs (benefits)* (sometimes called *indirect* costs or benefits) which involve less valued objectives.

Quasi-collective Goods: Goods produced by the private and public sectors which are specific but whose production has such significant spillover effects for society that their use and benefits are regarded as nonexclusive and collective.

Rational-Comprehensive Theory: A theory of decision making that claims or implies that there is consensus on policy problems: transitive choice; an exhaustive set of alternatives; complete knowledge of consequences; an exhaustive comparison of alternatives; and successful maximization of objectives.

Rationality: A self-conscious process of using explicit reasoned arguments to make and defend knowledge claims.

Rawls Criterion: A criterion of equity which states that one social state is better than another if it results in a gain in welfare for members of a society who are worst off.

Redistributional Benefits: Benefits that result in a shift in the income of one group to another. Redistributional benefits may be regarded as "pecuniary" and hence not productive of "real" or net efficiency benefits.

Responsiveness: A criterion according to which an alternative is recommended if it results in the satisfaction of the express needs, preferences, or values of citizens.

Shadow Price: A judgment about the monetary value of benefits and costs when market prices for certain intangibles are unreliable or unavailable.

Social Rationality: A characteristic of reasoned choices that involve the comparison of alternatives according to their capacity to maintain valued social institutions, that is, promote *institutionalization.*

Specific Goods: Goods produced mainly by the private sector which are exclusive, since their ownership is vested in specific individuals (including "legal persons") who have the sole legal right to limit others from their use or benefits.

Substantive Rationality: A characteristic of reasoned choices that involve the comparison of alternatives according to their capacity to promote the most *appropriate* choice among two or more forms of rationality.

Technical Rationality: A characteristic of reasoned choices that involve the comparison of alternatives according to their capacity to promote *effective* solutions for problems.

Transitive Choice: A choice where alternatives can be consistently ranked according to one or more attributes. If A_1 is preferable to A_2 in the choice set (A_1, A_2), and A_2 is preferable to A_3 in the choice set (A_2, A_3), then A_1 is preferable to A_3 in the set (A_1, A_3).

Value Premise: An assumption that in principle may be shown to be good or bad on the basis of some set of values or system of ethics.

STUDY SUGGESTIONS

1.   University of Chicago economist Milton Friedman argues for a *positive* (rather than normative) economics that focuses on the study of the factual premises underlying policy issues.

"Differences about economic policy among disinterested citizens derive predominantly from different predictions about the economic consequences of taking action—differences that in principle can be eliminated by the progress of positive economics—rather than from fundamental differences in basic values, differences about which men can only fight." [*Essays in Positive Economics* (Chicago: University of Chicago Press, 1953), p. 5].

Write a short essay that outlines the strengths and weaknesses of this position. In your answer refer to contrasts between designative, evaluative, and normative claims and the multiple forms of rationality underlying policy choices.

2. "If individuals can order their preferences in a transitive fashion, it should be possible to use majority rule to obtain a collective preference ranking which is also transitive." Comment.

3. Is rational choice possible? Write an essay on this question. In your answer be sure to distinguish between individual and collective choice, types of rationality, and alternative criteria for recommendation.

4. Indicate how you would measure the effectiveness of efforts to achieve the following goals:

   — Close the gap between municipal revenues and expenditures
   — Deter the commission of serious crimes in urban areas
   — Enhance the national security of the country
   — Improve the quality of life of citizens
   — Reduce national unemployment
   — Increase the income of poverty families

5. Return to Study Suggestion 4. Indicate how you would measure the *efficiency* of efforts to achieve these goals.

6. Many economists argue that equality and efficiency are competing objectives. For this reason, the relation between equality and efficiency is one that requires a trade-off where gains in equality must be sacrificed for gains in efficiency, and vice versa [see Arthur M. Okun, *Equality and Efficiency: The Big Trade-Off* (Washington, DC: The Brookings Institution, 1975)]. Other economists [see Jaroslav Vanek, *The Participatory Economy*, (Ithaca, NY: Cornell University Press, 1970)] and political scientists [see Carole Pateman, *Participation and Democratic Theory* (Cambridge, MA: Cambridge University Press, 1970)] argue that the "trade-off" between equality and efficiency is a consequence of the limited forms of democratic participation in politics and work. These writers argue that equality and efficiency do not have to be "traded" when politics and economics are fully democratic. What does this controversy imply about the appropriateness of some of the central concepts of modern cost–benefit analysis, including "opportunity costs," "pecuniary" versus "real" costs and benefits, and "net efficiency" versus "redistributional" benefits?

7. Return to Figure 7–3 and consider the following criteria for recommendation:

   (a) Maximize effectiveness at least cost [*Note:* Be careful—this is a tricky question].
   (b) Maximize effectiveness at a fixed cost of $10,000.
   (c) Minimize costs at a fixed-effectiveness level of 4000 units of service.

   (d)   Achieve a fixed-effectiveness level of 6000 units of service at a fixed cost of $20,000.
   (e)   Assuming that each unit of service has a market price of $10, maximize net benefits.
   (f)   Again assuming that each unit of service has a market price of $10, maximize the ratio of benefits to costs.

   Indicate which of the two main programs (program I and program II) should be selected under each of these criteria, and describe the conditions under which each criterion may be an adequate measure of the achievement of objectives.

8.   The estimation of risk and uncertainty is an essential aspect of making policy recommendations. While it seems obvious that the best way to obtain valid estimates of risk and uncertainty is to use the most highly qualified experts, there is evidence that "people who know the most about various topics are not consistently the best at expressing the likelihood that they are correct" [Baruch Fischoff, "Cost–Benefit Analysis and the Art of Motorcycle Maintenance," *Policy Sciences* 8 (1977), p. 184]. How can a policy analyst resolve this apparent dilemma?

9.   Discuss various ways to obtain shadow prices for clean air.

10.   Use procedures of value clarification and value critique to analyze value premises which underlie the following claim: "Increased energy production is essential to the continued growth of the economy. The government should therefore make massive investments in research and development on new energy technologies." Treat the first sentence as information (I) and the second as the claim (C).

11.   Calculate the discount factor (DF) at 10 years for a 5, 10, and 20 percent discount rate.

12.   Calculate the present value (PV) of the following cost and benefit streams (in millions of dollars) for two health programs. Use a discount rate of 20 percent. Which program has the highest present net efficiency benefits? Why?

| | YEAR | | | | | |
PROGRAM	1990	1995	2000	2005	2010	Total
I Costs	$60	$10	$10	$10	$10	$100
Benefits	10	20	30	40	50	150
II Costs	20	20	20	20	20	100
Benefits	10	20	30	40	50	150

13.   Construct an objectives tree on the basis of the following objectives of a crime control program:

   — Hire qualified police officers
   — Increase the frequency of police patrols
   — Make more arrests

— Purchase equipment
— Train police officers
— Increase citizens' sense of security

14. On the basis of the objectives tree just constructed, construct a constraints tree that displays the following limitations and obstacles:

— Costs per trainee cannot exceed $1000 per trainee
— All police officers must have at least two years of college education
— Vehicle maintenance costs cannot increase by more than 10 percent
— Protect citizens' civil rights

15. Select a newspaper editorial that makes a recommendation about some preferred course of governmental action (for example, national health reform, control of environmental pollution, shaping a New World Order). Conduct a plausibility analysis of the recommendation using the 10 threats to plausibility discussed in the text.

SUGGESTED READINGS

DUNN, WILLIAM N., "Values, Ethics and Standards in Policy Analysis," in *Encyclopedia of Policy Studies*, ed. Stuart S. Nagel. New York: Marcel Dekker, 1983, pp. 831–65.

FISCHHOFF, BARUCH, "Cost–Benefit Analysis and the Art of Motorcycle Maintenance," *Policy Sciences*, 8 (1977), 177–202.

GRAMLICH, EDWARD M., *Benefit–Cost Analysis of Public Programs*, 2nd ed. Englewood Cliffs, NJ: Prentice Hall, 1990.

HAVEMAN, ROBERT H., and JULIUS MARGOLIS, eds., *Public Expenditure and Policy Analysis*, 3rd ed. Boston: Houghton Mifflin, 1988.

MISHAN, EDWARD J., *Cost–Benefit Analysis*. New York: Praeger, 1976.

WHITTINGTON, DALE and DUNCAN MACRAE, JR. "The Issue of Standing in Cost–Benefit Analysis," *Journal of Policy Analysis and Management*, 5 (1986), 665–82.

8

Monitoring Policy Outcomes

> Recently . . . the concepts of cause and effect are being readmitted to the most sophisticated philosophy of science. Whatever stand one may take on this, it must be admitted that intentional projects designed to improve society (praxis, if you will) accept both the concept of cause and the concept of learning from praxis. Implementing social change efforts in natural settings is a praxis akin to experimentation, differing only in the equivocality of interpreting the outcome.
>
> —Donald T. Campbell, "The Experimenting Society," *Methodology and Epistemology for Social Science: Selected Papers* (1988)

The consequences of policy actions are never fully known in advance and, for this reason, it is essential to monitor policy actions after they have occurred. In fact, policy recommendations may be viewed as hypotheses about the relation between policy actions and policy outcomes: If action A is taken at time t_1, outcome O will result at time t_2.[1] While all hypotheses are based on prior experience and assumptions about cause and effect (otherwise they amount to blind speculation), they are no more than informed conjectures until tested against subsequent experience.

In this chapter we provide an overview of the nature and functions of monitoring in policy analysis and the policy-making process. After comparing and contrasting four approaches to monitoring—social systems accounting, social experimentation, social auditing, and research and practice synthesis—we describe and illustrate the application of methods used in conjunction with these approaches.

---

[1] See Jeffrey L. Pressman and Aaron B. Wildavsky, *Implementation* (Berkeley: University of California Press, 1973); and Erwin C. Hargrove, *The Missing Link: The Study of the Implementation of Social Policy* (Washington, DC: The Urban Institute, 1975).

MONITORING IN POLICY ANALYSIS

Monitoring is the policy-analytic procedure used to produce information about the causes and consequences of public policies. Monitoring, since it permits analysts to describe relationships between policy-program operations and their outcomes is the primary source of knowledge about policy implementation.[2] In one sense monitoring is simply another name for efforts to describe and explain public policies. As such, monitoring represents a way to make designative claims about past and present policy actions. Monitoring is therefore primarily concerned with establishing factual premises about public policy. While factual and value premises are in continuous flux, and "facts" and "values" are interdependent, only recommendation and evaluation are expressly concerned with the systematic analysis of alternative value premises. Finally, monitoring produces designative claims during and after policies have been adopted and implemented, that is, *ex post facto*. By contrast, forecasting seeks to establish factual premises in advance of action, that is, *ex ante*.

Monitoring plays an essential methodological role in policy analysis. When information about policy actions is transformed through monitoring into information about policy outcomes, we experience *problem situations*. Problem situations, as we saw in Chapter 5, are those systems of interdependent problems (messes) that are subsequently transformed through problem structuring into a policy problem. Equally important, information about policy outcomes is also transformed through evaluation into information about policy performance.

Monitoring performs at least four major functions in policy analysis: explanation, accounting, auditing, and compliance:

1. *Compliance*. Monitoring helps determine whether the actions of program administrators, staff, and other stakeholders are in compliance with standards and procedures imposed by legislatures, regulatory agencies, and professional bodies. For example, the Environmental Protection Agency's Continuous Air Monitoring Program (CAMP) produces information about pollution levels that helps determine whether industries are complying with federal air quality standards.

2. *Auditing*. Monitoring helps determine whether resources and services intended for certain target groups and beneficiaries (individuals, families, municipalities, states, regions) have actually reached them. For example, by monitoring federal revenue sharing we can determine the extent to which funds are reaching local governments.[3]

3. *Accounting*. Monitoring produces information that is helpful in accounting for social and economic changes that follow the implementation of broad sets of public policies and programs over time. For example, changes in the quality

---

[2] The best general source on implementation is Daniel A. Mazmanian and Paul A. Sabatier, *Implementation and Public Policy*, rev. ed. (Lanham, MD: University Press of America, 1989).

[3] Richard P. Nathan and others, *Monitoring Revenue Sharing* (Washington, DC: The Brookings Institution, 1975).

of life may be monitored with such social indicators as average education, percentage of the population below the poverty line, and average annual paid vacations.[4]

4. *Explanation.* Monitoring also yields information that helps to explain why the outcomes of public policies and programs differ. For example, social experiments in criminal justice, education, and social welfare help us find out what policies and programs work best, how they work, and why.[5]

Sources of Information

To monitor public policies in any given issue area we require information that is relevant, reliable, and valid. If we want to know about the consequences of programs designed to provide educational opportunity for disadvantaged children, we need information that not only documents problems of achieving educational opportunity in general but information that yields answers about specific factors that policymakers may manipulate to induce greater opportunity. The first type of information, as we saw in Chapter 3, is appropriately termed *macronegative*, while the latter is best described as *micropositive* (see the Glossary). Information acquired through monitoring must also be reliable, which means that observations should be reasonably precise and dependable. For example, we know that information on crime is unreliable by a factor of about 2:5 to 1; that is, there are some two to three times more crimes actually committed than reported to police.[6] Finally, we also want to know whether information about policy outcomes is actually measuring what we think it is; that is, whether it is valid information. If we are interested in violent crimes, for example, information on crimes in general (which includes auto theft and white-collar crimes) will not be a valid measure of the kinds of policy outcomes in which we are interested.[7]

Information on policy outcomes is regularly collected at various points in time at considerable cost to federal, state, and local governments, private research institutes, and universities. Some of this information is general— for example, information about the social, economic, and demographic characteristics of the population as a whole—and some is more specific since it deals with regions, states, municipalities, and other subpopulations within society. Consider, for example, the following sources of information about policy outcomes published by the U.S. Bureau of the Census, the

---

[4] See, for example, Office of Management and the Budget, *Social Indicators, 1973* (Washington, DC: U.S. Government Printing Office, 1974); and U.S. Department of Labor, *State Economic and Social Indicators*, Bulletin 328 (Washington, DC: U.S. Government Printing Office, 1973).

[5] See Alice Rivlin, *Systematic Thinking for Social Action* (Washington, DC: The Brookings Institution, 1971); and George W. Fairweather and Louis G. Tornatzky, *Experimental Methods for Social Policy Research* (Oxford and New York: Pergamon Press, 1977).

[6] See R. H. Beattie, "Criminal Statistics in the United States," *Journal of Criminal Law, Criminology, and Police Science*, 51 (May 1960), 49–51.

[7] See Wesley G. Skogan, "The Validity of Official Crime Statistics: An Empirical Investigation," *Social Science Quarterly*, 55 (June 1974), 25–38.

U.S. Bureau of Labor Statistics, offices and clearinghouses attached to federal agencies and institutes, and several nonprofit research centers:[8]

Historical Statistics of the United States	*United States Census of Population by States*
Statistical Abstract of the United States	*Congressional District Data Book*
County and City Data Book	*National Opinion Research Center (NORC) General Social Survey*
Census Use Study	
Social and Economic Characteristics of Students	*National Clearinghouse for Mental Health Information*
Educational Attainment in the United States	*National Clearinghouse for Drug Abuse Information*
Current Population Reports	*National Criminal Justice Reference Service*
The Social and Economic Status of the Black Population in the United States	*Child Abuse and Neglect Clearinghouse Project*
Female Family Heads	*National Clearinghouse on Revenue Sharing*
Monthly Labor Review	*Social Indicators, 1973*
Handbook of Labor Statistics	*Social Indicators, 1976*
Congressional Quarterly	*State Economic and Social Indicators*
Law Digest	
Current Opinion	

In addition to these sources federal, state, and municipal agencies produce reports on special programs and projects in education, health, welfare, labor, employment, crime, energy, pollution, foreign affairs, and other areas. Research centers, institutes, and universities also maintain data archives that contain a wide variety of political, social, and economic data, and there is a large stock of books, monographs, articles, and reports written by applied researchers throughout the country. Much of this information can now be accessed through several computerized information retrieval systems, including *United States Political Science Documents*, the *National Technical Information Service*, and the various information clearinghouses and reference services previously listed. When data and other types of information are not available from existing sources, monitoring may be carried out by some combination of questionnaires, interviewing, field observation, and the use of agency records.[9]

---

[8] For guides to available statistics, see Delbert C. Miller, *Handbook of Research Design and Social Measurement*, 3rd ed. (Chicago: David McKay, 1977); "Guide to the U.S. Census and Bureau of Labor Statistics: Data References and Data Archives," pp. 104–23; and "Social Indicators," pp. 267–80.

[9] A review of applied research methods is beyond the scope of this book. For reference materials, see Miller, *Handbook of Research Design and Social Measurement*; Clair Selltiz and others, *Research Methods in Social Relations* (New York: Holt, Rinehart and Winston, 1976); and David Nachmias, *Public Policy Evaluation: Approaches and Methods* (New York: St. Martin's Press, 1979).

Types of Policy Outcomes

In monitoring policy outcomes we must distinguish between two kinds of consequences: outputs and impacts. *Policy outputs* are the goods, services, or resources received by target groups and beneficiaries. Per capita welfare expenditures and units of home food service received by the elderly are examples of policy outputs. *Policy impacts,* by contrast, are actual changes in behavior or attitudes that result from policy outputs. For example, while units of home food service (meals) provided to the elderly is an appropriate output indicator, the average daily protein intake of elderly persons is a measure of impact. Similarly, the number of hospital beds per 1000 persons might be a good indicator of policy output. To monitor policy impact, however, we would have to determine how many members of a particular target group actually use available hospital beds when they are ill.

In monitoring policy outputs and impacts it is important to recognize that target groups are not necessarily beneficiaries. *Target groups* are individuals, communities, or organizations on whom policies and programs are designed to have an effect, while *beneficiaries* are groups for whom the effects of policies are beneficial or valuable. For example, industrial and manufacturing firms are the targets of federal programs administered by the Occupational Safety and Health Administration (OSHA), but workers and their families are the beneficiaries. At the same time the strict enforcement of health and safety standards may result in higher production costs and consequent cutbacks in employment. In this case certain groups (for example, unskilled and marginally employed workers) may be laid off, so that they are neither target groups nor beneficiaries. Finally, today's target groups and beneficiaries are not necessarily tomorrow's, since future generations are affected in different ways by present-day policies and programs. A good example is the effort to minimize the risk of cancer in adult life by protecting children from harmful chemicals and pollutants.

Types of Policy Actions

To account satisfactorily for variations in policy outputs and impacts, it is necessary to trace them back to prior policy actions. Generally, policy actions have two major purposes: regulation and allocation. *Regulative actions* are those designed to ensure compliance with certain standards or procedures, for example, those of the Environmental Protection Agency or the Federal Aeronautics Administration. By contrast, *allocative actions* are those which require inputs of money, time, personnel and equipment. Regulative and allocative actions may have consequences that are distributive as well as redistributive.[10] The regulation of liquor licenses by state liquor

---

[10] Theodore Lowi categorizes the impacts of public policies as regulatory, distributive, and redistributive. These categories may be treated either as attributes of actions or of outcomes, depending on how various stakeholders perceive needs, values, and opportunities (that is, policy

FIGURE 8–1   Regulative and allocative actions and their implementation through agencies, programs, and projects.

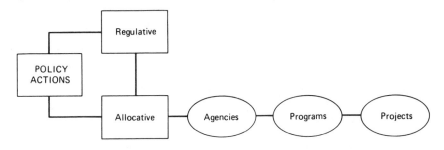

control boards affects the distribution of business opportunities, while the allocation of resources to the Social Security Administration results in the distribution of benefits to retired persons. By contrast the allocation of resources to federal revenue-sharing programs is designed in part to redistribute revenues from states to municipalities. Note, however, that all regulative actions require resource inputs. For example, federal occupational health and safety regulations require large resource allocations for effective enforcement. Regulative and allocative actions are implemented by federal, state, and municipal agencies in the form of programs and projects (Figure 8–1).

Policy actions may also be further subdivided into policy inputs and policy processes. *Policy inputs* are the resources—time, money, personnel, equipment, supplies—used to produce outputs and impacts. One of the best examples of policy inputs is the program budget, which contains a systematic account of resources allocated for program activities and tasks. By contrast, *policy processes* are the administrative, organizational, and political activities and attitudes that shape the transformation of policy inputs into policy outputs and impacts. For example, conflicts among agency staff and management, dissatisfaction with working conditions, or inflexible decision-making procedures may explain why programs that have the same resource inputs produce lower levels of outputs and impacts. The important point is to distinguish between inputs and processes, on the one hand, and outputs and impacts on the other. To fail to do so is akin to measuring "the number of times a bird flaps its wings without any attempt to determine how far the bird has flown."[11] Types of policy actions and outcomes are illustrated in three policy issue areas (Table 8–1).

problems) in particular contexts. See Theodore J. Lowi, "American Business, Public Policy Case Studies, and Political Theory," *World Politics*, 16 (July 1964), 689–90; and Charles O. Jones, *An Introduction to the Study of Public Policy*, 2nd ed. (North Scituate, MA: Duxbury Press, 1977), pp. 223–25. In the scheme used here all regulative action is also distributive or redistributive, no matter what the intent of the regulative action.

[11] Edward A. Suchman, *Evaluative Research: Principles and Practice in Public Service and Social Action Programs* (New York: Russell Sage Foundation, 1969), p. 61.

TABLE 8–1   Types of Policy Actions and Policy Outcomes: Inputs, Processes, Outputs, and Impacts in Three Issue Areas

ISSUE AREA	POLICY ACTIONS		POLICY OUTCOMES	
	Inputs	*Processes*	*Outputs*	*Impacts*
Criminal justice	Dollar expenditures for salaries, equipment, maintenance	Illegal arrests as percentages of total arrests	Criminals arrested per 100,000 known crimes	Criminals convicted per 100,000 known crimes
Municipal services	Dollar expenditures for sanitation workers and equipment	Morale among workers	Total residences served	Cleanliness of streets
Social welfare	Number of social workers	Rapport with welfare recipients	Welfare cases per social worker	Standard of living of dependent children

Definitions and Indicators

Our success in obtaining, analyzing, and interpreting data on policy outcomes depends on our capacity to construct reliable and valid measures. One way to construct measures is to specify the variables we are interested in monitoring. A *variable* is any characteristic of a person, event, or object that takes on different numerical values, while a *constant* is a characteristic that does not vary. For example, policy-impact variables include educational opportunity, public safety, and air quality. One difficulty with public policy analysis is that frequently we do not have precise definitions of these and other variables. For this reason it is useful to think about two kinds of definitions of variables: constitutive and operational. *Constitutive definitions* give meaning to words used to describe variables by using other synonymous words. For example, educational opportunity may be constitutively defined as "the freedom to choose learning environments consistent with one's abilities." Such definitions, while essential, provide us with no concrete rules or guidelines for actually monitoring changes in educational opportunity. In fact, it is impossible to measure educational opportunity directly, since constitutive or "dictionary" definitions provide only the most tenuous links with the "real world" of policy-making.

We experience policy actions and outcomes only indirectly, by using operational definitions and indicators of variables. An *operational definition* gives meaning to a variable by specifying the operations required to experience and measure it. For example, we can go much beyond our constitutive definition of educational opportunity by specifying that educational opportunity is "the number of children from families with less than $6000 annual income who attend colleges and universities, as documented by census data." In this case our definition is operational because it specifies the operation required to experience and measure educational opportunity. Here we are directed to locate and read those sections of the census on family income and educational levels of children. In so doing we experience educational opportunity indirectly. With this information in hand, we can proceed to monitor the impact of public policies.

Operational definitions not only specify procedures required to experience and measure something; they also help specify indicators of input, process, output, and impact variables. *Indicators* of variables—for example, average school enrollment, the number of drug addicts, or the amount of sulfur dioxide in the air—are directly observable characteristics that are substituted for indirectly observable or unobservable characteristics. We do not directly observe job satisfaction, quality of life, or economic progress.

There are many alternative indicators that may be used to operationally define the same variable. This creates problems of interpretation. For example, it may be quite difficult to know whether one, several, or all of the following indicators are adequate measures of the impact of crime-control policies: arrests per officer, arrests per known crime, the ratio of false to total arrests, number of crimes cleared, number of convictions, numbers of citizens reporting victimization by criminals, citizens' feelings of personal safety. Because the relationship between variables and indicators is complex, it is often desirable to use multiple indicators of the same action or outcome variable.[12] Sometimes it is possible to construct an *index*, that is, a combination of two or more indicators that together provide a better measure of actions and outcomes than any one indicator does by itself. Among the many types of indexes used in policy analysis are indices of cost of living, pollution, crime severity, energy consumption, health care, administrative centralization, and the quality of life.[13]

APPROACHES TO MONITORING

Monitoring is central to policy analysis. Yet there are so many ways to monitor outputs and impacts that it is sometimes difficult to distinguish monitoring from social research in general. Fortunately, monitoring can

---

[12] The general case for multiple indicators may be found in Eugene Webb and others, *Unobtrusive Measures: Nonreactive Research in the Behavioral Sciences* (Chicago: Rand McNally, 1966). For applications to criminal justice and other areas, see Roger B. Parks, "Complementary Measures of Police Performance," in *Public Policy Evaluation*, ed. Kenneth M. Dolbeare (Beverly Hills, CA: Sage Publications, 1975), pp. 185–218.

[13] On various kinds of indices, see references in Miller, *Handbook of Research Design and Social Measurement*, pp. 207–460; James L. Price, *Handbook of Organizational Measurement* (Lexington, MA: D.C. Heath and Company, 1972); Dale G. Lake and others, *Measuring Human Behavior* (New York: Columbia University Teachers College Press, 1973); Paul N. Cheremisinoff, ed., *Industrial Pollution Control: Measurement and Instrumentation* (Westport, CT: Technomic Press, 1976); Leo G. Reader and others, *Handbook of Scales and Indices of Health Behavior* (Pacific Palisades, CA: Goodyear Publishing Co., 1976); Lou E. Davis and Albert B. Cherns, *The Quality of Working Life*, Vol. I (New York: The Free Press, 1975); and Albert D. Biderman and Thomas F. Drury, eds., *Measuring Work Quality for Social Reporting* (New York: Wiley, 1976).

be broken down into several identifiable approaches: social systems accounting, social experimentation, social auditing and research and practice synthesis. These approaches may be contrasted in terms of two major properties (Table 8–2):

1. *Types of controls.* Approaches to monitoring differ in terms of the ways they exercise control over variations in policy actions. Only one of the approaches (social experimentation) involves direct controls over policy inputs and policy processes. The other three approaches "control" inputs and processes by determining after the fact how much of an observed variation in outcomes is due to inputs and processes, as compared to extraneous factors that are not directly connected with policy actions.

2. *Types of information required.* Approaches to monitoring differ according to their respective information requirements. Some approaches (social experimentation and social auditing) require the collection of new information. Social systems accounting may or may not require new information, while research and practice synthesis relies exclusively on available information.

Each of these four approaches also has certain common features. First, each is concerned with monitoring *policy-relevant outcomes.* Therefore, each approach deals with variables that are relevant to policymakers because they are indicators of policy outputs and/or impacts. Some policy-relevant variables can be manipulated by policymakers (for example, resource inputs or new processes for delivering services), while others cannot. These non-manipulable variables include preconditions which are present before actions are taken (for example, the average age or the cultural values of a target group) as well as unforeseen events that occur in the course of policy implementation (for example, sudden staff turnover, strikes, or natural disasters).

A second common feature of these approaches is that they are *goal-focused.* This means that policy outcomes are monitored because they are believed to enhance the satisfaction of some need, value, or opportunity— that is, outcomes are seen as ways to resolve a policy problem. At the same time some policy outcomes are monitored because they may inhibit the

TABLE 8–2 Main Contrasts Among Four Approaches to Monitoring

APPROACH	TYPES OF CONTROL	TYPE OF INFORMATION REQUIRED
Social systems accounting	Quantitative	Available and/or new information
Social experimentation	Direct manipulations and quantitative	New information
Social auditing	Quantitative and/or qualitative	New information
Research and practice synthesis	Quantitative and/or qualitative	Available information

satisfaction of some need, value, or opportunity.[14] Note also that non-manipulable variables, that is, policy preconditions and unforeseen events, are also goal-focused to the extent that they are known to affect policy outcomes.

A third feature common to these approaches is that they are *change-oriented*. Each approach seeks to monitor change, either by analyzing changes in outcomes over time; by comparing such changes across two or more programs, projects, or localities; or by using some combination of the two. While some approaches (social systems accounting) are oriented toward macro-level changes in societies, states, regions, and communities, other approaches (social auditing and social experimentation) are primarily oriented towards micro-level changes in programs and projects.

A fourth common feature of these approaches is that they permit the *cross-classification* of outputs and impacts by other variables, including variables used to monitor policy inputs and policy processes.[15] For example, such outputs as per pupil educational expenditures may be cross-classified with input variables (for example, teachers' salaries) and those intended to measure processes (for example, class sizes). Outputs and impacts may also be cross-classified by types of preconditions (for example, the average income of community residents) and unforeseen events (for example, frequency of strikes).

Finally, each approach is concerned with *objective as well as subjective* measures of policy actions and outcomes. For example, all approaches provide measures of such objective outcomes as units of health care received as well as such subjective outcomes as satisfaction with medical and health services. Objective indicators are frequently based on available data (for example, census materials), while subjective ones are based on new data acquired through sample surveys or field studies. In some instances objective and subjective measures are based both on available and new information. For example, past studies may be repeated (replicated) to obtain new information that may then be compared with old information in an effort to monitor the direction and pace of social change.[16]

Each of these common features contributes to a general definition of monitoring as the process of obtaining policy-relevant information to measure changes in goal-focused social conditions, both objective and subjec-

---

[14] There is also the special case in which outputs and impacts are neither enhancing nor inhibiting, but neutral. In this context, one of the objections to an exclusive concern with social indicators that have "direct normative interest" is that what is relevant to today's goals may not be so in later years. See Eleanor B. Sheldon and Howard E. Freeman, "Notes on Social Indicators: Promises and Potential," *Policy Sciences*, 1 (April 1970), 97–98. Note that if a goal-focused outcome is defined in terms of its potential effect on a policy problem—and if policy problems are artificial, dynamic, and interdependent (see Chapter 5)—then all outcomes, including "neutral" ones, may someday be of direct normative interest.

[15] Ibid., p. 97.

[16] This combination of old and new information is called *replication of baseline studies*. See Otis Dudley Duncan, *Toward Social Reporting: Next Steps* (New York: Russell Sage Foundation, 1969).

FIGURE 8–2   General framework for monitoring.

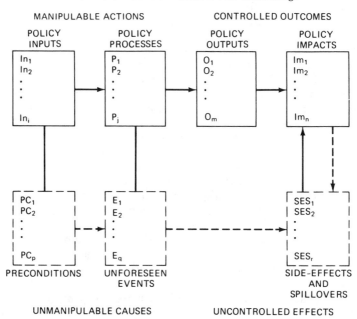

Note: The solid lines indicate effects on manipulable actions and controlled outcomes. The broken lines indicate unforeseen events, side effects and spillovers. Side effects and spillovers are uncontrollable secondary impacts that may enhance or inhibit the satisfaction of needs, values, and opportunities.

tive, among various target groups and beneficiaries.[17] Social conditions include policy actions and outcomes as well as policy preconditions and unforeseen events that affect actions and outcomes in the course of implementation. Impacts may be immediate (first-order impacts) or secondary (second-, third-, and nth-order impacts), as when policy actions produce "side effects" and "spillovers" beyond their intended effects. Side effects and spillovers may enhance or inhibit the satisfaction of needs, values, and opportunities. Elements of this general definition of monitoring are diagrammed in Figure 8–2, which represents a general framework for monitoring in policy analysis.

Social Systems Accounting

With this general framework in mind we can proceed to contrast the four approaches to monitoring. *Social systems accounting* is an approach and set of methods that permit analysts to monitor changes in objective and

---

[17] Compare the definition of social indicators offered by Kenneth C. Land, "Theories, Models, and Indicators of Social Change," *International Social Science Journal,* XXVII, 1 (1975), 14.

subjective social conditions over time.[18] The term *social systems accounting* comes from a report published by the National Commission on Technology, Automation, and Economic Progress, a body established in 1964 to examine the social consequences of technological development and economic growth. The commission's report recommended that the federal government establish a "system of social accounts" that would serve as a counterpart to national economic accounts.[19] Several years earlier a project undertaken by the American Academy of Arts and Sciences for the National Aeronautics and Space Administration explored the second-order impacts of the space program. One result of this project was the development of methods for monitoring social and political, as well as economic trends, and a major book was published in 1966 under the title *Social Indicators*.[20] While these efforts to develop social systems accounting occurred in the 1960s, they actually represent a continuation of work begun in 1933 under the auspices of the President's Research Committee on Social Trends. Under the direction of sociologist William F. Ogburn the Committee produced a two-volume report, *Recent Social Trends*, before its work was abandoned during the Depression.[21]

Work on social systems accounting continued throughout the 1960s and 1970s. Some of the major products of this period were produced by social scientists interested in objective and subjective indicators of social change.[22] Other major initiatives came from federal agencies, including the Department of Health, Education, and Welfare, the Office of Management and the Budget, and the Department of Labor.[23] In addition, several in-

---

[18] Much of the following account is based on Kenneth C. Land and Seymour Spilerman, eds., *Social Indicator Models* (New York: Russell Sage Foundation, 1974); and Land, "Theories, Models, and Indicators of Social Change," pp. 7–20.

[19] National Commission on Technology, Automation, and Economic Progress, *Technology and the American Economy* (Washington, DC: U.S. Government Printing Office, 1966). A primary influence on the Commission's recommendations was Daniel Bell, whose major work (*Toward Post-Industrial Society: A Venture in Social Forecasting*) was described in Chap. 2.

[20] Raymond A. Bauer, ed., *Social Indicators* (Cambridge, MA: MIT Press, 1966). Chap. 3, by Bertram M. Gross, is titled "The State of the Nation: Social Systems Accounting."

[21] President's Research Committee on Social Trends, *Recent Social Trends* (New York: McGraw-Hill, 1933). Ogburn's major work was *Social Change: With Respect to Culture and Original Nature* (New York: B. W. Huebsch, 1922).

[22] Two companion volumes were devoted, respectively, to objective and subjective dimensions of social change. See Eleanor B. Sheldon and Wilbert E. Moore, eds., *Indicators of Social Change: Concepts and Measurements* (New York: Russell Sage Foundation, 1968); and Angus Campbell and Philip E. Converse, eds., *The Human Meaning of Social Change* (New York: Russell Sage Foundation, 1972). For a recent review see "America in the Seventies: Some Social Indicators," *Annals of the American Academy of Political and Social Science*, 435 (January 1978).

[23] Relevant publications are U.S. Department of Health, Education, and Welfare, *Toward a Social Report* (Washington, DC: U.S. Government Printing Office, 1969); Executive Office of the President, Office of Management and Budget, *Social Indicators, 1973* (Washington, DC: U.S. Government Printing Office, 1974); and U.S. Department of Labor, *State Economic and Social Indicators* (Washington, DC: U.S. Government Printing Office, 1973). In 1974 the National Science Foundation funded a Center for the Coordination of Research on

ternational organizations (the United Nations and the Organization for Economic Cooperation and Development) have undertaken work on social indicators, as have the governments of France, the United Kingdom, West Germany, Canada, Norway, Sweden, and Japan.[24]

The major analytic element of social systems accounting is the *social indicator*. While there are various definitions of this term, the most useful is that which defines social indicators as "statistics which measure social conditions and changes therein over time for various segments of a population. By social conditions, we mean both the external (social and physical) and the internal (subjective and perceptional) contexts of human existence in a given society."[25] Social indicators, as has been suggested, are both objective and subjective, since they help monitor such objective conditions as urbanization as well as such subjective conditions as satisfaction with municipal services. Social indicators are used to monitor change at the national as well as state and municipal levels.[26] Social indicators are also available to monitor special aspects of social change such as pollution, health care, and the quality of working life.[27]

A list of representative social indicators is presented in Table 8–3. These representative indicators, drawn from several major sources, are grouped by area. Note, first, that many indicators are designed to monitor objective social states, for example, persons in state mental hospitals. Other indicators depend upon subjective responses, for example, persons afraid to walk alone at night. Second, most indicators are expressed in units of time and are cross-classified by various segments of the population, for example, persons afraid to walk alone at night are arranged in a time-series from 1965–1972 and cross-classified by race, age, education, and income. Third, some indicators are expressed in terms of present experience, while others are stated as future goals. For example, average annual paid vacation in manufacturing is expressed in terms of the 1967 value (two weeks) and a 1976–1979 goal (four weeks). Finally, many indicators are related to outputs and impacts of public policies. For example, the labor force participation rate for women aged 35–64 may be taken as an indicator of impacts of equal employment opportunity-affirmative action policies, while indices

---

Social Indicators, administered under the Social Science Research Council. The Center publishes *Social Indicators Newsletter*.

[24] For a comprehensive annotated bibliography, see Leslie D. Wilcox and others, *Social Indicators and Societal Monitoring: An Annotated Bibliography* (New York: American Elsevier Publishing Co., 1974). The major international journal is *Social Indicators Research: An International and Interdisciplinary Journal for Quality of Life Measurement*, published since 1974.

[25] Land, "Theories, Models, and Indicators of Social Change," p. 15.

[26] On social indicators at the community level, see Terry N. Clark, "Community Social Indicators: From Analytical Models to Policy Applications," *Urban Affairs Quarterly*, 9, No. 1 (September 1973), 3–36. On urban social indicators, see M. J. Flax, *A Study in Comparative Urban Indicators: Conditions in 18 Large Metropolitan Areas* (Washington, DC: The Urban Institute, 1972).

[27] See footnote 13. The most complete source on policy-relevant social indicators is Duncan MacRae, Jr., *Policy Indicators* (Chapel Hill, NC: University of North Carolina Press, 1985).

TABLE 8–3 Some Representative Social Indicators

AREA	INDICATOR
Health and illness	Persons in state mental hospitals[1]
Public safety	Persons afraid to walk alone at night[2]
Education	High school graduates aged 25 and older[1]
Employment	Labor force participation rate for women[1]
Income	Percent of population below poverty line[1]
Housing	Households living in substandard units[2]
Leisure and recreation	Average annual paid vacation in manufacturing[1]
Population	Actual and projected population[2]
Government and politics	Quality of public administration[3]
Social values and attitudes	Overall life satisfaction and alienation[4]
Social mobility	Change from father's occupation[1]
Physical environment	Air pollution index[5]
Science and technology	Scientific discoveries[6]

Sources:
[1] U.S. Department of Health, Education and Welfare, *Toward a Social Report* (Ann Arbor, MI: University of Michigan Press, 1970).
[2] Office of Management and Budget, *Social Indicators, 1973* (Washington, DC: U.S. Government Printing Office, 1974).
[3] U.S. Department of Labor, *State Economic and Social Indicators* (Washington, DC: U.S. Government Printing Office, 1973).
[4] Angus Campbell, Philip Converse, and Willard Rodgers, *The Quality of American Life* (New York: Russell Sage Foundation, 1976).
[5] Otis Dudley Duncan, *Toward Social Reporting: The Next Steps* (New York: Russell Sage Foundation, 1969).
[6] National Science Board, *Science and Engineering Indicators* (Washington, DC) (Bi-ennial). National Science Foundation.

of air pollution may be used to monitor the impact of programs implemented by the Environmental Protection Agency. In short, most social indicators are policy-relevant, goal-focused, change-oriented, cross-classified, and expressive of objective and subjective social conditions.

In using social indicators for purposes of monitoring, it is frequently necessary to make assumptions about the reasons for change in a social indicator. For example, if reported crime is used to monitor the output of crime control policies, official statistics from the Federal Bureau of Investigation (*Uniform Crime Reports*) indicate that reported crimes per 100,000 inhabitants declined by three-tenths of 1 percent between 1975 and 1976 but increased by 76.2 percent between 1967 and 1976. To attribute the decrease or increase to criminal justice policies, it is necessary to make the assumption that changes in crime are a consequence of policy actions undertaken by federal, state, and local law enforcement authorities. This assumption is highly questionable, even when we have accurate data on resource inputs (expenditures for personnel and equipment), since we ignore uncontrollable factors (a more youthful population following the postwar "baby boom") as well as the processes used to transform inputs into outputs. In effect, we are forced to treat the relation between inputs and outputs as a kind of "black box," that is, an unknown area that symbolizes what we don't know (and therefore must assume) about the relation between inputs into outputs.

The use of social indicators has several advantages. First, efforts to develop indicators appropriate for monitoring policy outcomes may alert us to areas where there is insufficient information. For example, while there is much information about municipal services, much of this information deals with outputs, that is, the number and types of services provided per capita. Information about the impacts of municipal service policies on citizens—for example, impacts measured in terms of satisfaction with transportation, sanitation, and recreational facilities—is inadequate in most cases.[28] Second, when social indicators provide reliable information about the impacts of policies on target groups, it becomes possible to modify policies and programs. Social indicators also provide information that helps structure policy problems and modify existing policy alternatives. We may find, for example, that the number of high school graduates aged 25 and over has increased, but that the social mobility of the educated population has not changed. In this case we may wish to restructure the problem of social inequality in a way that places less emphasis on educational opportunity as a vehicle for social mobility.[29]

Social indicators also have various limitations. The choice of certain indicators (for example, percent of households below the poverty line) reflects particular social values rather than others and may convey the political biases of analysts.[30] Given that policy problems are themselves artificial and subjective, it is doubtful that any social indicator can be totally free of the values of those who develop and apply it for purposes of monitoring. Second, social indicators may not be directly useful to policymakers faced with practical choices. One study of federal policymakers, for example, finds that social indicators are not seen as having great instrumental value.[31] Hence, while social indicators may help to conceptualize or structure problems, they are often so general that they cannot be used to find specific solutions for particular problems.

Second, most social indicators are based on available data about objective social conditions. While it is easier to use available data on objective conditions than it is to collect new information about subjective conditions, it may be just as important to monitor subjective conditions as it is to monitor objective ones.[32] For example, reported crimes per 100,000 inhabitants may

---

[28] See, for example, the Urban Institute, *Measuring the Effectiveness of Basic Municipal Services* (Washington, DC: The Urban Institute, 1974).

[29] See Christopher Jencks, and others, *Inequality: A Reassessment of the Effect of Family and Schooling in America* (New York: Basic Books, 1972).

[30] Thomas R. Dye, *Understanding Public Policy*, 3rd ed. (Englewood Cliffs, NJ: Prentice Hall, 1978), pp. 324–25.

[31] Nathan Caplan and others, *The Use of Social Science Information by Policy-Makers at the Federal Level* (Ann Arbor, MI: Institute for Social Research, Center for Research on the Utilization of Scientific Knowledge, University of Michigan, 1975).

[32] Vijai P. Singh, "Indicators and Quality of Life: Some Theoretical and Methodological Issues," paper presented at the Annual Meeting, American Sociological Association, August 25–29, 1975.

decrease, yet citizens' sense of personal insecurity may remain the same or even increase. Similarly, the number of poverty families may decrease without any appreciable change in perceptions of the quality of life.

Finally, social indicators provide little information about the various ways that policy inputs are transformed into policy outcomes. Claims about variations in policy outputs and impacts are based on observed correlations between policy inputs and outcomes, rather than on knowledge about the processes by which resource inputs are transformed into outputs and impacts. Policy inputs are measured, policy outputs are measured, and the two are related by establishing the degree of their association. Concurrently, efforts are made to determine whether preconditions and unforeseen events—that is, factors apart from the original policy inputs—enhance or inhibit the production of some output. Yet the process of accounting for these nonpolicy effects takes place after policy outputs have been produced and is based on the use of statistical controls; that is, techniques that permit analysts to observe the effects of inputs on outputs under carefully specified conditions. For example, the effects of educational expenditures on school achievement will be analyzed for poor and middle-class families separately.

Social Experimentation

One of the consequences of using social indicators is that it may take a very large number of successes and failures to find out what works best and why. Such an approach has been called random innovation and contrasted with systematic experimentation.[33] *Random innovation* is the process of executing a large number of alternative policies and programs whose inputs are neither standardized nor systematically manipulated. Because there is no direct control over policy actions, the outcomes of policies cannot easily be traced back to known sources. By contrast, *social experimentation* is the process of systematically manipulating policy actions in a way that permits more or less precise answers to questions about the sources of change in policy outcomes. Social experimentation is advocated as a way to find solutions for social problems by deliberately maximizing the differences between types of policy actions in a small and carefully selected group of programs and assessing their consequences prior to making large-scale investments in untested programs.[34]

Social experimentation is based on adaptations of procedures used in classical laboratory experiments in the physical sciences.[35] (1) *Direct control over experimental treatments (stimuli)*: Analysts who use social experimen-

---

[33] Rivlin, *Systematic Thinking for Social Action*; and Rivlin, "How Can Experiments Be More Useful?" *American Economic Review* 64 (1974), 346–54.

[34] See, for example, Fairweather and Tornatzky, *Experimental Methods for Social Policy Research*.

[35] See Donald T. Campbell and Julian C. Stanley, *Experimental and Quasi-experimental Designs for Research* (Chicago: Rand McNally, 1966); and Campbell, "Reforms as Experiments," in *Handbook of Evaluation Research*, Vol. 1, eds. Elmer L. Struening and Marcia Guttentag (Beverly Hills, CA: Sage Publications, 1965), pp. 71–100.

tation directly control experimental treatments (policy actions) and attempt to maximize differences among them in order to produce effects that differ as much as possible. (2) *Comparison (control) groups:* Two or more groups are used in social experiments. One group (called the experimental group) receives the experimental treatment, while other groups (called control groups) receive no treatment or a significantly different treatment than that received by the experimental group. (3) *Random assignment:* Potential sources of variation in policy outcomes other than those produced by the experimental treatment are eliminated by randomly selecting members of experimental and control groups and by randomly assigning treatments to these groups. Random assignment minimizes biases in the selection of members and groups who may respond differently to the experimental treatment. For example, children from middle-class families may respond to a special education program in a more positive way than children from poor families. This would mean that factors other than the program itself are responsible for such outputs as higher reading scores. These selection biases are reduced or eliminated through randomization.

Social experiments and quasi-experiments have been advocated as a way to monitor the outcomes of public policy since the New Deal years of the 1930s.[36] In the post–World War II period, social experiments have been conducted in many areas of public policy: public health, compensatory education, welfare, criminal justice, drug and alcohol abuse, population control, nutrition, highway safety, and housing.[37] One of the best known social experiments is the New Jersey–Pennsylvania Graduated Work Incentives Experiment, funded by the Office of Economic Opportunity to answer questions surrounding the reform of the social welfare system in the 1960s. A random sample of able-bodied men aged 15 to 58 from low-income families was selected from three sites in New Jersey (Trenton, Paterson–Passaic, and Jersey City) and one in Pennsylvania (Scranton). In each city some families received various levels of guaranteed income and tax breaks, while others received none. Altogether, some 1350 families participated in the experiment.

Critics of welfare reform expected that income supplements and tax breaks (called a negative income tax) would induce men from low-income families to work less. This expectation was not substantiated by the original experiment, which indicated that the experimental (income maintenance) and control (no income maintenance) groups did not differ significantly in their employment behavior, as reflected by changes in earnings before and after the experiment. In fact, the earnings of the experimental groups showed a slightly higher increase than those of the control group.

Social experimentation has the potential of showing in precise terms

[36] A. Stephen Stephan, "Prospects and Possibilities: The New Deal and New Social Research," *Social Forces* 13 (1935), 515–521. See *Readings in Evaluation Research,* ed. Francis G. Caro (New York: Russell Sage Foundation, 1971), pp. 37–42.

[37] See Carl A. Bennett and Arthur A. Lumsdaine, eds., *Evaluation and Experiment* (New York: Academic Press, 1975); and Fairweather and Tornatzky, *Experimental Methods for Social Policy Research.*

whether certain policy actions (for example, the provision of income maintenance) result in certain outcomes (for example, family earnings). The capacity of experiments and quasi-experiments to produce valid causal inferences about the effects of actions on outcomes is called *internal validity*. The greater the internal validity, the more confidence we have that policy outputs are a consequence of policy inputs. In fact, procedures for social experimentation are a way to reduce threats to the internal validity of claims about policy outcomes.[38] Among these threats to internal validity the most important are:

1. *History.* A number of unforeseen events can occur between the time a policy is implemented and the point at which outcomes are measured. For example, public disturbances, strikes, or sudden shifts in public opinion may represent a plausible rival explanation of the causes of variations in policy outcomes.

2. *Maturation.* Changes within members of groups, whether these be individuals, families, or larger social units, may exert an independent effect on policy outcomes. For example, with the passage of time individual attitudes may change, learning may occur, or geographical units may grow or decline. Such maturation may make it difficult to explain policy outcomes.

3. *Instability.* Fluctuations in a time series may produce unstable variations in outcomes that are a consequence of random error or procedures for obtaining information and not a result of policy actions. Since most time series are unstable, causal inferences about the effects of actions on outcomes are often problematic.

4. *Instrumentation and testing.* The very fact of conducting an experiment and measuring outcomes may sensitize members of experimental and control groups to the aims and expectations of the experiment. When this occurs, policy outcomes may be a result of the meaning attributed to policy actions by participants, and not the actions (for example, income guarantees) themselves.[39]

5. *Mortality.* Some of the experimental or control groups, or their members, may drop out of the experiment before it is completed. This makes it more difficult to make causal inferences. For example, in the New Jersey–Pennsylvania experiment some families broke up before the experiment was over.

6. *Selection.* In many situations random sampling is not possible, thus requiring a quasi-experimental design which does not fully eliminate biases in selecting respondents. For example, if one group of children in a quasi-experimental program designed to improve reading skills is drawn primarily from upper-class families where regular reading is more prevalent, the difference between reading scores before and after the program will be less pronounced than with

---

[38] For a fuller discussion of threats to internal validity, see Campbell and Stanley, *Experimental and Quasi-experimental Designs for Research*, pp. 5–6.

[39] The effects of interpretation and testing are sometimes known as the "Hawthorne effect," named after a series of experiments conducted in the Western Electric Company's Chicago–Hawthorne Plant in 1927–1931. The output of workers increased after working conditions and other factors (inputs) were changed. Later, output continued to increase even after working conditions (rest pauses, lighting, and so on) were changed back to their original state, largely because the experiment itself provided opportunities for workers' participation. See Paul Blumberg, *Industrial Democracy: The Sociology of Participation* (London: Constable, 1968).

those of children drawn from lower-class families. This may make the program look less effective than it really is and, in some cases, can even make the experiment look harmful.[40]

7. *Regression artifacts.* When members of experimental and control groups are selected on the basis of extreme characteristics (for example, poor children selected for an experimental reading program may be high achievers), artificial changes in reading scores may occur as a result of what is known as *regression toward the mean.* Regression toward the mean is the statistical phenomenon where extreme values of some characteristic of a population automatically regress toward or "go back to" the average of the population as a whole. For example, the height of children of very tall or very short parents tends to regress toward the arithmetic mean of all parents. Children of very tall and very short parents tend, respectively, to be shorter and taller than their fathers and mothers.

There are many ways to increase the internal validity of social experiments and quasi-experiments by carefully designing research. Generally, such research involves random selection, repeated measures of outcome variables over time, and measurement of the preprogram outcome measures for some of the experimental and control groups but not others. The latter procedure eliminates the possibility of testing effects for some groups, whose outcome measures after the program can be compared to equivalent groups whose outcomes have been measured both before and after receiving inputs.[41]

Social experimentation is weakest in the area of *external validity,* which refers to the generalizability of causal inferences outside the particular setting in which an experiment is conducted. Important threats to the external validity of claims about policy outputs are similar to those that threaten internal validity, including interpretation, testing, and selection. In addition, other threats are important to the generalizability of claims. The most important of these is artificiality. Conditions under which a social experiment is carried out may be atypical or unrepresentative of conditions elsewhere. For example, conditions in New Jersey and Pennsylvania are different from those present in San Francisco, Seattle, and Anchorage, making generalizations problematic.

Social experimentations is frequently unsuccessful in monitoring policy processes, including patterns of interaction among staff and clients and their changing attitudes and values. Many of the most important policies and programs are so complex that social experimentation results in the oversimplification of policy processes. For example, social experimentation is not well suited to broad-aim programs which involve high levels of conflict

---

[40] See Donald T. Campbell and A. E. Erlebacher, "How Regression Artifacts in Quasi-experimental Evaluations Can Mistakenly Make Compensatory Education Look Harmful," in *Compensatory Education: A National Debate,* Vol. III (New York: Brunner-Mazel, 1970).

[41] The design described here is the "Solomon 4-group design." The best overview of alternative research designs and their role in reducing threats to internal validity is Fred N. Kerlinger, *Foundations of Behavioral Research,* 2nd ed. (New York: Holt, Rinehart and Winston, 1973), pp. 300–377.

among stakeholders, or contexts where the same inputs of personnel, resources and equipment are perceived in altogether different ways by different groups.[42] For these and other reasons various qualitative methods
for obtaining the subjective judgments of stakeholders have been used to
uncover otherwise neglected aspects of policy processes. These methods—
which range from participant observation and the use of logs or diaries to
group sessions that resemble a policy Delphi—may be viewed as a way to
complement or replace social experimentation.[43]

Social Auditing

One of the limitations of social systems accounting and social experimentation—namely, that both approaches neglect or oversimplify policy
processes—is partly overcome in social auditing. *Social auditing* explicitly
monitors relations among inputs, processes, outputs, and impacts in an
effort to trace policy inputs "from the point at which they are disbursed to
the point at which they are experienced by the ultimate intended recipient
of those resources."[44] Social auditing, which has been used in areas of
educational and youth policy by analysts at the Rand Corporation and the
National Institute of Education, helps determine whether policy outcomes
are a consequence of inadequate policy inputs or a result of processes that
divert resources or services from intended target groups and beneficiaries.

The essential differences between social auditing and other approaches
to monitoring are most easily seen if we compare social auditing with social
systems accounting and social experimentation. Variations of the latter approaches have been used to monitor educational policies in two important
studies, *Equality of Educational Opportunity* and the Westinghouse Learning Corporation's evaluation of the Head Start program.[45] In the former
case, a variation of social systems accounting, the effectiveness of various
levels of school resources were monitored by measuring the relation between
resource inputs (teachers, textbooks, school facilities) and outcomes, measured in terms of the achievement levels of students. In the Head Start

---

[42] See Robert S. Weiss and Martin Rein, "The Evaluation of Broad-Aim Programs: A
Cautionary Case and a Moral," in Caro, *Readings in Evaluation Research*, pp. 287–96; and
Ward Edwards, Marcia Guttentag and Kurt Snapper, "A Decision-Theoretic Approach to Evaluation Research," in Streuning and Guttentag, *Handbook of Evaluation Research*, Vol. 1, pp.
139–82.

[43] See M. G. Trend, "On the Reconciliation of Qualitative and Quantitative Analysis:
A Case Study," *Human Organization*, 37, No. 4 (1978), 345–54; and M. Q. Patton, *Alternative
Evaluation Research Paradigm* (Grand Forks, ND: University of North Dakota Study Group
on Evaluation, 1976).

[44] James S. Coleman, *Policy Research in the Social Sciences* (Morristown, NJ: General
Learning Press, 1972), p. 18. See also Michael Q. Patton, *Utilization-Focused Evaluation*
(Beverly Hills, CA: Sage Publications, 1978).

[45] See James S. Coleman and others, *Equality of Educational Opportunity* (Washington,
DC: U.S. Government Printing Office, 1966); and Victor Cicarelli and others, *The Impact of
Head Start: An Evaluation of the Effects of Head Start on Children's Cognitive and Affective
Development* (Washington, DC: U.S. Government Printing Office, 1969).

study, which had several characteristics of a social experiment, the relations between special reading and skill-development activities (inputs) and cognitive and affective skills (outputs) of children exposed to the program were studied in a number of cities. The essential feature of these two approaches is that

> the policy inputs are measured, policy outcomes are measured, and the two are related (with, of course, the use of experimental or statistical controls to neutralize the effect of situational variables). Whatever institutional structure intervenes is taken in effect as a black box into which the input resources go and out of which the desired outcomes and side effects come. In the first research mentioned above [*Equality of Educational Opportunity*], the school was the black box. Inputs to it were teacher salaries, pupil–teacher ratio, age of textbooks, size of library, and a variety of other traditional measures of school resources. Outputs studied were achievement of students in verbal and mathematical skills. In the second study, the resource inputs were the additional resources provided by Head Start; the outputs were cognitive and affective measures on the children.[46]

In monitoring policy processes social auditing provides important information about what goes on inside the "black box." The processes monitored in a social audit are of two main types: resource diversion and transformation.[47] In *resource diversion* original inputs are diverted from intended target groups and beneficiaries as a result of the passage of resources through the administrative system. For example, the total expenditures for two manpower training programs may be equal, yet one program may expend a higher percentage of funds on salaries and other personnel costs, thus resulting in fewer staff members per dollar and a diversion of services from beneficiaries. Far more important is the process of *resource transformation*. Here resources and their actual receipt by target groups may be identical, yet the *meaning* of these resources to program staff and target groups may be altogether different. If the meaning of resources is in fact different, then resources may have been transformed in such a way as to enhance (or retard) their impact on beneficiaries. For this reason quantitative methods may be supplemented by *qualitative methods* designed to provide information about the subjective interpretations of policy actions by stakeholders who affect and are affected by the implementation of policies.[48]

A good example of the supplementary use of qualitative methods to monitor policy processes is that provided by a housing experiment con-

---

[46] Coleman, *Policy Research in the Social Sciences*, p. 18.

[47] The following account of social auditing differs from that of Coleman, which is confined to "resource loss." Coleman's account does not include resource transformation and is based on the restrictive assumption that social auditing is appropriate only for policies involving resource distribution.

[48] The best expositions of qualitative methodology are Barney G. Glaser and Anselm L. Strauss, *The Discovery of Grounded Theory: Strategies for Qualitative Research* (Chicago: Aldine Publishing Company, 1967); and Norman K. Denzin, *The Research Act* (Chicago: Aldine Publishing Company, 1970).

ducted in 1972 by the U.S. Department of Housing and Urban Development (HUD). This particular experiment was designed to find out whether direct cash payments for housing would help low-income families to obtain adequate housing on the open market.[49]

In this case, quantitative measures of inputs and outputs not only forced some analysts to treat policy-program processes as a "black box"; initially, it also prevented them from seeing that certain factors—for example, spontaneous assistance by housing counselors—accounted for program impacts. The supplementary use of qualitative methods yielded strikingly different results than those that might have been produced by focusing exclusively on quantitative measures of inputs and outputs. This case also shows that alternative approaches to monitoring are potentially complementary. Social experimentation and quantitative measurement were successfully combined with social auditing and the qualitative description of policy processes.

Research and Practice Synthesis

Social auditing and social experimentation require the collection of new information about policy actions and outcomes. Social systems accounting, while based chiefly on available information, also requires new data insofar as information about subjective social conditions is out of date or unavailable. In contrast to each of these approaches, *research and practice synthesis* is an approach to monitoring that involves the systematic compilation, comparison, and assessment of the results of past efforts to implement public policies. It has been used to synthesize information in a number of policy issue areas that range from social welfare, agriculture, and education to municipal services and science and technology policy.[50] It has also been employed to assess the quality of policy research conducted on policy processes and policy outcomes.[51]

There are two primary sources of available information relevant to research and practice syntheses: case studies of policy formulation and implementation; and research reports that address relations among policy ac-

---

[49] See Trend, "On the Reconciliation of Qualitative and Quantitative Analyses: A Case Study."

[50] See, for example, Jack Rothman, *Planning and Organizing for Social Change: Action Principles From Social Science Research* (New York: Columbia University Press, 1974); Gerald Zaltman, Robert Duncan, and James Holbek, *Innovations and Organizations* (New York: Wiley-Interscience, 1973); Everett Rogers and F. Floyd Shoemaker, *The Communication of Innovations* (New York: The Free Press, 1971); Robert K. Yin and Douglas Yates, *Street-Level Governments: Assessing Decentralization and Urban Services* (Santa Monica, CA: The Rand Corporation, October, 1974); U.S. General Accounting Office, *Designing Evaluations* (Washington, DC: U.S. GA Office, July 1984); and Richard J. Light and David B. Pillemer, *Summing Up: The Science of Reviewing Research* (Cambridge, MA: Harvard University Press, 1984).

[51] See, for example, Ilene N. Bernstein and Howard E. Freeman, *Academic and Entrepreneurial Research: The Consequences of Diversity in Federal Evaluation Programs* (New York: Russell Sage Foundation, 1975).

tions and outcomes. When research and practice synthesis is applied to case studies, it may be based on the *case survey method,* a set of procedures used to identify and analyze factors that account for variations in the adoption and implementation of policies.[52] The case survey method requires that the analyst first develop a *case-coding scheme,* a set of categories that capture key aspects of policy inputs, processes, outputs, and impacts. In one such case survey, analysts sought to determine the influence of political participation and other process variables on the delivery of municipal services, an output variable.[53] Other case surveys, focusing on public agencies and private corporations, have attempted to determine what factors account for successful and unsuccessful efforts to implement and utilize a variety of management innovations.[54] Representative indicators and coding categories from a typical case-coding scheme are illustrated in Table 8–4.

When research and practice synthesis is applied to available research reports, it is based on the *research survey,* research synthesis, or evaluation synthesis, a set of procedures used to compare and appraise results of past research on policy actions and outcomes.[55] Some of the more important applications of the research survey method have yielded insights into factors associated with the diffusion and communication of innovations, planned social change, and the outputs and impacts of public policies and programs.[56] The research survey method provides several kinds of information: empirical generalizations about sources of variation in policy outcomes; summary assessments of the confidence researchers have in these generalizations; and policy alternatives or action guidelines that are implied by these generalizations. Sample results of one application of the research survey method are illustrated in Table 8–5.

The research survey method, like the case survey method, requires the construction of a format for extracting information about research reports. The typical research report form includes a number of items that help analysts to summarize the research and appraise its quality. These items include variables measured, the type of research design and methods used, the issue area in which the research was carried out, and an overall assessment of the reliability and validity of the research findings. A sample research survey form is presented in Figure 8–3.

---

[52] See Robert K. Yin and Kenneth Heald, "Using the Case Survey Method to Analyze Policy Studies," *Administrative Science Quarterly,* 20, No. 3 (1975), 371–81; William A. Lucas, *The Case Survey Method: Aggregating Case Experience* (Santa Monica, CA: The Rand Corporation, October 1974); and Yin, *Case Study Analysis* (Beverly Hills, CA: Sage Publications, 1985).

[53] Yin and Yates, *Street Level Governments.*

[54] William N. Dunn and Frederic W. Swierczek, "Planned Organizational Change: Toward Grounded Theory," *The Journal of Applied Behavioral Science,* 13, No. 2 (1977), 135–58.

[55] See Rothman, *Planning and Organizing for Social Change;* U.S. General Accounting Office, *Designing Evaluations;* and Light and Pillemer, *Summing Up.*

[56] Rogers and Shoemaker, *The Communication of Innovations;* Gerald Zaltman, *Toward a Theory of Planned Social Change: A Theory-in-Use Approach,* prepared for the Second Meeting of the Network of Consultants on Knowledge Transfer, Denver, Colorado, December 11–13, 1977; and Rothman, *Planning and Organizing for Social Change,* Chap. 6, pp. 195–278.

TABLE 8–4   Case-Coding Scheme: Representative Indicators and Coding Categories

TYPE OF INDICATOR	INDICATOR	CODING CATEGORIES
Input	Adequacy of resources	[ ] Totally adequate [ ] Mostly adequate [ ] Not adequate [ ] Insufficient information
Process	Involvement of policy analyst(s) in defining problem	[ ] Makes decisions [ ] Influences decisions [ ] No influence [ ] Insufficient information
Output	Utilization of results of policy research	[ ] High [ ] Moderate [ ] Low [ ] None [ ] Insufficient information
Impact	Perceived resolution of problem(s)	[ ] Complete [ ] Partial [ ] No resolution [ ] Insufficient information

There are several major advantages of research and practice synthesis as an approach to monitoring. First, the case survey and research survey methods are comparatively efficient ways to compile and appraise an increasingly large body of cases and research reports on policy implementation.[57] Whether the focus is upon cases or research reports, research and practice synthesis allows analysts to systematically and critically examine different empirical generalizations and their implications. Second, the case survey method is one among several ways to uncover different dimensions of policy processes that affect policy outcomes. Generalizations about policy processes may be used to support arguments from parallel case and analogy, for example, by showing that policies and programs carried out under similar circumstances have similar outcomes. Finally, the case survey method is a good way to examine objective as well as subjective social conditions. The case survey method is an inexpensive and effective way to obtain information about the subjective perceptions of policy processes held by different stakeholders.[58]

The main limitations of research and practice synthesis are related to the reliability and validity of information. Cases and research reports not only vary in quality and depth of coverage but are often self-confirming.

---

[57] On case materials see *Cases in Public Policy and Management* (Boston: Intercollegiate Case Clearing House, 1979). This volume contains descriptions of 577 cases, 200 of which are accompanied by teaching notes. On research reports, see, for example, *United States Political Science Documents* (Pittsburgh, PA: Center for International Studies, 1978–79, and annually).

[58] See Zaltman, *Toward A Theory of Planned Social Change*; and Dunn and Swierczek, "Planned Organizational Change: Toward Grounded Theory."

TABLE 8–5   Sample Results of the Research Survey Method: Empirical Generalizations, Action Guidelines, and Levels of Confidence in Generalizations

GENERALIZATION[1]	ACTION GUIDELINES[2]	CONFIDENCE IN GENERALIZATION[3]
1. Current resource expenditures are strongly associated with past resource expenditures.	In determining the receptivity to new policies and programs, analysts should seek out situations where substantial resource expenditures have occurred in the past.	3
2. Policy outcomes are associated with the level of economic development of the municipality, state, or region where policy actions are undertaken.	In determining the receptivity to new policies and programs, analysts should focus attention on wealthy, urban, and industrial areas.	4
3. Outputs of educational policies in municipalities with professional city managers (reform governments) are greater than in municipalities without professional managers (nonreform governments).	Analysts should adjust recommendations according to information about the type of municipality where policy actions are intended to take effect.	2

Notes:
[1] Empirical generalizations are based on available research reports, including scholarly books, articles and government reports.
[2] Action guidelines are derived from empirical generalizations. The same generalization frequently implies multiple action guidelines.
[3] The numbers used to express the degree of confidence in a generalization are based on the number of reliable and valid studies that support generalization.

Source: Adapted from Jack Rothman, *Planning and Organizing for Social Change: Action Principles from Social Science Research* (New York: Columbia University Press, 1974), pp. 254–65.

For example, most available cases and research reports contain no explicit discussion of the limitations and weaknesses of the study, and frequently they put forth only one point of view. Similarly, available cases often report only "successful" efforts to implement policies and programs. Despite these limitations, research and practice synthesis is a systematic way to accumulate knowledge about policy actions and outcomes in many issue areas. Because it relies exclusively on available information it is less expensive than social auditing, social experimentation, and social systems accounting. At the same time these other approaches to monitoring have their own distinctive advantages and limitations. The strengths of one approach are often the weaknesses of another. For this reason the most persuasive generalizations about policy outcomes are those that have multiple foci (inputs, processes, outputs, impacts), use different types of controls (direct manipulation, quantitative analysis, qualitative analysis), and are based on a com-

FIGURE 8-3   Sample research survey form.

1. Title of Report ─────────────────────────────

2. Authors of Report ─────────────────────────

3. Abstract of Report (conceptual framework, hypotheses, research methodology, major findings)

4. Issue Area (for example, health, labor, criminal justice):

─────────────────────────────────────

5. Major Variables Measured (Describe):
   (a) Input ─────────────────────────────
   (b) Process ───────────────────────────
   (c) Output ────────────────────────────
   (d) Impact ────────────────────────────

6. Empirical Generalizations (List):

─────────────────────────────────────
─────────────────────────────────────
─────────────────────────────────────
─────────────────────────────────────

7. Research Design (for example, case study, social experiment, cross-sectional study)

─────────────────────────────────────

8. Research Quality (reliability of data, internal validity, external validity)

─────────────────────────────────────

bination of available and new information about objective and subjective conditions.

TECHNIQUES FOR MONITORING

Monitoring, unlike other policy analytic methods, does not involve procedures which are clearly associated with alternative approaches. Many of the same techniques are therefore appropriate for each of the four approaches: social systems accounting, social auditing, social experimentation, and social research cumulation. Techniques appropriate for the four approaches to monitoring are illustrated in Table 8–6.

Graphic Displays

Much information about policy outcomes is presented in the form of *graphic displays*, which are pictorial representations of the values of one or more action or outcome variables. A graphic display can be used to depict a single variable at one or more points in time, or to summarize the relationship between two variables. In each case a graph displays a set of data points, each of which is defined by the coordinates of two numerical scales. The horizontal scale of a graph is called the *abscissa* and the vertical scale is called the *ordinate*. When a graph is used to display a causal relationship,

TABLE 8–6   Techniques Appropriate to Four Approaches to Monitoring

APPROACH	GRAPHIC DISPLAYS	TABULAR DISPLAYS	INDEX NUM-BERS	INTER-RUPTED TIME-SERIES ANALYSIS	CONTROL-SERIES ANALYSIS	REGRESSION-DISCON-TINUITY ANALYSIS
Social systems accounting	×	×	×	×	×	○
Social auditing	×	×	×	×	×	○
Social experimentation	×	×	×	×	×	×
Research and practice synthesis	×	×	○	○	○	○

Note: ×, Technique appropriate to approach; ○, technique not appropriate to approach.

the horizontal axis is reserved for the independent variable (X) and called the X-axis, while the vertical axis is used to display the dependent variable (Y) and called the Y-axis. Since one of the main purposes of monitoring is to explain how policy actions affect policy outcomes, we usually place input and process variables on the X-axis and output and impact variables on the Y-axis.

One of the most simple and useful kinds of graph is the *time-series graph*, which displays an outcome variable on the vertical axis and time on the horizontal axis. If we wish to monitor the effects of police traffic control activities on motor vehicle deaths between 1970 and 1977, we might use time-series graphs like the ones presented in Figure 8–4(a) and (b). Note that graph (a) has a vertical scale marked off in units of 1000 motor vehicle deaths and an origin of 44,000 (the origin is the point where the horizontal and vertical axes intersect). By contrast, graph (b) is marked off in units of 5000 deaths and has an origin of zero. While both graphs display the same data—which shows a decrease in deaths after the implementation of the 55-mph speed limit in 1973—the decline in deaths is more dramatic in graph (a) than in graph (b). This example shows how the stretching or compression of values on the vertical axis can distort the significance of data. Since there is no clear rule to follow in selecting the size of intervals, it is essential to examine the underlying meaning of changes depicted in graphs.

Graphs may also be used to depict relationships between two or more variables at one point in time. Graphs of this kind, called *scatter diagrams*, were discussed in Chapter 6. We may use a scatter diagram to find out if one variable changes in the same direction as another, that is, whether two variables are correlated. If one of the variables precedes the other in time (for example, a new program precedes changes in the target population), or if there is a persuasive theory that explains the correlated variables (for example, economic theory posits that greater income results in a higher

FIGURE 8–4   Two graphic displays of motor vehicle deaths, 1970–1977.

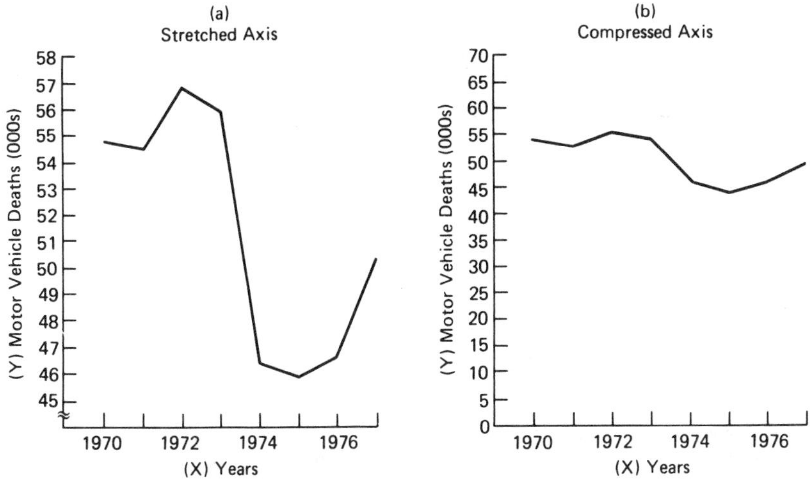

Note: Deaths include those involving collisions between motor vehicles and collisions between motor vehicles and trains, cycles, and fixed objects.

Source: National Safety Council.

propensity to save), then we may be warranted in claiming that there is a *causal relationship* between the variables. Otherwise, variables are simply *correlated*—that is, the values of two variables covary or "go with" each other—and one variable cannot be assumed to be the cause of the other.

A common problem in using graphs is *spurious interpretation*, a situation where two variables that appear to be correlated are actually each correlated with some other variable. A good example of spurious interpretation is that of the analyst who observes from an examination of data on municipal firefighting activities that the number of fire engines present at the scene of a fire (input variable) is positively correlated with the amount of fire damage (output variable). This observed correlation might be used to claim that the number of fire engines deployed does not reduce fire damage, since no matter how many fire engines are present, the amount of fire damage continues to rise at the same rate. This interpretation is spurious (false) because a third variable—the size of fires—is not taken into account. Once we include this variable in our analysis, we find that the size of fires is correlated both with the number of fire trucks deployed and fire damage. The original correlation disappears when we include this third variable in our analysis, and our interpretation is plausible, rather than spurious (Figure 8–5). Spurious interpretation is a serious problem since we can never be completely certain that we have identified all relevant variables that may be affecting the original two-variable relationship.

Another means for displaying data on policy outcomes is the *bar graph*, a pictorial representation that presents data in the form of separated parallel

FIGURE 8–5   Spurious and plausible interpretations of data on municipal firefighting
activities.

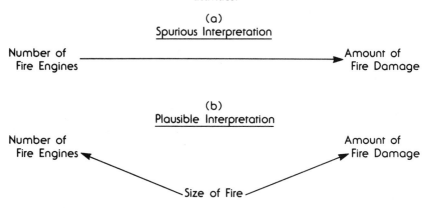

(a)
Spurious Interpretation

Number of   Amount of
Fire Engines ────────────────────────────────→ Fire Damage

(b)
Plausible Interpretation

Number of   Amount of
Fire Engines ◀   ▸ Fire Damage

◥ Size of Fire ◤

Source: Example adapted from H. W. Smith, *Strategies of Social Research: The Methodological Imagination* (Englewood Cliffs, NJ: Prentice Hall, 1975), pp. 325–26.

bars arranged along the horizontal (or vertical) axis. The bar graph presented in Figure 8–6 was used to display data on policy inputs (total municipal personnel costs per capita) as part of an analysis of the fiscal crisis of U.S. cities. Note that cities with growing population have the lowest per capita personnel costs, while cities that are losing population have higher costs. The bar graph also shows the somewhat special position of New York City in 1973.

Information about policy outcomes is often available in the form of *grouped frequency distributions* in which the numbers of persons or target groups in particular categories (for example, age or income) are presented graphically. For example, if we want to monitor the number of persons below the poverty line in various age groups, we might begin with the data in Table 8–7. These data can then be converted into two kinds of graphic displays: histograms and frequency polygons.

A *histogram* is a kind of bar graph that organizes information about a grouped frequency distribution of an action or outcome variable at one point in time. In a histogram the width of the bars along the horizontal axis is equal, and there is no space between the bars. The height of the bars in a histogram shows the frequency of occurrence in each group (called a class interval). The histogram illustrated in Figure 8–7a shows the numbers of persons below the poverty threshold in several age categories in 1977. The histogram can be easily converted into a frequency polygon (Figure 8–7b) by using the midpoints of each class interval as data points and connecting all points with a line. The difference between a histogram and a frequency polygon is that the latter uses a series of lines to represent the frequency distribution.

Another way to display information about policy outcomes is the *cumulative frequency polygon*, a graph which shows the cumulative frequen-

FIGURE 8–6   Bar graph showing total municipal personnel costs per capita for cities with growing and declining populations and for New York City.

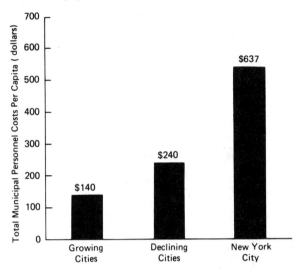

Note: Total personnel costs are for 1973. The growth and decline of population is based on a 1960–1973 average.

Source: Thomas Muller, *Growing and Declining Urban Areas: A Fiscal Comparison* (Washington, DC: The Urban Institute, 1975).

TABLE 8–7   Grouped Frequency Distribution: Number of Persons Below the Poverty Threshold by Age Group in 1977

AGE GROUPS	NUMBER OF PERSONS BELOW THE POVERTY THRESHOLD
Under 14	7,856,000
14 to 21	4,346,000
22 to 44	5,780,000
45 to 54	1,672,000
55 to 59	944,000
60 to 64	946,000
65 and over	3,177,000
Total	24,721,000

Note: The poverty threshold is based on an index that takes into account consumption requirements based on sex, age, and residence in farm or nonfarm areas. Poverty thresholds are updated to reflect changes in the Consumer Price Index. In 1977 the poverty threshold for all persons, irrespective of age and place of residence, was $3067 annually.

Source: U.S. Department of Commerce, Bureau of the Census.

FIGURE 8–7 Histogram and frequency polygon: number of persons below the poverty threshold by age group in 1977.

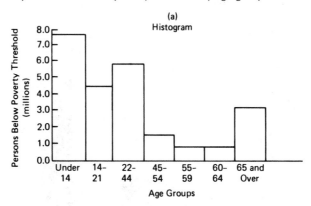

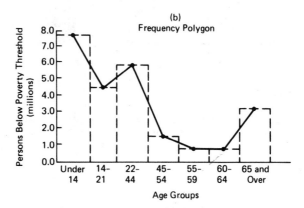

Source: U.S. Department of Commerce, Bureau of the Census.

cies of a distribution along the vertical axis. As one moves from left to right along the horizontal axis, the frequency of persons (or families, cities, states) in the first group is plotted on the vertical axis; the frequency of persons in the first and second groups is then plotted; and so on until we reach the end of the horizontal scale, which is the sum of all frequencies. In monitoring the effects of policies designed to alleviate poverty, a useful type of cumulative frequency polygon is the *Lorenz curve,* which can be used to display the distribution of income, population, or residential segregation in a given population.[59] For example, a Lorenz curve enables us to compare the share of total income earned by each successive percentage group in the population. These percentage groups are called *quintiles* or *deciles,*

---

[59] The original exposition of the Lorenz curve may be found in M. O. Lorenz, "Methods of Measuring the Concentration of Wealth," *Quarterly Publications of the American Statistical Association,* 9, No. 70 (1905), 209–19.

FIGURE 8–8   Lorenz curve showing distribution of family personal income in the United States in 1989 and 1975.

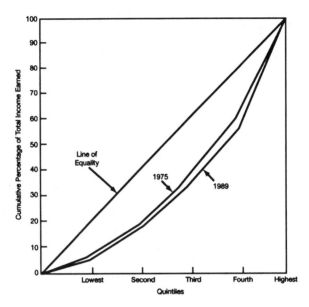

QUINTILES	1989		1975	
	Percentage	*Cumulative Percentage*	*Percentage*	*Cumulative Percentage*
Lowest	3.8	3.8	5.4	5.4
Second	9.6	13.4	12.0	17.4
Third	15.9	29.3	17.5	34.9
Fourth	24.0	53.3	24.1	59.0
Highest	46.7	100.0	41.0	100.0
	100.0		100.0	

Source: U.S. Department of Commerce, Bureau of the Census.

which are groups comprised of one-fifth or one-tenth of the population, respectively. Figure 8–8 shows the distribution of family personal income in the United States in 1947 and 1975. As the Lorenz curve moves closer to the diagonal (which represents perfect equality), family incomes become more equitably distributed. The curve shows that the distribution of family personal income was more equitable in 1975 than it was in 1947.

The Gini Index

The Lorenz curve illustrated in Figure 8–8 displays the distribution of income among families at two points in time. Lorenz curves may also be used to display the distribution of population or certain types of activities (for example, crime or racial segregation) among spatially organized units such as cities.[60] Lorenz curves can also be expressed in the form of the *Gini concentration ratio* (sometimes called simply the Gini index), which measures the proportion of the total area under the diagonal that lies in the area between the diagonal and the Lorenz curve. The formula for calculating this proportion is

$$GI = \frac{[(\sum X_i Y_{i+1}) - (\sum X_{i+1} Y_i)]}{\sum X_i Y_{i+1}}$$

where

X_i = the cumulative percentage distribution of the number of areas (for example, cities)

Y_i = the cumulative percentage distribution of the population or of some activity (for example, crime)

To illustrate the calculation of the Gini index, let us consider an example from the area of criminal justice policy. Suppose that we wish to depict the concentration of violent crimes in cities of various sizes in 1976. We would use the following procedures, illustrated in Table 8–8.

1. Place the number of cities and the total violent crimes reported for each class-size of cities in columns (1) and (2).

2. Compute the proportionate distribution of cities from column (1) and place in column (3). For example, 59 ÷ 7361 = 0.008.

3. Compute the proportionate distribution of violent crimes from column (2) and place in column (4). For example, 1095 ÷ 2892 = 0.379.

4. Cumulate the proportions of column (3) downward and place the results in column (5). For example 0 + 0.008 = 0.008, 0.008 + 0.015 = 0.23, and so on.

5. Cumulate the proportions of column (4) downward and place the results in column (6). For example, 0 + 0.379 = 0.379, 0.379 + 0.198 = 0.577, and so on.

6. Multiply the first line in column (6) by the second line in column (5), the second line by the third line, and so on. For example, 0.379 × 0.023 = 0.0087, 0.577 × 0.059 = 0.0340, and so on. Place the results in column (7).

7. Multiply the first line in column (5) by the second line in column (6), and so on. For example, 0.008 × 0.577 = 0.0046, 0.023 × 0.721 = 0.0166, and so on. Place the results in column (8).

8. Sum column (7) and record the total (that is, 1.3477). Sum column (8) and record the total (that is, 0.5322).

9. Subtract the total of column (8) from the total of column (7) and then divide by the total of column (7). That is, 1.3477 − 0.5322 ÷ 1.3477 = 0.8155 ÷ 1.3477 = 0.605 = 0.61. This result is the Gini index.

---

[60] For other indices, see Jack P. Gibbs, ed., *Urban Research Methods* (Princeton, NJ: Van Nostrand, 1961).

TABLE 8–8 Computation of Gini Concentration Ratio for Violent Crimes Known to Police per 100,000 Population in 1976

SIZE OF CITY	NUMBER OF CITIES (1)	VIOLENT CRIMES (2)	PROPORTION		CUMULATIVE PROPORTION		$X_i Y_{i+1}$ (7)	$X_{i+1} Y_i$ (8)
			Cities (3)	Crimes (4)	Cities (Y_i) (5)	Crimes (X_i) (6)		
250,000 and over	59	1095	0.008	0.379	0.008	0.379	0.0087	0.0046
100,000–249,999	110	573	0.015	0.198	0.023	0.577	0.0340	0.0166
50,000–99,999	265	416	0.036	0.144	0.059	0.721	0.1016	0.0494
25,000–49,999	604	338	0.082	0.117	0.141	0.838	0.2774	0.1306
10,000–24,999	1398	254	0.190	0.088	0.331	0.926	0.9260	0.331
Under 10,000	4925	216	0.669	0.074	1.000	1.000		
Totals	7361	2892	1.000	1.000			$\sum = 1.3477$	$\sum = 0.5322$

$$\text{Gini concentration ratio (GI)} = \frac{[(\sum X_i Y_{i+1}) - (\sum X_{i+1} Y_i)]}{\sum X_i Y_{i+1}}$$

$$= \frac{1.3477 - 0.5322}{1.3477} = \frac{0.8155}{1.3477}$$

$$= 0.605 = 0.61 \text{ (rounded)}$$

Source: Federal Bureau of Investigation, *Uniform Crime Reports for the United States,* 1976.

The Gini index shows the proportion of the area under the diagonal which lies between the diagonal and the Lorenz curve. It can be used to depict the concentration of wealth, income, population, ethnic groups, urban residents, crime, and other social conditions. The advantage of Gini index is that it is a precise measure of concentration that supplies much more information than the pictorial representation provided by the Lorenz curve. Further, the Gini index ranges from zero (no concentration at all) to 1.0 (maximum concentration). In the example of the concentration of violent crimes, note that approximately 2 percent of the largest cities (100,000 and up) have almost 58 percent of the violent crimes. If violent crimes were more or less equally distributed among cities of all class sizes, the Gini index would be approximately zero. In fact, however, violent crimes are heavily concentrated in large cities. The Gini index value of 0.61 shows that 61 percent of the total area is between the diagonal and the Lorenz curve. This is a substantial concentration with important implications for criminal justice policy in the United States.

Tabular Displays

Another useful way to monitor policy outcomes is to construct tabular displays. A *tabular display* is a rectangular array used to summarize the key features of one or more variables. The simplest form of tabular display is the one-dimensional table, which presents information about policy outcomes in terms of a single dimension of interest, for example, age, income, region, or time. In monitoring changes in energy demand in the United States over the period 1950–1970, an analyst might use a one-dimensional tabular display.

Information may also be arranged in tables with two dimensions, for example, levels of education by income, target groups by levels of education, or the income of target groups by time periods. An analyst concerned with the impact of the War on Poverty may wish to monitor changes in the number and percentage of families below the poverty level in the United States between 1959 and 1968. The following two-dimensional table (Table 8–9) would provide relevant information.

Another type of two-dimensional table involves the analysis of two or more groups by levels of some outcome variable, which might be employment, services received, or earnings. For example, social experiments are based on comparisons of groups that have received a particular type of treatment (experimental group) and groups which have not (control group). Table 8–9 was used to assess whether groups participating in a publicly funded alcoholism treatment program differed in the number of arrests following treatment (Table 8–10). The results indicate that a court-ordered policy of forced short-term referrals for treatment has no discernible positive effect on target groups.

In monitoring policy outcomes data may also be arranged in three-dimensional tables. For example, a three-dimensional table can be used to display the change between 1959 and 1968 in the number and percent of black and white families below the poverty threshold, while also taking into

TABLE 8–9   Race of Families Below the Poverty Level in the United States in 1959 and 1968 (Thousands of Families)

RACE OF FAMILY	YEAR		CHANGE (1959–1968)	
	1959	*1968*	*Number*	*Percent*
Black and other minorities	2135	1431	− 704	− 33.0
White	6185	3616	− 2569	− 41.0
Total	8320	5047	− 3273	− 39.3

Note: The threshold poverty level for a nonfarm family of four in 1968 was $3553 annual gross income. Data in 1959 and 1968 have been standardized to reflect changes in the definition of the poverty threshold in 1964.

Source: U.S. Bureau of the Census, *Current Population Reports,* Series P–60, No. 68, "Poverty in the United States: 1959–1968" (Washington, DC: U.S. Government Printing Office, 1969).

account the age of the head of household (the inclusion of age is called "controlling" for a third variable). The following three-dimensional display (Table 8–11) might be used to monitor the consequences of poverty policy between 1959 and 1968. The table shows that more white families than black families moved above the poverty threshold but also that the relative improvement of white families with a head under 65 years was considerably greater than any of the other three groups. This suggests that the position of black and elderly white families changed more slowly than that of younger white families.

Index Numbers

A useful way to monitor changes in outcome variables over time is to construct index numbers. *Index numbers* are measures of how much the value of an indicator or set of indicators changes over time relative to a base

TABLE 8–10   Number of Drunk Rearrests Among 241 Offenders in Three Treatment Groups

REARRESTS	TREATMENT GROUP			Total
	Alcoholism Clinic	*Alcoholics Anonymous*	*No Treatment*	
None	26 (32.0)	27 (31.0)	32 (44.0)	85
One	23 (28.0)	19 (22.0)	14 (19.0)	56
Two or more	33 (40.0)	40 (47.0)	27 (37.0)	100
Total	82 (100.0)	86 (100.0)	73 (100.0)	241

Source: John P. Gilbert, Richard J. Light, and Frederick Mosteller, "Assessing Social Innovations: An Empirical Base for Policy," in *Evaluation and Experiment: Some Critical Issues in Assessing Social Programs,* ed. Carl A. Bennett and Arthur A. Lumsdaine (New York: Academic Press, 1975), pp. 94–95.

TABLE 8–11 Change in Families Below the Poverty Level in the United States in 1959 and 1968 by Race and Age

	YEAR		CHANGE, 1959–1968	
FAMILY RACE AND AGE	*1959*	*1968*	*Number*	*Percent*
Black and other races	2135	1431	− 704	− 33.0
Head 65 years and over	320	219	− 101	− 31.6
Head under 65 years	1815	1212	− 603	− 33.2
White	6185	3616	− 2569	− 41.5
Head 65 years and over	1540	982	− 558	− 36.2
Head under 65 years	4654	2634	− 2011	− 43.3
Total	8320	5047	− 3273	− 39.3

Source: U.S. Bureau of the Census, *Current Population Reports*, Series P–60, No. 68, "Poverty in the United States: 1959–1968" (Washington, DC: U.S. Government Printing Office, 1969).

period. Base periods are arbitrarily defined as having a value of 100, which serves as the standard for comparing subsequent changes in the indicators of interest. Many index numbers are used in public policy analysis. These include index numbers used to monitor changes in consumer prices, industrial production, crime severity, pollution, health care, quality of life, and other important policy outcomes.

Index numbers differ in their focus, complexity, and degree of explicitness. Index numbers may focus on changes in prices, quantities, or values. For example, changes in the price of consumer items are summarized in the form of the Consumer Price Index, while changes in the quantity of pollutants are measured by various air pollution indices. Relatedly, changes in the value of goods produced by industry are summarized with the Index of Industrial Production. Whether they focus on price, quantity, or value, index numbers may be simple or composite. *Simple index numbers* are those that have only one indicator (for example, the quantity of crimes per 100,000 persons), while *composite index numbers* include many different indicators. A good example of composite index numbers are two Consumer Price Indexes used to measure the costs of some 400 goods and services. One index includes all urban consumers, while the other includes urban wage earners and clerical workers.[61]

Index numbers may be *implicitly weighted* or *explicitly weighted*. In the former case indicators are combined with no explicit procedure for establishing their value. For example, an air pollution index may simply aggregate various kinds of pollutants (carbon monoxide, oxidants, sulfur oxides) without taking into account the different costs in impaired health that

---

[61] In January 1978 the Consumer Price Index was revised. Since that time two indices have been produced. A new index includes All Urban Consumers, irrespective of whether they are employed, and covers 80 percent of the noninstitutional population. The old index includes Urban Wage Earners and Clerical Workers and covers approximately 50 percent of persons in the new index.

result from some of these pollutants (for example, carbon monoxide). An explicitly weighted index takes such factors into account by establishing the relative value or significance of each indicator.

There are two general procedures for constructing index numbers: aggregation and averaging. Aggregative indices are constructed by summing the values of indicators (for example, consumer prices) for given periods. Averaging procedures (or the so-called average of relatives method) require the calculation of average changes in the value of an indicator over time, while aggregate procedures do not. A useful and simple aggregative price index is the *purchasing power index*, which measures the real value of earnings in successive periods. A purchasing power index may be used to monitor the impact of wage agreements on the real income of employees as part of public sector collective bargaining activities. A purchasing power index is constructed by using values of the Consumer Price Index. This is done by locating the year (for example, 1977) for which we wish to determine the purchasing power of wages and converting this value into a *price relative*, that is, a value that expresses the price of goods and services in the year of interest (1977) relative to a base year (for example, 1967). If we then divide this price relative into one (this is called a *reciprocal*), we will obtain the purchasing power of wages in 1967 dollars.

In the following illustration (Table 8–12) the values of the purchasing power index for given years indicate how much every dollar is worth in real terms, relative to the Consumer Price Index base year of 1967. For example, in 1977 every dollar in wages buys about 55 cents of goods and services when compared with the purchasing power of one dollar in 1967. The purchasing power index can be directly converted into real wages by taking the nominal wages for given years and multiplying by the purchasing power index. This has been done in Table 8–13, which shows the real value of gross average weekly earnings in the textile industry for 1970, 1975, and 1977. Note that real wages in the textile industry declined until 1977, when a slight increase was evident.

Another useful aggregative index is the Index of Pollutant Concentration developed under the Continuous Air Monitoring Program (CAMP) of the Environmental Protection Agency. The concentration of various kinds of pollutants, measured in parts per million (ppm) or micrograms per

TABLE 8–12 Computation of Purchasing Power Index

	CONSUMER PRICE INDEX (1)	PRICE RELATIVE (2)	RECIPROCAL (3)	PURCHASING POWER INDEX (4)
1967	100.0	100.0 ÷ 100.0 = 1.0	1.0 ÷ 1.0 = 1.0	× 100 = 100.0
1970	116.3	116.3 ÷ 100.0 = 1.163	1.0 ÷ 1.163 = .859	× 100 = 85.9
1975	161.2	161.2 ÷ 100.0 = 1.612	1.0 ÷ 1.612 = .620	× 100 = 62.0
1977	181.5	181.5 ÷ 100.0 = 1.815	1.0 ÷ 1.815 = .551	× 100 = 55.1

Source: U.S. Department of Labor, Bureau of Labor Statistics.

TABLE 8–13   Computation of Real Gross Average Weekly Earnings in the Textile Industry

YEAR	NOMINAL EARNINGS (1)	PURCHASING POWER INDEX (2)	RECIPROCAL (3)	REAL WAGES (4)
1967	$ 87.70	100.0 ÷ 100 =	1.000 × $ 87.70 =	$87.70
1970	97.76	85.9 ÷ 100 =	0.859 × 97.76 =	83.98
1975	133.28	62.0 ÷ 100 =	0.620 × 133.28 =	82.63
1977	160.39	55.1 ÷ 100 =	0.551 × 160.39 =	88.37

Source: U.S. Department of Labor, Bureau of Labor Statistics.

cubic meter of air (mg/m^3), are punched into a recording tape every five minutes in various locations across the country. Pollutants fall into two main categories: gases and suspended particulates. The maximum concentration of pollutants reported in Chicago, San Francisco, and Philadelphia for two averaging times (five minutes and one year) in 1964 are displayed in Table 8–14. An averaging time of one year is the total quantity of pollutants reported in all five-minute intervals over a year's period divided by the total number of five-minute intervals for the year. An averaging time of five minutes is simply the maximum concentration of pollutants registered in any five-minute period. An implicitly weighted aggregative-quantity index can be developed to monitor the concentration of pollutants over time. The formula for this index is

$$QI_n = \frac{\sum q_n}{q_0} \cdot 100$$

where

QI_n = the quantity index for gaseous pollutants in a given time period n

q_n = the quantity of gaseous pollutants in period n of a time series

q_0 = the quantity of gaseous pollutants in the base period 0 of a time series

On the basis of this formula we can calculate index numbers to monitor changes in levels of pollutants (measured in millions of tons) between 1970 and 1975. We would begin by selecting 1970 as the base period (q_0) and calculate values of the quantity index for 1973, 1974, and 1975. These values are provided in Table 8–15 which shows that total pollutant emissions have declined since 1970.

The weakness of this implicitly weighted aggregative-quantity index of pollution is that it does not take into account variations in the concentrations of pollutants or their relative damage to health. By contrast the index developed as part of the Environmental Protection Agency's Continuous Air

TABLE 8–14 Maximum Concentration of Pollutants Reported in Chicago, Philadelphia, and San Francisco for Averaging Times of Five Minutes and One Year

| | TYPE OF POLLUTANT | | | | | | | | | |
| CITY AND AVERAGING TIME | Gases[1] | | | | | | | Suspended Particulates[2] | | |
	Carbon Monoxide	Hydro-Carbons	Nitric Oxide	Nitrogen Dioxide	Nitrogen Oxides	Oxident	Sulfur Dioxide	Lead	Organic (Benzene Soluble)	Sulfate
Chicago										
5 minutes	64.0	20.0	0.97	0.79	1.12	0.17	1.62	NA	NA	NA
1 year	12.0	3.0	0.10	0.05	0.15	0.02	0.18	0.6	15.1	16.6
Philadelphia										
5 minutes	43.0	17.0	1.35	0.37	1.50	0.25	1.00	NA	NA	NA
1 year	7.0	2.0	0.04	0.04	0.08	0.02	0.09	0.8	12.2	19.8
San Francisco										
5 minutes	47.0	16.0	0.68	0.38	0.91	0.29	0.26	NA	NA	NA
1 year	7.0	3.0	0.09	0.05	0.14	0.02	0.02	NA	9.2	6.2

Notes:
[1] Gaseous pollutants measured in parts per million (ppm) of air in 1964.
[2] Suspended particulates measured in micrograms per cubic meter (mg/m^3) of air in 1964.

Source: N. D. Singpurwalla, "Models in Air Pollution," in *A Guide to Models in Governmental Planning and Operations*, ed. Saul I. Gass and Roger L. Sisson (Washington, DC: U.S. Environmental Protection Agency, 1975), pp. 69–71.

TABLE 8–15 Implicitly Weighted Aggregative Quantity Index to Measure Changes in Pollutants in the United States, 1970–1975

POLLUTANT	QUANTITY			
	1970	1973	1974	1975
Carbon monoxide	113.7	111.5	104.2	96.2
Sulfur oxides	32.3	32.5	31.7	32.9
Hydrocarbons	33.9	34.0	32.5	30.9
Particulates	26.8	21.9	20.3	18.0
Nitrogen oxides	22.7	25.7	25.0	24.2
	229.4	225.6	213.7	202.2
Quantity index (1970 = 100)	100.0	98.34	93.16	88.14

$$QI_n = \frac{\sum q_n}{\sum q_o} \cdot 100$$

$$QI_{1970} = \frac{\sum 113.7 + 32.3 + 33.9 + 26.8 + 22.7}{\sum 113.7 + 32.3 + 33.9 + 26.8 + 22.7} \cdot 100$$

$$= \frac{229.4}{229.4} \cdot 100 = 100.0$$

$$QI_{1973} = \frac{\sum 111.5 + 32.5 + 34.0 + 21.9 + 25.7}{\sum 113.7 + 32.3 + 33.9 + 26.8 + 22.7} \cdot 100$$

$$= \frac{225.6}{229.4} \cdot 100 = 98.34$$

Note: In millions of tons of pollutants (gases and particulates).
Source: U.S. Environmental Protection Agency.

Monitoring Program provides explicit weights, since it permits analysts to examine the maximum concentration of pollutants in given periods (averaging times) and relate these concentrations to known health hazards. For example, while the overall quantity of pollutants has declined since 1970, some cities have registered very high levels of pollution in particular periods. Data on these periods are not reflected in the implicitly weighted quantity index illustrated in Table 8–15. Most important, the concentration of different types of pollutants per time period creates different kinds of health hazards. An explicitly weighted quantity index takes into account both the concentration of pollutants per time period (averaging times) and potential health hazards. While we will not construct an explicitly weighted aggregative-quantity index on the basis of averaging times reported by the Continuous Air Monitoring Program, it is important to consider relationships between the duration of exposure to pollutants and damage to health and the environment (Table 8–16).

There are several indexes widely used to monitor changes in policy outcomes. These include the two Consumer Price Indexes (CPI) already

TABLE 8–16 Duration of Exposure to Pollutants and Consequent Damage to Health and the Environment

DURATION OF EXPOSURE	CONSEQUENCE	POLLUTANT			
		Carbon Monoxide	*Oxidants*	*Particulates*	*Sulfur Oxides*
1 second	Sensation				
	Odor	–	+	–	+
	Taste	–	–	–	+
	Eye irritation	–	+	–	–
1 hour	Athletic performance impaired	–	+	–	–
	Visibility reduced	–	+	+	+
8 hours	Judgment impaired	+	–	–	–
	Stress to heart patients	+	–	–	–
1 day	Health impaired	+	–	+	+
4 days	Health impaired	+	–	+	+
1 year	Vegetation damaged	–	–	+	+
	Corrosion	–	–	+	+

Note: A minus (–) indicates no damaging consequences. A plus (+) indicates damaging consequence.

Source: N. D. Singpurwalla, "Models in Air Pollution," in *A Guide to Models in Governmental Planning and Operations*, ed. Saul I. Gass and Roger L. Sisson (Washington, DC: U.S. Environmental Protection Agency, 1975), p. 66.

noted above (one for all urban consumers and the other for urban wage earners and clerical workers); the Producer Price Index (PPI), before 1978 called the Wholesale Price Index (WPI), and used to measure changes in the prices of all commodities produced in the economy; and the Index of Industrial Production (IIP), published monthly by the Federal Reserve System and used to measure changes in the outputs of plants, mines, and utilities companies. The base period for all these indexes is 1967. In addition to these indexes there are those that measure the severity of crime, the quality of life, the quality of health care, and the quality of the environment (see footnote 13).

Index numbers have several limitations. First, explicit weighting procedures often lack precision. For example, estimates of the damage caused by different kinds of pollutants is partly subjective, and it is difficult to attach dollar costs to resultant health problems. Second, it is difficult to obtain sample data for indexes that are equally meaningful for all groups in society. The Consumer Price Index, for example, is based on a sample of more than 400 consumer goods and services purchased by urban residents. The sample is selected monthly from 56 urban areas, and data thus obtained are used to construct a composite national index. While the development of the two-part Consumer Price Index in 1978 makes index numbers more meaningful to retired, elderly, and unemployed persons, as well as to wage earners and clerical workers, the Consumer Price Index does not reflect price differences in many urban and rural areas. Finally, index numbers do not always reflect qualitative changes in the meaning or significance of index items over time. For example, as we learn more about the effects of various kinds of pollutants (for example, lead particulates or asbestos), their significance changes. The simple quantity of pollutants may not reflect the changing social value (or disvalue) attached to them in different time periods.

Index numbers may be used to monitor a wide variety of changes. Yet these techniques provide no systematic way of relating changes in policy outcomes to prior policy actions. We will now consider three sets of techniques that permit analysts to make systematic judgments about the effects of policy actions on policy outcomes: interrupted time-series analysis, control-series analysis, and regression-discontinuity analysis.[62] These procedures are used in conjunction with graphic displays and based on correlation and regression techniques discussed in the chapter on forecasting (Chapter 6). Although two of these procedures (interrupted time-series and control-series analysis) are equally applicable to social systems accounting, social auditing, and social experimentation, one of them (regression-discontinuity analysis) is exclusively applicable to social experiments.

Interrupted Time-Series Analysis

Interrupted time-series analysis is a set of procedures for displaying in graphic and statistical form the effects of policy actions on policy outcomes. Interrupted time-series analysis is appropriate for problems where an agency initiates some action that is put into effect across an entire jurisdiction or target group, for example, in a particular state or among all families below the poverty threshold. Because policy actions are limited to persons in the jurisdiction or target group, there is no opportunity for comparing policy outcomes across different jurisdictions or among different categories of the target group. In this situation the only basis of comparison is the record of outcomes for previous years.

The graphing of interrupted time series is a powerful tool for assessing the effects of a policy intervention on a measure of some policy outcome (for example, highway death rates, persons receiving medical assistance, job trainees employed, hospital mortality rates). As Figure 8–9 shows, some policy interventions have genuine effects on policy outcomes, while others do not. Interventions (a) and (b) indicate that the policy intervention is plausibly related to the increase in some valued outcome, since there is a practically significant jump in the value of the measured policy outcome after the intervention. Intervention (b), however, shows that the valued outcome was not durable—it began to "fade" after the fifth time period.

Intervention (c) also lacks durability, but it was also preceded by an extreme high in the measured policy outcome before the intervention. This suggests that there probably was "regression" toward the average value of

---

[62] The following discussion is based on Campbell, "Reforms As Experiments."

FIGURE 8–9 Interrupted time series showing effects and no effects.

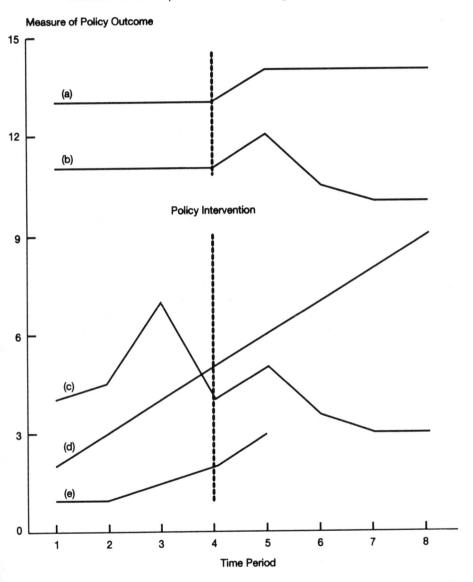

Source: Donald T. Campbell and Julian C. Stanley, *Experimental and Quasi-experimental Designs for Research* (Chicago: Rand McNally, 1967).

the time series after the intervention—that is, the increase between the fourth and fifth period probably would have occurred anyway (see below). Intervention (d) shows that the intervention had no effect since there is no difference in the rate of change in the value of the measured outcome variable. Finally, intervention (e) shows a slight increase in the measured policy outcome but one that was preceded by an increase already in progress. This weak effect is not sufficient to conclude that the intervention was responsible for the increase between the fourth and fifth periods. If data on subsequent time periods were available, the postintervention increase might prove to lack durability, or might increase at an increasing rate. Here it is simply not possible to know.

Interrupted time-series analysis is particularly appropriate for those approaches to social experimentation that are called "quasi-experimental" because they lack one or more characteristics of classical experiments discussed in the last section (that is, random selection of participants, random assignment to experimental and control groups, and measurement before and after the experimental treatment). The only feature that interrupted time-series analysis has in common with the classical experiment is measurement before and after some policy action (experimental treatment) is undertaken.

The best way to visualize interrupted time-series analysis is to consider a concrete illustration.[63] In 1956, after a record high number of traffic fatalities in 1955, the governor of Connecticut (Abraham Ribicoff) implemented a severe crackdown on violators of the state's speeding laws. At the end of 1956 there were 284 traffic deaths, as compared with 324 deaths the year before. Governor Ribicoff interpreted the outcomes of the crackdown on speeding in the following way: "With the saving of 40 lives in 1956, a reduction of 12.3 percent from the 1955 motor vehicle death toll, we can say that the program is definitely worthwhile." The apparent results of the speeding crackdown are displayed graphically in Figure 8–10. The values on the vertical scale have been deliberately stretched to exaggerate the magnitude of effects.

If we wish to monitor the outcomes of the Connecticut crackdown on speeding using interrupted time-series analysis, we will follow several steps:

1. Compress the values along the vertical axis so that the apparent observed effect is not so dramatic. Here we will use intervals of 25 rather than 10 deaths.

2. Obtain values of traffic deaths in multiple years before and after the implementation of the policy and plot them on the graph. This creates an extended time series from 1951 through 1959.

3. Draw a vertical line that interrupts the time series at the beginning of the year when the policy was implemented, that is, in 1956 (hence, an "interrupted time series"). Note that intervals used to display years in a time series denote the middle of each year (July 1), so that any point midway between two intervals is the value of the time series on January 1.

---

[63] See Campbell, "Reforms as Experiments," pp. 75–81; and Donald T. Campbell and H. Lawrence Ross, "The Connecticut Crackdown on Speeding: Time-Series Data in Quasi-experimental Analysis," *Law and Society Review*, 3, No. 1 (1968), 33–53.

FIGURE 8–10 Connecticut traffic deaths before and after
the 1956 crackdown on speeding.

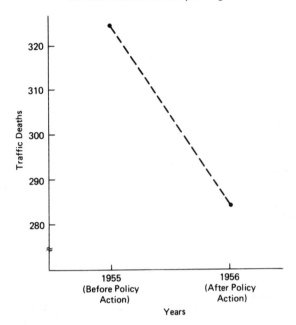

Source: Donald T. Campbell, "Reforms as Experiments," in
Handbook of Evaluation Research, Vol. 1, ed. Elmer L.
Struening and Marcia Guttentag (Beverly Hills, CA: Sage
Publications, 1975), p. 76.

The results of following these procedures are displayed in Figure 8–11,
which is called an interrupted time-series graph. Observe that this graph
creates an altogether different visual image of policy outcomes than that
presented in Figure 8–10.

The main advantage of interrupted time-series analysis is that it enables
us to consider systematically various threats to the validity of causal inferences about policy outcomes. The importance of these threats to validity,
already discussed in the last section (see pp. 351–352), can be easily seen
when we compare policy outcomes (traffic deaths) displayed in the interrupted time-series graph and Governor Ribicoff's causal inference that the
speeding crackdown definitely resulted in lowered traffic fatalities. Let us
now examine several threats to the validity of this claim by considering the
data displayed in Figures 8–10 and 8–11.

1. *Maturation.* Changes within the members of groups (in this case drivers) may
   exert effects on policy outcomes apart from those of policy actions. For example, death rates in Connecticut may have been declining for a number of
   years as a result of increased social learning among drivers who have been
   exposed to drivers' education programs or to public safety campaigns. The

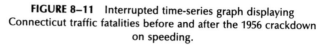

FIGURE 8–11   Interrupted time-series graph displaying
Connecticut traffic fatalities before and after the 1956 crackdown
on speeding.

Source: Adapted from Donald T. Campbell, "Reforms as Experiments," in *Handbook of Evaluation Research*, Vol. 1, ed. Elmer L. Struening and Marcia Guttentag (Beverly Hills, CA: Sage Publications, 1975), p. 76.

simple prepolicy-postpolicy graph (Figure 8–10) does not allow us to examine such possible independent effects. The interrupted time-series graph (Figure 8–11) enables us to rule out maturation as a plausible rival explanation, since the time series does not show a long-term secular decline in traffic fatalities.

2. *Instability.* All time series are to some degree unstable. The interrupted time-series graph permits us to display this instability, which is rather pronounced. The decline between 1955 and 1956 is only slightly greater than declines in 1951–1952 and 1953–1954, thus suggesting that the policy outcome may be a consequence of instability, and not the policy action. On the other hand there are no increases in traffic fatalities after 1956. Although this lends persuasiveness to the governor's claim, this argument would not have been possible without the interrupted time-series graph of Figure 8–11.

3. *Regression artifacts.* In monitoring policy outcomes it is often difficult to separate the effects of policy actions from effects exerted by the persons or groups selected for a program. If traffic fatalities for 1955 represent an extreme—as might be the case if we only have Figure 8–10 to go on—then the decline in traffic deaths in 1956 may simply reflect the tendency of extreme scores to regress toward the mean or general trend of a time series. Fatalities in 1955

are in fact the most extreme ones in the series. For this reason part of the decline from 1955 to 1956 may be attributed to regression artifacts, together with the instability of the time series. Regression artifacts are a particularly important threat to the validity of claims about policy outcomes for one important reason: Policymakers tend to take action when problems are most acute or extreme.

Control-Series Analysis

Control-series analysis involves the addition of one or more control groups to an interrupted time-series design in order to determine whether characteristics of different groups exert an independent effect on policy outcomes, apart from the original policy action. The logic of control-series analysis is the same as interrupted time-series analysis. The only difference is that a group or groups that were not exposed to the policy actions in question are added to the graph. Figure 8–12 shows the original data from Connecticut along with data on traffic fatalities from control states.

FIGURE 8–12 Control-series graph displaying traffic fatalities in Connecticut and control states, 1951–1959.

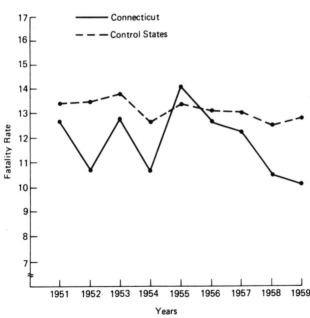

Note: The fatality rate is a population-based measure that represents deaths per 100,000 persons in the population of states.

Source: Donald T. Campbell, "Reforms as Experiments," in *Handbook of Evaluation Research*, Vol. 1, ed. Elmer L. Struening and Marcia Guttentag (Beverly Hills, CA: Sage Publications, 1975), p. 84.

Control-series analysis helps further to scrutinize the validity of claims about the effects of policy actions on policy outcomes. For example, rival claims based on history (sudden changes in weather conditions) and maturation (safety habits learned by drivers) would appear to be partly supported by the control-series data. Hence Connecticut and the control states show a similar general pattern of successive increases and decreases in traffic deaths between 1952 and 1955. Yet it is also evident that Connecticut traffic fatalities declined much more rapidly than control states after 1955. The control-series graph not only enables us to assess more critically the governor's claim about the success of his policy, but in this case allows us to rule out plausible rival interpretations. This has the effect of providing much firmer grounds for policy claims.

The use of interrupted time-series and control-series analysis, together with the various threats to internal and external validity, may be viewed as a policy argument. The original data on the decline in traffic fatalities between 1955 and 1956 represent information (I), while the policy claim (C) is "the program is definitely worthwhile." The qualifier (Q) expresses maximum certainty, as indicated by the term "definitely," and the *implicit* warrant (W) necessary to carry information to claim is that the policy action caused the reduction in traffic fatalities. What is important in the present case is the series of rebuttals (R) that may be advanced on the basis of the various threats to internal and external validity: history, maturation, instability, testing, instrumentation, mortality, selection, regression artifacts. These threats to the validity of claims have been put in the form of a policy argument in Figure 8–13.

The final procedure to be discussed in this chapter is an extension of regression and correlational procedures presented in Chapter 6. Since linear regression and correlation have already been described in some detail, we will not repeat the discussion of these techniques here, except to note that they are applicable to problems of monitoring as well as forecasting. Regression analysis may be used to explain past outcomes, rather than predict future ones, and the results of analysis are sometimes called "postdictions" to emphasize that we are predicting past events. Even where regression analysis is used to predict future events, the analysis is necessarily based on information acquired by monitoring past policy outcomes.

Imagine that we have obtained information about dollar investments in five manpower training programs, together with information about the subsequent employment of trainees who have completed these programs. The problem can be stated in the following way: How does the level of investment in manpower training programs affect the subsequent employment of trainees? A worksheet necessary to compute the regression equation $[Y_c = a + b(x)]$, the coefficient of determination (r^2), the simple correlation coefficient (r), the standard error of estimate $(S_{y \cdot x})$, and an interval estimate (Y_i) is provided in Table 8–17. The MYSTAT results, displayed below as Exhibit 8–1, should be self-explanatory. If they are not, you should return to Chapter 6 and review the section on correlation and regression (see pp. 231–40).

FIGURE 8–13   Threats to the validity of claims as a policy argument.

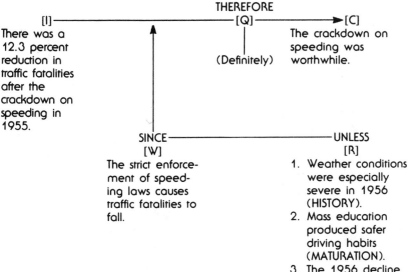

THEREFORE

[I] ─────────────────────── [Q] ──────────────→ [C]

There was a
12.3 percent
reduction in   (Definitely)
traffic fatalities
after the
crackdown on
speeding in
1955.

The crackdown on
speeding was
worthwhile.

SINCE ──────────────────────── UNLESS
[W]   [R]

The strict enforce-   1. Weather conditions
ment of speed-   were especially
ing laws causes   severe in 1956
traffic fatalities to   (HISTORY).
fall.   2. Mass education
                                produced safer
                                driving habits
                                (MATURATION).
                             3. The 1956 decline
                                reflects random
                                fluctuations in the
                                time series
                                (INSTABILITY).
                             4. Publicity given to
                                the crackdown
                                produced the
                                reduction in
                                fatalities (TESTING).
                             5. The system for
                                recording fatalities
                                changed in
                                1955–1956
                                (INSTRUMENTATION).
                             6. Many speeding
                                offenders left the
                                state in 1956
                                (MORTALITY).
                             7. 1956 was
                                unrepresentative of
                                the time series
                                (SELECTION).
                             8. Deaths in 1955
                                were extreme and
                                reflect regression
                                towards the mean
                                of the time series
                                (REGRESSION
                                ARTIFACTS).

TABLE 8-17 Worksheet for Regression and Correlation: Investment in Training Programs and Subsequent Employment of Trainees

PROGRAM	PERCENT OF TRAINEES EMPLOYED (Y)	PROGRAM INVESTMENT (MILLIONS OF DOLLARS)(X)	$Y - \bar{Y}$ (y)	$X - \bar{X}$ (x)	xy	y^2	x^2	Y_c	$Y - Y_c$	$(Y - Y_c)^2$
A	10	2	-20	-2	40	400	4	12	-2	4
B	30	3	0	-1	0	0	1	21	9	81
C	20	4	-10	0	0	100	0	30	-10	100
D	50	6	20	2	40	400	4	48	2	4
E	40	5	10	1	10	100	1	39	1	1
	$\overline{150}$	$\overline{20}$	$\overline{0}$	$\overline{0}$	$\overline{90}$	$\overline{4000}$	$\overline{10}$	$\overline{150}$	$\overline{0}$	$\overline{190}$
	$\bar{Y} = 30$	$\bar{X} = 4$								

$$b = \frac{\sum(xy)}{\sum(x^2)} = \frac{90}{10} = 9$$

$$a = \bar{Y} - b(\bar{X}) = 30 - 9(4) = -6$$

$$Y_c = a + b(X) = -6 + 9(X)$$

$$r^2 = \frac{b(\sum xy)}{\sum y^2} = \frac{9(90)}{1000} = 0.81$$

$$r = \sqrt{r^2} = 0.90$$

$$S_{y \cdot x} = \sqrt{\frac{\sum(Y - Y_c)^2}{n - 2}} = \sqrt{\frac{190}{3}} = 7.96$$

$$Y_{i(6)}(95\%) = Y_{c(6)} \pm 2Z(S_{y \cdot x}) = 48 \pm 1.96(7.96)$$

$$= 48 \pm 15.6 = 63.6 \text{ to } 32.4$$

EXHIBIT 8-1   MYSTAT Output for Table 8-11

DEP VAR: Y   N: 5   MULTIPLE R: .900   SQUARED MULTIPLE R: .810
ADJUSTED SQUARED MULTIPLE R: .747   STANDARD ERROR OF ESTIMATE: 7.958

VARIABLE	COEFFICIENT	STD ERROR	STD COEF	TOLERANCE	T	P(2 TAIL)
CONSTANT	-6.000	10.677	0.000		-0.562	0.613
X	9.000	2.517	0.900	.100E+01	3.576	0.037

ANALYSIS OF VARIANCE

SOURCE	SUM-OF-SQUARES	DF	MEAN-SQUARE	F-RATIO	P
REGRESSION	810.000	1	810.000	12.789	0.037
RESIDUAL	190.000	3	63.333		

Regression-Discontinuity Analysis

Having reviewed computational procedures for correlation and regression analysis, we are now in a position to consider regression-discontinuity analysis. *Regression-discontinuity analysis* is a set of graphic and statistical procedures used to compute and compare estimates of the outcomes of policy actions undertaken among two or more groups, one of which is exposed to some policy treatment while the other is not. Regression-discontinuity analysis is the only procedure discussed so far that is appropriate solely for social experimentation. In fact, regression-discontinuity analysis is designed for a particularly important type of social experiment; namely, an experiment where some resource input is in such scarce supply that only a portion of some target population can receive needed resources. Such experiments involve "social ameliorations that are in short supply, and that therefore cannot be given to all individuals.[64] At the same time randomization may be politically unfeasible and morally unjustifiable, since some of those who are most in need (or most capable) will be eliminated through random selection. For example, limited resources for job training cannot be allocated randomly among a sample of unskilled persons, since job training is intended for the most needy. Similarly, a limited number of schol-

---

[64] Campbell, "Reforms as Experiments," pp. 86–87.

arships cannot be distributed randomly among a sample of applicants of varying abilities, since it is the most meritorious student (and not the needy one) who is believed to deserve scholarship funds. Although randomization would help determine the effects of manpower training or of scholarships on the subsequent behavior of typical or representative members of a target population, randomization frequently violates principles of need or merit and is thus politically and morally unacceptable.

The advantage of regression-discontinuity analysis is that it allows us to monitor the effects of providing a scarce resource to the most needy or most deserving members of a target population that is larger than a given program can accommodate. Imagine a situation where large numbers of deserving persons (for example, those who obtain high scores on a law school entrance examination) are to be selected to receive some scarce resource (for example, a scholarship to law school). One of the aims of the admission policy is to select those persons who will succeed later in life, with "success" defined in terms of subsequent income. Only the most deserving applicants are awarded a scholarship, thus satisfying the principle of merit. But the most deserving students would probably be successful in later life even if they received no scholarship. Under these circumstances it is difficult to determine whether late success in life is a consequence of receiving a scholarship or of other factors, including the family backgrounds of applicants or their social position. Do scholarships affect subsequent success in life?

One way to answer this question is to conduct an experiment (called a "tie-breaking" experiment) where scarce resources are randomly allocated to a small number of persons who are identical or "tied" in their abilities or level of need. The easiest way to visualize a tie-breaking experiment is to imagine five individuals, all of whom have scored 100 on an examination. The problem here is to give awards to two of the most deserving students. Since all students are equally deserving, some procedure must be used to break the tie. One such procedure is randomization.

This same logic is extended to social experimentation through regression-discontinuity analysis. In a tie-breaking experiment we take a narrow band of merit or need (for example, as determined by entrance examination scores or family income) above some point that marks the cutoff between those who qualify for some resource and those who do not. To illustrate, imagine that this narrow band of ability is between 90 and 95 percent correct on a law school entrance examination. Persons with scores of 89 percent or less will not be given a scholarship; and persons with scores of 96 percent or more will be given a scholarship. But persons falling into the 90–95 interval (that is, the narrow band of ability) will be randomly divided into two groups. One group will receive a scholarship and the other will not. Note that this procedure can be justified only under conditions where there are more deserving or needy persons seeking a valued resource than can be accommodated within existing resource constraints.

Without this "tie-breaking equipment," we would be forced to choose only the top students. Under these conditions we would expect to find entrance examination scores to be strongly and positively correlated with subsequent success in life, as shown by the broken line in Figure 8–14. But by

FIGURE 8–14   Tie-breaking experiment
and regression-discontinuity analysis.

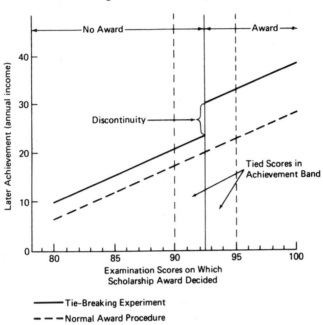

Source: Adapted from Donald T. Campbell, "Reforms as Experiments," in Handbook of Evaluation Research, Vol. I, ed. Elmer L. Struening and Marcia Guttentag (Beverly Hills, CA: Sage Publications, 1975), p. 87.

randomly selecting persons from the narrow band of ability (that is, the 90–95 interval), admitting some and rejecting others (the exact number depends on how many students can be accommodated in any given year), we can find out whether scholarships have an effect on later achievement over and above that of family background and social position. If entrance examination scores do have this augmenting effect, they will be displayed in the form of a discontinuous solid line that separates those who received scholarships from those who did not (Figure 8–14).

Regression-discontinuity analysis is based on principles of correlation and regression. The main difference is that regression-discontinuity analysis requires that we compute a regression equation $[Y_c = a + b(x)]$ for each of two groups, one of which receives some valued resource while the other does not. The standard error of estimate $(S_{y \cdot x})$, the coefficient of determination (r^2), and the simple correlation coefficient (r) may also be computed for each group. Note that the standard errors of regression estimates for the experimental and control groups can be converted into interval estimates that establish the significance of any discontinuity, for example, that displayed by the solid line in Figure 8–14.

Let us now use another hypothetical example to illustrate the application of regression-discontinuity analysis. Imagine that we want to monitor the effects of enforcement policies of the Environmental Protection Agency on the reduction of air pollution levels in various cities. Since enforcement is costly, it is not possible to mount programs in every city where pollution is a significant problem. A random sample of cities is not politically feasible because those areas with the greatest need for enforcement efforts would be eliminated simply by chance. At the same time we want to find out whether enforcement activities, as compared with no enforcement at all, reduce pollution.

Assume that 20 cities with moderate to high pollution levels have been selected for the enforcement experiment. These cities are ranked according to data on pollutants provided by the Continuous Air Monitoring Program (CAMP). The distribution of these cities by an index of pollution severity (100 = highest) is illustrated in Table 8–18.

Six cities in the interval between 81 and 85 have been identified as the "tie-breaking" group for purposes of the enforcement experiment. Three of these cities have been selected at random to receive the enforcement program, while the remaining three cities receive no program. Since these cities were chosen solely on the basis of chance, it is unlikely that charges of

TABLE 8–18   Distribution of Cities by Scores on a Hypothetical Index of Pollution Severity

POLLUTION SEVERITY		NUMBER OF CITIES
97		1
95		1
92		1
90		1
89		1
87		1
86		1
85		2
84		1
83	"Tie-breaking"	1
82	group	1
81		1
80		1
79		1
78		1
76		1
74		1
71		1
67		1
	Total	20

Source: Fictitious data.

favoritism will be advanced against policymakers, even though pollution severity scores for two of the control cities are slightly above those of the experimental cities. Imagine that air pollution levels in all 20 cities (10 each in the experimental and control groups) were monitored by CAMP one year before and one year after the conclusion of the enforcement experiment. Hypothetical results, displayed in Table 8–19, provide all data necessary to compute regression equations, standard errors of estimates, coefficients of determination, and simple correlation coefficients. Note that these calculations are made separately for the experimental and control groups. The MYSTAT output is displayed in Exhibit 8–2.

The results of the regression-discontinuity analysis help answer several questions about the outcomes of the enforcement experiment. First, observe the pre- and postenforcement means for the experimental and control cities. The pollution levels for both groups are lower in the postenforcement period, even though the control group received no enforcement program. Nevertheless, the difference between the pre- and postenforcement means is larger for the experimental cities ($88.6 - 84.7 = 3.9$) than for the control cities ($77.5 - 76.7 = 0.8$), suggesting that the enforcement program contributed to the decrease in pollution. Second, experimental cities have a stronger coefficient of determination ($r^2 = 0.971$) and simple correlation coefficient ($r = 0.986$) than those for control cities ($r^2 = 0.932$, $r = 0.961$). The standard error of estimate for the experimental cities ($S_{y \cdot x} = 0.76$) is also lower than that for the control cities ($S_{y \cdot x} = 2.27$). Hence, there is less error in the estimated relationship between enforcement and pollution levels for the experimental cities.

Finally, there is a partial discontinuity between the regression lines for the two groups. If we calculate interval estimates for the two "tie-breaking" cities with identical preenforcement scores of 85, we obtain the following results:

$$
\begin{aligned}
Y_i \text{ (experimental city 8)} &= Y_{c(85)} \pm 1.96(0.76) \\
&= 81.33 \pm 1.49 \\
&= 79.8 \text{ to } 82.8 \\
Y_i \text{ (control city 11)} &= Y_{c(85)} \pm 1.96(2.27) \\
&= 87.2 \pm 4.45 \\
&= 82.8 \text{ to } 91.7
\end{aligned}
$$

These interval estimates mean that the highest pollution level that is likely to occur 95 percent of the time in experimental city 8 is 82.8, while the lowest that is likely to occur 95 percent of the time in control city 11 is also 82.8. In other words, when we take the highest and lowest pollution levels that are likely to occur 95 percent of the time, the experimental city equals the control city. At the same time, the point estimates are closer for experimental city 10 (77.59) and control city 14 (80.2), indicating that the discontinuity is not as great for some cities.

Note that this kind of comparison would not have been possible without regression-discontinuity analysis. By randomly assigning "tied" scores

TABLE 8–19 Results of Regression-Discontinuity Analysis for Hypothetical Experimental and Control Cities

EXPERIMENTAL CITIES

City	Preenforcement Pollution Level (X)	Postenforcement Pollution Level (Y)	x	y	x^2	y^2	xy	Y_c	$(Y - Y_c)^2$
1	97	93	8.4	8.3	70.56	68.89	69.72	92.56	0.19
2	95	91	6.4	6.3	40.96	39.69	40.32	90.69	0.10
3	92	87	3.4	2.3	11.56	5.29	7.82	87.88	0.77
4	90	87	1.4	2.3	1.96	5.29	3.22	86.01	0.98
5	89	84	0.4	-0.7	0.16	0.49	-0.28	85.07	1.15
6	87	82	-1.6	-2.7	2.56	7.29	4.32	83.20	1.44
7	86	83	-2.6	-1.7	6.76	2.89	4.42	82.27	0.53
8	85	82	-3.6	-2.7	12.96	7.29	9.72	81.33	0.45
9	84	80	-4.6	-4.7	21.16	22.09	21.62	80.39	0.15
10	81	78	-7.6	-6.7	57.76	44.89	50.92	77.59	0.17
	$\overline{X} = 88.6$	$\overline{Y} = 84.7$	0	0	226.40	204.10	211.80	847.00	5.74

$$b = \frac{\sum(xy)}{\sum(x^2)} = \frac{211.80}{226.40} = 0.936 \qquad a = \overline{Y} - b(\overline{X}) = 84.7 - 0.936(88.6) = 1.8$$

$$Y_c = a + b(X) = 1.8 + 0.936(X)$$

$$S_{y \cdot x} = \sqrt{\frac{(Y - Y_c)^2}{n - 2}} = \sqrt{\frac{5.74}{8}} = 0.86$$

$$r^2 = \frac{b(\sum xy)}{\sum(y^2)} = \frac{936(211.80)}{204.10} = 0.97$$

$$r = \sqrt{r^2} = 0.98$$

CONTROL CITIES

City	Preenforcement Pollution Level (X)	Postenforcement Pollution Level (Y)	x	y	x^2	y^2	xy	Y_c	$(Y - Y_c)^2$
11	85	88	7.5	11.3	56.25	127.69	84.75	87.2	4.84
12	83	84	5.5	7.3	30.25	53.29	40.15	84.4	1.96
13	82	86	4.5	9.3	20.25	86.49	41.85	83.0	1.00
14	80	78	2.5	1.3	6.25	1.69	3.25	80.2	0.04
15	79	75	1.5	-1.7	2.25	2.89	-2.55	78.8	0.04
16	78	77	0.5	0.3	0.25	0.09	0.15	77.4	0.36
17	76	75	-1.5	-1.7	2.25	2.89	2.55	74.6	1.96
18	74	73	-3.5	-3.7	12.25	13.69	12.95	71.8	4.84
19	71	71	-6.5	-5.7	42.25	32.49	37.05	67.6	11.56
20	67	60	-10.5	-16.7	110.25	278.89	175.35	62.0	25.00
	$\overline{X} = 77.5$	$\overline{Y} = 76.7$	0	0	282.50	600.10	395.50	767.0	51.60

$$b = \frac{\sum(xy)}{\sum(x^2)} = \frac{395.5}{282.5} = 1.4 \qquad a = \overline{Y} - b(\overline{X}) = 76.7 - 1.4(77.5) = -31.8$$

$$Y_c = a + b(X) = -31.8 + 1.4(X)$$

$$S_{y \cdot x} = \sqrt{\frac{\sum(Y - Y_c)^2}{n - 2}} = \sqrt{\frac{51.60}{8}} = 2.41$$

$$r^2 = \frac{b(\sum xy)}{\sum(y^2)} = \frac{1.4(395.5)}{600.10} = 0.923$$

$$r = \sqrt{r^2} = 0.961$$

EXHIBIT 8–2   MYSTAT Output for Tables 8–13 and 8–14

Table 8–13

DEP VAR: Y   N: 10   MULTIPLE R: .985   SQUARED MULTIPLE R: .971
ADJUSTED SQUARED MULTIPLE R: .967   STANDARD ERROR OF ESTIMATE: 0.863

VARIABLE	COEFFICIENT	STD ERROR	STD COEF	TOLERANCE	T	P(2 TAIL)
CONSTANT	1.814	5.089	0.000	.	0.356	0.731
X	0.936	0.057	0.985	.100E+01	16.310	0.000

ANALYSIS OF VARIANCE

SOURCE	SUM-OF-SQUARES	DF	MEAN-SQUARE	F-RATIO	P
REGRESSION	198.142	1	198.142	266.030	0.000
RESIDUAL	5.958	8	0.745		

Table 8–14

DEP VAR: Y   N: 10   MULTIPLE R: .961   SQUARED MULTIPLE R: .923
ADJUSTED SQUARED MULTIPLE R: .913   STANDARD ERROR OF ESTIMATE: 2.408

VARIABLE	COEFFICIENT	STD ERROR	STD COEF	TOLERANCE	T	P(2 TAIL)
CONSTANT	-31.800	11.131	0.000	.	-2.857	0.021
X	1.400	0.143	0.961	.100E+01	9.771	0.000

ANALYSIS OF VARIANCE

SOURCE	SUM-OF-SQUARES	DF	MEAN-SQUARE	F-RATIO	P
REGRESSION	553.700	1	553.700	95.466	0.000
RESIDUAL	46.400	8	5.800		

FIGURE 8–15   Graphic display of results of regression discontinuity analysis for hypothetical experimental and control cities.

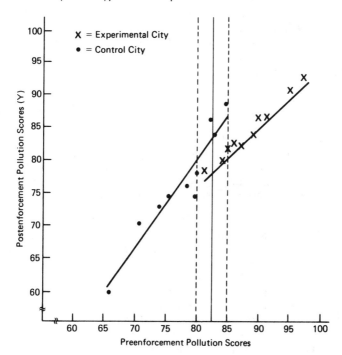

to experimental and control groups, we are able to determine the effects of the enforcement program on cities that are identical or very similar in their preenforcement pollution levels. The results of the regression-discontinuity analysis are more readily visualized if we display them in graphic form. In Figure 8–15 a partial discontinuity between the two groups is evident.

Regression-discontinuity analysis is a highly useful technique for monitoring the outcomes of social experiments that involve the distribution of some scarce resource. While our hypothetical example illustrates some of the calculations required to apply the technique, it also avoids some of its complexities. The application of the technique normally requires a much larger number of cases than that used here. For example, as many as 200 cases might have been required to do the kind of analysis just described. The need for a relatively large sample of cases is one of several conditions that must be satisfied in order to obtain valid results. These conditions, which include variables which are normally distributed, are discussed in available statistics texts.[65]

---

[65] See, for example, William Mendenhall and James E. Reinmuth, *Statistics for Management and Economics*, 3rd ed. (North Scituate, MA: Duxbury Press, 1978), chap. 11.

SUMMARY

This chapter has provided an overview of the nature and functions of monitoring in policy analysis, compared and contrasted four approaches to monitoring, and described and illustrated the application of techniques used in conjunction with these approaches. You should be able to discuss the following principles and generalizations:

1. Until policy recommendations are adopted, implemented and monitored, they are merely informed conjectures about the relation between policy actions and policy outcomes. Policy recommendations are similar to hypotheses: If action A is taken at time t_1, outcome O will result at time t_2.

2. Monitoring is a policy-analytic procedure used to produce information about the causes and consequences of public policies. Monitoring permits analysts to describe relationships between policy-program operations and their outcomes.

3. Monitoring is concerned with the production of designative claims and is therefore primarily concerned with establishing factual premises about public policy. While factual and value premises are in continuous flux, and "facts" and "values" are interdependent, only recommendation and evaluation are expressly based on value premises.

4. Monitoring yields designative claims after policies and programs have been adopted and implemented (*ex post facto*), whereas forecasting produces designative claims in advance of action (*ex ante*).

5. When information about policy actions has been transformed through monitoring into information about policy outcomes it is possible to experience problematic situations, that is, systems of interdependent problems (messes) that are subsequently transformed into policy problems through problem structuring. Information about policy outcomes is also transformed through evaluation into information about policy performance.

6. Information produced through monitoring performs at least four major functions: compliance, auditing, accounting, and explanation.

7. There are two types of policy outcomes: outputs and impacts. Policy actions are also of two types: inputs and processes. Policy actions have two major purposes: regulation and allocation.

8. Variables we wish to monitor may be defined constitutively and operationally. Operational definitions require that we specify the activities (operations) required to measure input, process, output, and impact variables.

9. Many alternative indicators may be used to define the same variable operationally. Because the relationship between variables and indicators is complex, it is frequently desirable to use multiple indicators of the same action or outcome variable. Multiple indicators are often combined in the form of an index. There are many kinds of indexes used to monitor policy outcomes.

10. Monitoring can be broken down into four identifiable approaches: social systems accounting, social experimentation, social auditing, and research and practice synthesis. These approaches may be contrasted in terms of two major properties: the types of controls over policy inputs and processes; and the type of information required.

11. Approaches to monitoring are concerned with policy-relevant outcomes, goal-

focused, and change-oriented. In addition each approach permits the cross-classification of variables and is concerned with objective as well as subjective measures of actions and outcomes.

12. Social systems accounting alerts us to areas where we have insufficient information and helps to structure problems and modify existing policies and programs. The limitations of social systems accounting include the difficulty of making the values underlying the choice of indicators explicit; the generality of indicators; the tendency to use available data that does not measure changes in subjective social states; the treatment of relations between inputs and outputs as a "black box"; and the absence of direct controls over policy actions.

13. Social experimentation attempts to follow procedures used in classical laboratory experiments: direct control over experimental treatments (stimuli); use of comparison (control) groups; and random assignment. Social experiments and quasi-experiments have been conducted in many issue areas: public health, compensatory education, welfare, criminal justice, drug and alcohol abuse, population control, nutrition, highway safety, and housing.

14. The capacity of social experiments to produce valid causal inferences is called internal validity. The most important threats to internal validity are history, maturation, instability, testing, mortality, selection, and regression artifacts. The capacity of social experiments to produce causal inferences that are generalizable to other contexts is called external validity. While many of the same factors that threaten internal validity also threaten external validity, one threat is especially important: artificiality of conditions under which an experiment is carried out.

15. Social auditing is a constructive response to limitations of social systems accounting and social experimentation. Social auditing explicitly addresses processes by which resource inputs are transformed into outputs and impacts and may involve the use of various qualitative methods designed to surface the subjective interpretations of policy processes held by stakeholders.

16. Research and practice synthesis uses available information in the form of case studies and research reports to compile, compare, and assess the results of past efforts to implement policies and programs. Research and practice synthesis is based on case survey and research survey methods. It is comparatively efficient, helps uncover various dimensions of policy processes, and may be used to support arguments from parallel case and analogy. The main limitations of research and practice synthesis are connected with the reliability and validity of information.

17. Monitoring, unlike other policy-analytic procedures, does not have clearly distinguishable sets of procedures that cluster around alternative approaches. Many of the same techniques are therefore appropriate for each of the four approaches. The major monitoring techniques are case and research survey methods, graphic displays, tabular displays, index numbers, interrupted time-series analysis, control-series analysis, and regression-discontinuity analysis. Each of these techniques has different uses, strengths, and limitations.

GLOSSARY

Allocative Action: A policy or program action requiring inputs of time, money, personnel, or equipment. Allocative and regulative actions may have consequences that are distributive as well as redistributive.

Beneficiary: A group for whom the effects of policies are beneficial or valuable. Beneficiaries (e.g., young children exposed to industrial pollution) are not necessarily a target group.

Case Survey Method: A set of procedures used to identify and analyze factors that account for variations in the adoption and implementation of policies and programs. The case survey method uses case studies and other records of experience.

Control-Series Analysis: A set of procedures that involves the addition of one or more control groups to an interrupted time-series design in order to determine whether characteristics of different groups exert an independent effect on policy outcomes.

External Validity: The generalizability of causal inferences outside the particular setting or area in which a social experiment is conducted. If an experiment is carried out under unusual or atypical circumstances (that is, it is artificial), it will have low external validity.

Gini Concentration Ratio (Index):   A measure of the proportion of the total area under the diagonal that lies in the area between the diagonal and the Lorenz curve.

Index: A set of multiple indicators. The Consumer Price Index (CPI) is a set of some 400 multiple indicators of prices for commodities and services.

Index Number: A measure of how much the value of an indicator or set of indicators changes over time in relation to a base period. An example of an index number is the Consumer Price Index (CPI).

Indicator: Directly observable characteristic substituted for indirectly observable characteristics and used as an operational definition of variables. British thermal units (BTUs) are an indicator of energy consumption.

Internal Validity: The capacity of social experiments to produce valid causal inferences about the effects of actions on outcomes. Threats to internal validity are history, maturation, instability, instrumentation and testing, mortality, selection, and regression artifacts.

Interrupted Time-Series Analysis: A set of procedures for analyzing policy actions as interruptions in an extended time series.

Lorenz Curve: A cumulative frequency polygon used to display the distribution of income, population, or residential segregation in a given population. Lorenz curves can also be expressed in the form of the Gini concentration ratio.

Policy Impact: An actual change in behavior or attitudes that results from a policy output. The improvement of the health of a target group (as contrasted with number of doctors per capita) is an example of a policy impact.

Policy Input: A resource (time, money, personnel, equipment, supplies) used to produce policy outputs and impacts.

Policy Output: A good, service, or resource received by target groups and beneficiaries. Per capital welfare expenditures is an example of a policy output.

Policy Process: The administrative, organizational, and political activities and attitudes that shape the transformation of policy inputs into outputs and impacts.

Price Relative: A value that expresses the price of goods and services in a given year relative to some base year.

Purchasing Power Index: An index computed on the basis of the Consumer Price Index that measures the real value of earnings in successive periods.

Qualitative Methods: Procedures designed to surface the subjective interpretations of policy processes and outcomes among stakeholders. Qualitative methods frequently involve participant observation, diaries, and logs.

Random Innovation: The process of executing a large number of alternative policies and programs whose inputs are neither standardized nor systematically manipulated. Many poverty programs carried out in the late 1960s are examples of random innovation.

Regression-Discontinuity Analysis: A set of procedures used to compare outcomes of policy actions undertaken among two or more groups, one of which is exposed to some policy treatment while the other is not. The central idea behind regression discontinuity is the "tie-breaking experiment" where scarce resources are randomly allocated to a small number of persons who are identical ("tied") in their abilities or needs.

Regulative Action: A policy or program action designed to insure compliance to certain standards or procedures, for example, those of the Federal Aeronautics Administration.

Research Survey: A set of procedures used to pool, compare, and appraise results of past research on policy actions and outcomes.

Social Indicator: A statistic that measures social conditions and changes therein over time for various segments of a population. Social conditions include objective as well as subjective contexts of human existence.

Spurious (False) Interpretation: A situation frequently encountered in interpreting data where two variables that appear to be correlated are both correlated with some other variable.

Systematic Experimentation: The process of systematically manipulating policy inputs in a way that permits more or less precise answers to questions about the relations of policy inputs and outputs. The New Jersey–Pennsylvania Graduated Work Incentives Experiment is an example.

Target Group: Persons, communities, or organizations on whom a policy or program is expected to have an effect. Target groups (e.g., industrial firms subject to federal environmental legislation) are not necessarily beneficiaries.

STUDY SUGGESTIONS

1. How is monitoring related to forecasting?
2. What is the relationship between ill-structured problems and approaches to monitoring?
3. What is the relationship between monitoring and the four types of policy claims discussed in Chapter 3?
4. Construct constitutive and operational definitions for any five of the following action and outcome variables:

Program expenditure	Equality of educational opportunity
Personnel turnover	National security
Health services	Work incentives
Quality of life	Pollution
Satisfaction with municipal services	Energy consumption
Income distribution	Rapport with clients

5. Listed below are several policy problems. For five of these problems provide an indicator or index that would help determine whether these problems are being resolved through government action.

Work alienation	School dropouts
Crime	Poverty
Energy crisis	Fiscal crisis
Inflation	Racial discrimination

6. The following table reports the number of criminal offenses known to the police per 100,000 population. Known offenses are broken down into two categories—total crimes against person and total crimes against property—over the period 1965–1989. Construct two curved-line graphs which display trends in crime rates over the period. Label the two graphs appropriately. What do these graphs suggest about crime as a policy problem?

Crime Rates in the United States: Offenses Known to Police per 100,000 Population,
1960–1976

	1965	1970	1975	1980	1985	1989
Violent	200	364	482	597	556	663
Property	2249	3621	4800	5353	4651	5077

Source: Harold W. Stanley and Richard G. Niemi, *Vital Statistics on American Politics,* 3rd
ed. (Washington, DC: Congressional Quarterly Press, 1992), p. 401.

7. In the following table are data on the percentage distribution of family income
   by quintiles in 1975 and 1989. Use these data to construct two Lorenz curves
   that depict changes in the distribution of income between 1975 and 1989. Label
   the two curves and the two axes.

Percentage Distribution of
Family Personal Income in the
United States by Quintiles,
1975 and 1989

QUINTILES	1975	1989
Highest	41.0	46.7
Second	24.0	24.0
Third	17.6	15.9
Fourth	12.0	9.6
Lowest	5.4	3.8
Total	100.0	100.0

Source: U.S. Bureau of the Census, *Current Population Reports,* Series P-60.

8. Calculate the Gini concentration ratio for 1975 and 1989 data in study suggestion 7. What do the Lorenz curves and Gini coefficients suggest about poverty as a policy problem? If poverty and other problems are "artificial" and "subjective," how valid is the information displayed by the Lorenz curves? Why?

9. Policy issue: Should average monthly benefits paid to mothers under the Aid to Families with Dependent Children (AFDC) program be increased?

YEAR	AVERAGE MONTHLY BENEFIT	CONSUMER PRICE INDEX (1982–1984 = 100)
1970	$183.13	38.8
1975	219.44	53.8
1980	280.03	82.4
1985	342.15	107.6
1988	374.07	118.3

Prepare a policy memo that answers this question. Before writing the memo:

(a) Prepare a purchasing power index for all years in the series, using 1970 as the base year.

(b) Convert the average monthly benefits into real benefits for these years.

(c) Repeat the same procedures, using 1980 as the base year.

10. You have been asked to monitor the outcomes of the 55 mph speed limit (National Maximum Speed Law of 1973). A leading proponent of the policy has stated that the policy is definitely successful in saving human lives. Here are data on the mileage death rate (deaths per 100 million miles) on intercity roads before and after the 1973 policy.

YEAR	MILEAGE DEATH RATE
1966	5.7
1967	5.5
1968	5.5
1969	5.3
1970	4.9
1971	4.7
1972	4.5
1973	4.3
1974	3.6
1975	3.5
1976	3.3
1977	3.4
1978	3.2
1979	3.3
1980	3.4
1981	3.1
1982	2.8
1983	2.6
1984	2.7
1985	2.6
1986	2.6
1987	2.5
1988	2.5

Source: National Safety Council.

(a) Construct an interrupted time-series graph that displays the decline in the mileage death rate between 1973 and 1974.

(b) Construct an extended interrupted time-series graph that displays the decline in the mileage death rate from 1966 through 1988.

(c) Identify and analyze possible threats to the validity of the claim that the 1973 policy is definitely successful in saving lives (for example, gasoline prices, safety improvements).

(d) Write a policy memo to the governor of your state. The memo should include your recommendation on whether the 55 mph speed limit should be retained and the evidence for that recommendation. Should it be retained? [*Note:* Be sure to take into account the long-term decline, which is probably due to a combination of improvements in automobile design, highway engineering, seat belts, driver education, and other safety factors.]

11. The War on Drugs was initiated in 1981 during the Reagan Administration and continued under President Bush. Although another policy—mandatory drug education in schools—had successfully eliminated the country's first cocaine epidemic at the turn of the twentieth century, the central focus of the Reagan–Bush policy is the interdiction of cocaine and crack cocaine before it enters the United States from other countries, especially South America. It is widely acknowledged that the policy has not reduced the quantity of cocaine and crack entering the country and that the street price of these drugs has actually declined since the early 1980s.

The following table provides data on some key policy outcome measures relevent to the War on Drugs. On the basis of these data, write a policy memo to the chief of the Drug Enforcement Administration that assesses the effectiveness of the War on Drugs.

Percentage of Cocaine Users in Past Month and Cocaine-Related Emergency Room Visits and Deaths Among Different Groups

GROUP	1982	1985	1988
High school seniors	5.0	6.7	3.4
College undergraduates	17.3	17.1	10.0
Age in general population			
12–17 years	1.6	1.5	1.1
18–25 years	6.8	7.6	4.5
26+	1.2	2.0	0.9
Emergency room visits			
Cocaine	NA	10,099	46,835
Crack	NA	1,000	15,306
Emergency room deaths	NA	717	2,163

Source: Drug Abuse and Drug Abuse Research (Washington, DC: National Institute on Drug Abuse, 1991).

12. Imagine that you are examining the effects of 10 scholarship awards on the subsequent performance of disadvantaged youths in college. There are fewer awards than applicants, and awards must be based on merit. Therefore, it is not possible to provide all disadvantaged students with awards; nor is it politically feasible to select students randomly since this conflicts with the principle of merit. You decide to allocate the 10 awards according to the following rules: No student will receive an award without scoring at least 86 on the examination; five awards will be given automatically to the top students in the 92–100 interval; and the remaining five awards will be given to a random sample of students in the 86–91 interval.

One year later you obtain information on the grade point averages of the 10 award students and 10 other disadvantaged students who did not receive an award. You have college entrance examination scores for all 20 students. Does the provision of scholarship awards to disadvantaged students improve subsequent achievement in college?

AWARD GROUP		NONAWARD GROUP	
Examination Scores	*Grade Point Average*	*Examination Scores*	*Grade Point Average*
99	3.5	88	3.2
97	3.9	89	3.2
94	3.4	90	3.3
92	3.0	86	3.0
92	3.3	91	3.5
86	3.1	85	3.1
90	3.3	81	3.0
89	3.2	79	2.8
88	3.2	84	3.0
91	3.4	80	2.6

(a) Construct a regression-discontinuity graph that displays examination scores and grade point averages for the award and nonaward groups. Use ×s and Os to display data points for the experimental (×) and control (O) groups.

(b) Construct a worksheet and compute for each group the values of a and b in the equation $Y_c = a + b(X)$.

(c) For each group write the regression equation that describes the relation between merit (examination scores) and subsequent achievement (grade point averages).

(d) Compute the standard error of estimate at the 95 percent estimation interval (that is, two standard errors) for each group.

(e) Compute r^2 and r.

(f) Interpret information contained in (a) through (e) and answer the question: Does the provision of scholarship awards to disadvantaged students improve subsequent achievement in college? Justify your answer.

13. Subtract 0.5 from each student's grade point average in the nonaward (control) group above.

(a) Does the Y intercept change for the control group? Why?

(b) Does the slope of the regression line change for the control group? Why?

(c) Does the standard error of estimate change for the control group? Why?

(d) Does r^2 and r change for the control group? Why?

(e) What do your answers show about the appropriateness of correlation and regression analysis for problems where pretest and posttest scores are highly correlated?

(f) What, then, are the special advantages of regression-discontinuity analysis?

14. Return to Study Suggestion 10. Using at least four threats to validity, construct rebuttals to the following argument: (B) The greater the cost of an alternative, the less likely it is that the alternative will be pursued. (W) The enforcement of the maximum speed limit of 55 mph increases the costs of exceeding the speed limit. (I) The mileage death rate fell from 4.3 to 3.6 deaths per 100 million miles after the implementation of the 55 mph speed limit. (C) The 55 mph speed limit (National Maximum Speed Law of 1973) has been definitely successful in saving lives. Study Figure 8–13 before you begin.

SUGGESTED READINGS

BARTLETT, ROBERT V., ed., *Policy through Impact Assessment: Institutionalized Analysis as a Policy Strategy*. New York: Greenwood Press, 1989.

CAMPBELL, DONALD T., in *Methodology and Epistemology for Social Science: Selected Papers*, ed. E. Samuel Overman. Chicago: University of Chicago Press, 1989.

COOK, THOMAS D. and CHARLES S. REICHARDY, eds., *Qualitative and Quantitative Methods in Evaluation Research*. Beverly Hills, CA: Sage Publications, 1979.

LIGHT, RICHARD J. and DAVID B. PILLEMER, *Summing Up: The Science of Reviewing Research*. Cambridge, MA: Harvard University Press, 1984.

MACRAE, DUNCAN, JR. *Policy Indicators: Links between Social Science and Public Debate*. Chapel Hill, NC: University of North Carolina Press, 1985.

MILES, MATTHEW B. and A. MICHAEL HUBERMAN, *Qualitative Data Analysis: A Sourcebook of New Methods*. Beverly Hills, CA: Sage Publications, 1984.

TROCHIM, WILLIAM M. K., *Research Design for Program Evaluation: The Regression-Discontinuity Approach*. Beverly Hills, CA: Sage Publications, 1984.

U.S. GENERAL ACCOUNTING OFFICE, *Designing Evaluations*. Methodology Transfer Paper 4. Washington, DC: Program Evaluation and Methodology Division, United States General Accounting Office, July 1984.

YIN, ROBERT K., *Case Study Analysis*. Beverly Hills, CA: Sage Publications, 1985.

Conclusion: Evaluating Policy Performance

"Evaluators should evaluate" is a value judgment itself but it also happens to be a tautology. So forget the idea that evaluations are a matter of opinion or taste. They are matters of fact and logic and more important than most.

—MICHAEL SCRIVEN[1]

As we saw in Chapter 8, monitoring is used to produce information about the causes and consequences of policies and programs. Monitoring is therefore primarily concerned with establishing factual premises about public policies. Evaluation, by contrast, is primarily concerned with establishing the value premises necessary to produce information about the performance of policies. Monitoring answers the question: "What happened, how, and why?" Evaluation answers the question: "What differences does it make?"

The purpose of this chapter is to address this important question by considering the policy-analytic method of evaluation. We first review the nature, aims, and functions of evaluation in policy analysis, showing that evaluation is based upon but is nevertheless different from monitoring. Second, we compare and contrast several approaches to evaluation in policy analysis. Third, we review methods used in conjunction with these approaches. Finally, we conclude the chapter and the book as a whole by returning to the problem of using policy analysis to improve policy-making.

---

[1] Michael Scriven, "Evaluating Educational Programs," *The Urban Review*, 9. No. 4 (February 1969), p. 22.

EVALUATION IN POLICY ANALYSIS

The term *evaluation* has several related meanings, each of which refers to the application of some scale of value to the outcomes of policies and programs. In general the term *evaluation* is synonymous with appraisal, rating, and assessment, words which imply efforts to analyze policy outcomes in terms of some set of values. In a more specific sense *evaluation* refers to the production of information about the value or worth of policy outcomes. When policy outcomes do in fact have value, it is because they contribute to goals and objectives. In this case we say that a policy or program has attained some significant level of performance, which means that policy problems have been clarified or alleviated.

The Nature of Evaluation

The main feature of evaluation is that it results in claims that are evaluative in character. Here the main question is not one of facts (Does something exist?) or of action (What should be done?) but one of values (Of what worth is it?). Evaluation therefore has several characteristics that distinguish it from other policy-analytic methods:

1. *Value focus.* Evaluation, as contrasted with monitoring, focuses on judgments regarding the desirability or value of policies and programs. Evaluation is primarily an effort to determine the worth or social utility of a policy or program, and not simply an effort to collect information about the anticipated and unanticipated outcomes of policy actions. Since the appropriateness of policy goals and objectives can always be questioned, evaluation includes procedures for evaluating goals and objectives themselves.[2]
2. *Fact-value interdependence.* Evaluation claims depend as much on "facts" as they do on "values." To claim that a particular policy or program has attained a high (or low) level of performance requires not only that policy outcomes are valuable to some individual, group, or society as a whole; it also requires that policy outcomes are actually a consequence of actions undertaken to resolve a particular problem. Hence, monitoring is a prerequisite for evaluation.
3. *Present and past orientation.* Evaluative claims, as contrasted with advocative claims produced through recommendation, are oriented toward present and past outcomes, rather than future ones. Evaluation is retrospective and occurs after actions have been taken (*ex post*). Recommendation, while also involving value premises, is prospective and occurs before actions have been taken (*ex ante*).
4. *Value duality.* The values underlying evaluative claims have a dual quality, since they may be regarded as ends and means. Evaluation is similar to rec-

---

[2] See Francis G. Caro, "Evaluation Research: An Overview," in *Readings in Evaluation Research,* ed. Francis G. Caro (New York: Russell Sage Foundation, 1971), p. 2; Michael Scriven, "The Methodology of Evaluation," in *Perspectives of Curriculum Evaluation,* American Educational Research Association Monograph Series on Curriculum Evaluation (Chicago: Rand McNally, 1967); and Gene Glass, "The Growth of Evaluation Methodology," *AERA Curriculum Monograph Series,* No. 7 (Chicago: Rand McNally, 1971).

ommendation insofar as a given value (for example, health) may be regarded as intrinsic (desirable in itself) as well as extrinsic (desirable because it leads to some other end). Values are often arranged in a hierarchy that reflects the relative importance and interdependency of goals and objectives.

Functions of Evaluation

Evaluation performs several main functions in policy analysis. First, and most important, evaluation provides reliable and valid information about *policy performance,* that is, the extent to which needs, values, and opportunities have been realized through public action. In this respect, evaluation reveals the extent to which particular goals (for example, improved health) and objectives (for example, a 20 percent reduction of chronic diseases by 1990) have been attained.

Second, evaluation contributes to the *clarification* and *critique* of values that underlie the selection of goals and objectives. Values are clarified by defining and operationalizing goals and objectives. Values are also critiqued by systematically questioning the appropriateness of goals and objectives in relation to the problem being addressed. In questioning the appropriateness of goals and objectives, analysts may examine alternative sources of values (for example, public officials, vested interests, client groups) as well as their grounds in different forms of rationality (technical, economic, legal, social, substantive).

TABLE 9–1   Criteria for Evaluation

TYPE OF CRITERION	QUESTION	ILLUSTRATIVE CRITERIA
Effectiveness	Has a valued outcome been achieved?	Units of service
Efficiency	How much effort was required to achieve a valued outcome?	Unit cost Net benefits Cost–benefit ratio
Adequacy	To what extent does the achievement of a valued outcome resolve the problem?	Fixed costs (type I problem) Fixed effectiveness (type II problem)
Equity	Are costs and benefits distributed equitably among different groups?	Pareto criterion Kaldor–Hicks criterion Rawls criterion
Responsiveness	Do policy outcomes satisfy the needs, preferences or values of particular groups?	Consistency with citizen surveys
Appropriateness	Are desired outcomes (objectives) actually worthy or valuable?	Public programs should be equitable as well as efficient

Note: See Chapter 7 for extended descriptions of criteria.

Third, evaluation may contribute to the application of other policy-analytic methods, including *problem structuring* and *recommendation*. Information about inadequate policy performance may contribute to the restructuring of policy problems, for example, by showing that goals and objectives should be redefined. Evaluation can also contribute to the definition of new or revised policy alternatives by showing that a previously favored policy alternative should be abandoned and replaced with another one.

Criteria for Policy Evaluation

In producing information about policy performance, analysts use different types of criteria to evaluate policy outcomes. These types of criteria have already been discussed in relation to policy recommendation (Chapter 7). The main difference between criteria for evaluation and criteria for recommendation is the time at which criteria are applied. Criteria for evaluation are applied retrospectively (*ex post*), while criteria for recommendation are applied prospectively (*ex ante*). These criteria are summarized in Table 9–1.

APPROACHES TO EVALUATION

Evaluation, as we saw above, has two interrelated aspects: the use of various methods to monitor the outcomes of public policies and programs and the application of some set of values to determine the worth of these outcomes to some person, group, or society as a whole. Observe that these two interrelated aspects point to the presence of factual and value premises in any evaluative claim. Yet many activities described as "evaluation" in policy analysis are essentially *non-evaluative*—that is, they are primarily concerned with the production of designative (factual) claims rather than evaluative ones. In fact, each of the four approaches to monitoring described in Chapter 8 are frequently mislabeled as approaches to "evaluation research" or "policy evaluation."[3]

Given the present lack of clarity about the meaning of evaluation in policy analysis, it is essential to distinguish among several different approaches to policy evaluation: pseudo-evaluation, formal evaluation, and decision-theoretic evaluation. These approaches and their aims, assumptions, and major forms are illustrated in Table 9–2.

Pseudo-evaluation

Pseudo-evaluation is an approach that uses descriptive methods to produce reliable and valid information about policy outcomes, without at-

---

[3] See, for example, the description of "evaluation" research in Marcia Guttentag and Elmer Struening, eds., *Handbook of Evaluation Research*, 2 vols. (Beverly Hills, CA: Sage Publications, 1975); and Leonard Rutman, ed., *Evaluation Research Methods: A Basic Guide* (Beverly Hills, CA: Sage Publications, 1977).

TABLE 9–2 Three Approaches to Evaluation

APPROACH	AIMS	ASSUMPTIONS	MAJOR FORMS
Pseudo-evaluation	Use descriptive methods to produce reliable and valid information about policy outcomes	Measures of worth or value are self-evident or uncontroversial	Social experimentation Social systems accounting Social auditing Research and practice synthesis
Formal evaluation	Use descriptive methods to produce reliable and valid information about policy outcomes that have been formally announced as policy-program objectives	Formally announced goals and objectives of policymakers and administrators are appropriate measures of worth or value	Developmental evaluation Experimental evaluation Retrospective process evaluation Retrospective outcome evaluation
Decision-theoretic evaluation	Use descriptive methods to produce reliable and valid information about policy outcomes that are explicitly valued by multiple stakeholders	Formally announced as well as latent goals and objectives of stakeholders are appropriate measures of worth or value	Evaluability assessment Multiattribute utility analysis

tempting to question the worth or value of these outcomes to persons, groups, or society as a whole. The major assumption of pseudo-evaluation is that measures of worth or value are self-evident or uncontroversial.

In pseudo-evaluation the analyst typically uses a variety of methods (quasi-experimental design, questionnaires, random sampling, statistical techniques) to explain variations in policy outcomes in terms of policy input and process variables. Yet any given policy outcome (for example, number of employed trainees, units of medical services delivered, net income benefits produced) is taken for granted as an appropriate objective. Major forms of pseudo-evaluation include the approaches to monitoring discussed in Chapter 8: social experimentation, social systems accounting, social auditing, and research and practice synthesis.

Formal Evaluation

Formal evaluation is an approach which uses descriptive methods to produce reliable and valid information about policy outcomes but evaluates such outcomes on the basis of policy-program objectives that have been formally announced by policy makers and program administrators. The major assumption of formal evaluation is that formally announced goals and objectives are appropriate measures of the worth or value of policies and programs.

In formal evaluation the analyst uses the same kinds of methods as those employed in pseudo-evaluation and the aim is identical: to produce reliable and valid information about variations in policy outputs and impacts that may be traced to policy inputs and processes. The difference, however, is that formal evaluations use legislation, program documents, and interviews with policy makers and administrators to identify, define, and specify formal goals and objectives. The appropriateness of these formally announced goals and objectives is not questioned. In formal evaluations the types of evaluative criteria most frequently used are those of effectiveness and efficiency.

One of the major types of formal evaluation is the *summative evaluation*, which involves an effort to monitor the accomplishment of formal goals and objectives after a policy or program has been in place for some period of time. Summative evaluations are designed to appraise products of stable and well-established public policies and programs. By contrast, a *formative evaluation* involves efforts to continuously monitor the accomplishment of formal goals and objectives. The differences between summative and formative evaluation should not be overemphasized, however, since the main distinguishing characteristic of formative evaluation is the number of points in time at which policy outcomes are monitored. Hence, the difference between summative and formative evaluation is mainly one of degree.

Formal evaluations may be summative or formative, but they may also involve direct or indirect controls over policy inputs and processes. In the former case evaluators can directly manipulate expenditure levels, the mix of programs, or the characteristics of target groups—that is, the evaluation may have one or more characteristics of social experimentation as an approach to monitoring (Chapter 8). In the case of indirect controls, policy inputs and processes cannot be directly manipulated; rather they must be analyzed retrospectively on the basis of actions that have already occurred. Four types of formal evaluation—each based on a different orientation toward the policy process (summative vs. formative) and type of control over action (direct vs. indirect)—are illustrated in Table 9–3.

Varieties of Formal Evaluation

Developmental evaluation refers to evaluation activities which are explicitly designed to serve the day-to-day needs of program staff. Developmental evaluation is useful "for alerting the staff to incipient weaknesses or unintended failures of a program and for insuring proper operation by those responsible for its operation."[4] Developmental evaluation, which involves

---

[4] Peter H. Rossi and Sonia R. Wright, "Evaluation Research: An Assessment of Theory, Practice, and Politics," *Evaluation Quarterly*, 1, No. 1 (February 1977), 21.

TABLE 9–3 Types of Formal Evaluation

CONTOL OVER POLICY ACTIONS	ORIENTATION TOWARD POLICY PROCESS	
	Formative	*Summative*
Direct	Developmental evaluation	Experimental evaluation
Indirect	Retrospective process evaluation	Retrospective outcome evaluation

some measure of direct control over policy actions, has been used in a wide variety of situations in the public and private sectors. Thus, for example, businesses frequently use developmental evaluations to distribute, test, and recall new products. In the public sector developmental evaluations have been used to test new teaching methods and materials in public education programs, such as Sesame Street and Electric Company. Such programs are systematically monitored and evaluated by showing them to audiences composed of children within specified age limits. Subsequently, they are "revised many times on the basis of systematic observations of which program features achieved attention and on the basis of interviews with the children after viewing the program."[5] Developmental evaluations, since they are both formative and involve direct controls, can be used to adapt immediately to new experience acquired through systematic manipulations of input and process variables.

Retrospective process evaluation involves the monitoring and evaluation of programs after they have been in place for some time. Retrospective process evaluation, which often focuses on problems and bottlenecks encountered in the implementation of policies and programs, does not permit the direct manipulation of inputs (for example, expenditures) and processes (for example, alternative delivery systems). Rather it relies on *ex post facto* (retrospective) descriptions of ongoing program activities, which are subsequently related to outputs and impacts. Retrospective process evaluation requires a well-established internal reporting system which permits the continuous generation of program-related information (for example, the number of target groups served, the types of services provided, and the characteristics of personnel employed to staff programs). Management information systems in public agencies sometimes permit retrospective process evaluations, provided they contain information on processes as well as outcomes.

Title I of the Elementary and Secondary Education Act (1965) was subjected to a form of retrospective process evaluation by the Office of Education, but with disappointing results. Title I provided funds to local school systems in proportion to the number of pupils from poor or deprived

---

[5] Ibid., p. 22.

families. Local school districts submitted inadequate and marginally useful information, thus making it impossible to evaluate and implement programs concurrently. Retrospective process evaluations presuppose a reliable and valid information system, which is often difficult to establish.

Experimental evaluation involves the monitoring and evaluation of outcomes under conditions of direct controls over policy inputs and processes. The ideal of experimental evaluation has generally been the "controlled scientific experiment," where all factors which might influence policy outcomes except one—that is, a particular input or process variable—are controlled, held constant, or treated as plausible rival hypotheses. Experimental and quasi-experimental evaluations include the New Jersey-Pennsylvania Income Maintenance Experiment, the California Group Therapy-Criminal Recidivism Experiment, the Kansas City Preventive Patrol Experiment, Project Follow Through, the Supported Work Demonstration Project, and various experiments in educational performance contracting.

Experimental evaluations must meet rather severe requirements before they can be carried out:[6] (1) a clearly defined and directly manipulable set of "treatment" variables which are specified in operational terms; (2) an evaluation strategy which permits maximum generalizability of conclusions about performance to many similar target groups or settings (*external validity*); (3) an evaluation strategy which permits minimum error in interpreting policy performance as the actual result of manipulated policy inputs and processes (*internal validity*); and (4) a monitoring system which produces reliable data on complex interrelationships among preconditions, unforeseen events, inputs, processes, outputs, impacts, and side effects and spillovers (see Figure 8–2). Since these demanding methodological requirements are rarely met, experimental evaluations typically fall short of the "true" controlled experiment, and are referred to as "quasi-experimental."

Retrospective outcome evaluations also involve the monitoring and evaluation of outcomes but with no direct control over manipulable policy inputs and processes.[7] At best controls are indirect or statistical—that is, the evaluator attempts to isolate the effects of many different factors by using quantitative methods. In general, there are two main variants of retrospective process evaluation: cross-sectional and longitudinal studies. *Longitudinal studies* are those which evaluate changes in the outcomes of one, several, or many programs at two or more points in time. Many longitudinal studies have been carried out in the area of family planning, where fertility rates and changes in the acceptance of contraceptive devices are monitored and evaluated over reasonably long periods of time (5 to 20 years). *Cross-*

---

[6] Walter Williams, *Social Policy Research and Analysis* (New York: Elsevier, 1971), p. 93.

[7] Note that three of the approaches to monitoring discussed in Chapter 8—that is, social systems accounting, social auditing, and research and practice synthesis—may also be considered as forms of retrospective outcome evaluation. Similarly, cost–benefit and cost–effectiveness analysis (Chapter 7) may be viewed as particular forms of retrospective outcome evaluation.

sectional studies, by contrast, seek to monitor and evaluate multiple programs at one point in time. The goal of the cross-sectional study is to discover
whether the outputs and impacts of various programs are significantly different from one another; and if so, what particular actions, preconditions,
or unforeseen events might explain the difference.

Two prominent examples of retrospective outcome evaluations that
are cross-sectional in nature are Project Head Start, a program designed to
provide compensatory education to preschool children, and the Coleman
Report. Indeed,

> almost every evaluation of the national compensatory education programs
> started during the middle 1960s has been based on cross-sectional data. Pupils
> enrolled in compensatory education programs were contrasted to those who
> were not, holding constant statistically such sources of competing explanations
> as family backgrounds, ethnicity, region, city size, and so on.[8]

Decision-Theoretic Evaluation

Decision-theoretic evaluation is an approach which uses descriptive
methods to produce reliable and valid information about policy outcomes
that are explicitly valued by multiple stakeholders. The key difference between decision-theoretic evaluation, on the one hand, and pseudo- and
formal evaluation on the other, is that decision-theoretic evaluation attempts to surface and make explicit the latent as well as manifest goals and
objectives of stakeholders. This means that formally announced goals and
objectives of policy makers and administrators are but one source of values,
since all parties who have a stake in the formulation and implementation
of a policy (for example, middle- and lower-level staff, personnel in other
agencies, client groups) are involved in generating the goals and objectives
against which performance is measured.

Decision-theoretic evaluation is a way to overcome several deficiencies
of pseudo-evaluation and formal evaluation:[9]

1. *Underutilization and nonutilization of performance information.* Much of the
   information generated through evaluations is underutilized or never used to
   improve policy-making. In part this is because evaluations are not sufficiently
   responsive to the goals and objectives of parties who have a stake in formulating
   and implementing policies and programs.
2. *Ambiguity of performance goals.* Many goals of public policies and programs
   are vague. This means that the same general goal—for example, to improve
   health or encourage better conservation of energy—can and do result in specific objectives that conflict with one another. This is evident when we consider

---

[8] Rossi and Wright, "Evaluation Research," p. 27.

[9] For accounts of these and other deficiencies see Carol H. Weiss, *Evaluation Research*
(Englewood Cliffs, NJ: Prentice Hall, 1972); Ward Edwards, Marcia Guttentag, and Kurt Snap-
per, "A Decision-Theoretic Approach to Evaluation Research," in Guttentag and Struening,
Handbook of Evaluation Research, pp. 139–81; and Martin Rein and Sheldon H. White, "Policy
Research: Belief and Doubt," *Policy Analysis*, 3, No. 2 (1977), 239–72.

that the same goal (for example, improved health) may be operationalized in terms of at least six types of evaluation criteria: effectiveness, efficiency, adequacy, equity, responsiveness, and appropriateness. One of the purposes of decision-theoretic evaluation is to reduce the ambiguity of goals and make conflicting objectives explicit.

3. *Multiple conflicting objectives.* The goals and objectives of public policies and programs cannot be satisfactorily established by focusing on the values of one or several parties (for example, Congress, a dominant client group, or a head administrator). In fact, multiple stakeholders with conflicting goals and objectives are present in most situations requiring evaluation. Decision-theoretic evaluation attempts to identify these multiple stakeholders and surface their goals and objectives.

One of the main purposes of decision-theoretic evaluation is to link information about policy outcomes with the values of multiple stakeholders. The assumption of decision-theoretic evaluation is that formally announced as well as latent goals and objectives of stakeholders are appropriate measures of the worth or value of policies and programs. The two major forms of decision-theoretic evaluation are evaluability assessment and multiattribute utility analysis, both of which attempt to link information about policy outcomes with the values of multiple stakeholders.

Evaluability assessment is a set of procedures designed to analyze the decision-making system that is supposed to benefit from performance information and to clarify the goals, objectives, and assumptions against which performance is to be measured.[10] The basic question in evaluability assessment is whether a policy or program can be evaluated at all. For a policy or program to be evaluable, at least three conditions must be present: a clearly articulated policy or program; clearly specified goals and/or consequences; and a set of explicit assumptions that link policy actions to goals and/or consequences.[11] In conducting an evaluability assessment, analysts follow a series of steps that clarify a policy or program from the standpoint of the intended users of performance information and the evaluators themselves:[12]

1. *Policy-program specification.* What federal, state, or local activities and what goals and objectives constitute the program?
2. *Collection of policy-program information.* What information must be collected to define policy-program objectives, activities, and underlying assumptions?
3. *Policy-program modeling.* What model best describes the program and its related objectives and activities, from the point of view of intended users of performance information? What causal assumptions link actions to outcomes?
4. *Policy-program evaluability assessment.* Is the policy-program model suffi-

---

[10] On evaluability assessment, see Joseph S. Wholey and others, "Evaluation: When Is It Really Needed?" *Evaluation*, 2, No. 2 (1975), 89–94; and Wholey, "Evaluability Assessment," in Rutman, *Evaluation Research Methods*, pp. 41–56.

[11] See Rutman, *Evaluation Research Methods*, p. 18.

[12] Wholey, "Evaluability Assessment," pp. 43–55.

ciently unambiguous to make the evaluation useful? What types of evaluation studies would be most useful?

5. *Feedback of evaluability assessment to users.* After presenting conclusions about policy-program evaluability to intended users, what appear to be the next steps that should (or should not) be taken to evaluate policy performance?

A second form of decision-theoretic evaluation is *multiattribute utility analysis.*[13] Multiattribute utility analysis is a set of procedures designed to elicit from multiple stakeholders subjective judgments about the probability of occurrence and value of policy outcomes. The strengths of multiattribute utility analysis are that it explicitly surfaces the value judgments of multiple stakeholders; it recognizes the presence of multiple conflicting objectives in policy-program evaluation; and it produces performance information that is more usable from the standpoint of intended users. The steps in conducting a multiattribute utility analysis are the following:

1. *Stakeholder identification.* Identify the parties who affect and are affected by a policy or program. Each of these stakeholders will have goals and objectives that they wish to maximize.
2. *Specification of relevant decision issues.* Specify the courses of action or inaction about which there is a disagreement among stakeholders. In the simplest case there will be two courses of action: the status quo and some new initiative.
3. *Specification of policy outcomes.* Specify the range of consequences that may follow each course of action. Outcomes may be arranged in a hierarchy where one action has several consequences, each of which itself has further consequences. A hierarchy of outcomes is similar to an objectives tree (Chapter 7), except that outcomes are not objectives until they have been explicitly valued.
4. *Identification of attributes of outcomes.* Here the task is to identify all relevant attributes that make outcomes worthy or valuable. For example, each outcome may have different types of benefits and costs to different target groups and beneficiaries.
5. *Attribute ranking.* Rank each value attribute in order of importance. For example, if increased family income is an outcome of a poverty program, this outcome may have several value attributes: sense of family well-being; greater nutritional intake; and more disposable income for health care. These attributes should be ranked in order of their relative importance to one another.
6. *Attribute scaling.* Scale attributes that have been ranked in order of importance. To do so, arbitrarily assign the least important attribute a value of ten. Proceed to the next most important attribute, answering the question: How many times more important is this attribute than the next-least-important one? Continue this scaling procedure until the most important attribute has been compared with all others. Note that the most important attribute may have a scale value 10, 20, 30, or more times that of the least important attribute.
7. *Scale standardization.* The attributes that have been scaled will have different maximum values for different stakeholders. For example, one stakeholder may

---

[13] See Edwards, Guttentag, and Snapper, "A Decision-Theoretic Approach," pp. 148–59.

give attribute *A* a value of 60; attribute *B*, a value of 30; and attribute *C*, a value of 10. Another stakeholder, however, may give these same attributes values of 120, 60, and 10. To standardize these scales, sum all original values for each scale, divide each original value by its respective sum, and multiply by 100. This results in separate scales whose component values sum to 100.

8. *Outcome measurement.* Measure the degree that each outcome is likely to result in the attainment of each attribute. The maximum probability should be given a value of 100; the minimum probability should be given a value of 0 (that is, there is no chance that the outcome will result in the attainment of the attribute).

9. *Utility calculation.* Calculate the utility (value) of each outcome by using the formula:

$$U_i = \sum w_j u_{ij}$$

where

U_i = the aggregate utility (value) of the *i*th outcome

w_j = the standardized scale value of the *j*th attribute

u_{ij} = the probability of occurrence of the *i*th outcome on the *j*th attribute

10. *Evaluation and presentation.* Specify the policy outcome with the greatest overall performance, and present this information to relevant decision makers.

The strength of multiattribute utility analysis is that it enables analysts to deal systematically with conflicting objectives of multiple stakeholders. This is possible, however, only when the steps just described are carried out as part of a *group process* involving relevant stakeholders. Hence, the essential requirement of multiattribute utility analysis is that stakeholders who affect and are affected by a policy or program are active participants in the evaluation of policy performance.

METHODS FOR EVALUATION

A number of methods and techniques can assist analysts in evaluating policy performance. Nearly all of these techniques, however, may also be used in conjunction with other policy-analytic methods, including problem structuring, forecasting, recommendation, and monitoring. Thus, for example, argumentation analysis (Chapter 5) may be used to surface assumptions about expected relationships between policy actions and objectives. Cross-impact analysis (Chapter 6) may prove useful in identifying unanticipated policy outcomes that work against the achievement of policy-program objectives. Similarly, discounting (Chapter 7) may be as relevant to policy-program evaluation as it is to recommendation, given that cost–benefit and cost–effectiveness analysis may be used retrospectively (*ex post*) as well as prospectively (*ex ante*). Finally, techniques that range from graphic displays and index numbers to control-series analysis (Chapter 8) may be essential for monitoring policy outcomes as a prelude to their evaluation.

TABLE 9-4 Techniques for Evaluation by Three Approaches

APPROACH	TECHNIQUE
Pseudo-evaluation	Graphic displays
	Tabular displays
	Index numbers
	Interrupted time-series analysis
	Control-series analysis
	Regression-discontinuity analysis
Formal evaluation	Objectives mapping
	Value clarification
	Value critique
	Constraint mapping
	Cross-impact analysis
	Discounting
Decision-theoretic evaluation	Brainstorming
	Argumentation analysis
	Policy Delphi
	User-survey analysis

TABLE 9-5 Interview Protocol for User-Survey Analysis

STEP IN EVALUABILITY ASSESSMENT	QUESTIONS
Policy-program specification	1. What are the objectives of the policy or program?
	2. What would be acceptable evidence of the achievement of policy-program objectives?[1]
Policy-program modeling	3. What policy actions (for example, resources, guidelines, staff activities) are available to achieve objectives?[2]
	4. Why will action A lead to objective O?[2]
Policy-program evaluability assessment	5. What do various stakeholders (for example, Congress, OMB, state auditor general, mayor's office) expect of the program in terms of performance? Are these expectations consistent?
	6. What is the most serious obstacle to achieving objectives?
Feedback of evaluability assessment to users	7. What performance information do you need on the job? Why?
	8. Are present sources of performance information adequate? Why? Why not?
	9. What is the most important source of performance information you will need in the next year?
	10. What key issues should any evaluation address?

Notes:
[1] Answers to this question yield operational measures of objectives.
[2] Answers to these questions yield causal assumptions about the relation between actions and objectives.

Source: Adapted from Joseph S. Wholey, "Evaluability Assessment," in *Evaluation Research Methods: A Basic Guide*, ed. Leonard Rutman (Beverly Hills, CA: Sage Publications, 1977), Fig. 3, p. 48.

The fact that various techniques may be used with more than one policy-analytic method points to the interdependence of problem structuring, forecasting, recommendation, monitoring, and evaluation in policy analysis. Many methods and techniques are relevant to pseudo-evaluation, formal evaluation, and decision-theoretic evaluation (Table 9–4).

Only one of the techniques listed in Table 9–4 has not already been described. *User-survey analysis* is a set of procedures for collecting information about the evaluability of a policy or program from intended users and other stakeholders.[14] User surveys are central to the conduct of evaluability assessments and other forms of decision-theoretic evaluation. The major instrument for collecting information is an interview protocol with a series of open-ended questions. Responses to these questions provide the information required to complete the several steps in an evaluability assessment previously described: policy-program specification; policy-program modeling; policy-program assessment; and presentation of evaluability assessment to users. A sample interview protocol for a user survey analysis is presented in Table 9–5.

UTILIZING PERFORMANCE INFORMATION

We began this book with a definition of policy analysis as *an applied social science discipline that employs multiple methods of inquiry, in contexts of argumentation and public debate, to create, critically assess, and communicate policy-relevant knowledge.* We also emphasized that policy analysis is essentially an intellectual process, while policy making is primarily political. Accordingly, many factors other than methodology shape the ways that information acquired through policy analysis is actually utilized in the policy-making process. Policy analysts are but one of many types of stakeholders in a policy system.

The distinction between two aspects of policy processes—the intellectual and the political—is critical for understanding the utilization, underutilization, and nonutilization of policy analysis. Indeed, the utilization of information produced by any of the policy-analytic methods discussed in this book—that is, problem structuring, forecasting, recommendation, monitoring, and evaluation—is significantly shaped by factors that are political, organizational, social, and psychological, and not merely methodological or technical in nature.[15]

The utilization of information is shaped by at least five types of factors.[16] These factors include (1) the characteristics of information, (2) dif-

---

[14] See Wholey, "Evaluability Assessment," pp. 44–49.

[15] See, for example, Carol H. Weiss, *Using Social Research in Public Policy Making* (Lexington, MA: D.C. Heath and Company, 1977); Charles E. Lindblom and David K. Cohen, *Usable Knowledge: Social Science and Social Problem Solving* (New Haven, CT: Yale University Press, 1979); and William N. Dunn and Burkart Holzner, "Knowledge in Society: Anatomy of an Emergent Field," *Knowledge in Society: The International Journal of Knowledge Transfer and Utilization*, 1, No. 1 (1988), 1–29.

[16] For an exploratory study of these factors, see William N. Dunn, "The Two-Communities Metaphor and Models of Knowledge Use: An Exploratory Case Survey," *Knowledge: Creation, Diffusion, Utilization*, 1, No. 4 (June 1980).

ferences in the modes of inquiry use to produce information, (3) the structure of policy problems, (4) variations in political and bureaucratic structures, and (5) the nature of interactions among policy analysts, policymakers, and other stakeholders.

Characteristics of Information

The characteristics of information produced by policy analyses frequently determine its utilization by policymakers. Information that conforms to the product specifications of policymakers is more likely to be utilized than information which does not, since product specifications are reflections of policymakers' needs, values, and perceived opportunities. Policymakers generally tend to value information that is embodied in personal verbal reports, rather than formal written documents, and expressed in a language that reflects concrete policy problems rather than the more abstract concerns of the social science disciplines.[17] Policymakers also attach greater value to information that is perceived as objective, that is, information that is accurate, precise, and generalizable to similar settings.[18]

Modes of Inquiry

The utilization of information by policymakers is also shaped by the process of inquiry used by analysts to produce and interpret that information. Information which conforms to standards of quality research and analysis is more likely to be utilized by policymakers. Yet there are widely differing views about the meaning of "quality." For many practitioners of policy research and analysis, quality is defined in terms of the use of social experimentation, random sampling, and quantitative measurement procedures.[19] The assumption here is that information utilization is a function of the degree to which policy research and analysis conforms to accepted scientific methods, provided that the resultant information is adapted to organizational constraints such as the need for timely information.

By contrast, other practitioners of policy research and analysis define quality in altogether different terms. Here quality is defined in terms which emphasize nonquantitative procedures designed to uncover subjective judgments about problems and potential solutions made by policymakers and other stakeholders.[20]

---

[17] See Mark van de Vall, Cheryl Bolas, and Thomas Kang, "Applied Social Research in Industrial Organizations: An Evaluation of Functions, Theory, and Methods," *The Journal of Applied Behavioral Science*, 12, No. 2 (1976), 158–77.

[18] See Nathan Caplan, Andrea Morrison, and Roger J. Stambaugh, *The Use of Social Science Knowledge in Policy Decisions at the National Level* (Ann Arbor, MI: Institute for Social Research, 1975).

[19] See I. N. Bernstein and H. E. Freeman, *Academic and Entrepreneurial Research* (New York: Russell Sage Foundation, 1975).

[20] See Rein and White, "Policy Research: Belief and Doubt;" Michael Q. Patton, *Alternative Evaluation Research Paradigm* (Grand Forks, ND: University of North Dakota, 1975); and H. Aeland, "Are Randomized Experiments the Cadillacs of Design?" *Policy Analysis*, 5 No. 2 (1979), 223–42.

Structure of Problems

The utilization of information by policymakers is also influenced by the appropriateness of the match between modes of inquiry and types of problems. Relatively well-structured problems involving consensus on goals, objectives, alternatives, and their consequences require different methodologies than do ill-structured problems. Ill-structured problems, whose essential characteristic is conflict, require methodologies which are holistic and which bring to bear multiple perspectives of the same problem situation in defining the nature of the problem itself.[21]

The distinction between well-structured and ill-structured problems is equivalent to the distinction between lower-level (micro) and higher-level (meta) problems. Meta-level problems involve issues of how to structure a problem, how to assist policymakers in knowing what should be known, and how to decide which aspects of a problem should be resolved on the basis of "conceptual" knowledge.[22] Most policy research and analysis is oriented toward the production of "instrumental" knowledge—that is, knowledge about the most appropriate means for attaining ends that are taken for granted. Such instrumental knowledge, since it is appropriate for well-structured problems at the micro-level, is less likely to be utilized by policymakers confronted by ill-structured problems which involve disagreement or conflict about the nature of problems and their potential solutions.

Political and Bureaucratic Structures

The utilization of information is also shaped by differences in the formal structures, procedures, and incentive systems of public organizations. The presence of policy-making elites, the bureaucratization of roles, the formalization of procedures, and the operation of incentive systems that reward conservatism and punish innovation all contribute to the underutilization and nonutilization of information produced by policy analysts. These and other factors which are external to policy analysis (external linkages) establish contraints and opportunities, creating a political and bureaucratic context for information utilization.[23]

Interactions among Stakeholders

The utilization of information by policymakers is also influenced by the nature and types of interaction among stakeholders in various phases

---

[21] Russell Ackoff, *Redesigning the Future: A Systems Approach to Societal Problems* (New York: Wiley, 1974); Ian I. Mitroff, *The Subjective Side of Science* (New York: American Elsevier Publishing Co., 1974); and Ian I. Mitroff and L. Vaughan Blankenship, "On the Methodology of the Holistic Experiment: An Approach to the Conceptualization of Large-Scale Social Experiments," *Technological Forecasting and Social Change*, 4 (1973), 339–53.

[22] See Nathan Caplan, "The Two-Communities Theory and Knowledge Utilization," *American Behavioral Scientist*, 22, No. 3 (1979), 459–70.

[23] See Robert F. Rich, *The Power of Social Science Information and Public Policymaking: The Case of the Continuous National Survey* (San Francisco: Jossey-Bass, 1981).

of the policy-making process.[24] Policy analysis is not simply a scientific and technical process; it is also a social and political process where the scope and intensity of interaction among stakeholders governs the way that information is produced, transformed, and utilized.

The interactive nature of policy analysis makes questions of information utilization highly complex ones. Policy analysts rarely produce information that is or can be used merely for "problem solving," in the narrow sense of discovering through analysis the most appropriate means to ends that are well defined and about which there is substantial consensus. Many of the most important policy problems, as we have seen in this book, are sufficiently complex, messy, and ill structured that the "problem-solving" model of policy analysis is inappropriate or simply inapplicable. For this reason policy analysis has been described throughout this book as an integrated process of inquiry where multiple methods (problem structuring, forecasting, recommendation, monitoring, evaluation) are used to continuously produce and transform information about policy problems, policy futures, policy actions, policy outcomes, and policy performance. Yet the interactive nature of policy-making also means that analysts critically assess and communicate policy-relevant knowledge as part of reasoned arguments and debates among competing stakeholders in the policy process.

SUMMARY

This concluding chapter has provided an overview of the nature, aims, and functions of evaluation, compared and contrasted three approaches to evaluation, and reviewed a number of specific techniques used in conjunction with these approaches. At this point you should be able to discuss the following principles and generalizations:

1. Monitoring answers the question: "What happened, how, and why?" Evaluation, by contrast, answers the question: "What difference does it make?"
2. While evaluation has several general meanings (appraisal, rating, assessment), evaluation in a more specific sense refers to the production of information about the extent to which policy outcomes contribute to the achievement of goals and objectives.
3. When policy outcomes do in fact contribute to the achievement of goals and objectives, we say that a policy or program has attained some significant level of performance, which means that policy problems have been at least partially resolved.
4. Evaluation has several characteristics that distinguish it from other policy-analytic methods: value focus; fact-value interdependence; present and past orientation; and value duality.
5. The main functions of evaluation in policy analysis are the provision of reliable and valid information about policy performance; the clarification and critique

---

[24] See Weiss, "Introduction," *Using Social Research in Public Policy Making*, pp. 13–15.

of values that underlie the choice of goals and objectives; and the provision of information for problem structuring and practical inference.

6.   Criteria for policy evaluation are the same as those for policy recommendation: effectiveness, efficiency, adequacy, equity, responsiveness, and appropriateness. The only difference is that in policy evaluation these criteria are applied retrospectively (*ex post*) to policy outcomes, rather than prospectively (*ex ante*) to policy actions.

7.   All evaluative claims involve factual as well as value premises. Yet many activities described as "evaluation" in policy analysis are essentially nonevaluative, since they are primarily concerned with the production of designative (factual) claims, rather than evaluative ones.

8.   There are three main approaches to evaluation in policy analysis: pseudo-evaluation, formal evaluation, and decision-theoretic evaluation. Each of these approaches has different aims, assumptions, and forms.

9.   Pseudo-evaluation is the equivalent of monitoring (Chapter 8), although formal and decision-theoretic evaluation presuppose that monitoring has already taken place.

10.   Decision-theoretic evaluation is a way to take into account and overcome several deficiencies of pseudo-evaluation and formal evaluation: underutilization and nonutilization of performance information; ambiguity of performance goals; and multiple conflicting objectives.

11.   Nearly all techniques for evaluating policy performance may also be used in conjunction with other policy-analytic methods. This highlights the interdependence of policy-analytic methods (problem structuring, forecasting, recommendation, monitoring, evaluation).

12.   Only one technique—user-survey analysis—has not already been described in connection with other methods. User-survey analysis is used in conjunction with evaluability assessment as one form of decision-theoretic evaluation.

13.   The distinction between cognitive and political aspects of policy processes is crucial for understanding the utilization, underutilization, and nonutilization of performance information by policymakers.

14.   The utilization of information is shaped by factors that are political, organizational, and social, and not those that are merely methodological or technical in nature. These factors may be grouped into five types: characteristics of information; differences in modes of inquiry used to produce information; the structure of policy problems; political and bureaucratic structures; and the nature of interactions among policy analysts, policymakers, and other stakeholders.

15.   The interactive nature of policy analysis makes questions of information utilization highly complex ones. Because most policy problems are complex, messy, or ill structured, the "problem-solving" model of policy analysis is inappropriate and inapplicable. For this reason policy analysis has been described throughout this book as an integrated process of inquiry where multiple methods are used to continuously produce, transform, and interpret information as part of reasoned arguments and debates among stakeholders in the policy process.

GLOSSARY

Evaluability Assessment: A set of procedures designed to analyze the decision-making system that is supposed to benefit from performance information and to clarify the goals, objectives, and assumptions against which performance is to be measured.

Evaluation Criteria: Particular rules or standards according to which policy outcomes are evaluated: effectiveness, efficiency, adequacy, equity, responsiveness, appropriateness.

Formative Evaluation: A type of formal evaluation that involves efforts to continuously monitor the accomplishment of formally announced goals and objectives.

Multiattribute Utility Analysis: A set of procedures designed to elicit from multiple stakeholders subjective judgments about the probability of occurrence and value of policy outcomes.

Summative Evaluation: A type of formal evaluation that involves the monitoring of efforts to achieve formal goals and objectives after a policy or program has been in place for a long period of time.

User-Survey Analysis: A set of procedures for collecting from intended users and other stakeholders information about the evaluability of a policy or program.

STUDY SUGGESTIONS

1. Compare and contrast evaluation and recommendation in terms of time and the types of claims produced by each policy-analytic method.

2. Many policy-program evaluations fail to recognize the latent purposes of evaluation, including a desire (a) to make programs look good by focusing on their surface characteristics ("eyewash"); (b) to cover up program failures ("whitewash"); (c) to destroy a program ("submarine"); (d) to engage in evaluation merely as a ritual that must be practiced to receive funding ("posture"); and (e) to postpone attempts to resolve problems ("postponement"). See Edward A. Suchman, "Action for What? A Critique of Evaluative Research," in *Evaluating Action Programs*, ed. Carol H. Weiss (Boston: Allyn and Bacon, 1972), p. 81. What problems does this raise for defining the objectives against which performance is to be evaluated?

3. Compare and contrast formative and summative evaluation. Which of these two types of evaluation provides performance information that is likely to be of most use to policymakers? Why?

4. What are the strengths and limitations of cost–benefit analysis as an approach to evaluation? (see Chapter 7). In your answer refer to contrasts among pseudo-evaluation, formal evaluation, and decision-theoretic evaluation.

5. Select a policy or program that you would like to evaluate. (a) Outline the specific steps you would take to conduct an evaluability assessment. (b) Outline the steps you would take in doing a multiattribute utility analysis of the same policy or program. (c) Indicate which of the two procedures is likely to yield the most reliable, valid, and useful results.

6. Select a program with which you are familiar, either because you have read about it or because you were actually involved. Prepare a short paper that outlines a plan, strategy, and procedures for evaluating this program. Refer to Appendix 1 in preparing your answer.

SUGGESTED READINGS

DOLBEARE, KENNETH, ed., *Public Policy Evaluation*. Beverly Hills, CA: Sage Publications, 1975.

DUNN, WILLIAM N., "Assessing the Impact of Policy Analysis: The Functions of Usable Ignorance," in *Advances in Policy Studies since 1950*. Vol. 10 of *Policy Studies Review Annual*, ed. William N. Dunn and Rita Mae Kelly. New Brunswick, NJ: Transaction Books, 1992, pp. 419–44.

GUTTENTAG, MARCIA and ELMER L. STRUENING, eds., *Handbook of Evaluation Research*. 2 Vols. Beverly Hills, CA: Sage Publications, 1975.

LINDBLOM, CHARLES E. and DAVID K. COHEN, *Usable Knowledge: Social Science and Social Problem Solving.* New Haven, CT: Yale University Press, 1979.

PATTON, MICHAEL Q., *Utilization-Focused Evaluation.* Beverly Hills, CA: Sage Publications, 1979.

RICH, ROBERT F., *The Power of Social Science Knowledge in Public Policy Making.* San Francisco: Jossey-Bass, 1981.

ROGERS, JAMES M., *The Impact of Policy Analysis.* Pittsburgh, PA: University of Pittsburgh Press, 1988.

RUTMAN, LEONARD, ed., *Evaluation Research Methods: A Basic Guide.* Beverly Hills, CA: Sage Publications, 1977.

WEBBER, DAVID J., "The Distribution and Use of Policy Knowledge in the Policy Process," in *Advances in Policy Studies since 1950.* Vol. 10 of *Policy Studies Review Annual,* ed. William N. Dunn and Rita Mae Kelly. New Brunswick, NJ: Transaction Books, 1992, pp. 383–418.

WEISS, CAROL H., *Evaluation Research.* Englewood Cliffs, NJ: Prentice Hall, 1972.

WEISS, CAROL H., ed., *Using Social Research in Public Policy Making.* Lexington, MA: D.C. Heath and Company, 1977.

Appendix 1

The Policy Issue Paper

A policy issue paper should provide answers to a number of questions. What actual or potential courses of action are the objects of conflict or disagreement among stakeholders? In what different ways may the problem be defined? What is the scope and severity of the problem? How is the problem likely to change in future months or years? What goals and objectives should be pursued to solve the problem? How can the degree of success in achieving objectives be measured? What activities are now under way to resolve the problem? What new or adapted policy alternatives should be considered as ways to resolve the problem? Which alternative(s) are preferable, given certain goals and objectives?

In answering these questions the analyst needs to acquire knowledge and skills in developing appropriate written materials and communicating results through policy presentations and other forms of interactive communication. Only recently have such knowledge and skills become integral parts of instructional programs in university departments and professional schools that deal with public policy. Policy analysis, although it draws from and builds on virtually all social science disciplines, differs from those disciplines because it seeks to improve as well as understand policy-making processes. In this respect, policy analysis has characteristics that make it an "applied" rather than "basic" policy discipline.[1] Analysts who want to be competent observers, interpreters, and critics must acquire much of the knowledge and many of the skills provided in basic policy disciplines. But the mission of policy analysis remains "applied" rather than "basic," a mission that places unusual responsibilities on analysts. Characteristics of the two kinds of policy disciplines are displayed in the following table.

Two Kinds of Policy Disciplines

CHARACTERISTIC	BASIC	APPLIED
ORIGIN OF PROBLEMS	• University Colleagues	• Governmental Clients and Citizens
TYPICAL METHODS	• Quantitative Modelling	• Development of Sound Arguments
TYPE OF RESEARCH	• Original Data Collection	• Synthesis and Evaluation of Existing Data
PRIMARY AIM	• Improve Theory	• Improve Practice
COMMUNICATIONS MEDIA	• Article or Book	• Policy Memo or Issue Paper
SOURCE OF INCENTIVES	• University Departments	• Government Departments and Citizen Groups

FOCUS AND FORMS OF THE POLICY ISSUE PAPER

The policy issue paper may address policy problems in a variety of issue areas: health, education, welfare, crime, labor, energy, foreign aid, national security, human rights, and so on. Papers in any one of these issue areas may focus on problems at one or more levels of government. Health and air pollution, for example, are international, national, and local in scope. The issue paper may take a number of specific forms, depending on the audience and the particular issue at hand. Thus, issue papers may be presented in the form of "staff reports," "briefing papers," "options papers," or so-called "white papers." An illustrative list of issues that may serve as the focus of a policy issue paper is presented below.

— Which of several alternative contracts should be accepted by a union bargaining team?

---

[1] The terms "basic" and "applied" are used for convenience only. It is widely acknowledged that these two orientations toward science overlap in practice. Indeed, there is much evidence to support the conclusion that many of the most important theoretical, methodological, and substantive advances in the "basic" social sciences originated in "applied" work on practical problems and conflicts. See, especially, Karl W. Deutsch, Andrei S. Markovits, and John Platt, *Advances in the Social Sciences, 1900–1980: What, Who, Where, How?* (Lanham, MD: University Press of America and Abt Books, 1986).

— Should the mayor increase expenditures on road maintenance?

— Should the city manager install a computerized management information system?

— Which public transportation plan should the mayor submit for federal funding?

— Should a state agency establish a special office to recruit minorities and women for civil service positions?

— Should a citizens' group support environmental protection legislation now before Congress?

— Should the governor veto a tax bill passed by the state legislature?

— Should an agency director support a plan for flexible working hours (flextime)?

— Should a legislator support a bill restricting the sale of hand guns?

— Should the president withhold foreign aid from countries that violate human rights?

— Should the United Nations General Assembly condemn the violation of human rights in a particular country?

— Should the United States withdraw from the International Labor Organization?

— Should taxes on foreign investments of multinational corporations registered in the United States be increased?

ELEMENTS OF THE POLICY ISSUE PAPER

A policy issue paper should be as complete as time and available information permit. An issue paper should "explore the problem at a depth sufficient to give the reader a good idea of its dimensions and the possible scope of the solution, so that it might be possible for a decision maker to conclude either to do nothing further or to commission a definitive study looking toward some action recommendation."[2] In this author's experience, most issue papers deal primarily with the formulation of a problem and possible solutions. Only rarely does the issue paper reach definitive conclusions or recommendations. While an issue paper may contain recommendations and outline plans for monitoring and evaluating policy outcomes, it is essentially the first phase of an in-depth policy analysis that may be undertaken at a later time.

In preparing an issue paper the analyst should be reasonably sure that all major questions have been addressed. Although issue papers will vary with the nature of the problem being investigated, most issue papers contain a number of standard elements.[3] These elements have been organized around the framework for policy analysis presented in the text.

---

[2] E. S. Quade, *Analysis for Public Decisions* (New York: American Elsevier Publishing Co., 1975), p. 69.

[3] Compare Quade, *Analysis for Public Decisions*, pp. 68–82; and Harry Hatry and others, *Program Analysis for State and Local Governments* (Washington, DC: The Urban Institute, 1976), appendix B, pp. 139–43.

ELEMENTS OF ISSUE PAPER	POLICY-INFORMATIONAL COMPONENT	POLICY-ANALYTIC METHOD
Letter of transmittal		
Executive summary		

I. Background of the problem
  A. Description of problem situation
  B. Outcomes of prior efforts to solve problem
	Policy outcomes	Monitoring

II. Scope and severity of problem
  A. Assessment of past policy performance
  B. Significance of problem situation
  C. Need for analysis
	Policy performance	Evaluation

III. Problem statement
  A. Definition of problem
  B. Major stakeholders
  C. Goals and objectives
  D. Measures of effectiveness
  E. Potential solutions
	Policy problems	Problem structuring

IV. Policy alternatives
  A. Description of alternatives
  B. Comparison of future consequences
  C. Spillovers and externalities
  D. Constraints and political feasibility
	Policy futures	Forecasting

V. Policy recommendations
  A. Criteria for recommending alternatives
  B. Description of preferred alternative(s)
  C. Outline of implementational strategy
  D. Provisions for monitoring and evaluation
  E. Limitations and unanticipated consequences
	Policy actions	Recommendation

References		
Appendices		

Observe that each element of the issue paper requires different policy-analytic methods to produce and transform information about policy outcomes, policy performance, policy problems, policy futures, and policy actions. A policy issue paper, however, has one major characteristic not shared by integrated policy analysis. The issue paper is essentially a prospective (*ex ante*) investigation that begins with limited information about past policy actions, outcomes, and performance and ends with as much information as possible about the nature of policy problems, policy futures, and policy actions to be taken in future.

A CHECKLIST

This checklist is designed as a practical guide to the preparation and self-evaluation of policy issue papers. Items in the checklist are based on guidelines for preparing policy issue papers presented earlier in this appendix. The checklist operationalizes these guidelines, provides brief examples, and contains a rating scale that may be used to evaluate the adequacy of specific elements of the paper. Remember, however, that some elements in the checklist may not be appropriate for each and every paper. The checklist should therefore be used in a flexible and creative manner.

RATING SCALE

1 = totally adequate

2 = adequate

3 = inadequate

4 = totally inadequate

0 = not applicable

ELEMENT OF POLICY ISSUE PAPER	EXAMPLE/NOTE	RATING
Letter of transmittal		
1. Are all relevant stakeholders expected to act on the paper addressed?	A paper on local law enforcement might be addressed to the chief of police, the mayor, and the director of public safety.	[ ]
2. Does the letter describe all attached materials?	"Enclosed please find a policy issue paper on options to increase the productivity of municipal employees. An executive summary of this paper is also included, along with relevant statistical materials appended to the text."	[ ]
3. Does the letter specify who is expected to take action, how, and when?	"We look forward to your reply well in advance of the meeting scheduled for June 15."	[ ]
Executive summary		
4. Are all elements of the issue paper described in the executive summary?	Every element of the issue paper (Source and Background of the Problem, the Policy Problem, and so on) should be included in the summary.	[ ]

ELEMENT OF POLICY ISSUE PAPER	EXAMPLE/NOTE	RATING
5. Is the summary clear, concise, and specific?	"This paper reviews problems of air pollution over the past ten years, showing that the level of industrial pollutants has increased by more than 200 percent in the 1968–1978 period. . . ."	[ ]
6. Is the summary understandable to all who will read it?	The point here is to avoid unnecessary jargon, long sentences, and complex arguments as much as possible.	[ ]
7. Are recommendations appropriately highlighted in the summary?	"In conclusion, we recommend that funds in the range of $15,000–20,000 be allocated to conduct an assessment of recreational needs in the Oakland area."	[ ]
I. Background of the problem		
8. Are all dimensions of the problem situation described?	Increasing crime rates may be analyzed in conjunction with data on unemployment, police recruitment, citizen surveys, migration, and so on.	[ ]
9. Have outcomes of prior efforts to resolve problems in the area been described?	"Similar training programs have been implemented in New York, Florida, and California, at a cost of $4,000–5,000 per trainee."	[ ]
10. Is there a clear assessment of past policy performance?	"Training programs in New York and California resulted in a 1 percent reduction in hard-core unemployment and were judged to be highly successful."	[ ]
II. Scope and severity of problem		
11. Is the scope and severity of the problem situation clearly described?	"Problems of industrial pollution are more severe today than at any time in our history and affect the physical well-being of 60 percent of the population. The resolution of these problems is an urgent matter that calls for timely and decisive action."	[ ]
III. Problem statement		
12. Is the problem clearly stated?	"The problem addressed in this paper is how best to satisfy the need for increased fiscal accountability among local governments in the region."	[ ]

ELEMENT OF POLICY ISSUE PAPER	EXAMPLE/NOTE	RATING
13. Is the issue clearly stated?	"The issue addressed in this paper is whether the state's Department of Community Affairs should increase its technical assistance to local governments in the area of financial management."	[ ]
14. Is the approach to analysis clearly specified?	"In addressing this issue we have employed cost-effectiveness analysis as a way to determine the levels of investment necessary to train 10,000 local officials in cash management techniques."	[ ]
15. Are all major stakeholders identified and prioritized?	The task here is to identify all persons and groups who significantly affect and are significantly affected by the formulation and implementation of policies. Stakeholders who are only marginally influential (or affected) may be dropped from the analysis, but this requires prioritization.	[ ]
16. Are goals and objectives clearly specified?	"The goal of this policy is to improve the physical security of the community. The objective is to reduce reported crimes by 10 percent or more in the 1979–80 period."	[ ]
17. Are measures of effectiveness clearly specified?	Here there are many choices: benefit-cost ratios, net benefits, distributional benefits, and so on.	[ ]
18. Are all sets of potential solutions outlined?	"Any effort to reduce crime in the area should take into account the effectiveness of law enforcement programs, the unemployment rate, population density, and urbanization."	[ ]

IV. Policy alternatives

19. Are alternative solutions specified?	"Three policy alternatives are analyzed in the course of this paper: educational programs to alert citizens to the role they can play in crime control; policy training programs; and advanced crime control technology."	[ ]
20. Are alternatives systematically compared in terms of their probable costs and effectiveness?	"Program A has a benefit–cost ratio which is twice that of program B."	[ ]

ELEMENT OF POLICY ISSUE PAPER	EXAMPLE/NOTE	RATING
21. Are relevant spillovers and externalities included in the analysis of alternatives?	"The early childhood educational program is not only cost–effective. It will also produce spillovers in the form of increased participation of family members in the school. At the same time there are important externalities in the form of increased costs for transportation to and from school."	[ ]
22. Are all relevant constraints taken into account?	These may be financial (for example, fixed costs), legal (for example, laws proscribing certain actions), or political (for example, lack of political support).	[ ]
23. Have alternatives been systematically compared in terms of political feasibility?	The point here is to make informed judgments about the probable support, relevance, and influence of key stakeholders in gaining acceptance for and implementing each alternative.	[ ]

V. Policy recommendations

24. Are all relevant criteria for recommending alternatives clearly specified?	Criteria may include: net welfare improvement; distributional improvement; cost effectiveness; and so on.	[ ]
25. Has the preferred alternative been clearly described?	"We therefore recommend that the second alternative be adopted and implemented, since it is likely to be more cost-effective and is politically feasible under present conditions."	[ ]
26. Is a strategy for implementation clearly outlined?	"The proposed policy should be implemented by the Department of Labor and state employment offices. Implementation should be phased over a period of three years and focus on cities with more than 50,000 persons."	[ ]
27. Are provisions made for monitoring and evaluating policies?	"The state employment offices should establish special units to engage in process and outcome evaluations, at intervals of 30 days. Results of monitoring and evaluation should be stored in a management information system and reports should be filed quarterly."	[ ]

ELEMENT OF POLICY ISSUE PAPER	EXAMPLE/NOTE	RATING
28. Are limitations and possible unintended consequences taken into account?	Here the point is to specify how limitations of the analysis affect the confidence one has in the conclusions. Possible unintended consequences (for example, abuses of social welfare programs, nuclear meltdowns, and so on) should also be thought through.	[ ]

References

29. Are references cited in the text included in the appropriate form?	It is preferable to use the "name–date" bibliographic form in a policy issue paper. Only the name of the author, the date of publication, and page numbers will be included in the text, with no footnotes at the bottom of the page. For example: (Jones, 1975: 20–23). The citation in the references will read: Jones, John (1975), *A Report on the Fiscal Crisis*. Washington, DC: Fiscal Institute.	[ ]

Appendices

30. Is relevant supporting information (statistics, legislation, documents, correspondence) included?	All statistical tables should be properly numbered and headed and the source of data specified at the bottom of the table. Legislation, documents, and correspondence should be identified as to its source, date, author(s), and so on.	[ ]

Appendix 2

The Executive Summary

The executive summary is a synopsis of the major elements of the policy issue paper. The executive summary typically has the following elements:

- Purpose of the issue paper or study being summarized
- Background of the problem or question addressed
- Major findings or conclusions
- Approach to analysis or methodology
- Recommendations(s)

The following executive summary provides a synopsis of a 90-page study titled *Freight Trucking: Promising Approach for Predicting Carriers' Safety Risks* (Washington, DC: U.S. General Accounting Office, Program Evaluation and Methodology Division, April 1991).

EXECUTIVE SUMMARY

PURPOSE

Freight trucks pose special safety risks. Over 4,000 people are killed annually in accidents related to heavy trucks. Fatalities are about twice as likely in accidents involving tractor-trailer trucks as in those involving automobiles only.

In recent years, the Congress has approved legislation to prevent situations that give rise to unsafe trucking operations. As a means toward this end, the House Committee on Public Works and Transportation and its Surface Transportation Subcommittee requested that GAO determine whether certain economic and other conditions could be used as predictors of safety outcomes. GAO's study had the following three objectives: (1) to formulate a predictive model specifying hypothetical relationships between safety and a set of conditions in the trucking industry; (2) to assess the availability and quality of federal data required to test the model; and (3) to use available data, to the extent possible, to develop a set of indicators that would predict safety problems in the freight-trucking industry.

The value of a workable model is that the Department of Transportation (DOT) could use it as an early warning system for predicting safety problems.

BACKGROUND

Although the Motor Carrier Act of 1980 codified the relaxation of federal economic control over the trucking industry, the Congress approved legislation in the 1980's designed to monitor and prevent situations that result in unsafe trucking operations.

GAO developed a model that hypothetically links changes in economic conditions to declining safety performance in the freight-trucking industry. (See pages 18 through 23.) The hypothesis is that a decline in economic performance among motor carriers will lead to declining safety performance in one or more ways, described by five submodels: (1) a lowering of the average quality of driver performance, (2) downward wage pressures encouraging noncompliance by drivers with safety regulations, (3) less management emphasis on safety practices, (4) deferred truck maintenance and replacement, and/or (5) introduction of larger, heavier, multitrailer trucks.

RESULTS IN BRIEF

GAO'S preliminary findings, using data on 537 carriers drawn from both DOT and the Interstate Commerce Commission (ICC), are that seven financial ratios show promise as predictors of safety problems in the interstate trucking industry. For example, three measures of profitability—return on equity, operating ratio, and net profit margin—were associated with subsequent safety problems as measured by accident rates. The data agreed with GAO'S model for five of seven financial ratios: Firms in the weakest financial position had the highest subsequent accident rates. GAO also used a number of other factors to predict safety outcomes, including the following. First, the smallest carriers, as a group, had an accident rate that exceeded the total group's rate by 20 percent. Second, firms operating closer to a broker model—that is, those that rely on leased equipment and/or drivers to move freight—had a group accident rate 15 to 21 percent above the total group's rate.

With regard to two of the submodels (driver quality

and compliance), driver's age, years of experience, and compensation were all good predictors of safety problems. GAO'S evidence is generally consistent with the model's hypotheses since younger, less experienced drivers and lower paid company drivers posed greater-than-average accident risks.

GAO'S study thus demonstrates the potential for developing preventive strategies geared to differences among carriers and drivers, and it also suggests the importance of monitoring by DOT of the variations in carrier accident rates in order to have a sound basis for developing those preventive strategies.

GAO'S ANALYSIS

Available Federal Data

To identify and evaluate data to test a carrier-safety model, GAO reviewed the literature, talked with industry experts, and conducted interviews with federal officials responsible for maintaining data sets. GAO then combined data provided by DOT and ICC to conduct analyses. GAO found that existing federal data sets did not bring together the necessary data to fully test this model. The federal collection of truck accident data was essentially independent of the gathering of economic data, and combining the two types of data from separate federal sources was generally impractical. Most importantly, the federal data allowing calculation of accident rates for individual motor carriers did not provide for a generalizable picture of a definable segment of the industry or an analysis of safety trends over time. The needed information about truck drivers and their accident rates was also lacking. As a result, GAO could test only two of the submodels (by obtaining data from two private surveys). One unfortunate implication of this is that even if all of the submodels do prove to have predictive validity, existing federal data bases still do not contain sufficient information to convert the model to an effective monitoring system. (See chapter 3.)

Economic Predictors

GAO judged that the best available accident rate data to combine with ICC's extensive financial data are those obtained from DOT's safety audits. Since the safety audits were discontinued after October of 1986, GAO's analysis was limited to the larger, for-hire ICC carriers with financial reporting requirements that were also audited by DOT during the years 1984–86.

GAO found evidence among these interstate carriers that carriers in different markets or different financial situations pose different safety risks. For example, carriers with losses of 0.3 percent or more on equity had a group accident rate (rates are defined as accidents per million miles) 2 years later that was 27 percent above the overall group's rate. (See pages 34 through 47.)

Predictors from the Driver Quality Submodel

One of the private surveys GAO used supplied data on approximately 1,300 interstate drivers serving Florida in 1989. As was predicted by the driver quality submodel, GAO found that younger and less experienced truck drivers were more likely to be in accidents. For example, the odds for drivers aged 21 to 39 having been involved in an accident in the prior 12 months were higher than the odds for drivers over age 49 by a factor of 1.6. (See pages 50 through 54.)

Predictors from the Driver Compliance Submodel

The other private survey GAO used yielded pertinent data from a national sample of drivers in rail-competitive trucking. GAO found that lower paid drivers were more likely than their higher paid counterparts to violate safety regulations, but only in the case of company drivers and excluding owner-operators (those drivers owning their own trucks). Among company drivers, those earning less than 18.5 cents per mile had about twice the odds of having received either speeding or hours-of-service citations (or warnings) in the past 90 days.

RECOMMENDATION TO THE SECRETARY OF TRANSPORTATION

The monitoring, enforcement, and policy-making value of much of the truck accident information gathered by DOT is lessened by the inability to construct accident rates. Although DOT already collects accident *data*, the mileage data required to calculate accident *rates* are not routinely collected from carriers. As a first step toward reducing the accidents of motor carriers, GAO therefore recommends that the Secretary of Transportation direct the Administrator of the Federal Highway Administration (FHWA) to require that mileage data on motor carriers falling under FHWA regulations be obtained annually to improve accident analysis. How such data are obtained may depend on a number of considerations, such as costs and respondent burden, but the foremost consideration should be that data obtained allow for the calculation of accident rates for carriers falling under FHWA safety regulations in order to support monitoring and enforcement efforts and to permit analysis of safety trends.

In implementing GAO's recommendation, DOT should consider further development of predictors of safety problems. For example, GAO's analysis suggests that indicators of financial health, market segment, and driver information may be useful to DOT in identifying higher risk groups of carriers for closer monitoring or enforcement efforts. More work needs to be done in validating these preventive indicators and identifying other predictors of safety outcomes. DOT should consider advancing this work on preventive indicators because, if successful, it would signal the policy changes needed to avoid or abate the predicted unsafe conditions. GAO's demonstration illustrates the kind of work that DOT will be able to do in prevention, particularly if better information on accident rates and economic and other intermediate factors is developed. (See pages 61 through 64.)

Appendix 3

Letter of Transmittal

The letter of transmittal accompanies the policy issue paper or study. The letter of transmittal usually has the following elements:

- The letterhead or address of the person(s) transmitting the issue paper or study
- The name, formal title, and address of the person(s) or client(s) who requested the issue paper or study
- A short paragraph stating the question or problem that the person(s) or client(s) expected the analyst to address
- A brief summary of the most important conclusions and recommendations of the issue paper or study
- A review of arrangements for further communication or work with the client(s)—for example, a scheduled briefing on the results of the issue paper or study
- A concluding statement indicating where and how the analyst can be reached to answer any questions
- A signature with the name and title of the analyst or the analyst's supervisor

A letter of transmittal used to forward *Science and Engineering Indicators, 1991* (Washington, D.C.: National Science Foundation for the National Science Board, 1991) is exhibited on the next page.

December 1, 1991

My Dear Mr. President:

In accordance with Sec. 4(j) (1) of the National
Science Foundation Act of 1950, as amended, it is my
honor to transmit to you, and through you to the
Congress, the tenth in the series of biennial Science
Indicators reports--*Science & Engineering
Indicators-1991.*
These reports are designed to provide public and
private policymakers with a broad base of quantitative
information about U.S. science and engineering
research and education and about U.S. technology in a
global context.
U.S. Government and industry have led the world in
recognizing the importance of science and technology
for achieving national objectives. Their support for
research and development (R&D), and especially basic
research, is reflected in the data in these pages. But
priorities and programs must be constantly redefined
and reshaped to adapt to rapidly changing global
economic, political, and social conditions. This
report pulls together in a convenient format much of
the data about science and technology pertinent to
these decisionmaking processes.
The coverage is broad. U.S. and comparative
foreign trends are tracked in precollege and college-
level science, mathematics, and engineering education;
scientists and engineers in the labor force; support
and performance of research and development, with
special detail on academic R&D; technological
innovation and the international competitiveness of
U.S. technology; and public attitudes toward, and
knowledge about, science and technology.
Mr. President, the National Science Board is proud
to call your attention to the fact that this tenth
edition of the biennial Indicators marks 20 years
since the Board initiated the report. It is widely
used around the world for policymaking as well as
serving as a model for national science policy data
compilations. My National Science Board colleagues and
I hope that your Administration and the Congress will

continue to find this report useful as you seek
solutions to our national problems.

Respectfully yours,

James J. Duderstadt
Chairman, National Science Board

The Honorable
The President of the United States
The White House
Washington, DC 20500

Appendix 4

The Policy Memorandum

It is widely but mistakenly believed that most policy analysts spend their time developing policy issue papers, studies, and reports. In fact, the primary activity of most analysts is the policy memorandum. Whereas the issue paper, study, or report is a long-term activity involving the conduct of policy research and analysis over some months, the policy memorandum is prepared over a short period of time—usually no more than one month, but often a matter of days. The difference between the issue paper, study, or report, on one hand, and the policy memorandum on the other reflect two contrasting styles of policy analysis. (See Appendix 1).

The policy memorandum beginning on the next page is a concise summary of a briefing report and accompanying backup documents titled *Budget Issues: Immigration to the United States—Federal Budget Impacts, 1984–1995* (Washington, DC: U.S. General Accounting Office, Accounting and Financial Management Division, August 1986). The policy memorandum, from a practical point of view, is an abbreviated executive summary (see Appendix 2).

B-223169

August 28, 1986

The Honorable Butler Derrick
Chairman, Task Force on the
    Budget Process
Committee on the Budget
House of Representatives

Dear Mr. Chairman:

In response to your letter of May 8, 1985, we have
examined the potential impacts of immigration on the
federal budget over the next 10 years. This effort was
undertaken with dual objectives: obtaining the best
possible estimate of budgetary impacts despite known
data inadequacies and beginning the development of a
methodology for dealing with long-term, crosscutting
issues of budgetary significance, of which immigration
is a prime example. On May 1, 1986, we presented a
briefing to you and other task force members and staff
on the results of our study. This report is a written
version of that briefing. We have also included
additional detail on the budgetary impact of
immigration on state and local governments.

Our study established fiscal year 1984 as a baseline.
We identified, and where necessary estimated, major
federal immigrant-related outlays and revenues for
that period. We then projected these data to yield
1990 and 1995 estimates under three different sets of
assumptions (scenarios) as to the future social,
economic, and political environment. These projections
are not intended as forecasts but were developed to
provide illustrative ranges. We also sought similar
data for selected programs and localities in the five
most impacted states, for illustrative purposes, but
we made no projections at this level.

Although there are constraints and limitations to our
analysis, it demonstrates that significant budgetary
impacts of immigration exist at the federal level, in
terms of both outlays and revenues. Dollar amounts can
be assigned to such impacts only if major assumptions
are made concerning immigrant participation in major

social and income security programs. This is due to
the uncertainties of population size and
characteristics in 1984, as well as to the lack of
direct information regarding immigrant-related outlays
and revenues, data gaps which are even more apparent
in the out year projections. We assumed, therefore,
that these participation rates would be comparable, on
the average, to those of U.S. citizens. We could not
test this hypothesis, and expert opinion varies.

Using these assumptions, we found that for fiscal year
1984 in the programs we examined

--per capita federal outlays for immigrants were
   roughly comparable to those for average U.S.
   residents;

--per capita, immigrants contributed fewer revenues
   to the federal government than average U.S.
   residents; and

--total immigrant-related outlays differed only
   slightly from total immigrant-related revenues.

Under all three scenarios examined, these observations
remain valid for 1990 and 1995, although uncertainty
increases.

Regarding the broader methodological interests which
it was designed to explore, this study of a
crosscutting issue has both value and limitations.
While specific total dollar amounts cannot be assigned
on any supportable basis, minimum outlays and revenues
can be identified, ranges can be estimated, and
comparisons can be drawn based on explicit
assumptions. Because both federal outlays and revenues
are significantly affected by immigration and remain
roughly in balance, the committee may wish to monitor
the key conditions and trends to determine whether
this balance is being maintained. Thus, we believe we
have demonstrated the feasibility of this approach,
but its usefulness will vary with the circumstances.

I would be pleased to discuss this information with
you further at your convenience. As agreed with your
office, we have not obtained agency comments on this
report. We are sending copies of this report to
interested parties, and copies will be made available
to others upon request.

If you or your staff have any questions on this report, please call me at 275-9455.

Sincerely yours,

Kenneth W. Hunter
Assistant to the Director

Appendix 5

Planning Oral Briefings

Written documents are only one of the principal means for communicating the results of policy analysis. The other is the oral briefing. Although the oral briefing or presentation has most of the same elements as the issue paper, the approach to planning and delivering an oral presentation is quite different. One of the best available sources of advice on how to plan an oral briefing or presentation is a software package called *Presentation Planner* (Pitsford, NY: Discus Electronic Training, Eastman Technology, Inc.).

The elements of an oral briefing typically include the following:

- Opening and greeting to participants
- Background of the briefing
- Major findings of issue paper, study, or report
- Approach and methods
- Data used as basis for the analysis
- Recommendations
- Questions from participants
- Closing

As we saw in Chapter 1, an essential aspect of oral communications—and the use of knowledge generated by means of policy analysis—is knowing the audience. Here a series of important questions should be asked prior to the briefing. How large is the audience? How many members of the audience are experts on the problem you are addressing in the briefing? What percent of the audience understands your research methods? Are you credible to members of the audience? Does the audience prefer detailed or general information? Where does the briefing fall in the policymaking process? At the agenda setting phase? The implementation phase?

Answers to these questions govern the strategy and tactics of communication appropriate for the particular audience. For example, if the audience is a medium-sized group with 20 to 25 persons, the diversity of the audience calls for specific communications strategies and tactics:[1]

- Circulate background materials before the meeting so that everyone will start from a common base.
- Tell the group that the strategy selected is designed to meet the objectives of the group as a whole but that it may not satisfy everyone's needs.
- Focus on the agendas of key policymakers, even if you lose the rest of the audience.

Another common problem in giving oral briefings is that policymakers may bring their own staff experts to the briefing. If a high percentage of the audience has expertise in the area you are addressing, the following strategies and tactics are appropriate:

- Avoid engaging in a "knowledge contest" with subject experts by focusing on the purpose of the presentation.
- Capitalize on the group's expertise by focusing on findings and recommendations.
- Avoid a lengthy presentation of background material and description of methods.
- Attempt to generate dialogue and a productive debate on policy options.

An equally important problem in oral briefings is understanding individual members of the group.[2] For example, it is important to know if the immediate clients for policy analysis are:

- Experts in the problem area.
- Familiar with your analytic methods.
- Influential participants in the policy-making process.
- Oriented toward detailed or broad information.
- Faced with high, medium, or low stakes in the problem.
- Politically important to the success of your recommendations.

Finally, oral briefings are based on various kinds of graphic displays.[3]

---

[1] Adapted from *Presentation Planner*, Group Analysis Menu.

[2] *Presentation Planner*, Individual Questions Menu.

[3] *Presentation Planner*, Graphics Submenu.

The most common of these is the transparency used with an overhead projector. In using overhead transparencies it is important to recognize that they are not appropriate if you want an informal style of presentation—overheads tend to make briefings very formal and make open dialogue difficult. It is also important to observe the following guidelines in using transparencies:

- Keep transparencies simple, with condensed and highlighted text.
- Use clear, bold, uncluttered letters and lines of text.
- Highlight important points and use different colors if available.
- Limit the text on any page to a maximum of 10 lines.
- Be sure the width of the screen is at least one-sixth of the distance between the screen and the farthest viewer.
- Make sure that the nearest viewer is a minimum of two screen widths from the screen.
- Remain on the same overhead for a minimum of two minutes to give viewers time to read plus an additional 30 seconds to study the content.
- Leave the room lights *on*—overheads are not films.
- Turn off the overhead projector when you want to redirect attention back to you and reestablish eye contact.

These are but a few of the strategies and tactics that are appropriate for different audiences and communications media. Given the goal of selecting communications media and products that match the characteristics of the audience, there is today a rich array of techniques for the visual display of information.[4] Appropriate computer graphics programs are also widely available.[5]

Many types of visual displays are available to the analyst who wishes to effectively communicate complex ideas. Examples of the following visual displays (created with *Harvard Graphics*) are provided below:

- Bar Charts
- Pie Charts
- Frequency Histograms
- Relative Frequency Histograms
- Ogives
- Scatter Plots
- Time-Series Graphs
- Graphs With Data Tables

These displays are useful for effectively communicating simple as well as complex aspects of policy variables. In most policy presentations, how-

---

[4] An excellent source on these questions is Edward R. Tufte, *The Visual Display of Quantitative Information* (Cheshire, CT: Graphics Press, 1983).

[5] An outstanding, user-friendly graphics program is *Harvard Graphics* (Mountain View, CA: SPC Software Publishing Co., Version 2.3, 1990).

ever, a key visual display is one that summarizes relationships between two or more alternatives and their respective impacts. The options–impacts matrix (see below), which is a rectangular array of policy alternatives by anticipated impacts, is well suited for this purpose. The matrix provides a concise visual map of the range of impacts associated with alternatives. The preferred impacts may be shaded, as below, so that participants in a presentation can easily examine the pattern of tradeoffs between impacts before they have been compressed into an index or ratio (for example, a benefit-cost ratio), which frequently obscures issues and prevents informed discussion.

Options–Impacts Matrix

POLICY IMPACT	POLICY ALTERNATIVES	
	55 MPH	65 MPH
TRAVEL TIME IN HOURS	22.6 Billion	20.2 Billion
GALLONS GASOLINE CONSUMED	81.6 Billion	87.1 Billion
CHANGE IN AIR POLLUTION	1 % Decrease	3 % Increase
TRAFFIC FATALITIES	45,200	54,100
INJURIES	1,800,000	2,000,000
PUBLIC SUPPORT	70 %	30 %

NOTE: Shaded boxes are preferred impacts.

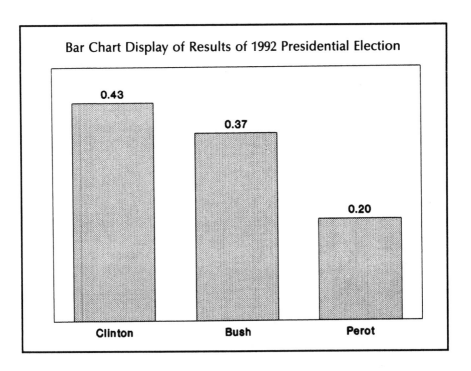

Bar Chart Display of Results of 1992 Presidential Election

0.43 Clinton
0.37 Bush
0.20 Perot

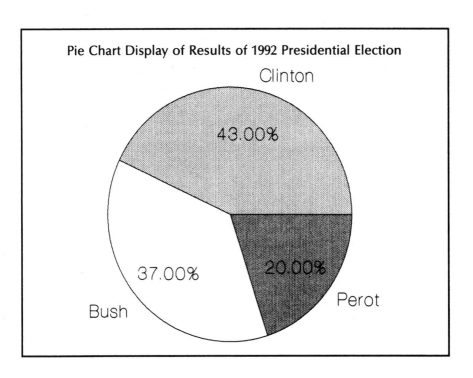

Pie Chart Display of Results of 1992 Presidential Election

Clinton 43.00%
Bush 37.00%
Perot 20.00%

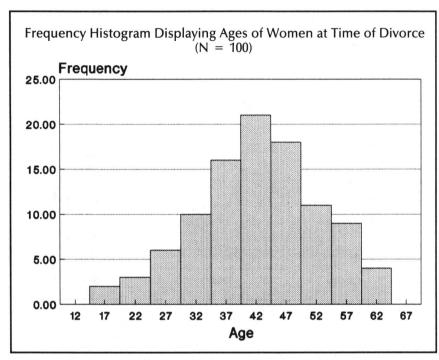

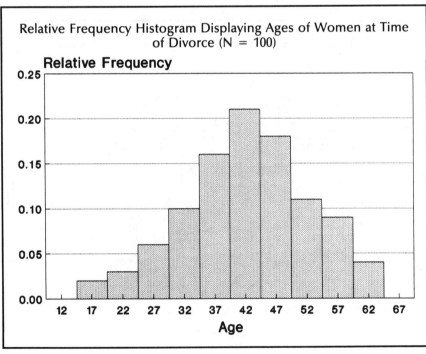

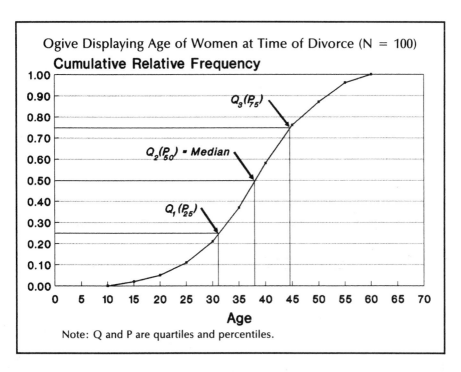

Ogive Displaying Age of Women at Time of Divorce (N = 100)

Note: Q and P are quartiles and percentiles.

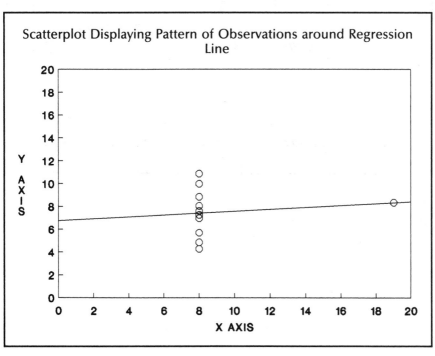

Scatterplot Displaying Pattern of Observations around Regression Line

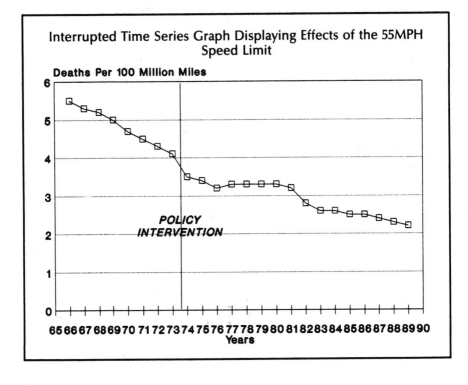

Interrupted Time Series Graph Displaying Effects of the 55MPH
Speed Limit

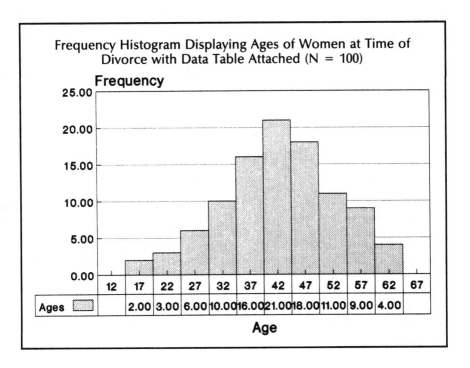

Frequency Histogram Displaying Ages of Women at Time of Divorce with Data Table Attached (N = 100)

	12	17	22	27	32	37	42	47	52	57	62	67
Ages		2.00	3.00	6.00	10.00	16.00	21.00	18.00	11.00	9.00	4.00	

Appendix 6

MYSTAT: Useful Routines for Policy Analysis

This appendix shows how to apply MYSTAT routines to some common statistical problems encountered in policy analysis. This demonstration of MYSTAT routines uses data on the 55 mph speed limit (National Maximum Speed Limit) available through government agencies such as the U.S. Department of Transportation and case materials published in articles and books on the subject.[1]

Some common problems to which MYSTAT routines may be applied include the following:

- Determining the average value of policy outcomes believed to result from one or more policies in different time periods.
- Examining the distribution or spread of policy outcomes believed to result from one or more policies.

---

[1] See, for example, U.S. Department of Transportation, *The Effects of the 65 mph Speed Limit through 1988: A Report to Congress* (Washington, DC: National Highway Traffic Safety Administration, U.S. Department of Transportation, October 1989); Charles T. Clotfelter and John C. Hahn, "Assessing the National 55 mph Speed Limit," *Policy Sciences* 9 (June 1978), 281–94; George M. Guess and Paul G. Farnham, *Cases in Public Policy Analysis* (New York: Longman, 1989), Chap. 6, pp. 177–206; Duncan MacRae, Jr., and James A. Wilde, *Policy Analysis for Public Decisions* (Belmont, CA: Wadsworth Publishing Co., 1979), pp. 133–52; and Edward R. Tufte, *Data Analysis for Politics and Policy* (Englewood Cliffs, NJ: Prentice Hall, 1974), pp. 5–30.

- Determining the correlations between the value of policy inputs and policy outcomes.
- Constructing visual displays of such distributions and correlations.
- Constructing two-way tables that show the presumed effects of policies on policy outcomes.
- Forecasting the future value of policy outcomes by making extrapolations with simple linear regression.
- Forecasting the future value of policy outcomes by making predictions with multiple regression analysis.

The MYSTAT routines demonstrated below do not include instructions on how to enter data, set program parameters, or save and call up files. These and other questions are covered in the MYSTAT help facility on your program disk and in the program manual that accompanies this text [Gary Simon, *Using MYSTAT* (Englewood Cliffs, NJ: Prentice Hall, 1989)].

TABLE A6–1   Data on the 55 MPH Speed Limit, 1966–1988

CASE	YEAR	POLICY	MDR	GPI	UNEMPLOY
1966	−11	0	5.7	15.0	3.8
1967	−10	0	5.5	15.5	3.8
1968	−9	0	5.5	16.0	3.6
1969	−8	0	5.3	16.3	3.5
1970	−7	0	4.9	17.0	4.9
1971	−6	0	4.7	18.2	5.9
1972	−5	0	4.5	18.3	5.6
1973	−4	0	4.3	21.1	4.9
1974	−3	1	3.6	33.2	5.6
1975	−2	1	3.5	36.4	8.5
1976	−1	1	3.3	38.8	7.7
1977	0	1	3.4	43.9	7.1
1978	1	1	3.2	46.2	6.1
1979	2	1	3.3	62.4	5.8
1980	3	1	3.4	86.1	7.1
1981	4	1	3.1	104.6	7.6
1982	5	1	2.8	103.4	9.7
1983	6	1	2.6	97.2	9.6
1984	7	1	2.7	99.4	7.5
1985	8	1	2.6	95.9	7.2
1986	9	1	2.6	77.6	7.0
1987	10	1	2.5	77.9	6.2
1988	11	1	2.5	78.1	5.5

Note: Years have been coded for purposes of time-series analysis according to conventions described in Chapter 6.

Sources: National Safety Council, U.S. President, *Economic Report of the President* (Washington, DC: U.S. Government Printing Office, 1991), pp. 322, 330, 351–54.

TABLE A6–2   State Population Density in 1980 and Mileage Death Rate in 1985

CASE	DENSITY[1]	MDR[2]	CASE	DENSITY[1]	MDR[2]
AL	76.7	2.5	MT	5.4	3.0
AK	0.7	3.1	NE	20.5	2.0
AZ	23.9	4.1	NV	7.3	3.4
AR	43.9	3.1	NH	102.5	2.5
CA	151.4	2.3	NJ	986.2	1.8
CO	27.9	2.2	NM	10.7	4.0
CT	637.8	2.0	NY	370.6	2.2
DE	307.6	2.0	NC	120.4	3.0
FL	180.0	3.3	ND	9.4	1.7
GA	94.1	2.6	OH	263.3	2.2
HI	150.1	1.9	OK	44.1	2.4
ID	11.5	3.3	OR	27.4	2.6
IL	205.3	2.2	PA	264.3	2.4
IN	152.8	2.4	RI	897.8	1.8
IA	52.1	2.3	SC	103.4	3.5
KS	28.9	2.5	SD	9.1	2.1
KY	92.3	2.5	TN	111.6	3.4
LA	94.5	2.8	TX	54.3	2.6
ME	36.3	2.2	UT	17.8	2.5
MD	428.7	2.2	VT	55.2	2.5
MA	733.3	1.9	VA	134.7	2.0
MI	162.6	2.3	WA	62.1	2.2
MN	51.2	1.9	WV	80.8	3.3
MS	53.4	3.5	WI	86.5	2.1
MO	71.3	2.4	WY	4.8	2.8

Notes:
[1] Population density expressed as population per square mile in 1980. Population density is relatively stable and changed little from 1980 to 1988.

[2] MDR refers to the mileage death rate (deaths per 100 million miles) on intercity highways regulated by the 55 mph speed limit.

Sources: U.S. Department of Commerce, Bureau of the Census; National Safety Council.

DEMONSTRATION DATA

Tables A6–1 and A6–2 display the data on the 55 mph speed limit used to demonstrate MYSTAT routines. These data include conventional policy outcome variables (for example, deaths per 100 million miles of intercity travel) as well as extrapolicy variables (for example, gasoline prices, unemployment, population density) that have been found to account for a small or large percentage of variance in policy outcomes. The selection of these variables is not merely a technical task—it requires the application of problem structuring methods that help discover variables to include within the boundaries of the problem (see Chapter 5).

DATA ENTRY AND FILE CREATION

The data in Tables A6-1 and A6-2 have been entered with the MYSTAT *edit* facility in two files created with the *save* command (see *USING MYSTAT*, pp. 7–11). These files were saved on a disk in drive A of an IBM-compatible computer. The files were named: "A: MDR6688.MYS" and "A: STATEMDR.MYS." A sample of the first 15 cases in the file named "A: MDR6688.MYS" is presented in Exhibit A6-1.

VISUAL DISPLAYS

It is essential to carry out a visual inspection of data *before* applying various statistical procedures. The visualization of data is essential because it allows us to see how a particular variable is distributed (for example, whether it is symmetrical or skewed) or how two variables are associated (for example, in a linear or curvilinear pattern). The visual display of quantitative data also permits us to identify extreme values (called "outliers") of a variable that could distort all subsequent analysis.

Exhibit A6-2 displays histograms (see Chapter 8) of the mileage death rate (MDR), the gasoline price index (GPI), and unemployment (UNEMPLOY). The GPI is a measure of the inflation of prices for gasoline, oil, and other petroleum products.

EXHIBIT A6–1   Sample of File

MYSTAT Editor

Case	YEAR	POLICY	MDR	GPI	UNEMPLOY
1	-11.000	.000	5.700	15.000	3.800
2	-10.000	.000	5.500	15.500	3.800
3	-9.000	.000	5.500	16.000	3.600
4	-8.000	.000	5.300	16.300	3.500
5	-7.000	.000	4.900	17.000	4.900
6	-6.000	.000	4.700	18.200	5.900
7	-5.000	.000	4.500	18.300	5.600
8	-4.000	.000	4.300	21.100	4.900
9	-3.000	1.000	3.600	33.200	5.600
10	-2.000	1.000	3.500	36.400	8.500
11	-1.000	1.000	3.300	38.800	7.700
12	.000	1.000	3.400	43.900	7.100
13	1.000	1.000	3.200	46.200	6.100
14	2.000	1.000	3.300	62.400	5.800
15	3.000	1.000	3.400	86.100	7.100

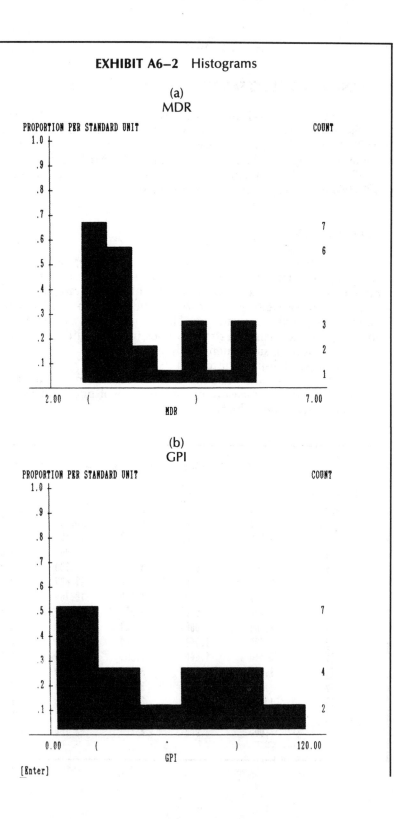

EXHIBIT A6–2 Histograms

(a)
MDR

(b)
GPI

[Enter]

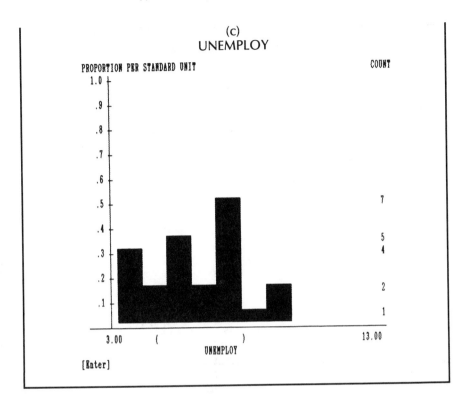

Exhibit A6–3 displays scatterplots of two sets of variables. The first (a) is a time-series display that plots deaths per 100 million miles (MDR) against time (YEARS). The second (b) plots MDR against the index of the price of gasoline (GPI). Observe that the first scatterplot (a) shows an essentially linear relationship, while (b) shows a strongly curvilinear relationship. As we learned in Chapter 6, nonlinear relationships such as that displayed in (b) must be transformed before linear regression analysis may be used. This has been done in (c), which shows the plot of MDR by LOGGPI (the gasoline price index transformed to its base *e* logarithm). [*Note:* The vertical axis has been stretched with the LINES = command for precision.]

STATISTICAL AND VISUAL SUMMARIES

After creating visual displays of variables it is important to obtain statistical (and combined statistical-visual) summaries of variables and their relations. Summaries include the mean, standard deviation, and range (MAXIMUM less MINIMUM), which are shown (Exhibit A6–4) for the time-series data in Table A6–1 [Command: >STATS]. A combined statistical-visual summary of deaths per 100 million miles (MDR) from 1966 through 1988 is shown in the bar graph displayed as Exhibit A6–5 [Command: >TPLOT].

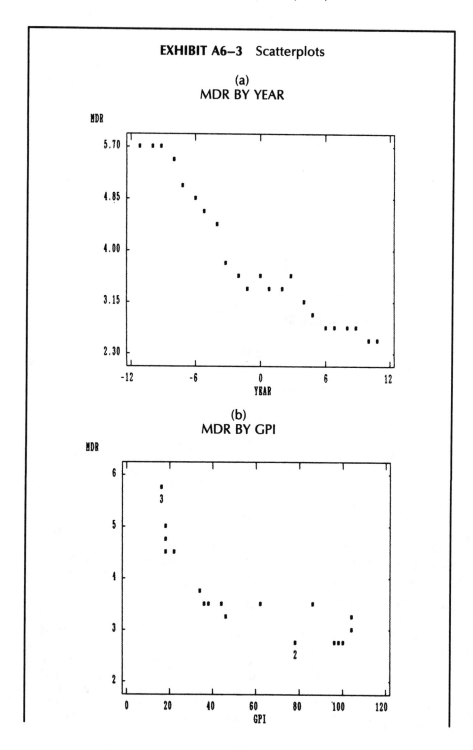

EXHIBIT A6–3   Scatterplots

(a)
MDR BY YEAR

(b)
MDR BY GPI

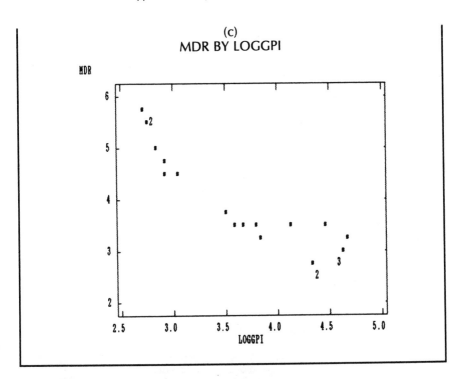

(c)
MDR BY LOGGPI

EXHIBIT A6–4   Basic Descriptive Statistics [>STATS]

TOTAL OBSERVATIONS: 23

	YEAR	POLICY	MDR	GPI	UNEMPLOY
N OF CASES	23	23	23	23	· 23
MINIMUM	-11.000	0.000	2.500	15.000	3.500
MAXIMUM	11.000	1.000	5.700	104.600	9.700
MEAN	0.000	0.652	3.717	52.978	6.270
STANDARD DEV	6.782	0.487	1.086	34.033	1.765

	LOGGPI
N OF CASES	23
MINIMUM	2.708
MAXIMUM	4.650
MEAN	3.729
STANDARD DEV	0.746

Exhibit A6–6 uses the data in Table A6–2 to display state population densities in 1980 as a stem-and-leaf display [Command: >STEM DENSITY]. The stem-and-leaf display provides information on the median (versus mean) population density in the 50 states in 1980, shows the shape of the distribution (strongly skewed toward high population density), and shows extreme or "outside" values of population density in some of the states (for example, New Jersey with more than 980 persons per square mile).

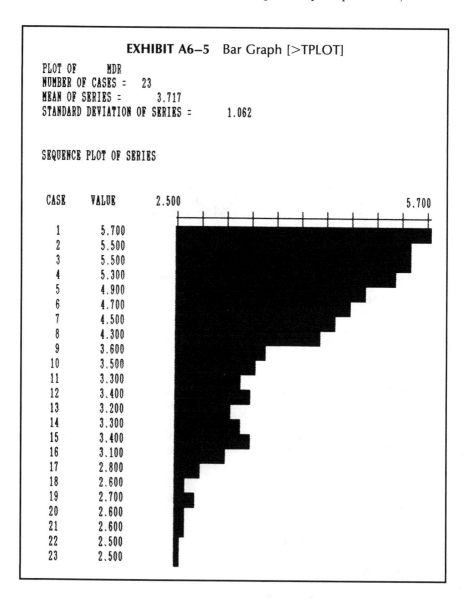

EXHIBIT A6–5   Bar Graph [>TPLOT]

PLOT OF   MDR
NUMBER OF CASES =   23
MEAN OF SERIES =   3.717
STANDARD DEVIATION OF SERIES =   1.062

SEQUENCE PLOT OF SERIES

CASE	VALUE
1	5.700
2	5.500
3	5.500
4	5.300
5	4.900
6	4.700
7	4.500
8	4.300
9	3.600
10	3.500
11	3.300
12	3.400
13	3.200
14	3.300
15	3.400
16	3.100
17	2.800
18	2.600
19	2.700
20	2.600
21	2.600
22	2.500
23	2.500

EXHIBIT A6–6 Stem-and-Leaf Display [>STEM]

STEM AND LEAF PLOT OF VARIABLE: DENSITY , N = 50

MINIMUM IS: 0.700
LOWER HINGE IS: 27.900
MEDIAN IS: 78.750
UPPER HINGE IS: 152.800
MAXIMUM IS: 986.200

```
0   000000111
0 H 222223
0   4455555
0 M 677
0   88999
1   001
1   23
1 H 555
1   6
1   8
2   0
2
2
2   66
2
3   0
***OUTSIDE VALUES***
3   7
4   2
6   3
7   3
8   9
9   8
```

The final form of data summary is the correlation matrix, which shows the association (positive and negative) between each pair of variables. Exhibit A6–7 uses data in Table A6–1 to create a matrix of Pearson correlation coefficients [Command: >PEARSON] among all variables in the data set, including the new variable LOGGPI (the GPI variable transformed to its base *e* logarithm).

EXHIBIT A6–7   Correlation Matrix [>PEARSON]

EARSON CORRELATION MATRIX

	YEAR	POLICY	MDR	GPI	UNEMPLOY
YEAR	1.000				
POLICY	0.826	1.000			
MDR	-0.958	-0.916	1.000		
GPI	0.894	0.786	-0.856	1.000	
UNEMPLOY	0.653	0.748	-0.777	0.735	1.000
LOGGPI	0.937	0.892	-0.935	0.976	0.768

	LOGGPI
LOGGPI	1.000

NUMBER OF OBSERVATIONS: 23

REGRESSION ANALYSIS

MYSTAT permits simple linear regression and multiple regression analysis. Exhibit A6–8 shows two simple regression analyses. The first (a) uses the file A: MDR6688.MYS to regress deaths per 100 million miles (MDR) on time (YEAR). This regression analysis assumes that MDR is the dependent (effect) variable, Y, and YEARS is the independent (causative) variable, X [Commands: >MODEL Y = CONSTANT + X and >ESTIMATE]. The regression equation (MDR = 3.717 − 0.153X) may be used to forecast the mileage death rate for a given year by substituting the coded time value for that year in the regression equation (see Chapter 6). For example, if we want to forecast MDR for 1997, we substitute the coded time value for that year (20) in the regression equation. The second regression analysis (b) uses the file A: STATEMDR.MYS to regress the 1985 mileage death rate (MDR) on population density (DENSITY) for the 50 states. In a full analysis the DENSITY variable, which is strongly skewed (see Exhibit A6–6), would be transformed or analyzed with a non-linear regression model (see Chapter 6).

Note that MYSTAT does not itself perform extrapolations—you must use a calculator to make this computation. You must also calculate your own interval estimate by using information on the STANDARD ERROR OF ESTIMATE provided in the MYSTAT output. To calculate an interval estimate, use the formula provided in Chapter 6.

MYSTAT also may be used for multiple regression. Exhibit A6–9 shows the results of a multiple regression analysis in which deaths per 100

EXHIBIT A6–8 Simple Linear Regression [>MODEL Y = CONSTANT + X; >ESTIMATE]

(A)
MDR Regressed on YEAR

DEP VAR: MDR   N: 23   MULTIPLE R: .958   SQUARED MULTIPLE R: .918
ADJUSTED SQUARED MULTIPLE R: .914   STANDARD ERROR OF ESTIMATE: 0.318

VARIABLE	COEFFICIENT	STD ERROR	STD COEF	TOLERANCE	T	P(2 TAIL)
CONSTANT	3.717	0.066	0.000	.	56.098	0.000
YEAR	-0.153	0.010	-0.958	.100E+01	-15.361	0.000

ANALYSIS OF VARIANCE

SOURCE	SUM-OF-SQUARES	DF	MEAN-SQUARE	F-RATIO	P
REGRESSION	23.832	1	23.832	235.968	0.000
RESIDUAL	2.121	21	0.101		

(b)
MDR Regressed on DENSITY

DEP VAR: MDR   N: 50   MULTIPLE R: .435   SQUARED MULTIPLE R: .189
ADJUSTED SQUARED MULTIPLE R: .172   STANDARD ERROR OF ESTIMATE: 0.527

VARIABLE	COEFFICIENT	STD ERROR	STD COEF	TOLERANCE	T	P(2 TAIL)
CONSTANT	2.726	0.091	0.000	.	29.874	0.000
DENSITY	-0.001	0.000	-0.435	.100E+01	-3.344	0.002

ANALYSIS OF VARIANCE

SOURCE	SUM-OF-SQUARES	DF	MEAN-SQUARE	F-RATIO	P
REGRESSION	3.111	1	3.111	11.183	0.002
RESIDUAL	13.354	48	0.278		

EXHIBIT A6–9   Multiple Regression Analysis: Effects of LOGGPI
and Unemployment on MDR (>MODEL Y = CONSTANT + X1 +
X2 . . . + Xi]

```
DEP VAR:    MDR    N:   23   MULTIPLE R:  .939   SQUARED MULTIPLE R:  .882
ADJUSTED SQUARED MULTIPLE R:  .871   STANDARD ERROR OF ESTIMATE:        0.391
```

VARIABLE	COEFFICIENT	STD ERROR	STD COEF	TOLERANCE	T	P(2 TAIL)
CONSTANT	8.748	0.426	0.000	.	20.539	0.000
LOGGPI	-1.202	0.174	-0.825	0.4096528	-6.887	0.000
UNEMPLOY	-0.088	0.074	-0.143	0.4096528	-1.191	0.248

ANALYSIS OF VARIANCE

SOURCE	SUM-OF-SQUARES	DF	MEAN-SQUARE	F-RATIO	P
REGRESSION	22.900	2	11.450	75.005	0.000
RESIDUAL	3.053	20	0.153		

---

million miles (MDR) is the dependent variable, Y. The independent variables, X1 and X2, are the logarithm of the gasoline price index (LOGGPI) and the unemployment rate (UNEMPLOY) [Command: MODEL Y = CONSTANT + X1 + X2]. Point estimates may also be made, as described above, by substituting the appropriate values of both variables in the multiple regression equation. For example, if we assume that a new gasoline tax or political instability in the Middle East will increase gasoline prices, or that unemployment will decrease in some future period, the multiple regression equation permits a *theoretical forecast* of the probable deaths that will occur under these new future conditions. According to the multiple regression equation, we may expect the death rate to fall as gasoline prices and the unemployment rate increase. The information on the STANDARD ERROR OF ESTIMATE provided in the MYSTAT output may be used to obtain an interval estimate, as described above.

CROSS-TABULATIONS

MYSTAT also permits cross-tabulations of frequency data that have been grouped into categories (for example, present–absent, before–after, high–medium–low). Exhibit A6–10 shows the cross-tabulation of three levels of

EXHIBIT A6–10　　Cross-Tabulation of MDR by Density

TABLE OF　　MDR　　(ROWS) BY　DENSITY　　(COLUMNS)
FREQUENCIES

	1.000	2.000	3.000	TOTAL
1.000	1	4	8	13
2.000	5	9	4	18
3.000	11	3	5	19
TOTAL	17	16	17	50

WARNING: MORE THAN ONE-FIFTH OF FITTED CELLS ARE SPARSE (FREQUENCY < 5)
SIGNIFICANCE TESTS ARE SUSPECT

TEST STATISTIC	VALUE	DF	PROB
PEARSON CHI-SQUARE	13.395	4	.009
LIKELIHOOD RATIO CHI-SQUARE	13.726	4	.008
MCNEMAR SYMMETRY CHI-SQUARE	.728	4	.867

COEFFICIENT	VALUE	ASYMPTOTIC STD ERROR
PHI	.5176	
CRAMER V	.3660	
CONTINGENCY	.4597	
GOODMAN-KRUSKAL GAMMA	-.5145	.15871
KENDALL TAU-B	-.3635	.12226
STUART TAU-C	-.3612	.12222
COHEN KAPPA	-.0492	.09456
SPEARMAN RHO	-.3930	.12990
SOMERS D　(COLUMN DEPENDENT)	-.3657	.12223
LAMBDA　(COLUMN DEPENDENT)	.3333	.11866
UNCERTAINTY (COLUMN DEPENDENT)	.1250	.06245

population density (high–medium–low) by three levels of mileage death rates (high–medium–low) for the 50 states in 1985. In order to use cross-tabulation, the original data on population density and death rates (Table A6–2) were converted into categories and saved in a file named A: STATECAT:MYS. This file is organized so that high population density has a value of 1, medium density has a value of 2, and low density has a value of 3. The same values (1, 2, 3) are also assigned to three levels of death rates. The organization of the file looks like this:

DENSITY	MDR	COUNT
1	1	1
1	2	5
1	3	11
2	1	4
2	2	9
2	3	3
3	1	8
3	2	4
3	3	5

The resulting cross-tabulation (Exhibit A6–10) shows a negative relationship between population density and death rates—that is, when population density is higher, death rates are lower. The commands necessary to cross-tabulate these data are as follows:

>USE "A:STATECAT:MYS"
>CATEGORY DENSITY
>CATEGORY MDR
>TABULATE DENSITY*MDR

Note that the MYSTAT output (Exhibit A6–10) provides a full range of descriptive and inferential statistics appropriate for tables. The chi-square value (PEARSON CHI-SQUARE) is used in standard tests of the statistical independence of variables in a table. The coefficients listed in the MYSTAT output are different measures of the strength of relations between these variables. In the present case (Exhibit A6–10), both variables are ordinally ranked categories (high–medium–low), which call for the use of the coefficient called GOODMAN-KRUSKAL GAMMA. To know when to use one (or more) of these coefficients requires that you ask your instructor, or consult a standard statistics text.

Author Index

467

Subject Index*

---

*Italicized page numbers refer to subjects which appear in chapter glossaries.

472

and "knowledge society," 51
multiple methods of inquiry in, 64–65
nineteenth-century background, 38–43
normative approach, 63
policy-analytic methods, 64
policy-informational components, 71
policy-informational transformations, 72
and policy sciences movement, 46–48
and "postindustrial" society, 51–57
and problem finding, 81
and problem solving, 81
and professionalization of social science,
  43–45
reason and ethics in, 126–30
and structure of policy arguments,
  92–100
in twentieth century, 43–50
usable knowledge in, 90–92
valuative approach, 63
within policy-making process, 15
Policy-analytic methods, 14
  definition, 30
Policy-analytic procedures, 14–15
  and appropriateness to phases of policy-
    making, 17
  definition, 30, 84
Policy-analytic techniques, 14, 30
Policy argument, 84
Policy argument, elements of, 66–68
  backing, 66–67
  policy claim, 66
  policy-relevant information, 66
  qualifier, 68
  rebuttal, 67–68
  warrant, 66
Policy argument, modes of, 100–126
  analycentric, 110–13
  authoritative, 101–4
  explanatory, 113–18
  intuitive, 106–10
  pragmatic, 118–24
  value-critical, 124–26
Policy arguments, structure of, 92–100
Policy assessment, 16, 19
Policy claims:
  definition, 92, 132
  types of, 92–93
    advocative, 92–93
    designative, 92–93
    evaluative, 92–93
Policy Delphi, 243–49
  contrasted with conventional Delphi,
    243
  polarization measures, 243, 248
  principles, 243–44
  procedural steps, 244–49
  questionnaire items, 245
Policy environment, 70, 85
Policy formulation, 16, 18, 85
Policy goal, 261
Policy implementation, 16, 19, 85
Policy-informational component, 71, 85
Policy-informational transformation, 72, 85
Policy impact, 396
Policy input, 396

Policy issue papers, 423–31
  checklist, 427–31
  elements, 425–27
  foci, 424–25
  forms, 424–25
  rating scale, 427
Policy issues, 142–44
  definition, 85
  hierarchy of types, 143–44
  operational, 144
  strategic, 144
Policy-making process:
  definition, 30
  phases of, 15–19
    agenda setting, 16
    policy adoption, 16
    policy assessment, 16
    policy formulation, 16
    policy implementation, 16
Policy memorandum, 439–42
Policy models, 152–61
  definition, 185
  descriptive, 153
  normative, 153–54
  perspective, 158
  procedural, 156–58
  surrogate, 158
  symbolic, 155–56
  verbal, 154–55
Policy objective, 261
Policy outcome, 69–70, 85
Policy output, 396
Policy performance, 70, 85
Policy problem:
  definition, 85, 185
  perspectives of, 150
  three classes of, 145–47
Policy process, 396
Policy-relevant communication, 30
Policy-relevant documents, 21–24, 30
Policy-relevant information, 12–13, 30,
  68–70, 132
  Types of, 68–70
    policy action, 69
    policy future, 69
    policy outcome, 69–70
    policy performance, 70
    policy problem, 68–69
Policy-relevant knowledge, 26–27, 30,
  91–92
  Uses of, 26–27
Policy Sciences, 50
  definition, 59
*The Policy Sciences: Recent Developments
  in Scope and Method* (1951), 46
Policy stakeholer, 70, 85
Policy Studies Journal, 50
Policy Studies Organization, 50
Policy system:
  definition, 85
  dialectical character, 70
  elements, 71
Political control, 59
Positive feedback loop, 261